THE HANDBOOK OF DIVORCE MEDIATION

THE HANDBOOK OF DIVORCE MEDIATION

LENARD MARLOW
AND
S. RICHARD SAUBER

PLENUM PRESS • NEW YORK AND LONDON

Library of Congress Cataloging-in-Publication Data

Marlow, Lenard.
   The handbook of divorce mediation / by Lenard Marlow, S. Richard
Sauber.
        p.   cm.
   Bibliography: p.
   Includes index.
   ISBN 0-306-43286-2
   1. Divorce mediation--United States. 2. Divorce counseling-
-United States.   I. Sauber, S. Richard.   II. Title.
HQ834.M32   1989
306.8'9--dc19   88-18791
                                                               CIP

© 1990 Plenum Press, New York
A Division of Plenum Publishing Corporation
233 Spring Street, New York, N.Y. 10013

Printed in the United States of America

God gave us children to make up for all of the other things that he also gave to us.

To our children (John and Leslie Marlow, and Teddy and Rachel Sauber) and to your children.

It is not always given to us to help people as we would like; sometimes we must content ourselves by helping them as we can.

Those who step forward to offer help in other people's lives should always remember to keep their hands in their pockets.

In most instances, the judgments that we make in other people's lives are irrelevant when they are not otherwise wrong. Worse yet, they are usually of no value to anyone, save perhaps ourselves.

One cannot expect to find perfect solutions to imperfect problems.

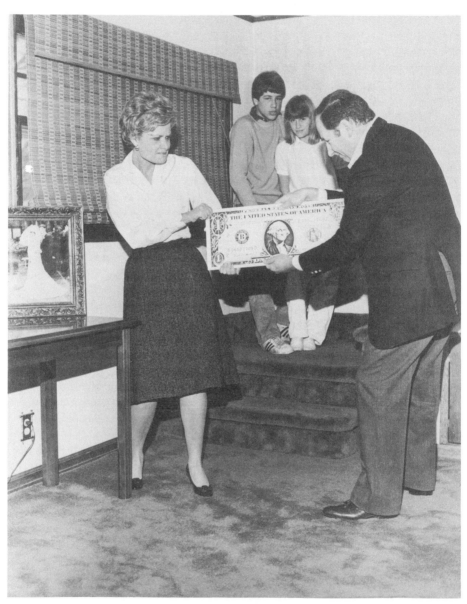

Divorce viewed as a legal event.

Divorce viewed as a personal event.

Preface

Mediation, as a procedure to assist couples in dealing with the problems incident to their separation and divorce, is still relatively new in the United States. For the would-be practitioner, that poses certain problems. Divorce mediation cannot provide a long history of generally accepted procedures. Nor is there even a body of information to which would-be practitioners can turn for instruction or guidance. And, of course, there are no established schools that can train or prepare a practitioner to do this work. To make matters worse, the situation is likely to remain in this state for some time to come. Given this fact, it was felt that it would be useful for practitioners (even for those already engaged in divorce mediation) to have a handbook which would trace a typical mediation from its inception to its conclusion and which would provide them with the substantive information they need to know in order to do divorce mediation. It is hoped that this handbook will fill this need.

Having said that, however, it must be acknowledged that the purpose of this book is very much beyond that. Until now, divorce mediation in the United States has been shaped principally by such books as O. J. Coogler's *Structured Mediation in Divorce Settlements: A Handbook for Marital Mediators*,[1] and John Haynes' *Divorce Mediation: A Practical Guide for Therapists and Counselors*.[2] Without attempting to detract from either of these works—and the contribution of both of these books, and particularly their authors, cannot be overestimated—it was felt that each of these works incorporated limitations that had to be challenged. From the standpoint of this book, the first of these presents divorce mediation as it would be practiced using the conceptual outlook of an attorney, while the second presents divorce mediation as it would be practiced using the conceptual outlook of a labor mediator. In contradistinction, the present book attempts to demonstrate how divorce mediation would be practiced using the conceptual outlook of a mental health professional. This is not to suggest that it is the thesis of this book that divorce mediation should only be practiced by mental health professionals. Rather, its thesis is that whether it is practiced by mental health professionals or not, the problems confronting the mediator should be viewed from the standpoint, and within the value system, of a mental health professional.

In setting forth the conceptual outlook of a mental health professional, and in then attempting to develop a model of divorce mediation based on that outlook, we were repeatedly confronted with certain problems. The first of these arose from the fact that, while divorce is unquestionably first and foremost a personal event in a couple's life, our attitudes toward it have in large measure been shaped by the view of it held by our legal system, and this is as true of mental health professionals as it is of society at large. We were also confronted with the fact that although divorce mediation has by and large been a response to what were seen as the very damaging effects of that view—the damaging effects of traditional adversarial divorce proceedings—it has, nevertheless, not seriously questioned the assumptions and, therefore, the view of divorce, upon which those proceedings are founded. This is expressed, for example, in the prevailing attitudes toward standards of practice and ethical requirements in mediation practice today which incorporate so many of the views that are reflective of adversarial assumptions and, therefore, adversarial concerns. It thus became one of our purposes, first, to question those assumptions and, having done that, then to attempt to enunciate what we thought should properly be the assumptions and concerns that should inform mediation practice.

In attempting to prepare a handbook on divorce mediation, and apart from constructing a model of it in keeping with the view which we hold of divorce, it soon became obvious that there were several additional questions that practitioners had not sufficiently addressed, and this despite the fact that they are very basic questions that confront both the couple and the mediator in almost every mediation. The first of these is, what obligation do two people, who were previously strangers, have to one another by virtue of the fact that they were married for a period of time?[3] The second is, how should the individual and joint efforts of the parties during their marriage affect the distribution of the property that either or both of them may own at the time of their divorce or that they may acquire subsequent to their divorce?[4] The third is, what is the role of a mediator in assisting a couple to address these and the other issues incident to their separation and divorce with which they will be faced and what interest and obligation does the mediator have in the resolution they come to?

Strange as it may seem, and as basic as these questions are, there has been little, if any, serious thought given to them. As to the first two—and this has been as true of divorce mediators as it has been of adversarial attorneys—it has summarily been assumed that the answer to them is whatever the divorce laws of the state in which the couple lives say that it is.[5] As to the third, divorce mediators have not only contented themselves by simply defining their role in keeping with assumptions implicit in adversarial practice, but worse, have bought a great deal of adversarial mythology in the process, and this has been as true of mental health professionals as it has been of attorneys. What makes this all the more difficult to understand is the fact that it was the rejection of many of those assumptions, and even some of that mythology, that brought them to mediation in the first place.

While we do not suggest that we have provided definitive answers to these questions, nevertheless, and in the belief that there must now be a starting point, we have attempted to initiate the necessary debate and to provide at least tentative ones. In considering those answers, the reader must keep in mind that, as with the model of divorce mediation itself which we have proposed, they only represent our present thinking and the conclusions to which that thinking has brought us. Undoubtedly, they will be subject to change in the future. We may even conclude that some of them were in error. And, of course, there is no one correct point of view, or method of doing anything, including the practice of mediation.

As for our model of divorce mediation itself, we would recommend, particularly for the beginning practitioner, that the procedures set forth in this book, and the assumptions upon which they are based, be accepted as a point of departure and be followed quite strictly, at least initially. After the practitioner has gained experience, and particularly after he has conducted to a conclusion ten or more mediations, he can begin to test those procedures, and our assumptions, against that experience to see how valid or invalid they have proved to be for him and, if he wishes, to experiment by modifying them to fit his own perceptions and his own style of conducting mediation. In any event, the one thing that we would ask that he not do—and this is particularly true for the experienced practitioner—is to dismiss them out of hand simply because they are inconsistent with accepted practice, and may therefore appear to be inappropriate and perhaps even irresponsible.

We acknowledge, in advance, that this will be difficult for many practitioners. As the reader will see, our assumptions and value judgments tend to result in a rather laid-back, hands-off, wait-and-see style. The assumptions and concerns that generally inform mediation today, however, being very different from our own, not only result in a different style, but also one that would be somewhat threatened by the approach we recommend. There is thus the danger, particularly for experienced mediators with entrenched ideas, that if we suggest, as we do, letting go of the reins to see what will happen and where the couple will end up if left on their own, that not having the confidence that our experience has given us, the minute the mediation appears to veer off course, they will immediately be overcome by the need to jump in and grab the reins again. Thus, rather than allow the mediation in question to test our assumptions, it will only have confirmed their own.

There is another consideration that complicates the matter further. A book—any book—can only teach the practitioner so much about doing mediation. To begin with, it is much easier to *show* someone how to conduct a successful mediation than it is to *tell* them how to do it. Recognizing this, and recognizing also that so much of that success depends upon intangibles that take place within the individual sessions, much of the "how-to-do-it" in this book is devoted to questions of attitude, tone, mood, and expression that, in our opinion, are critical to any intervention, be it an intervention in psychotherapy or in mediation. Nevertheless, it is just these intangibles that are so hard to convey with words alone. Secondly, it is not possible to give specific answers to each of the individual problems with which a couple and a mediator will be confronted, for the reason that each of these problems is unique unto itself, and because each incorporates varying, legitimate points of view. The most that we could hope to do, therefore, is to assist the practitioner, not by answering these questions in advance, but by preparing the mediator to deal with them himself when they arise. This has been done by walking the practitioner around these problems, so to speak, in an attempt to help him view them from a number of different possible positions. The hope is that the confidence the mediator will acquire in broadening his outlook and understanding with respect to each of these problems will stand substitute for any such ready-made answers and will provide him with the wherewithal to find resolutions for these issues on his own as he is confronted with them in his work. The hope, too, is that the procedure we have adopted will also force the mediator to lay bare and to question his own assumptions about these issues, and perhaps even his own prejudices, and to be more self-conscious of them.

———————

The book is divided into two sections. The first of these is entitled "Theory." Its purpose is to define and examine the assumptions implicit in the view of divorce mediation expressed in this book, as well as to question some of those that inform mediation practice, as well as adversarial practice, today. Quite deliberately, these assumptions have not been expressed in an expository, didactic fashion. Rather, they have been expressed in a series of seemingly separate, distinct essays about divorce mediation. In the course of a mediation, the practitioner will be called upon to ask certain questions of himself, about the goals of divorce mediation, and about his role in relationship to the couple whom he is assisting. What significance do rules of law have for the issues confronting the couple? What obligation does the mediator have to assure that the agreement concluded between them is fair? What obligation does he have to the couple's children, who are affected by, but are not a part of, the mediation? What is it that stands between the couple and an agreement, and how can the mediator best effectuate its resolution? What should be the relationship between the mediator and the attorney or attorneys whom the couple may consult? Time and time again, we have been called upon to address these and other questions. In fact, our understanding of divorce mediation, and the principles we have evolved in conducting our own practices of divorce mediation, are in large measure a by-product of our own struggle with these questions. What we have tried to do in these chapters, therefore, is to present the struggle of our own thinking with these questions as various issues we faced in the course of a mediation forced us to go back and give them renewed thought. This presentation is also reflective of our belief that successful media-tion will result more from the deepened understanding that the struggle with these questions will produce than from ready-made answers.

The second section is entitled "Practice." Its purpose is to take the practitioner through a complete mediation, and while intended for the experienced mediator as well as for the beginner, it nevertheless assumes that the practitioner is about to conduct his first mediation. It starts out by preparing the practitioner to engage in mediation generally, discusses each of the subjects that the mediator and the couple will be required to address in the course of the mediation—debts, real and personal property, custody (parenting), support, medical and life insurance, college education—and concludes with a discussion of the memorandum of understanding that will be prepared by the mediator, as well as the final agreement that will be signed by each of the parties. It is followed by an appendix that will provide some forms and some additional material that should be helpful to him in the course of his work.

Two final points must be made. The views that we have expressed in this book are born of our own personal experiences and reflect the conclusions that we have come to in wrestling with that experience. Obviously, that experience is limited rather than all-inclusive. In our case it is limited to couples from a certain stratum of society—generally upper middle-class white couples. It is also limited to our experience with those couples either in court-related (adversarial) proceedings or in private mediation. While we would resist the suggestion that the conclusions which we have reached can summarily be dismissed as inapplicable to other segments of society, or in other contexts, on that basis alone, nevertheless, since those conclusions can only be based upon our own experience, and since we have no authority to speak beyond that experience, we feel constrained to acknowledge this. Having said that, however, we would point out that the population served by private mediators in this country is in all likelihood the same as the population that served as the basis for our conclusions.

Secondly, the reader will find that we take exception to many of the views that are generally accepted as gospel in mediation circles today—what John Kenneth Galbraith called "the conventional wisdom." In fact, many of our conclusions will seem radically at variance with prevailing opinion. In judging those conclusions, and while acknowledging that they undoubtedly express our own values as well as judgments we have made based upon our previous professional experience, antedating our work in divorce mediation, we would like the reader to know that in each instance we have tested those conclusions, to the extent that we were able, in the course of the mediations which we ourselves have conducted over the last several years. While we would not, of course, suggest that this proves the correctness of those conclusions, we nevertheless submit that fact for whatever value it may have to the reader in considering them.

ACKNOWLEDGMENTS

We wish to acknowledge our deep appreciation to the following people who have contributed to this book: Max Cohen, whose insight and understanding, and particularly whose style of conducting therapy, informed so much of the book; Barbara Badolato, who lent her assistance at every stage of the book's development and who made invaluable contributions to many of the ideas expressed in its pages; Anthony Pizza and Andrew Horowitz, who researched and helped prepare the final text; and, finally, Doreen Dunne, Jacqueline Watters, Carolyn Patalano, and Jessica O'Malley, who prepared the manuscript and saw it through its many revisions.

CONTENTS

PART I. THEORY

1. WHAT IS DIVORCE MEDIATION? 3

2. LEGAL MYTHS 11

3. EQUITABLE DISTRIBUTION AND DIVORCE MEDIATION 23

4. IS THE AGREEMENT FAIR? 39

5. THE RULE OF LAW IN DIVORCE MEDIATION 63

6. IN WHOSE BEST INTERESTS? 73

7. CONTEXT 89

8. POWER IMBALANCES—THE PROBLEM FOR WOMEN IN MEDIATION 103

9. WHOSE FAULT IS IT? 121

10. CONDUCTING MEDIATION 127

11. A QUESTION OF CHOICE 153

PART II. PRACTICE

12. STARTING OUT 161

13. THE INITIAL MEETING 185

14. CHILDREN 211

15. MARITAL RESIDENCE 241

16. Assets and Liabilities 261

17. Support and Maintenance—Preliminary Considerations 285

18. Support and Maintenance—When, How Much, and How Long? 307

19. Medical and Life Insurance 359

20. College Education 373

21. Memorandum of Agreement 383

22. Income Taxes 417

23. The Cost of Raising a Child 435

Appendix: Forms and Letters 443

Notes 461

Bibliography 493

Name Index 497

Subject Index 501

About the Authors 507

PART I
Theory

CHAPTER 1

WHAT IS DIVORCE MEDIATION?

From the standpoint of the legal profession, divorce mediation is simply an alternative means of dispute resolution, and until now this has been the generally accepted view taken both by its advocates and by its opponents. Thus, divorce mediation has not questioned the legal nature of the dispute between the couple, or the fact that their divorce involves the determination of their respective legal rights and obligations flowing from their marriage. It simply questioned whether those legal rights and obligations had to be settled in an adversarial setting, and whether alternative procedures might not be both more appropriate and conducive to a resolution of the couple's differences.

What divorce mediation has represented, therefore, is an alternative procedure, one that will bring the couple to the same conclusion, but without exacting from them the cost, in terms of time, money, and emotional injury, that has invariably been its price. As a bonus, it has been its hope that agreements concluded between couples in a nonadversarial setting would be honored more than has been the case with agreements arrived at by more traditional adversarial proceedings.

On the face of it, this is a laudatory objective. Nevertheless, we will take strong objection to it. In fact, the central thesis of this book will be that to understand divorce mediation as simply an alternative legal proceeding is to misunderstand it. Just as importantly, it will be our purpose to replace this view with a radically different and, it is hoped, more useful understanding.

To appreciate fully our criticism of the prevailing view of divorce mediation, it will be necessary to retrace its development from its birth, just a few years ago, until the present time; to make explicit the assumptions upon which that view is predicated; and to then examine what, in our opinion, is a more appropriate set of assumptions.

THE ADVENT OF DIVORCE MEDIATION IN THE UNITED STATES

The mid-1960s saw a dramatic rise in the rate of divorce in the United States, and in the next ten years it more than doubled. With this sharp increase came an increased awareness and concern over the effects that divorce had on the families that it touched, particularly the children in those families. This concern soon extended to the procedures that couples traditionally employed to effectuate their divorce, as these were seen as exacerbating their problems.

Since divorce was regulated by law, and since it involved the determination of the respective legal rights and obligations of the parties arising out of their marriage, a couple's divorce took place within a legal setting, with each of the parties represented by separate

3

attorneys to protect their interests. Unfortunately, the legal system within which these attorneys worked was adversarial in nature and tended, in attempting to resolve the dispute between the parties, to make adversaries of them in the process. To compound matters, the adversarial struggle between the couple almost necessarily affected, and often involved, their children. Finally, these legal procedures were slow-moving and costly, adding further to both the emotional and financial cost of divorce.

By and large, divorce mediation represented a mental-health response to the problem of divorce. To be sure, there were lawyers who also expressed their concern, particularly lawyers from the academic community. In general, however, it was therapists, witnessing the effects of divorce upon the families they treated, who first insisted upon the necessity for more appropriate procedures, just as it was members of the mental health profession, such as Judith Wallerstein and Joan Kelly in *Surviving the Breakup*,[1] who first began to document the very damaging effects that divorce and the divorcing process had upon children.

The federal government also became concerned about the effects of divorce upon families and their children. As a result, the United States Children's Bureau gave a federal grant to the Association of Family and Conciliation Courts to study mediation's current status in the United States; and divorce mediation became the subject of the important annual conference held by that Association in late 1981. The growing attention given mediation was further reinforced just a few months later when the World Conference of the International Society on Family Law devoted its fourth annual conference, held in Cambridge, Massachusetts, to the question of resolving family disputes through the use of alternative methods of dispute resolution.

At about the same time, members of the legal profession began to take a fresh look at the emphasis which our legal system placed upon litigation as a means of resolving disputes between members of society generally. At the urging of leading jurists and academicians, such as Chief Justice Warren E. Burger of the United States Supreme Court, Chief Judge Lawrence E. Cooke of the New York Court of Appeals, and Derek C. Bok, President of Harvard University and the former Dean of its law school, serious questions were beginning to be asked about our reliance upon litigation as the primary means of resolving these disputes. The legal profession, and the law schools which would educate future lawyers, were urged to give thought to the skills used in negotiation, in addition to those used in litigation, as well as to the employment of such alternative procedures as conciliation, mediation, and arbitration.

Thus spurred on, major bar associations around the country began to form special committees to study "alternative means of dispute resolution" and, in June of 1982, the American Bar Association sponsored a conference in Washington to address the question of the use of such procedures in the resolution of family disputes.[2] In the academic community, and spearheaded by the Harvard Research Project and the influential book, *Getting to Yes*, by the directors of that project, Roger D. Fisher and William Ury,[3] law schools around the country began adding courses in alternative methods of dispute resolution to their curriculum, and to incorporate discussions of mediation, as well as an opportunity to conduct the negotiation of a matrimonial matter, into their regular curriculum—as Columbia Law School did with its revised course in Family Law. Stanford and Harvard Law Schools went even further and actually added courses on mediation.

It was into this setting that divorce mediation was born in the United States, and its growth has represented a blending of these two separate currents—the mental health profession's concern about the effects of the divorce process upon families, and the legal profession's concern with the overdependence upon litigation as a means of resolving disputes. And it was in this setting that divorce mediation came to be viewed as an alternative method of dispute resolution, and as simply that.

Yet the interest of the legal profession in alternative means of dispute resolutions has proved a mixed blessing. On the positive side, it has not only given credibility to divorce mediation, but may have actually saved it from fatal attack. As might be imagined, practicing attorneys, and bar associations which reflect their vested interests, have looked upon divorce mediation with both suspicion and disdain, for all of the proposed benefits to divorcing couples were viewed as being at the expense of the lucrative practices divorce lawyers had established. As a result, mental health professionals who entered the field stood subject to the charge of the unauthorized practice of law; and attorneys who attempted to assist separating and divorcing couples through mediation were liable to disciplinary proceedings based upon the legal profession's proscription against an attorney's representing parties having conflicting interests. And if attorneys and mental health professionals attempted to combine the skills of their respective disciplines, there were yet additional possible violations to be invoked.

Fortunately for divorce mediation, the demand of leading members of the legal profession that alternative methods of dispute resolution be found, and the legal profession's acceptance of this request, has tended to mute much of the criticism initially mounted against divorce mediation. In fact, had not the divorce mediation movement fallen under the protective umbrella of the alternative means of dispute resolution movement, it might well have died in its infancy. Certainly, its growth would have been impeded.

Unfortunately, there have been disadvantages as well. To begin with, in accepting itself as an alternative means of dispute resolution, the divorce mediation movement, rather than questioning what ought to be its assumptions and goals, has in large measure adopted and accepted the assumptions and goals laid down by the legal profession. Thus, divorce mediation did not question *where* it intended to lead a couple; it simply questioned how it intended to get them there. Secondly, it has left itself vulnerable to criticism based upon the view of divorce held by our legal system, and has been taken to task for failing to honor in its practice the assumptions upon which traditional adversarial divorce proceedings are based. This criticism has been expressed, for example, in the claim that the conflicting interests of the parties are not properly protected, that they are not sufficiently apprised of their respective legal rights, that there is not sufficient guarantee that the agreement concluded is fair, that there are inadequate standards of practice, and that there are no certification requirements to assure proper conducting of mediation by qualified practitioners. This criticism is summarized in the general charge that divorce mediation is simply concerned with getting it done, not with getting it right.

In responding to these charges, and having failed to question the assumptions on which they are based, divorce mediation has by and large accepted the legitimacy of the questions raised by the legal profession. As a result, it has attempted to defend itself, not by demonstrating that the criticism was misplaced, but by arguing that it has answered the objections, or, more often, that it is aware of the problem and is attempting to address it. In short, divorce mediation has generally accepted its role as subject to the legal profession's superior position, and as a stepchild to the legal process.

Divorce mediation must take a fresh look at these questions. More importantly, it must determine what assumptions about divorce and the divorcing process are implicit in those questions, and whether they are consistent with its view, if it is ever to define its own role. For it is only by doing this that it will ever be able to take its rightful place as truly an alternative to traditional adversarial proceedings.

DIVORCE AS A LEGAL EVENT

Adversarial divorce proceedings operate on certain assumptions which are generally accepted as accurately reflecting what divorce represents. It is through these assumptions (the categories of our understanding) that society has traditionally viewed divorce. And it is on the basis of these assumptions that we have defined an appropriate or inappropriate procedure in relationship to divorce. These assumptions are as follows:

1. That divorce, like marriage, is a *legal event:* one in which the state has an interest and, therefore, a right to control. Moreover, while a marriage will be freely granted (provided only that certain minimal requirements as to age, consanguinity, etc., are met), divorce is not granted as freely, even if both parties desire it. In other words, the state deems that it has a greater interest in the parties' divorce than it had in their marriage. Even today, when divorce is more freely granted, a couple is still usually required to demonstrate to the court—often by a showing of incompatibility based upon their having lived separate and apart for a certain period of time—that the divorce is legally justified. In short, while a couple has an absolute right to marry provided only that there is no legal impediment to their marriage, once married they may only divorce if they are first given the right to do so by the state.

2. That the marriage's failure, and the parties' consequent divorce, was occasioned by the misconduct of one of the parties. In the past, and since a divorce would not be granted unless one of the parties could prove marital misconduct, a great deal of judicial time and effort was directed to attempting to prove or disprove a party's guilt. While more liberal divorce laws, coupled with the enactment of equitable distribution statutes, have shifted the emphasis from marital misconduct to financial issues, the idea of divorce as being occasioned by one of the parties' misconduct, and therefore involving fault, is still deeply ingrained in our thinking. The result is that despite the enactment of our more modern divorce laws, the view of divorce that sees one of the parties as the victim of the wrong committed by the other continues to reinforce the belief that one of the principal purposes of divorce (and the judicial process) is to *right those wrongs.*

3. That the respective rights and obligations of the parties arising out of their marriage are defined by the law, and the purpose of the judicial process is not only to effectuate the parties' divorce, but to define, as well, these legal rights and obligations.

4. That the parties have adverse, conflicting interests. These conflicting interests not only characterize the dispute between the parties but also explain why it is so difficult for them to resolve it. Thus, from the standpoint of our legal system, it is these conflicting interests that stand between the parties and an agreement.

5. That the interests of each of the parties must be protected, and that it is the law's

function to do this. The law not only defines the parties' respective rights, but also provides the safeguards to protect those rights. The cornerstone of this protection is the judicial process itself and the representation, by separate attorneys, that it provides for each of the parties.

This view of divorce, which is the view of divorce as seen by traditional adversarial divorce proceedings, is characterized by us as the view of divorce as a legal event, and is expressed in the first of the two pictures (Figure 1) in the opening pages of this book. It is this picture that we have traditionally seen (and been trained to see) when we have looked at divorce.

DIVORCE AS A PERSONAL EVENT

Those who view divorce mediation as simply an alternative means of dispute resolution do not question these assumptions. They, too, wish to conclude an agreement between the parties that will protect their conflicting interests and be fair to each of them. They are simply concerned about the effects that doing this in an adversarial setting will have on the parties and their children, and wish to shelter them from these damaging effects. Thus, they question whether it is not possible, by the use of less adversarial proceedings, to accomplish the same ends.

As we noted at the outset, and on the face of it, this is a laudatory objective, and one that reasonable men could hardly fail to support. Nevertheless, it is our contention that to understand divorce mediation properly is to reject this view, and the assumptions upon which it rests, as an accurate representation of what divorce means for families. More to the point, we will argue that, in the final analysis, divorce mediation represents a shift— to use the terminology made popular by Thomas Kuhn,[4] a *paradigm shift*—in the way that we view divorce.

As Kuhn has pointed out, we discard the categories of our understanding not because they are no longer *true*, but because they are no longer *useful*—because their continued use begins to create as many problems as it solves. In such a case, it becomes necessary for us to find (create) new and more useful conceptual models. When we have done this, and although we may continue to look at the same experience, we no longer experience what we look at in the same way. We *look*, but what we now *see* is *different*.[5]

From our point of view, divorce mediation is, and must represent, such a paradigm shift. Traditional divorce proceedings are adversarial because of the way divorce is viewed by our legal system, and because of its assumptions about it. One is a function of the other, and it is not possible to separate them. If that is so, it is not sufficient simply to take these matters out of the courtroom, or even out of the hands of adversarial lawyers, and to put them into a mediator's office. Unless the *assumptions* upon which traditional adversarial divorce proceedings are *based* are questioned, and are replaced by a more appropriate set of assumptions, mediators will still consider it their primary function to assure that the rights of the parties, and their conflicting interests, are protected. And they will still be saddled with the inappropriate, counterproductive procedures which our legal system has imposed upon separating and divorcing couples based upon those assumptions.

Divorce mediation must insist upon a new view of divorce for yet another, and even more important, reason. The conceptual model that we have traditionally used to view divorce and the divorcing process, which sees it as primarily a legal event, is a terribly limited one. Thus, it not only has the effect of *categorizing* what it is that we do see, but, as with all conceptual models, it limits, as well, what we are *able* to see. In the case of divorce, the conceptual outlook of the law prevents us from seeing what is by far its most significant aspect—its human aspect. Nor will we be able to see this, and incorporate it into our understanding and into the practice of divorce mediation, unless there is first such a paradigm shift.

The view that we insist upon as being the only appropriate and useful view of divorce is characterized by us as the view of divorce as a *personal* event. The assumptions implicit in this view are the following:

1. That divorce is first and foremost an important *personal event* in the life of a couple and their family, and only secondarily a legal event. Divorce mediation rejects the idea that simply because the state regulates marriage and divorce that they become legal events, or that they should be viewed as such. On the contrary, it insists that the decision to divorce, like the decision to marry, is primarily a personal decision, one that has at most only certain legal implications.

2. That the divorcing couple, and the members of their immediate family, are in a *state of crisis*. The very structure of their lives has been threatened, and with it the social constructs that have given their lives meaning and their individual efforts validity. It is this being in a state of crisis that is the fundamental reality that should govern how a mediator attempts to help a couple with whom he is working.

3. That a couple must be helped to effectuate a *psychological* as well as a legal divorce. For most people, divorce represents one of the most stressful personal experiences they will ever be required to face. A mediator cannot ignore this, and it is thus not sufficient for him simply to assist them in obtaining a legal divorce. It is far more important that he assist them in putting the feelings of disappointment, of hurt, and of anger behind them if they are ever successfully to go about the important business of their lives.

4. That there are *no legal answers to personal questions*, and separating and divorcing couples should not be encouraged to believe that there are, or that there could be. The law has no special wisdom that will serve to solve the couple's problems, or to end their dispute. It cannot even provide them with an answer, except to impose one on them. Nor will it do to obfuscate this self-evident fact with misleading labels which refer to legal answers as legal rights, and to then send couples off on a fool's errand to find them.

5. That the ultimate determination of what is appropriate or inappropriate in the lives of the parties should be left to them. Outside agencies, whether they be the state, mental health professionals, or mediators, are poor instruments for judging, let alone regulating, the very delicate relationship that exists between family members. It is for this reason that the state declined to intervene during the couple's marriage except when the most minimal standards were breached. What was true in a couple's marriage is no less true in their divorce. A mediator is but an invited guest. More importantly, he was invited, not to judge, but simply to help.

6. In most instances, and particularly where they have children, the couple will be required to have an *ongoing relationship* following their divorce. In other words, while their divorce may end their marriage, it will not end their family. This being the case, it is not only necessary to resolve the dispute between the couple but, if possible, to resolve it in such a way that they will be able to do the necessary business with one another in the future that they must. In fact, divorce mediation was born in large measure of a recogni-

tion of the ongoing relationship between the couple and their children following their divorce, and of the importance in preserving it.

7. That separating and divorcing couples have important *interests in common*, as well as conflicting interests. Divorce mediation rejects as myopic a view of divorce, such as that held by the legal profession, which sees only the couple's conflicting interests, and not the far more important interests that they have in common.

8. That what keeps a couple from concluding an agreement between themselves is not their conflicting interests, as the law would have it, but rather their *feelings* of disappointment, hurt, anger, and fear. If that is the case, the dispute resolution procedure employed should be one that will address and assuage these very destructive feelings, and not, as is the case with traditional adversarial divorce proceedings, only exacerbate them further.

9. That divorce is not the occasion to assign blame or to bestow praise. Divorce mediation dismisses as naive and simplistic the traditional view that sees divorce as occasioned by the mistreatment of one of the parties by the other. On the contrary, viewing a family and its members from a systemic point of view, divorce mediation rejects the idea that individual elements in the very complex picture that makes up the life of a family can be singled out as the "cause" of the couple's separation and divorce. More importantly, it views the attempt to do this as pointless, improperly focusing a couple's attention where it does not belong, causing them to *look back to the past* rather than *forward to the future*.

10. That divorce is not the occasion to *right the wrongs*, whether real or imaginary, that have befallen the parties in their marriage. Not being able to see their own role in the drama that their divorce represents, it is commonplace for each of the parties to view themselves as the victims of what the other party has done to them. Understandably, they tend to view their divorce as the occasion to right these wrongs, and have been encouraged in this belief by the view of divorce held by our legal system. To encourage parties to hold these false expectations is simply to leave them twice disappointed, thereby adding yet a further impediment to the *necessary emotional closure* that their divorce must bring to each of them.

The view of divorce that reflects these assumptions is expressed in the second of the two pictures (Figure 2) in the opening pages of this book. What we see here, first and foremost, is a family. More importantly, it is a family that is in the process of a terribly painful period of transition. What has befallen them is not a legal event, but a personal tragedy, and it is to this that the mediator must respond if he is ever going to be of help to them in any meaningful way.

As one would expect, a set of assumptions such as this, which vary as sharply as they do from the assumptions implicit in the model of divorce accepted by traditional adversarial proceedings, will not only cause us to change the definition of what it means to be helpful in the first place, but, and just as importantly, will also change how we go about being of such help.

A QUESTION OF CHOICE

During the course of his work, a mediator will time and again be forced to ask some very basic questions about what it is that he is attempting to do for the couple and how he can best achieve it. Of necessity, this will in turn require him to define the *basic nature of their problem*, the *procedures* that should be employed in helping them resolve it properly, and the *obligations and limitations* inherent in his role as a third party who has stepped in to assist them. It will not be possible for a mediator to answer these questions without first clarifying and defining his assumptions about what divorce represents in the lives of a family and what his role should be if it is to be consistent with that understanding. In short, it will not be possible for him to answer these questions without first choosing between these two pictures, and between the conflicting assumptions implicit in them.

As we noted earlier, the traditional adversarial view of divorce has repeatedly attacked divorce mediation with the criticism that its only concern is to conclude an agreement between the parties—that its only concern is to get it done, not to get it right. Having failed, until now, to define its own identity, and having summarily accepted the assumptions implicit in the traditional adversarial view of divorce, divorce mediation has been left with no other choice but to accept this charge. Accordingly, it has defended itself by attempting to assure its critics that it is equally concerned with getting it right, and has even gratuitously saddled itself with procedures and standards of practice intended to assure this, despite the fact that they are inconsistent and at variance with its purpose.

The view of divorce mediation that we espouse will not accept this criticism. In fact, and rather than answering this allegation, it issues one of its own, based upon what it insists is its far more accurate view of what divorce represents. That criticism is that traditional adversarial divorce proceedings have been so blindly concerned with getting it right that they have long since ceased to concern themselves with whether they ever get it done. Worse yet, when faced with the human tragedy that divorce represents, the response of traditional adversarial divorce proceedings has been simply to encourage couples to make the most of it and not, as it properly should, to help them make the best of it.

Divorce mediation makes an even more severe criticism of traditional adversarial divorce proceedings, however, and that is that it is a myth, and worse, a deceitful myth, that traditional adversarial proceedings ever get it right in the first place. On the contrary, in failing to understand that to get it right also means to get it done, they always get it wrong. Divorce mediation was not born over a dispute as to whether or not agreements concluded by traditional adversarial divorce proceedings were fair or unfair. Rather, it was born in the belief that even if such agreements represented perfect justice, they were still not worth the time, cost, and emotional injury that were inevitably their price, particularly to the children who were the innocent victims in those proceedings.

If, as we maintain, the second of these two pictures, and the assumptions implicit in it, represent a more accurate view of what divorce represents in the lives of a family, then the supposed benefits that traditional adversarial divorce proceedings bestow upon each of the parties, even if received, simply do not compensate the parties, and particularly their children, for the injury they have suffered in the process. Like the ticket that Ivan Karamazov returns to God, if the price of such perfect justice is this human injury, the answer has to be thank you, but no thank you.

This is the ultimate indictment that divorce mediation lays at the feet of traditional adversarial divorce proceedings. Moreover, it is an indictment upon which it must insist if we are ever to be able to help separating and divorcing couples as we must, and if we are ever going to break the chain that now links one bad marriage to the next.

CHAPTER 2
LEGAL MYTHS

Couples rarely consult with lawyers when they get married. Nor do they have a battery of attorneys on hand during their marriage. Nevertheless, at the first suggestion that their marriage will terminate either in separation or divorce, their immediate thought is to seek legal counsel. Moreover, they are generally encouraged in this by the Greek chorus of well-wishers who immediately surround each of them, offering them advice and moral support, and urging them on. Thus, rather than being frowned upon for going out and employing hired guns to do battle for them, instead of sitting down as responsible adults and resolving these matters on their own, they are each encouraged in the belief that their decision to retain separate lawyers to be their champions is both appropriate and necessary.

Why is this? If a couple did not necessarily have to consult with attorneys when they decided to marry (when the legal rights and obligations that exist between them were created), why is it necessary for them to consult with attorneys when they decide to divorce (when those rights and obligations are being concluded)? Why, if they treated those matters as personal ones during the course of their marriage, and resolved them without resorting to legal assistance, can't they still treat them as personal ones, despite their decision to divorce?

The answer is because we view divorce as a legal problem, requiring a legal solution. It is viewed as a legal problem because it involves the termination of a legal relationship. It is viewed as a legal problem because it is assumed that it is the law that necessarily defines our respective rights and obligations to one another arising out of that relationship. And it is viewed as a legal problem because we believe that it is the law that will protect us and assure that the agreement concluded between us is fair.

Our assumptions notwithstanding, it is not so. In fact, the idea that a couple's separation or divorce leaves them with a legal problem, which requires a legal solution, is nothing but mythology. To make matters worse, and as the experience of all too many separating and divorcing couples has borne out, it is a very dangerous mythology as well.[1]

IS DIVORCE A LEGAL EVENT?

Why is divorce viewed as a legal event? The first reason is that it is regulated by law. However, the fact that the state regulates events in people's lives (such as when and whom they can marry, and the conditions under which they can divorce) does not change those events into legal ones. Rather, they still remain personal events which at best only have legal implications. The state, after all, regulates many kinds of activities, including even when boxing matches can be conducted. But the fact that the state regulates boxing matches does not make a boxing match a legal event, and the two contestants do not hire lawyers to sit and advise them in their respective corners. Nor are lawyers sent into the ring to judge the match. In short, if the presence of lawyers in the divorcing process is to be justified, it will have to be on some other basis.

There is a difference between a divorce and a boxing match, however. With a boxing match, the state only regulates the conditions under which it can be held. It does not suggest the rules that will be employed in deciding the match. With divorce, on the other hand, the state not only determines when and under what conditions a divorce can be had, but also prescribes the rules by which the contest will be determined. That is why lawyers are sent in to judge the dispute between divorcing couples and why they are not sent into the ring to decide disputes between contesting pugilists.

The argument misses the point, however. With boxing, you are obligated to have a boxing match to decide the contest because you cannot decide it in any other way. For two boxers to each contend that they are the best in the world means to have a match to determine who is right, and it will not do for them to say that they have decided the question by flipping a coin, or even by taking a poll of all of the sportswriters in the country. In fact, we would not even let them agree between themselves. Rather, there must be a fight to determine it.

With divorcing couples, on the other hand, there is no law that says that the parties must do battle with one another. On the contrary, it is only necessary for them to have a legal contest if they are unable to resolve the matter by some other means, in fact, by almost any other means. In short, the application of legal rules is not a necessary means to resolve a couple's dispute, and they are only applied when it cannot be resolved in some better way.

If divorce is not a legal event, what is it that has kept us from recognizing this self-evident fact? It is simply our mistaken belief that the divorcing process represents not just the resolution of a dispute between a couple, but, and more importantly, the determination of their respective rights and obligations. Just as two boxers cannot determine who is correct in each saying that he is the stronger and better fighter without having a boxing match, so, too, separating and divorcing couples cannot determine who is correct as to what their respective rights and obligations are without first resorting to the law.

Again, the argument misses the point. With boxers, the question in dispute is which is correct in saying that he is the stronger and better fighter. That is why it is necessary for them to have a boxing match to decide it. With separating and divorcing couples, however, their dispute is not over which of them is correct in their opinion of the law. They are simply in dispute over the questions that have arisen as a result of their decision to divorce—how long the husband will be required to provide support for the wife and whether she will have the right to move with the children to a different state—and are unable to resolve them without resorting to the law. However, the fact that we may have to resort to a set of rules to settle a question if we are unable to resolve it in any other way does not mean that those rules are otherwise important, let alone that we must first determine what they are, and how they would be applied, before we attempt to resolve it on our own. Nor do they gain in importance by referring to them as legal rights rather than simply as legal rules, for it is still the resolution of the dispute, and not the definition of these legal rules, that is ultimately at issue. (It would be as if, had the couple decided to settle their dispute by having a chess match, that we then began to talk of them as having a chess problem and claimed that what was at issue was their respective chess rights.) After all, while there may be some principle involved in a boxing match—that of determining who is right in contending that they are the better fighter—there is no principle involved in a couple's divorce. All that is at issue is the resolution of the issues that have arisen as a natural consequence of their decision to separate and divorce.

Having said this, there are still some misgivings. After all, there is a very basic difference between the rules of chess and legal rules. No one would suggest that the rules of chess are anything but arbitrary. Nor does it make any difference that they are. All that is important is that they are the same for both players—that each start out in the same positions. Legal rules are very different, however. To begin with, they are not arbitrary; they have been carefully thought out. More importantly, their very purpose is to correct the fact that the parties do not start out in the same positions as do two chess players—the husband here is left with a lucrative legal practice while his wife is left with none. That is why it is appropriate to talk of these legal rules—the rules that provide what the wife is entitled to receive to make up for the difference in her position compared to that of her husband's—as being legal rights, whereas it does not make sense to talk of the rules of chess as being chess rights. And that is why it is important for each of the parties to know what their legal rights are, and that their agreement accurately reflect them.

But is that really so? It may well be that a couple's divorce has left them in very disparate positions. It may also be that one of the purposes of their agreement is to correct that disparity. It may even be that legal rules provide guidelines that could help them to do this. But it is only legal mythology that those legal rules must be applied, or that a couple cannot come to an agreement without them.[2] And it is only a worse legal mythology that holds that the application of those rules will necessarily result in a fair and just resolution of the problem, let alone a better one than would be achieved without them.[3]

But of all of the legal mythologies, the most dishonest is the one that maintains that lawyers (or their clients, for that matter) actually employ legal rules for that purpose. Whether, as in chess, the rules are designed to put the players in an equal position at the beginning of the game or, as with the law, to make adjustments for the fact that they do not start out in equal positions, those rules do not, nevertheless, give us any assurance as to how the game will be played or where it will end. Nor do they provide us with any guarantee that the final outcome will not have more to do with the skill—and perhaps the persistence, luck, or even deceit—of the players than it does with the justice of their cause. Most importantly of all, given the fact that these rules are employed in an adversarial setting, the most likely outcome is not that justice will be done, but that one of the parties will come out a winner and the other a loser, as that, after all, is the object of the game.[4]

Legal Rights

If this is so, why have we persisted in placing so much importance in these legal rules? Because we have allowed ourselves to be persuaded that they are not just legal rules or guidelines, but legal rights, and that what is at issue in a couple's separation and divorce is first the determination and then the protection of these legal rights. Again, this is simply mythology, a mythology that stems from a failure to distinguish between two different kinds of laws that the state enacts.

The first category of laws is usually constitutional in nature and guarantees, for example, our right to vote, to speak, and to practice the religion of our choice. These laws and constitutional safeguards can appropriately be labeled legal rights, as they reflect values that are so deeply felt that we have attempted to safeguard them from attack based upon changing attitudes or the vagaries of time.

The second category comprises the numerous laws enacted to regulate society's conduct or simply to resolve disputes between its members. While these laws may embody society's conception of what is fair and appropriate at any given time, and while that is very important, and at times critical, in the resolution of their disputes, that is *all* that they do. Even so, they do this only in very *general* terms. As a result, and especially when they are applied to regulate our personal affairs, all too often they are not only very difficult to apply, but also appear to be very arbitrary in character, having little to do with the realities of our individual lives. To speak of them as representing legal *rights*, therefore, rather than simply as legal *rules*, is to endow them with a significance that they do not have and do not deserve.

The point is that the rules that society adopts in the form of the laws it enacts to resolve disputes between people are simply that, and no more. They are applied by society, not because they do justice, but because they are necessary to end the dispute that the parties were unable to end themselves. Since that is the case, they only become important when the dispute cannot be resolved by some other means. And any *other* means that the couple can agree upon will do—including even flipping a coin. (If the dispute was over who should receive the newer of two television sets, the most efficient and appropriate procedure might be to flip a coin. In fact, if they could agree on the division of the two television sets, it would not even be necessary to flip a coin at all.) Again, a dispute resolution procedure (flipping a coin) is not important in its own right. It is only important when people have a dispute and it is not possible for them to resolve it short of the application of that procedure.

Having said this, there will again be some misgiving. It will be argued, as we have previously noted, that the purpose of legal rules is not simply to resolve the dispute, but to resolve it in a way that will do justice to both parties. In fact, it is hard to read the history of the equitable distribution statutes enacted by the various states as being anything other than an attempt to do just this. Putting aside, for the moment, the question of whether or not legal rules are actually employed by attorneys in an adversarial setting to achieve any such justice, that does not alter the fact that it was the purpose of these statutes to do justice between separating and divorcing couples. That is why it is important that they be applied in the resolution of their dispute.

While this argument may seem compelling at first blush, it is not. The discussions between any two disputants, including separating and divorcing husbands and wives, take place, as one commentator has noted, *in the shadow of the law.* Since, if they are unable to resolve their dispute on their own, it will be resolved by the application of the law, what a court will or will not do very much affects the *climate* in which those discussions take place. Thus, if a court has no power to award a wife any portion of a business acquired by her husband during their marriage, he does not *expect* to have to share any portion of it with her. Similarly, if a court will award her support for the rest of her life, she does not *expect* to receive less.

With the tremendous increase in the rate of divorce in this country beginning in the early 1960s, more and more attention began to be focused on the *climate* created by our existing divorce laws for the resolution of disputes between separating and divorcing couples. Not only was it felt that the application of those laws failed to provide justice between the parties but, and more importantly, that they almost guaranteed that the result would be *un*fair and *un*just—that the law *stood between* a couple and a fair resolution of their dispute. What had to be done, therefore, was to change the law and, in the process, to change the climate that would influence the discussions that took place between them.

To be sure, the various legislatures, in enacting those statutes, and in changing the law that would be applied by courts in the resolution of matrimonial disputes, could not help but make judgments, if only in general terms, as to what an appropriate or inappropriate resolution should be. But the legislature did not pretend that the application of those principles would necessarily guarantee that justice would be done in a particular case, let alone that the result achieved by their application would be more appropriate than could be reached by the couple on their own.

For were it otherwise, those statutes would not have reserved to the couple the right to decide those issues on whatever basis they might choose, even in disregard of those principles.[5] Thus, and having created a more appropriate climate in which discussion could take place, those rules of law became important principally either to frame those discussions or when the parties were unable to agree on better ones.[6]

If this is so, why do we persist in referring to these legal rules as legal rights? Simply to hide this fact from ourselves. After all, people do not want their disagreements decided in an arbitrary manner. That is why they do not resolve them by flipping a coin or by playing a game of chess. They want the resolution of their disputes to be *fair*, and to represent what is just. Thus, if we are going to get people to resolve their differences by the application of legal rules—by agreeing to play a game of legal chess—when they come to find out how the game is played, it is far better for us to talk about their legal rights rather than simply about the rules of legal chess.

We also persist in this because of our failure to make yet a second distinction in our use of the word *rights*. Without question, people have an absolute right to refuse to settle a dispute other than on their own terms, and, if that is not possible, to insist instead that it be resolved by the application of legal rules and principles. It may be foolish for them to do this; at times it may even be irresponsible. Nevertheless, it is their absolute right.[7] However, the fact that they have the right to insist that their dispute be resolved by the application of legal rules does not convert those rules into legal rights.

For example, a wife may decide to resort to a court of law because she believes that she will be given maintenance for a longer period of time by a judge than she has been offered by her husband (just as he may resort to a court of law because he believes that he will be required to give it for a shorter period than she has asked); and, if the court is willing to give her what she is asking for, she will certainly view this as her right to receive it. But if the legislature were to enact a new law completely eliminating alimony or maintenance, or giving the court authority to award it to her only for a limited period of time and until she had become self-supporting, that would not represent any violation of her rights, as would be the case were the legislature to attempt to abridge her right of free speech.[8]

Again, the fact that the court will give the wife support for 10 years means that she has the absolute right to reject her husband's proposal and go to court and ask for support for 10 years, but it does not follow from this that one of her legal rights is to receive support for 10 years. Thus, even if a court were to award her support for this length of time, that would not mean that they could not later reduce both the amount and duration of that award, based on a change in either her or her husband's circumstances.[9] Nor would it represent any violation of her legal rights if they did.

Finally, the mythology also stems from our failure to distinguish between the rules that the court applies (what we call our rights) and the procedures that we must employ in order to get them to apply them. If the wife here had received notification that she had won the lottery, it would make sense to say that she had a right to the prize, as all that she would have to do to receive it would be to present her winning ticket. Does it make any sense, however, to say that her right to have her dispute resolved by the application of those legal rules which she believes will be of benefit to her is the same kind of right? For if she has the right to resort to a court of law for that purpose, her husband also has the right to fight her every step of the way. It may be ultimately pointless for him to do so. It may even be irresponsible on his part. Nevertheless, it is his absolute right, and in the adversarial setting in which our laws are applied, it is simply not possible to ignore this.

In short, it makes no sense to talk of abstract legal rights and to ignore the procedures that will have to be employed in order to obtain them when, in the adversarial world in which these rules are applied, they go hand in hand. Thus, and the mythology aside, what we are ultimately left with are simply two different procedures that a couple can employ in order to resolve their differences.

There is yet a further implication. If the application of legal rules simply represents the procedure the law provides when separating and divorcing couples cannot otherwise resolve their disputes, and if these rules are not legal rights embodying any necessary wisdom or guaranteeing any necessary justice, it is not necessary that the agreement to which the parties come *conform* to those legal rules. In fact, with but one important exception, it is not even necessary that they know these legal rules at all before they resolve their dispute.[10] (It would be as if, having agreed upon the division of the two television sets, they then flipped the coin anyway to make sure that they had divided them correctly.) Our problem, however, is that we have so confused the dispute between a separating and divorcing couple with the dispute resolution *procedure* traditionally invoked to resolve it, that we can no longer see the one without the other. In fact, we continue to do this even when we know better.

A simple example will demonstrate this. Let us suppose that a separating and divorcing couple has decided that the wife will have custody of their two children and that she will continue to live with them in their home. They have even agreed that the home will not be sold until the youngest child graduates from high school. Can one imagine the husband's attorney objecting to the agreement which the husband has concluded with his wife concerning the custody of their children, and the fact that they will continue to live in their home until they graduate from high school, on the grounds that there were important legal rules and principles (legal rights of the husband's) which he did not consider before he concluded that agreement with his wife?

The question is, or at least should be, rhetorical. Again, the fact that we may ultimately be required to resort to the law and to legal rules to resolve our personal disputes does not *change* them into legal ones. They remain personal problems that are still best resolved not by the application of arbitrary legal rules having little to do with our individual lives, but by the far more relevant personal considerations that we have always used in deciding them.

While the advocates of divorce mediation have so far failed to fully appreciate the implications of this fact, its critics, particularly the organized matrimonial bar, have not. On the contrary, they understand them all too well. After all, if disputes between husbands and wives can be resolved without the application of legal rules and principles, then they can be resolved without lawyers. [11]

Thus if lawyers are going to be successful in maintaining their monopoly over the divorcing process, they can only do so by insisting that it is a legal process involving the adjudication of a couple's legal rights, since it is only they who can advise the parties as to what those legal rights are. [12] If the legal mythology is pierced, however, then lawyers can claim no special province, since there is nothing in either their training or understanding that gives them any superior position here, and certainly no position superior to the understanding of the parties themselves.

Is there ever a situation where these legal rules would become critical? The answer is yes. Suppose, for example, that a husband advises his attorney that his wife has been a constant thorn in his side throughout his marriage and that he does not want to give her a penny more than he absolutely has to—a penny more, in other words, than the law allows. Suppose, in other words, that the husband here is more intent on *getting even* than in getting *done,* and that he is desirous of employing any weapon that he can. If that is the case, being advised of these legal rules and principles, and how he can use them to leave her with as little as he can, would indeed be extremely helpful to him.

There are important implications in this for mediation. As we know, couples who are in the process of separating and divorcing generally have little understanding of why it is and how it is that they have gotten to this point in their lives. On the contrary, they each tend to idealize themselves as being the innocent victim of what the other has done to them. Not uncommonly, they want the other person to pay for the crimes that they believe he or she has committed and look to their separation agreement as the vehicle to accomplish this. However, it is not the *purpose* of a separation agreement to correct the wrongs, whether real or imagined, that couples feel they have suffered in their marriages. Nor should they be encouraged to look to it for that purpose. Rather, its purpose is to help them to *put the past behind them* and to get on with the important business of their lives. Characterizing the dispute resolution rules that the law applies as being legal rights and obligations, as we have been taught to do, only tends to reinforce this unfortunate tendency to seek redress. Worse yet, it tends to encourage unrealistic levels of expectation that are then only followed by equivalent levels of disappointment. This, unfortunately, has been part of the legacy that our legal system has left separating and divorcing couples.

LEGAL ANSWERS

If divorce is *not* basically a legal event, and if the function of legal rules and principles is simply to help a couple resolve a dispute they cannot otherwise resolve—and not to vouchsafe any legal rights they have, or to guarantee any necessary justice—then we ask again, why is it necessary, or even necessarily appropriate, that we concern ourselves with these rules? If the law is going to justify its application, it must do so on some other basis. The only basis left is that the application of these rules and principles represents an effective way of deciding disputes between separating and divorcing couples. Unfortunately, the law fails this test, too.

Whatever else may be said about the use of a coin to resolve a dispute, no one can deny that it is both efficient and definitive. The same, unfortunately, cannot be said for the law. If it is mythology for couples to believe that their separation and divorce leaves them with certain legal problems, it is even worse mythology for them to believe that those legal problems have clear legal answers, or that those answers can be easily obtained.

Let us illustrate this with an analogy drawn from mathematics. To say that we have a mathematical problem is to say that if any number of mathematicians took the same problem and applied to it the same rules of mathematics, that they would not only be able to arrive at an answer but, and more importantly, that they would all arrive at the same answer. What if they were unable to come to a definite answer but, instead, only a range of possible answers? Or, even worse, suppose that they were able to come to a definite answer but that they each came to a different one? While we might still be grudgingly willing to acknowledge that the problem was a mathematical one, we would be hard pressed to understand what it meant to say that it *had* a mathematical answer—to say that the application of mathematical rules and principles would *solve the problem*.

This, of course, is exactly the state of the law. Not only are legal rules and principles unable, in most instances, to provide separating and divorcing couples with answers that will settle their disputes but, although it is not generally appreciated, the way lawyers apply those legal rules and principles only adds further to their dispute. In fact, it would not be too much to suggest that the way their lawyers apply those rules actually *creates* the dispute.

What happens when a husband and wife each consult with attorneys in a traditional adversarial setting? Generally, the question that the wife asks her attorney is "What are my legal rights?" That is not what her lawyer hears her ask, however. He does not consider that she has come to him out of intellectual curiosity, or that she is there to pose him academic questions. On the contrary, she has come to him to represent her and to be her advocate. What he hears her ask, therefore, is "How much can I get?" In other words, "By applying those legal rules to my best advantage, how much will I receive?" Similarly, when the husband consults with his attorney and asks, "What are my legal obligations?" what his attorney hears him ask is "How little will I have to give?" Needless to say, the parties each come away with very different answers.

The application of these legal rules and principles has thus *not* provided the couple with an answer to their problems. In fact, if one wished to parody the legal profession, one could suggest that the couple only has a problem in the first place because their attorneys have given them different answers to the same question. To make matters worse, by framing those answers in terms of rights and obligations, they have then sprinkled legal holy water on them. In doing this, however, they have not thereby aided in the resolution of the problem. On the contrary, they have only made its resolution all the more difficult, for while their reference to legal rights and obligations may have added to the sanctity of their answers, it has also had the effect of causing the parties to take *fixed positions* from which it is then difficult for them to budge. After all, it is a lot more difficult to compromise one's legal *rights* than it is one's legal *answers*.

Let us illustrate this. Suppose, for example, that the attorney with whom the wife has consulted has advised her that in his opinion she should receive support for herself for seven or eight years and that he is going to start out the negotiations by asking that she receive support for 10 years. Fearful as to how she is going to provide for herself following her divorce, the wife is very anxious to get support for as long as she can—certainly for at least seven or eight years and perhaps even longer. Moreover, fueled by her anger toward her husband, she may even believe that he owes that to her. As a result, she comes away from the meeting with her attorney confirmed in the belief that even if she will not receive support for 10 years, as she would like, it is at least her absolute right to receive it for seven or eight.

The husband, of course, has also consulted with an attorney. However, he has been given a very different answer. In fact, he has been told that he is probably not obligated to provide her with support for more than four or five years. To make matters worse, and since we are talking abut his legal obligations, he has been left with the impression that he would be a fool to give her more. To start out the negotiations, his attorney advises him that he is going to offer her support for two or three years.

What happens when, after meeting with her husband's lawyer, the wife's attorney informs her that he is only prepared to provide her with support for two or three years? Does the wife conclude that her husband's position is based on the fact that he has been given a different answer to the same question? Does she even conclude that it simply represents a bargaining position which he has taken as part of the negotiations, similar to her own? Unfortunately, she does not. Rather, her fear in being on her own and her comparison of her own position with his, fueled by her attorney's encouragement that she is *legally entitled* to receive support for at least seven or eight years, causes her to view the offer made by her husband with anger and perhaps even outrage.

Sprinkling legal holy water on the answers her attorney has given to her has thus not helped the situation, and it certainly has not resulted in a resolution of the problem. Rather, all that her attorney has accomplished is to cause her to look distrustfully toward her husband—to view him as her adversary—and to further fan some of the very destructive feelings she has brought to the discussions, and that make a resolution of their differences so difficult. And, of course, her husband's attorney has only added further to the problem by doing the same thing.

CONFLICTING INTERESTS

If the problem is that we have tended to *sanctify* legal rules, and then to apply them in a manner that makes it *more* difficult, rather than less, to resolve the couple's differences, perhaps the answer is not simply to ignore legal rules, but to look to them, and to apply them, differently. After all, those who turned to divorce mediation did not do so due to any complaint over legal rules, or even any dispute as to their importance. Their objection was to the fact that those rules were being applied in an adversarial setting, and it was that that they wanted to change.

To be sure, our laws may not represent perfect justice or necessarily be relevant to the circumstances of our individual lives. Nevertheless, they do represent societal norms which can *aid* a couple in the resolution of the issues with which they are faced. If that is so, and particularly if we look to those rules and principles simply for *guidance* rather than for precise answers, would it not be appropriate for the couple to refer to them? Not, of course, by resorting to separate lawyers who will simply give them different answers. And not by resorting to a court of law—getting an answer, to be sure, but one that is hardly worth the price; rather, by having the parties sit down with *one* lawyer who will tell them what the law is, answer their questions, and send them on their way.[13]

Unfortunately, this simple solution sends shudders down the spines of adversarial lawyers as it calls into question the mythology that justifies adversarial proceedings.[14] But why is it that one attorney cannot do this? The explanation generally given by lawyers for their inability to do this is very curious. It is because the parties have conflicting interests.[15] In actual fact, this explanation is simply verbal sleight of hand designed to hide the fact that the lawyer representing the husband and the lawyer representing the wife do not apply the same rules in the same way—that they look at the problem with two very different sets of glasses. It is this double standard that lawyers employ, and not any conflicting interests the parties have, that makes it impossible for one attorney to answer the husband's and the wife's question. The attorney cannot answer the question simply because he does not know which set of glasses to put on.

Nothing could be stranger than the legal system's view of conflicting interests save perhaps the unexamined assumption that the presence of conflicting interests dictates that divorcing couples must have separate attorneys to represent them. In fact, the idea that conflicting interests demand that the parties each have separate lawyers stems more from *habit* than it does from any necessary logic. (If we think about it, the presence of those conflicting interests, which can do so much damage if left unbridled, just as logically calls for the presence of but one attorney to guarantee that they are properly kept in check.) More to the point, we have persisted in this habit to such a point that we have long since ceased questioning the logic that supposedly supports it. The result is that separating and divorcing couples continue to be roasted on the legal system's sacred skewer of conflicting interests, which insists that they are adversaries and thereby makes adversaries of them in the process.

We must therefore ask again, why is it not possible for a couple to sit down with one lawyer who will give them answers to their questions? A lawyer, after all, is not incompetent to express legal opinions; on the contrary, that is his proper function. Nor does he become incompetent because the question is posed to him by two people rather than one. Rather, our legal system only deems him to be incompetent for that purpose when those two people would like to hear *different answers to the question*.

However, a lawyer's incompetence to express a legal opinion cannot be based on what each of two parties would like to hear. It is only based on the fact that our legal system is organized as an adversarial struggle in which the law is used by each of the contestants to gain a personal advantage. However, that does not mean that the law must be so employed, or that a lawyer should be foreclosed from providing legal answers to people who wish to use them, not as legal weapons, but as a means of resolving a dispute between themselves. (This would be akin to prohibiting them from choosing a single business appraiser to value the husband's business, and insist instead that they must each choose separate appraisers, one of whom will evaluate the husband's business as high as he can, for the wife's benefit, and the other of whom will evaluate it as low as he can, for the husband's benefit.) Nor will it do to invoke the concept of conflicting interests as a smokescreen to hide this obvious fact, or worse, to use it as an excuse to insist that it is *improper* to employ legal opinions other than as adversarial weapons. For this is no less absurd than it would be to suggest that while it is appropriate to use hard metal to make a sword, it is not appropriate to use it to make a plowshare.

There is nothing particularly unique in the idea of conflicting interests. After all, all of us have them. What is unique is simply the fact that our legal system has *elevated* those conflicting interests to a level of sanctity, when common sense and experience tell us just the opposite. Society does not function by each of us insisting upon the supremacy of our individual, conflicting interests. Rather, it functions, if it functions at all, in our willingness to subordinate those *conflicting* interests to the far more important interests that we have *in common*.

It is only our legal system that elevates those conflicting interests to an absolute, and insists that, regardless of the damage done to the parties and their children, that they do battle with separate lawyers to protect those interests. What makes this charade all the more offensive is its dishonesty, for the truth of the matter is that it is not *possible*, as the law pretends, to protect the conflicting interests of both of the parties, for the very reason that they are in conflict. All that can be done is to compromise them.

There is an even more important point that must be made. It does not follow, as night follows day, that because parties to a dispute have conflicting interests that they must resolve their dispute on the *basis* of those conflicting interests, let alone that they should be encouraged to do so. On the contrary, they have every right to ignore their conflicting interest and to decide their dispute on the basis of the far more important interests that they have in common.

In fact, in most instances sanity dictates that they do nothing but that. If two countries were to sit down at a conference table to negotiate a peace treaty on the basis of their conflicting interests alone, their talks could lead to nothing but war. If their talks are ever going to lead to peace, they will have to be predicated instead on the far more important interests they have in common, and on their willingness to abandon the limited pursuit of those conflicting interests.

In the real world, as opposed to the legal world, we do not choose between our conflicting interests and the interests we have in common. Rather, in each instance we perform a delicate, subtle operation of balancing the two to achieve what is in our *overall* best interests. Unfortunately, the myopic vision of the law, which cannot see beyond the termination of a couple's marriage, combined with the law's insistence that what is at issue are their respective legal rights, triggers a no-holds-barred attitude. From that point forward anything and everything is justified in the name of vouchsafing their conflicting interests, regardless of the cost and injury to them.

The legal profession's strange attitude toward the parties' conflicting interests is perhaps best mirrored in the difficulty that it has had to date in accommodating itself to divorce mediation, and the questions it has asked itself in the process. Since the only reality the law recognizes *is* the parties' conflicting interests, and since one lawyer cannot represent parties whose interests are in conflict, the legal profession cannot decide who the lawyer is supposed to represent in mediation, whether both parties or neither of them, and countless hours have been spent in this pointless debate.

In either event, the law is left with the dilemma of determining whether or not it is ethical for one attorney to assist a separating and divorcing couple who, by definition, have conflicting interests. Worse yet, it endlessly preoccupies itself with this question when it has never once stopped to ask a far more important question, namely, whether or not it is ethical for two lawyers to take members of a family who have had a long history together, who are at a point of great stress in their lives, and who must, despite their separation and divorce, maintain a relationship with one another, and, simply in the name of those narrow interests that divide them, make adversaries of them. For in truth, there is something rather unsettling about the spectacle of bar associations around the country, and the legal community generally, worrying about the possible adverse effects of mediation upon separating and divorcing couples when, despite all of the evidence before them, they have never once expressed any concern about the real damage that the adversarial system, in the name of protecting those limited conflicting interests, has done to the families it touches.

CHAPTER 3

Equitable Distribution and Divorce Mediation

Until recently, and in particular until the tremendous increase in the rate of divorce that occurred in this country starting in the early 1960s, the overwhelming majority of marriages ended in death, not in divorce.[1] Thus, if the law wished to assure that a fair allocation of the property that had been acquired in the marriage was made to each of the parties upon the termination of their marriage, what was necessary was to assure that our *estate* laws were equitable, not our divorce laws. If a significant number of marriages did not survive to the death of one of the parties, however, this was no longer sufficient, and it now became necessary to assure that our divorce laws were equitable as well.

The Problem

What was it that rendered our divorce laws so inequitable? Principally the fact that whereas, upon the death of a husband, the court had the right to assign his wife (widow) a share of his estate (his separate property), the court did not usually have that same right upon their divorce. On the contrary, and with the exception of community property states, the property that was held in the husband's name generally constituted his sole property, and his wife had no direct claim upon it. As a result, the court was without authority to divide it between them or to assign any portion of it to her. What made this particularly inequitable, especially in upper middle-class families, was the traditional division of labor between husbands and wives. These were not only the families that were most likely to experience an accumulation of capital as time went by, beyond simply the equity in their home, which was generally in the wife's name as well as in the husband's. They were also the families in which the traditional division of labor, with the wife specializing in child rearing and other domestic activities and the husband specializing in the production of income, was most prevalent. Given this division of labor, however, the husband generally controlled the money that came into the family. As a result, the capital accumulation tended to remain in his name alone, particularly where that capital accumulation was represented by the business that he owned or by investments that he had made.

A couple's divorce thus left the parties in very disparate positions economically, for, and again putting the value of their home aside, the husband was not only left with the superior earning capacity, but with most of the accumulated wealth as well. The remedy for this inequity mirrored the traditional view of men and women, which saw men as independent and self-sufficient, and women as dependent and not able to provide properly for themselves. And that remedy was to require the husband to continue to use his income and capital to support his wife following their divorce for the balance of her life.

Unfortunately, and again particularly in upper middle-class families, this still left the husband with far more of the income and, again putting the equity in their home aside, almost all of the capital. To make matters worse, the previous household responsibilities of the wife often continued following the couple's divorce, at least if there were minor children, and thus left the wife incapable of making any real financial contribution that would alter this inequity. Even if she were not so disabled, however, the fact that she had devoted her energy and skill to making a home rather than making a living, left her at a severe disadvantage relative to her husband in that respect.[2]

Putting aside for the moment the question of just how equitable this traditional solution to the problem was, and the implications that solution had for each of the parties—the wife being left dependent upon her ex-husband and the faithfulness of his payments for the rest of her life, and her husband being required to support his former wife for the remainder of his own—the solution at least tended to recognize the wife's future entitlement, in the form of permanent alimony, for her past contributions to the marriage, just as it recognized the husband's, in the form of his retention of his capital, for his.[3]

Unfortunately, however, the rapid increase in the rate of divorce brought with it a new consideration that rendered this traditional solution even more inequitable than it had been originally. In fact, and although it is rarely mentioned as such, it was this factor more than any other that mandated a change in our divorce laws.

The rough kind of justice that our older divorce laws effectuated may have been sufficient when there were few divorces, and even fewer remarriages. But it ceased being even rough justice when the divorce rate increased, for that increase also brought with it an increase in remarriage, and at the present time about half of all women who divorce while still relatively young remarry within three years.[4] More significantly for our purposes, the median duration of their second marriages is only 5.3 years.[5]

To understand the problem posed by the phenomenon of remarriage, and why that phenomenon rendered our former divorce laws unjust, it is again perhaps instructive to compare the effects of a wife's remarriage when her previous marriage was ended by divorce rather than by death. When a wife's marriage was ended by her husband's death, she normally received all of the property that she and her husband had owned together in which she had a survivorship interest, and this generally included their home. She also commonly received the proceeds of whatever policies of life insurance he had maintained on his life. Finally, if he had not left her the bulk of his remaining estate (his separate property), which was usually the case, the law provided that she was at least entitled to receive a certain portion of it. More significantly for our purposes, what she received was hers to keep forever, which meant that her right to it was not affected by her later remarriage.

If a wife's marriage ended in divorce, however, the situation was quite different. Although the wife was granted permanent alimony in lieu of an interest in her husband's estate (separate property), that right was a limited one; and it generally ended upon her remarriage, as did her interest in his life insurance, had he been required to maintain any for her benefit.[6] Thus, while her husband's right to retain the benefits, in the form of his increased income and his accumulated capital, that were the by-products of his efforts during the lifetime of their marriage was not affected by his future remarriage, his *wife's* right to retain her interest in those benefits, in the form of alimony, *was.*

For reasons not germane to our purposes, and not particularly flattering to the view traditionally held of women in any event, the wife's right to retain her interest in those benefits was also affected, as her husband's was not, by her future conduct, as well as by the fact of her remarriage, as many states had statutes that deprived the wife of her right to alimony if she was found to be living with another man, particularly on a long-term basis.[7]

Again, the irony here was in the fact that a wife's very divorce, which created her problem in the first place, only added to that problem, since the circumstances of unmarried couples living together has become far more prevalent in recent years, at least in part as a result of the increase in the rate of divorce.[8] In short, the solution which had been traditionally employed to compensate wives for their contribution to their marriage, and for the inequities in their divorce, only tended to further increase those inequities as the rate of divorce and remarriage climbed.

One final factor contributed to this inequity. As we noted, the wife's remarriage, and sometimes even relationships short of her remarriage, generally terminated her husband's obligation for her support. At that time, the rationale that predicated a husband's obligation to support his wife upon her past contributions to the marriage, and on the disparity in their respective economic circumstances at the time of their divorce, was pushed aside in favor of the theory that held that a husband should not be obligated to support a wife whose services he no longer enjoyed and that the burden of her support should be upon the shoulders of the man who was presently receiving the benefit of those services.

Whatever may have been the logic of this argument—and it was based, not on any logic, but on a traditional, and again rather unflattering, view of women—it at least had the benefit of assuring that there was a male figure upon whom the wife could rely for her support. The problem, however, is that the wave of change that brought about divorce in the first place carried second marriages in its wake as well.

In fact, the risk of divorce for the wife in her second marriage was as great or even greater than it had been in her first.[9] And yet, even though her first husband was still left far better off economically than was she, and even though the logic that had obligated him to support her for the rest of her life should she require it, based upon her past contributions to their marriage, still applied with equal force, her second divorce did not revive his obligation. On the contrary, regardless of how long her first marriage had lasted, or how short the duration of her second one, once her first husband was relieved of his obligation to support her, he was relieved of it forever.[10]

But wasn't the wife now entitled to support from her second husband, based upon that same logic? Perhaps, but usually not to the same extent, for the change in attitude that predicated a wife's right to support more on her contribution to the marriage than upon the fact of her dependency worked to her disadvantage. To begin with, particularly with older women, it was less likely that there were children of that second marriage. Secondly, the life expectancy of that second marriage was generally shorter than the first.[11] Thirdly, there was also the greater probability that the wife was working at the time of her second divorce.[12] Finally, she being older,[13] it was far more likely that her second husband was financially established at the time of their marriage, which made it more difficult for her to show any contribution toward his improved economic position, even indirectly; and all of these factors combined to impose a lesser obligation upon the wife's second husband than had been imposed upon her first.

Furthermore, and perhaps even more importantly, the wave of change in the rate of divorce, and in our attitudes about divorce generally, affected the traditional attitudes toward second marriages before it affected legislative change concerning first marriages; and this too was to women's disadvantage. Thus, a court faced with a wife's second divorce, even if it was predicated upon her husband's so-called fault, had to feel less protective toward her than it had the first time around. After all, multiple divorces are simply not consistent with the stereotyped view of women as innocent, helpless dependents. Nor is it easy to be as sympathetic to someone who has gotten themselves in trouble, so to speak, a second time, as it was the first. All of these factors tended to contribute to a court's having to question whether or not her second husband's obligation was not a far more limited one.

The Solution

How has the law dealt with the problem of divorce in modern marriage? It has done this by resorting to principles of partnership law. Starting out from the premise that marriage was now to be considered a total partnership, an economic as well as an emotional one, the legislature then invested the court with the power to distribute the partnership assets of the marriage between the husband and the wife at the time of the dissolution of their partnership—in other words, at the time of their divorce.

What were those partnership assets? To answer this question the legislature created a legal fiction. It was called marital property, and was generally defined to be all property that was acquired during the marriage as a result of the effort of either or both of the parties, whether as a wage earner, homemaker, parent, or companion.[14] Since marital property was only that property that had been acquired through marital effort, it did not generally include property that either of the parties had acquired prior to their marriage and owned at the time of their marriage. Similarly, it also did not generally include property, even if it was acquired during the marriage, if that property was the result of the effort of someone other than the husband or the wife, as would be the case, for example, of a gift or inheritance that either of the parties received during the marriage from, for example, his or her parents. Instead, those assets were considered to be the separate property of the party who had owned it at the time of the marriage or who had acquired it through gift or inheritance during the marriage.

The distinction between marital and separate property was in most instances critical. The reason for this was that while the court had the power to distribute marital property (usually equitably) between the parties at the time of their divorce, it had no power to touch the property that either or both of the parties owned separately. Those were not partnership assets. Accordingly, upon the dissolution of the partnership, they were generally not part of the partnership accounting.[15]

Before examining how these legal fictions have been applied to deal with the problem of divorce in modern marriage, there is a second consideration reflected in these same statutes that must also be mentioned. For while the equitable distribution statutes enacted by the various states may have opened with the declaration that marriage was now to be considered a total partnership, those same statutes also strongly reflect the awareness that that partnership is, nevertheless, a *limited* one.

Thus, and while the reality of marital dissolution may justify women in expecting more out of their divorce, it also warns them to expect less out of their *marriage*. In short—and this is particularly true of those marriages that were contracted from the late 1960s on—women who enter into marriage today are charged with the responsibility of knowing that there is almost a 50% possibility that their marriage may end in divorce. Further, it charges them with the responsibility of knowing that their divorce may well leave them in a position of financial inequality in relationship to their husbands if they allow themselves to be dependent upon their husbands for their support. Most important- ly, it tells them that they cannot look to the courts to correct that inequity. On the contrary, they are increasingly going to have to look to themselves, and to the income that they can earn from their labors outside of the home, for that purpose. Nor, it tells them, will it do to argue whether this is fair or unfair. Rather, it is a factor that they must consider before undertaking marriage and even during their marriage.

The result has been that a condition that at first permitted women the luxury of terminating marriages they did not like—in 1982 one out of two married women were working or looking for work as compared to only one out of seven in 1940[16]—became a necessity when there was a divorce, and this regardless of whose decision that divorce may have been. This second consideration is reflected in the new concept of temporary or rehabilitative maintenance which appears, either expressly or implicitly, in virtually all of the new equitable distribution statutes.[17]

The Application of Equitable Distribution

As we have noted previously, the law's solution to the problem has been to create certain legal fictions drawn from partnership law. As a result, the court's concern has principally been with two questions: (1) what constitutes property that is subject to dis- tribution, and (2) what constitutes an equitable division of that property between the parties.

It is not our purpose here to provide a review of the answers that have been given under the equitable distribution statutes enacted by the various states. Rather, it is to raise a question, namely, what are the implications of those answers on the practice of divorce mediation?[18] More specifically, it is hoped to free divorce mediators from the mistaken belief that an appropriate resolution can be achieved only by a slavish duplication of what courts and lawyers do in applying equitable distribution statutes. It is also the hope that it will help them to recognize that the judicial resolution of these matters must, at least in part, be understood in terms of the limitations that act upon all judicial interventions and all judicial solutions, rather than, as is all too often the case, viewed as the road that must necessarily be taken to reach the correct result, let alone some perfect justice between the parties. Finally, it is to underscore the fact that whereas these legal fictions may have been created simply to solve a problem, once born, they have taken on a life of their own that has created as many problems as they have solved.

To illustrate this, we will use as an example the decision in *O'Brien v. O'Brien* handed down by the highest court of the State of New York in 1986.[19] The couple was married in April 1971. At the time of their marriage both were employed as teachers at a private school. The husband had completed only three and one-half years of college, but shortly after the couple's marriage returned to school at night to earn his bachelor's degree and to complete sufficient premedical courses to enter medical school. In September 1973, the parties moved to Mexico where he became a full-time medical student. While he pursued his studies, his wife held several teaching positions and contributed her earnings toward their living expenses.

The couple returned to New York in December 1976 so that the husband could complete the last two semesters of medical school and his internship training. Following their return, the wife resumed her former teaching position. In October 1980 the husband was granted a license to practice medicine in the State of New York. Two months later, he commenced an action against the wife for a divorce. At the time of the trial, he was a resident in general surgery. While both parties had contributed toward their living and educational expenses, and had received additional help from both their families, apart from a $10,000 student loan which the husband had obtained, the wife had contributed 76% of their income. The wife's expert witness testified that the present value of her contribution toward her husband's medical education was $103,390.

The case presented an almost classic example of the problem of modern divorce. Nearly all of the parties' nine-year marriage had been devoted to improving the career potential of the *husband*, and his wife had played a major role in that project. She had worked throughout the marriage, had contributed all of her earnings to their joint efforts, and had even sacrificed her own educational and career opportunities in the process by deferring obtaining permanent certification as a teacher. Now, however, by reason of their divorce, she was to be deprived of the benefits of her efforts in the form of sharing with her husband his increased future earning capacity.

The situation cried out for relief.[20] Unfortunately, the court's hands were almost completely tied. New York, like most other jurisdictions, had already determined that a medical practice acquired during a couple's marriage was marital property, the value of which could be distributed upon a couple's divorce. Unfortunately, however, Dr. O'Brien had no medical practice. On the contrary, at the time of the commencement of the action, he had just obtained his license to practice medicine and was but a resident in surgery.[21] In other circumstances, the court could have solved the problem by giving Mrs. O'Brien all, or substantially all, of the other marital property. Unfortunately, there was no other marital property here of any real value. Nor could the court solve the problem by requiring Dr. O'Brien to support his wife. In keeping with the more modern view, New York law provided that support was only to be awarded where there was need. Here, however, Mrs. O'Brien had been self-supporting throughout the marriage, and continued to be. There was thus no need or, therefore, occasion for an award of re-habilitative maintenance. Nor, given the fact that Dr. O'Brien was still but a resident, was there such a disparity in their respective incomes as would have permitted the court to have found need, and to have made a maintenance award, on that basis. To make matters worse, even if maintenance had been justified, it might only terminate in but a short period of time should Mrs. O'Brien remarry, which was actually what happened in this case.[22] Thus, though the facts seemed to cry out for relief, the court was without an apparent remedy.

To solve the problem, the court did two things. First, it expanded the concept of marital property and held that the husband's license to practice medicine, apart from any medical practice that he may or may not have had, itself constituted marital property, and this regardless of the fact that such a license did not fit within traditional property concepts, since it could not be sold and therefore had no market value. The court held that it was property, nevertheless, the value of which was reflected not only in the money, effort, and lost opportunity for employment that had been expended in acquiring it, but, and even more importantly, in the enhanced earning capacity that it provided.[23]

The second action the court took was to place a value on the husband's license, arrived at by comparing the average income of a college graduate (which the husband would have been but for his medical education) and that of a general surgeon (which the husband would be at the end of his residency), between that latter date and the date when he would reach the age of 65. After taking into consideration federal income taxes, an inflation rate of 10%, and a real interest rate of 3%, the difference was capitalized in average earnings and the amount reduced to present value. Accepting the testimony of the wife's expert witness, who gave a present value of the husband's medical license on this basis, the court found it to be worth $472,000. It then awarded the wife $188,000, representing 40 percent of its present value, and directed the husband to pay this amount to her over a period of years, in eleven annual installments of various amounts.

The Law and Divorce Mediation

What effect, if any, should the decision in *O'Brien* have upon a divorce mediator? To put it another way, would it be irresponsible for him to approach the problem here without any concern as to whether or not the husband's medical license was marital property, let alone about its value? Not in any state other than New York, or possibly Michigan.[24] At least at the present time, the decision of the New York Court of Appeals is a distinctly minority opinion, as the courts in literally every other state that has considered the problem have held that neither a professional degree nor a license is marital property.[25]

It is important for mediators to consider this. It is even more important that they understand its implications. The concept of marital property is simply a legal fiction (the Court of Appeals in New York called it a "statutory creature"). It exists, not because it is a part of nature itself, but because the law says it exists. More importantly, it was created by the law simply to solve a problem, and if the law could have solved that problem in a simpler way, and without straining the concept of property to the extent that it did, it certainly would have done so; for in stretching that concept it has created as many problems as it has solved. (For example, is a teacher's or a plumber's license also marital property? And what about the medical degree itself? Obtaining the degree was what took years and years of effort, not the license, which was probably obtained after only a few months of study. And what about a master's degree in business administration, or a college degree, for that matter? The problems are endless.)[26]

Unfortunately, given the fact that a mediator practices in but one particular jurisdiction and is thus often insulated from the laws of other states, the solutions adopted by the courts in his own state soon begin to lose their fictitious character. Thus, after a period of time, it simply becomes a given, for example, that a professional license is marital property and is worth what the courts have said it is worth. Worse yet, it is soon forgotten that this was simply a judicial solution to a problem that must be understood more in terms of judicial limitations than as the result of any necessary logic.[27]

A mediator does not operate under the same constraints that a judge does, however. It may well be that the Court of Appeals in *O'Brien*, bound by the principle of precedent and by a concern for the effect that its decision would have on future cases, was not able to solve the problem by giving Mrs. O'Brien maintenance because the facts did not warrant such an award and because, even if they did, it would have been constrained to terminate her maintenance upon her remarriage.

However, the couple themselves, and therefore the mediator, do not operate under those same constraints. Thus, they could have solved the problem much more easily and, as we will see later, far more equitably, by simply providing that Mrs. O'Brien would receive support from her husband over a fixed number of years in an amount which could have been based upon his actual earnings during the period in question. As for the problem of her remarriage, the agreement could have just considered that fact irrelevant and provided that the payments would continue over the period in question, regardless of her possible remarriage.[28]

Let us take the argument one step further. Let us assume that the mediator and the couple live and work in New York State. To prejudice the question further, let us also assume that, in a rash of understanding, every other state in the United States has now seen the wisdom of the decision of the Court of Appeals in New York and has not only held, without exception, that a professional license is marital property, but has also adopted New York's method of valuing it.

How should this affect the mediator's thinking and his conduct of the mediation? Must he not now accept the fact that a professional license is marital property and, before proceeding with the mediation, have its value determined by an expert? More to the point, and given the fact that it has now become the law of the land that a professional license is marital property, would it not be irresponsible of him to do otherwise? After all, if the mediator were to allow the parties to proceed without having the license evaluated, would this not be to leave them buying a pig in a poke?

The answer is still no. Again, a court of law may be required to employ legal fictions in order to reach an appropriate result, and they may even have the need to take those legal fictions seriously. But that does not mean that those of us who are not so required to employ them must, or should, do the same. Nor are we compelled to do this simply because these fictions have become universally accepted.

Having said that, it must be acknowledged that there will be many who may have difficulty with this. After all, if every court in the land declares that a professional license is marital property, how can we continue to maintain that it is nothing but a fiction? It is, nevertheless, even though it will admittedly become far more difficult to see that. In fact, it is difficult even now, for although the legal concept (construct) of marital property is only of recent origin, we have already come to think and act as if it existed from time immemoriam.

If our argument is to be persuasive, therefore, we are going to have to direct it elsewhere. That being so, let us consider the question again. The fiction created by the Court of Appeals in *O'Brien* consisted of two elements: firstly, that a professional license is marital property, and secondly, and perhaps even more importantly for our purposes, that it had an ascertainable value. Is that true, however, or is that too simply another convenient fiction created by the court? The answer is the latter, for if there was anything more fictitious than the Court of Appeals' determination that Dr. O'Brien's medical license constituted a species of property, it was its finding that the present value of that license was $472,000.

Consider how that value was arrived at. Without question, and being personal in nature, the value of Dr. O'Brien's medical license could only be its value to *him*. (Which value, for the sake of argument, we will accept as being the difference between what Dr. O'Brien would have earned as a college graduate and what he will earn as a general surgeon.)[29] But wasn't that the value the Court of Appeals ascribed to it? Absolutely not. The Court of Appeals, quite obviously, could not possibly know how valuable that license would prove to be to Dr. O'Brien, even by its own definition. It didn't even know how valuable his bachelor's degree was, based on such a standard. To know that, it would have needed a crystal ball. Accordingly, it simply ascribed to Dr. O'Brien the average income of a general surgeon and subtracted from this amount the average income of a college graduate. That Dr. O'Brien's income might turn out to be more or less than that average was simply deemed irrelevant and, therefore, ignored.

Again, since the court did not have the vaguest idea how long Dr. O'Brien would actually practice, or be able to practice, medicine, it arbitrarily assumed that he would practice until he reached the age of 65. That he might become disabled, or even die, years before then, or that he might continue to practice long after, again became irrelevant. Since the amount that the court arrived at was before taxes and based on the present value of the dollar, it was next necessary to factor in future income taxes that Dr. O'Brien would have to pay, as well as the increased cost of living. Once again, the fact that the court had absolutely no idea whether income tax rates or the rate of inflation would be higher or lower in the future was again deemed irrelevant and completely ignored.[30]

But can it really be believed that a court, let alone the highest court of the State of New York, would predicate its decision on a value as speculative as this? After all, if instead of studying medicine, Dr. O'Brien had spent the same time preparing to be a pharmacist (or a businessman) and had just opened his first pharmacy (business), would the court have concluded that the value of his training was what the average pharmacist (businessman) earned?[31] And, if it did, would that be any the less buying a pig in a poke, than for a mediator simply to disregard the value of that license?

The answer is that the Court of Appeals did just that. More importantly, they *acknowledged* it. As Justice Bernard Meyer stated in his concurring opinion:

> Yet the degree of speculation involved in the award made is emphasized by the testimony of the expert on which it was based. Asked whether his assumptions and calculations were in any way speculative, he replied: "Yes. They're speculative to the extent of, will Dr. O'Brien practice medicine? Will Dr. O'Brien earn more or less than the average surgeon earns? Will Dr. O'Brien live to age 65? Will Dr. O'Brien have a heart attack or will he be injured in an automobile accident? Will he be disabled? I mean, there is a degree of speculation."[32]

In fact, it was just this very degree of speculativeness that led the Court of Appeals of Kentucky to reject the idea that a professional license is marital property, let alone that a court could determine with any degree of reliability what its value was. As that court stated:

> Although studies have been propounded by which this potential is to be measured, as yet we find too speculative and general for our reliance. By necessity such

evaluations are based upon factors such as means and norms. The result may well inform us of what Mr. Average Pharmacist may expect to draw from his practice, but it sheds insufficient guidance upon what Mr. Moss will receive.[33]

Nor is this the end of it. Quite the contrary, there is an even more serious problem, for while a court may have engaged in a kind of hocus-pocus in placing a value on the husband's license, at least it was a hocus-pocus that could perhaps be applied in future cases. Thus, and as speculative as the results in these various cases may be, since they would have been arrived at by the application of the same formula, the results would at least be consistent.

But what about the amount awarded to Mrs. O'Brien in this case? What formula did the court apply there, and how could that formula be applied by the mediator, or by another judge for that matter, in another case? The simple answer is that there was no formula, and that there is absolutely nothing in the *O'Brien* decision that could possibly assist a mediator or judge to decide another case in the future. Does the decision in *O'Brien* mean that all wives are entitled to receive 40% of the present value of their husband's medical licenses? Obviously not. If equitable distribution means anything, it means that the distribution of marital property is to be based upon the circumstances of the particular case, and not on cookie-cutter formulas. And this is certainly so where what is being distributed as marital property is not property that presently exists, like money in the bank, but property that is nothing more nor less than future earnings.[34]

What were the facts in *O'Brien* that led the Court to award Mrs. O'Brien 40% of the present value of her husband's license, rather than 10%, 20%, 30%, or 50%? And what in those facts would serve to assist a judge (or a mediator) to make an appropriate determination in the future? Frankly, it is very hard to tell. The only facts that the court mentioned are the following:

1. The parties had been married for approximately 9 years.
2. During this time the wife had contributed approximately 76% of the parties' income.
3. In assisting her husband to obtain his medical license, Mrs. O'Brien had relinquished the opportunity to obtain permanent certification as a teacher.
4. Between December of 1980, the date of the commencement of Dr. O'Brien's action for a divorce, and 1985, he would continue his studies as a resident in surgery.
5. For the next 27 years he would practice surgery and enjoy the benefits of his medical license.
6. The present value of Mrs. O'Brien's contribution toward her husband's medical education was $103,390.

What value did or could the court ascribe to each of these factors which would lead it irresistibly to the conclusion that Mrs. O'Brien's interest should be 40%? Again, it is very hard to say. While the court noted the fact that Mrs. O'Brien's earnings accounted for 76% of the couple's income, this is actually an irrelevant consideration, as no one would suggest that Dr. O'Brien, as a medical student, did not work as hard, if not harder, than his wife during this period of time, even if that effort was not reflected in present dollars. More importantly, and relying upon a presumption that more commonly favors women than men, the court in its opinion reaffirmed the fact that martial contributions "should ordinarily be regarded as equal," regardless of the fact that some of those efforts were financially more remunerative than others. Nor can it be said that the fact that Mrs. O'Brien had relinquished the opportunity to obtain permanent certification was really such a relevant factor, as there was nothing in the court's opinion to suggest that she had foregone obtaining this certification rather than just postponing its attainment.

What we are left with then is simply the fact that Dr. O'Brien and his wife worked equally hard for 9 years to obtain his medical license and that he would be working alone for the next 32 years to convert that license into spendable dollars. How the court proceeded from these facts, however, to 40% is a mystery. To be more accurate, it is more akin to a judicial leap of faith than to a result reached by logic, let alone any necessary logic. Unfortunately for other judges and would-be mediators, however, like all leaps of faith, there is nothing in the logic that brought the person in question to the point of departure that will suggest with any degree of accuracy where that leap should end. [35]

As if the problem of the value of Dr. O'Brien's medical license, and Mrs. O'Brien's interest in it, is not confounded enough, consider how the court directed Dr. O'Brien to pay Mrs. O'Brien her interest in its value. Did the court's determination that the present value of Dr. O'Brien's medical license was $472,000, and that Mrs. O'Brien was entitled to 40% of that value, result in a present award to Mrs. O'Brien of $188,000? The answer is no. The determination by the highest court of the State of New York that Dr. O'Brien's medical license was presently worth $472,000 did not, of course, mean that he actually had the $472,000 to pay her. Legal fictions may have the power to stretch our imaginations, but as the Court of Appeals acknowledged in its decision, they do not have the same power to fill our pockets.

Thus, all that the court could do was to direct Dr. O'Brien to pay it out over a period of time. In arriving at a present value of $472,000, however, the court had already discounted the value of Dr. O'Brien's potential future earnings. Did that mean that the award of $188,800 made to Mrs. O'Brien would then be augmented to take into account the fact that it would be paid out over a 10-year period, rather then at the present time? No. Did it even mean that Mrs. O'Brien would receive interest on the deferred payments? Again the answer was no. What did it mean? It simply meant that the payment that Dr. O'Brien was directed to make to Mrs. O'Brien was no less arbitrary than either the value that had been placed upon his license or the interest in that license that was assigned to her.

What then are we to make of the decision of the Court of Appeals in *O'Brien*? When all is said and done, was the result reached by the court really very different than would have been the case had it simply made an award of maintenance to her for a period of years that would be unaffected by her possible remarriage? In fact, doesn't it look embarrassingly close to just that, despite the fact that the court had no power to do this? Even more importantly for our purposes, should a mediator be concerned that he assisted a couple to come to this same result, or even another result equally equitable, simply because he did not go through this same hocus-pocus?

Obviously not. Perhaps it should be of concern to him if the fictions employed by the courts and the law lead to some necessary result, or could be thought of as guaranteeing some necessary equitable judgment. But if that is not the case—and it clearly is not— then it is not necessary for a mediator to be slavishly bound to the procedures that a court employs. After all—and it is critical that we understand this—courts employ these fictions not because they are right or just but simply because they are limited in what they can do in order to arrive at a just result. They are limited in that they must employ procedures that can be followed by subsequent courts in the future, limited in that they are not permitted to use certain other procedures, given the nature of their statutory grant, limited by the need for consistency with prior judicial decisions, and limited, finally, by the effect that their decision will have on future judicial determinations.

Neither the mediator nor the couple are so limited, however. There is absolutely no reason, therefore, for them to have to apply those same fictions. More importantly, there is absolutely no reason to believe that they would achieve a more equitable result if they did.

FACT AND FICTION

Up to this point the question that we have addressed is whether or not a mediator is bound to follow the same procedures that a court would follow in order to reach the same equitable result. Our argument has been that if a mediator is not obligated to work within the same constraints that bind a judge, and that if all that the Court of Appeals really did was to give Mrs. O'Brien a fixed, tax-free alimony (maintenance) payment for a period of years; if a mediator can get to the same result without having to indulge in the judicial sleight of hand employed by the Court of Appeals, is there anything wrong in that and should he be concerned by it?[36]

We now want to ask a further question. Suppose that a couple, not having followed the same legal procedures, comes to a different—perhaps even a far different—result. Should that bother the mediator? Before addressing this question, however, let us advance the argument a step further. Perhaps it is unfair to use a professional license, or even a professional practice, for that matter, as the basis for the argument. After all, if we were dealing with a one-family private home in Shaker Heights, Ohio, no court would suggest that its value was the average of the amount that all one-family private homes in Shaker Heights would bring on the open market, as found by an expert real estate appraiser. On the contrary, the appraiser would be sent out to give his estimate of the value of the particular house in question. Nor would anyone seriously suggest that the value of the home, as so determined, was a mere legal fiction. Let us assume, therefore, that we are dealing, not with Dr. O'Brien's medical license, but with an asset, like a private home, that has a value that is reasonably ascertainable.

To prejudice the matter even further, let us also assume that the whole problem of what represents an equitable distribution of marital property has been resolved uniformly by the various states and that, without exception, they each now hold that, in every case, an equitable distribution is an equal distribution. There is no cause, therefore, for the mediator to concern himself with whether what a court would consider to be fair in the instant matter would be 20%, 30%, 40%, or some other number. In each case the answer is the same. The court would hold that the wife should receive 50% of the present value of the marital property. If all of the marital assets were of this kind, wouldn't the mediator then be justified in insisting that an equitable distribution of those assets be the same distribution that a court would direct—in this case, 50%? In fact, wouldn't it be negligent, and perhaps even irresponsible, for him to accept less?

At first blush it would seem that it would. Nevertheless, that is still not the case, for even if all of the states were uniformly so to hold, thereby dispelling any questions one might possibly have as to whether or not the property in question was marital property or what the law felt was an equitable distribution of it, there still remains embedded in the law's solution to the problem of modern marriage yet another disturbing fiction. Worse yet, it is one that has never been made explicit. And that is the fiction that husbands and wives cease to be individuals simply because they marry.

Consider the following: a mediator is consulted by a couple who had been married for approximately eighteen years. The husband is a psychologist and is employed by a mental health agency. His wife is a college instructor. They have two teenage children and own their own home. Although they were both active parents, the majority of the household duties, as well as the care of their children, are the responsibility of the wife. Though not necessarily expending more effort in the process, the husband has earned the bulk of the money that has gone toward their living expenses. In her free time, the wife has written a textbook and presently derives royalties of approximately $6,000 a year from it. The textbook had been written within the last few years of the parties' marriage, and it is anticipated that the wife will continue to receive these royalties for the next four or five years.

When the question of the royalties that the wife derived from this textbook was raised, the husband inquired of the mediator whether they were not marital property in which he had an interest. The wife looked in amazement at her husband's suggestion. What did their marriage have to do with her book? She could have written that book at any time; it just happened to have been written during their marriage. She could also have written it at any place; it just happened to have been written in their home. In fact, it had been written in her head, and her husband had had nothing, but nothing, to do with it. The book was the result of her individual effort—and a very considerable effort as well—and to suggest otherwise was a travesty.

To be sure, there were many times when the wife had closeted herself in her study, working on her book, and the husband had thereby been deprived of her company. But should he be compensated for this inconvenience, any more than she should be compensated for the fact that she had been left at home alone on numerous occasions while he was out playing tennis in the early morning hours, or after work at night? Was it ever intended when they got married that they would share all of their waking moments, let alone all of their thoughts, together, or that they would not have individual lives—and could their marriage have ever survived this long had they not? And if these were inconveniences that they had each suffered so that the other could pursue his or her own individual interests, was it necessary or appropriate for either of them now to have to compensate the other for those inconveniences? After all, weren't such inconveniences implicit in the fact of their marriage?

Suppose, instead, that the parties here had been business partners rather than marital partners. They owned the local bookstore in town, and although they had different functions (he being principally concerned with the ordering of new books and she being principally concerned with their sale), they considered the contributions they each made to the business to be of sufficiently equal value, despite the fact that they were different in kind, and even sometimes different in effort. Suppose further that he had written a book in his spare time, that was later published. Would she have any legal or moral claim to any portion of the royalties received from that book?

To be sure, it was implicit in their understanding that neither of them would do anything detrimental to their common efforts, such as opening a competing bookstore in the next town or devoting less than their full time and efforts to the business. But was it ever expected that they would not also have individual lives simply because they were partners or that, despite the fact that it was strictly a business partnership, that their individual lives might not on occasion interfere with their partnership efforts? (On one occasion, he was unable to attend to his business duties due to a death in his family; on another, she was gone for several days when she took her daughter to look at colleges. In each instance, it was the fact that the other was there, doing his or her job, that permitted them the luxury of being able to do this.)

The question, of course, is a rhetorical one. Common sense tells us that people can be partners for certain purposes and still remain individuals for others. Nevertheless, our modern divorce laws, in their effort to remedy certain of the abuses of previous practice, have created a fiction that flies in the face of this commonsense reality. Why has it done that? Simply because it had no alternative. With the normal business partnership, such as that between the couple who ran the local bookstore, the partners are *limited* partners. They are only partners for the purposes of the particular business enterprise, and that enterprise is clearly defined.

With partners to a marriage, however, the limits of that partnership enterprise are not as easily drawn. In fact, couples rarely draw them at all. As a result, it is a lot harder to see where the partnership's efforts end and the individual's efforts begin. This is particularly difficult because, in many instances, the same effort could be viewed as partnership effort for certain purposes and individual effort for others. For the court to attempt to undertake the delicate process that would be required to separate these efforts into their respective parts would be to get lost in an endless quagmire.

The law's response to the problem, therefore, has been to deny it. It has done this by throwing up its hands and declaring that from the moment two people marry, individual effort no longer exists and all effort is marital effort. And if that declaration, and the fiction embodied in it, does violence to the reality that husbands and wives still remain individuals despite their marriage, then so much the worse for that reality.

But that does not mean that the couple themselves, or the mediator, for that matter, must ignore that reality. And it certainly does not mean that their result will be more equitable if they do. Unlike a court of law, they are not faced with the problem of what would happen if they attempted, in each case, to separate what should rightfully be considered the individual effort of each of the parties and what should rightfully be considered marital effort. They are only concerned with doing what is appropriate in this particular instance. Nor is it necessary to insult our common sense to do that.

The husband in this instance, as a psychologist, has accumulated a very substantial personal library of books, most of them during his marriage. In fact, he has spent several thousand dollars over the years for that purpose. Must those books too be thrown into the marital pot, and would it really offend our sense of justice if they weren't? Because the law does not distinguish between individual effort and marital effort, does it mean that a couple is not free to make that distinction?

Before answering this question, there is yet one final problem with the application of equitable distribution statutes that must be discussed, and that concerns the factors the court will consider in making its award. More to the point, it concerns the factors the court will *not* take into account.

Consider the following: a couple has been married for almost 20 years and has two teenage children. Although the wife is a fine person, and has been a good wife to her husband and mother to his children, he is nevertheless very unhappy in his marriage. In fact, he has been unhappy for some time and has increasingly found himself looking outside of the marriage for emotional support. For the last nine months he has been seeing a woman whom he would like to marry. Fixed in his decision, the husband has announced to his wife that he would like a divorce.

The wife is shaken by her husband's announcement. Although she was aware that there were problems in the marriage, she never fully realized the depth of her husband's dissatisfaction, let alone the fact that he was seriously considering divorcing her. To make matters worse, and unaware of his emotional involvement, she cannot understand why he is not willing to join with her in seeking professional help to save their marriage. Depressed and overwhelmed with grief, all that the wife can see is her world shattered around her.

Being a basically decent man, her husband is aware of where his decision has left his wife and of the disparity in their respective circumstances, for while she cannot see beyond the fact of her divorce, he has already planned a new life for himself to which he looks forward. For these and other reasons he has decided to deed his interest in their home to her. While, on one level at least, he is aware that he is no more responsible for their divorce than she, it was, nevertheless, his decision and not hers, and it is she who has been left where she is and does not wish to be. He cannot change that, but he would at least like to do something in recognition of this fact.

How should the mediator view the husband's decision? To put it another way, should it bother him that the wife will receive the entire interest in their home, which is by far their largest asset? Is that equitable? If the decision had been made by a court, that certainly would not have been the result. She might have been permitted to continue to live in the home for a period of time, but upon its sale the proceeds would have been divided between them, probably equally.

But what about all of the factors taken into consideration by the husband in making his decision? Aren't these human elements important at all? They may be, but not as far as the law is concerned. On the contrary, as with almost all of the factors that affect human conduct, they would be considered totally irrelevant by the court. Why is this? After all, most equitable distribution statutes provide that the court, in making a distribution of marital property, may, in addition to the factors specifically enumerated by the statutes, take into consideration such other factors as it deems appropriate under the circumstances.[37] Aren't these just the kinds of factors that these statutes had in mind? The answer is no. On the contrary, and in reviewing its grant of authority, the question that the courts have repeatedly posed themselves is simply whether or not those other factors included marital fault.[38] By and large, their answer to this question has been no.[39]

If fault is not a relevant factor, then how relevant are all of the other human considerations—the hurt, the anger, the feelings of betrayal and disappointment, the guilt and the tremendous sense of loss, that one or both of the parties feels? After all, are not these the feelings that comprise the very lives that we live? That may be, but as far as the court is concerned, they are totally irrelevant and, therefore, are not factors taken into account in arriving at its determination.

Before drawing any conclusions from this, it is important to remember that judicial relevancy, like judicial truth, is different from human relevancy and human truth. The fact that these are not considerations a court can put into the balance in weighing its decision does not mean that they are not relevant considerations that the parties themselves can, and perhaps should, take into account in making their own. In fact, from their standpoint they may be among the most relevant considerations of all.

But does this not mean that the result in two mediations, having almost identical fact patterns, may be very different? And does this not mean that the result in both these cases may be very different from that that would have been determined by a court of law? But why should that bother a mediator? To be sure, it would suggest a miscarriage of justice if the two determinations had been made by a court of law. But they were not made by a court of law. They were made by couples who, despite their almost identical fact patterns, were nevertheless very different.

One final point: given the fact that people are different, and therefore view the same things differently, it is more than likely that a mediator may be confronted with a wife who is not interested in her husband's professional license, his library of books, or his tennis trophies, notwithstanding the fact that money was expended to acquire them and they are considered by the law to be marital property in which she has an interest. Before mediators, in their zeal to be responsible, replicate the practice of adversarial lawyers of intimidating the wife here with a lesson in the law, and make her feel uncomfortable, and perhaps even foolish, for not demanding everything that the law allows, they should remind themselves of a rather obvious fact. The Court of Appeals of New York made an award to Mrs. O'Brien simply because she asked them for one. To be sure, in making such an award, the Court of Appeals held that all spouses, similarly situated, were now entitled to an award should they wish one. But the Court of Appeals certainly never held, or intended to hold, for that matter, that if, based upon other considerations, these other spouses should decline to seek an award that they would be making a mistake, let alone breaking the law.

It is important that mediators remember this. As the Court of Appeals did not question Mrs. O'Brien's motives in seeking recompense for the efforts she felt that she had invested in helping her husband obtain his medical degree and license, so too a mediator should not question her motives if she decides not to seek compensation for those efforts. Nor, for the same reason, should he concern himself with whether the compensation she asks, or to which the parties agree, is the same that would have been awarded her by the court.

A *mediator and a judge are not trying to do the same thing.* They are not even trying to solve the same problem. The judge is trying to make a determination that is equitable, one that resembles, as closely as is possible, the criteria established by the legislature and by prior judicial decisions. A mediator, on the other hand, is trying to conclude an agreement between two people, one that comports, as closely as is possible, with their own personal conception of what is appropriate or inappropriate, and is one they feel they can live with.

CHAPTER 4

Is the Agreement Fair?

What obligation does the mediator have to assure that the agreement concluded between the parties is fair? Critics of divorce mediation have been quick to raise this question. The mediator's obligation, they charge, is simply to conclude an agreement between the parties. Thus, it is the fact of the agreement and not its quality that most concerns him. For lawyers who have functioned in a more traditional adversarial setting, therefore, the cost of the benefits of a mediated settlement may be an agreement that is unfair to one of the parties, usually the weaker one. From their standpoint, without the presence of separate lawyers to champion each of the parties' conflicting interests, and thereby protect them, there is little likelihood, let alone any guarantee, that the resulting agreement will be fair.

Advocates of divorce mediation have generally been stung by this criticism and have therefore summarily accepted it at face value. As a result, their response has been to echo this concern for the quality of mediated agreements. This has been expressed in a number of concrete ways: (1) the requirement that mediators assess a couple's *suitability* for mediation before undertaking the procedure, (2) the incorporation into mediation practice of procedures designed to *empower the weaker* of the two parties, (3) standards of practice that impose upon the mediator the obligation of *rejecting* agreements that are not fair, and (4) the requirement that the agreement be *reviewed* (and sometimes drawn) by separate attorneys.

From our point of view, this criticism has been accepted much too quickly. In doing so, divorce mediation has not stopped to consider its objectives or what obligation it has to each of the parties. Worse, it has unquestioningly accepted the assumptions implicit in the adversarial view of divorce traditionally held by the law and by lawyers, rather than questioned those assumptions, as it should have.

Different Standards

Before proceeding to consider the mediator's obligation to conclude a fair agreement, however, it is perhaps in order to make some general observations about the question of fairness and, more particularly, about the criticism leveled at divorce mediation, generally by matrimonial attorneys, that it fails to assure that the final agreement will be fair. The first of these is that in insisting that mediated settlements be fair to both parties, matrimonial attorneys are imposing upon divorce mediators a very different standard, and a very different obligation, than they impose upon themselves.

What obligation does an adversarial lawyer have to conclude an agreement that is fair? A well-known matrimonial attorney told the story of a woman he had represented in the negotiation of a separation agreement. When the matter was concluded, he turned to his client and observed that he thought that the agreement that she had signed was a fair one. Rather than thanking him for his efforts, the woman replied, "I didn't hire you to get me a fair agreement. I could have done that myself. What I hired you to do was to get me as much as you could."

Most matrimonial lawyers do not have to be reminded of this. It is not their obligation to conclude an agreement that will be fair to both parties. In fact, it is their inherent inability, in an adversarial setting, to consider the needs of both parties at the same time that accounts for the fact that the parties have separate lawyers to begin with. Their obligation is simply to protect their own clients' interests, for to worry whether the agreement that is being concluded is fair to the other party (or, as one critic of mediation has said, even fair to the children, who, after all, do not pay his fee) would be a derogation of his duty.[1]

To talk of an attorney's having an obligation to conclude a fair agreement in this context is thus an inconsistency in terms. If the wife's attorney is able to secure more for her than she deserves, he does not chasten himself by saying that the agreement was unfair to the husband. He doesn't even say that it was too fair to the wife. He simply congratulates himself on the fact that he has done a very good job in representing his client.[2]

The critics of mediation are thus left with a dilemma. In insisting that mediators have a duty to assure that agreements concluded by the couple are fair to both, they are either imposing on mediators an obligation they do not impose upon themselves, or they must solve the problem of how two attorneys, each of whom is simply concerned about reaching an agreement that is in his own client's best interests, will nevertheless come away with an agreement that is fair to both parties.

If pressed on this point, one would assume that the answer lawyers would give would be that it is the adversarial nature of our legal system that guarantees that the agreement will be fair. Unfortunately, this is far easier to say than to demonstrate. If the critics of divorce mediation are correct, the parties come to the contest with unequal bargaining powers. One may be strong and the other weak. One may be sophisticated and the other naive. One may be possessed of more than sufficient financial and emotional resources for the contest, and the other bereft of both. One may be willing to fight long and hard, and totally without restraint, and the other not.

By what legal hocus-pocus will their two attorneys be able to correct these imbalances? By none. In fact, they may only add to them, for what guarantee is there, after all, that the two attorneys are possessed of equal skill and understanding, that one is not more dogged or persevering than the other, or that one may not engage in conduct no less reprehensible than his client's? In short, what guarantee is there that the stronger of the two parties will not also have the stronger of the two attorneys?

Perhaps it is the judge who guarantees that it comes out fairly in our adversarial system. But where is the judge in all of this, and how does he provide this protection? The judge, after all, does not sit in on the settlement discussions conducted by the parties and their attorneys. On the contrary, he is only called in when those settlement discussions prove unsuccessful and it is therefore necessary to decide the matter. However, and as matrimonial lawyers like to boast, probably 90% of the time a settlement is concluded without the necessity of a trial—without a judge being required to decide the matter. How then does the judge function to assure that the agreement is fair? The answer is that, except in those few instances when he is called in to decide the issues, he doesn't.[3]

There is yet a further flaw in the argument. If the procedures of our adversarial system were such as to guarantee that agreements concluded between separating and divorcing couples were fair, we would expect to find many couples who would bear witness to this. Unfortunately, they will not be easily found. As anyone who has functioned in a traditional adversarial setting can testify, very few, indeed, are those who conclude agreements between themselves because they think they are fair. They sign their agreements, not because they are satisfied with them, but because they want to get done with them. In fact, in most instances it is only possible to conclude an agreement between separating and divorcing couples in an adversarial setting when they have finally *given up* their unrealistic expectations that what they will be left with is an agreement that they believe is fair.

What is true of agreements concluded through negotiations is even more true of agreements concluded for the parties by the court. If *fair* means anything, it would have to mean fair as seen by the judge—the impartial, objective instrument of the law. Yet rare is the case when that opinion is shared by both parties. In fact, rare is the day when one if not both of the parties does not walk away from the court feeling anything but aggrieved by the agreement that has been imposed upon them by the court.

Different Yardsticks

There is a second problem with the question of fairness, one which, for some strange reason, is almost never mentioned. Moreover, it is a particularly vexatious one in terms of the principle of autonomy that normally acts as a restraint upon the state's interference in the lives of others, particularly in their private affairs.

Whether we realize it or not, by insisting that the parties' agreement conform to a certain standard, we are infringing on their right to make the decisions that affect their lives on their own, free of third-party interference. It is no defense to this to say that all we are trying to do is assure that they are being fair with one another, or that we are simply trying to protect them and their children, as these are always the excuses given by outside intermeddlers. More importantly, these arguments will not suffice unless we first come to terms with the question of why these reasons are accepted as sufficient justification now when they were never accepted as sufficient before. To put it another way, if we have never subjected the parties' conduct to a standard of fairness (particularly a standard of fairness as defined by the law) during their marriage, or at its inception, why are we justified in doing so now simply because they are getting a divorce?

Consider the following example. A millionaire falls in love with a very beautiful woman. Before agreeing to marry him, she insists that he settle upon her the sum of 1 million dollars which is to constitute her sole and separate property, to which he agrees. The money having been transferred, the couple then marries. Regardless of how we might personally view each of the parties' conduct in this instance, is there any among us who would seriously question that they should have the right to enter into this marriage under these conditions, if they choose to? More to the point, would we be justified in making inquiry concerning the terms of their agreement, and whether it is fair, at the time that they applied for a license to marry, before we allowed it to be granted to them? Needless to say, the question is a rhetorical one.[4]

Let us take the example a step further. Shortly following the marriage, the gentleman in question has second thoughts about the decision that he has made, particularly about the consideration that he paid for his wife's hand, and whether it was fair that he should have had to do so. He, after all, brought millions to the marriage. She, on the other hand, brought only her good looks, which will fade in time, as his wealth continues to increase. Concluding that he has grossly overestimated the worth of her good looks, which have no monetary value in any event, he seeks to have the prenuptial agreement set aside as being, if not unconscionable, at least grossly unfair. Should we have the right to step in and relieve the husband of the burden of his inopportune bargain and require his wife to return the money she has received? Again the question is a rhetorical one.

Let us take the example yet one further step. The husband complains that the contributions he and his wife make to the marriage are grossly disparate and, therefore, unfair. Because of the nature of his business, he is required to devote long hours to work, often until late in the evening. His wife, on the other hand, is not obligated to work at all (and would earn very little if she did), and instead spends her time in leisure, shopping, lunching with friends, or relaxing at the country club to which they belong. To make matters worse, his wife does not share his interest in the opera or in chamber music, and he must either forego their pleasure, or go alone. Once more we will ask the question. Would we be justified in passing judgment on the contributions each of the parties makes to the marriage and determine whether they are fair or unfair? And would it be appropriate for us to intervene to adjust them, if they are not? Once again the question is a rhetorical one.

Why is it, then, if we left these matters to the parties' individual determination at the time of their marriage, and during their marriage, should we not do so at the time of their divorce? Why, in other words, if we did not subject their conduct to a legal yardstick then, are we justified in doing so now? It is hard to find an answer, and those that might be offered are not sufficient.

The first has to do with protection, particularly of women, for the law rarely enters to protect the interests of men. Unfortunately, this explanation is grounded in the rather unflattering and infantilizing notion that women, like children, need the special protection of the law—not when they enter into a marriage (when they come under the protective wing of a stronger, self-sufficient husband) but at the time of their divorce (when they lose the security of his presence). It also represents the equally curious and antiquated view that divorce is occasioned by the husband's desire to move on, usually to greener pastures. Whether born of male conceit or male insecurity, in the world in which we presently live, where half of married women work, and where as many or more divorces are initiated by wives as are by their husbands, this explanation will not suffice.[5]

The second reason given is the presence of children. Unfortunately, this reason is equally wanting. To begin with, the couple's children were present during their marriage as well as at the time of their divorce, yet that was never deemed sufficient justification for our intervening in their lives, or setting standards for their conduct. More importantly, and although an agreement can certainly be unfair to children as well as to wives, when we talk of unfairness, we are generally talking about whether the marital assets the wife will receive, and the amount and duration of her support, are fair, neither of which directly concern the parties' children. If further proof be needed it is in the fact that those who express their concern about the fairness of the agreement will be no less concerned were they to be advised that the parties do not have children or, if they do, that they are all grown and self-supporting.

The third argument relates to competency. A couple's divorce is generally a very stressful period in their lives and their conduct is thus often affected by very powerful feelings. Given this fact, it is only appropriate that we intervene to assure that the important decisions the parties have made concerning their lives, and perhaps those of their children, were not made on the basis of strong, but, nevertheless, transitory and impermanent emotions that rendered them less than competent at the time. Unfortunately for this argument, most, if not all, of the important decisions that people make in their lives are based upon just these kinds of emotions. That was certainly true in the case of their marriage. And yet we did not intervene then. If that is so, why are we justified in doing this now?

There is one final argument that must be addressed. While the parties were married to one another, there were certain natural restraints that acted as governors upon their conduct, and their dealings with one another, given their desire to maintain an ongoing relationship. Now that they are divorcing, those restraints no longer exist. Quite the contrary, each party is simply concerned with getting as much as he or she can, regardless of the good opinion of the other. If proof be needed for this, one has only to turn and observe how they do battle with one another at the time of their divorce.

Although this argument may, at first blush, seem persuasive, it does not stand up to analysis. While it would certainly be fair to assume that the decision to divorce effects a change in the relationship between the couple, it is nevertheless not sufficient to support the conclusion expressed in this argument. To begin with, it places too great a burden on that decision, at the expense of the myriad other factors that determine the relationship between the parties. Thus, the fact that a decision had not previously been made to separate or divorce was no guarantee that one of the parties would not be unfair, and perhaps even abusive, to the other. Nor is the fact that such a decision has now been made proof that such conduct will necessarily follow.

More importantly, the view of the relationship between the parties expressed in this argument is rather naive. The strong interdependencies that are built up in a marriage do not disappear in a moment simply with the decision to divorce. Nor does a party's need to continue to maintain a certain image of himself, not only in his own eyes, but in the eyes of the other as well. Quite the contrary, that relationship is a continuum that often extends for years beyond the parties' divorce, and as anyone who has worked with separating and divorcing couples can testify, the adhesive factors in that relationship are more often than not painfully strong at this time.

Nor do the battles that separating and divorcing couples have traditionally engaged in refute this. On the contrary, they only demonstrate what effect adversarial proceedings have upon those adhesive factors and the painful feelings that are inevitably their by-product. Thus, the fact that such conduct occurs, and that such attitudes are expressed, in an adversarial setting is not proof that they will also be the condition in mediation.[6]

Does this mean that there is no danger that the agreement concluded between the parties in mediation may be unfair? Of course not. It simply means that the possibility of such inequity—or, to be more accurate, conduct that a third party will view to be inequitable—is always present in their relationship. But the possibility of that inequity still does not answer the question as to why the principle of individual autonomy deserves less respect now, simply because a couple is separating or divorcing, than it did at every other point in their lives. For better or for worse, those who would impose upon mediators an obligation to assure that agreements concluded by separating and divorcing couples are fair will have to come to terms with this question.

Fair to Whom?

One final observation (or question, if you will) must be asked, and this concerns the mediator's own interest in the mediation. Unfortunately, the word *fair*, like the concept of justice, evokes such an immediate, positive response that it is very hard to consider this question objectively. Nevertheless, it is an important question, and one that must be asked by a mediator over and over again if he is to be true to his purpose. That question is, *why* does he care whether the agreement concluded by the couple is fair? Why should it matter to him that it is, or offend him if it is not? After all, for many years the couple has lived together, and done business together, with one of the parties perhaps feeling that he or she was being unfairly treated. It did not concern the mediator then; why should it concern him now?

The obvious answer to this question is because he did not *know* about it then, but he does now. But what difference should that make? The conduct is the same, whether he knows about it or not. Nor does it change the issue, which is still whether or not his being offended by the parties' agreement gives him the right to step in and attempt to change it. For in allowing himself to become offended by the conduct of the parties (in this case, the unfair agreement that they have concluded), a mediator is still guilty of improperly interjecting himself, and his *own* needs, into the parties' private affairs.

We are offended by injustice after all, not simply because of what it does to others, but also because of what it does to us. While we may live in a world that is oblivious to our purpose and irreducible to our understanding, we are nevertheless incapable of living in a world that has no meaning and makes no sense. And so our lives are a constant effort to shelter ourselves from the ultimately irrational and alien world in which we live. For this purpose we adopt social conventions to make it seem familiar; we invent scientific laws to make it seem predictable; we adopt legal rules to give it order and to prevent it from being left to arbitrary caprice; and we create religious and moral rules to make it seem just and fair, and to help us explain it and live with it, when it is not.

Since each of these stratagems is designed, in its own way, to hide from us its true character, and to make of it a world in which our actions seem to make sense and to have meaning, an attack upon any of them is very threatening to us. In a way, it is the most serious threat of all, for it poses the possibility that we will be hurled back into a meaningless, chaotic existence which would quite literally drive us mad. It is for this reason that we are so often more upset at what happens to others than they are themselves. For them, what happens is only a statement about their own individual lives; for us, it is a statement about life itself.

Whether he wishes to acknowledge it or not, a mediator is thus affected by the outcome. But this does not justify his interest in it, let alone his right to dictate the criteria by which it is to be determined. What is happening in the lives of the parties has nothing to do with him. He has no right, therefore, to project his own needs onto their agreement or to permit it to affect him emotionally, for if he does, he will be of no help to anyone other than himself. Nor will it do to attempt to avoid this predicament, or worse, to deny the problem entirely, by protesting that all that he is trying to do is simply what is *fair*.

FAIRNESS AND THE LAW

Up to this point, we have attempted to question some of our thinking about the question of *fairness* and, more particularly, a mediator's obligation to assure the quality of the agreement concluded between the parties. Let us assume, for the sake of argument, that a mediator is under such an obligation, and that he thus has a duty to conclude agreements that are fair, even if adversarial lawyers do not. This does not end the matter, however, for we are still left with the question, what is a fair agreement? It is one thing, after all, to impose an obligation on a mediator to conclude an agreement that is fair to both parties; it is quite another, as we will see, for him to know such an agreement when he sees it.

Mediators have not generally addressed this problem for the simple reason that they have summarily and unthinkingly adopted as the measure of fairness the definition provided by the law. Thus, when we ask of an agreement whether it is fair or unfair, what we really mean is whether it bears sufficient resemblance to an agreement the parties would have received had they gone to court. In doing this, however, we have picked a far more arbitrary, and far more questionable, definition than we realized. Worse yet, we have picked a definition that is burdened with endless problems. Let us consider some of them.

Firstly, to insist that agreements concluded between separating and divorcing couples resemble agreements that they would have received had they gone to court presupposes that there is something special about court-dictated agreements. But is there? More to the point, are such agreements necessarily fair? If we assume that they are, this is only because we have endowed the legal rules courts apply to conclude them with far more significance than they deserve.

How have we done this? To begin with, we talk of our laws as representing legal rights rather than simply legal rules, thereby investing them with a special wisdom that is supposed to guarantee that their application will result in necessary justice. More importantly, we have severed those laws from the political setting in which they were born, thereby denying and ignoring their very arbitrary quality.

It is naive to believe that our laws are necessarily fair or just, for if they were, we would not forever be proposing changes in them. The most that can be said for our laws is that they represent what is considered to be fair at any particular time. In fact, we cannot even say this, for the laws we enact do not represent what society considers to be fair; rather, they represent what the diverse elements of society are willing to accept at any point in time. We cannot forget that our laws are born of a political process. That process is not an even flow of reasoned judgment about what is fair or unfair in society. Rather, it represents a process of compromise between the various elements of society—the vocal, but often minority group, pushing for change; the entrenched, also minority group, resisting that change; and the larger, often indifferent group, standing between them, which each of the two minority groups attempts to arouse and enlist on its behalf.

Given this situation, it is very likely that none of these diverse groups considers the particular law that has been enacted to be fair. In short, its enactment represented not what was right, but simply what was possible. For the same reason, laws often continue on our books, despite the fact that none of these groups consider them to be fair, simply because they are not able to agree, in the political process, on a new law to change them. Thus, given the fact that it is not possible to separate our laws from the political process in which they were born, even if they reflect what society considers to be fair, they do so very imperfectly.[7]

There is another problem in using the law as a yardstick of what is fair or unfair, for not only do our laws vary over time, they also vary from place to place at the same time. The laws of different states, after all, are not the same. Thus, while the various states generally subscribe to the same principles in the distribution of marital property and in the granting of spousal and child support, there are still significant differences from state to state.

A wife who is found to have been guilty of fault may not be awarded support in Louisiana,[8] although she may be in Michigan.[9] A husband is not obligated to maintain a policy of life insurance on his life for the benefit of his wife, as part of his obligation to support her, in Virginia,[10] although he may be obligated to do so in New York.[11] Property received by a spouse, either by gift or inheritance, during the marriage is marital property, subject to division between the parties at the time of their divorce, in Delaware[12] and North Dakota,[13] while it is not in New Jersey.[14] Fault may not be considered in the equitable distribution of property in Illinois,[15] although it may be in Alabama[16] and must be in Missouri.[17]

A parent is obligated to support his or her children until they reach the age of 21 years in New York,[18] but only until they reach the age of 18 years in Florida.[19] The court cannot require one spouse to support the other following their divorce in Texas,[20] while it can in Pennsylvania.[21] The court has the power to require a husband to support his wife following her remarriage in Washington[22] and Nebraska,[23] while it does not in Utah.[24]

A professional license is not marital property subject to distribution upon divorce in New Jersey[25] or Arizona,[26] while it is in New York.[27] A court can consider the possible future inheritance of one of the parties in fixing support or in making an equitable distribution of their marital property in Pennsylvania,[28] Kentucky,[29] and Connecticut[30] while it can not in Washington, D.C.[31] Thus, to make "fair" synonymous with what a court will do may simply mean to say that fair depends on where a couple happens to live at the time of their divorce.

There is a third problem in using this definition. In making the judgments it does, the law is simply incapable of considering all the elements and nuances that make up the fabric of our individual lives. As a result, it deals in more general, all-inclusive principles. For the same reason, it tends to deal more with concrete realities than with intangibles. In doing this, however, it often ignores just those emotional factors that are most significant to us and that most affect what we consider to be fair or unfair. Thus, legal rules, particularly as they are applied to the resolution of our personal disputes, often appear to be very arbitrary, having little to do with the realities of our individual lives.

The final, and perhaps most troublesome problem in using the law as a yardstick of what is fair or is not fair, however, concerns the law's unpredictability. To say that *fair* is what the law says it is assumes that we know, or can know, how the law would be applied in a particular case. This is not always as simple as it sounds, however. After all, if lawyers could agree on what a court of law would do, it would not be necessary for them to go to court to find out. Put another way, it is precisely because it is so difficult for lawyers to make accurate predictions as to what it is that a court will or will not do that leaves the couple with a problem in the first place.

The problem of the law's unpredictability has become accentuated with the enactment of equitable distribution statutes, which provide for the distribution of property between the parties at the time of their divorce. Ironically, that is precisely because the courts have been charged with the responsibility of attempting to achieve an equitable distribution of that property; for the goal of achieving such an equitable distribution is necessarily at variance with the goal of having a predictable result, just as the goal of predictability ultimately undermines the attempt to do justice in each particular instance.

This can perhaps best be illustrated by comparing equitable distribution statutes with those that generally provide for the distribution of property, not upon divorce, but upon death. The extent to which a wife has a right to share in her husband's estate upon his death is generally dependent on the number of children that her husband has.[32] Thus, in the State of New York, for example, if her husband has no children, a wife is entitled to receive one-half of his estate. If he has two children living at the time of his death, she is only entitled to receive one-third.[33] Since the only relevant circumstance is the number of children the husband had who are alive at the time of his death, and since that is generally easily ascertainable and rarely in dispute, it is not very difficult to determine (predict) just what portion of her husband's estate a wife is entitled to receive upon his death. Unfortunately, however, since the number of children the husband had is the only relevant circumstance, the application of the law can result in tremendous inequities.

For example, a wife in a childless marriage of but one year is entitled to receive a greater percentage of her husband's estate than is a wife who has been married to her husband for 30 years and borne him four children. By the same token, and just as unfairly, in neither case is the wife's entitlement dependent upon the contribution she made to the marriage, or how devoted she was to her husband. All wives are entitled to the same portion of their husband's estates, whether they were the best of wives or the worst of wives, whether they be old and infirm or young and healthy.[34]

Under equitable distribution statutes, all wives are obviously not treated the same. Quite the contrary, all the factors irrelevant in determining a wife's entitlement to share in her husband's estate—for example, the length of the parties' marriage, the age and health of the parties, the extent of their own separate estates, the contributions each made to the marriage—are critical to the court's determination as to her entitlement to share in her husband's estate upon her divorce, since it is only a consideration of those various factors that will result in an equitable distribution.[35]

Unfortunately, and while this may result in a fairer determination in each case, it also makes that determination far more difficult to predict, since by definition it is dependent upon the unique facts of each case. To put it another way, while our inheritance laws may not be particularly fair in that they treat all wives the same, to the very extent that they are unfair, their application is very predictable. Conversely, while our equitable distribution laws may be much *fairer*, in that they judge each wife on her own merits, to the very extent that they are fairer, their application is *less* predictable.[36]

All the problems involved in using the law as a standard of fairness were illustrated in a course on family law given at the Columbia University School of Law. In an attempt to teach family law in a setting closer to that in which it is practiced, the student lawyers were divided into two law firms, one to represent a cardiovascular surgeon in the midst of divorce and the other to represent his wife. Each law firm was broken down into ten or more teams of lawyers, who were charged with the responsibility of negotiating a settlement for their respective clients. In each instance, the teams of student lawyers from the two firms were given the exact same factual information about their respective clients and negotiated their settlements with the exact same set of laws as their yardstick. Yet in no instance were the final agreements concluded by the student lawyers the same. [37]

Did this mean that all but one of the teams had concluded the wrong agreement— had concluded an agreement that was unfair? Of course not. All that it meant was that *fair* means different things to different people, even when they use the same yardstick of the law and apply it to the very same set of facts.

Is "Fair" What the Mediator Considers to Be Fair?

If a legal yardstick of what is fair or unfair is not sufficient, what yardstick can we use? Perhaps a fair agreement is one the mediator considers, based upon his experience and judgment, to be fair. Unfortunately, with this definition there are even more problems than with the last, not the least of which is that it is no less presumptuous for a mediator to state with assurance what is or is not fair in the world than it is for an adversarial attorney. In fact, it is even more presumptuous, given the fact that the mediator claims to be speaking for both parties.

There is a far more serious problem in using the mediator's judgment as the appropriate yardstick. While mediators may assert their views as to what is fair or unfair with great assurance, in the final analysis that assurance is only proof of the strength of their convictions, not their correctness. To make matters worse, mediators are no more unanimous in their view of what is fair or unfair than are adversarial lawyers, or any other group, for that matter. Worse yet, and whether they wish to acknowledge it or not, they bring their own prejudices with them to mediation. There are their prejudices based upon their sex. There are their prejudices based upon their profession of origin. There are their prejudices based upon their own personal life experiences. And there are their prejudices that are simply a reflection of the prejudices of the society in which we live and even the logic in our thinking.

Let us illustrate this. It is simply a fact of life, for example, that our idea of fairness is affected by certain views we hold about men and women. Men are considered to be strong and to be able to take care of themselves. Women, on the other hand, are considered to be dependent and in need of care. Thus, if it is suggested that the proceeds of the home owned by the parties be divided between them equally, we will generally feel that this is fair. Let us suppose, however, that the husband comes forward and says that the wife can keep more than half. Our response will generally be to say that this is "more than fair."

Suppose, however, it is the wife who suggests that the husband can keep more than half of the proceeds. While we might not object, the suggestion will still probably make us feel a little less than comfortable and question in our mind whether it would be "fair." (We will also probably question her motive in making this suggestion, and whether or not she will later regret it.) Of course, if the husband were to suggest that he should receive more than half of the proceeds, there would be no question in our minds. That would be "completely unfair."

The difference in our attitude toward men and women was reflected in a mediation conducted between parties who had agreed to a joint custodial arrangement in which their son would live one week with his mother and one week with his father. There was a great disparity in the incomes of the parties despite the fact that they were both equally well educated, except that in this instance it was the wife who had the larger of the two incomes. She was employed by a large firm and earned approximately $48,000 a year. Her husband, however, as a free-lance designer and instructor at a vocational training institute, earned only $21,000 a year. At the outset of the mediation, the husband said that he wanted no interest in his wife's pension, or, for that matter, anything else that she had; nor was he looking for any contribution from her for the support of their child. This was accepted by the mediator without objection.

Had the situation been reversed, and had it been the wife who had made such a statement, would the mediator have felt quite so comfortable? In fact, would he not have felt under an obligation to assure himself that the wife knew the implications of renouncing her interest in her husband's pension and would he not have questioned whether an agreement that did not contain provision for the husband to make payment to her for the support of their child would be in her best interests? Why did the mediator not feel compelled to step in and question the husband's statement here? Because what he heard speaking was the husband's pride as a man in not wanting to be dependent upon a woman. Being a man himself, he understood this, and did not stop to question whether the result was fair or unfair.

Curious at his reaction, the mediator presented the same fact pattern to another mediator, who was a female. She was not bothered by the situation at all. On the contrary, she was mildly angry at the man. Why didn't he make more money? After all, he was a man, and a well-educated one at that. His career had not been interrupted by the necessity of having to give birth to his son, as had his wife's. In fact, her reaction was that if the husband's circumstances were as they appeared, then he had no one to blame but himself. After all, he was a man.

Nor will differences of opinion among mediators be confined to unusual cases. They will be just as prevalent in the ordinary, everyday issues with which mediators are presented. Take the following example. A husband, 49 years of age, and his wife, who is 45, have been married for 25 years. Their one child, 21 years of age, has just graduated from college and is self-sufficient. The husband, who is an accountant, is employed and earns $55,000 a year. His wife, who is an interior designer, earns $33,000. Does the husband have any obligation to support his wife and, if he does, what should be the amount of his support payments and how long should he be obligated to make them?

How is a mediator to determine this? Is the answer based upon whether or not the wife is sufficiently able to provide for her own support? If it is, then she is probably not entitled to support, because it cannot be said that a single woman is not capable of supporting herself on $33,000 a year, as interior designers who are not married obviously do. Is it instead to be based on the disparity in their incomes? If it is, and since her husband earns 66⅔% more than she does, she is probably entitled to support. Even if we are to assume that a support payment is justified, however, how much should it be? Is it fair that, after a marriage of 25 years, her husband should be left better off than she is? If it is not, then she should probably receive $11,000 a year, or one-half the difference between their incomes.

Is it fair, on the other hand, that her husband should never be better off than she, even though his earning potential is greater? If the answer is no, then the payments should probably be less than $11,000 a year. But how much less? Finally, how long should he be obligated to support her? Should her husband be obligated to support her until she has rehabilitated herself and is able to achieve her maximum potential? If that is the case, he may not have any obligation to support her at all, since she has already achieved that level of competency. Should he be required to support her so long as there is a significant disparity in their incomes? If that is the case, and since there will probably always be such a significant disparity, he may be obligated to support her forever.

If neither of these criteria is appropriate, what criteria can we properly apply? Like the teams of law students who negotiated different settlements for the cardiovascular surgeon and his wife, there will be as many answers to this question as there are mediators to whom it is posed, and we are left with the dilemma that what is "fair" may ultimately depend upon the particular mediator that a couple gets.

Perhaps the difficulty in determining what was fair or unfair in the last example had little to do with differences of opinion among mediators. Perhaps, instead, it had to do with the complexity of the fact situation. After all, it is admittedly very difficult to make judgments such as this in marriages of long duration, where the lives of the parties are so intertwined with one another and where one may have substantially changed his or her position based upon the fact of their marriage. But that is not to say that it is not possible to make such judgments in cases where the facts are less complicated, or that experienced mediators will not be able to agree on what is fair in those instances.

Let us see if this is so. In a particular case, a mediator was confronted by a couple who had been married for 10 years. Neither of the parties had changed their positions as a result of their marriage either to have children (they had no children) or for any other reason. Although they had both worked throughout the course of their marriage, there was a substantial disparity in their incomes. At the time of their divorce, they had combined savings of approximately $90,000 which, aside from an inheritance of approximately $35,000 which had been received by the party having the larger of the two incomes, was their only property of any value. (They did not own a home.) When it came to the question of the disposition of these savings, the party with the larger income suggested that they be divided between them 70–30, in exact proportion to the incomes which each of them had contributed to the marriage.

Was this suggestion fair? More importantly for our purposes, will any number of mediators agree upon whether it is or not? There are certainly at least two very different, and perhaps legitimate, ways of viewing the situation. This was not a situation where each of the parties had made different contributions—for example, one as a homemaker and the other as a wage earner—that were difficult to compare. Their contributions had been of the same kind and, without question, there was a substantial disparity in the quantity of those contributions. In fact, but for the contribution of the larger wage earner, there would not have been any savings at all, as the income of the smaller wage earner, when matched by an equal contribution from the larger wage earner, was just sufficient to meet their living expenses. Why, in a situation such as this, should one of the parties be unjustly enriched, and get more than he or she gave?

That, of course, is how the situation looks from the standpoint of contributions. But how does it look when the marriage is viewed as a partnership? The two parties did not start out with an agreement that they were to be treated differently in the marriage. Rather, they started out as equal partners. To be sure, either of them had the right, at any time, to raise his or her hand and complain that there was an inequity in the relationship—that the financial, emotional, intellectual, or other contributions each made to the marriage were inequitably disparate—and to end it so as not to continue to be shortchanged in the future.

But that does not mean that the party who raised his or her hand had the right to turn back the clock and ignore the fact that, at least up to this point, they were equal partners; and if the party with the smaller of the two incomes had known that the other would later assert that right, he or she might never have entered into the marriage in the first place. Furthermore, would it be fair for the parties to leave the marriage in such unequal positions, with the one having the greater ability and future prospects being given the added advantage of the larger of the two stakes as well?

Which of the arguments is the better one? Or, to put it in terms which we better understand, could it be said that only one of these points of view had validity?[38] More importantly for our purposes, do we have any reason to assume that different mediators will be of the same opinion here? The mediator who had been presented with this problem was a man. To test out his own reaction, he decided to present the facts to another mediator who was a woman. She had very great difficulty with the problem. Why was that? Because, unlike the mediator who had been confronted with the problem, she did not know whether the party with the larger of the two incomes was the husband or the wife.

To complicate matters, and although she suspected that the fact that the problem had been presented to her in the first place might suggest that the fact pattern was an unusual one—that it was the wife who had the larger of the two incomes—she was afraid to rely on that. In fact, she was so fazed by the question—by the risk that in conceding that a larger share of the savings should go to the larger wage earner that it might have been the wife that she left with less, or that by conceding that their savings should be divided equally, she may have given the husband more—that she was literally unable to answer the question.

"Would it make any difference," he continued, "if I told you that the party with the smaller of the two incomes had agreed to accept a 70–30 division of the assets?" Unfortunately, it did not, for now she had the added problem of worrying about the circumstances that had caused the wife to permit her husband to walk away with a lion's share of the savings, if in fact it was the wife whose income was smaller. (In actual fact, the couple had already agreed upon a 70–30 division of their assets before they came into mediation. Nor was the mediator particularly bothered by that arrangement—perhaps for the reason that it was the wife who had the larger of the two incomes. His only problem was that at the time that they came into mediation, her income was almost four times that of her husband—78% of their combined incomes—and he couldn't help but wonder what his reaction would have been had the situation been reversed.)

Until now we have only considered the different yardsticks that a mediator might reasonably apply, based upon the different views that society holds concerning men and women. But what about the other nonrational considerations that affect a mediator's judgment as to what is fair or unfair? If we acknowledge that we are each influenced by our experience, then is it anything less than naive to pretend that our judgments, even our judgments as to what is fair or unfair, will not be influenced by that experience?

Is it realistic, for example, to believe that a mediator who has been divorced, and who receives child support from her former husband that she considers to be inadequate, will necessarily have the same opinion as to what constitutes adequate support as will a mediator who has never been married, or has been married but has never been divorced? Similarly, would it be reasonable to expect that these opinions would necessarily conform to the one held by a mediator who was himself divorced and obligated to make child support payments? And can we ignore the possibility that a mediator might unconsciously resist seeing a wife receive more by way of alimony or child support then she herself receives, or a husband's paying less than he himself pays? Is it really possible to rule out these and the many other emotional considerations that affect our judgments, and might, for the same reasons, affect the judgment of a mediator as to what is fair or unfair?

In short, we cannot solve the problem of what is fair by saying that it is what experienced mediators say it is. Perhaps this is because the concept of fairness is too elusive and too hard to pin down. Perhaps we cannot rid our judgments of our own particular biases and points of view. Perhaps the very concept of *fair* is not a given that can be applied at all times and at all places, but is one that is forever being revised. Whatever the reason, it is simply not possible to arrive at an objective yardstick that can be applied by all mediators in all instances, or even one that they will all apply in the same way, and with the same result, in any particular instance.

Is "Fair" What a Couple Considers to Be Fair?

On the face of it, the problem of fairness could be solved quite easily by defining a fair agreement as one which the parties themselves consider to be fair, and a number of people in the field of mediation have proposed such a subjective yardstick as far more appropriate than, for example, the objective yardstick that the law provides. [39]

Unfortunately, however, this definition is not without its problems either. To begin with, to say that fair is not what the law says it is, or even what experienced mediators say it is, but what the couple themselves feel is fair, is not to solve the problem, for we are again just left with many different opinions as to what is fair and what is not fair, and not a necessary set of criteria by which to judge between them.

There is another, even more serious, problem in using this definition of *fair*. To suggest to the parties that the object of mediation is to conclude an agreement that each of them will consider to be fair is also to suggest to them that they will be left with such an agreement. It is irresponsible to make such a suggestion. Worse yet, to do so is simply to mimic the failings of traditional adversarial divorce proceedings. At least one of the reasons separating and divorcing couples who resort to adversarial proceedings are left as hurt and angry when they get through as they were when they began is because their lawyers have all too often given them very unrealistic expectations. Nor does it make any difference that these expectations were justified by their attorneys with the claim that all that they were trying to get for them was what was fair. On the contrary, it only makes their disappointment worse, for having received or been left with less, the necessary implication is that the agreement they received was an unfair one.

While it may be discomfiting to say so, the truth is that their agreement will not be fair, at least as they see it. There is nothing about their divorce that is fair, and it makes no sense to suggest to them that there is. What has happened to them is a terrible thing, and it will not do to pretend otherwise. It certainly will not do to suggest that mediation will correct that wrong—that it will make it all right by leaving them with an agreement that is fair to each of them. On the contrary, one of the hardest jobs that the mediator will have is to get the parties to accept the situation despite the fact that, at least from their standpoint, it *must* seem so *un*fair.

What the mediator seeks, therefore, is not an agreement that each of the parties considers to be fair, but, and far more modestly, simply one that they are each willing to *accept* and feel they can *live with*. To be sure, it is not an agreement that they accept in anger or out of frustration, because this too would be simply to duplicate the kinds of agreements that are so often concluded through adversarial proceedings. Nor, however, is it one that they accept because it represents some perfect, or even approximate, justice. There *is* no justice in the *situation*, as they see it, and for them to be able to conclude an agreement means that, at least on some level, they are willing to accept *this*. *That* is why their personal judgments of what is fair or unfair *cannot* be the final arbiter, even if they are necessarily relevant. And that is why they will not serve as an adequate yardstick, or solve the problem.

Fairness as the Absence of Coercion

Lacking either an objective or subjective yardstick to turn to, it is sometimes thought that the definition of a fair agreement is one that is concluded without coercion. After all, an agreement concluded, not because one wanted to, but because one *had* to, is not an agreement at all, and as we have outlawed shotgun weddings, so too should we outlaw shotgun divorces. That is all very well and good. The problem, however, is that the coercion exerted by one or both of the parties is never a shotgun. Rather, it is your everyday, garden-variety type of coercion, and it is simply not possible to get rid of it.

If a husband, though convinced of the necessity of his decision to leave his wife, is plagued by feelings of guilt in having abandoned his children, and if his wife, due to her anger, reinforces those feelings, that is not coercion, that is simply a fact of life. If a husband is an imposing person who tends to intimidate his wife, that too is a fact of reality. These are simply aspects of each of the parties' personalities that the other has had to live with in their marriage, and they are the same aspects of their personalities that the mediator is going to have to live with in their divorce. Nor will it do to complain that the presence of these emotional components makes it impossible to conclude an agreement. It doesn't. It just makes it more difficult.

Suppose, in the middle of a mediation, the wife threatens that if the husband will not desist from the demands he is making that she will terminate the mediation and proceed to court. Is that coercion? Or is it simply the expression by the wife of her bottom line? Anytime one of the parties takes a stand and says, in effect, "I will not be pushed beyond this point," it has a coercing effect. But is that necessarily bad or inappropriate? After all, isn't that simply part of the reality with which the other party will have to deal?

There is a final point that must be made. Even when coercion is not characterological in origin, the situation may have such a coercing effect. The wife is at a disadvantage not because her husband is more persistent and dogged than she; she is at a disadvantage because she desperately wants to end the marriage, which he does not. The husband is at a disadvantage not because his wife necessarily has a stronger personality than he, but because he is locked in a marriage to a borderline personality. The wife is at a disadvantage not because her husband is necessarily more knowledgeable and astute than she, but because he has a rigid, inflexible personality.

One could have very interesting (and unfortunately very lengthy) discussions as to whether or not it is fair that one of the parties should have to bargain in a context such as this. Unfortunately, these discussions are as irrelevant as they would be inconclusive. In any event, that is the reality, and the mediator is not going to change it. In fact, the more intransigent and difficult to deal with the other party is (in conventional characterization, the more *power* that he or she has), the *less effective* the mediator will be. For while the mediator may be able to effectuate change if one of the parties is only mildly intransigent, if he is a borderline personality, he may not be able to change him at all.

What If the Price of Mediation Is an Unfair Agreement?

Let us advance the argument one step further. We will now assume, at least for the sake of argument, that a mediator is under an obligation to assure that the agreement concluded by the couple is fair to each of them. We will even assume, again for the sake of the argument, that it is possible to judge whether or not an agreement is fair by a yardstick that has been freed of all of the problems with which we have wrestled up to this point. To prejudice the matter further, we have purposely reduced that standard to a minimal level to guarantee that there will be absolutely no dissent as to whether the agreement in question is fair or is not fair. Now suppose that it is not possible to conclude an agreement that meets even this standard? In fact, suppose that the price that one of the parties will have to pay to conclude any agreement at all is to accept one that is manifestly unfair?

It is the concern that this is just the kind of an agreement that one of the parties may well be left with without the benefit of the safeguards our adversarial system provides that is behind all the criticism of divorce mediation. And since it is a concern to which mediators are very sensitive, the standard answer they have given is that a mediator has an obligation to disassociate himself from the mediation when he believes either that one or both of the parties is not proceeding in good faith or, worse yet, that the agreement that is being concluded is not fair to one of them.

Before mediators throw the couple out into the cold, however, they ought to give more serious thought to the question. In fact, mediators should consider whether or not they have been asking the right question in the first place. For, as we will argue, the question that a mediator should properly ask himself at that point is not whether he is willing to be a party to an agreement that is manifestly unfair to one of the parties but, rather, how he will have helped the party whom he wishes to protect if he refuses to do so.

Consider the following example. A couple consults a mediator in San Francisco. They had originally come from Philadelphia, but had moved to San Francisco with their daughter, who is now eleven years of age, when the husband was reassigned by the corporation with whom he was employed. The husband has a passive-aggressive personality and while, on the surface, he presents himself as a pleasant, reasonable and, at times, even jocular person, this veneer is very thin. Beneath it seethes a constricted, angry man who has on more than one occasion been guilty of minor, but nevertheless inappropriate, physical abuse of his wife.

The wife is anxious to leave San Francisco and return with their daughter to Philadelphia, where her family lives. Time and time again throughout the mediation she has had to suffer her husband's attempts to be less than fair with her. When she rejected her husband's initial proposal for support of their child, his response was that there would simply not be an agreement between them and that they would have to fight it out in court. Although the mediator was able to increase the suggested amount slightly, it was still inadequate, and the husband resisted each further advance by stating that he would not be left with an amount that was insufficient for his needs, refusing to consider that this so-called "insufficient" amount was still substantially more than the wife would have for herself and their child, even with her own earnings.

Although he did not presently live in their marital residence in San Francisco, and although it was the wife's intention to vacate it and move to Philadelphia, he refused to permit the sale of the home, which constituted their principal asset. It was his intention to put in for a transfer back to the East Coast, and although it might take some two years for that transfer to be approved and accomplished, he preferred to rent the home rather than to sell it because if he owned the home at the time of his transfer, his employer would pick up all of his expenses in connection with its sale and his relocation. Nor would he share this reimbursement with his wife (who had to pay her own expenses to get back to Philadelphia) in exchange for her willingness to hold off the sale and to defer having the use of her equity in the home.

Even when it came to the distribution of the proceeds of the home upon its sale, the husband kept trying to get the edge on his wife. Initially, he had held out for two-thirds of the increase in the value of the home between the present time and the time that it was sold, arguing that this was only fair because he would have the "headache" of selling it after she had gone and because he was going to be inconvenienced by his wife's move to Philadelphia and his not being able to see his daughter on a regular basis. He also wanted deducted from the selling price his expenses in making certain repairs to the home, which he insisted be based upon his present, inflated estimates rather than their actual cost.

Later on, he switched tactics and decided that he would prefer a "clean break," and wanted to freeze his wife's interest in the home by valuing it at the present time and buying her out at that price—even though she would not receive her share until he actually sold the home, perhaps two years later. Even here, he tried to lowball the selling price as between the two of them by insisting upon being permitted to deduct prospective brokerage commissions from the price (despite the fact that he might not sell it through a broker at all) and by inflating his anticipated closing costs. (When the mediator, who was an attorney, advised him that the seller never paid the cost of title insurance or a mortgage recording tax, he dismissed this information by stating that although the mediator was a lawyer, he was not a real estate lawyer.)

At each session, the husband arrived with a huge notebook of material. Invariably, he would open up the notebook and take out three copies of a long, computerized sheet of information that he had prepared for the session, handing one of the copies to his wife and one to the mediator. Referring to the sheet, he would then set forth his jagged logic to support the position he had previously taken, and to oppose that suggested by his wife. As if all of this were not difficult enough, when the meetings did not seem to be proceeding at the pace or in the direction he intended, he would send a message to his wife by turning to the mediator and observing that time was very important here as his wife had already made plans to move.

What should the mediator have done here? More to the point, should he have allowed himself to be a party to all of this by sitting by and permitting the husband to take advantage of his wife? For, all the niceties and polite talk aside, that is certainly what he was doing. The mediator pondered this question over and over. He knew that the husband was as anxious to get this done as was the wife to get to Philadelphia. He also knew, however, that the husband had a far more rigid personality. While the wife's dilemma was that she did not wish to allow what she thought was fair to get in the way of what she was trying to achieve, the husband's characterological flaw was that he inevitably did. Worse yet, the kinds of arguments that the husband advanced (when he advanced arguments at all) did not admit of any resolution, only an endless and meaningless debate.

If there was going to be any movement here, it could only be by the mediator's calling a spade a spade and letting the husband know that he felt that he was trying to take advantage of his wife. Unfortunately, and although the mediator could not prove this, he was firmly convinced that the only effect that this would have would be to give the husband cause to claim that the mediator was biased and upset the mediation.

The mediator was thus in a dilemma. If he threw down the gauntlet and let the husband know he felt that he was trying to take advantage of his wife, or if he refused to continue with the mediation and be a party to this, the mediator ran the risk of jeopardizing the mediation. However, if he did nothing, he would thereby permit the husband to take advantage of his wife, and in doing so be a party to it.

Then there was the hardest question of all. Suppose the mediator decided to confront the husband. For whose benefit would he be doing this? If he was doing this simply because it offended his own personal conception of what was right and what was fair, and because he did not wish to be a party to anything that was not, he was allowing his own personal interests and needs to interfere with his professional responsibility. His job, after all, was to attempt to help the parties (in this case, the wife), not to make moral judgments. But how would he be helping her if he simply intervened and caused the mediation to end, and where would that have left her?

And what of the wife? How did she view her husband's coercion? Much the same way as she would have had he been a stranger who had abducted her child. She could have complained that it was unfair that, in order to obtain her daughter's release, she was going to have to pay the ransom that he was demanding. Only a fool would waste his time in such meaningless philosophizing, however, and the time would be far better spent attempting to raise the necessary money to secure her release. (When the child was returned, there would be time enough for such intellectual moralizing, if anyone was still interested.)

The wife here (the weaker spouse) was in the same position. From her standpoint, her husband held her life for ransom, and she wanted to reclaim it. She could have made a case (at least she could have persuaded herself) that to have done business with her husband over the length of their marriage was always to have come out on the short end of the stick. In fact, at least one of the reasons she wanted a divorce was to end what she felt was this injustice in their relationship.

Put another way, on some level at least, her divorce represented an acknowledgment on her part that it was impossible for her to change her husband or, therefore, the inequity in their relationship. For better or for worse, this was the reality, and, at least from her standpoint, it meant that she might have to come out on the short end of the stick one last time. While, at least intellectually, it might be proper to say that her decision to divorce had been made because she no longer wished to come out on the short end of the stick, even only one more time, and that having made that decision, she no longer should, the reality was that their relationship was not yet over, and that until it was—until an agreement had been concluded—she was still burdened with the disabilities of that relationship.

To be sure, she could have resorted to adversarial proceedings in an attempt to get her husband to do what was right, but that was not what she wanted. She wanted to get done with it and, as her husband correctly suggested, get on a plane to Philadelphia; and to resort to such procedures might only have prolonged the matter interminably. Nor was there any guarantee that those proceedings would have resulted in a fair agreement. Those who have insisted that a mediator must disassociate himself from an agreement when he does not consider it to be fair have unwittingly lent support to the rather naive belief that if a mediator refuses to go along with an agreement when it is not fair, that a fair one is available for the asking—simply by resorting to adversarial proceedings. This, unfortunately, is not the case.

While one may *wish* to assume that the agreement would be fairer, in actual fact it might not be; and it would certainly be a mistake to assume that it would be fair in the sense that we are talking about here. Difficult people are difficult in any setting, and while it may offend us to accept the fact that they come off better than reasonable people, the fact is that they sometimes do, even if, in order to make this unpleasant fact more palatable, we add "but only in a limited sense." The cost of doing business with them is simply too great. That being the case, it is even possible that this wife might have come away with the same agreement when, after months and perhaps years of an unresolved situation, she only then conceded to her husband what she was unable or unwilling to concede to him now.

But even if she did come away with everything she wanted, and rightfully deserved, what about the price she would have had to pay—not only in getting it, but also in having gotten it? It is wonderful for a mediator to walk away satisfied that he has concluded an agreement that is fair to the wife, and if he can do that with but a little persuasion exerted on the husband, that is fine. However, if he can only accomplish this by beating him at his own game, what price will he later exact (and what price will the wife later have to pay) for having done this? In the real world these are real questions, and they will not go away simply by invoking the stock answer that it is a mediator's obligation to conclude an agreement that is fair to both of the parties.

THE PRICE OF AN AGREEMENT

There is one last problem that must be addressed in connection with the question of fairness. It is not sufficient that the critics of divorce mediation have faulted it for a sin of which they are equally guilty, nor that they have attempted to saddle divorce mediation with both an imprecise and arbitrary standard. It is not sufficient that they are improperly imposing conditions on the parties at the time of their divorce that they very properly refrained from imposing upon them either at the commencement of or during their marriage. It is not even sufficient that in judging agreements by the standard of fairness alone, and by then elevating that standard to a shibboleth, they have eliminated as a relevant consideration the *cost* that the parties may well have to pay to obtain such an agreement. The final insult is that, in claiming that the price that couples may well have to pay by resorting to mediation is that they will be left with an unfair agreement, they have improperly suggested that agreements concluded through adversarial proceedings are not only necessarily fair, but are also cost-free.

Whether they wish to admit it or not, there will be a *price* involved in obtaining *any* agreement, and the critics of divorce mediation, in concentrating only on the possible costs of concluding an agreement in mediation, simplistically and disingenuously ignore this. As we have noted, to reject an agreement in mediation as unfair is *not* to be given a *better* one, just for the asking. On the contrary, it will come only at a price, and usually a very high one. Thus, the proper question is not what price a party will pay in attempting to conclude an agreement through mediation, but, rather, what price will he pay if he is unable or unwilling to conclude an agreement in that way?

There is a further point that must be made. In decrying the price that one of the parties may have to pay in order to conclude an agreement through mediation, the advocates of adversarial proceedings have prejudiced the issue by very narrowly defining what will be considered as included in the price that they will have to pay should they turn instead to adversarial proceedings. Will that price include the financial cost of those proceedings? Will it include the time those proceedings will take? Will it include the emotional trauma that the parties and, more importantly, their children, will suffer? The answer is no. The tunnel vision of adversarial lawyers is such that there is only one consideration, namely, will the agreement be fair—will it resemble the agreement the parties would have been left with had they gone to court.

But what would an adversarial lawyer say if pressed about the costs of obtaining such an agreement? His answer would be a very curious one—moreover, one that permits him the luxury of ignoring all of the other relevant considerations. For him, those other factors are simply the price that the wife may have to pay in order to enforce her legal rights, and he does not consider it within his province to judge whether that price is worth paying. It may be very unfair that the wife in this instance may have to subject herself to months, and perhaps even years, of costly litigation in order to obtain custody of her daughter, and the right to move to Philadelphia with her, without having to pay the ransom that her husband is demanding in the negotiations for her release; but that is the price that one pays to secure what one wants in the real world. It may not be fair, but then no one ever suggested that it would be.

But if adversarial lawyers do not question that price, let alone the wife's absolute right to decide whether or not it is an acceptable one for her to pay for what she wants, if she resorts to traditional adversarial divorce proceedings, why then is that price now questioned simply because she has turned to mediation?

The answer, of course, is that it should not be. If we are willing to sit by and allow a wife to take whatever steps she deems necessary to obtain what she considers to be a fair agreement, regardless of its cost, why should we object if she accepts an agreement that she considers to be less than fair because of those costs? The answer is that we do not, provided only that her decision is made in an adversarial context. If the wife's lawyer is unable to secure for her what she wants (what she considers to be fair) through negotiations, and if her only recourse will be costly litigation, if she ultimately decides to settle for what she can get rather than to fight on, he will not take exception to the fact that it is her right to do so. He may advise her that he feels that the settlement is unfair. He may even recommend that she reject her husband's offer and take the matter to court. But he does not dispute the fact that it is ultimately her decision to make.

In complaining, therefore, that agreements concluded in mediation may be unfair to one of the parties, the critics of divorce mediation are not only simplistic and inconsistent, but also disingenuous. For when all is said and done, it is not that they object to unfair agreements; it is simply that they object to unfair agreements that are not concluded in an adversarial setting.

CONCLUSION

What then is the mediator's obligation in relationship to the agreement concluded by the parties? In particular, what obligation does he have to assure that it is fair?

Nothing that we have said should be construed to suggest that a mediator can forsake the attempt to conclude an agreement that is fair (or, to be more accurate, that he can forsake the *attempt* to avoid concluding an agreement that is *un*fair), despite the many limitations in the concept of fairness as a yardstick, and despite the numerous other problems to which we have referred. As considerable as those limitations may be, the parties nevertheless invest with importance the fact that what they are attempting to achieve is an agreement that will be fair to them. Thus, if they are to give their assent to that agreement, they must either be persuaded that it is, or be made to understand why it cannot be, and helped to accept it if that is the case.

What we would insist upon, however—and this is the whole thrust of our argument—is that the mediator's quest for an agreement that is fair must, of necessity, be undertaken in a world of competing values, conflicting considerations, and different points of view. Nor is it possible to advance one except at the expense of the other. The most that a mediator can hope to do, therefore, is to reach an appropriate balance between them; and there is no guarantee that he will be able to do even that. In short, it will not do to expect perfect solutions to imperfect problems.

That is why a mediator cannot simplistically accept as his goal, and only goal, the effectuation of an agreement that is equally fair to both of the parties. Nor can he, just as simplistically, reject all those that are not. This is a luxury that neither he nor the parties can afford, and it will not do for him to attempt to lighten his burden by employing such a narrow-minded, singular definition of his obligation to the parties he is seeking to help. That, after all, is exactly the defense that adversarial lawyers have traditionally given for their refusal to consider the broader aspects of the problems with which they are confronted, and the terrible personal price that divorcing couples and their children have paid in the process—namely, that what they are concerned with is *justice*, and the conclusion of an agreement that is *fair* to their clients.

Consider the following situation. The decision to divorce had been made by the wife, over her husband's objection. He was furious at the decision she had made, a decision he did not want, did not understand, and was having an even more difficult time accepting. In fact, he was so overwhelmed by his hurt and anger that all that he wanted to do was somehow to make her feel the terrible pain that she had caused him. To add to the problem, he saw himself as the only one who was going to have to pay for that decision. From his standpoint at least, that would be the case if, as a result of their agreement, it was he, and he alone, who was forced to leave his home, his children, and his community, and left faced with the difficult task of rebuilding his life, while his wife simply went on very much as before.

Thus, he did not see why she should be permitted to continue to live in their home, and to sit on his considerable equity there, while he was forced to endure far less commodious accommodations. He therefore felt that it was only right that their home be sold so that he too could enjoy the benefit of the equity tied up in it by rolling it over into new living accommodations. (In fact, if he waited for his money, as his wife suggested, he might never have that benefit as, losing his rollover benefits under the tax code, he would be required first to pay approximately one-third of that profit in income taxes.) Nor, given his terrible hurt and anger, was he able to consider the consequences to his wife, or even to his children, in any of this.

For similar reasons, he also could not accept his wife's suggestion that she should receive a portion of his retirement benefits, thereby also invading the savings that he had worked to secure for his future. In fact, this was only to add insult to injury. From his standpoint, his pension was a benefit that she was supposed to enjoy if she stayed married to him, not if she left him. Nor was his opinion very much changed when his wife advised him that under the law his pension was marital property in which she had an interest as a result of their marriage.

It would never have occurred to the mediator to worry whether it was fair or unfair had the wife consented to the sale of their home or to give up her interest in her husband's pension. Such a concern would presuppose that the mediator could know what was fair here—that he could adjudicate between the competing points of view of the husband and the wife. The fact that our judicial system pretends that it can do this did not mean that the mediator should be similarly guilty of such arrogant nonsense. That is why he was not particularly concerned with whether or not the agreement that the parties concluded would have been the same as would have been imposed upon them by a judge in a court of law. And it certainly would not have occurred to him to assume that any such judgment would have represented a definite determination of what was fair or unfair in their lives.

Nor would it have occurred to him to object, should the wife have agreed to this, on the grounds that it was not in the best interests of her children. To be sure, he believed that it would be very unfortunate, and in fact very traumatic, for the children to be uprooted from their home. And if he could help the couple find a solution that would not require this, he would have very much liked to do so. But he would have also very much liked to see the parties save their marriage, in part for the same reason.

That did not mean, however, that he objected to the wife's decision to divorce her husband, or felt that he had a right to do so, simply because that decision would force these same children to suffer the trauma of their parents' separation. He did not pretend to know the consequences of all of the possible decisions that each of the parties could make in their lives. Nor did he pretend to know which of those possible decisions would be best for them (or for their children). Thus, and as he accepted the wife's feelings then, and the decision those feelings had led to, so too did he now accept her husband's.

The fact that the mediator did not pass judgment on the parties' feelings, or the reasons that they employed to justify them, did not mean that he was not *concerned* about the decisions that they made in their lives, or that he did not try to get them to take into account what he believed to be the appropriate considerations that should properly inform them. That is why he tried as hard as he did to get the husband to consider the effects upon his children if they were forced to move from their home, their friends, and their community. Nor did this mean that he was not concerned with the conditions under which those decisions were made. In fact, he considered that to be his principal responsibility.

Thus, while he was not ultimately concerned with whether or not the wife secured the right to live in the home, what did concern him was whether or not she knew that she had a right to do so—knew that a court of law would have most certainly given her the right to continue to live in the home with her children until they had at least graduated from high school. Aside from the fact that he believed that he had an obligation to assure himself that she was aware of this, as an act of responsibility, and although he could never know for sure how future considerations might affect their ability to live with the agreement they had concluded, he could not ignore the fact that if the wife gave in to her husband's demands, and later found out that she was not so required by law, that might well affect her ability to do so.

The answer here might have been to suggest that the wife consult with an attorney before she agreed to this. (Since the mediator was himself an attorney, he could have given her the same information—her attorney would have told her what her rights were; the mediator would have given her an answer.) This, too, would not have occurred to him. His problem, after all, was that he wanted to assure himself that she was aware of the law, not because rules of law necessarily represent what is fair, but because they are a reality and because her knowledge or lack of knowledge of those rules might well later affect whether or not she would be able to live with that agreement. Thus, though he wanted her to have the answer (or, in this case, assure himself that she was aware of it), he did not want to lay down those rules in a manner that would necessarily be determinative of the issue.

Why was that? Because to him the way the husband felt was also a reality and of equal force. It is fine to say that it is in the best interests of children that they not be required to experience the trauma of being uprooted from their home coincident with having to deal with the trauma of their parents' separation and divorce. Suppose, however, that this was accomplished only at the expense of the husband feeling that he had been dealt the terrible injustice of alone being asked to pay the price of his and his wife's divorce. Who is to say what consequences might flow from this that would also affect these children's best interests? That, too, was a reality. Nor was it any answer to this to say that, in allowing his own interests to take precedence over his children's, the husband was acting unreasonably. (Any more unreasonable than the wife had been in deciding to seek a divorce?) If the husband continued to feel as he did, then that too was part of the reality that his wife and children, and the mediator as well, had to live with. And that too, therefore, had to be a concern of his.

In short, the complexity of the world in which the mediator worked did not admit of the simplicity of one-dimensional yardsticks, even those that bore the legend "fair," or answers that were intended to end the discussion because they came packaged as "legal rights." For those yardsticks did not alter the fact that the parties came to the mediator with very different feelings and, therefore, very different points of view. For the mediator to conclude an agreement that both of the parties felt was fair would probably require him to get them to adopt a common point of view. But he knew that he was not going to be able to do this. (They had not been able to do it in their marriage, and he was not going to be able to do it in their divorce.) In fact, his job was somehow to get them to an agreement in spite of this.

CHAPTER 5
THE RULE OF LAW
IN DIVORCE MEDIATION

Mediators do not generally give much thought to the place and function of legal rules in mediation. They know that the negotiations between the parties take place in "the shadow of the law," to use the phrase coined by Mnookin & Kornhauser.[1] They also know that these negotiations somehow involve legal rights and obligations that each of the parties have. Nevertheless, they view these legal rights and obligations as somewhat mysterious and beyond their understanding. As a result, they leave these matters in the hands of lawyers, and dutifully instruct the parties that they should each have separate counsel of their own choice to advise them of their respective legal rights.

Nor does a mediator understand how lawyers actually determine the legal rights and obligations of the parties. Thus, when the couple returns from consulting with their lawyers and reject the proposed agreement (the husband saying that his attorney advised him that he had given too much, and the wife that her attorney advised her that she had gotten too little), the mediator has no idea how the two lawyers came to these conclusions—which only deepens the mystery. Nevertheless, the mediator does not question the fact that the procedure he has recommended, and the couple has dutifully followed, makes sense and is necessary to protect their respective interests, even though he would be hard pressed to tell you why. Again, it is better not to think about it.

It is important, nevertheless, that mediators give thought to the place of these legal rules in mediation. Time and time again, the mediator will be confronted with the fact of these rules. How should he deal with them? What effect do they or should they have upon the mediation? Is it important that the mediator assure himself that the parties are familiar with these rules, and how should he do this? What if the couple's agreement does not conform to these rules? It is not possible for a mediator to discharge his obligation unless and until he has first come to terms with the question of *the place of these legal rules* in mediation.[2]

THE USE OF LEGAL RULES IN TRADITIONAL ADVERSARIAL DIVORCE PROCEEDINGS

As has been suggested previously, the failure of divorce mediation to come to terms with the question of the role of legal rules in mediation is based in large measure upon a misunderstanding of what legal rules are. Even more importantly, however, it is based on a misunderstanding of how they are applied in traditional adversarial divorce proceedings. This misunderstanding is compounded by the fact that the law is viewed as embodying not legal rules but, rather, legal rights. This gives our laws an immutable, etched-in-granite character and endows them with a special importance. Rather than being simply the expression of the considerations that a court would use in making its determination, they take on the aura almost of God-given rights with which each of us is born. Obviously, if they have this significance, it is important for the parties to know what they are. In fact, to ignore them is to allow the couple to proceed at their peril, and to risk coming away with less than is their due.

Our beliefs notwithstanding, these are not what legal rules are. More importantly, this is not how they are *employed* in adversarial proceedings. These substantive legal rules, together with the numerous procedural rules of the law, simply represent *benefit and detriment cards—pawns*, if you will, in the game of legal chess. Some of these rules represent advantages and some disadvantages for the respective players. It is the lawyer's job, based upon his understanding of these rules, and his experience and his skill, to use as many of these advantage cards as he can to advance the interests of his client and as many of these disadvantage cards as he can to impede the progress of his opponent. The other lawyer uses them in the same way and for the same purpose for *his* client's benefit. Thus, the substantive and procedural legal rules—the advantage and the disadvantage cards—simply become legal *weapons* that the two lawyers use to get or keep as much as they can for their respective clients.[3]

Nor could it be otherwise. The two attorneys do not view their clients as having come to them for help to resolve a serious problem in their lives. Rather, they view their clients as having come to them to be their representative and to advocate their cause. Moreover, since these proceedings take place in an accepted adversarial setting, this only tends to reinforce this attitude. In such a setting, it is not an attorney's function to question whether the rules of the game make sense or are fair. Nor is it his function to question whether his client will come out with more than he deserves. Rather, it is simply to apply those rules to his client's best advantage, and so long as he conducts himself ethically (observes the etiquette of the game), he has discharged his responsibility. In fact, for him to ask questions beyond this is to exceed his province. He was not hired to make moral judgments; he was hired to be his client's *champion*. Thus, if the use of those legal rules will leave his client with everything and his or her spouse with nothing, so be it. That only means that his client had a very good lawyer—and that, after all, was what he was paid to be.[4]

As we have said, adversarial lawyers do not question their role as hired guns. Nor do they question the fact that the name of the game they play is simply to get as much as you can and to give as little as you have to, and that the rule is that there are *no* rules—that it is anything and everything that the law will allow. Most importantly of all, there is no misconception in their minds as to what legal rules are or what their role is in applying them.

THE APPLICATION OF LEGAL RULES IN DIVORCE MEDIATION

Divorce mediation, quite naturally, rejects the idea that legal rules should be used simply as weapons in a game of legal chess to improve one party's position at the expense of the other. Similarly, it rejects the idea that these legal rules and principles embody any necessary wisdom or logic. In fact, it views them as rather arbitrary principles, having little to do with the realities of a couple's life and certainly not superior to the judgments that they could make on their own. What relevance, then, do these rules and principles have in mediation, and why is it necessary to know them?

To understand how mediation uses legal rules and principles, it is necessary first to take off the hat of an advocate and put on the hat of a mediator. Wearing that hat, what does one see? To begin with, and whether our laws are fair or unfair, the parties endow them with significance, and they therefore shape their expectations. That is a fact of life. If the law of a particular state says that if a husband has inherited property and it is in his name alone, that his wife does not have any interest in it, then the husband does not expect to have to give her any portion of it—and this is so whether the wife feels this to be fair or unfair. That is a reality with which a mediator will have to deal. However, unlike a lawyer in an adversarial setting, he is not bound by it. He does not believe that those rules embody any necessary logic, let alone guarantee any necessary justice. They may be limiting factors, but they are not absolutes. In fact, from his standpoint, the problem is that the expectations created by these rules and principles may just as easily produce an agreement between the parties that is unfair as it will one that is fair.

(Here, the property, which is the parties' only asset of any real value, was inherited recently by the husband. The wife's earlier inheritance, of about the same value, was used to put their three children through college and graduate school, and to finance trips and vacations which the parties took over the years, and has been completely dissipated.) In this instance, the law may be an obstacle to a fair agreement because it prevents the husband from looking at the facts of his and his wife's lives on their own terms and causes him instead to see them in terms of artificial categories that have little to do with the reality of their life together. The mediator's job, then, may be to see whether he can effectuate a fairer agreement than the law would provide—despite the expectations that the husband has based on the law. To be sure, he will not always be very successful in this. Legal fictions being what they are, the parties will all too often attach more significance to them than they deserve. Worse, they will also confuse them with equity and forget that they are only the vehicle by which the law attempts to do equity.[5] However, unless a mediator is willing to abandon the attempt to strive for equity in favor of simply parroting the law, he will have no choice but to try.

In other instances, the mediator will use the law as a reality principle. Instead of viewing it as an obstacle to be overcome, he will use it as a protective shield. In this case, the lack of agreement between the parties is occasioned by the fact that they disagree as to whether it is fair that the wife should have an interest in her husband's business. As arbitrary as the law may be in its determination (at one time it may have said no, at another time it may have said yes), the mediator can nevertheless invoke it as a means of resolving the disagreement when all else fails. When the husband refuses to concede that his wife should have any interest in his business, despite the inequity that would result if she did not, the mediator intervenes and says, "But that is the law." In this instance, he invokes the law, not for the purpose of deciding the disagreement between them, but for the purpose of ending it. The law is a reality, and although it may rub against the husband's intentions, he cannot, nevertheless, deny it.

From the standpoint of the mediator, what he is primarily trying to do is to effectuate change—in this case, a change from a lack of agreement to an agreement. At the same time, of course, he would like that agreement to be fair to each of the parties. However, since he does not view these legal rules and principles as constituting a guarantor of this, he does not believe that they represent a necessary yardstick by which to judge the agreement that he has helped the parties conclude. Rather, these legal rules and principles are simply realities that either *limit* what he is *able* to do or *aid* him in accomplishing what he *wants* to do.

How does this view of the law affect the way a mediator would treat legal rules and principles? To begin with, if a mediator suggested to a couple that they seek legal counsel, it would not be so that they could each determine their rights and obligations, to assure that their agreement accurately mirrored those rights and obligations. Knowing what he does about legal rules and how they are applied by lawyers, he would not believe that they could ever find out exactly what their rights were anyway—that they could ever find out, save by going to court, exactly how a court would apply those legal rules in their particular case. Nor does he believe that their agreement would necessarily be a better one because it conformed to the one a court of law would give them. Maybe it would and maybe it wouldn't.

If the mediator did suggest to the couple that they consult with an attorney, it would be for very different purposes. The first would be to avoid concluding an agreement that one or the other of the parties would later feel was unfair. Perhaps it would be extremely unfair in a particular instance for one of the parties to share in the other's pension. (The husband does not have a pension. However, his parents are extremely wealthy and he will be well provided for in his old age. The wife, on the other hand, will need every penny of her own pension to support herself when she retires.) Before he waives his interest in his wife's pension, however, it would be best that he knows that the law says that he has an interest in it. It is not that the disposition that the law would make in this case would be fairer. (Since the court in the particular jurisdiction could not take cognizance of the husband's future inheritance, or therefore consider it,[6] it might be far less fair.) It is simply that the mediator does not want to jeopardize the efficacy of the agreement as one both parties can live with, and this might well occur if the husband concluded an agreement without being aware that the law said he had a right to assert an interest in his wife's pension, and later found this out. Again, since legal fictions are realities in a very important sense, it would be irresponsible for a mediator to deny this fact, or to act in disregard of it.

Another instance in which the mediator would recommend that the parties consult with an attorney would be as a strategy to break an impasse. The couple disagrees as to whether it is fair that the wife should share in her husband's pension. It is not the purpose of mediation to have endless philosophical debates as to what is ultimately fair or unfair in the world, and there will be as many answers to that question as there are people who are asked their opinion. If the couple does not start out with a common view of what is fair or unfair, and if the mediator is unable to produce a common view, then there must be some way to break the impasse.

Here, referring the couple for legal counsel (to find out what the law says) may serve to do that, since the couple will feel obligated to accept what the law says whether they like it or not. However, since this is the only reason the mediator is referring the couple for legal counsel, it is not necessary that they consult with separate attorneys, as would be the case if legal rules and principles were viewed as rights that had to be championed. The only question at issue is whether the law in the particular jurisdiction would give the wife an interest in her husband's pension. One attorney will do. In fact, one lawyer will do better, since what the mediator wants is an answer, not just so many legal opinions that will decide nothing.

Since legal rules and principles are therefore simply a means to an end, and are used by a mediator as an intervention or strategy to achieve a desired result, the mediator does not consider himself slavishly bound by them. Rather, he is free to deal with them in a far less constricted manner. Suppose, for example, that there is a dispute between a husband and a wife as to how long she will have the right to live in their marital residence with their children. The husband turns to the mediator (who happens to be a lawyer) and says, "How long do I have to let her live in the home?"

What he is of course asking is how long the law will allow her to live there. The husband is now attempting to use the law as a strategy, not because he feels that the answer the law will give makes sense or is right, but simply because he believes that it will tend to side with his position. The mediator, of course, does not believe that there are or should be legal answers to personal questions. More importantly, he believes it is his job to bring home this fact to the husband. Instead of answering the question, therefore, he turns to the husband and asks one himself.

"Tell me," he says, "how are your children taking your separation? If they were required to leave their home and be uprooted from their community at this time, do you think that it might make it more difficult for them? And what about your son who is in the 10th grade? Do you think it would be a good idea to disrupt the continuity of his high school experience by being required to relocate to a new school district before he graduates?"

What the mediator is doing here is trying to get the husband to deal with the resolution of this issue on the basis of the same kinds of practical considerations that the couple used during their marriage (when they bought their home because they felt it would be a good place to raise their children, and because they wanted them to have the benefit of the schools in the area), rather than on the basis of the application of arbitrary legal rules and principles having little to do with their actual lives.

Nor would the situation be any different even if the parties' children were not involved. The youngest child will graduate from high school in about a year and there is nothing in his circumstances that would require maintaining the home beyond that date. Nevertheless, the wife is very threatened by such an imminent sale of the house and would like to be able to postpone it for another year or two. It might well be that a court would direct its sale when all of the children have graduated from high school. But that does not mean that the husband may not find it in himself to agree to permit his wife to live in the home beyond that date and thereby allow her a bit more time to adjust to the fact of their divorce should she need it. Nor does it mean that a mediator should not help him to do this if it seems warranted under the circumstances.

SELF-DETERMINATION

To say that legal rules are simply a means to an end—a strategy or intervention used by a mediator to achieve a desired result—raises a serious question. If a mediator employs legal rules in this fashion, is he not guilty of attempting to manipulate the couple and to influence them in a direction he himself has chosen? And isn't his attempt to do this in derogation of the principle of self-determination which a mediator, or any third party who intervenes in the life of another, ought to respect? In fact, isn't respect for the principle of self-determination the strongest argument in favor of the application of legal rules and principles to the resolution of a couple's dispute? They may not represent perfect justice and they may at times even be irrelevant to the realities of a couple's life. But by resolving a couple's dispute on the basis of those rules, and those rules alone, we at least assure that the important decisions of their lives are not left to individual caprice or, in this case, the manipulative efforts of a mediator.

Before addressing this question, we would first like to bring it into sharper focus. At the same time, we would like to make certain observations about the principle of self-determination and lay bare and make more explicit our own attitudes toward it.

It could be argued that while the principle of self-determination deserves our respect when we are dealing with individuals, or a collection of individuals, such as a family, that it should no longer deserve our respect when we find that one of the members of that group is being unfair to another, or is trying to take unfair advantage of him, and our purpose in intervening is to prevent this from happening. For many, this will be the most compelling argument of all. We are, of course, not talking about a situation where the conduct of one of the members of the group toward the other is so flagrant that it breaches minimal societal standards, as the principle of self-determination is obviously not deserving of our respect in a situation such as that.[7]

However, we would argue that when those minimal standards have not been breached, the self-determination of the members of the group—as expressed in the balance in their relationship with one another—should be respected. To be sure, given the differences in the personalities of its members and their relative positions within the group, the balance between them will not be a perfect one. It may even appear very imbalanced. It is their balance, nevertheless, and it represents the compromises they have felt justified in making between themselves in order to maintain it. More importantly, if that compromise does not cause *them* to complain, then it should not offend *us*, and we have no right to let it.

But suppose that it is so offensive? Admittedly, not so offensive as to breach minimal societal standards, but offensive nevertheless. Even so, a third party intervener, whether he be a therapist or a mediator, must proceed with caution. It is *their* relationship—how they each view what takes place between them—that the mediator is attempting to affect. If that is the case, then the principle of self-determination is still deserving of our respect, for in the final analysis it is still their collective judgment as to the acceptability of that relationship to themselves, and not to a third party observer, that is at issue.

It could also be argued that the restraint that is required, based on the principle of self-determination, to a group of individuals with an ongoing relationship is not required when, as is the case in a couple's separation or divorce, that relationship is coming to an end. Again, we would reject this argument. Nor would we wish to do so on the ground that, particularly if the couple have children, they will be required to continue to have an ongoing relationship following their divorce. (That may be true, but in an important sense it will be a very different relationship.)

Rather, we would reject the argument for a different, but equally important, reason.

A person—in this case each of the parties individually—also has a relationship to *him or herself*. This is occasioned by the fact that it is necessary for each of us to explain our life, and what occurs in it, to ourselves. At times, particularly when people are going through periods of stress and major personal change, the balance in their own personal relationship with themselves is as delicate and tenuous as is that between them and their spouse. Our deference to the principal of self-determination—which is grounded first in our respect for the integrity of individual life and the fact that it is not given us to know what is best for others and, secondly, in our understanding that, even if we did, we nevertheless cannot guarantee what the ultimate effects of our intervention will be— requires that we show great restraint in interfering with this balance. It also requires that if we intervene at all, we do so delicately and with great care.

This brings us to a final point. There are those who would solve the problem, not by calling into question the respect that should be shown the principle of self-determination, but by claiming that the act of intervening is not inherently inconsistent with it. Thus, they would argue that the problem could be solved through the careful training of mediators to assure that, when they intervene, they do so in a completely neutral manner, thereby guaranteeing that they do not impose their own values on the parties they are attempting to help.

At least to the extent that this argument is advanced to deny the problem, we would reject it out of hand, because we would consider it dishonest to suggest that a mediator could ever do this completely. It is inherently impossible for a third party intervenor to be absolutely neutral and not, in the very act of intervening, impose his own values upon the parties.[8] It is for this very reason that the act of intervening is always a threat to the principle of self-determination. A mediator may certainly *minimize* this potential risk by being ever mindful of it, but he can never completely *eliminate* it.

We are left, therefore, with the dilemma that the principle of self-determination and the act of intervention are inherently inconsistent with one another, and we would summarily reject any attempt—even the attempt of would-be do-gooders—to solve the problem by denying this. Does this mean that we are thrown back on a strict reliance on legal rules as the only way of avoiding the problem? The answer is no, for as we have seen, those rules will not solve the problem either. Legal rules are not, like those of mathematics, rules that can be applied by all lawyers in precisely the same fashion, leading to one and only one answer. Since adversarial lawyers will not agree on how those rules should be applied, there is only one way that legal rules can be employed to solve the problem, and that is by submitting the matter to a court of law. Unfortunately, and as even the most diehard advocates of adversarial proceedings will acknowledge, this is a procedure to be recommended only as a last resort.

More importantly for our purposes, however, resort to the judicial application of legal rules will not vouchsafe the principle of self-determination, and protect the parties from would-be third-party intervenors, in this case their divorce mediator. In fact, it will only be to compound the problem, for the power a judge has, and a mediator does not, is the very power most violative of the right of self-determination. Nor is it an answer to say that the right of self-determination is being overridden to assure that *justice* is done—in this case to assure that the parties are not left with an unfair agreement. That may be so, but the right of self-determination is nevertheless a casualty in the process.

There is an even more serious problem with this answer, however. As we have seen, legal rules are not applied by judges in an abstract academic setting. They are applied in an adversarial tug-of-war between two lawyers who view them simply as legal weapons to be used to get, not what is fair to their clients, but what is best for them. Thus, the problem posed by the principle of self-determination will not be solved by applying impersonal legal rules to resolve the couple's dispute, for we will still be forced to choose between lawyers and mediators and how they each manipulate those legal rules. And this, of course, brings us back to where we started.

What accommodation, if any, can we then make between these two principles? More importantly, how will this accommodation affect the way a mediator intervenes and how he uses legal rules and principles as an intervention or strategy? We would propose the following compromise. Consistent with his primary concern for self-determination, a mediator should not use legal rules as an intervention, or should in only a very limited way, if the couple are in agreement. In other words, they should be used by him as an intervention to help the couple conclude an agreement, not to undo one they have already concluded.

If the couple has reached an agreement on a particular issue—that the wife will have custody of the children or that she will waive her interest in her husband's pension—the mediator's concern is simply to assure that each of the parties has made an informed judgment based upon all of the relevant considerations. Thus, it is not the mediator's concern that the wife may have waived her interest in her husband's pension. It is only his concern that in doing so she was aware she had a right under the law to assert an interest in it. Similarly, since it is not his function to judge their agreement, it is not a mediator's concern that the agreement concluded by the parties may differ from what *he* would consider to have been appropriate, and perhaps even fair. It is simply to test out whether that agreement is one that they feel they can accept and live with. However, since his purpose is simply to *test* this, and not to *question* it, he must do this carefully.[9]

The mediator's role is of course very different if the parties do not start out in agreement and are unable to come to one. Here, his function is to help them come to that point. Nor is it easy to do this in terms of their own view of what is appropriate, since, by definition, they are not of one mind here. Obviously, a mediator will attempt to resolve the issue on whatever common ground he can find, and that must be his first and foremost obligation.

Again, this is because his concern is to conclude an agreement that is consistent, not with some objective yardstick, no matter how fair it may be, but rather one that, even if not totally acceptable to them, is one that they are nevertheless willing to sign and accept. When all else fails, the mediator can turn to legal rules. While they may not be a substitute for the far more appropriate considerations we ought to resort to in making the decisions we must in the conduct of our lives, they do, nevertheless, exist as a reality if we are unable to agree upon the appropriateness of those other considerations. Thus, they frame the discussions between the parties and also serve as a reminder of what they will be left with if those discussions prove unsuccessful.

But if a mediator uses legal rules in this fashion, is this still not manipulation? And is there still not the danger that, in doing so, he may impose his own values on the parties, if only his belief in the importance of their coming to an agreement? There can be no question but that this is a real danger and it would be as dishonest as it would be irresponsible to suggest otherwise.

What then is the answer? There is none. Like the very hardest questions we are posed in life, it is not possible for us to answer them. All that we can do is struggle with them. This—the inevitable conflict between these opposing principles—is the very fine line that anyone who intervenes in the life of another, be he a therapist or a mediator, is required to walk. For a responsible mediator, that means that he must always be on his guard against the inevitable intrusion of his own values. Just as importantly, it means that he must always be careful that he does not permit those values, even in the name of justice or equity, to subvert the principle that reserves to the couple the right ultimately to determine what they are willing to accept and not accept. And he must bind these concerns, like a signpost on his door, as a constant reminder of the dangers in his enterprise.

CHAPTER 6

In Whose Best Interests?

What ought to be the role of the mediator in disputes between husbands and wives concerning their children?[1] Activists in the field of family mediation, who are concerned that the benefits of mediation are not at the expense of the husband's and wife's legal rights, or at the expense of a fair agreement between them, believe that the mediator's role is *more* than simply to conclude an agreement between the parties. They insist that the mediator also has an obligation with respect to the quality of that agreement. In the area of child custody mediation, this is expressed in the belief that it is the mediator's obligation to be the advocate of the *children*, and to assure that the agreement concluded between the parties is in *their* best interests.

On the face of it, it seems only reasonable that the mediator should be charged with this responsibility. Nevertheless, we will take strong objection to this, and will argue that its good intentions are not sufficient to save it from mischief, and dangerous mischief at that. More to the point, we will argue that this position once again reflects the failure of family mediation to question its assumptions, and to test them against those that generally inform its understanding. Worse, it represents an unthinking acceptance of the attitudes and assumptions of our legal system in relation to its determination of custody disputes.

To understand why and how family mediators have been charged with this responsibility, and what the implications of that responsibility are, it will first be necessary to review how custody determinations have traditionally been handled by the courts and the criticism that has been leveled at its procedures.

Custody Determinations in Traditional Adversarial Divorce Proceedings

Disputes between husbands and wives concerning their children's custody have always been dealt with by the courts in a rather curious way. If a couple was able to resolve their dispute, little attention, if any, was ever given by the courts as to what that resolution was, or how it came about. Rather, if it was embodied in either a written agreement or oral stipulation, it was generally summarily accepted by the court. To be sure, if the agreement was not in keeping with the then prevailing normative standards (e.g., if it provided that the father, rather than the mother, was to get custody of the children), the court might engage in a very cursory inquiry to satisfy its own prejudices or to determine that this was at least being done with the full consent of both of the parties. However, as more and more uncontested divorces were granted without either of the parties having actually to appear in court, and as custody arrangements between separating and divorcing couples began to show greater variation, even this practice fell into neglect.

The court's acquiescence in the determination made by the parties, and its exercise of judicial restraint in reviewing that determination, was not generally based upon principles of family autonomy, or even a concern for the court's ability to make a better determination than had been made by the couple themselves. Rather, it was based on the presumption the court generally applied to all disputes, namely, that out-of-court settlements were to be favored over litigated determinations.

If, on the other hand, the parties were unable to resolve their dispute, something very interesting occurred. While, at least up to this point, the dispute had simply been between the parties themselves, the court now took the position that there were actually three parties in interest, the father, the mother, and their children. Having elevated the children to a party in interest, however, the court now found itself in a dilemma, for not only was one of the parties unrepresented, but, and by virtue of their age alone, incompetent as well. The court's answer to this dilemma was to say that it would act to represent the children's interests, as part of the state's function to be the guardian of minors and other incompetents.

The nature of legal adversarial proceedings being what it is, it is hard for an advocate to see anything other than his client's own best interests, and the court, as newly appointed counsel for the children, quickly adapted itself to its new role. Whereas, up until this point, the court's function had been to decide the custody dispute between the husband and wife, or at least to protect their respective interests, those interests now became not only secondary, but, indeed, largely irrelevant. From this point forward the court's only concern was with its own client, and pulling a yardstick from its drawer upon which was engraved the words "the best interests of the child," the court then embarked upon an inquiry to find the result that would best measure up to that standard.

In taking on its new assignment as advocate for the children, the court did not do so with any real assurance that it knew what those best interests were, or that it could even accurately define them. Nor did it do so because it possessed the necessary qualifications even to recognize those best interests if it found them—although, not infrequently, judicial arrogance tended to stand substitute for any such informed understanding.

By the same token, it did not do so based on any appreciation of the very subtle interdependent relationship between family members that would justify singling out the interests of the children as being separate and apart from, let alone superior to, the interests of the other family members. Nor, finally, did it do so based upon any firm conviction that it would be able to vouchsafe, in the long days ahead, the decision it would leave each of the family members. Rather, it did so simply because it had the *power* to, and this regardless of whether or not its exercise of that power was in *anyone's* best interests.

The new role of the court now put the couple in an unusual position. Their decision to fight for custody was not, in truth, predicated upon any deep conviction that their children's interests would best be served by being with one of them rather than with the other. It was based simply on their desire to have custody of their children. In truth, it cannot be said that it was always based even on this, as not uncommonly the quest for custody by one of the parties had more to do with his or her desire to punish the other party than it did with serving their own legitimate purposes, let alone those of the children.

It would do no good, of course, for either of the parties to admit this. The court, after all, had not only established itself as the proper arbiter of the dispute on behalf of the children, but had made it clear that all arguments for custody of the children would be measured and judged against the yardstick of their best interests alone. Thus, if one of the parties was to prevail in the custody dispute, he or she would have to demonstrate to the court that it was in the best interests of the children that they did so.

But what was in the children's best interests? It was certainly not a custody determination made by the court, for in most instances the procedures employed in making that determination were far more damaging to the children than almost any decision that could be made by the court, even one made by the flip of a coin. Furthermore, in invariably awarding sole custody to one of the parents, and in then relegating the other parent to a minimal, secondary role, the court by definition ruled out the one result truly in the best interests of the children, namely, a substantial ongoing relationship with both of their parents. And how were either of the parties to demonstrate to the court just what the children's best interests were, given the fact that they were no more qualified than the judge to speak for those best interests? Nevertheless, if they were to prevail in the contest, a case would have to be made.

And so it was. Following the very limited understanding of the law, which has always tended to view divorce as a grade-B western, divided into good guys and bad guys, each of the parties set out to demonstrate, not that it was in the best interests of the children that their custody be awarded to them, but that it was in their best interests that it *not* be awarded to the *other*. In short, and lacking any meaningful understanding as to what the children's best interests were, the attempt was instead made simply to disqualify the other party as a fit custodian—to make him the bad guy.

What had started out as an inquiry in aid of the best interests of the child thus quickly turned into something that was anything but. In fact, it is hard to imagine anything more injurious to the best interests of the children than the hearing ultimately conducted by the court to determine those best interests, for if there was ever any ray of hope that the parties might join together in common cause for the benefit of their children, in most instances, when the trial was finally concluded, it was extinguished forever.

The most casual occurrences were taken out of context and exaggerated in the reporting in each of the parties' attempt to discredit the other. Was it the wife's habit to have an occasional glass of wine with one of her girlfriends in the late afternoon? Then she was made out to be an alcoholic. Had the husband, on one occasion, slapped one of the children as a punishment? Then he was made out to be a child abuser. Wasn't it the wife's habit occasionally to leave the children with a baby-sitter when she spent the evening out with some of her girlfriends? Then she was made out to be a neglectful parent. Had the husband been guilty of the casual use of marijuana on a few occasions? Then he was made out to be a drug addict. Had the wife lost her temper and used less than befitting language to her children? Then she was made out to be an irresponsible mother. Did the husband spend long hours away from his family, devoted to his work? Then he was made out to be a workaholic, and less-than-interested parent. And, worst of all, had the wife been emotionally (sexually) involved outside of her marriage? Then she was made out to be immoral, a bad influence on her children, and clearly unfit to be their custodian.

And what about the children in this barrage of charges and countercharges? If it was their best interests that were truly at issue, then certainly it was appropriate that they be heard from, if not to give testimony for or against either of their parents, then at least to express their feelings about them. (This was politely described by the court as taking into consideration their wishes.) We will never know the damage that was done to children in being made unwitting parties to these proceedings, and in being subjected to the pressure that each of their parents invariably placed upon them, knowing just how important their opinion might well be. "If both your parents were drowning and you had just one life preserver to throw to them, to whom would you throw it?" A wonderful question to be symbolically asking a child, all in the name of guaranteeing his or her best interests.

On occasion, either at the urging of the court or perhaps on their own, the parties would once again attempt to settle the custody dispute themselves before the court was called upon to decide it. If that was the case, the hearing was usually interrupted for a short period, the yardstick of the children's best interests was returned to its drawer, and the parties were encouraged by the court to continue with their negotiations. If those discussions began to falter, the yardstick was once again hesitatingly taken from its place of safekeeping, only to be returned for good when the parties' agreement was securely concluded. Turning once again to its belief that it was far better to settle the dispute than to decide it, the court summarily concluded that it was no longer necessary to represent the children, or to determine their best interests, and turned to the parties and congratulated them on their successful resolution of the issues.

Custody Mediation as an Alternative

If it is not too much to suggest that divorce mediation represents a reaction against the damaging effects traditional adversarial divorce proceedings have had on families and their children, it is also not too much to suggest that it was equally born of a distaste for the manner in which the law concluded disputes between separating and divorcing couples concerning their children. Nor was there very much in those proceedings to commend it. By *definition*, the judge was absolutely *incompetent*, both by previous training and often by disposition, to make the judgments necessary for a proper determination of the case. On occasion, the judge was aided by the auxiliary services of the court, but more often than not they simply did not have the time or the manpower to do the matter justice. Worse yet, in many instances those evaluations were seriously affected by the prejudices, and at times even incompetence, of the persons assigned to do the investigation. Except for this, all that the court was left with was the testimony of the parties themselves, which was usually worthless, or that of their paid experts, which was almost always inconsistent. As for the children themselves, rarely did they have any real representation in the proceedings and rarely were their interests ever served in any meaningful way.

To its advocates, therefore, custody mediation came to be viewed not simply as an alternative to contested custody litigation, but, and more importantly, as a way to correct what were considered to be its shortcomings. No longer would the interests of children be subjected to biased or unprofessional judgments. No longer would they be affected by the lack of proper representation. And no longer would they be sacrificed to whatever arbitrary arrangement their parents might conclude on their own. Now, finally, their best interests would be served, and it was the mediator's job to see to it that they were.

In redefining its role, the advocates of custody mediation did not question the assumptions of traditional adversarial custody proceedings that the object was to achieve a result which was in the best interests of the children. They simply took issue with the *procedures* employed by adversarial proceedings for that purpose. And they took particular issue with the fact that children had never been *properly represented* in those proceedings, and this notwithstanding the lofty language of the court that was intended to suggest that they had.

For these advocates of custody mediation, its goals are perhaps best expressed by Donald T. Saposnek, a clinical child psychologist, in his book *Mediating Child Custody Disputes.*

> Above all . . . the mediator must remain the *advocate for the children.* Although this point seems obvious, it is worth considering more carefully. The traditional adversarial approach to child custody determination has failed to provide meaningful advocacy for the children of divorcing parents. Attempts have been made to provide legal counsel for children in custody proceedings . . . but the legal system so far has not been able to find an appropriate place for the needs and wishes of the child in the adversarial scheme. Moreover, the lawyers who typically are assigned the task of legal advocacy for the child usually have no special training for this task, and therefore are not necessarily more knowledgeable about, or sensitive to the needs and feelings of children than are the judges or the parents' own attorneys. Hence, the attorney for the child most often functions only to slow down the legal process, and to confuse rather than clarify the issues.[2]

Although the underlying assumptions of our legal system would have logically led to the conclusion that the children (and, for that matter, *each* of the children) should be provided with counsel to represent their separate, conflicting interests, to the credit of our legal system, it has generally resisted that logic. This is not to say that there have not been those who have seriously suggested this from time to time, and on occasion that suggestion has been followed. After all, if we do not send the parties into the ring without first providing each of them with a pair of gloves and with a trainer, should their children, who are equally interested parties, be less equipped? Nevertheless, the spectacle of having children pitted against their parents in an adversarial relationship carried logic just a little too far.

Custody mediation, following the model of our legal system, now proposes to correct this by giving the children assigned counsel. And that counsel will be the mediator himself. Of course, it will not accomplish this without a very curious result. Decrying the adverse effects of adversarial custody proceedings, custody mediation now proposes to entice separating and divorcing parents to leave the court, and the protection of their separate attorneys, and to come into the mediator's office and sit down together in a common effort. What they have not been told, however, and what they do not know, is that when they enter the mediator's office they will be greeted, not by a warm ally, but by their children's attorney and advocate.

QUALIFICATIONS

Having defined the mediator's role, it next became necessary to set forth the qualifications that the mediator must possess in order to discharge his responsibilities. If the primary function of the mediator is simply to resolve the custody dispute between the parties, then the ability to do this would be qualification enough. Having assigned him a much larger role, however, these qualifications are now no longer sufficient.

> While it may be true that such general mediation skills are necessary for child custody mediation work, they clearly are not sufficient . . . The mediator must be competent to give valid, current, and helpful information about child development, about children's typical and atypical responses to family conflicts, about family members' needs and feelings, about family dynamics, about the divorce process (emotionally, structurally, and legally) and about the likely future outcomes for children and parents of a variety of different postdivorce family structures. The mediator should be knowledgeable about individual psychodynamics, interractional dynamics, family systems, and behavior change, and have a broad general knowledge of psychological functioning. Child custody mediators who are not specifically trained in these areas may seriously compromise the benefits of child custody mediation.[3]

How will mediators who are not specifically trained in these areas seriously compromise the benefits of child custody mediation? Because they will not be qualified to make the *judgments* that must be made to resolve child custody disputes in the best interests of the child. One of the problems with our legal system had always been that the ultimate determination was left to someone who, in training and professional background, lacked the qualifications necessary to make the judgments involved. In insisting upon these standards, custody mediation now proposes to correct this abuse.

STANDARDS

Having determined that it is the mediator's obligation to be the children's advocate, and having set forth the qualifications that the mediator must possess to be a proper advocate, custody mediation next had to provide the mediator with appropriate standards to guide him in that advocacy. Here again, and seeking not to remedy the ills of traditional adversarial custody proceedings, but to improve upon them, custody mediation summarily accepted as its goal the court's yardstick of the children's best interests. The problem as they saw it was not that this yardstick was inappropriate, but simply that it was ill-defined and therefore elusive. It thus became the task of custody mediation to provide mediators with appropriate criteria by which to determine the children's best interests. This was done, for example, by the Maine statute that brought divorce mediation to that state in 1984. Thus, in conducting custody mediations, the Maine statute directs the mediator to be guided by the following considerations:

A. The age of the child;

B. The relationship of the child with the child's parents and any other persons who may significantly affect the child's welfare;

C. The preference of the child, if old enough to express a meaningful preference;

D. The duration and adequacy of the child's current living arrangements and the desirability of maintaining continuity;

E. The stability of any proposed living arrangements for the child;

F. The motivation of the parties involved and their capacities to give the child love, affection and guidance;

G. The child's adjustment to the child's present home, school and community;

H. The capacity of each parent to allow and encourage frequent and continuing contact between the child and the other parent, including physical access;

I. The capacity of each parent to cooperate or to learn to cooperate in child care;

J. Methods for assisting parental cooperation and resolving disputes and each parent's willingness to use those methods;

K. The effect on the child if one parent has the sole authority over the child's upbringing; and

L. All other factors having a reasonable bearing on the physical and psychological well-being of the child.[4]

On the face of it, this is all very reasonable and appropriate. In actual fact, however, it is *not*; for in proposing these standards, and in demanding the qualifications that it prescribes, the advocates of custody mediation have unwittingly done a dangerous thing. They have not only established standards for the family *independent of those to which family members may subscribe*, but have made themselves *more qualified* than the family members themselves to make the necessary judgments which affect *them*. Nor is that the end of it. In insisting upon these qualifications as a prerequisite to make the judgments involved, they have, with one broad stroke, disqualified the most appropriate persons of all—the children's parents—as competent for that purpose.

But that is not all; nor is it the worst of it. In adopting the vague standards that it has, which in large measure only replicate the ill-defined concept of the best interests of the child used by the courts, custody mediation has but incorporated one further abuse of our legal system. And that is to provide a standard so imprecise that it has rendered it as *difficult to apply* as it is *impossible to question*. Custody mediation, however, has carried this abuse one step further. With a judge, there could never be more than the *pretense* that he really knew, or could know, what was in the children's best interests. With a custody mediator, however, the mediator's impressive qualifications are now to be such that he will have a strong weapon at his disposal to quell those doubts, no matter how well founded they may be.

Custody Mediation's Proper Role

Where has this view of custody mediation brought us and what has it accomplished? All that it has done is to bring us full circle, for is there any difference, after all, between the arrogance of ignorance and the arrogance of knowledge? Are they not each dangerous in their own way? While the judge may have been guilty of seeking to impose a determination upon the parties, he was at least willing to forego that obligation, if not on the basis of principle, then at least on the basis of convenience, if the parties were able to come to an agreement themselves. The mediator, however, is not so willing to bend to this convenience. Rather, accepting his mission as advocate for the children and their best interests, and convinced that his superior expertise gives him the right to determine what those best interests are, he will see it through to the end.

How is it that we have come to this curious result—that what started as an attempt to *do away* with adversarial custody proceedings, and to return to family members the power to make the decisions that affect their lives, has ended up simply transferring that power from one group of professionals to another? It has come about, first, because the advocates of custody mediation have unquestioningly accepted the assumptions implicit in the very legal model that it rejects and, second, because it has failed to fashion procedures consistent with its own understanding.

What is that understanding? It is, quite simply, the assumptions implicit in the view of the family held by mental health professionals in their dealings with them. Those assumptions are the following:

1. Wherever possible, the conduct and control of a family's affairs should be left *in the hands of family members themselves*. While it may become necessary for the state to intervene in the affairs of a family for the protection of one of its members, if minimal standards affecting the physical or mental well-being of one of its members is breached, the general rule should be one of self-restraint. Thus, the state does not ask whether the parties are "good" parents, but simply whether they are "good enough" parents.

2. Judicial restraint is not based simply on a commitment to individual autonomy. It is also based on the understanding that it is not possible for the state to *regulate* the affairs of a family without, at the same time, *interfering* with its affairs. Thus, and no matter how lofty its pretensions, when the state intervenes it does so at the risk of *undermining the very delicate relationship that exists between family members*.

3. In most instances, it is simply not given us to be able to make the kinds of determinations necessary to justify our substituting our judgments for those made by the parties themselves, whatever they may be. It is even more difficult for us to do this without imposing on them our own personal prejudices or—and equally wrong—the *normative prejudices* that society holds at any given time.

4. It is one thing for the state to make determinations binding upon the parties, in their best interests; it is quite another for the state to be able to vouchsafe those determinations. The fact remains that it is simply impossible for outside agencies, whether they be the court, mental health professionals, or even mediators, to regulate the very subtle relationship a family represents. All that they can do is make judgments binding upon the parties, and then wash their hands of the problem. Outside interference is born of arrogance; outside restraint should be born of humility.

5. The crisis that the family members, and particularly their children, are experiencing, calls for a swift and expeditious resolution. Indeed—and this is true of the overwhelming majority of custody disputes—the *fact* of its resolution is *as* important, if not *more* important, then the *manner* of its resolution. Separation and divorce brings with it a disruption in those patterns of interaction between family members that serve as the necessary security base for children's continued successful development. Added to this initial trauma is the continued lack of security that stems from a failure to reassemble those pieces into a new, stable pattern. Since the parents' failure to reestablish new patterns of interaction between themselves and their children is usually a function of the unresolved dispute between them, it is necessary to effectuate at least some minimum accommodation between the parties. Most importantly for the sake of the children, this accommodation must be made as *quickly* as possible.

6. The needs of the family must be considered as a whole. Children's needs (what the law calls their "best interests") cannot be considered as separate and apart from the needs of the other family members, and except where minimal standards are breached, it is improper to do so.

7. The needs of children are always the same—to be able to maintain an ongoing relationship with both their parents, free of interference and free of any undue tension between them. Thus, their needs are never served by making judgments between their parents, as the law would have it, as to which is more fit to be their custodian. On the contrary, their needs can only be served by effectuating an accommodation between their parents that will avoid the necessity of any such choice.

8. That the application of the foregoing principles are no less valid at the time of a couple's separation or divorce than they were during their marriage. To be sure, the family is going through a traumatic and painful reorganization. But it remains a *family*, nevertheless—the same as it would have had that reorganization been as a result of the death, incarceration, permanent institutionalization, disability, or the induction into military service of one of its members, rather than their separation. While any of those events would have left the family less able to minister to its own needs, they would not have so changed its *fundamental nature*, or the relationship between its members, as to justify the application of new and different principles. And they certainly would not justify outside interference into its affairs.

The Invited Guest

One would have expected that the logic of these principles, which brought those concerned with the effects of divorce and the divorcing process upon children (be they judges, lawyers, academicians, mental health professionals, clergymen, or members of the public) to mediation as an alternative to traditional adversarial custody proceedings, would have likewise guided them to develop *programs* for child custody mediation consistent with those principles. This, unfortunately, has not been the case. On the contrary, and as has been the experience with divorce mediation in general, the assumptions implicit in the legal model of divorce have been summarily, and unthinkingly, carried over into mediation practice—and this is true whether the custody mediation is being conducted privately or, as is becoming more commonly the case, in conjunction with court-related facilities. As was noted earlier, this has been expressed in (1) the goals of child custody mediation, (2) the qualifications needed to conduct child custody mediation to a successful conclusion, and (3) the criteria to be applied in assessing the final outcome.

What, then, ought to be the role of the mediator consistent with the principles enunciated above? It is submitted that the mediator's role—and this is true whether the dispute relates to a custody-related or noncustody-related issue—should be one of *restraint*. It is summarized by us in the phrase "the invited guest."

The mediator, after all, has been invited to help, not to judge. And he will *help most by judging least*. It is not his function to reorganize the couple's lives, any more than it would have been his province to rearrange their furniture had he been invited into their home as a guest. It is not simply that the mediator has had the couple extend an invitation to him under false pretenses—by not making it explicit that he reserves the right to make judgments about them and their children, superior even to those they might make on their own. It is that the mediator *will not help them*, or the cause of their children, in making those judgments.

In this respect, the mediator must constantly keep in mind that the couple's real problem is not the issue in dispute between them concerning their children. The real problem is that they have lost the ability to deal successfully with that issue on their own. The mediator will not solve this problem by deciding the issue for them. In fact, by adding the weight of his decision to the already delicate balance that exists in their relationship, he may only compound it. In short, in setting their goals, in laying down the qualifications that a mediator must possess, and in establishing the criteria to be applied, the advocates of custody mediation have only encouraged mediators to lose sight of what should be their primary objective, namely, to help *restore* the couple's ability to deal successfully with the problem themselves.

In attempting to achieve this, the mediator would be well advised to keep certain principles in mind. The first of these tells him that it would be error to accept the problem at face value. In a bad marriage—one in which the parties have not been able successfully to negotiate their differences—they often argue out in their divorce the very issues that they were unable to resolve in their marriage. Moreover, the real issues are usually camouflaged; as a result, the arguments between the parties are rarely about the issues over which they are really fighting. This situation is further complicated by the fact that the decision to separate and divorce has unleashed painful and overwhelming feelings that not only become problems in their own right but that also fasten on, as it were, to already existing areas of contention, further burdening their possible resolution.

What this tells a mediator attempting to resolve a dispute between a couple concerning the custody of their children—or any dispute relating to their divorce, for that matter—is that though the dispute may be *over* the custody of their children, it is not necessarily *about* the custody of their children. As an advocate for the children who is concerned with their best interests, and aided by his considerable knowledge and understanding concerning their psychological well-being, a mediator could immediately set out on a quest for the answer, and thereby solve the problem. He would do this, however, only at the risk of missing the point, for since the answer he finds may have nothing to do with the real problem, it will not resolve it.

At times, the dispute is not even between the couple. It may be a struggle that one of the parties is having with himself. On one occasion, a mediator was confronted with a couple who had two children, a boy and a girl. When the issue of the children was raised, the father voiced the opinion that he felt that his daughter should continue to live with her mother following their separation, but that his son should live with *him*. Although the mediator was surprised that the husband, who seemed a responsible and concerned parent, would want to separate his children, he did not raise the issue. Instead, he sat and listened. The decision to separate and divorce here had been the husband's, and it was one with which he was still having great difficulty. As the discussions proceeded, the mediator became convinced that the husband was guilt-ridden over his decision, particularly as it affected the children, and he began to wonder whether the husband's suggestion that the parties split up their children was an attempt on his part to assuage his feeling that he was abandoning his children.

Gaining the wife's permission to speak with her husband privately, the mediator told him that he could not help but notice how overwrought he was and how painful the question of his children's future seemed to be for him. He then carefully shared with the husband the question that he had in his mind about his dilemma, and how he was possibly attempting to solve it. When the mediator was through, the husband broke down and told the mediator how guilt-ridden he felt over his decision and how difficult it was for him to face his children. When he had unburdened himself, the husband turned to the mediator and told him that he did not want to split up his children and that they should continue to live in their home with their mother. Again, a mediator who, on hearing the husband's proposed solution, had simply set out on a quest for the right *answer*, might never have stopped to consider what was really the *right question*.

This example is illustrative of the second principle, a corollary of the first, and also derived from the practice of psychotherapy. That principle is that people do not solve their problems in therapy; on the contrary, if therapy is successful, the problems will simply go away. Thus, if the mediator is able to touch upon, and address, those emotional issues standing between the couple and their ability to resolve the issues concerning their children on their own, they will no longer have a problem, or, if they do, it will no longer be one that will require his intervention. As the example illustrated, the same is true if he is able to touch upon the *internal* conflicts that are making it so difficult for one of the parties to accept what would otherwise be an appropriate solution. Needless to say, that should properly be his goal.

In this regard it is important to remember that separating and divorcing couples do not, after all, have disputes concerning their children that are grounded in different intellectual opinions as to what is in their best interests, let alone competing theories of child and adolescent development. To be sure, they may, on occasion, invoke these opinions and theories in defense of their respective positions. But their *positions* always come first, and the opinions and theories that support them come later. Since that is so, mediators will have little success in shaking those opinions and theoretical assumptions. Nor would they be successful in changing the parties' positions, even if they could. Rather, they will only be met by a new intellectual or emotional line of defense.

Let us suppose that the mediator is able to dispel the emotional considerations fueling the custody dispute. Let us further suppose that neither of the parties attempts to defend their positions based upon either their own considered opinions or on psychological theory. Would it not then be appropriate for the mediator, rather than just to help them resolve it in whatever manner they find acceptable, to act as advocate for the children and, if need be, to decide the dispute in their best interests, based upon his considerable expertise? The answer is still no.

What, after all, is the dispute between the parties? In almost every instance it is whether the father or the mother will have custody of the children or whether there will be some variant of shared parenting. On occasion there may also be ancillary issues, such as the children's exposure to the present or future lover of one of the parties; the right of one of the parties to live with the children beyond a stated distance; or the right of the custodial parent to live with his or her girlfriend or boyfriend in the marital residence.

To justify that the mediator, or any other person, for that matter, object to the parties' determining the issue as they wish, and to substitute as a criterion for that determination the principle of "the best interests of the child," requires, of necessity, that the mediator or other third party be able to demonstrate that the solution of choice is clearly, or at least likely, to be in the better interests of the child than the random, perhaps even haphazard, settlement that the couple would otherwise conclude on their own. The only way the mediator can do this, however, is either to demonstrate that the decision of choice is mandated by sound psychological principles or that it is justified based on the demonstrated superior beneficial consequences for the child in the future. Unfortunately, the mediator can do neither.

Let us take the first of these tests, namely prevailing psychological opinion. All a mediator can say with any degree of certainty about prevailing professional opinion on the subject is that it is not of one mind, since for every authority who comes forward to speak in favor of a proposition, there will be another to speak against it. In fact, open-minded observers of the scene can only conclude that it is an area where reasonable men can disagree. It might be otherwise in a period of social equilibrium. During such periods of time, social change is so slow that our theories of human behavior seem to be based on immutable principles. Similarly, at such times it is hard even to see, let alone demonstrate, their normative quality.

In periods of social change, such as our own, the effect is very different. We are constantly reminded of the arbitrary quality of our social constructs and the theories that we elaborate to support them. We are reminded of an even more interesting fact, however, which is a kind of social variant of Heisenberg's law of indeterminacy (which in physi s states that the very act of attempting to determine—predict—the place of a particular phenomenon in a physical continuum has the effect of changing the place of that phenomenon): our very act of violating sound, normative principles, changes the soundness of those normative principles.

Not too many years ago, if a qualified child psychologist or psychiatrist had been asked, for example, whether it would be detrimental to children to be placed in the custody of their father rather than their mother, to live in a home occupied by their mother and her unmarried boyfriend, or to alternate their residence between their father's and their mother's homes, etc., he might well have concluded, and perhaps with some reason, that it was not in the children's best interests.

While in most instances this would have been justified in terms of certain psychological principles, in point of fact, those principles were only correct in the context of the given normative standards (i.e., it was only in a world in which custody was always, or at least usually, granted to mothers, that it would not be in a child's best interests if his custody were granted to his father). However, the very act of questioning those normative standards—by awarding custody to fathers, by permitting children to live in a home with their mother occupied by her lover, by alternating their residence between the home of their father and their mother—has tended to change the normative base from which those former principles were derived.

The debate began with those who sought change attempting to demonstrate that the proposed alternative arrangements were in the child's best interests, or at least not adverse to those best interests—an impossible task in a normative setting which, by definition, had to *prejudice the consequences* of such an arrangement. By persuading certain members of the public that it was permissible, or even appropriate, to engage in these alternative modes of conduct (or, to be more accurate, by providing them justification for what they had already decided to do), the advocates for social change slowly began to alter the acceptable normative base, and with it the conclusions psychologists and psychiatrists had to draw from the social norms with which they dealt.

Thus, what may not have been consistent with sound psychological theory ten or fifteen years ago may not necessarily be inconsistent with it today. The result is that mental health professionals who would have answered these questions in the negative only five or ten years ago are now not so sure. Put another way, man's considerable ability to adapt to the conditions of life is such that even if there are immutable principles of psychological development, they do not mandate one, and only one, human response.

If it is not easy to justify a custodial determination as in the best interests of a child based upon immutable principles of psychological development, it will be even harder for a mediator to do so on the basis of his being able to make an accurate prediction of the future consequences of any one or more of the options being debated. The analogy of Heisenberg's law of indeterminacy should serve to demonstrate part of the problem in attempting to make any such accurate prediction. If that analogy and the other teachings of modern physics are not sufficient to dispel any such belief, there is an analogy closer to the thinking of family therapists that should.

The paradigm on which the generally accepted principles of family therapy are based is derived from systems theory and, more specifically, from the rejection of linear causality in favor of circular causality. For our purposes, that means rejecting the idea that it is possible to understand present phenomena or occurrences in terms of past individual, isolated occurrences (causes). Rather, those occurrences are the result of a complex of events that act upon, and react back upon one another in such an ongoing reciprocal way that it is not possible to isolate individual elements from this continuum as constituting, in one case, the cause, and in the other, the effect.

There is a corollary to this principle that is less generally recognized in theoretical terms, although most family therapists, at least those not overcome with the arrogance of knowledge, understand it. That is that it is not possible to make accurate predictions of the future outcome of events, particularly of those affected by a complex of antecedent considerations. While this corollary follows from the accepted premises of systems theory, it is generally less appreciated than the rule. The reason for this is that our *confidence* in science, *combined with our misunderstanding of science*, has contributed to our belief to the contrary.

If it is not possible to isolate an individual event as having been causative, or responsible for, a present occurrence, then it is similarly impossible to state that a present isolated event will inevitably lead to a particular future occurrence. In short, it is *impossible to make linear predictions in a world of circular causality*. Nor is it impossible because we do not know all the existing causative factors that will impinge upon the future outcome. It is impossible because we cannot know how the *interaction* of all the present causative elements (and others that we do not and cannot know, e.g., the personal circumstances of other men and women who will enter the parties' lives in the future) will tend to create yet additional causative factors that will affect the result.

In short, there is simply no basis for the mistaken belief that mediators or other third parties are able to know what determination will be in the child's best interests, or that their opinions in such regard are a better guarantee than the random conclusion which the parties may arrive at themselves. Quite the contrary, there is every reason to believe that they will be worse. Again, following the principle of Heisenberg's law of indeterminacy, outside agencies are not simply making judgments about the families they investigate. Their very act of investigation, as well as their judgment, is an intrusion into the lives of these families. And, except where the most minimal standards are being breached, those intrusions are more often than not in derogation of the children's best interests.

Is it possible for a mediator to suspend his judgment and, in contenting himself simply with helping a couple come to a resolution of the dispute, allow them to come to whatever resolution they may? Putting aside the question of whether or not the result will be in the best interests of the child, isn't it possible that the result will actually be harmful to the child, and doesn't the mediator have an obligation to protect the child from this? (To put this in the context of the debate concerning the court's relationship to mediated custody settlements, should the court simply rubber-stamp whatever agreement the couple has arrived at? Doesn't the court at least have the obligation to make inquiry to assure that minimal societal standards have not been breached?)

Again, the answer has to be no. To justify that intervention—to deviate from the principle of individual autonomy in the regulation of a family's affairs—it must be demonstrated that there is some factor in the reorganization of the family occasioned by the family's separation and divorce that justifies an intervention that was not justified at any other time throughout the previous life of the family. However, and as we have already noted, there is nothing so uniquely different about the reorganization of the family that takes place at the time of separation or divorce, as distinct, for example, from the reorganization that takes place in the event of the death, incarceration, or institutionalization of a family member, that justifies this, unless the parties themselves are unable to agree on the manner in which that reorganization will occur.

(To be sure, in most of these other instances the occurrence that requires the family's reorganization does not, at the same time, require a choice between the parents in terms of with whom the children will live. Even so, any one of these occurrences, as well as others that might be thought of, might cause the parent left with the primary responsibility of the child to consider placing the child in the home of a relative or friend, either temporarily or on an extended basis, and he or she would be free to do so without being required to justify the act, let alone obtain the court's approval.)

There is an even more practical reason. What divides the couple is not a dispute over the kinds of minimal standards that would activate the state's concern, and justify their intervention. The dispute between the parties, after all, is not whether either the mother or the father, or both, should be permitted sexually to abuse their children. Rather, it is whether the children will live with their father, with their mother, or with both. While it would seem that this is a self-evident fact, which would in turn lead to a self-evident conclusion, the opinions being expressed as to the standards to be applied in resolving the dispute between the parties, the qualifications of those employed to assist them, and the court's review of the settlement, once concluded, would belie this.

Is this to suggest that a mediator will never be confronted with a problem concerning the parties' children which will require greater expertise than they themselves possess? Suppose, for example, that they announce to the mediator that they have found, or at least have the strong suspicion, that one of their children is using drugs. Isn't this just the kind of situation that would require a mediator to have the qualifications insisted upon by the advocates of child custody mediation? Again, the answer is no.

It is not the purpose of mediation to deal with the ongoing problems people have in their lives. (The couple could have just as easily informed the mediator that one of their children had a serious medical problem. Would this mean that the mediator could not properly discharge his obligation to the parties, and to their child, unless he was also a qualified physician?) Its purpose is to help them get on with their lives—to help them, once again, to be able to deal effectively, or perhaps not so effectively, with the problems they will be confronted with in their joint and individual lives. Thus, and unless there is an issue concerning their child's use of drugs or their child's health that is preventing the couple from resolving the issues that stand between them and an agreement, there is absolutely no reason that the mediator need concern himself with them.[5]

CONCLUSION

In assigning the mediator a lesser role, as we do, he has not been given one any less important, or that less serves the best interests of the children. In fact, it serves their interests best. It is *parents*, after all, and not outside agencies, who *must raise* their children. Mediators must never forget this. Nor should they forget that the object of every successful mediation is to assure that they will be left *able* to do this. For mediators concerned with what is truly in the best interests of children, this is a sufficient enough task. If that is so, then it is the *understanding* necessary to do this—and not any academic conversance with psychological theory—that is truly the necessary qualification for successful custody mediation.

CHAPTER 7
CONTEXT

How is it that separating and divorcing couples are able to resolve disputes in mediation that they are unable to resolve in traditional adversarial divorce proceedings? What is it about mediation, and the setting in which mediation takes place, that facilitates this? While there are obviously a number of factors, two stand out. The first is the relationship that develops between the mediator and the couple and, more importantly, the trust that they come to repose in him. The second is found in the context in which mediation takes place.

Context is everything. You can take a couple, even a couple who is in the process of separating and divorcing, and place them in one context, and despite their disappointment, hurt, anger, even their fear, you can help them to be the decent people who they would prefer to be if they were only given a chance. Or you can place them in another context and, given time, each of them will begin to act in ways that, even by their own sense of what is appropriate, will be out of character for them. Similarly, you can take this same couple and place them in a context that will tend to facilitate a resolution of the issues with which they are faced. Or you can place them in a context that will make it almost impossible for them to conclude an agreement between themselves, despite their desire to do so. Again, it all depends upon the context in which they find themselves.[1]

THE CONTEXT IN WHICH TRADITIONAL ADVERSARIAL DIVORCE PROCEEDINGS TAKE PLACE

What is it about the context in which traditional divorce proceedings take place that makes it so ill-suited to a resolution of the issues with which separating and divorcing couples are faced? It is, quite simply, that it is an adversarial one. Traditional divorce proceedings proceed on the assumption that the parties are adversaries, having conflicting interests. As a result, and like every self-fulfilling prophecy, it places them in a setting (context) that then tends to make adversaries of them.

How does this self-fulfilling prophecy work? A simple example will demonstrate this. One of the most basic tenets of traditional adversarial divorce proceedings is that they are designed to protect each of the parties and their conflicting interests. In fact, it is in large measure because separating and divorcing couples have been subtly and not so subtly persuaded that they need this protection, and that the law will provide them with it, that they turn to adversarial lawyers in the first place. But why do they need this protection? Ironically, they need it only because the context in which traditional adversarial divorce proceedings take place causes each of them to feel *threatened*.

A husband is told by his wife that she is intent on divorcing him, and learns that she has consulted with an attorney. Does he assume that his wife and her attorney are meeting together to plan a party for him? Obviously not. It may be a surprise, but it will hardly be a surprise party. On the contrary, he assumes that they are planning to take him for everything that they can get. Quite naturally, this leaves him apprehensive. Since the discussions his wife has had with her attorney have taken place behind closed doors, and in his absence—the polite words the law uses to describe this is to suggest that these discussions took place in confidence—the husband's suspicions are only fanned further. To protect himself, he too now consults with an attorney.

What is the wife's reaction upon learning that her husband has seen an attorney? Does she say to herself that he has consulted with an attorney simply to find out about the technical procedures of their separation or divorce, or to obtain information he does not have, just as she did? Of course not. Rather, she assumes that he has consulted with an attorney in order to protect himself—to see to it that she will get as little as the law will allow. Does this tend to assuage any of the wife's fears? Obviously not. On the contrary, it reinforces them and persuades her that she was wise to have found herself a good attorney first. Thus, while legal mythology would have it that the parties retain separate attorneys to protect themselves, the truth that it is only because they have gone out and retained separate attorneys that they each now find themselves in *need* of protection.

But is it fair to say that it is the parties' separate attorneys, or even our adversarial system, for that matter, that has made the wife feel threatened and in need or protection? Isn't it really her divorce that has done so? While, at first blush, that may appear to be the case, in actuality it is not. To be sure, the wife's impending separation and divorce has presented her (as it has her husband) with an overwhelming problem—the knottiest, in fact, that she has probably ever had to face. In addition, it is a problem that she will now have to face almost completely on her own. Understandably, that has left her feeling insecure and fearful. But those feelings were born of the situation she now finds herself in, not of anything that her husband has necessarily done. What is it, then, that has caused her to direct those fears at her husband, and to feel that she needs protection *from him*? It is the adversarial proceedings to which she and her husband have turned to resolve the issues between them. And what has been the effect of this? It has been to make her *husband* her problem, rather than her divorce.[2]

This brings us to another aspect of the context in which traditional adversarial divorce proceedings take place that further adds to the problem. As we have noted, the discussions between each of the parties and their attorneys take place behind closed doors, and the other party is not present. That might be well and good if the wife and her attorney were only talking. But they are doing more; they are also planning to take action. Unfortunately, and like a surprise attack in warfare, much of the effectiveness of that action will be lost if it is announced in advance. As a result, almost all actions in traditional adversarial divorce proceedings take place at a distance and without the other party's prior knowledge.

What effect does this have on each of the parties' conduct? The following example will illustrate this. When the wife first consulted with her attorney, she informed him that she and her husband maintained a joint bank account of $10,000. She was concerned about this. She had no idea what her husband might be planning, or what he might do. That left her between a rock and a hard place. If she decided to protect herself by going to the bank and withdrawing the money from that account, that would make her a thief. On the other hand, if she did not wish to step out of character simply because she had decided to divorce her husband, and therefore left the money where it was, if her husband then took the money instead, that would make her a fool. That was the wife's dilemma, or, rather that was the dilemma that our legal system's view of the parties (that they are adversaries), and the context in which they are placed (one in which they deal with one another only from a distance, and without the other's prior knowledge), had created for the wife.

This is the consequence of the context in which traditional divorce proceedings take place. Rather than being open and aboveboard with one another, the parties face off against one another guardedly, and with their hands under the table, so to speak. The inevitable effect is to cause each of them to feel threatened and to worry what the other may be doing with their hands. The insecurity this breeds increasingly tends to lead to, and then to justify, preemptive action on each of their parts to protect themselves. Unfortunately, the only effect of this preemptive action is to reinforce the other party's belief that he too needs protection, and to cause him to take action either to offset that taken by the first party or simply to retaliate. In either event, each preemptive step taken by one of the parties in an attempt to protect himself inevitably leads to what soon becomes a never-ending cycle of action and reaction.

This brings us to yet another problem created by the context in which traditional divorce proceedings take place. Invariably, the separate attorneys with whom the parties consult compound the problem by reinforcing their fears. After all, they have seen how husbands and wives act when they get divorced, and therefore know what to expect. (Actually, they have only seen how husbands and wives act when they resort to adversarial proceedings, but not knowing better, they assume that such conduct is a function of the divorcing process itself rather than simply a function of adversarial proceedings.)[3] It is quite natural, therefore, that they should want to protect their clients from this conduct. That, after all, is what they have been hired to do. This means deciding for the wife whether it is better for her to be a thief rather than a fool. Without question, her attorney will decide *thief*, for if she is to be left a thief or a fool in any event, better to be left a thief with the money than a fool without it.

The separate attorneys with whom the parties have consulted all too often add to the problem in yet another way. They are not there just to give advice. They are also there to sell themselves and their services, and this may be the only opportunity they will have. The whole context of traditional divorce proceedings is such that each party believes it is in his best interest to have a *tough* attorney. Quite naturally, therefore, the attorneys with whom they consult will each try to persuade them that that is the case. In doing this, they will often proceed on the assumption that if their prospective client hears tough talk and sees tough action that he will be so persuaded.

This is especially true of the wife's lawyer. He will often make unflattering comments about her husband, reinforce her feelings that he has been less than fair with her and announce, in graphic terms, what he intends to do to him. To let her start to see some action, he then concludes with a list of the things he intends to do, usually followed by instructions as to what he wants her to do. These latter may range from simply preparing a budget for her necessary needs, to the emptying of safe deposit boxes and the closing of bank accounts. They may also extend to going through her husband's books and records and even, possibly, secretly into his office. For his part, he may serve her husband with a summons, and then subpoena his books and records. In the adversarial world in which their affairs will be determined, some of this information can be very helpful. Unfortunately, and given the context in which those proceedings will take place, it may now also be necessary. In the meantime, however, and while her attorney's words of advice and warning may prove of some comfort to her, they will also reinforce her fears, for they will tend to confirm her view of her husband as, if not her enemy, then at least someone who cannot be trusted. And what is the result of this? It is to have created a climate in which the rule quickly becomes that there are no rules, that it is every man for himself, and anything goes. It is to have created a climate in which each party truly feels threatened and in need of protection.[4]

There is another element in the context in which adversarial proceedings take place that makes them so ill suited to resolve the outstanding issues, and that is its tendency to encourage each party not only to take fixed positions but then also to exaggerate them. The wife's lawyer has informed her that she is entitled to receive support for at least ten or eleven years; her husband's attorney has informed him that he is not obligated to give her support for more than five or six. However, rather than viewing these statements as the expression of different legal opinions or adversarial positions, each of the parties comes away feeling that they have been given an expression of their God-given legal entitlements. Needless to say, if these indeed *are* their legal entitlements, they would of course be fools to give more or to accept less.

What has been the effect of this advice? Has it been to resolve the differences between the parties? Has it even been to create an atmosphere that will help promote such a resolution? The answer is no. On the contrary, the only effect of characterizing the dispute in terms of legal rights has been to have dipped each of the parties in legal cement, and, as they will soon find, it is also very fast-drying cement.

The myth is that the two attorneys are now going to sit down together and negotiate these differences. The truth is that having encouraged the parties to take unrealistic, fixed positions, and then in having sprinkled legal holy water on those positions, they really have little if anything to talk about. After all, the wife's attorney is not going to come back from that meeting and recommend to her that she accept support for eight or nine years when he has just told her that she has a right to expect to receive it for ten or eleven. Nor can the husband's attorney go back with that recommendation, when he has, in effect, told the husband that he would be a fool to give her support for more than five or six. Thus, all that the two attorneys will do will be to meet, lay their respective demands on the table, and then leave.

Unfortunately, the two attorneys have done something else that will make it all the more difficult for the parties to resolve their differences. Given the nature of adversarial proceedings and the context in which they take place, neither attorney has stated his true position. On the contrary, and to give themselves ample negotiating room, the wife's attorney has asked for more than he really expects to get and the husband's attorney has offered less than he really expects to give. This, of course, has only widened the gap between them. It has also tended to poison further the atmosphere in which those negotiations will take place and to reinforce the fears of each party.

Rather than viewing the other's demands as stratagems in the adversarial negotiating process, the husband and wife each take these positions to represent the true expression of what the other feels entitled to receive or obligated to give. Colored by the strong emotions with which each of the parties is struggling, it is not possible for either to view these demands other than with a sense of outrage. Whatever shred of trust either still had in the other has been destroyed, and each has been absolutely convinced of the other's malevolence and, therefore, of his or her own need of protection.

By now, the parties' positions are so far apart that each of their attorneys begins to feel that the gulf may be impossible to bridge, and each is less and less inclined to take the first step toward doing so. As a result, the negotiations between the parties literally come to a standstill. Given this, and after but a short time, one or both attorneys feels the need to invoke the aid of the court, and to initiate legal proceedings, in order to give the negotiations impetus and to provide their respective clients with a way out should they prove unsuccessful. While the critics of divorce mediation tend to ignore the fact of this litigation, and its importance as a weapon in the negotiating process, it is as much a part of the context in which adversarial proceedings take place as is the meeting room a divorce mediator uses.[5]

This brings us to a final point. While divorce lawyers are prone to congratulate themselves on how often they are able successfully to negotiate an agreement between the parties in an adversarial setting, in doing this they give themselves credit they rarely deserve. In the overwhelming majority of instances, the agreements in question are not concluded through negotiations. Rather, they are concluded largely through attrition. After months, and often years, of literally going nowhere, the parties become so tired and worn down, and so anxious to get on with their lives and past their pain, that they are willing to accept less, or to give more, than they believe they should. Whereas before, prodded on by their attorneys, all that they wanted was what was right, now all they want is to be done.

There are certain unfortunate consequences in concluding an agreement in this manner. While their agreement may have *settled* the matter, it has *not* necessarily *concluded* it. On the contrary, in first giving them unrealistic expectations and in then denying them, those adversarial proceedings have left in their wake bitter feelings of hurt and resentment that come back to haunt the parties and, all too often, their children as well. This is the legacy of the context in which traditional adversarial proceedings take place. And this is the legacy that divorce mediation hopes to revoke.

THE CONTEXT IN WHICH DIVORCE MEDIATION TAKES PLACE

What is it about the context in which divorce mediation takes place that makes it so effective in resolving issues that are so difficult to resolve in traditional divorce proceedings? To begin with, the tendency, which is ever-present in adversarial divorce proceedings, to fear that the other party may resort to self-help, and therefore to take preemptive action to protect oneself, is simply not present to any great extent. Conferences are not held in secret, behind closed doors. Everything takes place in the open. As in the analogy we previously used, the parties' hands are always on top of the table rather than under it. Further, clandestine conduct is not expected or, therefore, subtly approved, as is the case in adversarial proceedings.

On the contrary, mediation, by presenting itself as a responsible, rational way to deal with these problems, clearly makes it known that such conduct is not appropriate. Also, the parties are each required to come and meet with one another, usually on a weekly basis, to discuss the issues between them. Thus, neither can avoid the other, or let a third party do the accounting for them.[6] Rather, if one party acts inappropriately, he is going to have to face his accuser. Furthermore, he is going to have to hear those accusations made before a third party whose good opinion he probably would not like to lose. Lastly, it simply does not make sense to waste the mediation sessions in endless harangues about a matter which, if an agreement can only be concluded, will in all likelihood no longer *be* an issue. After all, it is only going to take but a short time, and not months or perhaps years, for each of the parties to put the matter behind them if they will only use that time constructively.

Secondly, instead of being placed in a context that suggests that the object is simply to get as much as you can and to give as little as you have to, and in which legal rules are used as weapons in that cause, the parties are provided with a setting that conveys that their enterprise is a problem-solving one. Thus, and rather than being pitted against one another in a struggle that has as its stated object to leave one a winner and the other a loser, they are invited to sit down in an attempt to conclude an agreement that they will both feel they can live with.

Thirdly, the context in which divorce mediation takes place is not one that leaves each party feeling the helpless *victim* of a *process over which he has no control.* In entering into mediation, they have not *surrendered authority* over their affairs to judges, to lawyers, or even to the mediator. Rather, they have reserved that authority to themselves, to whom it rightfully belongs. Thus, they do not have to worry, as they constantly do in adversarial proceedings, *where* the mediation will take them, or, therefore, where they will be left. It will only take them where they choose to go. They therefore proceed throughout the mediation with the very comforting knowledge that should it ever get to a place where they do not wish to be, they are not bound by it on that account. On the contrary, they can end it simply by standing up and leaving.

Perhaps the most important benefit of the context in which divorce mediation takes place, however, is the fact that it tends to separate the problems at hand from the overwhelming feelings with which the couple is struggling. As we have noted, it is not the practical problems with which the couple are confronted that make a resolution of the issues between them so arduous. Rather, what makes it so difficult are the painful feelings with which one or both are struggling that have become encrusted around these practical problems. While the context in which adversarial divorce proceedings take place tend both to exacerbate these wrought-up feelings and, at the same time, to cause the parties to lose sight of those practical problems, the context in which divorce mediation takes place tends to do just the opposite. More importantly, it brings home the reality that those feelings have *nothing to do* with the practical problems in question, and helps them to separate the two.

That context is critical to a resolution of the problems separating and divorcing couples have is demonstrated by an interesting phenomenon that occurs in traditional divorce proceedings but is literally never present in mediation. One of the reasons it is extremely difficult to negotiate settlements between the parties in adversarial divorce proceedings is that each of the parties has been given such very different answers to the question, "What are my legal rights and legal obligations?" Moreover, each of the parties recognizes this, and therefore knows that it will be a long, and perhaps bitter, struggle before the matter is concluded. As a result, each digs his heels in and prepares himself for a long fight.

This does not mean that the parties will hold their lives in abeyance in the meantime, however. On the contrary, they will each try to go about their business as best as they can. Unfortunately, and because the matter has not been concluded, that means that to a great extent they will each have to resort to self-help. The husband, for example, cannot wait to get on with his life for some nine months to a year (and perhaps even longer), until the matter is finalized, and so he decides to leave on his own. Not wishing a confrontation with his wife, and when she is not in the home, he packs his bags and leaves, removing certain items of personal property that he wishes to take with him, including the stereo equipment and the color television set. Also, now that he has established a separate residence for himself, he cannot continue to turn over the bulk of his paycheck to his wife as he previously had, and instead gives her what he can, after he has made provision for his own needs. Unfortunately, his actions take place at a distance and without consultation, and it leads to a reaction on his wife's part, in what soon appears to be a never-ending cycle. After all, what assurance does she have that he will not come back into the house and remove other things? (Changing the locks may prevent that.) And what assurance does she have that he will not reduce her support even further? (Perhaps withholding access to the children will put pressure on him not to do this.)

Since the two attorneys have been unable to resolve the larger issues and conclude the matter, their time is taken up in endless attempts to deal with *all* of these problems. In fact, and as any matrimonial attorney can testify, much of their time is spent attempting to put out the brush fires that repeatedly ignite simply because the principal matters at issue remain unresolved.[7] And, since they are rarely able to deal with them very effectively, the parties become increasingly frustrated and feel totally unprotected by the law, which in turn creates the need, and then the justification, to resort to further acts of self-help to protect themselves. In time, and as each action triggers yet another reaction, it is hard even to remember how it all began. And, of course, it is even harder to stop.

This brings us to the final problem. The husband is frustrated and wants to get on with the business of his life. Unfortunately, the negotiations are at a standstill and nothing is happening. How can the husband get his wife to move? The adversarial proceedings to which he has turned have not provided an answer to his problem. They have not even provided an effective forum in which to resolve his and his wife's differences. In fact, they have left him no further ahead now then he was before. Hamstrung, often angry, and left with no better way to get his wife to budge, he finally does the only thing left. He resorts to pressure. The pressure he resorts to is not always wise, nor very becoming. Nevertheless, there seems little else that he can do, and so he feels justified in applying it.

As we noted, this conduct has become so endemic in traditional divorce proceedings that it has come to be seen as simply a natural by-product of the divorcing process. In actual fact, however, it is only a by-product of the context in which traditional adversarial divorce proceedings take place. This has only recently been generally appreciated. Since divorce, and the adversarial context in which a couple's divorce was resolved, were so inextricably bound together, it was often difficult, if not impossible, to see one apart from the other. It has now become more apparent, however, by the fact that such conduct literally never takes place in divorce mediation.

A mediator will almost never be confronted with a wife who presents him with a letter from a bank threatening foreclosure proceedings, or a notice from a utility company threatening to disconnect service. Nor will he be confronted by a husband who complains that his wife has denied him access to his children, or closed out a joint bank account and appropriated the funds. The context in which divorce mediation takes place simply does not lead either party to believe that such action is necessary or appropriate.

It could be argued that this difference stems from the fact that divorce mediation is a self-select process. While that is undoubtedly true, and while divorce mediation probably tends to weed out the most unhealthy segment of the separating and divorcing community (just as traditional adversarial divorce proceedings tend to reward this segment the most),[8] this is not a sufficient explanation. For it does not take account of the fact that from time to time a mediator will be presented with a couple who has first resorted to traditional adversarial divorce proceedings and found themselves engaged in just such conduct, but who, having finally turned to divorce mediation, not only act in an entirely different manner now that they are placed in the context in which divorce mediation takes place, but also act exactly as do couples who initially self-selected mediation rather than adversarial proceedings.

Context and the Debate about Mediation

The importance of context, and the failure of both the critics and advocates of divorce mediation to recognize its importance, is reflected in certain recurrent debates in mediation circles. More accurately, they represent criticisms of mediation made by the matrimonial bar and the response of divorce mediators to that criticism. The first of these concerns the issue of discovery. From the standpoint of practicing matrimonial attorneys, mediation is wanting in that it does not properly incorporate into its procedures, as does adversarial practice, the financial discovery necessary to assure that there has been full and complete disclosure, and that the agreement concluded between the parties is based upon a correct picture of their respective financial conditions.

Why is such disclosure necessary, however? Wouldn't it be sufficient simply to ask each of the parties, either separately or together, to complete a financial statement or affidavit that they would then represent to be true and accurate, and that would be attached to their agreement? The answer that will be given by matrimonial attorneys, of course, is that there is no guarantee that the parties will tell the truth. In fact, they will argue that it is only the financial discovery built into traditional adversarial proceedings that keeps each of the parties honest, and finds them out when they are not.

Unfortunately, this is not a sufficient answer. To be sure, people do lie on occasion, but they also tell the truth. Thus, the question is not whether people are honest or are liars, but rather under what circumstances and conditions (in what context) they are more likely to lie or more likely to tell the truth.

Without question, the context in which traditional adversarial divorce proceedings take place can only tend to promote the former, as it places a *premium on deception* and *penalizes honesty*. The *entire tone* of adversarial divorce proceedings is one of *exaggeration*.[9] Fearful that the truth will hurt, and even more fearful that the other side will exaggerate that truth in their favor, there is *no alternative but to play with that truth* oneself. If, for example, it would be appropriate for a husband to pay his wife $1,200 a month for her support and that of their children, it would be foolish for him, in an adversarial setting, to propose that amount, for instead of being greeted as a responsible offer, it will simply be viewed as a point of departure. (It is for this reason that matrimonial attorneys traditionally dance around with one another in an effort to get the other to make the first move, and to avoid having to declare their own position before the other's is known.) Thus, what normally happens is that the husband offers only $900 and the wife asks for $1,500.

The same phenomenon occurs when it comes to the parties' disclosing their income and assets. The husband is in business for himself, and has cash income of approximately $20,000 a year. Fearful that she and her children will be left destitute, his wife has tried to depict to the court a resplendent life-style, dropping the names of well-known pricey restaurants that they had once or twice visited as if these were weekly occurrences. To be honest in this context, and to acknowledge the existence of cash income of $20,000 a year, would be foolhardy. Aside from the fact that the husband could only expect the wife's attorney to claim, once the admission had been made, that the cash actually amounted to a great deal more (since it was in cash, how could the husband prove that it was not?), he will probably only be thanked for his honesty by having his undeclared income held over his head as a threat in his wife's effort to settle the litigation more favorably to herself.

The lesson, of course, is don't be foolish—which in the context of adversarial divorce proceedings means *don't be a fool by being honest*. The result is very curious. The discovery proceedings that have been paraded as one of the *advantages* of traditional adversarial divorce proceedings turns out to be simply one of its *necessities*, for having cast the proceedings in a context that encourages the parties to dig deep holes in which to hide their valuables, it then becomes necessary to provide each of them with shovels to uncover them.

That this conduct is a function of the context in which traditional adversarial divorce proceedings take place is demonstrated by the manner in which these same discussions proceed in mediation. To begin with, and at least if mediation is conducted properly, since the parties are not encouraged to take positions, or feel the necessity of protecting themselves by doing so, they do not. This is not to suggest that husbands and wives necessarily agree on the appropriate level of maintenance or child support. But their disagreements are simply that, and since in more cases than not they only represent legitimate differences of opinion, and nothing more, they can rather quickly be resolved. The same is true when it comes to cash income. It is never mentioned as a threat, for what might be considered an appropriate or necessary strategy in the context of adversarial proceedings is not in mediation. And since this is understood, it simply does not occur. What is more interesting, however, is how openly cash income is discussed. In fact, it is discussed as openly (and often as casually) as any other item of business that is put on the table.

Does this mean that the context in which divorce mediation takes place is a guarantee that each of the parties will disclose all of his or her income and assets? Of course not. However, that does not mean that they will be uncovered by the elaborate disclosure and discovery procedures of which matrimonial attorneys boast. To begin with, matrimonial attorneys, and even the accountants they occasionally hire, are poor financial detectives. More importantly, there is no reason to believe that a husband who has lied about his income and assets is likely to reveal them in disclosure. Rather, he will simply show his wife's attorney what he wants her to see. True, there may be internal inconsistencies that may partially give him away, and the wife's attorney may even find clues that will lead to some of the things that the husband has hidden.[10] But they will not find very much. The world is a very big place in which to hide things, and it is a lot easier to hide them than it is to find them.

Thus, and notwithstanding the virtues of these proclaimed procedures, rare indeed is the wife who comes away feeling that she has found out all that there was to know about her husband's true financial circumstances. On the contrary, her frustration in not being able to prove all that she knows or believes to be there, plus her anger at sitting by and watching what she believes is her husband's dishonest presentation of his true financial picture, only tends further to fuel the vicious adversarial cycle.

The point is that in a world in which guarantees are not given, decisions must be made on the basis of comparative risks and costs. In this instance, it must be based upon a choice between the context provided by traditional adversarial divorce proceedings and that provided by divorce mediation. Even putting aside for the moment the other benefits that mediation offers separating and divorcing couples, for practitioners who have worked extensively in both contexts, there can be little choice. It is far better to work in a context that does not encourage or reward dishonesty than in one that attempts to ferret it out.

What has been said about the question of disclosure is equally true with respect to the question of power. Husbands whose families are dependent upon them obviously have the power to withhold necessary support during the course of the proceedings, just as wives who are left with the custody of their children no doubt have the power to withhold them from their husbands. If this power is exercised by either of the parties, the law does provide procedures to protect them from its occurrence, or at least its repeated occurrence. But that protection is far less effective than it is represented to be.

Firstly, it is always after the fact, for the court, after all, does not have the power to turn back the clock. Secondly, it is almost always less generous (in terms of the amount of money or the amount of visitation that is awarded) than was the voluntary contribution previously made by the other party. Most importantly of all, however, that protection, no matter how effective, is never as good as the protection afforded the parties when this conduct simply does not take place. Thus, the question is not whether one or both parties has power at their disposal. Rather, it is whether the context provided by traditional adversarial divorce proceedings or by divorce mediation is more likely to act as a restraint upon the exercise of that power or more likely to encourage its use. Again, for those who have worked with separating and divorcing couples in both of these contexts, there can be no question about this. Judged by this test, mediation provides far greater protection than do adversarial proceedings.

SOCIAL CONSTRUCTS

There is one final lesson that the concept of context teaches us, and that is that it is not a given but, rather, a construction of our imagination. If certain contexts are conducive to a successful resolution of a problem, others are even better. Thus, and by analyzing those elements that tend to promote a more successful resolution of the problem, it is possible to create an even more ideal context. If properly understood, this awareness should also answer a question that has repeatedly been asked in mediation circles, and, it may be hoped, resolve the debate it has engendered.

In considering mediation, it is repeatedly asked whether or not it is a negotiating process. From the standpoint of an understanding of context, however, that is not the proper question. The question is not whether mediation is a negotiating process, but whether a negotiating process is the most effective means of resolving disputes between separating and divorcing couples. It is the same question that mediation asks of traditional divorce proceedings, namely, not whether divorce is an adversarial process, but whether an adversarial process is the most effective means of dealing with the issues separating and divorcing couples face. As we have previously noted, if we conclude that adversarial proceedings are the most effective ones, then that is what we will be left with. The same is no less true with divorce mediation. If we consider it to be a negotiating process, that is what it will become.

But what is wrong with that? Negotiations, after all, are one of the most widely respected forms of dispute resolution, particularly between disputants who, like labor and management, have an ongoing relationship. More importantly, it has proven to be a successful procedure, as evidenced by the numerous agreements which have been concluded by the application of its principles. The same, however, could also be said about traditional adversarial divorce proceedings. After all, and as matrimonial lawyers are quick to boast, the vast majority of couples seeking a divorce conclude agreements between themselves without going to trial. If we reject those procedures nevertheless, as we do, it is because that is not a sufficient answer. In short, the question is not simply whether a particular procedure ultimately works; the question is first, whether it is an appropriate procedure in terms of its costs in relationship to its benefits, and second, whether it is the best procedure available.

Adversarial divorce proceedings were rejected not only because they were ineffective (in terms of time and money) but also because of their terrible side effects (in terms of the human injury that was also part of their cost). This, of course, is not true with negotiations. They are far more effective and have far less damaging side effects. Nevertheless they are still not as effective as the procedure that, for lack of a better label, we term "mediating in a common cause."[11]

On what basis do we accept or reject a particular procedure as being most effective in resolving the problem a couple has at the time of their divorce? Simply on the basis of the assumptions that we hold about the nature of that problem and what it is that stands between the parties and its resolution. From our standpoint, negotiations, preferable as they may be to adversarial proceedings, still share with those proceedings the basic view of divorce as a legal event in a couple's life rather than, as we maintain, primarily a personal event. Thus, central to the concept of negotiations is the belief that the mediator is faced with a dispute between the parties as to their legal rights and obligations and that what stands between them and the resolution of that dispute is the informed bargaining process that good negotiations provide.

From our standpoint, however, what the couple has is not a dispute at all, and certainly not a dispute about their legal rights and obligations. Rather, it is a problem— or, to be absolutely accurate, what we consider it more productive to view as a problem rather than as a dispute—and what stands between them and a resolution of that problem are not their conflicting interests but rather the very difficult feelings that are the by-product of their decision to divorce. The context we would create, therefore, is one best designed to deal with these feelings if and when they arise. This would not only cause us to adopt very different procedures in conducting mediation than we would if we viewed it as a negotiating process. It would also cause us to view as inappropriate procedures inconsistent with that understanding and that work at cross-purposes with it.

The context we would consider appropriate for the conduct of divorce mediation would be one that created an atmosphere both accepting and emotionally protective. In fact, the first meeting, and sometimes the second meeting as well, will be designed to set the necessary tone, to enlist each of the parties' trust, and to permit the expression of those feelings that are so overwhelming for one or both of them. In disregard of this, the proponents of divorce mediation as a negotiating process devote the first two and some-times three meetings in explaining procedures, obtaining agreements as to the rules that will prevail in mediation, preparing budgets, collecting financial information, detailing issues and setting forth each of the parties' proposals and counterproposals—all in prepa-ration for the ultimate negotiations that will follow.

From our viewpoint, this not only creates a less than ideal context, but, and by ignoring what is central to the dispute between the couple and the means by which it will be addressed, can actually impede its resolution. To bottle up the emotional component of the dispute between the parties, as this negotiating process does, is not without its consequences. As one of the leading advocates of divorce mediation as a negotiating process has acknowledged, mediators who follow this procedure can expect an emotional explosion to occur after about the third meeting. Unfortunately, and rather than under-standing the implications of this, it has simply been accepted as a given.

Secondly, by viewing it as a dispute (to be resolved, to be sure, by an alternative dispute resolution procedure), the parties are each still encouraged first to explain, then to justify, and finally to defend their own positions. For us, this process creates a coun-terproductive atmosphere that only makes a resolution of the problem more, rather than less, difficult. In contrast, the atmosphere we would create is one in which each of the parties will be able better to understand and, it is hoped, be more sympathetic to, the other's point of view—something that is difficult if you are forever preoccupied with defending your own.

Thirdly, negotiations tend to emphasize each of the parties' *positions*, rather than, as we would have it, simply their different *points of view*. In doing so, they lend themselves to the same kinds of exaggeration as do adversarial proceedings, even if not to the same extent. Thus, one of the leading proponents of divorce mediation as a negotiating process has warned mediators to be on the lookout for add-ons that the parties may attach to their proposals—the things that they do not expect to get but nevertheless add on simply in order to have something nonessential to concede in the negotiating process. If mediation is not set up as a negotiating process, however, and if it is instead established as a problem-solving process where the couple meets together in common cause, so to speak, the questions that a mediator will ask will be very different and will not lend themselves to this same kind of exaggeration. There is a difference, after all, in a mediator asking one of the parties, "How do you feel about that?" rather than, "What is your position on that?" And there is a difference in the answers he will get, since people do not tend to exaggerate their points of view as they do their demands.

The question, therefore, is not what kind of a process divorce mediation is; it is what kind of process we wish it to be. This, as we have noted, will depend on our view of divorce, and what it means and represents to separating and divorcing couples. From our standpoint that view is critical, for once again, what you see is what you get.

Conclusion

An appreciation of the importance of context in the resolution of the issues separating and divorcing couples face is thus critical to an appreciation of the benefits of mediation and to an understanding of the inadequacies of traditional divorce proceedings. It is critical for yet a further reason, and that is because it will tend to cut through so much of the debate that has gone on between the advocates and the critics of divorce mediation.

Consider, for example, the opposition of many women's groups to divorce mediation.[12] On the face of it, that opposition is based upon the belief that mediation is not in women's best interests—that women will not fare well in mediation. Not that these groups feel that women's interests are necessarily well served by traditional adversarial divorce proceedings. Quite the contrary, most of their efforts have been, and still are, devoted to trying to change what they consider to be the gross inequities for women in those proceedings.

Why then are they opposed to mediation? Because they believe that it will not only lead women down a blind alley in which they will get lost, but will also distract them from what should be their principal objective, namely, to improve the existing system so that it will do justice to women. In other words, the problem with adversarial proceedings is not that women are sent into the ring to do battle with their husbands. Rather, the problem is that it is an unfair contest because their husbands have been better prepared for it than they have and because the rules are slanted in their favor. For these groups, therefore, the remedy for the critical problem that divorce poses is not to get women out of the ring so that they will not have to do battle with their husbands. It is to assure that women are as well prepared for the contest as are their husbands and that the rules are changed so that they go into the ring on an equal footing. In short, the remedy is to improve traditional adversarial divorce proceedings by making our laws fairer, and by assuring that they result in justice between the parties.[13]

It is only a failure to understand the effects of the context in which traditional divorce proceedings take place that could permit women's groups, or anyone else for that matter, to persist in this fantasy. It is not possible to correct the ills of adversarial proceedings by changing the rules of the game. That is akin to suggesting that the ills of boxing could be eliminated by seeing to it that organized crime is kept out and by assuring that the rules do not permit low body blows. None of this will change the fact that a boxing match is, by definition, a knock-down, drag-out fight and that the object of the game is to win by doing bodily injury to your opponent. That is what it means to go into a boxing ring. The same, unfortunately, is also true of adversarial divorce proceedings, and all of the legislative enactments in the world will not change that.[14]

There is one test, and one test alone, that is acceptable in choosing between these two competing procedures (contexts); and that is which of them will tend to facilitate an agreement between the parties by *bridging* the distance that stands between them and such an agreement, and which of them will only tend to widen the breach and make the possibility of such an agreement even more remote. If that test is applied, traditional adversarial divorce proceedings would have to be summarily dismissed and seen as the dismal failure that they are. In fact, and judged by that standard, it is hard to imagine a set of procedures as ill conceived to assist separating and divorcing couples as are those provided by the law.

CHAPTER 8

POWER IMBALANCES—THE PROBLEM FOR WOMEN IN MEDIATION

For many observers, the most serious problem in mediation concerns the imbalance of power between the parties, and it is as impossible to listen to a critic of mediation without being confronted with this problem as it is to attend to a training program for would-be mediators, or a conference of experienced ones, without being presented with a workshop designed to assist them to deal with it.

How did the question of power imbalances become such a large issue in mediation practice? For the critics of mediation, it became an issue because they made it one. Even for diehard advocates of adversarial divorce proceedings, it was hard to deny what had become the almost universally accepted view of the damaging effects of those proceedings, particularly upon children, and was not particularly politic to try, given the pressure exerted on the legal profession by some of its most influential members to seek alternatives to the judicial resolution of disputes. Thus, if adversarial proceedings were to be defended, it was best to do so, not by denying their price, but by emphasizing their benefits. Those benefits, it was claimed, were that each of the parties had his own attorney to represent him and to advance his interests.

But why did the parties each need separate attorneys for that purpose? After all, they had been able to live their lives together in the past without the presence of separate attorneys. Why did they need them now? To answer this question the critics of mediation created the myth of the astute, financially sophisticated, domineering husband and the ignorant, unsophisticated, submissive wife. And like the human contortionist and the bearded lady who are dragged out and presented to the audience by every traveling circus, the strong man and the weak lady become the center of attraction at every performance put on by all of those who professed their serious concern about the dangers of mediation.

To make matters worse, the same concern was echoed by the advocates of mediation themselves, albeit for different reasons. In many instances, these were the people who were concerned with the place of women in society, and who had fought to raise their consciousness as they had fought to raise their salaries. They were also the ones who had waged a campaign to improve their positions at the time of their divorce by pressuring for the enactment of equitable distribution statutes, and they did not now want to see those hard-won gains lost in mediation. Since they could not help but view women's inequitable position somewhat in class terms, which saw men's advantage at the expense of women's disadvantage, this criticism struck a very sensitive nerve. So they too climbed on the bandwagon and added their voices to those who professed their concern with the fate of women in mediation.

There has been a third group of people who have also unwittingly added to the problem, and these are certain mental health professionals who became involved in divorce mediation. When the critics of divorce mediation and those concerned with the protection of women's rights raised their voices over the question of power imbalances, these mental health professionals misinterpreted what they heard and unthinkingly nodded their assent. After all, they too were often confronted with power imbalances in the relations between the parties whom they saw in family and marital therapy. In fact, a good deal of the therapy in these cases often consisted in addressing this very issue. Unfortunately, the nod of recognition these mental health professionals gave to those concerned with the problem of power imbalances in mediation was misinterpreted by them, and concluding that correcting the imbalances in power that existed between husbands and wives, as they understood it, was also a threshold issue in family therapy, the advocates of divorce mediation were only encouraged further in their concern. As a result, the question of power imbalances between husbands and wives has become almost universally accepted as constituting a serious problem in mediation.

Is it really, however? Does the strength of one of the parties and the weakness of the other necessarily taint the outcome in mediation as it has been suggested that it does? In short, is the imbalance in power between the parties the Achilles' heel of divorce mediation? Unfortunately, this has been so summarily assumed that we have long since passed the point where it is considered necessary, or even appropriate, for that matter, to interrupt the parade of concern and ask what is still the fundamental question: namely, does the emperor really have clothes on at all? Nevertheless, it is a question that must be asked. For in truth he does not, and this notwithstanding the testimony of the many witnesses who claim that they have seen them.

KNOWLEDGE VS. IGNORANCE

As we have previously noted, the myth created by the critics of divorce mediation not only sees the husband as strong and domineering, and the wife as weak and passive, but also attributes to him a financial sophistication which she generally lacks. This too, so those who express their concern complain, leaves the couple in unequal bargaining positions and gives the husband more power than his wife.

There is absolutely no merit to this argument. To begin with, there is almost nothing in mediation that requires sophistication on the part of the parties themselves. After all, mediation does not see a couple involved in weighty debates about the problems of deficit spending or the theory of supply-side economics. On the contrary, it involves rather mundane questions, such as the cost of fuel and electricity and of a new pair of sneakers. But the resolution of these questions is not dependent on knowledge that is unique to men as opposed to women, or on knowledge that they cannot readily obtain should it be necessary. Nor are the numerous other questions that husbands and wives must decide, such as whether or not the wife's remarriage will affect her right to continue to live in the marital residence, whether she shall have the right to move with the children beyond a stated distance, whether her future earnings will affect the amount of support that her husband will be required to pay her, and if so, by how much, etc. In fact, most of the questions that require special expertise, such as the tax implications of payments made by a husband to his wife for her support or that of their children, or the law of the particular jurisdiction, are routinely provided to both of the parties, by either an accountant or an attorney, as part of every mediation.

To be sure, questions of valuation may arise during the course of a mediation—as to the value of the husband's pension, his dental practice, or perhaps his business. But husbands are not necessarily better authorities on these questions than their wives, and no mediator would accept their opinion without outside corroboration even if they were. In short, the idea that husbands have an edge over their wives because they are men of commerce or industry while their wives are simply homemakers, or that they are possessed of some special knowledge that gives them an advantage in the discussions, is simply without foundation. Men who are in business may well have knowledge of business affairs that their wives do not. However, this is not what is involved in the mediation of their separation or divorce, any more than it was a factor in their marriage.

THE STRONG MAN VS. THE WEAK LADY

If a husband's power does not reside in the fact that he has more of the knowledge necessary to participate in mediation than his wife does, perhaps it resides in the fact that he has a stronger personality or is more overbearing; and it certainly cannot be denied that there are people in this world who are stronger, just as their are those who are more fragile. Having said this, however, those who express their concern over this supposed problem in mediation somehow assume that they have proven their point beyond any reasonable doubt, and then simply rest their case.

Nevertheless, the fact of individual strengths and weaknesses, standing alone, is not a sufficient premise upon which to predicate the argument. To begin with, such strengths and weaknesses are not neatly arranged by sex, as this stereotype would suggest; nor are they determined by whether a person is a breadwinner or a homemaker. To be sure, those who express their concern over this question will also acknowledge that it is possible that a weak husband might also be taken advantage of by his strong wife. However, they do this simply to be consistent, for not once has it ever been seriously suggested that this is also a serious problem in mediation, and the example always put forward is the stereotyped one of the dominant husband and subservient wife.

Secondly, and even when such strengths and weaknesses exist, as they admittedly do, it does not follow that they will necessarily be *used* as the argument suggests. It cannot be denied that if a husband is given power by his wife, he will most certainly exercise it. But it does not follow from this that he will use that power to dominate *her*, or worse, to take *unfair advantage* of her. It may only mean that, as between the two of them, it will be he who sets the tone in their relationship, and while it might offend our democratic sensibilities to say so, the truth is that a great many marriages are somewhat imbalanced in this way. Nor are they necessarily the worse for it.

That such imbalances exist is not a reflection of the fact that marriages are necessarily made up of weaker and stronger people, and certainly not that they are made up of domineering and subservient ones. It is simply a reflection of the fact that they are made up of *different* people. It may well be that these differences were the ingredients that held the relationship together. They may also have been the ingredients that eventually rocked its delicate balance. But it is only mythology, and a simplistic mythology at that, that sees those differences as resulting in a relationship where the needs of one of the parties are met only at the expense of the needs of the other, who is always left wanting.

Thirdly, and perhaps most importantly, very weak people are *not as tractable* as the mythologies of the critics of divorce mediation would have it, which sees them dutifully marching off into mediation at the direction of their husbands, who intend to take advantage of them once they get them there. On the contrary, they are insecure and afraid, and tend to seek out more powerful people to protect them. In fact, this is probably why they picked their husbands in the first place, and that strength is often the price that they have had to pay for his protection.

To be sure, some women such as this will undoubtedly find their way into mediation. There is no reason to be concerned about them, however, and certainly no reason to believe that they will need the mediator's protection from their husbands. Women such as this come into mediation very tentatively and, at least initially and until their fears are assuaged, they are always there with one foot out of the door. Contrary to the conventional mythology, their insecurity does not make them compliant lambs. Rather, their insecurity makes it very difficult for them to let go. This is particularly so if they were not the ones who initiated the divorce in the first place. Again, these women put up with their marriage and its disabilities primarily because of the security that their husband's strength afforded them.[1] However, if their husbands are going to be able to persuade them to forego the protection of their strength in their divorce, they will have to come forward with something very tangible and secure that will stand substitute for it. On the other hand, if it is the wife herself who has initiated the divorce, then by definition she is no longer quite the weak, dependent woman she once was. On the contrary, the fact that she has found the strength to end the relationship also means that, to some extent at least, she has finally tapped the sources of her own strength.

But what of the second group of women, those who have not just lived with stronger, more powerful husbands, but those who have lived with husbands who have dominated them, and perhaps even brutalized them? Notwithstanding the concern voiced by all those who have raised this issue, it is simply unrealistic to believe that women such as this are going to resort to mediation or be comfortable with it. They had a difficult enough time in their marriages with their husbands' power; they certainly do not want to stand naked before it in their divorce. If they are no longer going to have the dubious benefit of their husbands' strength to protect them against the world, then they are going to want to have *someone* to defend them against that strength. In short, it is the very women for whom this concern is expressed who are most likely to feel the need for protection (and to buy the legal system's mythology of protection), and turn to adversarial attorneys for that purpose rather than to mediation.

There is an even more serious error in the thinking that underlies this argument, however; and that is that it improperly and incorrectly assumes that what was a problem in the couple's marriage will also necessarily be a problem in their divorce. In doing this, the argument misses the very essential difference in the position of the wife during her marriage and at the time of her divorce, regardless of her strengths and weaknesses. During her marriage, and unless her husband's conduct breached minimal societal standards, such as would be the case if he struck her or refused to support her, the wife was by and large left without recourse, since the law will not generally intervene to regulate the relationship between a husband and his wife.

It may be inappropriate that a husband treats his wife as he does, that he keeps a close rein on the money that she is allowed to spend, that he is overbearing and a bully, that he is indifferent to his children and cavalier in his treatment of her, and that he squanders the family's monies and is profligate in his ways. It makes no difference. If the wife is not prepared to end their relationship, then she will simply have to do her best to put up with his conduct. It may be unfair that she is required to live under these conditions, but if she is not prepared to divorce him, or even to abandon him, then she will simply have to work this out with him in whatever way she can.

The minute that the decision to separate and divorce has been made, however, all of this changes. Nor does it make any difference whether it was he or she who made that decision. In either event, the previous restraint upon the law's intervention immediately drops and either party is now free to call upon the law to intercede in his or her behalf. It is no longer necessary for the wife to suffer in silence as a condition of maintaining her marriage, as was previously the case. Nor is it necessary for her to accept less than is her due in order to avoid a confrontation with a husband whom she will be forced to live with for the rest of her life. The law, previously reluctant to enter into what it viewed as the private relationship between the wife and her husband, is now willing to intervene simply for the asking. That means that the wife is no longer forced to accept the short end of the stick.

Whether she resorts to mediation or instead retains an attorney to negotiate an agreement for her, if she does not like what her husband is offering, she is always free to reject it and go to court and ask for more. Thus, the very fact of the couple's divorce immediately empowers the wife, since there now stands on the sidelines the force of the law which she can at any time call upon to enter the field on her behalf. Even more importantly, her husband understands her new power, even if he does not like it. Thus, he may be able to persuade her to consider mediation as an option. But she is not obligated to accept it. Nor is she forced to stay there when she has arrived. On the contrary, she is free to leave any time she wishes.

To maintain their argument, therefore, those concerned with the question of power imbalances in mediation have thus had to picture a woman so dominated by her husband's power that she will allow herself to be led into mediation as a lamb is led to slaughter. Nor will the mediator pose any real threat to her husband once he gets her there, for if her husband really has the power that the argument presupposes, there is nothing that the mediator will be able to do to get the wife to accept *his* strength as a weapon against her husband, let alone substitute that strength for her fear of him.

Can it be said that there are no women at all such as this? It may well be that there are, even if they are extremely rare, rather than the rule, as the argument impliedly suggests. But their existence does not represent a flaw in divorce mediation, as it is summarily assumed that it does. It may be unfair that a woman in this position will come out with less than will a woman who is not married to a bully. It is also unfair that a woman who is married to a decent, generous husband will come out with more than a woman who is not. However, that is a condition of *life*, not of mediation. More importantly, it is not a condition that traditional adversarial proceedings will be able to correct either. Thus, while the critics of divorce mediation would suggest that the safeguards built into adversarial proceedings will adequately deal with these imbalances, the sad history of those proceedings proves just the opposite. Turning to those proceedings did not mean that these women were no longer bullied by their husbands. All that it meant was that they were now bullied in different ways.

Negotiating Skills

Quite commonly, the argument is not predicated upon the husband's superior knowledge or even his superior power. Rather, it is predicated upon his superior negotiating skills. The argument is then sealed, and all possible objection nullified, with the observation that it is common knowledge, after all, that men are better negotiators than women. [2]

Again, the question is not whether men are more knowledgeable, more powerful, or better negotiators than their wives. The question is whether these are the factors that regulate a husband's and a wife's relationship or determines what takes place between them. [3] The answer is that they do not, and it is only a very simplistic view of the relationship that exists between husbands and wives that sees it in terms of superior power or superior negotiating skills.

Let us illustrate this by carrying an example to the extreme. A husband and a wife are in disagreement as to the custody of their children. Based on his superior negotiating skills, the husband has presented an argument that overwhelmingly and irresistibly leads to one conclusion and one conclusion alone, namely, that the children should be in his custody. Is there anyone who seriously believes that the ultimate outcome here will depend on the wife's ability to construct an argument of her own that just as powerfully and irresistibly leads to the conclusion that their children should be with *her*? More importantly, is there anyone who seriously believes that, if she is unable to do this, she will be forced to concede custody of her children to her husband?

But what then will the wife here do if she is unable to marshal as convincing an argument as her husband? She will simply say *no*. Her husband may attempt to take her to task for not supporting her conclusion with a valid argument of her own. He may even say that she is acting unreasonably or irrationally, and it is possible that the wife may feel somewhat uncomfortable in not being able to defend herself better than she has. But the one thing that she is not going to do is concede the argument on that account. On the contrary, and if what is at issue is of real concern to her, she will protect herself by whatever means she must.

There is a second serious flaw in the argument. The wife, after all, is not forced to sit and be overwhelmed by her husband's superior negotiating skills, any more than she is obligated to sit and be overwhelmed by his superior knowledge or power. On the contrary, she is always free to get up and leave and, armed with her own lawyer, go to court and have the matter determined in her favor by someone who is neither bound nor intimidated by the traits in her husband that so overwhelm her. Just as importantly, her husband knows this. Thus, if he employs his superior power and skill simply to drive his wife into a corner, that may well be the price he will have to pay for it. And he knows that too.

One final point: as one would expect, those who see a husband's superior negotiating skills as being a problem in divorce mediation are those who assume that mediation is a negotiating process. (As far as the advocates of divorce mediation are concerned, it is those who set it up as a negotiating process.) However, and as we have noted elsewhere,[4] although negotiations may take place on *occasion* during the course of a mediation, mediation is not *by definition* a negotiating process. Nor should it be made into one.

DIVORCE MEDIATION VS. ADVERSARIAL PROCEEDINGS

This brings us to yet another unfortunate consequence of the debate engendered by the misplaced concern over power imbalances in mediation; and that is that is has unthinkingly reinforced certain assumptions implicit in adversarial thinking. In suggesting, as they have, that people may be left powerless in divorce mediation, without their own separate attorneys to advance their interests, the critics of divorce mediation have fallen back on the myth that traditional adversarial divorce proceedings, and the separate attorneys which it provides each of the parties, gives them this power. Unfortunately, even the advocates of divorce mediation, who should know better, have unwittingly reinforced this myth in their concern for balancing the supposed imbalances in power between the parties.

It is a myth, nevertheless. A divorce lawyer, after all, does not have a magic wand that he can wave to protect a woman such as this. Nor is he a threat to her husband. He may be a nuisance to him. He may even be an impediment to him. But her husband will find a way to get around him, even if his *wife* has to pay for it. In fact, and if the adversarial lawyer whom she has retained is not careful, he may only find that he has made her position *more* difficult rather than less. For in the very act of attempting to protect her, he may only set in motion procedures that will escalate the conflict, and with it the husband's wrath and unbridled anger. The rather naive view of power, implicit in the exaggerated concern over power imbalances between the parties, may not understand this, but in the real world it is a fact.

As with the use of other magical words, such as legal rights, justice, or fair and equitable, routinely invoked in defense of traditional adversarial proceedings, the symbolic strength of the word *power* is such that we never pause to consider this, let alone ask just *how* the wife's lawyer will provide her with this power, or what emotional price she will have to pay in order to get it. For in truth, the idea that the wife's problems will all be over if she turns to adversarial proceedings, and that the lion that her husband was in mediation will now become a lamb, is again simply myth, albeit a convenient one.[5]

The myth aside, the parties have no power whatsoever in traditional adversarial divorce proceedings. The only power that they have is to initiate them. Having done that, however, they quickly lose all control over those proceedings, or ability to direct their outcome. On the contrary, they soon find that they are but bit players consigned to the wings of the drama. Nor do their attorneys, who are center stage, have any more control over them, even though they may appear to. Rather, the proceedings take on a life of their own, and the couple and their attorneys are simply dragged along to its inexorable conclusion. In fact, it is this feeling of helplessness in the face of these proceedings that makes each of the parties feel so powerless, and so unable to control their destinies, that is one of the most common complaints expressed by husbands and wives caught in the legal process of divorce.

The exact opposite is the case in mediation. Rather than leaving either of the parties powerless, mediation is an *empowering* procedure. Unfortunately, in being so obsessed with the supposed problem of power imbalances in mediation, the advocates of divorce mediation have overlooked this fact. In doing so, they have also overlooked one of mediation's most significant virtues—that it is a process that *invests* each of the parties with power instead of robbing them of it, as do traditional adversarial divorce proceedings. Instead of being left feeling helpless, each of the parties has complete control over the outcome. Neither is forced to sit and endure the slings and arrows of outrageous fortune flung at them by the other simply because they are on a judicial conveyer belt over which they have no control. Quite the contrary, they have the most important power of all, and that is to be able to stand up and terminate those proceedings at any point should they be unhappy with the direction in which they are going, including the power to turn to adver.arial attorneys to do the job for them should they feel that it is ever in their best interest to do so.

PROTECTION

The concern with power imbalances in divorce mediation has, unfortunately, reinforced adversarial mythology in yet another way. It has done this by blurring the very important distinction between *power* and *protection*.

While the advocates of divorce mediation concern themselves with imbalances in power between the parties, adversarial divorce lawyers, ironically, never talk about power. Rather, and in a curious Freudian slip of the tongue, they talk instead about protection. Unfortunately, the advocates of divorce mediation have taken the two terms to be synonymous. In doing this they have overlooked the subtle, but critically important, difference.

What the Freudian slip acknowledges, and what the advocates of divorce mediation have so far failed to understand, is that the reason our adversarial system sells protection is because it has left each of the parties feeling so very powerless. Conversely, it is the very sense of powerlessness each of the parties feels in the face of those adversarial proceedings that causes them to feel the need to buy this protection. After all, people who feel powerful do not buy protection; it is only sold to those who do not.

What is it that makes the wife, for example, feel so powerless? The mythology says that it is the superior power of her husband. Unfortunately, this answer will not do. To begin with, it does not explain why her husband also feels powerless, despite his supposed superior strength, and why he also feels the need to go out and hire an attorney to protect himself. Nor does it explain why the wife does not feel powerful once she has retained an attorney to advance her interests. She does not simply because her attorney has not given her that power, *only his protection*. But since it is incomplete, and only partial protection at best, she is left feeling almost as powerless as before. In time, and as the adversarial process begins to proceed on its way, she may even feel less so.

There is an even more serious problem with the argument, however. A person does not feel that he needs protection simply because another person has power. Rather, he feels the need of protection because he fears that the other person will use that power against him. In other words, it is not power, but the *unbridled use* of power, that is threatening. And there's the rub. Adversarial divorce lawyers sell protection, and each of the parties feels compelled to buy that protection, precisely because adversarial proceedings encourage the unbridled use of power. Why is this? Because, contrary to the official mythology, those proceedings only leave each of the parties feeling more threatened than they did before. In a world where the old rules no longer apply, where all action takes place at a distance and proceeds unannounced, and where the only rule is that it is each man for himself, self-help and preemptive action quickly take the field. They also very quickly appear to be a necessity.

Having left each of the parties exposed to the unbridled power of the other, do adversarial proceedings then protect the parties from it? The answer, of course, is that they do not. If the idea that adversarial proceedings provide each of the parties with power is mythology, it is even more fantastic mythology to believe that it provides them with protection from the other's power. In fact, and in one of the cruelest ironies of all, the very proceedings that cause each of the parties to feel in need of protection in the first place then leaves them feeling threatened and almost totally unprotected.

Nor could it be otherwise. After all, adversarial proceedings are adversarial in nature because the parties have each been led to view one another as adversaries and to treat one another as such. Thus, and as the parties learn all too late, the best protection that each of them can be given is not the protection that adversarial attorneys hawk, which at best only salvages the damage that has already been done to one of them by the other. It is the protection that comes from having the far greater assurance that such damage will not occur in the first place. That is the kind of protection that mediation provides.[6]

POWER IMBALANCES AND MENTAL HEALTH PROFESSIONALS

As we have noted, the concern about power imbalances in divorce mediation has unwittingly been reinforced by certain mental health professionals who have expressed their sympathy for the issue being voiced. This is particularly unfortunate since, of all those who have raised their voices in concern, they are the group who should have known better.

To begin with, a mental health professional would view as naive the understanding of the critics of divorce mediation and, unfortunately, even of some of its advocates, as to the relationship between husbands and wives, let alone how they exert their influence on one another. The critics of divorce mediation see their influence as being raw, arm-twisting power, with the imbalances in power resulting in the weaker party being overwhelmed by the stronger party. Translated into the context of mediation, that means that the stronger party will be able to force the weaker party to accept less than is her due, and to give away more than she should.

Contrary to this mythology, however, the husband's superior power does not convert the wife to his point of view. It simply leaves her unable to convert him to hers. It may be that other considerations will persuade the wife not to fight the husband any further; but these have nothing to do with his power. They have to do, instead, with the myriad existential realities that act as limiting factors on the options available to us in life and our willingness to exercise those options. In the end, it is not that the wife is intimidated or persuaded by her husband's power or logic. It is that she decides, for other (and usually sensible and valid) reasons, not to do further battle with him.

A mental health professional would also view as simplistic the attempt to explain the very complex interrelationship between people, particularly husbands and wives, and how they influence one another, on the basis of strengths and weaknesses alone. To do so would be to ignore the attachments, the interdependencies, the world of meaning and the personal validation that are all such a significant part of their relationship. Nor are these considerations only factors in their marriage, as the argument presupposes. To be sure, and for the critics of divorce mediation, who only see couples in an adversarial setting that unleashes destructive feelings that tend to do violence to these considerations, it may seem so. For anyone who has worked with separating and divorcing couples other than in an adversarial setting, however, there can be little question but that this is not the case. Quite the contrary, these attachments and interdependencies can continue to be painfully strong. In fact, it is the very strength of these feelings that so often makes their divorce as difficult as it is.

To look at strengths and weaknesses in such a one-dimensional way, as this argument does, is also to miss what is often one of the relationship's most significant aspects. Thus, while someone who cannot see beyond the apparent strength of one of the parties, or the apparent weakness of the other, may simply see a strong man and a weak woman, a more sophisticated eye may well discern a woman who has learned to *use* those other aspects of the relationship, and even her own apparent weaknesses, as *strengths* to balance out the power of her more secure husband. At times, he may even find that this weak woman has quite effectively learned to *control* the relationship by carefully deploying her weaknesses.

There is a further limitation in the view that sees only a strong man and a weak woman: that is its inability to explain what held the relationship together and, even more importantly, why it fell apart. If the marriage permits the husband to control his wife, and if that is all that he wants to do, why then does he seek a divorce? By the same token, if the wife only stays in the marriage because she is so intimidated by her husband's strength, how does one explain her decision to leave him? Strengths and weaknesses alone do not answer these questions, any more than they explain the complexities of close interpersonal relationships, or why people marry and divorce.

Finally, when a mental health professional talks about the problem of power imbalances, he is generally talking about something that is a problem in the successful *continuation* of a couple's marriage, not in the successful conclusion of their divorce. In large measure, however, the problem of power imbalances is no longer a problem once the decision to end the marriage has been made. In terms of the concerns expressed here, power is only a problem in the marriage because the wife *feels* powerless. She is not powerless, however, because she *lacks* power. She is powerless either because she has not *tapped the sources* of her power, and is therefore not aware of her own power, or because, for any one of a number of other possible reasons, she has been unable or unwilling to *exert the power* that she has.

In a very important sense, what the couple's divorce represents is a recognition that it is not going to be possible for them to work out a successful adjustment in their relationship so as to permit the wife to exert her influence in the marriage. Again, this is not because the wife is powerless in the marriage; it is because any attempt by the wife to exert her own influence will, of necessity, require a countervailing change on the part of her husband. More often than not, however, he is unable to effectuate that change. Ironically, and contrary to the conventional mythology, he is unable to change not because he is strong, and unwilling to give up his power. He is unable to change because he is insecure, and *afraid* to let go of it.

However, and again contrary to conventional mythology, what was true in their marriage is not true in their divorce. While, to be sure, the factors in the husband's personality that caused him to attempt to resist the wife's expression of her own influence may not have changed, they will not have the same limiting effect that they previously did. By definition, there is not going to be the same kind of ongoing relationship between the parties. For the husband, that means that controlling the wife's power may not necessarily be the same life-and-death issue that it was formerly. More importantly, for the wife it means that she may not necessarily be under the same constraints, and may be freer to assert her own needs.

It would therefore be a mistake for mediators to conclude that when they express their concern over power imbalances between the parties, they are simply responding to the same problem in mediation that mental health professionals are responding to in family therapy. To begin with, a mental health professional would consider the view held by those who are concerned with this problem, as to how influence is expressed and exerted in the relationship between a husband and a wife, as being simplistic. More importantly, he would take issue with the suggestion that the constraints that created a problem for a wife in her marriage would necessarily create the same problem for her in her divorce. In short, he would not accept as valid the underlying assumptions that support this concern.

The Issue of Power Imbalances and the Practice of Mediation

Until now, we have simply concerned ourselves with the misunderstanding and confusion in the debate between those who profess their concern with the problem of power imbalances in divorce mediation. We must now turn our attention to what is by far our most serious concern—the effect that this debate, and this thinking, has had upon mediation practice.

The first ill effect that this preoccupation with power imbalances has had on mediation practice has been to make it a threshold issue. To be sure, a mediator may encounter imbalances in power between the parties that he will feel it necessary to address in the course of the mediation, just as he may find such imbalances in power were he to see the same couple in family counseling. But the exaggerated concern over power imbalances has imposed upon mediators the obligation to *go out and look for them*. It is no longer sufficient for a mediator, as it is for a family therapist, to sit back and watch the drama unfold, making note of the problems or potential problems as he goes along. The protectionist thinking that misguidedly informs so much of mediation practice today insists, instead, that the mediator go into each mediation armed with a checklist of potential problem areas that he must satisfy before he undertakes the mediation. The name that has been given to this is called *assessing the couple's suitability for mediation*.[7]

Is the husband an alcoholic? Has he been guilty of sexually molesting his daughters? Has he physically abused his wife? Are there imbalances in power in the couple's relationship? These are the kinds of concerns that mediators have been charged with and which they have been led to believe they must satisfy before it is appropriate for them to undertake the mediation. At the least, this kind of inquiry is rather insulting, in that it presupposes that people are somehow criminals, or at least less than responsible, simply because they have decided to get divorced. Furthermore, it inappropriately invades the privacy of people who are but strangers to the mediator. Finally, by again incorporating, and then underscoring, *adversarial* concerns, it establishes an atmosphere exactly opposite to the one most conducive to successful mediation.

A second and even graver problem is the very real danger that mediators who are so concerned, and even obsessed, with the issue of power imbalances between husbands and wives, will see almost everything that goes on in mediation as an expression of those imbalances. Let us give an example. During the course of the mediation, the question comes up as to whether or not the wife will have the right to live in the home after the children graduate from high school, and until they have completed their college education. The husband insists, perhaps even angrily, that he wants his equity in the home when they graduate from high school and, if his wife does not have the money to buy him out, that the home will have to be sold. The wife says nothing, or perhaps just quietly indicates that she would like to have the right to live there until they graduate from college, and then says no more.

Has the husband used his power to intimidate the wife? Even more importantly, has she *been* intimidated by it? A mediator could certainly interpret this exchange between them as the basis for this conclusion. He might be making a mistake, however, if he did. To begin with, he would be overlooking a lot of other evidence that would call this interpretation into question, not the least of which is the fact that the husband has already *agreed* that the wife can continue to live in the home until the children have graduated from high school. Secondly, he may have converted what was only a legitimate difference of opinion into the exercise of power simply because those opinions were expressed in different ways or even different tones of voice.

There is an even more serious problem with the mediator's judgment, however, even if it is accurate. Worse, it is a problem only compounded further if the mediator then intervenes to correct it, as he is urged to do by those who express their concern over the problem of power imbalances. For in doing so, he will have *frozen the action*. A road takes many turns before it reaches its final destination and it would be wrong for a mediator, as it would be wrong for a driver proceeding down a highway, to judge where it will ultimately lead simply on the basis of a single bend in the road. If a mediator rushes in at this point and attempts to straighten out the situation by correcting what he perceives to be the imbalance in power between the parties, he will never get to see where the road might have taken the couple had he left them on their own. Unfortunately, mediators who see the expression of power at every turn, and who explain every turn in terms of the exercise of power, will not feel comfortable doing this. From their standpoint, if these imbalances in power are not corrected immediately, then, and from the very outset, the direction of the road can only be downhill for the weaker of the two parties.

The effect of this kind of thinking upon mediation practice can be no less stifling than it would be in the practice of family therapy. The relationship between a husband

and a wife represents a complex of factors—the existential givens, if you will, that constitute the coercive facts of life in the real world in which we live. The name that a mental health professional gives to this complex is called reality, and he knows that he must remain open to that reality, and to his experience, rather than to judge it or, worse, prejudge it. However, the concern with power imbalances, which has the mediator categorize what takes place before him in terms of power and imbalances in power, causes him to do just that.

There is a third problem with the concern over power imbalances, and that is that it segregates, and improperly distinguishes, one aspect of the multifaceted complex that represents human personality and human interaction from all of its other aspects, giving it a priority it ill deserves. Moreover, in doing this, it attempts to justify a response on the mediator's part which is not only inappropriate here, as it would be in all other instances, but which is also inconsistent with what should be his basic stance when confronted with this variety of human expression.

During the course of his work, a mediator will be faced with the full panoply of human feelings and expressions. Nor will they always be pleasant or helpful. He will be confronted by people who are insensitive, unthinking, and self-righteous. He will meet others who are foolish, immature, unrealistic, inconsistent, and, at times, even irrational. There will be some who are small-minded, annoying, and frustrating, not to mention obstinate and intransigent. At times they may even be rude, abrasive, insulting, and offensive, not only to one another, but to the mediator as well. And, of course, he will always have to deal with the fact that they are hurt and angry, and sometimes even vindictive and vengeful.

It is precisely at that point, when he is faced with the display of these all too real emotions, that the skill of a mediator will be tested. In fact, his art, to the extent that mediation is an art, will be expressed in his response to this display, as his own character will be reflected in the understanding, carefully honed and refined, that is expressed in that response.

There are two principal components to that understanding. The first can perhaps best be expressed by the term *acceptance*. The mediator will not always *like* what he sees and hears during the course of a mediation. Nor will he always feel that the positions taken by the parties, or the arguments they advance to justify them, necessarily have merit. On the contrary, they will often seem petty and unreasonable, and at times even ridiculous. They will also invariably reflect a rather limited and one-sided understanding of what has happened to the two of them and, therefore, a rather distorted sense of what is appropriate or inappropriate under the circumstances.

But that, nevertheless, is how they *feel*. To be sure, the mediator could take exception to those feelings, and argue that they are neither justified nor appropriate. However, he knows that the parties in question did not come to him for that, and his better understanding tells him that it will serve no useful purpose for him to do this. Accordingly, he accepts the fact that their feelings and attitudes are part of the reality with which he must deal. Reality is a terrible weight, impeding our progress, that we are forever burdened to carry on our shoulders. It is not subject to reason and is impervious to moral exhortation. It is simply part of the givens, and the mediator therefore accepts it.

The second component of that understanding, born of the first, is expressed by the term *human limitation*, and it has to do with what we have a right to expect and not expect of our lives and the very inadequate, and at times maladaptive, strategies that we devise and employ in dealing with them. It also has to do with what we have a right to believe we will be able to effect, let alone guarantee, in the lives of others.

Life is a high-wire act. More to the point, it is a dangerous high-wire act requiring us carefully to maintain our balance as we proceed from one end of it to the other. Nor will it be possible for any of us to achieve a perfect state of balance. Thus, and as careful and skillful as we may be, we will never get to our destination without faltering. That being so, our position will always be somewhat precarious, and the most that we can ever hope for is to attain a state of *balanced imbalance*. For those less careful or fortunate, the crossing can be even more difficult. They may even completely lose their footing and their lives end in tragedy.

What should the mediator's response be when faced with the fact of human limitation? It should be one of restraint, a restraint born of the understanding that it is not given us to *guarantee* that the strategies that we would devise, or the decisions that we would make, in other people's lives are more appropriate or will necessarily turn out to be any better than their own. In fact, we have no guarantee that they may not even turn out to be worse. It is not just that the outcome is subject to considerations that we can no more accurately predict than can the parties themselves. It is not even that the appropriateness of those decisions is dependent on an emotional congruity that only the parties themselves can say is right. It is also born of the fact that even if our decisions are right in some abstract sense, this does not mean that the parties in question will be capable of *following* the advice that we give them, let alone effectuate the personal transformation that may often be required for them to do so.

To be sure, there will always be those who will be certain that they know better, and who will therefore want to intervene and try their hand at it. Furthermore, they will have no end of reasons and excuses to justify their doing so. Lawyers will excuse themselves by saying that they are just trying to assure that the parties' agreement is fair and just. Friends and relatives will excuse themselves by saying that they are just trying to make sure that it is appropriate. Mental health professionals will justify themselves by saying that they are simply trying to guarantee that the decisions that the parties make are healthy ones. And mediators will excuse themselves by saying that they only wish to assure that the parties agreement was not the result of coercion or an imbalance in power between them. We must not be fooled, however. These are always the reasons given by those who would meddle where they do not belong. Nor can we forget that the claim of those who maintain that they know better what is right for other people than they do themselves, by whatever name it is called, is still arrogance.

How does this understanding affect the attitude of the mediator toward the parties and their agreement? It affects it by causing him to balance whatever weight he might give to his own insight and understanding with an equivalent level of humility, a humility born of an awareness that places a restriction on what he will be able to do, or even has a right to attempt. The mediator is there because he believes that he will have been of some small benefit to the couple if he can help them get from where they are to the distant shore. He does not know what their individual fates will be when they get there. Nor does he have any illusions as to the difficulties that may await them when they do. Since human limitation is a very part of the condition of life, it would be naive for him to think otherwise or to expect more. Nevertheless, he believes that they can only get lost in the troubled waters on which they are now adrift and that, whatever their future fates may be, he must get them past where they now are. Nor can he permit anything to distract him or interfere with the obligation that he has assumed. To be sure, the swelling waters may at times engulf and overwhelm the parties. But if the mediator permits them to take control of him as well, then the ship will certainly founder and they will all be lost.

Does anything that we have said mean that a mediator will never see power being exerted by one of the parties, or the other party feeling constrained by the exercise of that power? Obviously not. He will see it just as he will witness the many other factors that characterize the parties and affect their relationship. And will he sit by and do nothing when he is confronted with it? Again, we have not suggested that. But seeing the problem differently, and bringing a very different understanding to that problem, he will also act differently. To begin with, he will not view the expression of power as being separate and distinct, or necessarily different, from the rest of what he sees during the course of a mediation. While, for those obsessed with the problem of power imbalances in mediation, it represents a special problem, for him it is but one expression of many and, as such, deserving of no different treatment.

Secondly, and as we have said previously, he will not necessarily be that quick to act when he does see it. Unlike those who see power, and the abuse of power, at every turn, he does not draw inevitable conclusions from every flexing of muscle by one of the parties, even when that flexing is not met by an equal response from the other. Most importantly of all, unlike those who feel compelled immediately to rush in and wipe the slate clean whenever they are confronted by any of these considerations, he does not expect the couple to conclude an agreement free of these human expressions, or one untainted by these factors. On the contrary, he understands that they will affect the ultimate agreement that they conclude, just as they have affected everything else in their lives together. And he accepts this.

Finally, and when he does intervene, he will do so very differently, and for a different purpose. As we have repeatedly stated, in rejecting traditional adversarial divorce proceedings, divorce mediation must reject as well the assumptions upon which those proceedings are based.[8] In terms of our present discussion, that means to reject the understanding of the very complex relationship that exists between people, particularly members of a family, in simplistic terms of power. That is all adversarial lawyers see because that is all they have been trained to see and because that is their stock-in-trade. It is a naive and simplistic view of the world, however, and it becomes no more accurate simply because, like pulling marionettes on a string, they can cause each of the parties to act toward one another on that basis.

When a mediator is faced with the expression of power—or with the expression of stubbornness, insensitivity, selfishness, or unrealistic expectations, for that matter—he does not consider it productive to counterbalance the scales with equal quantities of power, stubbornness, insensitivity, selfishness or unrealistic expectations. That is the way of the adversarial lawyer. On the contrary, he views these as existential realities with which he must deal, and perhaps circumvent, if he is to be able to conclude an agreement between the parties. Will the mediator feel the need to act as a balance in situations such as this? He undoubtedly will. But it will not be the kind of balancing that simply throws a weight on one end of the scale to offset that on the other. Rather, it will be the very delicate act of balancing that every skilled mediator learns to perform as he carefully and patiently edges his way along the very narrow tightrope that leads the couple to an agreement.

There is one last point that must be made. The understanding that brings the mediator to the point where he is willing to accept what takes place in front of him, and not pass judgment upon it, does not mean that he is not *concerned* with the decisions the couple ultimately make. It simply means that he does not become *invested* in those decisions. His concern, therefore, is with *procedure, not with outcome.* It is his job, to the extent that he can, to help the parties make informed, intelligent decisions, and to call to their attention all of the considerations that he believes should affect those decisions. But he knows that he will have to do that in the face, and within the context, of the constraints imposed by their individual attitudes, and the characteristics of their particular relationship. And, as we have said, he accepts this. As a result, he does not view himself as the guarantor of that agreement. Nor, for the same reason, will he permit himself to become invested in it.

"CLASS STRUGGLE"

There is one last unfortunate consequence of the concern with power imbalances that must be mentioned. As we have noted, and despite the polite lip service to the contrary, the imbalances in power which both the critics and advocates of divorce mediation are concerned about are always the power imbalances that supposedly exist between the strong husband and the weak wife. (Although the demanding wife and the milquetoast husband are as much a part of our inherited mythology as the strong man and the weak woman, those concerned with the problem of power imbalances have never proffered them as an example of their concern.) The effect has been to fuel what is already an unfortunate tendency to see disputes between husbands and wives as a class struggle, thereby promoting an almost Thurberian war of the sexes. This tendency has been further reinforced by women's advocates who, in their zeal to promote the cause of women, and to be on guard against anything that they feel might be disadvantageous to them, have been slowly but surely effectuating a politicalization of divorce.

How has this been accomplished? Firstly, it has been asserted that the economic realities of divorce fall only on the shoulders of women and children, and not their husbands. Thus, we have been told by Lenore J. Weitzman, then a professor of Sociology at Stanford University, that whereas the standard of living of women and children in the first year following their divorce decreases by approximately 73%, the same standard of living of their husband's increases by 42%.[9] The same is supposedly true in the area of child custody. It is common knowledge that the vast majority of children remain in the custody of their mothers following their parents' divorce. However, the attempt by men's groups to challenge the logic that inevitably leads to this result has sent tremors through women's advocates groups, who have now marshalled their defenses in complaint about the difficulty that "good enough" mothers are facing in attempting to assert their right to custody of their children.

This supposed fact has now been documented by psychologist Phyllis Chesler, who reports the result of a six-year study she conducted of several hundred cases in which she found that 82 percent of the fathers had obtained custody of their children either in court or by extralegal means such as kidnapping. [10] Finally, and although the numerous equitable distribution statutes that were enacted in the last number of years had as their purpose the fairer distribution of property to women upon their divorce, matrimonial attorneys Harriet Cohen and Adria Hillman report that their study of the application of that statute in New York clearly demonstrates that women are *not* sharing equitably, let alone equally, in the distribution of marital property. [11] It makes no difference that these conclusions are drawn from a biased and distorted reading of the facts. Nor does it make any difference that their authors started out with an ax to grind, and then ground it to their liking. In each case, the effect has been to draw sharp lines between men and women, and to cause a politicalization of divorce in the process.

Unfortunately, that politicalization has now invaded divorce mediation as well. As a result, and even though it is not particularly flattering to women, buying the mythology that mediation will simply represent the opportunity for husbands to take economic advantage of their wives, who will find themselves defenseless and without the aid of an attorney to protect them, many of these groups strongly object to divorce mediation. [12] It is not that divorce mediation is bad; it is simply that it is bad for women.

Is the opposition of these groups really based on the fear that mediation will not be fair to women, however? When the discussion is about finances, it is of course hard to tell. But these groups are almost as uncomfortable about the mediation of child custody disputes, for they see the mediation of child custody as simply resulting in more agreements providing for joint custody. But what is wrong with that? Is there anything wrong with the idea that children should have the opportunity of a meaningful, ongoing relationship with both their parents? Is it unfair for men to have as important an effect on their children's lives as their wives? And are there no instances in which joint custody or, more accurately, shared parenting, would be an effective and appropriate way to accomplish those objectives? Unfortunately, that is apparently not the point. Joint custody may possibly be more fair to children and to men in certain instances, but women's groups do not feel that it is best for women, and when the yardstick of fair conflicts with what is best for women, that yardstick is simply discarded. In short, and apparently like the stereotyped male with whose attitude they take issue, these groups do not want what is fair for women; they only want what is best for them.

While men and women are not born antagonists, as some would apparently have it, the unfortunate tendency on the part of women's groups (and, it must be noted, certain men's groups as well) to ask only for what is fair when that is to their advantage, but to reject it when it is not, cannot help to do anything but tend to fulfill the prophecy of this assumption. Mediation must resist this very narrow understanding of the effects of divorce, which is unfortunately one of the legacies of traditional adversarial divorce proceedings. Divorce is not bad only for women, as women's advocates would have it, or bad only for men, as some men's groups would insist. Nor is it even bad only for children, as those concerned with the effects of divorce upon children contend. It is a tragedy for all of them, for each in their own way. It is upon this understanding that divorce mediation must insist.

CHAPTER 9

WHOSE FAULT IS IT?

Until recently, the prevailing view in our society saw divorce as occasioned by the misconduct of one of the parties, and numerous factors conspired to promote and to reinforce this view. To begin with, and since both the state and organized religion tended to promote marriage, and therefore to discourage divorce, divorce was not freely allowed. On the contrary, it was deemed justified, if at all, only by conduct that went to the very heart of the commitments made by each of the parties in their contract to marry. Thus, divorce was not granted unless one of the parties was found to be guilty of conduct that violated an essential aspect of the relationship—adultery, cruel and inhuman treatment, abandonment, etc.

Our Judeo-Christian tradition further added to the problem in that it tended to view conduct that it did not like or approve of as misconduct, caused by human failing. Thus, conduct viewed as grounds for one of the parties to obtain a divorce became a divorce occasioned by the misconduct, and therefore fault, of the other party. It is this understanding that has traditionally characterized the law's view of divorce and has, therefore, historically informed adversarial divorce proceedings. Moreover, it is a view that, despite our more liberal divorce laws—which, after all, are more reflective of society's desire to permit divorce than they are of any real change in their understanding of it—still informs so much of our thinking about divorce.

What effect has this understanding had on the law's attitude toward divorce? It has been to cause our legal system to view divorce as a melodrama made up of villains and heroes. This has had many unfortunate consequences, not the least of which was that, particularly in the past, divorce proceedings were characterized as attempts to establish the guilt or innocence of the respective parties. Divorce actions thus tended to resemble quasi-criminal proceedings, which had as their object the determination, and then punishment, of the guilty party.[1] This in turn tended to reinforce the misplaced sense of guilt that one of the parties sometimes felt, as it did the exaggerated sense of innocence, and therefore betrayal, just as often felt by the other. The result was that instead of helping each of the parties to effectuate some kind of *emotional closure with the past*, and the basis for a *working relationship in the future*, those legal proceedings only tended to exacerbate further the feelings which made this so difficult, if not impossible.

To be sure, and particularly in recent years, there has been a significant change in the law's attitude, and state after state has now adopted no-fault divorce laws which permit parties to end their marriage simply because there has been an irretrievable breakdown in their relationship.[2] So too, and even before the advent of the concept of rehabilitative maintenance, there were frequent expressions of judicial opinion to the effect that alimony was not to be granted as a reward or imposed as a punishment.[3] Be that as it may, the concept of fault has been dying but a slow death, and it is still with us.[4]

Why is that? Principally because the practices that the law discarded, based upon the old thinking, have not been replaced by any new understanding. Thus, while our new equitable distribution statutes may have signaled that recognition that there must be a more modern attitude toward marriage to replace the old and now outdated one, it did not at the same time also herald in a new understanding of divorce. Quite the contrary, the idea that divorce was occasioned by the fault and misconduct of one of the parties was rejected, not because it was found to be incorrect, or because it was superseded by a better understanding, but, in large measure, simply because it had become unpopular and was no longer in fashion. In short, our divorce laws were changed simply because more people wanted to end their marriages, not because they came to have a better understanding of their divorces. The result has been that whether it is still explicitly a factor that a court must take into consideration in awarding support or distributing marital property—and it still is in a number of states[5]—the idea that divorce is occasioned by the misconduct of one or both parties is still deeply ingrained in adversarial thinking.

Divorce mediation represents not only a rejection of adversarial proceedings, but of this understanding as well. How would a divorce mediator view divorce? Again, through the eyes of a therapist. To begin with, and given the very complex relationship that exists between family members, he would view the idea that a couple's divorce had been occasioned by the misconduct, and therefore fault, of one or both of the parties as being simplistic at best. To be sure, he has known wives who have divorced their husbands because they committed adultery or were guilty of cruelty to them. But he has also known wives who did not divorce their husbands despite the fact that they committed adultery or were guilty of cruelty. By the same token he has known wives who have divorced their husbands even though their husbands had never committed adultery or been guilty of cruelty. He would thus find it very difficult to explain divorce based upon such conduct, or at least difficult to explain it based on such conduct alone. This is not to say that he would consider acts of adultery or cruelty to be irrelevant, let alone appropriate. It is to say that he would make a sharp distinction between the propriety of an act and its necessarily being the cause of a couple's divorce.

Secondly, and perhaps even more importantly, he knows that the conduct being complained of is more often than not really a symptom of the problem rather than its cause. To be sure, there are acts of adultery that have nothing to do with any problem in the marriage. But in a very important respect these acts of adultery also have nothing to do with the marriage, in the sense that the person committing the act of adultery is not making a statement about his spouse, is not using the adulterous relationship as a bridge to transport him out of his marriage, and does not intend or expect that it will in any way affect his life with his spouse. Paradoxically, it is even possible that the adulterous relationship is unconsciously employed as a means of maintaining the marriage, even though it can, quite obviously, also represent serious risk to it, particularly if it becomes known to the other spouse.

The acts of adultery that lead to divorce are generally of a very different nature. These are acts in response to the serious problems that already exist in the relationship and are reflective of them. More often than not, they represent the desperate attempt of one of the parties to fulfill perceived needs that they feel are being denied to them in the marriage. To look to this conduct as the cause of the divorce is therefore simply to miss the cause. Thus, a therapist would make a very sharp distinction between the problems that caused one or both of the parties to be unhappy in the marriage and to become dissatisfied with it, and the conduct that he or she then engaged in once that level of unhappiness and dissatisfaction had set in. Being ignorant of the former, and being angered and often outraged by the latter, the parties and, with them, traditional adversarial divorce proceedings, have tended to focus on the latter. For the therapist, however, and while these acts may, admittedly, render it impossible for the marriage to continue, they nevertheless are not the *cause* of its demise.

A therapist would reject the view that divorce is occasioned by misconduct for yet a further reason, which is grounded in the radically different perspective that the therapist employs in understanding human conduct. Our Judeo-Christian tradition, embedded in the story of Adam and Eve, views human conduct as being initially, and therefore potentially, perfect. If human conduct as we see it is less than perfect, that is simply due to human failing, as is the disharmony that exists in the world, as opposed to the harmony that existed before Adam and Eve's fall from grace. From this understanding, harmony will be restored when human conduct is purged of its transgressions, and the last 2,000 years of Western religion has dedicated men to this purpose and chastised them, in one form or another, for failing to achieve it. From this standpoint, the difference between the conduct of men as we see it, and perfect conduct, is explained simply as personal failure.

The therapist's understanding of human conduct is dramatically at variance with this view. Rather than seeking his understanding in the story of Adam and Eve, he would be far more inclined to explain the disharmony between man and nature as being inherent, and as part of the human condition, as was expressed, for example, by Freud in *Civilization and Its Discontents*.[6] For the therapist, man lives in a world that is both oblivious to his intentions and insensitive to the very things that are most dear to him. It is man's fate to have to live in, and adapt to, this world and all of his conduct can be understood as his attempt to do this. In fact, and as Jay Haley[7] and others have pointed out, even those actions that fail of their purpose, and lead to the kind of symptomatology that therapists are called upon to deal with, can be explained as misdirected attempts to do this, attempts that have led, not to adaptation, but to maladaptation. However—and this is what is most critical in the therapist's understanding—the gap between human conduct and perfect harmony is not explained by human failure. It is explained by human limitation. Thus, and while all life on earth has shown an incredible ability to adapt to the circumstances within which it has found itself, that ability is not unbounded. On the contrary, it is in every instance affected by the biological and environmental givens that exist at any point in time, and that forever set limits on our human endeavors.

There is yet a further aspect to his human limitation. We approach the decisions in our lives with less than adequate resources and always burdened by the heavy weight of past circumstances and the effects that they have had upon us, most of which we cannot change and are not even aware of. We are then given but limited options from which to choose. Even then, we are forced to make our decisions with less than adequate information. To add to the problem, our judgment is often affected and overshadowed by powerful but nevertheless immediate considerations having no lasting significance. We must then make those decisions without any real ability to know or predict the consequences of our actions or, therefore, the ultimate effects that they will have. Finally, and as if these were not burdens enough, our best-laid plans are always subject to the whims of others, and to chance occurrences beyond our control. Is it any wonder then that our plans so often go astray? Is it any wonder that the strategies we employ in our lives so often prove inadequate? And is it any wonder that our lives turn out to be less than perfect, and so often filled with disappointments?

It is this understanding of human conduct as being explainable more in terms of limitation than in terms of fault that informs the therapist's understanding of the couple's marriage and their divorce. A marriage brings to it two very different people. In fact, and as Ivan Boszormenyi-Nagy has observed,[8] in a very real sense all marriages are mixed marriages in that they bring together two people having very different histories, characteristics, and expectations. Their marriage is their ongoing act of negotiating those differences. In fact, one might separate successful and unsuccessful marriages into two groups. In the first would be those couples who have been able, on some reasonable basis, to negotiate those differences over a lifetime of personal development, change, and, at times, even tragedy. The second would be made up of what we call unsuccessful marriages—those couples who have not been able successfully to negotiate those differences over the period of their life together.[9]

The differences we are talking about are not differences in individual interests or even, for that matter, our inherent characterological differences. In fact, and contrary to conventional mythology, those differences, particularly the former, have little to do with successful or unsuccessful marriages. Rather, they are the deep-seated psychological differences generally referred to by mental health professionals as *defenses.*[10]

It is common knowledge that people choose mates with comparable levels of maturity but possessing opposite defense systems. While it may well have been that it was these defense systems that initially attracted the parties to one another, it is also true that those same differences represent the areas of friction between them. This is why it is not uncommon to find that couples sometimes divorce one another for the very reasons that they married one another. To be sure, and while these defense systems characterize people very definitely, they are only one portion of a much larger spectrum that makes up what a person is. Nevertheless, and while the other components that characterize their personalities, and account for their similar and dissimilar likes and dislikes, tend to make their relationship more or less enjoyable, they do not usually constitute the bedrock upon which their marriage will fail or succeed. Rather, it is over these dissimilar defenses that the critical negotiations in their marriage will take place.

Although it should not be necessary to say so, the negotiations that we are talking about here, and that take place in the marriage between two people, are not the same kinds of negotiations that mediators talk about when they talk about mediation being a negotiating process. Nor do these negotiations take place formally between the parties as they do in mediation. On the contrary—and this is one reason they prove so unsuccessful—they are usually disguised and masked with arguments that rarely have anything to do with what is ultimately at issue between the parties.

When those negotiations are successful, it is possible for each of the parties to see the other in their wholeness. In fact, when they are successful, even failings and limiting traits can be viewed through the feelings of affection that one party has for the other and appear, not as irritants, but simply as amusing characteristics. When those negotiations are unsuccessful, however, those same traits tend to be viewed instead as fatal crimes. Worse yet, it becomes difficult for either of the parties to see the other except through the very limiting facets that those irritating defenses increasingly tend to present. In fact, in time they become almost all that either of the parties is able to see in one another.

Each of the parties has a very strong investment in maintaining the relationship, and time and time again they will go back to try to find their way around the impasse—to find their way, within the limitations the other party's defense system imposes, to meet what they conceive to be the necessary conditions for their continuing in that relationship. Unfortunately, and as hard as they try, they can neither change the offending characteristics nor live with them. From the standpoint of the one initiating the divorce, it occurs because no matter how he twists or turns, and no matter how many times he walks around the problem, he simply cannot find a solution to it. In another sense, however, it might be just as fair to say that the divorce occurs because he is not able to alter those needs and defenses of his own that become limiting factors in the face of the other party's own coping mechanisms.

At the end, almost all that one or both parties is able to see is those extreme differences in character, those areas of friction that so sharply divide them. Unfortunately, these character differences are not viewed simply as that. On the contrary, the frustration and irritation that they have caused have made them appear to be grievous crimes to the injured party. For, in time, these traits tend to deny what to him are the very minimum conditions under which he can continue to live. He is left angry by this fact and just as angry that, to change it, he is going to be compelled to end his marriage and throw over the very structure of his life. To complicate matters further, it is difficult, and at times impossible, for the injured party to see, let alone accept, his own role in what has happened. His hurt, his anger, and his resentment over the fact of where this has left him are simply too great.

These are the considerations that inform the mediator's understanding of what has brought the couple to the point where they now find themselves, and how they got there. Moreover, it is an understanding too complex to admit of the simplification implicit in the view that sees one of the parties as guilty, and alone responsible for the marriage's demise, and the other as innocent, and having had nothing to do with it. Does this mean that the mediator believes that the party who has initiated the divorce therefore has no obligation to the other party by reason of his decision? Not necessarily. But if the initiating party has such an obligation, it is not because he alone has been responsible for the marriage's demise, but because it is his decision that has left the other party where he did not wish to be, and with problems he never expected to have. Does this mean that the other party may not consider himself an innocent victim, and his spouse guilty of fault? Obviously not, and one of the mediator's jobs will be to try to understand and accept this. But this does not mean that he is obligated to agree with it. Nor does it mean that he is obligated to factor it into the agreement the couple ultimately reach.

Let us suppose that the mediator practices in a state in which, by statute, fault is still a factor to be considered by the court in making an award of alimony,[11] or in the distribution of marital property.[12] Is not the mediator then under an obligation to consider fault as a factor in the discussions between the parties, regardless of his own personal views? For those who follow a knee-jerk attitude toward the law, and who summarily assume that if the law announces something to be so that it must be so, and that this automatically forecloses all discussion, there will seem to be one, and only one, answer, and that is that if the law says that fault is a relevant factor then it is a relevant factor. Nevertheless, the answer to the question is no. A mediator may not be able to change the fact that legal thinking in the state in which he practices cannot get beyond the idea that divorce is occasioned by the misconduct, and therefore fault, of one of the parties; but that does not mean that *he* is *bound* by the *law's ignorance*.

Nor is there any reason that he should be. To be sure, either of the parties may decide to submit the matter to a court of law, rather than to resolve it through mediation, because they feel that the issue of fault which the court is obligated to consider may improve their positions. And, like taking the low road over the high road, that is a decision that they have an absolute right to make. However, that does not mean that the mediator is obligated to make those roads one and the same. On the contrary, and so long as he makes it absolutely clear that fault will not be considered as a guidepost along the road he travels, and each of the parties understands this before they proceed, then he has discharged his responsibility to them, and he has no obligation beyond that. In short, the mediator is under no obligation to incorporate into his procedures considerations and attitudes reflective of the assumptions of adversarial divorce proceedings, particularly when those considerations and attitudes are inconsistent with his own, simply in the name of assuring that the results in both cases will mirror one another and be the same.

Again, this is not to suggest that either of the parties may not consider fault as a factor, and that it may not color their thinking. Nor is it to suggest that a mediator has any right to object to this. It is to say that he has no *obligation* to adopt that point of view for the purposes of the mediation.

CHAPTER 10

CONDUCTING MEDIATION

How a mediator will conduct divorce mediation—the procedures he will employ and the style that he will adopt—are in large measure a function of the answers that he gives to the following questions: (1) What is the problem that has brought the couple to mediation? (2) What is it that stands between them and a resolution of that problem? (3) How can a mediator aid in its resolution and what procedures would be most helpful for that purpose? and (4) What responsibility does the mediator have to each of the parties, to their children, and to the agreement they will ultimately sign?

From our standpoint, and although these issues have been previously discussed and even debated in mediation circles, until now this has been done against the background of a set of assumptions which, though they have not always been made explicit, have nevertheless been implicitly accepted. As one would expect, those assumptions have had a great influence on the procedures and standards of practice that have been accepted as appropriate and responsible in mediation practice.

If the role of a mediator, and the procedures he employs, are derivative of the answers he gives to these questions, then it is essential that they be addressed. More specifically, and aside from making clearer the relationship between the answers that a mediator gives to these questions and the procedures that he will adopt, it is our purpose to make explicit the assumptions that underlie the procedures now generally employed and recommended for mediators and, more importantly, to contrast them with those that would be employed by mediators if the answers to these questions were based instead on the assumptions that inform our understanding of the problem that brings a couple to mediation.

THE PROBLEM

The prevailing view of divorce mediation in the United States shares with more traditional adversarial divorce proceedings the belief that the problem a couple's separation or divorce presents them is primarily one of defining and determining their respective legal rights and obligations to one another flowing from their marriage, and then concluding an agreement that will resolve their dispute concerning those rights and obligations. It does not question that the parties have conflicting interests—that their interests are adverse to one another. It does not even question that it is these conflicting interests that stand in the way of an agreement. It simply takes issue with the assumption that these conflicting interests must be resolved in an adversarial setting, where the parties tend to deal with one another from fixed, all-or-nothing positions, and that all too often finds a resolution of their dispute in the declaration of one of them a winner and the other a loser.

If the couple's conflicting interests are not to be resolved in an adversarial setting, how then are they to be resolved? The answer conveyed by the prevailing view of divorce mediation is through an informed negotiating process, based on the model of negotiations in, for example, labor mediation. This view of divorce mediation, which sees it as a negotiating process, is premised on the belief that most negotiations fail because they are not informed by a proper analysis and clarification of the dispute between the parties. It is also premised on the belief that if the demands and counterdemands of the parties can be put aside, if the essential needs of each can be understood, and if the facts necessary for an intelligent resolution of these issues can be developed and verified, then, in most instances, it will be possible to assist the parties to develop solutions to meet these essential needs. In short, the assumption implicit in this view is that what keeps the parties from a resolution of the dispute between them is simply the lack of this kind of clear, organized analysis of their dispute, which is then followed by such a creative bargaining process.

Viewed from this standpoint, the mediation of disputes between separating and divorcing couples, like the negotiation of disputes between any two people, involves a process of first defining the outstanding issues between the parties, collecting and developing the factual information necessary to discuss these issues intelligently, determining the positions of each of the parties with respect to these issues, analyzing the essential needs of the parties expressed in these positions, and exploring the possible options open for a resolution of these issues—all of which is then followed by a bargaining process in which these positions are modified in an exchange of give-and-take between the parties.

No one can take exception to such an informed bargaining process as a means of resolving disputes between people, and divorce mediation can certainly benefit from the kind of analysis of the negotiating process that was expressed, for example, in *Getting to Yes*, by Roger Fisher and William Ury.[1] Thus, negotiations of any kind will benefit from an understanding of the fact that what is essential in any successful negotiation is, first, the definition of what is really of concern to each of the parties beneath the fixed positions they have taken; second, the ordering in importance of each of these concerns; and lastly, a bargaining process that sees as its objective a resolution that will permit each of the parties to come away from the negotiating process with enough of those things that are of significance to them to enable them to accept the agreement they have concluded.

Nevertheless, our view of divorce mediation is radically at variance with the view that sees it as basically a negotiating process. More importantly, it is radical in the sense that it takes issue with the assumptions that underlie that view. It is not that these assumptions are incorrect when applied to disputes between parties generally. It is that they are inaccurate when applied to disputes between separating and divorcing couples. To be more specific, it is that we see as very different the couple's underlying problem and what stands between them and its resolution.

What is the essential problem that brings a couple to a divorce mediator? From our point of view—and this is one of the two cardinal principles of divorce mediation, as we see it—the couple comes to a mediator, not with a dispute, and certainly not with a legal dispute, but with a serious life problem, and that problem is that they are in a personal state of crisis brought about by the decision, usually by one of them, to separate or divorce. To be sure, this problem has created issues they must address and resolve in order for each of them to get on with the important business of their lives.

It is also true that in some instances what stands between a couple and the resolution of those issues is simply the kind of analysis and informed bargaining procedure employed by those who see divorce mediation as basically a negotiating process and, if that is the case, these should rightfully be applied.

In most instances, however, that is not the case. Rather, the matter remains unresolved because there is something interfering with this kind of orderly, commonsense analysis: the feelings of disappointment, rejection, hurt, anger, misunderstanding, abandonment, fear, and sometimes even vindictiveness that are the inevitable by-products of the crisis in the couple's life that the decision to separate and divorce has precipitated.

This belief that what ultimately stands between a couple and an agreement are these *feelings* is the second cardinal principle in our view of divorce mediation. It is a cardinal principle because it not only informs our understanding of what keeps separating and divorcing couples from an agreement, but, as we have said, because it also prescribes the *manner* in which a mediator will attempt to guide a couple to an agreement and the procedures that he will employ for that purpose.

But aren't strong feelings present in all disputes between contending parties, whether they be two superpowers, labor and management, or simply a separating husband and wife? The answer is yes, as there is an emotional component of varying degrees in all disputes between people. However, there is still an important, fundamental difference. Disputes between separating and divorcing couples are different in kind from disputes between all other people, and to fail to understand this is to acknowledge one's ignorance of the nature of the divorcing process. With all other disputes, the emotionality that exists is by and large a *function* of the dispute. With separating and divorcing couples, on the other hand, *the dispute is primarily a function of that emotionality.*

What distinguishes the disputes between separating and divorcing couples from all others is that theirs is first and foremost an emotional relationship, and this fact simply cannot be *ignored or minimized.* Each of the parties has invested his hopes, his expectations, and even his self-worth in the relationship. Each has developed strong emotional attachments and dependencies based upon the relationship. Each has been left with a sense of personal failure in the fact that the relationship has come to an end. And, particularly if it is the party who does not want the divorce, he has also been left with a terrible sense of loss, and sometimes even betrayal.

Nor is this the end of it. The matter is further complicated by the fact that in finding themselves where they are, each of the parties cannot help but tend to view themselves as the victim of what the other has done to them. It is simply not possible for either of the parties to see their own role in the drama that has unfolded. Rather, they believe that they are where they are because, in one case, of what the other has *failed* to do, and in the other, because of what he or she has *decided* to do. And since *they did not get married to get divorced*—since they did not expect or intend to be where they are, and are not happy to now find themselves there—they are hurt and angry.

This emotional climate is further complicated by the fact that in the overwhelming majority of instances the decision to separate and divorce is *not a mutual one*—which means that the couple are *not emotionally apace.* For one of the parties, the decision to separate and divorce is one he has been considering for some considerable time, usually for at least a year. As a result, he has had the time to *prepare* himself for the decision he has now announced and intends to carry out. For the other party, however, and despite all the signs that might have been apparent to an outsider, more often than not he is caught totally unprepared. The decision thus not only takes him by surprise, but also leaves him overwhelmed with feelings of rejection and abandonment. In many cases, this is compounded by the fact that his spouse is, or perhaps has been, emotionally involved with someone outside of the marriage, which of course only further lowers his self-esteem and adds to his distressed state as he looks forward to his own future single life. Last, but certainly not least, are the terrible feelings of helplessness and fear, particularly if the party who suffers the other's decision to separate is the one who is the financially dependent one. In fact, it is this fear, born of a sudden sense of feeling helpless and alone, that can at times be the most overpowering of all.

These are the feelings that so overwhelm the parties at the time of their separation and divorce and make a resolution of the issues between them so difficult. And these are the feelings that will often have to be identified, acknowledged, and addressed if the mediation is going to result in an agreement between them.

This is not to suggest, however, that our view of mediation considers it to be therapy, or sees as the mediator's function the resolution of these very difficult feelings that so overwhelm one or both of the parties. The trauma that the decision to separate and divorce has caused each party, and the damage that it has done to their life-coping mechanisms, will often take years to repair to the point where they are again functional. More importantly, it is not the mediator, but rather the ongoing flow of life itself, that will serve to effectuate this. Before that flow can continue, however, and before they can get on with the business of their lives, it is necessary for each of the parties to effectuate an emotional closure with the past. Their agreement and their divorce, which together bring their marriage to a legal conclusion, are necessary preconditions to this. Unfortunately, the very feelings that stand between the parties and this closure also often stand between them and that agreement. That is why the mediator views these feelings, and the state of crisis that produced them, to be the primary problem that the parties bring to him. And that is why it may be necessary for him to deal with these feelings, albeit in a limited way, in the course of the mediation.

It is in this sense then that mediation is therapeutic, while not at the same time therapy. The couple have come to the mediator for a specific purpose, and his function is therefore a limited one. While he would hope that the agreement they conclude would help to resolve the emotional conflicts that exist between them so as to permit them to get on with their lives, he views this to be the *by-product* of a successful mediation rather than its specific *goal*. Since the couple has not come to him requesting such help, the mediator would consider it presumptuous of him to invade their privacy and to enter where he has not been invited. Given this fact, he deals with these underlying emotional issues to the extent, and only to the extent, that they *interfere* with the couple's *ability to address the practical questions* that must be resolved by them in their mediation. But he does this in the knowledge that if he can resolve these practical issues and get them to an agreement, that he has helped them *beyond* that.

STYLES OF CONDUCTING MEDIATION

As one would expect, the definition of the problem the couple has, and what stands between them and its resolution, will greatly affect the view a mediator, or any third-party intervener, has as to his role and his responsibilities. If, from the standpoint of traditional adversarial divorce proceedings, what is principally at issue is the determination of each of the parties' legal rights and the protection of their conflicting interests—and, particularly if these considerations are given precedence over all others—the procedures that will be employed to assist separating and divorcing couples to resolve their disputes will be those traditionally employed for that purpose. Similarly, if the problem is seen from the stand-point of the prevailing view of divorce mediation, which generally accepts these assumptions but sees the problem as that the couple has been encouraged by our adversarial system to take fixed, and at times inflexible, positions rather than to engage in informed, meaningful negotiations that will help them clarify the issues and find solutions that will meet their respective needs, then the answer to their problem will be seen as providing them with a structured and enlightened negotiating process, as is expressed in *Getting to Yes*, with standards of practice being built into the mediation process that will protect the legal rights of the parties and their conflicting interests. If, on the other hand, the problem is seen from the standpoint we insist upon as being a more accurate view of what divorce represents in the lives of each of the parties, the procedures employed will be far different. Similarly, in each instance these different processes will not only assign different roles to the mediator, but will also call upon him to bring to the mediation different skills and, as we will argue, even different understandings.

For our purposes, we will categorize the composite of these differences under the heading of different *styles* of conducting mediation. While recognizing that the actual style a mediator employs may be heavily influenced (and limited) by his own personality, his profession of origin, and the training he has received to do mediation, for our purposes, and since we wish to idealize these styles for illustrative purpose, we are more concerned with how they reflect a mediator's attitude (often unexpressed) as to the nature of the problem faced by the parties in their divorce, the procedures he considers to be most appropriate in addressing and resolving that problem, and the view he holds as to his own role and obligation in that process. We recognize that all of these considerations do not lend themselves to easy categorization, let alone classification into but two styles of conducting mediation. We recognize also that, in actual fact, mediators who hold different views of the problem a couple's divorce poses for them will nevertheless bring to the process attitudes and skills that, if not exactly alike, certainly overlap. Nonetheless we still believe that such a classification is useful—at least, if it is not taken too literally.

With all this in mind, and while acknowledging that some mental health professionals sound and act more like attorneys once they begin to do divorce mediation, just as some lawyers begin to sound and act more like mental health professionals, we would nevertheless divide all mediators into two groups. The first we will call attorney/labor mediators, or activists; the second we will call therapist mediators, or passivists. The former corresponds to mediation conducted in keeping with the prevailing view of divorce mediation at the present time held by both its advocates and by its critics, which we have characterized as divorce viewed as a *legal event*. The latter corresponds to mediation conducted in keeping with the view of divorce mediation we advance, which we have characterized as divorce viewed as a *personal event*.

Attorney/Labor Mediators

For the attorney/labor mediator, the problem is seen as one of attempting to negotiate an agreement between two people to a dispute, much as disputes are mediated between labor and management. However, whereas disputes between labor and management are only marginally bounded by the law, the dispute between the divorcing couple is, to a great extent, *about* the law, and more particularly about the legal rights and obligations each has flowing from their marriage. The object of the mediation is thus not only to conclude an agreement between the parties, but also to conclude one that is fair, and in the best interests of their children.

For the attorney/labor mediator, therefore, a successful mediation must do two things: (1) assure that the parties are informed participants in the mediation process—have been individually apprised of their respective legal rights, and furnished with all of the factual and financial information necessary to participate meaningfully in the mediation; and (2) provide the parties with an informed negotiating process that will identify the issues in dispute and the positions taken by each of them, examine the proposals they have each made for their resolution, and then seek accommodations between the parties that will satisfy each of their essential needs. From the standpoint of the attorney/labor mediator, therefore, the key to the mediation is accurate information and sound procedure.

For the attorney/labor mediator, the parties are like passengers embarking on an ocean liner, and the mediator its captain. The trip has been initiated by the couple themselves, and they have selected both its destination and their mode of transportation. The mediator's job is to get them there, and it is he who gets the ship under way, regulates its speed, and carefully plots its course. Before permitting the passengers to embark, however, he must see to it that the ship has been properly provisioned and all of the equipment necessary to secure the passengers' safety properly checked. For while the passengers are his guests, and while he treats them as such, he is nevertheless the captain of the ship, and it is he who prescribes the rules and sets the standard for acceptable conduct.

In similar fashion, attorney/labor mediators believe that the mediation will not get under way without their impetus, or proceed properly without their direction. Their attitude is perhaps best expressed in the approach that leaves to the couple themselves *what* their agreement will be, but leaves to the mediator the *procedures* that will be employed to *reach* it. In short, while the couple controls their *agreement*, the mediator controls the *mediation*.

Given their view of the problem, attorney/labor mediators tend to replicate the procedures employed by attorneys in traditional adversarial divorce proceedings. Just as a divorce lawyer would not proceed to trial before he has prepared his case and completed his pretrial discovery proceedings, so too an attorney/labor mediator will not commence the negotiations until the financial information has been assembled and verified, the parties' budgets prepared, the issues defined, and their positions clearly stated. At times he will not proceed unless and until each party has consulted with separate attorneys, which may be required at varying times through the mediation and, most certainly, at its conclusion. From his standpoint, these procedures are essential if the parties' conflicting interests are to be properly protected, and the first two or three sessions are generally devoted to these housekeeping chores.

THERAPIST MEDIATORS

From the standpoint of the therapist mediator, what the couple has is *not a dispute but a problem*. More importantly, that problem is *not* a *legal* one, but rather a *personal* one, born of the present crisis in their lives. He also views very differently what it is that stands between them and a resolution of that problem. For the therapist mediator, what is central to his understanding is the *emotional component* in the relationship between the parties. It is this emotional component that gave birth to their relationship; it is this emotional component which has left them with a problem; and it is this emotional component that stands between them and a resolution of that problem.

Up to this point, the couple has generally been able to make most of the important decisions affecting their lives together—whether they would have children, and how many; where they would live; what their respective obligations would be; how they would spend their leisure time. More importantly, they have been able to do this without resort to the law or to legal rules. Why is it that they are unable to decide and agree upon these things now?

From the standpoint of the therapist mediator, it is not because they lack sufficient information about their legal rights and obligations. Nor is it because they lack the necessary information concerning their financial circumstances. And it is not because they are unable clearly to define the issues between them. It is because they are over-whelmed with feelings of hurt, disappointment, fear, and the myriad other emotions confronting a couple at the time of their separation and divorce. Each of them, albeit for different reasons, would like to get past the pain that their separation or divorce represents. From time to time, however, they get stuck on these feelings, and cannot get beyond them. It is the mediator's job to help them do this.

For the therapist mediator, the couple is like a model ship floating down a shallow brook. The brook, and the couple floating down it, have an impetus and natural direction of their own, and do not need him to get them started. However, the couple is unable to control that flow, or prevent it from at times overwhelming, and even overturning, them. Like someone walking along the bank of the brook, following the model ship on its course, it is only necessary for him to intervene when it comes too close to the bank, gets stuck on a jutting rock or overturns in midstream. Once having righted the ship or freed it from the obstacle that has impeded its forward movement, however, he can put his hands back in his pockets and continue to observe its progress until it comes into danger again.

The therapist mediator's understanding of the couple's problem will also directly affect how he approaches the mediation. He views himself and, in fact, the whole setting in which mediation takes place as simply a facilitator. To begin with, he facilitates best by facilitating least—by first allowing the couple to resolve the matter on their own and by intervening only when they are having difficulty. Secondly, and while he carefully controls what takes place in the mediation, he does so more by his presence, by the subtle structure he gives it, and by his casual interventions, than by any specific rules or procedures he insists upon following. (He provides the setting, he sets the tone, and he sits by and listens carefully to the discussions.) Thirdly, he has a limited conception of his function, born of a limited conception of what is possible. It is not a perfect world, and one cannot expect to find perfect answers.

Thus, he does not expect to resolve in their divorce the conflicts that the couple were unable to resolve in their marriage. If he could do that, it would not be necessary for them to get divorced in the first place. Nor does he believe that their divorce represents the occasion to make judgments about their marriage (let alone correct what are, from their individual perspectives, its abuses and injustices), and he feels that such judgments—like most judgments as to what is fair or unfair—are simplistic where they are not otherwise wrong, and dangerous when they are not otherwise irrelevant. Thus, he sets a far more modest goal for himself—simply to help the couple through the crises of their divorce and address those conflicts standing between them and an agreement.

A couple and the mediator usually begin as total strangers. Additionally, they have come to discuss matters that are not only very personal, but also very painful. Understandably, there is a natural hesitancy on the couple's part to lay it all out on the table. At least initially, therefore, they only present to the mediator what they want him to see. The mediator knows, however, that what he sees is only a very small portion of the whole. It is as if they have given him a map of their lives, but have only drawn in one or two of the major highways. Part of him would like to have a more accurate picture, showing the other troubled roadways and how they intersect with one another. The better part of him, however, holds back. Since he has respect for the parties, and particularly the pain they are experiencing, he does not want to invade their privacy any more than is necessary. Nor does he want to cause these trouble spots to be revealed prematurely, and before he will be able properly to deal with them. And so he sits and waits, and carefully watches.

As he watches, he keeps reminding himself that, like an iceberg, there is far more beneath the surface than has been shown to him. Perhaps one of the parties was, or still is, emotionally involved outside of the marriage. Perhaps one of the parties is dependent on alcohol or drugs, or has put the family into debt due to heavy gambling losses. Perhaps one of the parties has been inconsiderate of, or physically abused, the other. There is a great deal of emotionality encrusted around these occurrences. In many instances, the party pained by these events would like to air them, if only to be able to share his hurt with the mediator. The mediator knows this, but waits nevertheless, for the aggrieved party may find a way of dealing with these painful feelings on his own.

When does the mediator intervene and probe those feelings? He does this, firstly, when he feels that it is necessary to do so to enlist the *support* and engender the *trust* of one of the parties. Not infrequently one of the parties becomes somewhat upset during the initial meeting, and to the watchful eye of the mediator that discomfort is readily apparent.

"This is very difficult for you, isn't it?" he asks. While respecting that party's dignity and integrity, the mediator nevertheless attempts to share his humanity with him. If carefully handled, there is little danger that the emotional release will result in a tirade of anger or vituperative accusations, even if there is some slight, fleeting reference to a grievance felt at the hands of the other. Rather, the response of the party will generally be in keeping with the tone of the question posed by the mediator. In this manner, the mediator will not only have found a way to make contact with the pained party, but will also have provided that party with a protective setting in which to express it. In doing this, and in relieving at least some of that pain, he will have enlisted the party's *trust in the process*, and that is the primary thing that he wants to do.

A second instance when the mediator will intervene and probe beneath the surface is when it becomes apparent that there are hidden issues, carefully wrapped around hidden feelings, below the surface, that are interfering with what must be accomplished. Not uncommonly, couples argue out in their divorce the very issues that they were unable to resolve in their marriage. Just as commonly, the subject of their argument is not necessarily the real issue in dispute—which accounts for the saying that married couples rarely argue over the things that they are really fighting about. It is for this same reason that the lengthy discussions that they had in their marriage ended in such disappointment, with neither of the parties feeling that the other had understood a word that they had said. When the mediator senses this, it is important that he intervene and locate the real issue. At that point, it must be addressed, put on the table and dealt with.

Given their view of the problem, therapist mediators do not tend to replicate the procedures employed by attorneys in traditional adversarial divorce proceedings. In fact, in most instances, they would not feel that those procedures would advance the purposes of mediation, and might actually impede them. Just as importantly, they would not want to waste the valuable time that the first number of sessions provide them on the house-keeping chores with which attorney/labor mediators busy themselves. From the stand-point of the therapist mediator, there will be time enough for them, if and when they are needed. After all, aside from the necessary determination of the respective incomes, assets, and liabilities of each of the parties, which can be sketched in as needed and completed at a later time, these procedures are only employed because they are seen as necessary to resolve the dispute between the couple. In point of fact, and particularly if the problem is viewed as primarily a personal one, rather than a legal one involving first the determination and then the protection of the parties' respective legal rights and obliga-tions, they are only necessary when the couple is unable to resolve the dispute by some other means. Thus, the therapist mediator does not feel bound by these concerns and he will come back to them later, if that should prove necessary.

ACTIVISTS AND PASSIVISTS

Lawyer/labor mediators and therapist mediators tend to be activists, on the one hand, and passivists on the other. They each have a very definite sense of direction, which in both cases is to bring the couple to an agreement. They differ, however, both in their view as to the function and nature of that agreement, and how it is to be reached.

Activists tend to feel more of a responsibility for the quality of the agreement being concluded by the parties, and they consider the procedures that they have set for them-selves as very important, since they look to those procedures as a necessary guarantee of the quality of that agreement. That being the case, they tend to take a more active role in controlling the course of the mediation and its direction.

Passivists, on the other hand, tend to look upon the agreement more as an end in itself. It is not that they are not concerned about the quality of the agreement concluded by the parties, and whether it is fair or unfair. It is simply that this concern is outbalanced by the conviction that such judgments are not always relevant, let alone helpful, in the complex which the relationship between the parties represents. More importantly, it is born of a conviction that it is ultimately presumptuous, and worse, dangerous, for a mediator or any third party to attempt to make such judgments in other people's lives. Lastly, it is a reflection of the mediator's view as to the limited nature of his role, and of the limited role of mediation itself for that matter. What has happened to the couple is a tragedy, and he is not going to change that. He does not expect the parties to view their agreement as being fair—there is nothing fair in what has happened to them. Instead, he will be quite content if he can somehow get them to accept their agreement in spite of this.

The Mediator

Up to this point we have concerned ourselves with how the different views of divorce will affect the model of divorce mediation that is considered appropriate and how, in turn, that model will influence the style a mediator will employ in conducting mediation. We must now add to this the mediator himself and the skill and understanding he brings with him. Whether a mediator is an activist or a passivist is not, after all, dependent alone upon the view he holds as to the proper function and purpose of mediation. It is also dependent on the skills and understanding he brings to the process. Some mediators, whether due to a lack of previous training or simply by disposition, do not feel comfortable dealing with the human emotions involved in a couple's separation and divorce.

Not infrequently, they avoid having to do so, at least to the extent possible, by structuring the mediation more formally, usually as a negotiating process, and by then strictly controlling the procedures to be followed. Then too, and like initiates to therapeutic practice, they may feel at a loss, and that they are not doing anything unless they are continually doing something. Lacking confidence in themselves, they are not sure how they will handle the situation if one of the parties should be carried away by his emotions, or what they will do if the couple comes to an impasse and there seems to be no way either through it or around it.

Passivists usually bring a different array of skills to mediation. To begin with, they are either natural counselors or they have had a great deal of formal training in counseling. Secondly, they usually bring with them a certain human understanding that permits them empathetically to engage and be helpful to the parties with whom they deal. Lastly, they bring a sense of confidence in themselves. It is not that they will necessarily have all the answers, though not infrequently that confidence may, at least in some measure, be grounded in their considerable experience in dealing with the kinds of problems, both practical and emotional, that the couple is experiencing.

More often, however, it is simply a confidence in themselves. They do not necessarily know what they will do when faced with an unexpected occurrence. What they know is that, in all likelihood, they will somehow find a way to deal with it when it occurs and that if they deal with it less effectively than they might have, or perhaps not even very effectively at all, they will think about it, and learn from it, and deal more effectively with it in the future. It takes this kind of confidence to be a passivist—to be able not to *have* to be in control at every moment for fear that you will *lose* control. In short, this confidence does not preclude failure; nor will it be shaken by it.

Even when passivists intervene, as they will over and over again during the course of the mediation, their intervention is of a different kind. While activists may also bring a great array of skills with them which they will employ during the course of the mediation, their very view of the problem is such that they tend to fall back on certain fixed, standardized procedures, since they believe that it is these procedures that will best guarantee a proper result.

Passivists, on the other hand, would eschew any such set procedures. To begin with, they do not share the activists' belief in the efficacy of these procedures. Secondly, they would consider it their function, as well as part of their skill, to make an assessment in each instance of what procedure would be most effective in the particular case. Finally, they would tend to view the procedures that they will follow much as a therapist would view an intervention, not as a procedure employed to lead to a specific result, but as a procedure employed to get past a particular impasse.

These differences in approach can be summarized, and expressed in the third cardinal principle of divorce mediation, and that is the principle that the flow in mediation should always be from the couple to the mediator rather than from the mediator to the couple. As we have noted previously, the therapist mediator views himself as basically a facilitator, which means that he views his role as a limited one. Thus, as he would not, as a therapist, consider it his function to rearrange the couple's lives, neither does he consider it his function, as a mediator, to arrange their divorce.

That means that he does not start out with an agenda of his own. If he assumes that his function is to assist them to conclude an agreement between themselves, that is only because that goal is implicit in the fact that they have come to him. Even here, however, he keeps an open mind and waits to see what will happen. Thus, if both parties are still struggling with the question as to whether or not they should separate in the first place, his openness will permit him to hear this when they initially meet, and to respond to it.

The therapist mediator's belief that the flow should be from the couple to him will be the guiding principle that he will follow in conducting mediation. It is, after all, the flow of their lives that is at issue, and he does not believe that it is his function or province to direct it or even to redirect it. Far more modestly, it is simply to intervene when that flow becomes interrupted or misdirected. Thus, instead of rushing in to do a job, he will always wait and see what job, if any, needs his attention. Again, the couple do not need him when they are not having a problem, they only need him when they are. Even when he does intervene, it will not be to take over the mediation or to attempt to solve the problem. It will be simply to remove the impediment preventing the couple from doing this themselves or to provide them with the assistance that they will need to do so.

Suppose, for example, that the issue the mediator wishes to discuss next is the question of the custody of the parties' children. Since the mediator's limited purpose is to test the waters, so to speak, all that he need do is to initiate the conversation with a simple question such as, "Have you given thought to where your children will be living following your separation?" The response to that question (or even, in the rare instance, the lack of response to it) will tell the mediator whether there is a problem that needs his assistance and, if there is, what it is.

Even if he senses that there may be a problem here, however, that does not mean that he will immediately intervene. Before doing this, he would first like to see how the couple address the question on their own. If he is patient for but a short period of time, he may find that they are able to discuss it to a conclusion without him. Even when that is not the case, his restraint may prove helpful to him. In many instances, and simply by listening to them discuss the problem, he may avoid misinterpreting what is really at issue, which might have been the case had he jumped in too quickly. Just as importantly, by sitting back and listening, he may learn a great deal about how they feel, and how they express their feelings to one another, all of which will be of great help to him when he *does* intervene.

There is one last point that must be made. It would be a mistake to conclude that activists are more involved in the mediation than are passivists, or that they do more. Passivists are as busy during the mediation as are activists. They are just busy doing different things. What they are primarily doing is carefully watching and listening to what is going on. Paradoxically, and once he decides to intervene, the therapist mediator will often become more of an activist than the attorney/labor mediator.

The type of person who has the confidence necessary to be a passivist, and who does not need the security of fixed, formal procedures, is also generally someone who has developed a vast array of skills that he will employ at this time. Like a workman who comes laden with numerous boxes of equipment in his hands and under his arms, the passivist has an almost unlimited number of tools that he can carefully pick and choose from in each instance. His skills are born of his experience in helping other couples in the past to find solutions to the same problems. They are born of his imagination and his ability to construct new solutions for the immediate problem. And they are born of his understanding of why it is the couple is stuck in the first place, and what he must do to free them.

THE MEDIATOR'S UNDERSTANDING

We have previously referred to the understanding a mediator brings to his task and emphasized that this understanding is critical to the view of divorce mediation we propose. Again, and while acknowledging that it would be simplistic to suggest that this understanding is unique to mediators who view divorce as a personal event rather than a legal event in a couple's life, or that it does not also inform, at least to some extent, the attorney/labor mediator's practice of divorce mediation, the fact remains that it is not central to their view of divorce or, therefore, to their conduct of divorce mediation. Like adversarial attorneys, whose conduct is also informed, albeit only to a limited extent, by this understanding, their conduct of mediation is more influenced by the procedures they employ and look to as the guarantee that the mediation will be properly conducted. For the therapist mediator, on the other hand, it is this understanding, and not these procedures, that are critical, and to which he will turn time and time again.

The understanding we are talking about is not simply a technical or formal understanding. It *is* that, but it is much more. It is an understanding of human possibility, but also of human limitation, including one's own limitations. It is an understanding of human worth and a respect for that worth. And it is an understanding of the human community and the fact that we are all members of it. It is the kind of understanding that slowly and laboriously gives form to who it is we have become, how we view the world we live in, and how we relate to the people whom we meet, particularly those whom we serve professionally.

The quality of the understanding we are talking about, and its importance in the dynamics that take place between the mediator and each of the parties, was expressed, in an analogous situation, by Lewis Browne Hill, in an article entitled *On Being Rather Than Doing in Psychotherapy:*

> My thesis is that *being* and *doing* in therapy cannot be in fact separated. A therapist is what he does. Conversely put, what the therapist does is an expression of

what he is. Being and doing are not two disparate things, separate and isolated from each other. There cannot be a real choice between being and doing, that is, a choice of one or the other in therapy. The choice of what to do, what patients to treat, what goals to set, what techniques to use, or the choice from moment to moment whether to say something or not, or to do something or not; the choice of strategy for the long pull or the tactic of the moment is a choice which is made by the therapist as a predetermined expression of what he *is*, as a person and as a therapist . . . The late Louis Cholden . . . could establish potent therapeutic situations with schizophrenic patients. I, and others, asked him how he did it. He answered with obvious sincerity and simplicity that schizophrenic patients were very nice to him, they told him things. I understand that this was as far as Cholden went in explaining his transactions with patients, or his reasons for what he did. It was apparent that his behavior with the patient was appropriately an expression of what he was, of what he felt, thought, and experienced in participant observation with patients. And to this, as one might expect of schizophrenics in the presence of a benevolent and interested therapist, they responded by being nice to him and telling him things he needed to know.[2]

In divorce mediation also, the principal device the mediator employs is simply the trust that each of the parties reposes in him. From the very outset, he has conveyed to the couple that he believes them to be decent people, far better than their present circumstances permit them to appear. He knows how difficult this is for each of them, and they have come to trust him and to believe that he very much wants to help them through these difficult times. Sometimes his simple physical presence serves as a sufficient balance to keep up the necessary flow. In one instance a husband, recently separated, commenced each mediation session with the announcement that it was necessary to leave some time at the end in order to discuss the question of visitation with his children, since it was impossible for him to discuss this with his wife outside the mediator's office. When the allotted time came, the discussion between the couple proceeded without incident, and although much of their pain and hurt was focused in these discussions, the mediator was never once required to say a word, let alone intervene.

Many times all that the mediator need do is to let one of the parties know that he is aware of how they feel. In a particular mediation, the couple appeared so bottled up in their feelings that they were unable to address the issues at hand. The decision to divorce had been the husband's, and the wife was still wrestling with her hurt and pain. She desperately wanted her husband to know just how great that pain was, but he did not want to hear of it—the last thing he would permit her to do was to lay the guilt for their divorce upon him.

Almost without consciously thinking about it, the mediator found himself expressing to the husband, probably in more eloquent terms than the wife herself would have been able to summon, just how she felt. There was nothing judgmental in the mediator's words, however, and the husband thus permitted the mediator to say what he would not have allowed his wife to say. When the mediator was through, and the wife had finally been heard, the mediation could begin, and it proceeded from that point without incident. As the mediator knew, there was only one thing worse for the wife than to suffer, and that was for her to suffer silently and alone. Reaching into his bag of tools, the mediator found the way to address the wife's hurt without at the same time offending the husband, thereby setting the necessary stage for the continuation of their mediation.

Time and time again the mediator becomes a storyteller. Each of us spends our lives telling stories to ourselves about ourselves. It is our way of understanding our lives and what it is that has happened to us. Those stories are not always useful stories, however. Far too often they tend to preserve rather than relieve our failures and the pain and anger they have engendered. The mediator tells the parties different stories, better stories. He must replace the stories that they are holding onto, that tie them to their hurt and anger, and prevent them from getting on with the business of their lives, with a story that will restore their sense of dignity and will help them look forward rather than back.

Usually, there is a common theme to the stories he tells. The stories they have told themselves have been borrowed from the conventional mythology that views divorce as if it were a crime involving guilt and innocence. His story talks instead of two basically decent people who did the best they could. Neither of them got married to get divorced. Neither of them wanted their lives to come to this point. Neither of them views with anything but great trepidation the prospect of picking up the pieces of their lives and starting anew. If they have failed it was not because they did not try, each in their own way. They failed because they were simply two different people who did the best they knew how, but who were just unable to negotiate those differences beyond this point. To say more than this is to add nothing that is constructive. In fact, it is to add nothing at all. It is simply to look for causes or explanations that do not exist and will not help. It is simply to ask for easy answers to very complex problems.

It is not possible at this point for either party to see the other as they actually are. Their tremendous disappointment, and their hurt and anger, prevent this. They are only able to see the other through those narrow lenses of disappointment. Hopefully, if they can be helped to put these feelings of hurt and anger behind them, they can come to a more complete understanding and again be able to see one another more clearly, and more completely.

It is said in therapy that the therapist helps his patient in spite of his theories. While it is these theories that are helpful for the therapist's understanding, it is the therapist who is helpful for his patient's understanding. The same is true in mediation. The difficulty is that the couple feel too much and understand too little. Nor will the mediator, at least at the outset, always be able directly to improve that understanding, for quite often those feelings will not permit him to do this. Rather, he will have to wait the parties out and address these feelings indirectly. To do this, however, it is first necessary for him to create the appropriate setting and to build the rapport and trust between himself and each of the parties that this will require.

The mediator must also act as a balance to these feelings. To do this, he has to give of himself, at times literally to lay his humanity on the table. All that he is and all that he knows is spread out before the couple. To the extent possible, he shares their problem with them, and while keeping the necessary distance he must if he is ultimately to be helpful to them, he nevertheless conveys to them that he is at one with them, and that they are all there in a common cause. In an understanding, nonjudgmental manner, the mediator repeatedly pushes the couple forward.

"We must get on." "Let's get it done." These are the messages that the mediator continually reinforces. There is a problem that must be solved. It is not possible for each of them to look at it in the same way. But it is a common problem nevertheless. Somehow, a way must be found to solve that problem so that each of them can get on with the business of their lives. Beneath their present feelings of hurt and disappointment, they each know that the mediator is right. They know, also, that he genuinely wishes to help them to do this. The mediator comes to stand as a symbol of sensibility in all of this. Not infrequently, he, and the mediation itself, come to appear as a small island of sense and sanity in an otherwise troubled sea. And the couple comes to rely on this.

Very often, each of the parties is able to do for the mediator what they cannot do for one another. Not uncommonly, what stands between the request made by one of the parties and the assent given by the other is not the inappropriateness of the request, or even the inherent difficulty on the part of the other party to accept it. What makes an agreement impossible is simply the label that one of the parties has put upon it.

"If I give in to that, I would really be a fool." Whether correctly, or incorrectly, that is how the party views it. In such instances, the mediator will help separate the act from the label. "She's getting everything that she wants, and I'm coming away with nothing," is how he looks at it. So long as the act of agreeing is viewed as an act of defeat, he cannot entertain the request on its merits.

"No one is really coming away with what they want," the mediator quietly says. "I know how difficult this is for you," he continues, "but it is difficult for her too. You are not wrong in asking that your home be sold in two years, when your youngest child graduates from high school. This is a reasonable request. It is just that your wife feels very threatened with the idea that she will have to find a new home for herself in such a short period of time. In six months or a year from now she may have no difficulty considering the sale of the home. But right now it is just very threatening to her. If she could have just another year or two, it would make it a great deal easier for her. She may decide to sell the home when your daughter graduates from high school. She is simply very terrified right now by the thought that she will have to do that. Do you think that you could see your way clear to give her the option of living there just a little longer?"

Changing for the husband what it *means* to agree with the wife's request can make all the difference. This and the fact that the mediator has personalized the request as coming from him rather than from his wife. In doing this, the mediator draws on the line of credit he has established with the husband. He also changes the focus of the request, for, as we have said, not uncommonly one of the parties is able to do for the mediator what he still has difficulty doing for his spouse.

Again and again the mediator reinforces the reality that it is not possible to conclude an agreement that will leave either of the parties without risk. "It is as if we have been given a tablecloth that is too small for the table," he tells them. "If we pull it down so that it completely covers the table at your end, this end of the table will be completely exposed. If we pull it down to completely cover this end, you will be left with too little. All that we can do is spread it out in such a way that each of you is given some protection, and neither of you is left too exposed."

Throughout, the mediator stands as a reality principle as to what is possible and what is not possible. He does not pretend that he is going to solve all of their problems, because he will not. He does not even pretend that he will be able to explain it sufficiently, because that is to suggest that it is somehow rational and understandable, when in a most basic sense it is not. What he can do, however, is help them to understand that they can only get *lost* in their hurt and anger, and in these unanswerable questions, and that the price that they will have to pay for holding onto them is simply too great. To do this he will, at times, have to act as the adult to the child which one or both of the parties is expressing. Even then, however, the judgments he expresses will only be about the positions they have taken, and not about the persons who have expressed those positions. This is how the mediator hopes to help them, if they will trust him and if they will let him do that for them.

This is easier to do with the person who has made the conscious decision to separate or divorce. That person has struggled for some time with the decision, a struggle made all the more difficult by the fact that there were usually strong ties that held him to the marriage, despite its deficiencies. He did not wish to end his marriage. Quite the contrary, for the longest time, and sometimes for years, he has walked around the problem of his marriage over and over again in an attempt to find some key to unlock it. No matter how hard he tried, however, and no matter how much effort was expended, the problem would simply not lend itself to any solution. In deciding to end the marriage, he had no illusions that he would be ending his problems. Quite the contrary, he knew that he was simply exchanging one set of problems for another. In fact, it was this knowledge, at least in part, that kept him so long from making the decision to separate.

In the end, that decision was made because he became convinced that no matter how much more time and effort was expended, and no matter how many more times he walked around the problem of his marriage, it still would not lend itself to a solution. And though he knew, to be sure, that his divorce would only leave him with a new set of problems, he believed somehow that if he applied his efforts to them, and struggled with them, in time his situation would improve. He knows this; all that it is necessary for the mediator to do is to remind him of it.

But what does the mediator say to the party who did not choose to separate and divorce? The mediator knows that if the marriage was as bad as it was for the party whose decision it was to divorce, it could not have been without its problems for the other party either. Nevertheless, the other party chose to live with those problems rather than to end the marriage. That meant that his attachments and dependency upon the relationship, coupled with the fear he had about assuming the new problems resulting from a divorce, were such that it was easier to suffer the marriage's deficiencies than to end it. Now, however, and with one swift act, his *worst* fears have been realized. Of the two sets of problems—the one he did not like but felt that he could live with, and the one that so frightened him that he could not face it—he has been left with the latter.

Again, if the mediator is to succeed here, he must be absolutely *honest*. Nor can that honesty be expressed in words alone. At times that honesty can only be conveyed by acknowledging that there are no words that are appropriate, let alone sufficient, for the purpose. Words are human constructs that we have created to attempt to make sense of the world that we live in, and to help us to understand it. However, and unless we are extremely careful, when we attempt to use those words in a situation that makes no sense, and is neither understandable nor acceptable to us, we may not only end up perverting their proper use, but also call into question our credibility. In such a situation it is far better to have no answer and to say nothing. This is particularly true in those situations where the hurt and shock are still so great that nothing that the mediator could say by way of explanation, no matter how honest, could be *heard*.

When the mediator cannot use words, however, he can still use *time*. The mediator knows two things. The first is that the majority of the things that we most fear in life are far worse in the expectation than they are in reality. Secondly—and this, of course, is the other side of the same coin—faced with certain realities, even those that we have dreaded most, given time, we find a way to create defenses to better protect ourselves and thereby learn to live with them. Knowing this, the mediator falls back on *time*, knowing that if he can wait out the parties' questions, rather than attempting to answer them, he will use that time to solve the problem (and thereby answer the question) that he cannot.

ASSUMPTIONS, OPINIONS, AND JUDGMENTS

There are certain principles the mediator must attempt to honor religiously throughout the course of the mediation. The first of these, which has particular application during his initial discussions with the couple, is that he must *assume nothing*.

When the mediator and the parties first meet, they will usually be total strangers. The mediator knows that the mere act of meeting with him, let alone engaging in the discussions which they must, will be difficult and at times even painful for one or both of the parties. Nor will it always be possible for them to exempt him as a possible target at which to direct some of the feelings with which they are struggling.

The problem for the mediator, particularly at the outset, is that he does not know what those feelings are or where they are hidden. Thus, while he may want to reach out in order to help the parties, there is always the danger that in doing so he may become so actively involved that he may inadvertently get caught in the crossfire. To avoid this, it is essential, at least until he has won their trust, that he intervene as a somewhat neutral presence.

The mediator can assume nothing, save perhaps that surface appearances are almost always deceiving. What the couple will present to him, especially at the outset, is only a small portion of what is actually there. The most significant aspects of their lives, particularly the painful feelings that one or both of them are struggling with, will usually be hidden beneath the surface. Before the mediator wades into these troubled waters, it is essential that he first locate these feelings and determine what and where they are.

In this respect, the mediator should approach the parties as he would a field he had reason to believe was mined with explosives. Although the terrain may appear tranquil and inviting, it would be foolhardy for him to assume that it was safe for him to walk wherever he might choose. Before he commits himself or takes any step, he would be well advised to test carefully that he does not unintentionally put his foot down on dangerous ground only to set off an explosion.

Let us illustrate this. During the course of the initial meeting, and in an attempt to contrast the positive benefits of mediation with the more harmful effects of adversarial proceedings, the mediator refers to the damage that is so often done to children caught in the adversarial struggle between their parents. Drawing to a conclusion, he turns to the couple and tells them that even in the brief time that they have been together he can tell that they are both responsible persons, concerned with the well-being of their children, and that they would certainly not want to expose their children to this. With this, the mediator is greeted with a barrage from the wife.

What mistake did the mediator make? His mistake was in assuming that the wife viewed her husband as responsible, let alone primarily concerned with the best interests of their children. She does not believe this at all. If he were, he would not, after nineteen years of marriage, have left her and their three children for another woman, one who not only lives in the same community as the parties, but who was a friend of the wife's as well. He would have attempted to save their marriage, as the wife begged him to, rather than have abandoned his family as he has. As far as the wife is concerned, it may be easy for the mediator, who is also a man, and in the business of divorcing couples as well, lightly to dismiss this. But then he is not going to be left with the responsibility of having to raise these three children, or explain to them what has happened to their father.

Nor is she willing to accept the mediator's suggestion that what they must do now is sit down and resolve their differences sensibly, and without rancor, so that they can conclude an agreement that is fair to both of them. There is nothing fair here, and for the mediator to suggest to the wife, let alone to her husband, that he can make up to her and their children for what he has done, is an insult. Nor is she particularly concerned with how her husband will manage following their divorce. He should have thought about that before he started this.

Thus, before the mediator makes any statement, even the most casual one, he must first ask himself whether or not that statement contains any assumptions about the parties themselves, their attitude toward their separation and divorce, or their feelings toward one another. If he concludes that there is such an assumption implicit in the statement, he must then carefully probe to determine whether or not that assumption is well founded before he proceeds further and puts it on the table. Should he fail to do this, he runs the risk of finding himself at odds with one of the parties.

This brings us to the second principle, which is somewhat a corollary of the first. That principle holds that the mediator must carefully avoid expressing opinions of his own or taking issue with those expressed by either of the parties. In the previous example, the mediator might well take exception to the oversimplified explanation the wife gave of what happened in her marriage, or how it got to where it is. He knows that while another woman can play a large part in the breakup of a bad marriage, she will have little if any effect on a good one. He also knows that someone who becomes emotionally involved with his next-door neighbor probably never intended to go very far. He knows too that in all likelihood the husband would have greatly preferred for the matter to have come to a very different conclusion than it has. Finally, he knows that the wife here has probably had more to do with what has happened in their marriage than she is able to acknowledge or to take responsibility for. But does this mean that the mediator should give expression to these opinions, let alone take issue with those expressed by the wife?

Before answering this question, let us consider the expression of a different kind of opinion. While attempting to work out the periods of time that a couple's two children, ages six and eight, will spend with their father, a dispute arises between the parties. Because the wife will have custody of the children, the husband has insisted upon the right to visit with them every weekend. Moreover, he has indicated that he wants each weekend to commence on Friday evening before dinner and to end on Sunday evening following dinner. Because she would like to spend some time with the children on the weekend herself, the wife has objected to this arrangement and has suggested that her husband have the children either three out of four weekends or, if he insists on having them every weekend, that the children be returned to her on Sunday morning after breakfast on two of the four weekends.

The husband will not hear of this. He maintains that it is essential for the proper well-being of their children that they develop and maintain a strong relationship with him and insists that this cannot be accomplished only on intermittent occasions or for but short periods of time. In further defense of his position, he states that he has read numerous articles about children of divorce, and has spoken to a number of professionals in the field, and that all of these authorities agree that it is essential that children be with their fathers for meaningful periods of time such as he has suggested. To buttress his argument, he concludes by stating that this is particularly important here, where the children in question are boys, as it is common knowledge that boys fare less well than do girls in divorce and need the sustained role model of a father.

While the mediator would certainly not take issue with the importance of a strong ongoing relationship between these two young boys and their father, he knows that the strength of that relationship, and the influence of the father here, is not dependent on whether he will be able to see them for the periods of time he has demanded. Furthermore, he knows that his relationship with them will not be undermined were they to spend Sundays with their mother every other weekend as she has requested.

Finally, he knows that no matter how sincere the husband's desire to maintain an ongoing relationship with his sons may be, his proposed visitation schedule probably has more to do with his feelings toward his wife, who has initiated this divorce over his objections, than it does with sound psychological theory. In fact, these feelings are so strong that they have blinded him to the legitimate needs of his children who, by his proposed arrangement, may be unable to spend any portion of their weekends with their own friends. (When this was pointed out to the husband, he simply brushed it off by saying that it was far more important for them to be with him than with their friends and that, like other children of divorced parents, they will have two sets of friends, weekday friends and weekend friends.)

Let us now go back to the question that was left unanswered. Should the mediator take issue with the opinions expressed by the wife in the first case or by the husband in the second? The answer is no. Their opinions and conclusions do not represent objective judgments to which they have come, dispassionately, and only after careful study. Rather, they represent the expression and justification of strongly felt emotions that were born, and are the by-product, of the considerations that have brought each of them to where they are.

More importantly, in most instances nothing that the mediator will say is going to change them. Further, were the mediator to take issue with these opinions, he will do so only at the risk of drawing himself into a personal debate with the party in question. Nor, as we have said, is it a debate that will lead to any resolution. Rather, it will lead only to a standoff, and perhaps even to a loss of face on the part of one of the two protagonists. Moreover, in allowing this to happen, the mediator will have stepped aside from his professional role and responsibility, not to aid either of the parties, but simply to take up *a cause of his own.*

The mediator has no right to do this. Neither the wife nor the husband have come to him for an expression of his own personal opinions, no matter how astute they may be. Rather, they have come to him to help them conclude an agreement on terms that they consider to be appropriate. And that, of course, is the mediator's primary obligation. But if he indulges himself, either by allowing himself the luxury of giving expression to his own personal opinions or by taking issue with those expressed by the parties themselves, and thereby gets dragged into a personal confrontation, the only thing that he will have accomplished will be to have jeopardized the possibility of their ever concluding such an agreement, or of his being of any help to them at all.

The mediator's job, then, is not to take issue with these expressions of opinion, but to find a way to conclude an agreement between the couple in spite of them. Does this mean that the agreement concluded by the mediator will leave the husband in the second example with the right to have his children each and every weekend and his wife with no portion of any? We have not suggested this. All that we have said is that in each instance the mediator will have to find his way to some common ground—to an agreement that both the husband and the wife can live with and accept—other than by taking issue with the opinions expressed by the parties.

Perhaps, in this case, he will be able to do this by getting the husband to see how his feelings are coloring his demands and expectations. Perhaps he will be able to get him to reconsider his positions by means of a gentle, nonjudgmental, Socratic exchange of questions and answers. Perhaps he will be able to use the wife's refusal to accept this solution as a reality principle that the husband will have to come to terms with if he is going to conclude an agreement with her. Perhaps he will be able to underscore that reality, and cut through the husband's tortured logic at the same time, by bringing home to him the fact that a court of law will be no more likely to give him the right to be with his children for the periods of time that he is demanding than his wife is.

Perhaps what he will do will be to postpone a further discussion of this issue until later in the mediation, when all of the other issues have been resolved and when it may be possible to address this issue more productively. Perhaps he will accomplish this by employing one of the many other tools in his arsenal of skills. The one thing that he must not do, however, is to attempt to resolve it by confronting either of the parties and taking issue with the opinions they have expressed.

This brings us to the third principle, which is related to, but is nevertheless distinct from, the second. During the course of the mediation one or both parties may request or insist on the inclusion of certain provisions in the agreement that the mediator feels are unjustified and perhaps totally unreasonable. They may even give voice to their demands in demeaning and offensive language, and accompany them with derogatory verbal and facial expressions that the mediator finds to be as inappropriate as the demands themselves.

They may further frustrate the mediator's attempt to effectuate some rational resolution to the problem by defending their positions with illogical and even inconsistent arguments, and make silly and petty remarks that lead nowhere and only cause the discussions between the parties to degenerate and to get lost. Finally, and when pressed, they may end the discussion, and complete the mediator's frustration, by falling back on nothing more than the fact that that is *how they feel*.

This raises a question. Is it the mediator's business whether or not the demands made by the parties are justified or how they give expression to them? Put another way, to what extent is it appropriate for the mediator to pass judgment on the parties or to be affected by the relationship between them and how they do business with one another? The answer is that it is not his function to make these judgments and that he has no right to do so. In fact, and as hard as it may at times be for him, part of his training must be to teach himself not to be affected by, or to make judgments about, what takes place in front of him. The parties have not invited him into their lives for that purpose. Nor will he be of any value to them if he does. That being the case, he must forever be on his guard lest he indulge himself in a privilege that is not his to take and that will benefit no one but himself.

Let us illustrate this with an example. The mediator is consulted by a couple who have been married for 28 years and have two grown children. The husband is employed as a blue-collar worker and earns approximately $36,000 a year. The wife, who has certain physical problems that prevent her from either standing or sitting for extended periods of time, has not worked in many years and would have difficulty finding employment. Aside from the husband's pension, the parties' only asset of any value is their home. Because it is the wife's intention to relocate, and because it is her desire that her grown children continue to live in their home with their father, the home will not be sold presently. Rather, the wife will receive rent from her children that will offset the rent she will be required to pay on her new apartment. In addition, she will receive support from her husband equal to one-third of his gross salary.

The divorce has been initiated by the wife, who claims that she was forced to separate from her husband because of his mistreatment of her. This has greatly colored the wife's feelings and the demands she has made in the course of the mediation. Moreover, those demands have been expressed in highly emotional terms by the wife, and underscored in each instance by a reference to the fact that she would not be where she now finds herself but for her husband's mistreatment of her. While her husband would take exception to what, to him, is his wife's one-sided and oversimplified view of what has happened in their marriage, he has nevertheless backed away from any confrontation with her since he feels that it will lead nowhere and will only end up in yet a further onslaught of wronged feelings on her part.

The first of these demands concerns the support payments her husband has agreed to pay to her. Being religious, she feels that she has been left in a predicament. She is only 48 years of age and does not wish to live alone the rest of her life. Nor do her religious beliefs permit her to live with someone outside of marriage. If she marries, however, she will lose the support payments she is to receive from her present husband. What will happen if her second marriage does not work out, and she is forced to divorce again? Particularly if that divorce occurs after only a very short period of time, and she does not receive support from her second husband, that will leave her without any support at all. She therefore insists that if she does not receive support from her second husband equal to that to be paid to her by her present husband, then, and unless she receives a settlement upon her second divorce of a stated amount, her present husband's support obligation should revive. When her husband objects to this, she becomes very upset and tells him that it is in his best interests for her to remarry since, if she does, he will not be required to make support payments to her for the duration of her second marriage.

The second issue concerns the husband's pension. The husband, who is 52 years of age, will retire in approximately 13 years. While the wife has an interest in the benefits he has accrued in the 26 years that he has been employed at his present place of employment during their marriage, under the law of the jurisdiction where the parties live, she has no interest in the benefits that will accrue following their divorce. This, in effect, will give the wife an interest in approximately two-thirds of the total benefits, and the husband has agreed to share those equally with her. The wife is not satisfied with this and insists on receiving one-half of his total pension benefits. When the husband objects to this, the wife becomes very emotional and points out to him that if they had remained married until his retirement, as she would have but for his mistreatment of her, she would be entitled to one-half, rather than only one-third, of those benefits. At this point the wife becomes overwhelmed and starts to cry uncontrollably.

The third issue concerns the husband's social security benefits. Again the wife is concerned about the possible effects of her hypothetical remarriage. Despite the fact that she has been married to her present husband for 28 years and would clearly be entitled to receive social security benefits at the appropriate age based upon that fact, if she remarries she will irrevocably lose those benefits. By the same token, and unless she is married to her new husband for the requisite period of time, she will not receive benefits based on her second marriage and will be left with no benefits at all. She therefore wants the agreement to include provision that should she remarry and divorce, and should she not be entitled to receive social security benefits as a result of her second marriage, her husband will pay her a portion of his social security benefits. When the husband objects to this, the wife again becomes very upset and tells him that he should stop thinking only of himself and should start thinking of her for a change.

A court of law in the jurisdiction in which the parties reside would not have the legal authority to grant the wife any of the relief she has requested, a fact the husband knows. Moreover, and even if a court were to find that the husband had mistreated the wife, as she claims, the conduct complained of (which, without excusing it, was little more than the garden variety of misconduct present in almost all unhappy marriages of this kind) would be legally irrelevant in terms of the relief that they would have the power to grant to her. More importantly, in all likelihood a court would not give the wife any more than the husband has voluntarily offered, a fact the husband also knows. Nevertheless, the husband eventually accedes to all of his wife's demands.

Should this bother the mediator, and if so, why? (If, in the final analysis, it does not bother the husband—in the sense that he is willing to agree to it rather than to draw the line and refuse to—why should it bother the mediator?) The answer is that it should *not*. If there is any objection to be made here, there is one and only one person who has a right to make it, and that is the husband. It is he who has lived with the wife these many years, not the mediator, and it is he who will have to live with whatever agreement he may conclude with her now. It is therefore for *him* to decide what obligation he is willing or unwilling to assume, just as it is for her, in making the demands of him that she has, to make that same decision.

Does this mean that the mediator should be uninterested in the agreement ultimately concluded by the parties and that he has no responsibility toward it? We are not suggesting this. All that we are saying is that there are *limits* to that interest and responsibility based upon competing, but in the final analysis more important, considerations. Principal among these considerations is what we would call the parties' right to seek their own level—the right to conclude an agreement on their own terms and by their own means, to determine what is important to them and just how important those things are, and to decide what they are willing, or unwilling, to pay for what they want. That level may not be one of which the mediator personally approves. It may not be one that complies with some objective yardstick of what is considered to be "just" or "equitable." It will probably not even be one that is in accord with the mediator's own private sense of what is fair and therefore, one that he accepts without some reservation. But it is their level, nevertheless, and the mediator must therefore always balance his concern for the quality of the agreement concluded by the parties with his respect for that level.

What is the appropriate balance between these competing considerations—between the mediator's responsibility and the parties' right of self-determination with respect to the things that ultimately affect their lives? First, we would suggest that the mediator's responsibility is a *procedural* one, not a *substantive* one—that while he has a responsibility for the road that the parties travel, he is not responsible for their final destination. Second, we would suggest that while the mediator has an obligation to be *concerned* with the couple's agreement, he has no right to become *invested* in it. It is not a perfect world; nor can we expect it to be. People do not always make decisions that are necessarily in their best interests. They may not have done this at the time of their marriage and they may not do this now at the time of their divorce. However, this does not justify our stepping in to second-guess their decision. And it certainly does not justify our usurping their right to make those decisions.

The mediator's responsibility, then, is simply to provide each of the parties with the conditions that will best enable them to make what they consider the most appropriate decisions under the circumstances. That being the case, and since he has no right to become invested in the decisions they will then make, he cannot allow himself to be affected by what they may decide. He has a job to do, and although it is limited by certain considerations, it is, nevertheless, a very important one. Furthermore, he wants to perform that job professionally, since that, in the final analysis, is his first obligation. Thus, as he goes about his business, he cannot allow himself to be affected by what takes place in front of him, and thereby be distracted from that responsibility.

Let us illustrate this with the following example. A couple has been married for some 26 years and have two grown children. The husband earns $50,000 a year and the wife $11,000. The wife, who initiated the divorce, has asked her husband to provide her with support equal to her rent of $650 a month, to which he has agreed. When the question of the duration of the husband's obligation to make these payments was raised, the husband stated that he thought two or three years was appropriate. The discussion that then followed between the parties were framed by three considerations: (1) a certain timidity on the wife's part based upon the fact that her husband did not want the divorce, and was still having difficulty accepting it, (2) the husband's resistance to obligate himself legally for an indefinite, and even extended, period of time, and (3) ignorance on the part of two basically decent people who wanted to do the right thing, but really did not know what the right thing was.

It was the mediator's job here to recognize and then to address each of these issues. He had an obligation to address the wife's timidity, and to reinforce her appropriate sense of entitlement, by putting on the table the fact that there were certain obligations that flowed from a relationship of this duration and that they were unaffected by the fact that it was the wife, rather than her husband, who had decided upon the divorce. He also had an obligation to address the husband's resistance, and to reinforce the fact that the husband's obligation could not be defined simply in terms of his discomfort in committing himself legally, as understandable as that might be. Finally, and though he obviously could not suggest what was right or wrong, if they had no sense of this of their own, then he had an obligation to provide them with a *yardstick* that would at least indicate to them what was considered normatively appropriate under the circumstances. To be sure, what was considered normatively appropriate, as defined by what it could be expected that a court would or would not do, was extremely arbitrary, and the mediator certainly did not believe that it represented any final judgment on the matter.

Thus, it would not have occurred to him to draw any conclusion about the agreement ultimately reached by the parties because the duration of support was either more or less than would have been the case had it been determined by the application of such a yardstick. But, as normative as legal judgments may be, and particularly given the fact that the parties here had no independent sense of what was appropriate under the circumstances, it was the mediator's obligation to provide them with the benefit of that yardstick, for whatever value it might have.[3]

In another instance, what is being proposed by one of the parties is not based on any ignorance on his part. Nor can it even be said to represent a judgment on his part as to his marriage or the circumstances that have led to his divorce. Rather, it is based simply on a niggardly attitude, and on a desire to keep as much as he can and give as little as he has to. This will occur, for example, when a husband attempts to justify what is obviously an inadequate level of child support by a distorted and tortured reading of the wife's budget designed to demonstrate that the actual needs of the children (apart from those of the wife), as expressed in that budget, amount to no more than a very small percentage of the total. Again, and if necessary, the mediator has an obligation to step in here and underscore the inappropriateness of the proposed level of child support, both in relationship to the husband's ability as well as the amount that he has allocated for his own needs. For that purpose, he may resort to normative yardsticks, thereby putting on the table for the wife's benefit something which, if she seems unable to answer the husband's argument, will at least enable her to cut through it and, at the same time, support her own resolve not to accept less than she deems appropriate.

There is another consideration that will also cause the mediator to step in. The mediator is guided in his work by the principle that his role is to help the couple conclude an agreement they can live with, both emotionally and financially. This is in keeping with his desire to help them effectuate some closure to the strong feelings that have been a by-product of their relationship and their decision to separate and divorce. To be sure, it is a lot easier to state that goal than it is to know whether or not the agreement concluded by them fulfills its conditions, particularly since, at least ideally those conditions should be fulfilled, not only in the present, but in the future as well.

Whether or not the agreement is one the parties feel that they can live with at the present time is relatively simple to determine, for if one of the parties feels that it is not, he will not sign it. But what about the future? It is easy enough if what is at issue is an agreement that will require the husband to turn over 90% of his salary to his wife for her support and that of their children. Regardless of what the husband's reasons or motivations may be in agreeing to this, the fact remains that he cannot, and therefore will not, be able to *live* with that obligation. That being the case, the mediator is doing no one, including the wife, a favor by sitting by silently and allowing him to conclude such an agreement.

Suppose instead, however, that the husband has proposed to give her 60% of his salary rather than 90%. Suppose also that, instead of limiting her right to continue to live in their home until their youngest child has graduated from high school or college, he is willing to permit her to continue to live there for as long as she may wish, even should she remarry. It may be that these are conditions that the husband will be able to comply with in the future. But are they such that he may not later feel that the agreement is so grossly unfair that he cannot continue to live with it? And what will be the price that the parties, and perhaps their children, will be required to pay on that account? It is not possible for the mediator to know the answers to these questions, and it would be dishonest of him to pretend that he can. Thus, as concerned as he may be about these questions, and while he has an obligation to *raise* them, he has no right to *answer* them. Nor does he have the right to object to the answers the parties themselves may give.

Finally, the mediator must be concerned that the agreement concluded by the parties, as reasonable or unreasonable as it may be under the circumstances, does not run so far afoul of prevailing normative standards that it stands in jeopardy of being set aside by a court. It makes no difference that normative standards are simply that. If the couple's agreement deviates too far from those standards, one of the parties may later look back and conclude that it was grossly unfair and perhaps even unconscionable. More importantly, a court of law may well agree with him, and step in and set it aside.[4] Again, the mediator does none of the parties a favor by sitting silently by and allowing them to conclude such an agreement.

Having said this, it is necessary to return to the principles that initiated this discussion. The concern that the mediator properly has for the agreement concluded by the parties cannot be used by him as a back door to admit views and opinions that he was not invited to bring with him through the front door. Nor can it be used as an excuse to pass judgment on those held or expressed by either of the parties. Again, his right to be concerned about their agreement does not give him the right to become invested in it. Nor will it justify or excuse his attempt to deny the inevitable limitations of his undertaking that are born of the inherent conflict that exists between these opposing principles.

Is there a line here that the mediator can draw that will clearly distinguish for him what is and what is not permissible? Unfortunately, there is not. The very delicate balance that that line represents is one the mediator will have to establish, and then carefully walk, in each and every instance. Furthermore, and since it represents a compromise between competing principles, it will necessarily be somewhat arbitrary and therefore always subject to dispute. It is a critical line, nevertheless, for it is the one that distinguishes the professional from the amateur, the person who truly wishes to help from the mere intermeddler.

CHAPTER 11

A QUESTION OF CHOICE

Is divorce mediation a perfect procedure? Obviously not. There are no perfect solutions to imperfect problems in the world. Nor can we expect there to be. Why then do we turn to it? Because in the real world, where we are left with but imperfect alternatives, choices must be made.

This is easy enough, and no one will quarrel with that. Nor do we believe that any responsible person who has had experience with the alternatives available to separating and divorcing couples will have any difficulty in making that decision. Clearly, divorce mediation has to be the choice of preference.

Nevertheless, and having acknowledged that, for some there will still be a problem. And it is a problem with which even the advocates of divorce mediation seem obsessed. If we acknowledge that divorce mediation is not a perfect procedure, shouldn't we be concerned with its imperfections? In fact, if we ignore them, are we being anything less than irresponsible? Further, if mediators are right in being concerned with divorce mediation's imperfections, and if they seek to build into its procedures practices that will at least minimize, if not eliminate, these problems, shouldn't their efforts be supported?

The answers to these questions are obvious. Unfortunately, however, this is not the end of it. If mediation were like an automobile, intended simply to get us from one place to another, and if we chose it as a vehicle over a motorcycle because we considered it to be inherently safer and more practical, we would not stop there. On the contrary, and recognizing its limitations and imperfections, we would still consider it appropriate to further improve it as a vehicle—perhaps with steel-belted radial tires, power-assisted disc brakes, three-point seatbelts, etc.—to assure that we were brought to our destination more safely and securely.

The choice between divorce mediation and traditional adversarial divorce proceedings, however, is not just a choice between two different vehicles to get us to the same place. To be sure, to the critics of divorce mediation that is all it is. Unfortunately, this is also true for many of its advocates. Nevertheless, it is not. It is a choice between different value systems—a choice, if you will, between two very different ways of looking at divorce and of seeing what it represents in the lives of the families that it touches. Just as importantly, it is a choice between two very different views of what it means to be of help to people who are struggling with the problems incident to their separation and divorce.

The advocates of divorce mediation have not had any difficulty in choosing between these alternatives. What they have had difficulty doing, however, is understanding and accepting the implications of that choice. And this has resulted in a kind of failure of nerve.

How has this failure of nerve expressed itself? First, in divorce mediation's willing-

ness to accept as relevant questions that have been posed by the critics of divorce mediation based upon values implicit in adversarial proceedings. Secondly, in adopting yardsticks to judge its performance that incorporate adversarial measurements. And, finally, in
saddling itself with ethical requirements derivative of adversarial practice and adversarial
thinking, but inconsistent with its own.

Let us give an example. Our legal system's principal concern is the conflicting
interests of the parties. As a result, adversarial attorneys have insisted in their proposed
standards of practice that provision be built into mediation to assure that those conflicting
interests will be vouchsafed.[1] What is the reaction in mediation circles to the question of
how the couple's conflicting interests will be protected? Is divorce mediation's response to
reject the question as based upon a different set of concerns, as, for example, a marriage
counselor undoubtedly would if the legal profession were to criticize him for not making
the protection of the conflicting interests of the husband and wife whom he was seeing in
family therapy his primary obligation? Is it even to ask the critics of divorce mediation a
question of its own, namely, how do adversarial lawyers, in their zeal to insure that the
parties' conflicting interests are protected, also insure that they protect the other important
interests they have, not the least of which is to resolve the matter expeditiously, with as
little emotional toll as possible?

The answer, unfortunately, is no. Rather, it is to assure its critics that it is concerned
with the problem and that it has incorporated into its procedures practices that will insure
that it is properly dealt with. And so, mediators continue routinely to send couples off into
the adversarial world to consult with separate lawyers, despite the fact that the practice is
inconsistent with mediation principles and intended only to serve adversarial ends.

Let us suppose instead that divorce mediation had posed the question, and asked its
critics how they proposed to protect those interests the parties have in common, such as
their desire to avoid having their conflict adversely affect themselves and their children.
How would the advocates of traditional adversarial divorce proceedings have responded to
it? Would they have formed a bar association committee to study the adverse effects of
traditional divorce proceedings upon the parties and their children? Would they have
issued an opinion that it was unethical for attorneys to participate in those proceedings if
there was reason to believe that they would be unduly traumatic? Would they have
adopted rules designed to place a limit on those possible adverse effects by, for example,
requiring that if those proceedings did not prove successful within a reasonable period of
time, perhaps four to six months, that they had to be suspended and the parties directed to
an alternative procedure, such as mediation? Needless to say, these are all rhetorical
questions.

What then would have been their response? In a very real sense adversarial attorneys
would not have *understood* the questions. Perhaps even more importantly, they would not
have considered it *relevant*, even if they had. In fact, it would make no more sense to ask
an adversarial attorney this question than it would be to ask a general whether he was
concerned about the possibility of American casualties were we to go to war. Casualties,
after all, are a part of war, and it is not possible to separate the one from the other. In any
event, that is not his concern, but rather the concern of Congress who declared war.

The same is true of an adversarial attorney. If his client wishes to fight for custody of
his children, it is for his client, and not for him, to decide whether the emotional and
financial costs such a fight will entail are acceptable. By the same token, if his client feels

that the price is too high, then he will not pay it. Again, that is his client's decision to make, not his. For an adversarial attorney, those emotional and financial costs are not an *objection* to adversarial proceedings. They are simply their *price*, and everything, after all, has its price. But that price doesn't call into question the values that adversarial proceedings are intended to serve, any more than American casualties call into question the value of the freedom for which they have died. In short, the fact that adversarial proceedings are not perfect is not an objection, and certainly not a fatal objection, for an adversarial lawyer, and he does not question whether or not he should be a party to them, or have a failure of nerve, on that account. Since he believes in the values they serve—in this case the protection of the parties' conflicting interests—he does not question the cost.

There is another point to be made. An adversarial attorney does not pass judgment on the decision that his client has made to fight or not fight for custody of his children, let alone his right to make it. He may privately question his client's reasons or motives. He may even attempt to have his client reconsider them. But he recognizes and accepts the fact that it is ultimately his client's decision to make, and not his, and that he would be overstepping his bounds were he to interfere with his client's right to make it. Nor does he waver from this principle because that decision may have consequences detrimental to his client's children, or, for that matter, to his client as well.

Most importantly of all, he does not judge that decision against a yardstick of what is fair or just or right, or insist that it proceed from motives untainted by the hundred and one considerations, some good and some bad, that affect all of our actions. Rather, and so long as the actions contemplated by his client are neither illegal nor unethical, he respects his client's right to decide upon them, whether for better or for worse.

Do divorce mediators have the same respect for the principle of self-determination? Unfortunately, no. Though they know, probably far better than do adversarial lawyers, the tightrope they must walk between assuring, on the one hand, that the parties make knowledgeable and informed decisions and, on the other, that they reserve to them the ultimate right to make those decisions, whatever their reasons, their failure of nerve has left them intimidated by the insistence of their critics that they assure that the parties' reasons and motives are as pure as fresh-fallen snow and their decisions as fair and just as Solomon's. As a result, mediators have been led to discard their better judgment. Nor are they even able to see the irony in the fact that, in doing so, they have been persuaded by adversarial lawyers that they are under an obligation to make judgments that adversarial lawyers themselves do not make, and do not feel they have any obligation to make.

Divorce mediation's failure of nerve is also revealed in the yardsticks by which it judges its performance. By definition, any agreement that a couple concludes between themselves in mediation should ultimately be measured against the assumptions implicit in mediation practice. For divorce mediation, that test should be whether the agreement is one that both parties feel they can accept and can live with. Are divorce mediators content to leave it at that? Unfortunately, no. On the contrary, their failure of nerve is such that they are unwilling to accept an agreement that measures up to their own standards unless and until they have first looked over into the adversarial world to test out whether or not they got it right in terms of adversarial standards as well. To make matters worse, they then send the couple off to adversarial lawyers to do the testing.

Needless to say, adversarial lawyers do not suffer this failure of nerve. It does not concern them that the only reality they recognize is that of obtaining an agreement that will give their clients as much as they can get and require them to give as little as they have to. Nor does it concern them that, in the process, they may have left the parties as hurt and angry when they got through as when they began, and less able to effectuate the necessary emotional closure that they must if they are to be able to proceed with their lives. And they certainly do not send their clients off to mediators to make sure that they did not get it wrong.

Is this to suggest that divorce mediation would be justified in simply brushing off as irrelevant the questions posed by its critics? And if it did this, wouldn't it be as guilty in the process as are the advocates of traditional adversarial divorce proceedings? Quite obviously, divorce mediation does not wish to replicate the history of traditional adversarial divorce proceedings which, in more than one hundred years, has never once stopped to assess the damage that it has caused, or even acknowledged that damage, let alone offered the slightest constructive suggestion as to how to minimize it. What we are simply suggesting is that it must judge that criticism, as it must judge all of its efforts, in terms of its own values and its own assumptions.

Why has it failed to do this? There are a number of reasons. The first is that divorce mediation has failed to define itself sufficiently—to answer the basic question, what *is* divorce mediation? As a result, it has been forced to accept the identity assigned it, largely by its critics. From the standpoint of traditional adversarial divorce proceedings, divorce mediation is simply an alternative means of dispute resolution. In other words, it is simply a different vehicle to get to the same place. Implicit in this is the view that divorce is basically a legal process involving the application of legal rules and principles to the facts of the parties' lives. Unfortunately, divorce mediation has not questioned this assumption. It has simply questioned whether those legal rights and obligations had to be settled in an adversarial setting and whether alternative procedures might not be more conducive to a resolution of the couple's differences.

As we have said, that is not what divorce mediation is. Rather, it represents a radically different view of what divorce represents in the lives of families that it touches and what it means to help those families through that personal crisis. It also represents a radically different view as to what stands between the couple and an agreement, and how such an agreement can best be achieved.

The second reason is not as easy to categorize and is even more difficult to explain. By and large, the divorce mediation movement has been spearheaded by lawyers and mental health professionals. Unfortunately, although the lawyers in question recognize the bankruptcy of traditional adversarial divorce proceedings, they did not fully appreciate how the assumptions *implicit* in those proceedings contributed to the problem.[2] Thus, when they left the arena of adversarial practice and moved over to mediation, they brought with them their baggage of adversarial concerns. This is reflected, for example, in their preoccupation with the issue of confidentiality and, of course, the parties' legal rights and their conflicting interests.[3]

With mental health professionals, on the other hand, it is not what they brought with them but what they left behind. For some strange reason, when mental health professionals took off their hats as marriage counselors and, walking across the room, put on their hats as divorce counselors, they left the better part of themselves behind them. Surely, if there was any group it might have been expected would have understood what divorce represents, and asked the right questions, it would have been the mental health profession. And yet, when they crossed over into divorce mediation it was as if they had come into a totally different world. Questions that they would never have thought to ask had the same couple consulted them in marriage counseling now seemed to be urgent and necessary because they had come instead for divorce counseling.

Moreover, judgments that they would have considered it inappropriate to make as mental health professionals they now did not hesitate to express or impose as mediators. Thus, if it is suggested that a mediator has an obligation to raise, as a threshold issue, whether either of the parties is involved emotionally outside of their marriage or has been guilty of misconduct to his or her spouse, mental health professionals do not object to this. Similarly, if it is urged that a mediator is obligated to assure that the parties' relationship with one another, as expressed in their agreement, conforms to the mediator's expectations, or even to certain objective criteria, mental health professionals do not take exception to this either, despite the fact that in each instance they thereby violate basic tenets of therapeutic practice. As if this is not bad enough, and though they know that in therapy it is *they*, and not their *theories*, who help their clients, and that, in fact, they often help their clients *in spite of* their theories, having moved over into mediation, they come to their task weighed down with unnecessary busywork and homework assignments, and theories of negotiation and conflict management, which they then allow to monopolize their efforts and misdirect their proper focus.

The third, and perhaps most important reason is—again—simply a failure of nerve. Divorce mediation has not had the courage of its convictions. This is expressed, for example, in the recurring suggestion that, before commencing mediation, mediators are under an obligation to *screen* a couple to determine their suitability for mediation. Does an adversarial divorce lawyer have this failure of nerve?

For example, suppose he is consulted by a less than decent or honest husband whom he finds is simply intent on using the adversarial process to punish his wife for all the crimes, real and imagined, that he believes she has committed against him during their marriage. Can one picture the attorney declining to accept the client because he does not believe that he will be honest and forthright and that, as a result, the ultimate agreement might be unfair, or because he believes that his insistence on fighting for custody of his children is intended to serve purposes other than their best interests and may well prove to be against them? The question, unfortunately, is a rhetorical one. Divorce lawyers cannot be accused of any failure of nerve. Quite the contrary, and absolutely convinced of the virtues of adversarial proceedings and the goals they serve, they take all comers.

Not so with divorce mediation. Because it has blindly accepted the mythology that those adversarial procedures incorporate safeguards that are *lacking* in mediation practice, and that there is therefore always the danger that divorce mediation will go awry, those who come to us must be carefully screened to assure that they are *suitable*—to assure, in other words, that they will get to the right place even without these important safeguards.

If there are imperfections in mediation practice, as there undoubtedly are, they will not be corrected by adding adversarial baggage. They will only be corrected by bringing that practice closer to the principles that should properly guide it. To do this, however, divorce mediation must first properly define itself and answer the important questions that it has yet to *ask*. To do this, it must gain the courage of its convictions. Finally, to do this it must make the necessary choice.

PART II

PRACTICE

CHAPTER 12
STARTING OUT

Couples rarely come to the decision to divorce at the same time. On the contrary, the decision is usually that of one of the parties alone. In many instances the other party is not even aware that a decision was being contemplated at all and is taken terribly by surprise. This is not to suggest that the initiating party is acting lightly, and without forethought. Quite the contrary, he has probably been seriously contemplating his decision for at least a year before he actually acted upon it. However, though his dissatisfaction with his marriage is very real, there are, nevertheless, strong dependencies that still tie him to his home, to his children, and even to his spouse. It is only because the price that he has to pay to hold on to the benefits of the marriage has simply become too great that he has finally concluded, usually very reluctantly, that he has no other choice. The decision to divorce is thus one of the most difficult decisions a person will ever have to make and, understandably, it takes a great deal of time to come to it.

What this means is that in most instances the couple do not come to their divorce emotionally apace or equally of the same mind. Rather, one usually wants the divorce while the other does not. The party whose decision it is has been preparing himself for some time, and has already gone through a great deal of the questioning and soul-searching. He may even have looked outside of the marriage for emotional support—first to meet some of the needs that were not being met in the marriage and then to assist him in letting go of it—and may have already established a new relationship with someone else. He now wants to get on with it and get it over. The other party, however, is resistant. He may not yet be ready to accept the fact that it is over and still holds on to the idea that perhaps it may not have to be. Not uncommonly, he is very resentful that the other party is not willing to work to try and save the marriage. At other times, and even when he knows that there is no possibility that it will be saved, he may still be afraid to let go and go out on his own.

This is usually the emotional climate that exists when the couple come to mediation, even, surprisingly, when they have already been separated for some period of time. It may also be one of the first problems that the mediator will have to address.

THE INITIAL TELEPHONE CALL

The initial contact with the mediator is made by a telephone call. In most instances, the caller is the person who is interested in obtaining the divorce. At times, however, he may be the party who does not want the divorce, and may be calling simply because he has been prodded by his spouse, or because he is less threatened by the prospect of mediation (which he views as perhaps offering the hope of a reconciliation) or at least a device to stave off the inevitable, than more formal divorce proceedings. The caller may have read an article about divorce mediation. He may have learned about it from a television or radio program. He may have been directed to mediation by a friend who has gone through a similar experience. Or he may have seen a small advertisement placed by the mediator in a local newspaper or the yellow pages of the telephone book. In most instances, and because mediation is still not widespread, he may have many questions and his telephone call may simply be for information. Although he has called and made contact with the mediation facility, in all likelihood he would still like to keep his distance. He is still thinking about divorce and this telephone call is but one of a number of tentative forays he will make into the world of divorce before he actually enters it. It would therefore be most helpful if the mediation facility had a brochure, or some other material explaining mediation, that could be sent to him without obligation.

Without threatening the caller, nor forcing him to make a commitment that he is not yet prepared to make, the mediator must, nevertheless, reach out and make contact with him. Unfortunately, however, all that the mediator knows is that the caller is either a male or a female who is married and who is considering divorce. Initially, he does not even know *that*, since it may be the caller's spouse who is the one considering the divorce. Then too, the caller may be a relative or friend of the person in question. What the mediator wishes to do at this point is to draw the caller into a conversation. It would be helpful, however, if he knew something more about the caller. Surprisingly, one or two simple questions, which will not be threatening to the caller, will be sufficient. "How long have you been married?"; "Do you have any children?"; "Is this your decision or the decision of your spouse?"; "Are you and your spouse still living together?"

A competent mediator will now have enough information to initiate a discussion with the caller. From the mediator's standpoint that conversation should convey three things: first, that the mediator understands the very difficult emotional problem that the caller is, or has been, struggling with; second, that the mediator is a concerned person who would like to help; and third, that mediation is the only sane, intelligent procedure to be employed in dealing with the kind of problem the caller and his spouse have. (If the caller is the one who does not want the divorce, but it becomes obvious to the mediator that the caller's spouse has come to a fixed decision to separate and divorce, the mediator can also gently act as a reality principle. His job then is to try to get the caller to realize that the question is not whether they will divorce but simply how they will divorce.) If the mediator can succeed in this, then, and in a sea of troubled waters, he will begin to sound like a safe harbor of refuge.

Not uncommonly, the caller will indicate that although he would like to come in and mediate the issues relating to his divorce, his spouse will not do so. This is a very difficult problem. In fact, it is probably the most difficult problem that divorce mediation faces today, for whereas it only takes one to start an adversarial divorce proceeding, it takes two to start a mediation. To make matters worse, it is a problem the mediator will not be able to deal with very effectively. The caller's spouse does not want the divorce and is not ready for it, and is probably working under the maxim "Never put off for tomorrow what you can put off for the next day." It is his hope that if he does not acknowledge the problem, that it will perhaps go away.

Also, he may have some reason to believe in the efficacy of this strategy. After all, the party initiating the divorce may well have talked like this before. Those talks did not lead to a divorce then, and perhaps they will not lead to a divorce now. Besides, to ask the reluctant spouse to come in and participate in the mediation is like asking him to come in and help build the scaffold from which he will later be hanged. Even if he is to be divorced, it may be just too much to ask him to participate in it in this way. The mediator's dilemma, then, is that he is talking to the wrong party. All that he can hope to do is to attempt to talk to that other party *through* the caller.

What is it that the mediator can say to the caller that may be of help to him? The situation is that the caller would like a divorce but has been unable to get his spouse to cooperate with him in obtaining it. At least until this time, his spouse has effectively avoided having to deal with the problem by leaving it with him, thereby making it *his* problem. Operating on the understanding that one should never try to solve another person's problem and that, on the contrary, one must always bring home to the other person the fact that it is he who has a problem, the mediator tells the caller that what he must do is make the problem his *spouse's* rather than his own. To accomplish this, the first thing that he must do is to make it clear to his spouse that he *intends* to get a divorce. Until now, and although he may have said this, he has not done it, and since his actions belie his words, his words have not been taken at face value. In fact, his actions may have only reinforced his spouse's natural tendency to deny the reality of the situation.

How can the caller bring this reality home to his spouse? The first thing he can do is reinforce his words with consistent conduct. Thus, and while it is never justified intentionally to hurt another person, the caller must be made to understand that in failing to act consistently toward his spouse as if they really were divorcing, he may only be encouraging his spouse's fantasy that a divorce is perhaps not inevitable, which can be the cruelest kindness of all. Accordingly, and if he really *does* intend to divorce his spouse, he must begin to act as if this were so.

If the person involved is the husband, it might even be useful for him to indicate that it is his intention to move from the home, and establish a separate residence for himself, by a specified date.[1] However, before he leaves he would like to conclude the necessary business that they must, since that is the responsible thing to do. By the same token, he would much prefer to do this in a sane, civilized manner, by employing, for example, the procedures that mediation offer. However, if his wife will not cooperate with him in this, then he will have to do it in whatever manner he can, since it must get done.

"How," he asks his wife, "would you like to do it?" If she does not answer, or if her answer is not affirmative, he must go on. "I can only assume that you are not willing to mediate these issues with me, and as much as I do not want to do so, I have no alternative but to retain a lawyer. Do you want me to retain a lawyer, because if that is what you want me to do, that is what I will do." To be sure, his wife may respond to this, but in the wrong way, and may turn, not to mediation, but to adversarial proceedings. That is a risk that he will have to take. Since he is not willing or able to wait the time that it may take for his spouse to accept the reality that their marriage is over and participate in its dissolution, he will be forced to take matters into his own hands and resort to self-help.

Perhaps when his spouse receives a letter from his attorney, or is served with papers in the action he institutes, the realization may finally come home to her and she will then be willing to turn to mediation before too much damage has been done; and the caller must always be instructed to continue to hold that out as an option. Thus, if he turns to adversarial proceedings, it will not be because he wants to, but because his spouse has left him with no alternative.

There is yet another factor that may be holding back the caller's spouse, and that is fear. Particularly if the spouse is the person who is the financially dependent partner in the marriage, the thought of divorce may be very frightening, for it brings with it the threat of being completely on one's own. This fear can not only cause the caller's spouse to attempt to deny the reality of the divorce but, and when it is no longer possible to continue to do that, to seek protection from that fear. Given the mythology our legal system has created, it is more than likely that the caller's spouse may well assume that such protection can only come by having his own attorney to champion his cause.

Again, all that the mediator can do is attempt to educate the reluctant party through the person who has called him to inquire about mediation. This will not be very easy to do, as the mythology that lawyers protect their clients is so ingrained in our thinking that we never question it, let alone stop to ask ourselves how they actually do this—how one attorney will be able to get more for his client when the other is trying just as hard to see to it that his client will be able to give less. The mediator will nevertheless attempt to dispel this mythology as best he can. He will point out that the presence of separate attorneys will not increase the available dollars and that, on the contrary, all that they will do is fight over how to divide them. He will also try to explain that the only way that lawyers can really protect their clients is to prepare them for the inevitable fight, when in fact their best protection would be to avoid it altogether.

Finally, he will try to convey to the caller that it is a lot easier to *start* adversarial proceedings than it is to *stop* them; that once begun, they tend to have a life of their own and that each of the parties quickly become but bit players, lost in the wings of the drama; that since our legal system is adversarial in nature, it will tend to see the parties as adversaries and will thereby make adversaries of them in the process; and that the ultimate price that they will each pay in abandoning sense and sensibility in the name of this illusive protection is that the very painful feelings that make any discussion between them so difficult will soon become exacerbated to the point that it will be impossible for them to effectuate a settlement until both of them have become so worn down that they are forced to give up. And how will mediation protect each of them? By helping them conclude an agreement between themselves without becoming the victims of these kinds of senseless and destructive proceedings.

It cannot be suggested that these attempts to reach the reluctant spouse will be overly effective. To begin with, the message is being delivered by probably the worst person who could be employed for that purpose. The very fact that he has decided upon a divorce means, from his spouse's standpoint, that he is not to be *trusted*; and if his spouse consults with friends and relatives or, worse yet, with an attorney, this distrust will only be magnified. Unfortunately, however, and unless the other party can be induced to call the mediator directly, there is no other messenger available, and the mediator will have to do the best he can.

To be sure, in time, and as divorce mediation becomes a more accepted method, many of these problems will lessen. Today, when the thought of divorce occurs, a person's immediate reaction is to consult with his or her own attorney and the appropriateness of this response is reinforced by both friends and relatives. In the future, and as divorce mediation becomes more widespread, this will hopefully change, and when a person announces his intention to retain an attorney to represent him, the reaction that he will get may well be, "Why do you have to go out and get hired guns to do this? Can't the two of you sit down and resolve these problems like adults?" But this will still take some time.

While the initial telephone call may result in an appointment, more often than not it will simply be for information. The caller may have had the mediator's name and telephone number (or his brochure or a copy of his advertisement) for months before he made his initial contact, and it still may be weeks, and perhaps months, before the decision to go ahead is made. The decision to divorce, as we have noted, is a process involving factors that are pulling the initiating party toward a divorce and factors that are holding him back, and these opposing considerations may still continue to pull at one another without final resolution. In fact, so strong are the factors that continue to militate against the divorce that even if the caller makes an initial appointment, in many instances it will be canceled before the scheduled meeting.

PREPARING FOR THE INITIAL CONFERENCE

It is neither necessary nor appropriate for the mediator to attempt to get a great deal of information about the parties over the telephone before he meets with them. Nevertheless, it would be helpful to have at least enough information so that he can begin to engage the couple in a discussion when they meet, and this he can accomplish with but a few questions. If the mediator knows how long the parties have been married, the number and ages of their children, whether they own a home or live in an apartment, whether either has been married previously, their occupations, and whether they are already separated or still living together, he will have enough information for that purpose.[2]

Having obtained the information that he will need for his own purposes, the mediator must now address the question of how he will transmit to the couple the information that he feels they should know about mediation generally, and his procedures in particular, before they actually proceed. The initial consultation, after all, is for the couple to have an opportunity to learn more about mediation, to decide whether or not they wish to employ it, and whether they wish to use this particular mediator. While the mediator may also wish to use this meeting for other purposes as well, he must nevertheless still provide them with the information they will want and have a right to know. This includes whom they will be meeting with, when the meetings will be scheduled, how long the meetings will last, how they will obtain the information that they need to know as they go along, how their legal questions will be answered, how their final understanding will become a legally binding agreement, how they will obtain a divorce, and what the various charges for the mediation and the other services that they will be provided will cost.

The mediator's problem is that he does not wish to allow the *informational* aspects of his initial meeting with the couple to interfere with the far more important business that he has to transact. Moreover, if he starts this meeting by going over this information with them, and answering their questions in a very businesslike manner, he may not only ignore these important issues, but may impart this information in such a businesslike way that he creates a negative emotional climate between himself and one or both of the parties rather than the positive one that he had hoped to establish. And, given the couple's state of mind, it is more than likely that the mediator may employ this procedure only to have been rewarded for his efforts by finding that one or both of the parties may not have heard more than half of what he has said.

The mediator can handle this problem in one of two ways. He can prepare, in advance, a short three- or four-page type-written set of materials, preferably bound in a neat, simple cover, which he can give to each of the parties to read in his waiting room before he takes them into his office. Or he can wait until the end of the session and then verbally provide this information, or at least such as did not already come out in their discussion.

The disadvantage of the first procedure is that it tends to add to the impersonality of the couple's initial contact with the mediator. Nevertheless, it is probably the preferable one. The mediator's job during his first meeting with the couple will be to break the ice, and he will not want all these business matters to interfere with that goal. He certainly will not want them to impose a formal or didactic orientation on a meeting that he would like to keep unstructured and easygoing. While this written material may initially start the meeting off in the wrong direction, a good mediator will be able to overcome this trend, and redirect it, once he and the parties sit down together in his office.

Secondly, the parties are far more likely to comprehend this information if they *read* it at *their own pace* rather than have it spoken to them. Thirdly, and since it has been prepared in advance, the mediator is assured that he has imparted to the couple everything that he feels that it is important for them to know, and that it has been said in a way that gives the desired impression. Fourthly, there is a sense of professionalism in being dealt with in an organized, even if somewhat impersonal manner, and that, together with the other more formal procedures the mediator will employ, can go a long way toward building the couple's *confidence* in the mediator. Last but not least, it gets all this material out of the way, and permits the mediator to use the first meeting for his own purposes.

If this approach is employed, it is suggested that when the mediator first meets the couple in his waiting room, and after he has introduced himself, that he take a seat and explain to the couple that before he and they come inside to talk with one another, he would like to give them an overview of mediation and the procedures that they will follow, and to that end he has prepared some material he would like them to read before they begin. He can then tell them that he has found that this material will not only stimulate certain questions they may then want to ask him when they meet together but that it will also answer many of their questions in advance, thus giving them the opportunity to use their time together to discuss some of the more important things that are on their minds.[3]

FORMAL MATERIAL

While a mediator does not *need* to provide the couple with any formal material, other than a financial information sheet that they will later complete, it is nevertheless recommended that such formal material be employed. This material should be prepared in advance, shown to the parties during their initial consultation, and given to each of them if they decide to go ahead with the mediation. This packet (again, typewritten, and bound in a neat, simple cover), should contain at least a copy of the financial information sheet, a form budget, and a list of the basic questions that the couple will be asked to address in the course of their mediation.[4] Ideally, it should also contain a summary, in layman's terms, of the laws pertaining to divorce in the state in question; actual copies of the relevant statutes; a summary, again in layman's terms, of the relevant sections of the Internal Revenue Code pertaining to the transfer of property between spouses, payments made by one of the parties to the other, the exemptions for the children, etc.;[5] a general discussion of the effects of divorce on children, and how to handle the problems it may pose for them;[6] a general outline of the emotional stages of divorce;[7] and any ethical opinions of state or local bar associations pertaining to divorce mediation that the mediator feels it would be appropriate to provide the couple. Where appropriate, this information should be preceded by a short explanation indicating its function and how it is to be used.

While it is not essential that a couple be given all this information, it nevertheless serves many useful purposes. Again, it lends a quality of professionalism to the proceedings. As we have noted, the mediator is anxious to enlist the couple's trust and confidence, and this is one of the main purposes of their initial meeting. To be prepared, and to be organized, enhances this confidence. Secondly, the mediator can use this material to ease the concerns of the more fearful party. He explains that it is very important in mediation that couples make informed and intelligent decisions and that no important considerations be neglected or overlooked. The material he will provide them is designed to assure this.

It is also a way for the mediator to counter the impression, which adversarial lawyers repeatedly reinforce, that more traditional proceedings have certain safeguards built into them that will better protect each of the parties and assure that their agreement is fair. Without necessarily referring to those procedures, the mediator can convey the impression that mediation *also* employs procedures designed to provide this kind of protection.

Thirdly, this material can tend to provide the mediation with a built-in structure and direction that will then permit the mediator to adopt a more informal and less directed approach during the actual sessions. Thus, if all the questions the parties must answer in order to come to an agreement have been set out in advance, it is not necessary to have specific agendas, or worry that a discussion tangential to the main issues will misdirect the mediation, for there are always these questions to come back to, to get the mediation back on track.

There is an even more important reason to use this formal material; it tends to solve a major problem for the mediator. Since this is not an adversarial proceeding, the couple do not each have attorneys to point out to them all the factors that might, or perhaps even should, be of concern to them. The mediator, quite obviously, wants to assure that each of the parties is aware of this information and has given thought to these considerations. Aside from the fact that not to call it to their attention would be irresponsible, there is always the risk that if an agreement is concluded under such circumstances, the efficacy of that agreement will be undermined.

There is an inherent problem, however, if the mediator is the source of this information; for he cannot impart it without running the risk that one of the parties may feel that he is not being impartial. For example, if the mediator should advise the wife during the course of the mediation that under applicable state law her husband's pension is property in which she has an interest arising out of their marriage, then, whether correctly or incorrectly, her husband, who may well be sensitive to begin with about the issue of his pension, may feel that the mediator has taken sides with his wife.

By imparting all of this information in the material he presents the couple at the outset, however, the mediator effectively solves this problem and at the same time avoids the risk that the wife may not be aware of this fact. This is particularly true if, in addition to being contained in the more didactic sections of this material, it is also made a part of the questions. Thus, rather than telling the wife in the presence of her husband that she has the right, under the law, to assert an interest in her husband's pension, and asking her whether she wishes to, the mediator can instead simply direct the couple's attention to the question in the material which states, "Will either of you have any interest in the other's pension?", and then ask whether they have had an opportunity to give thought to this.

Because the information is presented to the couple in this way, it no longer seems to come from the mediator. Nor can it be interpreted as being personal to this couple, or directed to this specific husband's wife. It is simply part of the given, like the woodwork in the room, and no matter how sensitive the husband may be about his pension, it will be as difficult for him to direct his annoyance at the mediator as it will be for him to object to its being put on the table for discussion. Similarly, and to the extent that the wife may be hesitant to raise the question of her husband's pension on her own, despite her feeling that she should have an interest in it, it lifts from her shoulders the burden of having to do so. She did not bring it up; it was just there. In short, in the hands of an experienced mediator, this formal material can be used very effectively to put issues on the table, or to impart relevant information about issues that are already on the table, which the mediator would like to have it appear came other than from himself.

The Advisory Attorney

Particularly if the mediator is not an attorney, but even if he is, he will have to determine in advance his relationship to the other attorney or attorneys who will function in the mediation. Will he simply mediate all of the issues himself and then, when these are resolved and he has summarized the couple's understanding in writing, have them take that understanding to separate attorneys of their own choice (or perhaps to a single attorney) to have it reduced to writing? Will he provide them with a list of attorneys they may choose for that purpose? If he is an attorney, will he himself prepare the final agreement or, if he is not, will he direct them to an attorney with whom he works? Will he insist that each of them consult with separate attorneys prior to the commencement of the mediation, or at its conclusion? These are questions that the mediator must address. More importantly, they should be addressed and answered within the conceptual framework of mediation itself, and based on the assumptions that inform the mediator's efforts, and not, as too often has been the case, the assumptions that inform an adversarial view of divorce.

It is our very strong recommendation that if the mediator is not a lawyer himself, that he form an association with an attorney with whom he will work. Even if the mediator has provided a couple with information concerning the federal and state laws that impact upon their discussions, there are bound to be questions of a legal nature that will arise during the course of the mediation. Just as importantly, the mediation must ultimately result in a formal agreement, prepared by an attorney, that the parties must sign. In short, attorneys (or at least one attorney) are an essential element of the mediation, since there are necessarily legal functions to be performed. That being so, the question then is simply

how these functions are to be integrated into the mediation process and, more importantly, whether they will be integrated in a way that is consistent with the objectives of
mediation or at variance with them.

At the present time, it is still the widespread practice of mediators to disassociate
themselves from the legal function and to insist that each of the parties consult with
separate attorneys, either prior to the commencement of the mediation or at its conclusion; and that their separate attorneys prepare the ultimate agreement that they will sign.
While supposedly intended to protect each of the parties, and to meet certain objections of
the critics of mediation, this practice, rather than representing an appropriate compromise
between adversarial and nonadversarial procedures, only attempts to combine procedures
that are basically inconsistent with one another.

Thus, and as mediators have come to learn, the only thanks that they usually receive
for sending husbands and wives off to separate attorneys is to have them come back and
complain that they have been advised, on the one hand, that they got too little, and on the
other, that they gave too much—which, after all, is the most that the mediator had the
right to expect, in the first place, of attorneys who do not ask whether an agreement is *fair*
to their client, but only whether it is *best* for them.

The same is true if the mediator insists that the parties each review the finished
agreement, prepared by the lawyer with whom the mediator is associated, with their own
attorneys—not to pass judgment on the terms of the agreement, but to assure that it
properly reflects their understanding. When they return, the mediator will usually be
presented with numerous suggested changes in language. On occasion these suggested
changes may be very helpful. This will be the exception, however, particularly if the
mediator is working with a skilled attorney who has had a great deal of experience
preparing agreements of this nature. In fact, in most instances, they will do little but pose
gratuitous and, at times, difficult problems for the mediator.

These suggested language changes generally fall into two groups. In the first group
are those changes in language that literally effect no change at all. Although the mediator,
and even the attorney with whom he is associated, cannot help but wonder whether the
proposed changes stem from ignorance or, worse, whether they are an attempt on the
attorney's part to suggest to his client that he is actually doing something significant for
him when he is not, thereby justifying his fee, the client will usually put great stock in the
suggested changes, even if he does not understand them, which will more often than not
be the case.

The mediator now has a problem. In fact, he has a multitude of problems. If he does
not make the changes suggested by the party's attorney, why did he insist, or even
recommend, that the party consult with an attorney in the first place? If he takes issue with
the suggested changes, he may create a greater problem for himself, since the party may
feel that the mediator is attacking someone in whom he has confidence, and who is trying
to protect him. Finally, if he makes each and every change that has been suggested by the
attorney in question, he is allowing that attorney to dictate the language, if not the terms,
of the agreement. He is also creating a problem for the other party, who is forced to sit
there, undefended, and watch the agreement being altered at the direction of the other
party's attorney.

Suppose, instead, that the mediator attempts to resist the proposed change. To do
this, however, he must give a reason, which must either explicitly or implicitly call into

question the advice and recommendation, and perhaps even the competence, of the attorney in question. Moreover, he does this at the risk of finding himself viewed as acting as the other party's attorney, or at least appearing as if he is. It simply makes no sense for a mediator to insist that the parties seek separate representation only to be left with this dilemma. If the person left with this problem is the attorney/mediator himself, or the advisory attorney associated with him, it can be particularly vexatious; for it often leaves his own competence challenged by the incompetence of the attorney whom one of the parties has consulted.

In the second category are those changes of a more substantive nature. On the face of it, one would assume that these are just the kinds of changes that the mediator would welcome, and that might well be the case if they were the kind that took the understanding of the parties and expressed it in clearer language, thereby guaranteeing that it would be interpreted correctly. Unfortunately, however, these are rarely the kinds of substantive changes with which the mediator or the advisory attorney will be greeted. Rather, they will be the kinds of changes that adversarial attorneys spend their lifetime making, namely, changes in language that are calculated to improve the positions of their respective clients. However, it is precisely this kind of narrow-minded thinking, and the conduct it encourages, that mediation means to question.[8]

But isn't this a risk the mediator takes any time either or both parties consult with separate attorneys? More importantly, does he have a right to attempt to avoid that risk by making it a rule of mediation that the parties may not consult with separate attorneys? Obviously not. Aside from the fact that such instructions might well expose the agreement concluded by the parties to subsequent legal attack, it would be extremely inappropriate for a mediator to prevent either of the parties from obtaining whatever information or advice they may consider appropriate or necessary, regardless of the problems it may later pose for the mediator and perhaps even for the mediation itself. However, it is one thing to advise the parties that they have an absolute right to consult with attorneys of their own choice; it is quite another to institutionalize this requirement into mediation.

How then can one explain the fact that this requirement has so often been built into mediation practice? It is simply born of the naive belief that, despite all of its infirmities, adversarial proceedings do somehow protect each of the parties, and the unexamined assumption that, no matter how small the value of that protection, and how great the risk in attempting to obtain it, that it is nevertheless always justified. It is also encouraged by the failure of mediation to come to terms with the fact that what it is attempting to do for the couple is not only very different from, but even inconsistent with, the goals of traditional adversarial proceedings.

There is yet another problem involved in having each of the parties seek separate counsel at the conclusion of the mediation to prepare their final agreement, and that is that the mediator may lose control of the mediation. Procedurally, the two attorneys will not each prepare a draft agreement. Rather, one attorney will prepare the draft and send it to the other for his consideration. It will be rare that the second attorney will not want to make changes. Whether because he would resent the mediator's intrusion at this point, or because he would simply consider it wasteful to involve the mediator in these language changes, he will in all likelihood discuss them directly with the other attorney. It is possible that they will resolve them between themselves without incident. It is also possible that if there is a substantive disagreement that they will honor the mediation procedure and send each of their clients back to the mediator to discuss it further. There is also the danger, however, that both the clients and the mediator will be bypassed in the process and that the considerations that so often tend to affect attorneys' thinking will slowly but surely undermine the mediator's efforts and turn the whole matter into an adversarial proceeding.

There is only one way to minimize this risk, and to guarantee that the legal aspects of the proceedings will proceed consistent with the assumptions and goals of the mediation; and that is to incorporate both the legal and nonlegal aspects into the mediation procedure. If the mediator is an attorney, that means that he should himself discharge all of those obligations. If he is not, it means that he should associate himself with one, and that the services of that attorney should be incorporated as an integral part of the process. In other words, the couple should be informed from the outset that, in addition to meeting with the mediator, who will conduct the mediation, they will also be meeting with a knowledgable attorney who will answer whatever legal questions they have during the course of the mediation, and who will later prepare the final agreement they will eventually sign.

Does this mean that the mediator is subtly, and perhaps not so subtly, discouraging the use of outside attorneys, even if, at the same time, he is advising the parties that it is their absolute right to have separate attorneys? The answer is yes. Mediation represents a commitment to the idea that the interests of the parties and their family are best vouchsafed by the resolution of these issues in a *nonadversarial setting,* just as divorce lawyers are committed to the idea that the individual interests of the parties are best protected by the use of adversarial proceedings. If it is not a criticism of adversarial lawyers to say that they employ adversarial proceedings or that they encourage separating and divorcing couples to resort to them, then the same is equally true of divorce mediation. Unless divorce mediation wishes to continue to incorporate procedures into its practice that are inconsistent with its purpose, it is going to have to both understand and accept this.

If the mediator decides to associate himself with a particular attorney, the next question is: What should he look for in the attorney whom he selects? The mediator must be very careful here. While it is very important that he be conversant with the matrimonial law of the jurisdiction in question and, even more important, that he be an extremely careful and experienced draftsman, these credentials are not sufficient. To begin with, much of what an attorney knows and uses in his traditional practice has no place in mediation. Pleadings are not going to be prepared, motions are not going to be made, and a trial is not going to be conducted. The knowledge and skill that is required for the proper performance of these legal tasks is therefore largely irrelevant. Even in terms of knowledge of the substantive law, it is principally confined to the rather small body of legal rules that define the interests each of the parties have in their property, and their obligations to one another, as well as to their children, for their support.

What then are the skills that the mediator should look for in addition to those enumerated? To begin with, the attorney should be one who, to paraphrase the words of Chief Justice Warren E. Burger, would prefer to see himself as the healer of human conflict rather than as an advocate of that conflict.[9] By definition, that means that he has been able to distance himself enough from adversarial principles and procedures as to be able to see them as simply a means to an end—and only *one* or *many means* to that end—and not as a quasireligious set of beliefs. Secondly, he must be someone who has good counseling skills and who is comfortable in that role. Even though the role of the mediator and the advisory attorney should be sharply delineated, it is as impossible as it is unnecessary to make such a delineation absolute.

Thus, and while it is certainly not necessary that a mediator be an attorney, or even expert in matrimonial law, he must be generally conversant with the divorce law in his jurisdiction, and even with tax law for that matter, at least to the extent that it bears upon the issues before him. If the law in the state in which the mediator practices says that a husband's pension is considered to be property in which both of the parties have an interest arising out of their marriage, the mediator must know this so that this pension can be put on the table as an item of business to be discussed.

Similarly, and although the attorney need hardly be a trained mental health professional, let alone have the counseling skills of one, when he answers the questions the couple pose, and particularly when he reviews with them the draft agreement he has prepared, he will often be presented with the same nonlegal (emotional) issues with which the mediator was confronted; and to do his job properly he will have to be able to recognize and possess the basic skills necessary to deal effectively with them. Lastly, the attorney must be one who either has, or can be taught, the assumptions implicit in the mediator's view of the problem separating and divorcing couples face, and who can come to learn to look at the couple's problem from that set of assumptions.

Having selected an appropriate attorney with whom to work, the mediator must then decide how their separate duties will be discharged. While this will vary from mediator to mediator, and may well change in time as the mediator and the attorney develop a working relationship with one another, and as their skills begin more and more to overlap, it is nevertheless suggested that the following procedure be employed as a starting point. At least in the beginning, the linchpin in the procedure should be the mediator, and the couple should be encouraged to view the attorney simply as a resource person who will be employed during the course of the mediation when and as needed, and at the conclusion of the mediation when it is necessary to reduce their understanding to a formal written agreement. In short, the mediation should be conducted by the mediator without the attorney present.

There are a number of reasons for this. First, it is simply a waste of time, effort, and money for both the mediator and the attorney to be employed at the same time. Second, the attorney may tend to have greater status in the eyes of the couple than the mediator. To incorporate the attorney as a coequal participant in the mediation may thus only detract from the power of the mediator himself, a power important for him to retain if the mediation is to proceed effectively. Finally, they may simply get in one another's way.

Ideally, the best procedure would be for the advisory attorney to be present at the first or, preferably, the *second* meeting with the couple, to be introduced to them by the mediator, to allow him briefly to explain his role to the couple and to give them an opportunity to ask him whatever questions they may have prior to the commencement of the mediation. The advisory attorney would then advise each of the parties that he will be available to answer whatever other questions may arise for them in the course of mediation. Following this he would then excuse himself, and the mediator proceed with the mediation.

Unfortunately, ideal as this procedure may be, it is not very practical. Even if the mediator and the attorney share the same offices, which is unlikely, to do this will require that they coordinate their separate schedules for what will, in all likelihood, be but a brief appearance by the attorney. As a result, this procedure will rarely be employed. Being unable to adopt this procedure, many mediators who work hand in hand with an advisory attorney go to the other extreme and postpone the meeting between the couple and the attorney until the mediation is concluded and it is time for the attorney to prepare the agreement. As we will see, this is not the best solution.

We would recommend the following. After the couple has decided to proceed with mediation and been given whatever material the mediator provides, they should be instructed to schedule a joint meeting with the advisory attorney before the actual mediation begins. Aside from the fact that it makes far more sense for a couple to learn what they may feel they need to know, and to have an opportunity to have their questions answered, *before* the mediation begins, rather than after it is concluded, if properly handled, this meeting can aid the purposes of the mediation. Again, it adds an aura of professionalism to the procedure which, hopefully, will tend to support the suggestion of thoroughness that the mediator wishes to convey and add to the confidence each of the parties will then place in the process.

Furthermore, meeting formally with an attorney in this way may tend to blunt the distinction between the two procedures and encourage the parties in the belief that their interests are being protected in much the same way that they would be had they resorted to adversarial proceedings. To be sure, in an adversarial setting they would each be meeting with separate attorneys rather than with one attorney; but a skilled advisory attorney can easily turn this distinction into an advantage.

For example, he can point out that while in adversarial proceedings everything takes place secretly, behind closed doors, in mediation everything is open and above board. He can also emphasize the fact that since an adversarial attorney uses legal rules as weapons, and does not give the same answer to a wife that he gives to a husband, he could not meet with both parties together. That is not the case in mediation, however. On the contrary, since his purpose is to *educate* them as to the law, and to help them *use it constructively*, he *wants* each of them to hear the answers that he gives to the *other's* questions—which is why he is meeting with them together and never meets with them separately.

The advisory attorney must conduct this meeting very skillfully. On the one hand, he wants to be warm and engaging, and to have each of the parties feel comfortable, creating the same sense of confidence the mediator imparted in his initial meeting with them. However, he must be very careful not to interfere with the role of the mediator or worse, to usurp his power. On the contrary, he must use this opportunity to *enhance* the mediator in the couple's eyes. For example, he should explain to them that not only has he worked with the mediator for a considerable period of time, but specifically chose to work with him because of his skill and experience. He should also reinforce the fact that although the mediator is not an attorney, for which reason it is he rather than the mediator who is answering their legal questions, this does not mean he is not conversant with the law. He is actually very familiar with the legal rules and principles that affect their discussions even if he is not permitted, as a matter of law, to express *legal opinions*.

In all likelihood, it will not be necessary for the couple to meet with the advisory attorney again until the mediation is concluded, though they should be afforded the opportunity to do so if either of them considers it desirable. The only rule that must be followed is that, regardless of who has a question to ask, *both* parties must be present at each and every meeting with the advisory attorney.

The principal function of the advisory attorney will be performed after the couple have come to a tentative understanding and it is time for him to prepare a draft of their agreement. Here, one of two procedures can be employed. The advisory attorney can prepare the draft of the agreement from the notes sent to him by the mediator and then call the couple in to go over that draft. Or he can meet with the couple before he begins the draft to go over those notes, to make sure that he completely understands their agreement and to fill in any gaps.

This is probably a question of style, and perhaps also a function of how lengthy are the notes the mediator provides him. Mediators who do not work consistently with an advisory attorney, and who therefore do not know who the attorney will be who will ultimately draft the agreement, tend to prepare a very lengthy summary of the parties' agreement, which has become known as a memorandum of understanding. That memorandum is then given to each of the parties to take to their respective attorneys, or perhaps to a single attorney chosen from a list provided the couple by the mediator.

Preparing these lengthy memoranda is, unfortunately, very time-consuming and, in many ways, a wasteful process, born of necessity. For a mediator who works consistently with the same advisory attorney, however, experience, and the procedures which they employ, can greatly reduce the time the mediator will have to spend in the preparation of these memoranda, without any loss in terms of the thoroughness or quality of the ultimate agreement.

Whichever of the two procedures is employed, once the agreement has been prepared by the advisory attorney, a copy of that agreement should be sent to each of the parties for them to review, in their own home and at their own pace, before they come in to meet with the advisory attorney to go over it. Moreover, they should be clearly advised that the agreement they have received is a draft, and a draft only, and that in no event will they ever sign it. They should be instructed to read it over carefully and to make any notes or comments directly on the draft. They should also be told that it is expected that there may well be changes that they may wish to make in that agreement—not because either they or the advisory attorney got it wrong, but simply because anytime an understanding is reduced to writing it may appear different than they expected, or because one or both may have second thoughts about the agreement. That is why it has been prepared as a draft and that is why, though it is a *complete* agreement in all respects, it has not been prepared for them to *sign*.

When the advisory attorney meets with the couple to review the draft agreement, he can again follow one of two procedures. He can review the agreement with the couple and, if there are any changes either of them wish to make that they are not in agreement about, can then discuss those suggested changes with them himself, one by one, in much the same way that the mediator did during the course of the mediation and, it would be hoped, resolve them. Or he can simply go over the agreement with them, make a list of the open issues, and then send the couple back to the mediator to discuss them with him.

Again, this is mainly a question of style. Some attorneys may feel more comfortable staying closer to the traditional role of a scrivener and in relying upon the greater counseling experience of the mediator to address these issues. Others may feel very comfortable dealing with these issues, particularly if they are not too complex, and may in fact have been drawn to mediation because they wished to balance their regular practice by employing their skills in this area. It may also be a question of experience as well as style and, in time, and particularly as the mediator and the advisory attorney work more closely together, the advisory attorney may assume more of the mediation functions in wrapping up the agreement at this point.

An Agreement with the Couple

It is common practice for many mediators to enter into a formal, written agreement with a couple prior to the commencement of the mediation. Ostensibly, the purpose of this agreement is to *set forth the goals* of the mediation and the *procedures* that will be employed by the mediator. From the mediator's standpoint, it may also serve to set forth the *ground rules* to be followed in the course of the mediation. Thus, mediators have traditionally used it for the purpose of obtaining an agreement between the parties that they will at all times be fair with one another; that they will not engage in negative patterns of communication or indulge in emotional outbursts during the course of the mediation; and that they will make full and complete disclosure of all of their income and assets. Not infrequently, it will also contain a provision granting the mediator the right to terminate the mediation should he conclude that either or both parties have violated any of their obligations, or if he feels that the agreement they have reached is unfair to one of them.

While born of the same concerns that inform so much of the protectionist attitude that exists in mediation circles today, the fact remains that these agreements serve *no useful purpose*, are *ill-informed* and, in many instances, *counterproductive*.

To begin with, it is not for the mediator to set the rules and conditions of the mediation and, except in rare instances, all these decisions should be left to the parties themselves. Unlike traditional adversarial proceedings, or even arbitration, with but very few exceptions, the *rule in mediation* is that there are *no predetermined rules*. This leaves the autonomy in the hands of the couple themselves, where it belongs, and it should be left at that. Secondly, to exact these kinds of commitments from the parties is akin to asking a five-year-old to promise that he will be a good boy. He either will or he will not, and after but a short time his promise will have very little to do with it.

Lastly, and perhaps most importantly, in certain instances the conduct the mediator is attempting to proscribe is not necessarily as improper or counterproductive as he assumes, notwithstanding the pejorative labels, such as "negative" or "inappropriate," that he attaches to it. Thus, and while a mediator may not wish to *encourage* emotional outbursts, this does not mean that they may not well be understandable, appropriate, and worse, even productive. Sometimes these emotional outbursts serve as necessary escape valves for pent-up emotions. Sometimes they are necessary means to bring home a certain reality, such as the fact that there is a line beyond which a party will not be pushed. Sometimes they serve merely to clear the air. And sometimes they signal to the mediator the true bottled-up emotional issue that underlies, and is distorting, the discussion that is taking place.

This is not to suggest that it is inappropriate to have an agreement with the parties. It is only to take issue with many of the items that mediators routinely include in those agreements. Thus, it is often useful to have a formal agreement as to the *fees* that the couple will be charged and how and when they will be required to pay them. This is perhaps less important where a mediator, functioning very much like a mental health professional, simply charges the couple by the session and collects his fee at the conclusion of each meeting. However, if the mediator is going to be working with an advisory attorney, whose fees the couple will be agreeing to pay at the same time, it would be best to commit all of this to writing at the outset so as to avoid later misunderstanding. This is particularly true if the mediator and the attorney will be charging different hourly or per-session rates, or if the attorney will be working on a fixed-fee basis to be paid in install-ments.

The second purpose that a writing serves is to protect the mediation process itself. There is certain information that the mediator wishes to assure that the parties have heard and understood, not only because they should properly have this information, but also because he does not want one of them to be able to complain later that he was not aware of it at the time. Thus, if the mediator does not want to be faced with a party who may later have second thoughts about the agreement that he has signed and who claims that he had not been told, for example, that he could consult with an attorney of his own choice before signing it, it would be advisable to have each of the parties sign a letter acknowledg-ing that they have been specifically informed that they had this right.

The mediator, obviously, will not present this letter to the couple with the suggestion that he is asking them to sign it to protect the mediation process, and perhaps even himself. He will use it to advance the purpose of the mediation. Thus, he tells them that to insure that he has not forgotten to tell them anything important for them to know, and also to insure that they have heard and understood it, he has adopted the procedure of summarizing certain of the discussions they have had at their initial meeting in a letter he will send them before their first mediation session and which he will ask them to sign at that time, acknowledging that they have read it and understand it. This is also an appropriate procedure to follow at the conclusion of the mediation, and before the couple sign their final agreement, to record, for example, the couple's acknowledgment that they have each had an adequate opportunity to read over their agreement, and to discuss it with whomever they wished, before signing it.

THE SPACING AND LENGTH OF THE MEDIATION SESSIONS

Although the scheduling of meetings is discretionary with the mediator, it will be our recommendation that, at least as a general rule, the meetings be scheduled about a week apart if possible. The spacing of the meetings stems from two considerations. On the one hand, the mediator wishes to leave enough time between the meetings to permit each of the parties to *digest* what has taken place at the previous session and to think about the issues they are discussing. At the same time, he does not wish such a lapse of time between meetings that *continuity* is lost or the issues under discussion are no longer fresh in the parties' minds. From our experience, spacing the meetings about once every week tends to serve both purposes.

The second question the mediator must address is how long each session will last. Some mediators, particularly those from a mental health background, who are used to working within a forty-five minute to an hour period, favor shorter sessions. They believe that by keeping the sessions to a definite, fixed length (never less than an hour, however), they add a certain discipline to the proceedings and thereby force the couple to use their time more constructively. Other mediators conduct more open-ended sessions and terminate the meeting, usually after two or three hours, when they feel that attention is waning and time is not being used as valuably as it should.

We would recommend a compromise between these two positions. For most mediators, the issues under discussion do not lend themselves to the time limitations of a therapeutic session. At the same time, they find two- or three-hour sessions too exhausting for mediator and couple alike, and not justified in results. They prefer a fixed session of about an hour and a half in length. From our experience, this length of time represents a healthy balance between these two competing considerations. Obviously, there will be situations in which these general guidelines will be varied. A husband will be shortly transferred by his employer and it is imperative that the couple and the mediator meet twice, and perhaps even three times, a week in order to conclude an agreement. A particular issue may prompt a discussion which a mediator does not want to have to cut off abruptly, particularly when the discussion is leading to fruitful results.

On other occasions, the mediator may himself vary these general rules for his own purposes. For example, he may feel in a particular situation that enormous amounts of time are being used to discuss minute and trivial details. He may therefore attempt to make the couple more appreciative of the time they have by advising them that, because of other commitments, he will not be able to give them more than an hour at their next meeting. In some instances, the mediator may feel that the couple is simply using the sessions as the occasion to ventilate their hurt and anger at one another. He may therefore advise them that he will not be able to meet with them the following week and that the next appointment he can make with them will have to be in two weeks.

While, to a great extent, the spacing and the length of sessions is appropriately discretionary with the mediator, and perhaps even a question of style, there is one procedure that we must comment upon, and take exception to, even though it is admittedly rarely employed. This is the *marathon* mediation session. While such marathon sessions may be understandable in labor mediation, and while it may be appropriate in those instances to take advantage of the participants' worn-down condition to bring home the reality of the importance of an agreement, and perhaps even the *triviality* of the issues that are standing between them and that agreement, such conduct is absolutely inappropriate in divorce mediation.

Divorce mediation is not an EST meeting or a marriage encounter. Nor is it ever appropriate to create *artificial emotional environments* that either stimulate or overpower one or both of the parties, or that serve as a means of empowering the mediator. This is not to suggest that the mediator does not have power or that he will not use it; nor is it to deny that there will be powerful emotions in play during the course of the mediation. It is simply to proscribe any attempt artificially to fan those emotions, or to substitute for them surrogate emotions. It is also to deplore a mediator's attempt to use his power charismatically.

SETTING AND ATTIRE

If at all possible, the mediator should meet with the couple in an informal setting. Ideally, the mediator and the couple will sit in a circle with perhaps a small coffee table in the middle. Given that there is a certain amount of work with papers, as well as note taking on the part of the mediator and perhaps on the part of the couple, some mediators like to work around a table. If that is the case, it should be a simple, round table. Plain, conference-type chairs with arms, that both swivel and tilt, are particularly good since they combine a businesslike setting and an informal and comfortable atmosphere at the same time.

While dress is admittedly a question of style, it will be our strong recommendation that the mediator dress in a businesslike manner—in either a business or sports suit with a jacket and tie—rather than in slacks and a sport shirt, as is increasingly becoming common practice in the mental health profession. People who consult with a professional do so because they have a problem, often a very serious one, and because they want help. Certainly that is the case of the couple who have come to the mediator. They not only want to deal with someone who is qualified, and capable of taking care of their problem; they also want to *feel* that they are dealing with such a person, and they have a right to this.

It is no answer to say that a surgeon is as competent in a T-shirt and pair of shorts as he would be if he were dressed in surgical garb. The fact remains that if a professional wears the attire that the person ascribes to his profession (be it a clerical collar, a doctor's white jacket or an attorney's business suit), the person seeking help feels more reassured that he is getting *professional advice* and *professional service*. And he is *entitled* to that assurance. If the professional gives less than this, he is doing so because it meets his *own* convenience, or because it serves his own purposes rather than the needs of those he is supposed to serve. Worse, his casual attire tends to deny the seriousness of what to the couple is very serious business indeed. This is particularly so in the case of divorce mediation, and everything about the mediator, both verbally and nonverbally, should convey his *awareness* of just how *serious* is the concern that has brought the couple to him. At times during the course of the mediation, one or the other party will look to the mediator for guidance through the shoals of the troubled waters they are navigating. They want to be able to trust him and to rely on his assurance that it is safe for them to proceed and move forward. He must do everything in his power to make it possible for them to be able to do this, including presenting himself in a way that will reinforce that confidence.

This is not to suggest that the mediator should be formal or unapproachable. That will not do either. Rather, he should try to strike the kind of balance that is expressed in the saying that he should never be *so professional as to be unfriendly*; nor should he ever be *so friendly that he ceases to be professional*.

Co-Mediation

At the present time, a number of models of mediation are employed. In part, this diversity stems from the fact that mediation is still in its infancy, and there is thus understandably a certain amount of experimentation. In part, it simply represents a question of style. In part also, however, it represents a *misunderstanding* of what divorce mediation *is* and *how it works*.

Since the issues that will be raised in mediation obviously call upon the skills of many professionals (the legal profession, the accounting profession, the mental health profession, etc.), some practitioners initially felt that a *team* consisting of professionals from these various fields would provide the best mediation. This is *not* the case, however. These various professionals are needed simply as *resource* people to address specific, and usually limited, issues, much as a real-estate appraiser would be called in if there were a question as to the value of a piece of real property owned by the parties. To have these various professionals sitting around during the entire mediation, however, is an unnecessary expenditure of both talent and money. It is also awkward when they have little if anything to contribute, and counterproductive when they join in (or interrupt) when they should not. They should be employed, therefore, only on a when-and-if-needed basis, and not as co-mediators, or permanent members of the mediation team.

Another co-mediation model has been borrowed from sex therapy, where, and principally for reasons of gender identity, a team consisting of a male and female therapist is generally employed. There is something to be said for this approach, since the use of a single mediator leaves one of the parties potentially outnumbered and possibly feeling that the mediator cannot understand the problem from his or her perspective. This is not a critical factor, however, only a limiting one, and competent mental health professionals who do conjoint family therapy deal with this problem day in and day out.

More importantly, and while there are potential advantages to this procedure, there are also possible disadvantages. To be sure, a team of mediators who work with one another over an extended period of time will develop a sense for one another that will enable them to blend their contributions. But it is just as likely that they will at times get in one another's way. Most of what a mediator does is based, not on a preestablished set of procedures, but on his sense of what is appropriate or inappropriate at the time. No matter how attuned two mediators may be to one another, it is very unlikely that their individual senses at any given point in time will always be the same. There is thus always the danger that they may get in one another's way.

Accordingly, and while there is certainly nothing wrong in this approach, it has to be questioned whether its benefits are not outweighed by its detriments, particularly given the fact that it requires a duplication of time and effort on the part of two mediators and, therefore, a greater cost to the couple.

A team of co-mediators, consisting of a therapist and either an accountant or an attorney, also arose from the conviction that mediation involves both technical as well as practical issues. However, and as anyone who has done any amount of mediation knows, the financial and legal questions that are at issue are really in no way as complex as they may at first appear, and most mediators quickly pick up all the technical information they will need to know on a day-to-day basis to do mediation. Should something out of the ordinary occur, and if the mediation facility does not have an attorney or an accountant on staff, the couple can easily be referred to one for that purpose, and this is again a far more sensible and economical way of employing these professionals.

In our view, the model that should ideally become the prevailing one for divorce mediation in the future is that of the single mediator, just as the single psychotherapist is the more prevalent model in the mental health field. A mediator has his own sense and his own style. It is not necessarily right or wrong; it is simply a style that he is comfortable with and that works for him. No matter how effective his co-mediator's style may be, more often than not it will simply get in his way. Rare indeed will be a team of mediators so attuned to one another that they will conduct themselves, and appear, as one, like two synchronized Olympian swimmers. Within a short time, these differences will become apparent and, while they may not actually undermine the trust that the mediators hope the couple will repose in them, they will certainly do nothing to reinforce it. More importantly, they may only tend to detract from one another's power or to defuse it, and that power—the trust that each of the parties has in the mediator—is often the critical factor in the success or failure of the mediation.

Children in Mediation

Since what occurs in mediation affects the parties' children, it is sometimes felt by mediators that they should be involved in the mediation, at least to a limited extent. Some mediators go so far as to recommend, and even mildly insist, that the children be present during at least one session so that the parents and the mediator can express to them the fact that they are attempting to conclude, or have concluded, an agreement that will properly provide for them in the future, and to assure them of both of their parents' contii.uing concern for their well-being.

On the face of it, this may seem all well and good, and even responsible conduct on the part of the mediator. We would question it, however, and question as well whether it is not simply part of a tendency to *romanticize* mediation, rather than accept it as the responsible procedure that it is assumed to be. Parents, as adults, have a responsibility to take care of their children, and their children have a need to be taken care of and protected. Their children do not want or need to know *how* that will be done, however. What they want and need to know is simply that it *will* be done. In fact, to embroil them too much in how it will be done is only to lay bare the fact that getting it done is to some extent a problem, in fact a far greater problem than they realize, and to rouse their fears and feelings of insecurity. It is not that one wants to keep children in ignorance; it is simply that it serves no purpose to *educate them prematurely* about problems that they do not understand and cannot solve.

Obviously, parents must assure their children that all will be well, and that they will be taken care of, despite their divorce. However, children should receive this assurance from their parents, and not from their parents' mediator. More importantly, they should be told this in the protective environment of their home rather than in the strange and perhaps even frightening environment that the mediator's office represents. In fact, to receive this assurance in a mediator's office may only be to give the children a double message, and thereby increase the very anxiety that the mediator and the parents are attempting to assuage. This is not to suggest that there is never an occasion in which it would be appropriate to include the children, or one or more of them, in a meeting with the mediator. It is only to suggest that this should not be done as a matter of course. And no pressure should be placed upon a parent to include a child if he or she feels uncomfortable about doing so.

When a child is brought into the mediation, it is usually at the request of one or both of the parents. What should the mediator do if one of the parties would like the children brought into the mediation but the other does not? We would advise a mediator never to bring the children into the mediation over the objection of either of the parties, and that he should refuse to do so. Nevertheless, he must be careful how he handles the request. If the mediator turns down the suggestion, and since the party who has made it may well have a great deal of his self-esteem invested in the suggestion, he may take it as a personal judgment about himself. There is also the risk that he may view the mediator's opinion as a sign that the mediator has taken sides with his spouse. The mediator must thus be very careful how he handles this. The procedure to follow is simply to say that the mediator has a rule he consistently follows, and that is that he will never do anything—in this case bring the children into the mediation—unless they are both in agreement that they want him to do it. In this manner the mediator can best deal with the problem without offending the party who has made the suggestion.

RELATIONS WITH THE PARTIES' ATTORNEYS

On occasion, the mediator may receive a written communication from one of the party's attorneys. These communications can take various forms. It may be a communication requesting that the mediator include certain provisions in the couple's agreement. It may simply be a communication informing the mediator that the attorney has advised his client that he has no legal obligation to make a payment in the amount, or for the duration of time, that has been suggested by the wife, or perhaps even agreed to by his client. It may even be a communication to the effect that unless the mediation concludes in conformity with the advice he has given to his client, he has instructed his client not to sign the agreement, and that litigation will immediately ensue.

How should the mediator deal with communications such as this? Completely to ignore the communication would perhaps be impolite, and might even cause the party whose attorney has sent the letter to become annoyed with the mediator on that account. On the other hand, for the mediator to respond to the substance of the communication is only to create an even greater problem. Each of the parties is at liberty to consult with whomever they wish—their parents, their friends and neighbors, their lovers, or their attorneys—concerning any of the matters at issue in the mediation. The advice they get may not be very helpful. In fact, it may be misguided, or tend to undermine the mediation. Nevertheless, it is their absolute right to seek and, should they be so advised, to listen to this advise.

While this is a party's absolute right, however, it has nothing to do with the mediator or with the mediation. In short, while it may affect how the party who has received the advice may feel and what he may decide to do, and while the mediator may have to deal with that fact, he mut not allow the party in question, or his attorney, to make it *his* problem. In each instance, and whether that advice comes simply from a friend or from an attorney, the party will have to decide whether or not he wishes to act upon it. That is *his* problem and not the mediator's, and by *refusing* to make it his *own* problem, the mediator must underscore this fact.

The mediator should politely communicate this to the party whose attorney has communicated with him, or to the attorney directly, depending on the circumstances. [10] If he responds to the attorney directly, a copy of that letter should be sent to the attorney's client to avoid the possibility that the attorney may inaccurately report the contents to his client.

Should a copy of this letter be sent to the other party? This represents a dilemma for the mediator. On the one hand, he is treating the attorney's communication as a noncommunication—as something that has nothing to do with the mediation, and is not a part of it. To send the other party copies of the communications from and to the attorney in question, however, is only to introduce the attorney's communication into the mediation through the back door. On the other hand, to fail to advise the other party of these communications (that the mediator has not only received a communication from the other party's attorney but has responded to that communication) is improperly to keep information from the other party that, though not relevant to the *issues* under discussion, is nevertheless relevant to the *mediation*, since it creates a potential issue in the *relationship* between the mediator and the other party.

Perhaps the best procedure, though admittedly not an ideal one, is simply to send the other party a copy of the mediator's reply to the attorney's letter but not a copy of the communication to which it refers. While the curiosity of the other party cannot but be aroused by the omission of the original communication, it is perhaps better to suffer the consequences of this offended curiosity than it is to suffer the consequences that may follow from a reading of that original communication.

What if the communication from the party's attorney is a telephone call? This poses an even more difficult problem for the mediator, and he must be very careful here. He does not wish to be impolite or to offend the attorney in question, who may be acting in good faith. Nor, however, does he wish to allow him to interject himself into the mediation. If he does not hear the attorney out, at least to a certain extent, he may appear curt and abrupt. On the other hand, if he permits the attorney completely to have his say, then he may find himself stuck with the information. To make matters worse, and since the attorney is an advocate for one of the parties and has, therefore, probably not thought out the problem from the mediator's standpoint, let alone appreciated his predicament, the mediator must be very careful in what he says, for he cannot offend the attorney without also running the risk of offending the party whom the attorney represents.

Perhaps the best procedure to follow is to put the problem in adversarial terms that the attorney will understand. Thus, the mediator should explain to the attorney that although he would like to have his help and assistance, he has a problem in speaking with him privately, as there is always the danger that the other party may *misinterpret* their conversations, feel that he is being *improperly influenced* by him, and perhaps even come to feel that he has lost his *impartiality*. Thus, he has adopted the procedure of requesting that all communications from either of the parties' attorneys be in writing. This way, and in keeping with the spirit of mediation, everything is on the table for both of the parties to see. He would therefore appreciate it if the attorney would send him a letter incorporating his suggestions. The mediator might also consider following up the telephone call with a letter to the attorney summarizing their conversation. It will not only serve to minimize the risk that the attorney's client may receive a distorted impression of their conversation, through poor translation, but will also serve to reinforce, in the other party's mind, the mediator's integrity and forthright conduct.

Suppose, instead, that the communication that the mediator receives from the attorney is for permission to attend the next mediation session. Suppose even that this request comes from one of the parties themselves. Suppose further that both of the parties request the presence of their attorneys. This poses an extremely difficult problem for the mediator. The parties, again, have an absolute right to whatever assistance they wish, and the mediator certainly does not wish to put himself in a position where it appears, or could be reasonably suggested, that he is attempting to prevent them from availing themselves of such assistance. There is a big difference, however, if that assistance is offered outside of his office than it is if it is given during the course of the mediation itself.

To begin with, and despite the quaint conceit of some matrimonial lawyers that what they have been doing all of these years in negotiation agreements for clients with other attorneys is really to have been mediating them, there is a fundamental difference between adversarial negotiations and mediation, whether they recognize it or not. If the couple wish to engage in negotiations, they have every right to do so. This does not mean, however, that the mediator is under an obligation to provide them with his office for that purpose, let alone to convert the mediation into an adversarial proceeding, which is inevitably what will happen if the parties appear with their own attorneys.

The problem becomes compounded even further if the request comes from only one of the parties. On the face of it, the problem here is that the other party is left undefended, and having to fend for himself. In actual fact, however, this is not as great a problem as it may at first appear, and a competent and experienced mediator could easily handle it. The real problem is that in doing so the mediator is cast in the role of the other party's defender. This is an extremely awkward position for the mediator to be in and he must not permit it to occur.

In short, the mediator cannot permit the mediation to be *turned into something other than it is supposed to be*. If that means that the mediator is setting limits on the assistance that one of the parties is able to receive, and only permits him to receive that assistance between the sessions but not at the sessions, so be it. The party in question will then have to decide which procedure he wishes to employ, mediation or adversarial negotiations. But he *cannot have both*.

Is this to suggest that there is never an appropriate occasion for the parties' separate attorneys to be present during any portion of the mediation? It is dangerous to make blanket pronouncements, as there may well be instances when their participation would not only be appropriate but perhaps even helpful. Certainly that would be the case if the two lawyers came to the mediation with the attitude of meeting together in an effort to solve a common problem rather than simply to come out with what is best for their respective clients, and perhaps in time attorneys may learn to adopt such a constructive attitude. But they do not approach their representation with this attitude at the present time, and a mediator must understand this in making his decision.

The problem posed by the parties' separate attorneys is not simply occasioned by the fact that their respective adversarial positions are inconsistent with the nonadversarial character of mediation. It also stems from the fact that the mediator may well have sanctioned, and even encouraged, each of the parties to seek separate representation. But why has the mediator suggested that they do this if he is not then willing to accept the recommendations of the attorneys with whom they have consulted? The mediator is between a rock and a hard place, and he must be very careful. The party in question views his attorney as his ally. It is impossible, therefore, for the mediator to attack the attorney's recommendation without attacking that party as well. Nevertheless, he cannot permit the attorney in question to control the mediation or dictate the terms of the couple's agreement. The mediator will therefore have to feel his way through the thicket very carefully. Sometimes, and particularly if he feels that his relationship with the party in question is secure, he can openly discuss his dilemma. If he does this, he can also underscore the situation by indirectly asking him how he would feel had the suggested changes come, not from his attorney, but from his spouse's attorney.

THE INITIAL MEETING

Having prepared the material he will need and established the procedures he will follow, at least initially, the mediator is now ready to meet with the couple. This will probably be the most important meeting he will have with them and it is critical to the mediation that it be conducted carefully.

How the mediator conducts this initial meeting, just as how he will conduct the mediation in general, will again be a function of how he answers the questions posed in the opening paragraph of Chapter 10. If he follows the prevailing view of divorce mediation, and apart from providing the couple with information about how the mediation will proceed and answering whatever questions they may have, the initial meeting, and usually the next one or two meetings, will be concerned with *assessing the relationship* between the parties and their suitability for mediation; collecting whatever information he considers necessary for the proper conduct of the mediation; determining the *issues* in dispute and the positions of each of the parties with respect to these issues; and seeing to the preparation of their respective *budgets*. It may also include arranging for the *valuation* of certain of their property, such as their home, a business or professional practice either of them may own, and any retirement benefits to which they may be entitled.

Because we would answer these questions very differently, the procedures we would recommend will also be very different. From our standpoint, and since the success of the mediation will depend, not upon all of this information, but on the *rapport* the mediator establishes between himself and each of the parties, and the trust that they come to repose in him, the initial meeting will be used principally for that purpose. At the same time, and since the mediator knows that what stands between the parties and the conclusion of an agreement between themselves are the painful feelings with which one or both of them is struggling, it will also be used subtly to ferret out these emotional trouble spots and even to begin to address them. Finally, he will try to make each of the parties feel comfortable with the mediation process itself, and attempt to assuage whatever fears or misgivings they may have about it.

THE COUPLE ARRIVES

When the parties arrive, the mediator will often immediately notice their discomfort, or at least the discomfort of one of them. This is a very difficult experience and it is awkward for them to be there. It is doubly awkward for them to be there together, and to have to attempt to deal, in an impersonal, businesslike manner, with something that is so acutely painful and has so many personal emotional overtones. Also, the mediator is a stranger to them, which only adds to the couple's discomfort. At least initially, the mediator should simply note this discomfort but not comment upon it. Instead, and in a warm and reassuring manner, he should introduce himself and, after he has given them an opportunity to read whatever material he has prepared for them in advance, invite them into his office.

Throughout the mediation, the mediator follows two somewhat inconsistent truisms. The first tells him that beneath the surface of what he sees, and often of what is being discussed, is a world of emotions that critically affect what is taking place before him. The second truism is that both as a practical matter, and because he wishes to respect the parties' privacy, he does not address or even outwardly acknowledge these feelings unless they interfere with the course of the mediation or the ability of the parties to participate meaningfully in what is being discussed.

The initial interview with the couple represents an exception to that second rule. At a later point, the mediator may well have to call upon the trust that each of the parties has reposed in him to help them over certain of the trouble spots they will encounter. To do this, however, he must first gain that trust. That, in turn, means addressing at least a measure of that emotionality and bridging some of the distance between them.

As we have noted previously, and although the mediator will always take an active part in the mediation, he will be more the responder than the initiator. Having set forth the goals of the mediation, and defined its structure in broad outline, his role will not be so much to lead the mediation as to set it in motion, to redirect it when it becomes misdirected, and to free it up when it becomes stuck. In his initial meeting with the couple, however, the mediator has a specific job to do. He wants to establish a relationship between himself and each of the parties. He wants to convey to them that he understands just how difficult what they are doing is, and that it is his sincere desire to help them. Finally, he wants to begin to create the setting and emotional environment which will enable him to do that. His immediate concern is to get a personal sense of the couple. Most importantly, knowing as he does that one of the parties probably does not even wish to be there, he wants to identify that party's pain and address it.

At the time that the initial consultation was scheduled over the telephone, the mediator obtained some general information about the couple to help him initiate the discussion. He now wants to use that information to identify them more exactly so that he will know what it is that he has to do and how to proceed to do it. One or two questions will be sufficient for that purpose. "I know from my experience," he begins, "that the decision to separate and divorce is usually not a joint one. Is that the case here?" This, or any one of a number of other possible questions, will not only enable the mediator to identify the person in pain but will also serve as an opening for him to reach out to that person.

Having begun to do this, however, the mediator may immediately be confronted with an issue he must resolve. Now that their respective interests are out in the open, the mediator may have a problem in that they would each like to proceed in a different direction, the one to discuss attempting to work out the problems in their *marriage*, and the other to discuss working out the problems in their *divorce*. The mediator must be very careful here. Most mediators, be they mental health professionals or attorneys, came to mediation out of a concern for the *family* and the effects that the divorcing process has upon it. Understandably, therefore, their bias is usually in favor of maintaining the marital relationship if that is possible.

Nevertheless, it would be very wrong for the mediator to put the party who is seeking the divorce in the awkward position of having to defend himself against both his spouse and the mediator. He did not come to the mediator for that purpose; nor did he expect to be put in that position. The mediator must therefore respect his decision. At the same time, it is equally important that the mediator convey to the party who would like to save the marriage that he *understands* that desire; that despite the fact that he is a divorce mediator, his primary interest lies in marriage and not in divorce; and that if both of the parties wish him to do so (but only if they *both* so wish), he will be glad to refer them to a competent family therapist to discuss these issues.

Suppose both parties express a willingness to discuss the problems in the marriage with a view to resolving them. Assuming that the mediator is professionally qualified to do so, should he undertake to do this himself? Without wishing to lay down a hard-and-fast rule, it would nevertheless be our suggestion that he refrain. To begin with, if his efforts are unsuccessful—and at this point the probability of success is slight—he does not want the disparate feelings that each of them may come away with to undermine his effectiveness as a mediator. Secondly, he is anxious to reinforce the fact that his office is the place where they will address the problems incident to their *divorce*, not the problems that they had in their *marriage*, and he does not want anything to distract from that fact, which he is trying so hard to bring home to the resistant party. Thus, we would suggest that it is the better rule that the therapist keep his different roles separate, and not wear two hats at the same time.[1]

The mediator now knows where the parties are emotionally. There are perhaps one or two other pieces of information that he would like to have in order to locate them still more accurately. He will next ask them whether either of them has consulted or retained an attorney. There are many purposes to this question. The mediator knows that whenever someone is considering a divorce there quickly arises around them a Greek chorus of well-wishers who comment from the sidelines on what is happening, offering advice, urging them on, and providing them with information—much of it ill-advised, misinformed, and even inconsistent. Generally, this Greek chorus is comprised of friends and relatives. However, it can even include attorneys whom one or both of the parties have consulted.

Not uncommonly, the mediator will note some surprise on the face of one of the parties when the other acknowledges that he has consulted an attorney. If he had not wanted to tell his spouse this, should the mediator have put him in the position where he was required to do so? While the mediator should obviously respect each party's privacy, and never place either of them in an embarrassing position, this exception can perhaps be excused. The mediator will subtly use this question to demonstrate the difference between adversarial divorce proceedings, which are all conducted in secret (as evidenced by this consultation of which the other spouse was not aware) and divorce mediation, where everything is done aboveboard and in full view of all parties concerned. It will also again give the mediator an opportunity to deal with some of the emotionality that may surface when these facts are disclosed.

Having asked this question, and particularly if the mediator feels that the response has not elicited all of the information he wishes, he should proceed further. He is anxious to know on what information each of the parties is operating, and what they have been told by the Greek chorus, as it may well influence their thinking and, therefore, the mediation; and unless it is put on the table the mediator may not have an opportunity to deal with it. "Have either of you advised any of your friends or relatives that you are considering divorce mediation?" he asks. This, and one or two other questions, will quickly elicit this information as well as the impressions and underlying assumptions which each of the parties has about divorce mediation, both positive and negative. In addition to giving the mediator an opportunity to correct some of this negative misinformation, it will also provide him with an opportunity to contrast how things are done in traditional adversarial divorce proceedings with how they are done in mediation, and to reinforce mediation's positive benefits.

The following example will perhaps illustrate this. On a particular occasion, and in response to the mediator's inquiry as to whether either of the parties had discussed the fact that they were considering mediation with anyone, the wife responded that she had, and that her friends had uniformly warned her against it. She knew that if her husband had consulted with an attorney, he would have attempted to hide his assets and misrepresent his true financial circumstances—that is what had happened with one of her best friends, and with another woman she knew—and so she did not know whether she could trust him.

There was nothing in the way that the husband presented himself that suggested to the mediator that he was not trustworthy. On the contrary, the wife acknowledged his good character, and the husband, who had been the one who had initiated the divorce over his wife's objection, clearly indicated his desire and intention to provide responsibly for her and their children. The wife really knew this. What she was expressing, however, was her fear that she could not trust that *knowledge*, for her trust was undermined by what she had been told, and by how she had seen men—even supposedly decent men—act once they got involved in a divorce.

Now that the problem was out in the open, the mediator was able to deal with it. Turning to the wife, he pointed out that if her husband had really wanted to be deceptive, and to try to take advantage of her, he would have gone out and hired a hard-nosed lawyer to represent him, and to help him accomplish this. But he had not done that. Rather, he had come with her to mediation. Besides, there was no truth in the suggestion that husbands changed their character when they become involved in a divorce. That was simply what happened—to wives as well as to husbands—when they turned to adversarial proceedings to resolve their problems. In fact, that was one of the worst aspects of traditional adversarial divorce proceedings—that it took basically decent people and made them act so inappropriately and irresponsibly, and so out of character.

It wasn't necessary for her to take his word for this, the mediator continued. She could judge for herself. Had her husband engaged in any of the conduct she had been warned about? Had he taken away her credit cards or sent letters to department stores disaffirming his obligation to pay for purchases she made? Had he raided any of their joint bank accounts? Had he withheld support from her? The questions, as the mediator knew, were all rhetorical ones.

More importantly, he went on, when her friends retained adversarial lawyers, did that prevent their husbands from engaging in the conduct they complained of so bitterly? On the contrary, all that the lawyers accomplished was to cause each of the parties to become fearful and suspicious of the other, and to feel the need to defend themselves by resorting to this type of preemptive conduct. The irony was that though her friends had warned her against divorce mediation, and of her need to protect herself against her husband, divorce mediation was really the best protection she had, since such conduct was not sanctioned in divorce mediation, as it routinely was in traditional adversarial divorce proceedings. Nor did husbands or wives who mediated their differences consider it either appropriate or necessary to engage in such conduct.

Is there anything else that the mediator would like to know or ask either of the parties? While the mediator may have inquired whether or not the couple had sought professional help to deal with the problems in their marriage, either individually or together, he will generally avoid delving further into this. To be sure, he would very much like to know some of the circumstances that have brought them to this point in their lives, as it might help him to address some of the emotional issues beneath the surface. If he discusses them openly, however, with both of the parties present, he may simply create a problem for himself. It is only *one* of the parties—usually the aggrieved party—who considers all of this information important. For the other party, and regardless of how awkward it may be for him, it is usually either inaccurate or irrelevant. In either event, it is always only half of the story. Nor does the mediator consider it to be important, for he knows that what is ultimately relevant at this point is the fact that they are there, not how they got there. Thus, he does not want to reinforce the mistaken impression that this is what is really important by getting involved in long-winded discussions about events which are irrelevant to his purpose and which will only tend to take the couple and the mediator far afield.

On the other hand, if he were to discuss these matters privately with each of the parties separately, particularly at this point, he may only create a climate opposite to the one he intends, since each party will assume, and perhaps not incorrectly, that the other has used the time so afforded to him merely to set forth his list of grievances. Under the circumstances, it is perhaps best to leave these matters alone, at least for the time being, and to wait for the time when they can be discussed in a more positive atmosphere, if it is still necessary to do so.

There are mediators, nevertheless, who follow a different procedure. Borrowing from the practice of matrimonial attorneys, and usually concerned with issues of protection, they make specific inquiry during the initial meeting as to the causes of the parties' divorce and, for example, whether either of them is, or has been, romantically involved with someone outside of the marriage; whether there has been any family violence; whether proper support payments are being made, etc. In fact, for those who employ this practice, they would consider it extremely irresponsible on their part were they *not* to ask these questions.

We cannot express too strongly how misguided and ill-advised we consider this practice to be. Putting this information on the table protects neither of the parties from anything. Its only effect is to embarrass them, and improperly to invade their privacy. There are things that the very best of people say and do in a marriage, particularly in a marriage that ends in divorce, that they would never say or do under normal circumstances. Since it is not possible to reconstruct in the mediator's office the conditions that gave rise to this conduct, and that will properly characterize it, to bring it up at this point is only to distort it at the expense, and to the embarrassment, of the offending party. If it is truly relevant to the purposes of the mediation, the mediator will learn about it soon enough. He may even learn about it anyway. If it is not relevant, there is no reason why it should be placed on the table and made an issue. The mediation will be successful, after all, if the mediator is able to reinforce each of the parties' sense of worth and self-respect. It will not be served, therefore, by his asking questions that will only tend to embarrass them and undermine their dignity.

There is another reason why it is improper to ask questions such as these, for in doing so the mediator is only encouraging each of the parties to tell their story, much as they would tell it to a lawyer whom they had retained to commence or defend an adversarial proceeding. Adversarial lawyers normally ask these kinds of questions because, being historically grounded in *fault,* our divorce laws have required each of the parties to prove the other's guilt or their own innocence. These stories were told in private, however, and the two lawyers were not required, as the mediator now will be, to attempt to reconcile them, let alone to deal with the emotionality they will trigger. Nor will the mediator be successful in doing this. On the contrary, it is the very fact that the parties are no longer able to tell themselves a sufficiently consistent story about their life together that has brought them to this point in their lives, and the mediator is not going to *correct in their divorce* what they were *unable to correct in their marriage.* Thus, all that the mediator will get for his efforts is to reopen wounds that he cannot heal and to inflame hurts that he cannot soothe. The fact that adversarial attorneys feel the need to make these inquiries is irrelevant, as this is one of the legacies of traditional adversarial divorce proceedings that divorce mediation hopes to revoke.

The tendency of the law to encourage parties to view divorce in terms of misconduct, and as a function of that misconduct, coupled with its view that divorce is the occasion to define and to protect the legal rights of each of the parties, has had yet another unfortunate consequence. It has encouraged separating and divorcing couples to view their divorce as the occasion to right all of the wrongs, both real and imagined, that have been done to them during their marriage, and to look to their separation agreement as the vehicle to accomplish this, rather than, as it properly is, simply the means of concluding the necessary business of their marriage. This too is one of the inevitable legacies of traditional adversarial divorce proceedings that mediation hopes to revoke.

Thus, to encourage the parties to tell their stories is to head them in the opposite direction from the one they need to go. One of the things that the mediator must convey to each of the parties is that there is *no future in the past*—that they cannot change it and that all that they can do is to learn to accept it, to let go of it, and to get on with their individual lives. Moreover, and in contradistinction to the practice employed in traditional adversarial proceedings, the mediator must also help the couple understand that the resolution of the issues incident to their divorce have nothing to do with, and must be separated from, the circumstances that have lead them to that divorce. If that is the case, the practice of concentrating the parties' attention on these issues can only tend to undermine one of the intended purposes of mediation.

Occasionally, the need for self-vindication being what it is, one of the parties may nevertheless let the mediator know what he did not ask, and the mediator will be left with the problem of how he should deal with this information. The mediator does not know the couple, nor they him, very well at this point. He will therefore have to make a judgment whether to address the issue that has been raised or simply to take note of it and let it pass for the time being. If the remark was more of an offhanded one, it is probably better to follow the latter of these two procedures.

If it is more pointed, however, and particularly if there is a noticeable response from the other party, the mediator may feel the need to address it. His objective here, however, is not to allow the occasion to be used as a sounding board for the aggrieved party's complaint. Rather, it is to afford him the opportunity to acknowledge that party's hurt and anger, but to do so in a way that is not confrontational as far as the other party is concerned. It is also his purpose, at the same time that he acknowledges the feelings in question, to begin to educate the party expressing them that those feelings are serving him no useful purpose and that, while the hardest thing for him to do may be to let go of them, in the final analysis *that is what his divorce must represent.*

By this point in time, a great deal of the underlying emotionality has probably been expressed. Before concluding the initial meeting, it would perhaps be best to try to effectuate an emotional closure to some of those feelings. This can perhaps best be accomplished by the mediator's turning to the couple and simply saying to them, "Tell me a little bit about your children." There is more than some truth in the suggestion that God gave us children to make up for everything else that he also gave to us. Not uncommonly, we look to our children to fulfill in their lives some of the things that were denied to us in ours. Just as commonly, they become idealizations that give purpose and meaning to our individual efforts. The mediator knows, therefore, that most people like talking about their children. More importantly, turning the discussion to the couple's children may also help to take their minds off some of the more painful things that they have been discussing up until this point. Additionally, it may help to *reinforce the commonality* that still exists between them, despite the conditions which have led to their separation.

This question can also serve another purpose. At their next meeting, and when the mediation itself begins, the first question the mediator will wish to address is that of their children. It may be that they are both deeply invested in their children and that their attitudes are almost identical. On the other hand, they can have sharp differences of opinion here. It is even possible that their different attitudes, perhaps even the indifference of one of the parties toward their children, has been a source of disappointment for one of them, if not of actual contention between them. The mediator would like to have a preview of those attitudes, since it will help him in approaching these discussions. It may also help him to locate each of the parties more accurately and better to understand them and the issues that have brought them to this point.

At other times, the question may not have the desired effect. One of the parties, usually the one who does not want the divorce, is not shaken from his preoccupation with his hurt and anger by the mediator's reference to his children. On the contrary, his hurt and anger is such that he simply cannot get beyond it. Nevertheless, the question was an important one because it underscored for the mediator the depth of those feelings and his need to address them. The couple's divorce, after all, must have as its ultimate objective a closure of these feelings. Unfortunately, this poses a problem for the mediator, and leaves him with a dilemma. To effectuate that emotional closure, he knows that he must first get the couple to an agreement and a divorce. On the other hand, he also knows that he will not be able to get them to that point unless and until he can first initiate at least some, if not all, of that closure. Given this, most of his hard work will be done in the very eye of those crosscurrents that both pull the parties forward and at the same time hold them back.

CONFIDENTIALITY

Mental health professionals do not generally give much thought to the question of confidentiality in their practice. Rather, they simply take it for granted that what is said to them in the course of treatment is said in confidence, and that they would never repeat it.

It may well be that the law protects such statements, and provides that a therapist cannot be required to divulge them. But that is really of no significance to him, as he would not divulge them even if that were not the law. On the contrary, he respects the confidentiality of what has been told him simply as a matter of professional responsibility, and because of the trust that the client or patient reposes in him. By the same token, it would make no difference to the therapist whether he had learned the information in a private session, with just one of the parties present, or in a joint session, that included both of them. It is all the same.

Lawyers, on the other hand, worry a great deal about confidentiality. In fact, it is one of their most sacred cows. To make matters worse, they know that many of the assumptions upon which mental health professionals proceed are legally erroneous. To begin with, most mental health professionals labor under the belief that the privilege is theirs— that if they are called as a witness in a trial that they can refuse to disclose what has been told to them during the course of treatment on the grounds that it was a privileged communication. They are not aware that the privilege belongs to their client or patient, and not to them, and that they can be required to disclose what they were told, whether they want to or not, unless the client asserts his claim of privilege by objecting to the testimony and unless his objection is sustained by the court. If the patient should fail to object to the question asked of the therapist, however, the therapist will be required to disclose what was told to him by the client, even though in the strictest of confidence, and even though to do so may violate one of the most basic tenets of his profession.[2]

Similarly, lawyers know that while statements made to a therapist by a client are generally privileged, that privilege is not absolute. On the contrary, there are many public policy considerations that will be deemed to override it.[3] Thus, and in certain jurisdictions, if the issue before the court is the custody of the parties' children, those interests can be deemed to take precedence over the privilege.[4] Similarly, and in other jurisdictions, the privilege does not exist in criminal proceedings, where what is at issue before the court is the guilt or the innocence of the defendant.[5] Even where no judicial proceedings are involved or contemplated, there can still be exceptions to the privilege, such as is the case with child abuse reporting statutes, which require those who learn of acts of child abuse in the course of their work to report and testify to the acts in question, despite the confidential relationship that exists between the person making the statement and the person hearing it.[6] Finally, the privilege does not apply simply because the statement was made to a therapist. It only applies if the statement was made in connection with treatment the therapist was rendering to the patient or intended to render to him.[7]

Given this, and particularly given the fact that the relationship between the mediator and the couple is *not* that of a therapist and patient or an attorney and client, much concern has been expressed by lawyers that confidentiality does not exist in mediation, and that a mediator may later be required to disclose what one of the parties has unwittingly told him. As a result, mediators have been routinely cautioned that each of the parties must be warned of this fact before they begin mediation, and that it would be professionally irresponsible of them not to do this. This warning usually includes the requirement of contrasting for the parties the different treatment that will be accorded statements that they make in the course of mediation with those that they might make in a meeting with their own separate attorneys. In fact, the obligation on a mediator's part to discharge this responsibility has become as much a tenet of faith in divorce mediation as is the tenet of confidentiality in therapy.

What sense does it make to impose this obligation upon a mediator? Absolutely none. On the contrary, the exaggerated concern about confidentiality in mediation is nonsense, and it becomes *no more* responsible simply because it is *legal* nonsense. It represents but one more example of the unthinking incorporation into mediation practice of concerns based upon adversarial principles, principles that have nothing to do, and which are inconsistent, with those that should properly inform divorce mediation.

Consider the following. Now that therapists have been educated to the fact that their understanding of the privilege that attaches to communications made to them in the course of treatment is misinformed, what changes should they make in their practice? The therapist now knows, for example, that when he meets with a married couple in family therapy (perhaps the very same couple who will later come to him for divorce mediation), that should his efforts prove unsuccessful and they later divorce, and particularly should custody of their children ever become an issue, he may be required to testify as to the fitness of each of them to be the custodian of their children; and for that purpose disclose statements that were made by one or both of them to him in confidence.

Does this mean that the therapist will now preface each of their conjoint sessions with a recitation, carefully drawn by his attorney, as to the risks that are involved for each of them should they undertake family therapy with him? (Suppose, for example, that the wife acknowledges that she is having an affair, and her husband later calls the therapist as a witness to testify to the relationship between the wife and her boyfriend on the issue of whether or not she has disregarded her duties to her children in furtherance of that relationship, or has perhaps exposed her children to it, all in support of his contention that she is unfit to be their custodian.) Or will he decide that, even should his sessions be prefaced with such a careful recitation, that the risks to each of the parties is simply too great, and give up the practice of family therapy altogether?

But would his problems necessarily be over if he did this? The therapist has now limited his practice to individual therapy. Suppose that he practices in one of the many jurisdictions that hold that considerations of public policy can on occasion override the principle of confidentiality. Does this mean that every time a patient or client consults with him that before undertaking treatment he must first warn the patient or client of all of the kinds of statements that he would be under an obligation to disclose and the conditions under which he will be required to disclose them?

Lawyers, no doubt, would probably consider this to be a serious problem. One would hope, however, that therapists will not be so persuaded. A therapist, after all, is trying to help. And he helps most if his client or patient trusts him and has confidence in him. If that is the case, what sense does it make for him to start out the treatment by warning them that they should very carefully consider whether they really can afford to do so?

The mediator, like the family therapist, is also attempting to help. And as with the therapist, there are certain conditions that must obtain if he will be able to do that. First and foremost is the trust that each of the parties come to repose in him. Second is the atmosphere he will try to create so that their discussions can profitably take place, an atmosphere that he will subtly contrast with the atmosphere, and with the assumptions, that characterize adversarial divorce proceedings. That being the case, it will serve no useful purpose for the mediator to undermine that trust with warnings and disclaimers, or the positive atmosphere that he is trying to create by underscoring adversarial considerations.

But what of the potential risks to each of the parties? The husband is in business for himself, and a substantial portion of his income is in cash that he has not reported for income tax purposes. If he discloses this to the mediator and his wife during the course of their mediation, and if he and his wife are unable to resolve their differences and must ultimately settle them in court, the mediator may be called as a witness and forced to disclose the damaging confession made by the husband to him that was not protected by the privilege of confidentiality. Should this not be of concern to the mediator? Absolutely not.

The husband has a choice. He can sit down with his wife, openly and honestly, and, in a responsible manner, attempt to resolve the questions incident to their separation or divorce. Or he can decline to do this and, hiring an adversarial lawyer, play legal games with her where the rules are that she will get, not what is fair, but what she can find. To be sure, the husband has the absolute right to choose the second of these alternatives. But that does not mean that a mediator should concern himself about this, let alone worry that in choosing the responsible path, the husband may not have clearly thought through the possible advantages to himself in being deceptive, and perhaps even a criminal. Nor should the therapist worry that he has permitted the husband to make this choice without first having read him a Miranda warning as to the possible consequences to himself in speaking freely.[8]

The truth is that the problem of confidentiality in mediation that so concerns the critics of divorce mediation and, unfortunately, even some of its advocates, is not a problem at all, let alone a defect in mediation, as is so often suggested. On the contrary, it represents but one more example of exaggerated adversarial concerns that have unthinkingly been carried over into divorce mediation. Furthermore, it represents yet another instance of legal hypocrisy. Our divorce laws—and this is true in community property as well as in equitable distribution states—require that there be a full accounting between husbands and wives at the time of their divorce, that they each disclose to the other all of the assets that they have acquired during their marriage, and that the value of their interest in that property be determined. If that is the case, why should a mediator be concerned that the husband in this instance may do just that, or whether, before he does, that he has fully considered all of the implications—fully considered the possible advantages to himself, and the disadvantages to his wife, should he instead decide to play the legal game of hide-and-seek and catch me if you can?

Does this mean that a mediator, like a mental health professional, should not concern himself with the question, or not advise the parties that the privilege of confidentiality does not attach to the discussions that will take place between them? Unfortunately, no, and at least at the present time, it is necessary that each of the parties be so advised. But, and as strange as this may at first blush appear, in so advising each of the parties, a mediator is not really doing this for their protection. (After all, society's interest is in encouraging people to be responsible, not to warn them about the dangers in being so, or of the advantages of being irresponsible.) It is to protect the mediation process itself.

In conducting mediation, a mediator must always act to protect the agreement that the couple will ultimately conclude between themselves. If either of the parties should later seek to set that agreement aside, based upon considerations recognized by the law, then it is the mediator's job to assure, at least to the extent that he can, that he has followed procedures designed to minimize, if not eliminate, that possibility. Thus, and while it is extremely unlikely that a court would ever set aside an agreement simply because one of the parties was not aware of the fact that discussions which took place in mediation were not privileged, it is nevertheless possible that this fact, combined with other facts, just might prove sufficient for that purpose. To prevent this from happening, and at least until agreements concluded through mediation, perhaps with the participation of but one attorney, are more securely protected by the courts than they now are, it is best for the mediator to follow a counsel of caution.

If the purpose is primarily to protect the mediation process itself, and not the parties, however, this will dramatically affect how the mediator will impart the information. All that is necessary is that the parties each be apprised that confidentiality does not exist in mediation; not that this fact be highlighted in such a way as to undermine the very purposes that mediation tends to serve. If that is the case, it is both unnecessary and inappropriate for the mediator to address this with the parties directly, let alone to make an important issue of it. Rather, the information should be imparted to them in a way that satisfies the requirement while at the same time minimizing its significance.

One way to accomplish this is for the mediator to advise the parties at the conclusion of the initial meeting that to assure himself that there is nothing of importance that he may have forgotten to tell them during their meeting, he has adopted the practice of incorporating all of the information he considers it important that they know in a letter he will send them following the meeting and before the commencement of the mediation. When they return, he will ask each of them to sign a copy of this letter acknowledging that they have both read it and understood it, and have had an opportunity to ask him any questions that they may have had concerning it.[9] There are few things that a court will find more binding upon a party than a writing that he has signed, particularly one that bears a legend above his signature that he has read it and understood it. At the same time, there is nothing better than such a letter, which will be read and signed by each of the parties simply as a matter of course, to satisfy the necessary requirement without undermining the purposes of the mediation in the process.

Assessing a Couple's Suitability for Mediation

Under what conditions should a mediator decline to undertake a mediation? In answer to this question, an attorney gave the following response. "Whenever both of the parties are not interested in a divorce. If one of the parties, for example the husband, is opposed to it, and particularly if he does not feel that his wife has grounds for divorce,[10] he should be told that he has a right to fight it and advised to consult an attorney for that purpose should he so desire. Only if he too wishes to obtain a divorce—or at least has decided not to oppose his wife's intentions in obtaining one—should the mediator proceed with the mediation."

It is tempting to pass this quaint opinion off as merely the reflection of a misguided adversarial mentality. It becomes far less humorous, however, when one learns that the remark was made, not by an opponent of mediation, but by one of its leading advocates in her community. And it serves as a reminder of how irrationality can come to seem like common sense when it becomes institutionalized and part of our everyday thinking.[11]

Suppose this issue had arisen in therapy rather than in mediation. When faced with a husband who is unable or unwilling to join with his wife in obtaining a divorce, a therapist could, to be sure, advise the husband in many ways. He could tell him that he could throw a mild temper tantrum. He could tell him that he could threaten to move thousands of miles away. He could tell him that he could challenge his wife for custody of their children. He could tell him that he could reduce her support to the minimum provided by the law, or otherwise simply be hard to do business with. And he could no doubt tell him other things as well, all in the name of attempting to make her decision more onerous, and to dissuade her from her intended course of action.

The question, however, is not whether he could give him this advice, but whether he has any obligation to do so. More importantly, would it be responsible on his part if he did? One would like to think that if the wife in this case had come to the fixed decision to divorce her husband, and particularly if the therapist felt that there was little, if any, prospect that she would change her mind, that it was his job to help her husband accept this reality and learn to live with it, not to encourage or endorse self-destructive conduct on his part that could only serve the purpose of attempting to deny it.

It is hard to believe that there will be many who will disagree with this. It is even harder to believe that there will be any who will feel that a responsible therapist should so advise the husband. If that is the case, why should this same counselor feel compelled to do so now, simply because the parties are in mediation rather than therapy, or simply because one of the options available to the husband—in this case, fighting his wife's action for divorce—is one that is granted to him by the law? The answer, of course, is that he should not. This fact shouldn't make the slightest difference, and if we feel that it does, that is again simply a reflection of a misguided thinking that *sanctifies options* because they are *legally permissible.* After all, there is nothing illegal in a husband's threatening to move thousands of miles away or to fight his wife for custody of their children either, and in that sense, those options are no less legally sanctioned than is the threat to fight her by opposing the divorce itself. That does not mean that a mediator is under an obligation to remind the husband of this fact, however, or that it would be irresponsible on his part if he did not.

In most instances, however, the question of whether or not the mediator should decline to undertake the mediation is not posed in this way. Rather, it is posed as the inquiry of whether or not the couple is suitable for mediation, since it has unthinkingly been accepted that before a mediator undertakes a mediation, he is obligated first to make this determination. Moreover, it is an obligation that has been imposed upon him by his friends as well as his critics. In fact, it has come to be such a standard requirement that it has almost ceased to be questioned at all.

Question it we must, however, for it represents yet another example of divorce mediation's unthinking acceptance of certain of the assumptions implicit in adversarial thinking, with the result that there has been incorporated into mediation practice procedures intended to vouchsafe adversarial considerations that are inconsistent with its purpose. Unfortunately, the advocates of divorce mediation do not see this, and it has not been an easy matter to open their eyes to it. When seeing the emperor's clothes becomes institutionalized, and when we come to accept even what our eyes and our common sense tells us is not there, it is not easy to correct our thinking, for, by definition, an appeal to our common sense will no longer work. In such a situation, the extreme of parody may be necessary, and we must be excused, therefore, if we resort to it. And so, we will answer the question by asking a question.

Under what conditions should an adversarial divorce lawyer decline to undertake to represent a client? To put it another way, are lawyers obligated to screen potential clients to determine their suitability for adversarial divorce proceedings? And what obligation are they under to define adversarial proceedings in context so that the client understands the differences between adversarial proceedings and other means of conflict resolution, such as mediation, that are available to him?

Suppose, for example, that an adversarial attorney is consulted by a less than decent or honest husband who, he finds, is simply intent on using the adversarial process to punish his wife for all of the crimes, both real and imagined, that he believes she has committed against him during their marriage. Can one imagine the attorney here declining to accept the client because he does not believe that he will be honest and forthright and that, as a result, the ultimate agreement might be unfair; or because he believes that his insistence on fighting for custody of his children is intended to serve purposes other than their best interests and may well prove to be against them? Similarly, can one imagine an adversarial attorney advising a client whom he has just met and who, he finds, is a very decent and responsible person, concerned with the welfare of his children and even of his wife, that he is concerned that if he and his wife become embroiled in adversarial proceedings that much of these healthy feelings may be destroyed, and their children adversely affected in the process?

More importantly, can one imagine the American Bar Association's Committee on Ethics handing down an opinion that when faced with a client such as this, an attorney is under an obligation to inquire of him whether his wife is of the same disposition and, if she is, to advise him of the dangers of adversarial proceedings and suggest that he consider nonadversarial procedures first before he undertakes them? Needless to say, these questions are rhetorical ones, as no adversarial lawyer would do this. On the contrary, secure in the conviction that they are on the side of truth and justice, adversarial lawyers take all comers. In fact, given that conviction, they would have great difficulty even understanding the question.

Why should it be any different for a mediator? After all, if he is convinced that the setting in which mediation takes place is a far more conducive one, and far better designed to help couples conclude an agreement between themselves than the setting provided by adversarial proceedings, why should he impose upon himself this precondition of suitability, or feel obligated first to screen the parties to determine whether they meet this test? Or why should he be obligated first to compare the advantages and disadvantages of adversarial divorce proceedings to assure himself that the couple is not making a mistake in choosing mediation?

The answer, of course, is that he should not. On the contrary, he has every right to proceed on the assumption that a suitable couple is one he will be able to assist in concluding an agreement and that, accordingly, all couples are therefore potentially suitable for mediation. Similarly, he has every right to proceed on the assumption that mediation is always the procedure of choice.

Does that mean that a mediator will be successful in concluding an agreement between every couple, or that mediation will prove to be more successful than adversarial proceedings in every instance? Of course not. But then, what assurance does a divorce lawyer have that he will be able to conclude an agreement for the same couple through adversarial negotiations? And what assurance does he have that adversarial proceedings will prove more successful than mediation? Absolutely none. But he does not reject them in advance on that account. Nor should a mediator. What will happen, then, to a couple who turn out not to be suitable for mediation? The same thing that will happen to a couple who turn out not to be suitable for adversarial negotiations. They will be condemned to go to court and have a judge impose an agreement on them.

Is our suggestion that all couples are to be presumed suitable for mediation to be taken literally? After all, won't there be couples with whom the mediator will simply not be able to work? Obviously there will, just as there may be clients with whom a divorce lawyer may later find he is unable to work. If that is the case, they will simply part company. But that is not a judgment that either the divorce lawyer or the mediator must make at the commencement of the undertaking, let alone one that they have an *obligation* to make.

But wouldn't it still make sense for a mediator to make this judgment at the *outset*, rather than simply to waste his or the couple's time and effort in a pointless exercise? Maybe it would and maybe it wouldn't. There is no question but that certain people are far more suitable for mediation than others. And it is also true that there are some who do not lend themselves to it very well at all. But it does not follow from this that a mediator should waste his time classifying the couples he meets, let alone that he should automatically discard those who do not fall into the desired category. To be sure, certain people (be they borderline personalities, neurotically conflicted, angry and vindictive, or merely fearful) will pose special problems for the mediator. This does not mean, however, that the mediation will not prove successful or that the mediator will not be able to conclude an agreement for them. It may only mean that it will be more *difficult* for him to do so.

For those who are concerned about the suitability of a couple for mediation, and about the mediator's obligation to first determine this, this may not be a sufficient answer. After all, they are not simply concerned with whether or not the mediator will be able to conclude an agreement between the couple. Rather, and expressing protectionist attitudes that have so invaded mediation thinking, their concern is over the *quality* of that agreement. For them, the statement that any couple able to conclude an agreement through mediation is suitable for mediation is tantamount to saying that any *agreement* concluded in mediation is an acceptable one.

That is not the case. We are not suggesting that any and all agreements are acceptable in mediation. We are simply saying that it is neither possible nor necessary for the mediator to attempt to prejudge what a particular couple's agreement will look like in advance. It is certainly possible that the circumstances of the case may be such that a mediator may wish to disassociate himself from the matter, and have no part in the couple's agreement, just as one would assume that an adversarial attorney might become so dissatisfied with his client or his client's conduct that he would choose to withdraw from the case. But again, this does not mean that he is obligated to make this judgment in advance, let alone that he should.

This is perhaps even more true in mediation than it is in adversarial proceedings. In adversarial proceedings, a lawyer by and large accepts his clients' attitudes and conduct as he finds them. His job, after all, is not to change his client, but to defend him. In mediation, on the other hand, at least part of what the mediator may have to do is to set those feelings and attitudes against the reality of what that divorce represents, and the adjustment that each of the parties will have to make in their lives in the face of it, so that at least *some* of those feelings and attitudes will change. In short, if the mediator is successful, some of the problems that might now cause him to reject the couple may, at a later time, no longer be obstacles.

On occasion, a mediator may be tempted to reject the couple, not on principle, but simply for his own convenience. This might be the case, for example, if the mediator comes to the conclusion that the husband is simply too difficult or irrational for him to deal with. If he does this, however, it is important that he understands what he is doing. In a very important sense no one is ever irrational. The problem is not that their conduct is irrational; the problem is that we are unable to make sense of their conduct within the constructs of our own understanding. If that is true, we attach the label that we do, not to make judgments about the person in question, but to make excuses for ourselves. ("I can't help him because he is crazy.") To be sure, and whether the limitation is in the maladaptive conduct of the party or in the understanding of the mediator, it may be impossible to work with the couple and conclude an agreement. However, these are not the cases that the mediator should summarily reject, since it is these cases that will also help him develop his skills.

In an ironic way, the very people whom a mediator has been told he has a duty to protect by rejecting their spouses as unsuitable are perhaps the ones who would most benefit from mediation if it proves successful. By the same token, they are probably the last people the mediator should reject and send off to do adversarial battle with their unsuitable spouses. As has been noted, one of the worst aspects of traditional adversarial divorce proceedings is that they tend to reward the least healthy people in society. As a result, unhealthy people have a distinct advantage over healthy people in those proceedings. In an adversarial setting, each of the parties sets out to obtain what he or she believes is fair and just. In the course of those proceedings, however, the desire to obtain what is fair and just becomes pitted against the terrible price involved in getting it. For healthy people, faced with the human costs that are invariably involved, a reassessment must be made. However, because they are healthy, they are able to find a way to do this and to live with a settlement that is somewhat less than fair or just, at least as they see it, and thereby find a way out of the morass of adversarial proceedings.

For less healthy people, however—in fact, the very ones whom a mediator has been told he has an obligation to reject as unsuitable—that is not so easy. On the contrary, and precisely because they are unhealthy, getting even is more important than getting done. In fact, getting even is so important that compared to that, it may not be important whether they ever get done at all.

Nor is it possible for these people to weigh the cost to the members of their family, and even to themselves, in the process. As a matter of principle, they will see it through to the end, whatever the price. Thus, to reject a couple because one of the parties seems to be unsuitable for mediation is not necessarily to protect the healthier party, as the mediator intends. On the contrary, it may be simply to subject that party to a procedure in which his spouse has even more of an advantage precisely because his personality is such that those proceedings will afford him wider latitude than would mediation.

Let us assume that a mediator follows our suggestion and does *not* reject a couple just because he believes that they are unsuitable. Is this to say that the agreement the mediator will be able to conclude in this situation will be as good or as fair as an agreement that he might be able to conclude in another? Again, maybe it will and maybe it won't. But even if it won't be—and this, of course, is a very distinct possibility—this again is no reason to reject that agreement, let alone to reject the couple. Agreements concluded by divorce lawyers through adversarial proceedings, after all, are not all the same either, and some are obviously better than others. If that is not a sufficient reason for a divorce lawyer to reject a particular agreement concluded through adversarial proceedings, then it is not a sufficient reason for a divorce mediator to reject one concluded through mediation.

Is it fair that a wife should be forced to deal with an unreasonable, and perhaps even irrational, husband in attempting to mediate an agreement? Probably not. But is it any fairer that she will have to deal with this same difficult husband if she attempts to conclude an agreement with him through adversarial proceedings? Again, the answer is the same. Nevertheless, and except for those who blindly accept adversarial rhetoric, and naively believe that adversarial proceedings will somehow mysteriously protect the wife from a husband whom life itself has been unable to protect her from, she will only have to deal with the same difficult husband there that she will have to deal with here. In fact, she may have to deal with a far *more* difficult husband, since, oftener than not, adversarial proceedings, and the context in which they take place, tend to make difficult people more difficult.

Why, then, has the duty to assess the suitability of a couple been imposed upon divorce mediators, and why have they so willingly assumed this responsibility? It has been imposed upon them because of the mythology that adversarial proceedings have built into them certain safeguards that will protect each of the parties and assure that they get it right. Since mediation, quite obviously, does not contain these same safeguards, there is always the danger that it will go awry and that the parties will get it wrong. It is therefore necessary to protect the couple by incorporating this requirement into mediation practice. Lacking the courage of their convictions, divorce mediators have unfortunately bought this mythology. In doing so, they have once again incorporated into their practice procedures that are at variance with their assumptions and inconsistent with their goals.

MEETING WITH THE PARTIES SEPARATELY

Implicit in the discussion up to this point is the assumption that the mediator will meet with both of the parties at the same time during their initial meeting. Is this necessary? In fact, isn't it placing an unnecessary burden, and imposing unnecessary limitations, on the mediator? After all, if the mediator had an opportunity to meet with the parties separately, he could perhaps get to know each of them better, learn from them the history that has brought them to this point, and address with them certain of the emotional issues that it might be more difficult to address in the other's presence.

Whatever may be the advantages in doing this, it is nevertheless recommended that the mediator avoid this practice. One of the mediator's goals in his initial contact with the couple is to create a setting in which the discussions between them will take place and implicitly to contrast that setting with the one in which adversarial divorce proceedings take place. If the mediator starts out by meeting with each of the parties separately, he cannot help but duplicate in the parties' minds the secretive atmosphere in which the consultations between clients and attorneys take place. Each of the parties has to view with concern, and perhaps even suspicion, what is taking place between the other and the mediator, wondering whether the other is simply using the occasion to make a case for himself or herself.

Furthermore, since they do not subscribe to the other's point of view, each also has to believe that the mediator is being presented with a biased and distorted picture, one they will then feel the need to correct. Nor can they help but worry whether the mediator may have been taken in by the other's story, or be partial to the other's point of view, a feeling only reinforced by the impression of trust and confidence the other party may exhibit after meeting privately with the mediator.

Unfortunately, separate meetings with each of the parties tend to reinforce certain of the very attitudes that the mediator is trying to alter. Except to the extent that it will help him understand some of the underlying emotionality, the mediator is really not interested in the stories that each of the parties want to tell him, no matter how important they may be to *them*. While these are the stories that they may have told themselves to explain their divorce and how they came to it, he does not subscribe to them. Rather, he knows that they are where they are simply because they are two very different people who rubbed up against one another's differences, who after a period of time were unable to negotiate those differences, and who eventually were only able to see one another *through* them. And he also knows that it will do little good to try and go any deeper than this.

The parties, unfortunately, are each wrapped up in their own stories and have a need to tell them. They still cling to the belief that those stories will explain how it is and why it is that they have been brought, usually because of the failings of the other party, to this point in their lives. And, just as assuredly, they will each have a great need to vindicate themselves. To meet with the parties separately at this point, and to permit each of them to tell enough of their stories so as to enable the mediator to learn what he would like to know may, to be sure, help *them* ventilate some of the terrible feelings they are experiencing. To permit this, however, is only to risk reinforcing their belief in the relevancy of these stories, when what the mediator wants to impress upon each of them is the fact that those stories are not only history, but useless history as well.

While one or both of the parties may wish to use their initial meeting for this purpose, the mediator has set a far different goal for himself. First and foremost, he wishes to establish the fact that he understands just how difficult what they are experiencing is, and that he sincerely wishes to help them through it. Secondly, it is to gain their confidence by convincing them that he has the necessary skill and experience to do this. Lastly, and perhaps most importantly, he wants to start to build the trust that he hopes they will come to repose in him. This is not to say that it is impossible for the mediator to accomplish this in separate meetings with each of the parties. It is simply to say that it is too important an undertaking for him to take the risk involved in attempting to do this.

Once the necessary trust has been established between the mediator and each of the parties, the mediator will have a much freer hand. When he has clearly established the fact that he can be trusted, and that he would never take any action with respect to one of the parties without the full knowledge and consent of the other, it will *then* be possible for him to meet with them separately, should the need arise, and there may well be an occasion when he may wish to do this.

Time and time again the mediator will find himself confronted with a situation in which the ongoing progress of the mediation is being impeded by feelings expressed by one of the parties that he would like to address. In most instances, and particularly if the mediator is adept and tactful, he will be able to address those feelings even in the presence of the other party. Occasionally, however, he may fear that were he to attempt to do this he might cause embarrassment to one of them.

The following example will illustrate this. A couple who had been married for over 35 years came into mediation. Some nine months earlier the husband had announced his desire to separate and subsequently moved out of the marital residence. Despite the lapse of time, the wife was still smarting from the hurt attendant to her rejection. The husband, who had graduated from a prestigious graduate school, and who was in business for himself, presented himself as a worldly man of finance and often found it necessary to expound at length on matters of little significance. In actual fact, however, he was really a business failure and had only been able to maintain his business over these many years because his wife's own earnings, supplemented by money she had inherited, had helped support their family. Even then, his business repeatedly required small capital contributions from time to time, again made by his wife from her inheritance. As it was, their separation occurred shortly after the wife refused, for the first time, to provide him with additional funds for that purpose.

Throughout the mediation, and despite the husband's sense of guilt and his wife's sense of wrong, surface appearances were maintained, and the husband addressed each of the issues, pencil and paper in hand, in his characteristic businesslike manner. Although the wife had great difficulty overcoming her hurt and anger, only once did she threaten to unmask those appearances. At the initial session, and in response to the mediator's inquiry as to whether there was anything concerning the health of either of the parties or their children that he should know, when the husband responded "No," the wife looked at him askance and inquired of him whether there wasn't something that he had not told the mediator. Improperly assuming that the wife's comment referred to the husband's physical health, the mediator asked the wife to what she was referring, whereupon she informed him that her husband had been previously hospitalized for depression. (The husband's response to this was simply to brush off his wife's statement with the comment that this had been years ago and that he was now fine, and the mediator decided that it was better simply to let the matter pass without further comment.)

In the course of the mediation, and in large measure because of the guilt that he felt, the husband had agreed that his wife could continue to live in their home for as long as she wished. Moreover, and in recognition of his indebtedness to her in connection with the loans she had made to his business, he had agreed that upon its sale she was to receive a much larger share of the proceeds. After giving second thoughts to this, and because he realized that he would be left with little, if any, liquid assets, the husband attempted to renegotiate his understanding with his wife to the end that she would presently use some of her inheritance to buy out his interest in their home.

At this point the hurt and anger that the wife had in large measure kept under control exploded. For 35 years she had supported her husband, time and time again, only to be rewarded in the later years of her life by having him walk out on her, and this was all that she could see or feel. In fact, she was so consumed by these feelings that despite her tremendous sense of dignity, and her desire to comport herself as the lady that she was, her husband's present suggestion, which once again touched upon her inheritance, could not but trigger a release of these feelings.

Up to this point, and because these feelings had not interfered in any appreciable way with the conduct of the mediation, the mediator had respected each of the parties' privacy and had simply observed all of this without comment. Now, however, those feelings were standing as a barrier to the mediation and had to be addressed. Unfortunately, the mediator had a problem in doing this.

What the mediator wanted to tell the wife was a very different story from the one she had been telling herself. Her husband was not the man he presented himself to be, a fact that she, on a certain level, well knew. This was something that she and her husband could not talk about, however. Rather, he continued to pretend to himself and to everyone else that he was a successful man of the world, and she quietly, though often grudgingly, supported his efforts to maintain this facade. They really both knew better, however. Over and over again that illusion had been pierced by his need to turn to her for additional financial help. In fact, in time she could not help but come to represent to him a mirror reflecting his failure. While her hurt stemmed from her feeling that the support she had given him these many years had only been repaid by rejection, it was as true to suggest that he left her because of his *own* feelings of rejection or, perhaps to put it more accurately, because he could not be the man in her eyes that he had to be in order to maintain their relationship. By the same token, and whether she wished to acknowledge it or not, it was not possible for her to view him as a man or, therefore, to support the illusion that he was. This is why he had left her and why their marriage had come to an end. In short, what the mediator wished to convey to the wife was that what had happened to them was not a crime but a tragedy.

It was not a story that the mediator could easily tell, however. It would have been highly inappropriate for the mediator to have told this to the husband, or even the wife in his presence. The husband's defenses may well have been inadequate and maladaptive, but they were the only defenses he had; and unless the mediator was in a position to guarantee him better ones (which he clearly was not), he had no right to tamper with them. Nevertheless, if the mediator could have helped the wife replace the counterproductive story that she insisted upon telling herself with a better story, one that would help diffuse the tremendous rejection that she was feeling, this would not only aid the progress of the mediation but, even more importantly, help her manage more effectively feelings with which she was struggling.

Using the occasion of the wife's emotional outburst (and the husband's discomfort in the face of it) as a pretext, the mediator turned to the husband and asked if he would have any objection if he spoke to his wife alone for just a few minutes. At this point in the mediation, the mediator knew that the husband both trusted and respected him and he had little doubt that the husband would accede to his request and not misinterpret it. In actual fact, he not only readily agreed to the suggestion, but actually welcomed it as a reprieve from what had become an uncomfortable situation for him.

Left alone together, the mediator was able to discuss these factors openly with the wife. Despite her sense of rejection, she still had a strong attachment to her husband. In fact, his sense of failure, and his need to defend himself by posturing as he did, was very upsetting to her. Unfortunately, her feelings of rejection and abandonment did not permit her to give expression to those feelings. Relating their separation to *his* failings, rather than to her own, enabled her to defuse some of those feelings of hurt and anger. When that was done, the mediation was able to proceed to a conclusion.

In each instance, the mediator must make a judgment. Mediation is not shuttle diplomacy, and the mediator does not want to create a situation in which he encourages the parties to take fixed positions which he then negotiates in a series of private meetings with each of them. It is not even labor mediation, where the tenor of the discussions is affected by the fact that the parties are each aware that their present negotiations are only part of an ongoing series of negotiations that have taken place in the past and will continue to take place in the future. In fact, and from the very outset, the mediator has attempted to dispel the attitude that they are negotiations at all—to dispel the idea that mediation is the act of bargaining from preset, fixed positions.

On the contrary, what the mediator continually attempts to reinforce is the fact that he and the parties are simply meeting in an attempt to make some sense of their present situation, and to solve a common problem that they have. Sitting together, as they do at each of their meetings, reinforces this. Nevertheless, and particularly if that setting becomes a limiting factor, the mediator can and should meet with the parties separately if he feels that it is appropriate. Again, the only precondition is that his doing so will not taint the atmosphere he has attempted to create, or undermine the trust that either of them has in him. That, of course, means that both of the parties must feel comfortable with his meeting with them privately and agree to it. This is in keeping with the rule that the mediator always follows—that *he will never do anything unless both parties agree.*

Concluding the Initial Meeting

The balance of the initial meeting will be spent explaining to the couple the procedures that the mediator and they will follow in addressing, one by one, the questions that must be resolved in their separation agreement. If the mediator is not an attorney, this will include a discussion of how the necessary legal functions will be performed: whether by an attorney with whom the mediator works, or by the attorney(s) whom the parties may themselves consult and retain for that purpose.

This is a crucial phase of the initial interview. The couple is attracted to the idea of using mediation. Nevertheless, they may still have some reservations. Whatever problems they might have should they each retain separate attorneys to resolve the problems incident to their divorce, it will provide each of them, at least initially, with a sense that they have handed the problem over to someone *else*, and it is no longer theirs to worry about. And, particularly for women, there is the feeling, again at least initially, that they have someone in their corner to protect them. Accordingly, and even if they may feel that mediation is a more rational procedure, they may still have some misgivings. It is therefore critical that the mediator address these concerns. He will do this best by underscoring his own professionalism and that of the mediation process itself, and he should spend some time with the couple doing this.

What are the essential elements of that process? First, and perhaps foremost, the mediator will provide the couple with an *appropriate setting* in which the discussions between them can take place. Secondly, he will provide them with the *necessary information* to assure that those discussions are informed ones and that they are each able to participate in them intelligently. Thirdly, he will provide them with his own *experience, understanding, and professional background* to assist them where they have difficulty.

The mediator must reinforce the importance of the setting in which mediation takes place. He can do this best by contrasting that setting with the one provided by traditional adversarial divorce proceedings. In those proceedings, as has been noted, everything is done secretly, and behind closed doors, which only feeds the feelings of fear and insecurity of each of the parties. (It is as if the parties meet and face one another with their hands under the table, neither sure of what the other's hands are doing, and afraid on that account.) As a result, each feels the need to take preemptive action in anticipation of what the other is or may be planning, conduct that inevitably only leads to a vicious cycle of usually pointless and counterproductive actions and reactions. In mediation, on the other hand, everything is open and aboveboard, and the parties face one another with their hands on the table. Since that is so, neither feels threatened or has the need to protect themselves in such destructive ways.

In traditional divorce proceedings, the parties have no control over the process. They may have control over it before it begins, but once they set it in motion, it then takes on a life of its own. Worse yet, they will quickly find that they are but bit players, lost in the wings of the drama. In fact, not even their attorneys, who are center stage, really have any control over it. In divorce mediation, on the other hand, each of the parties has complete control over the process. In fact, all that either one of them has to do to stop it is simply to stand up, open the door and leave.

One of the worst aspects of traditional adversarial divorce proceedings is the fact that there are no rules to the game and that it is simply each man for himself. As a result, even decent people soon find themselves doing and saying things that are totally out of keeping with their character. To make matters worse, there is literally no accountability. Neither has to answer to the other and each can simply hide behind their attorneys who will defend and justify whatever they have done. This never happens in mediation. Such conduct is not considered appropriate, is totally inconsistent with the spirit of the proceedings and, as a result, quite literally does *not* occur. When couples employ mediation, they want to spend their time constructively, addressing the problems that must be resolved. They do not want to come to the sessions simply to have to meet their accuser and to waste time discussing issues that have nothing to do with their ultimate agreement. More importantly, mediation permits each of the parties to be the decent people they would prefer to be, and encourages them in this.

The second thing that the mediator will do will be to provide the couple with information. Mediation is an informed process and it is extremely important that the couple participate in it intelligently. Part of the mediator's job is to assure that they will have available to them any and all information which they will need in the course of their mediation. For example, it will not be necessary for them to concern themselves with whether or not they have considered all of the things that must go into their agreement, let alone worry that they may have forgotten something. It is the mediator's job to assure that this does not happen, and as they will see, he will direct their attention, one by one, to each and every issue that must be resolved by them and included in their agreement. In fact, this is perhaps even more important in mediation than it is in traditional divorce proceedings. Mediation is not simply concerned with helping a couple effectuate a legal divorce. It is concerned with helping them effectuate an emotional divorce as well. It will not do, therefore, for them to sign an agreement and only later find that there were issues that they had not properly addressed and resolved in their agreement. If this were to happen, that would only tend to rake up feelings that had previously been laid to rest, and undermine one of mediation's most important purposes. On the contrary, if an issue should arise in the future, they should be able to open their agreement and find the answer to it. One of them may be slightly disappointed, but there can be no dispute because that is what they agreed to. This is the kind of agreement with which the mediator intends to leave each of them.

Thirdly, they will have the mediator's assistance, and the experience which he has acquired over these many years in helping separating and divorcing couples. There is a mistaken belief that separating and divorcing couples are so hurt and angry that they cannot communicate with one another. That is not the case. It is simply that they may not be able to communicate with one another alone, for all too often when they attempt to sit down and discuss the issues themselves, the feelings of hurt, anger, disappointment, fear, and sometimes even betrayal tend to creep up through the "cracks in the woodwork" and overwhelm their discussions. If those conversations take place in the mediator's presence, however, he will help to assure that this does not happen. In fact, at least part of his job will be to help to clear the lines of communication between them.

When the mediator is through outlining these procedures, and if he has done this carefully, each of the parties should feel secure in the process and in the fact that they need not concern themselves that they will be discussing these issues directly, and without the aid of separate attorneys.

FEES

Before the meeting is concluded, the mediator should discuss his fee arrangement with the couple and how payments are to be made. When the question of fees come up, some mediators follow the procedure of also discussing the allocation of the payment between the parties. Some go even further and follow a rule that the parties must contribute equally. We recommend neither practice. In most instances, the question of who will pay the mediator's fee, or whether or how it will be allocated between them, will not be raised as an issue unless the mediator raises it. With rare exception, if the issue has not already been resolved by the parties themselves, it will get resolved without the mediator's intervention. Thus, his thanks for doing this may simply be to raise an issue that will otherwise not become one. Even if it is raised, however, it would be far better for the mediator to finesse the issue at this point than to address it. Thus, rather than discussing it, he should simply state that this too is one of the questions that they will have to resolve in the course of their mediation. To begin with, the question of who should pay the fee may not even be the *real* issue. Even if it is, however, it is probably too early in the mediation to address it. Finally, and perhaps most importantly, even if the payment of the mediator's fee is raised as an issue at the initial meeting, in more instances than not it will get resolved without the mediator's intervention before the mediation begins.

In this respect the mediator must remember that the purpose of the initial meeting is not to resolve the issue between the parties. It is not even to determine what those issues are, and, as a general rule, the mediator must resist any attempt by the parties to get into the *substance* of these matters. His purpose is merely to afford the couple an opportunity to meet with him, to learn how it is that he hopes to help them, and to come to feel comfortable with him. From the mediator's standpoint, it is also to permit him to get to know each of the parties better and to preview, so to speak, what will be the attitudes expressed by each of them during the course of the mediation.

In no event should the mediator insist that the fee be paid by the parties based upon any particular allocation. At its best, this practice again represents a tendency to romanticize divorce mediation. At its worst, it represents arrogance on the part of the mediator who, after all, has no business telling the parties how they should conduct their lives. At times, this practice is defended on the basis that it would be *unfair* for one of the parties, perhaps the party who wants the divorce or who wants to employ divorce mediation rather than adversarial proceedings, to have to bear the brunt of the mediator's fee on that account. At other times it is defended on the basis that it tends to establish, right at the outset, the fact that mediation is based on the principle of equality—that the parties are equals, have made equal contributions to the marriage, will share equally in its benefits and should, therefore, share equally in its obligations.

Unfortunately, this attitude does violence to an opposing principle that the mediator must steadfastly honor throughout the course of the mediation, and it will not do for him to violate it at the very outset. That principle is, first, that the parties must seek their own level, and, second, that their level is not inappropriate simply because it fails to conform to some objective, but nevertheless irrelevant, yardstick, or because it is at variance with some preconceived notion of what is fair or unfair held by the mediator, or even by society. That it was appropriate for a couple to share equally the cost of the mediation in another case does not mean that it is appropriate for them to do so here. Even more importantly, it is far better to let them work this out themselves by whatever means they may employ for that purpose—even by default, if need be, with one of them paying for it simply because the other won't—than it is for the mediator to interfere with how they would otherwise resolve the issue.

Having concluded a discussion of his fees, and having answered whatever questions the parties may have, it is now time for the couple to decide whether they wish to use divorce mediation and to employ the services of the mediator. This is not necessarily a decision that they will want or perhaps be able to make at this time. Some couples may wish to discuss it between themselves before they leave, and if the mediator senses this, he can excuse himself for a few minutes to give them an opportunity to do so. Other couples will not hesitate to discuss it right in front of him, and will usually quickly decide that they wish to go ahead. In other instances the mediator may sense that there is some reservation on the part of either or both of them, and he will simply tell them that they should talk about it after they leave and, if they decide to go ahead, to call him to schedule another appointment.

Regardless of whether a decision is made to proceed with the mediation, and before concluding the initial meeting with the couple, it would be useful for the mediator to obtain a bit more information from them, and he should have a folder, which contains a prepared form, ready for this purpose. [12] Aside from providing the mediator with name, rank, and serial number information that he may need at a later time, this will again re-emphasize the professional, businesslike nature of the mediation. More importantly, however, it will provide the mediator with information that will be helpful to him in the course of his initial sessions with the couple. To be sure, if they decide to go ahead with the mediation, he will provide them with forms for them to fill out that will contain much of the specific information that will be needed as the mediation proceeds—for example, the bank accounts they maintain, the stock they own, etc. [13]—but he will not wish to use their first one or two meetings on such business matters, that can be attended to at a later time, when those meetings can be used for far more important purposes.

Nevertheless, he would like to have at least some of this information at his disposal—for example, whether both of the parties work, their respective incomes, and whether they are self-employed or employed by others; the cost of maintaining their apartment or home and, if they own it, the equity that they have tied up in it; the number and ages of their children and whether either of them have children by a previous marriage; and whether there are any health or other special problems that will be relevant to their discussions.

Knowing, for example, how much it costs to maintain the marital residence and, if it is one that they own, how much equity there is in relationship to its value, will give the mediator an opportunity to give some thought to one of the critical questions that will often arise in the course of the mediation, namely, whether to maintain the home as the residence of one of the parties and the children or to sell it. Having this information at hand before this topic is taken up for discussion will give the mediator an opportunity to give consideration to these questions. Similarly, if either of the parties has an obligation to a former spouse or children, this too should be known at the outset so that the mediator does not incorrectly assume that the earned income of the parties is all available to them and to the children of this marriage.

The Last Word

Before the couple leave, there is one final point that the mediator would like to convey, and that is that he is not suggesting that mediation is going to be easy. If their divorce represents a personal tragedy in their lives, as he knows it does, there can be nothing pleasant about it, and it would be as dishonest as it would be insulting for him to pretend otherwise. He does what he does, not because he believes that mediation is perfect, but because, given the alternatives, there can be no other rational choice.

Nor will he be able to do what has to be done all by himself, simply handing the parties a completed agreement when he is through. It will require their effort as well. The mediation will not be difficult because the parties are faced with unusual or complex problems. Rather, they will be the same kind of practical problems that they have had to deal with throughout their lives. More importantly, they are the kinds of problems that they have dealt with in the past, on their own, and without the mediator's help.

What, then, will make the mediation so difficult? It will be the fact that there has become encrusted around these practical problems the terrible feelings of hurt, disappointment, anger and sometimes fear that are the inevitable by-products of their decision to separate and divorce. The mediator will not take issue with those feelings, let alone suggest that they are not justified. Nevertheless, if the mediation is going to be successful, each of them is going to have to learn to let go of those painful, and unfortunately, destructive feelings, at least to some extent. They have a choice. They can hold on to their feelings, and can even justify their right to do so, if they wish. However, if they do that, then they will surely get lost in those feelings. Or, and as hard as it will be for them to do, they can try to put those feelings aside so that they can get done with it and get on with their lives. Again, that will be their choice.

Does it make sense for the mediator to share this with the couple at this point? As we have stated previously, one of the principal purposes of the first meeting is to establish a relationship with the couple and to enlist their trust and confidence. If the mediator is to do this, he must be forthright and honest with them at all times. By doing this at the very outset, he sets the tone of their discussions and indicates what they can expect of him in the future. He could have painted them a pretty picture. But that is not his way. He will always tell it to them straight. That being the case, they can rely on him and on what he says. Just as importantly, he has made it clear that they too have an interest in and responsibility for what will take place during the course of the mediation. At a later time he may well have occasion to call upon that card and to remind them of the obligation that they assumed. Since that is so, he wants to establish that line of credit as early as he can.

CHAPTER 14

CHILDREN

When the couple returns for their second meeting with the mediator, the formal mediation begins. While it is common practice for mediators to assure themselves at this point that all of the financial information requested of the parties has been compiled, and their budgets completed, it is recommended that these questions be put aside for the moment, and that the mediator turn instead to the question of the couple's children.

There are a number of reasons for this. The initial meeting was an informal one, designed primarily to give the mediator and the couple an opportunity to get to know one another and to begin to establish the rapport and the feeling of trust so vital to the mediation. It would be helpful to sustain this informality, and therefore to play down the more businesslike aspects of the mediation. It would also be useful to afford the mediator yet another opportunity to smoke out and address some of the underlying emotional issues before these other questions are put on the table. There may be a great deal that one or both of the parties is feeling and would like to share with the mediator, and, while not necessarily encouraging it, he does not want to stifle it either.

Secondly, and to the extent possible, the mediator would like to build on the commonality the couple still maintains, despite their decision to divorce, before he gets into these questions. That commonality is best expressed in their children and, as one usually finds, particularly with couples who seek mediation, the shared interests they have with respect to those children. Thus, rather than emphasize areas of more marked disagreement, the mediator should first address those issues where their interests are more in concert.

Finally, it is not really possible to address, let alone resolve, the other important issues involved in a couple's mediation—the disposition of their home, support, etc.—until the basic questions concerning their children have been settled. The mediator is attempting to create a picture for himself of this family following their divorce. It is not possible even to begin to sketch that picture until the place of the children is first determined.

In most instances, and though there may be questions concerning the children that will have to be addressed and resolved, there will not be any basic disagreement concerning the children. Moreover, there may be other issues that one or both of the parties feels is more pressing and would prefer to address. Is it appropriate, therefore, for the mediator always to start out by addressing the issue of the parties' children? Would it not be better for him to inquire, right at the outset, what those issues are?

The answer to the second of these questions is no. The mediator has started with the question of the couple's children because he believes the interests of the mediation will be best served by doing so. However, he is not insisting that the parties must resolve this question before any other issues are addressed. Rather, he is simply using the question of the parties' children as a means of setting the mediation afloat and putting it in motion. Having done that, he will then sit back and note the direction it takes and when and where it gets into troubled waters.

There are a number of reasons for this, aside from those already mentioned. To begin with, the very fact that the parties are willing and able to discuss the question of their children, even though it does not represent a serious issue between them, will often provide a preview for the mediator as to whether or not he should expect to run into troubled waters further on along the way. Furthermore, if these other issues are truly pressing, there is little danger that he will not learn about them or that one of the parties will not interrupt the discussion and raise them. Finally, if they are raised by one of the parties himself, rather than by invitation, the mediator will have far more latitude in determining when and how it is most appropriate to address them.

There is a second reason, and that is that by subtly discouraging the public airing of issues (grievances) that one of the parties considers important, the mediator is thereby makii.g a distinction between how problems are dealt with in an adversarial setting and how they are dealt with in mediation. In adversarial proceedings, when one of the parties has a problem (grievance), he is encouraged in the belief that it is appropriate for him to bring it to his attorney and that his attorney will solve it. After all, that is why he hired an attorney in the first place. The mediator, of course, knows that this is a blind alley, that neither of the parties' attorneys can really do this, and that these ultimately are problems they must solve themselves. Certainly he wants to *help* them do this if that is necessary. And if issues are raised, and if he can help the couple resolve them, it would be remiss of him not to do so. But there is a difference between their handing over the problem to him, and in a sense making it *his* problem, as they would to an adversarial lawyer, and his helping them with a problem that remains essentially their own. The mediator wishes always to underscore this distinction.

Finally, the mediator knows that it is the mediation process itself, as distinct from the act of addressing a specific question in the course of the mediation, that will help most to affect a resolution of the issue in question. As we have noted elsewhere, mediation is not simply a technique for resolving disputes between separating and divorcing couples. It is also a *process*, one that attempts to *change the attitudes* each party has about their separation and divorce, and to reeducate them as to what is *possible* and *realistic* to expect and what is not; and the success of a mediation is as dependent on this as on any of the techniques the mediator will use to bridge the differences between the parties. However, the process is, by definition, something that takes place over time. And since the mediator needs that time for the process to be effective, it may not always be efficacious for him to address the issues that one or both of the parties would like to raise *when* they wish to address it.

LABELS

Until recently, it followed almost as night follows day that the wife would have custody of the couple's children, and there were certain presumptions in the law—for example, that children of tender years were best suited living with their mother rather than with their father—that supported this assumption. However, while the vast majority of children still remain with their mothers following their parents' divorce, without question there has been a change both in society's attitude and in the court's thinking in this area.

As society has been forced to grapple with the question of divorce and its effects upon children, numerous alternative arrangements have been proposed to the traditional one that gave mothers custody (full control over the decisions affecting) of their children and gave fathers merely visitation (entertainment) rights on Sunday from 10 o'clock in the morning until 6 o'clock in the evening. These alternative arrangements have been given names, and it is not uncommon for couples to come into mediation inquiring about "joint custody," "shared parenting" or some other arrangement about which they have heard.

Labels do not change reality, however. Also, they are often very confusing, and at times even threatening. Not uncommonly, a mediator will find that a dispute between a couple concerning their children has little to do with any disagreement they have as to the future living arrangements of their children. Rather, it is really only over the label that one of the parties, often the husband, wishes to put on that arrangement. The husband comes into the mediation and announces that he wants joint custody of his children. Not exactly sure of what he means, but feeling threatened nevertheless, the wife responds that she will not even consider this. It would be an error on the mediator's part to assume that he is faced with a dispute concerning custody. There may be no dispute at all over the arrangement, but simply over the implications, for both of the parties, of the label that has been attached to it.

It is thus best for the mediator to eschew labels, or any discussion about them. Accordingly, he should initiate the discussion by asking the couple, "Have you given any thought as to where your children will live following your separation and divorce?" (Even though the mediator means "with whom" it is better to say "where." Into the bargain he may get an answer to a question that he has not asked yet.) To underscore the attitude that has characterized their discussions, he may continue by stating, "What I would like to know is where the children will be leaving for school from on Monday morning, and where they will be sleeping on Saturday night?"

DISPUTES AS TO CUSTODY

In most instances, the mediator will find that there is no real issue here and that, for example, the couple will quickly advise him that the children will continue to live with their mother in their home. Very often, particularly if the couple has already been separated for some period of time, their present living arrangements—he has moved out of the home and she continues to live there with the children—will provide the implicit answer to this question.

Let us suppose that the introductory questions posed by the mediator do not suggest an agreement between the parties, however. Let us suppose, further, that the mediator is told outright that the parties cannot agree where the children will reside, the husband maintaining either that they should live with him (or should perhaps share their residence with him and their mother), and the wife maintaining that they should live with her.

It would be wrong for the mediator summarily to conclude from this that the dispute between the couple really concerns a disagreement as to where their children should live. Maybe it does and maybe it doesn't. The separation from one's family that divorce represents is one of the most difficult adjustments that a person will ever have to make. It is particularly difficult for husbands, who have traditionally been required to separate not only from their wives, but from their children, their home, and their community as well, for in doing so they lose so much of what constitutes the very structure of their lives. Thus, what is being expressed is not necessarily the fixed determination on the husband's part to have custody of his children, or to have them live with him, whether in their home or somewhere else. It may only be the tremendous difficulty that he is having in separating from his children and his home. Accordingly, and before concluding that there is a genuine dispute as to custody, the mediator must first determine in his mind whether or not what is really being expressed is simply this loaded emotional issue.

On other occasions, though admittedly less often, the mediator may sense that there is common agreement that the children would be better off continuing to live with their father, but that the wife has difficulty acknowledging, let alone accepting, this. This is the other side of the coin. As difficult as it is for a responsible, concerned father to "walk away" from his children, it is perhaps even more difficult for a mother to do so. Any parent who leaves his home and children risks being left with the feeling that he has abandoned his children. For many fathers, the hardest job they will ever be required to do is to deal with this—to face their children and tell them that they are separating from their mother and "leaving" them. In fact, not infrequently husbands remain in their marriages, long after it makes any sense to do so, simply because they do not know how to do this.

Whatever a father's difficulty may be in confronting this issue, it is only magnified when the party required to do this is the mother, given the norms that have existed over these many years and that the implications for a father and mother are not the same. Additionally, our courts, which have a long history of awarding custody to mothers in almost all instances, except when they were found to be unfit, have only reinforced this problem. If the divorce left the wife with her children, no one gave it a second thought. However, if it left the children with her husband, the inference was that there must have been good reason for this. Moreover, and since women did not generally give up custody of their children, and were not expected to, those implications were no different when the husband was left with custody by an agreement between the parties rather than by a court order.

How the mediator will deal with these emotional issues is to a certain extent a question of personal judgment. In some instances he will initially pretend to ignore them and, particularly where the parties seem able to discuss the questions incident to their divorce without too much emotionality, play out with them for a while how they see their living arrangements with the children working out. In other instances, he will feel it necessary to address them at the very outset.

As a general rule, the mediator will not meet with the parties separately. Particularly at the outset of the mediation, to do so might only be to breed distrust. This is one of those occasions, however, when an individual meeting might be both warranted and helpful. The mediator may, for example, wish to share with the husband his awareness of how trying his separation from his children is for him. He may also want to let the husband know that he is aware of his struggle to do what is best for his children and his feeling that he is abandoning them or perhaps even losing them. If the mediator is to be successful in addressing the emotional issues that underlie the surface conflict between the parties, it will be necessary for him to help the husband acknowledge and address these feelings. In some instances, it may be easier for the husband to do this with the mediator alone, and without his wife present. (This is not to say that these issues cannot be addressed in a conjoint meeting, with both of the parties present, or that it would be inappropriate to do so. On the contrary, it might be very constructive. While this will obligate the husband to express certain feelings in front of his wife, which may be difficult for him, it may also enable her to understand them better, and to be more empathetic towards him.)

On the other hand, the situation may be such that, should the mediator meet separately with the husband at this point, even with the wife's permission, that, and particularly if the individual meeting does not end in a resolution of the problem acceptable to the wife, the wife may only come away convinced of her husband's absolute intransigence, and the futility of the mediation. In each instance the mediator will have to make a judgment on the limited information he possesses as to which procedure would be best to follow under the circumstances. As a general rule, the mediator should not suggest an individual meeting with one of the parties unless he is convinced that the issue of custody is not the real issue, and that the party in question can be honest with himself, and is not so overwhelmed by feelings directed at his spouse that he will be able to acknowledge this.

Throughout the mediation, the mediator will have a problem. He knows that there are emotional issues that underlie all of the discussions between the parties. He will deal with them the way a therapist would deal with resistance—he will not go looking for them, and will ignore them unless they begin to interfere with what he is trying to accomplish. When they do surface, however, he must address them. That is the mental health component of divorce mediation—the ability to recognize and address those feelings that are preventing the couple from dealing effectively with the practical issues that must be resolved in order for them to separate and divorce. Whether that counseling is done in his conjoint sessions with the couple, with both of them present, or whether it is occasionally done with one of them alone, in both instances it is not only a necessary part of the mediation, but represents the ultimate exercise by the mediator of his skill and understanding.

Joint Custody

Joint custody was born of a concern for the fact that upon divorce, one of the parties, usually the husband, was automatically "divorced" from his children as well as from his wife. Increasingly, divorced fathers began to question why this onus should be placed on them. As women raised their voices to seek greater financial equality for wives upon divorce, husbands joined in to point out that gender-neutral statutes were also those that did not arbitrarily favor mothers over fathers; and that this too had been the legacy of laws and customs that placed women in a more subordinate, but at the same time somewhat more protected position. This protest was reinforced by the argument that all children, and particularly the children of divorce, require a strong relationship with both of their parents if they are to deal effectively with the trauma that their parents' separation occasioned.

No one can question the importance of the relationship children have with their parents, not only to the children themselves but to their parents as well. Nor is there any question that any arrangement involving a couple's children should seek to maintain, not simply a relationship in name between the children and each of their parents, but a relationship in fact as well. The problem simply is how to do this in the face of their parents' divorce, and the fact that their parents will now be living in separate households, consistent with the somewhat changed needs of both the parents and their children.

Unfortunately, joint custody has become a cause. In addition, it uses as a shibboleth a term that started out meaning one thing but now has very different meanings for different people. (That is why many thoughtful persons have attempted to substitute the term "shared parenting".) As a result, and instead of sitting down in each instance and attempting to work out an arrangement that makes sense for the children and for the parties, the issue too often turns on the question of whether one is in favor of or opposed to joint custody. These philosophic arguments only tend to obfuscate what is really the important issue, and should be avoided.

In each instance the attempt should be made to work out the living arrangements for the parties and their children on the basis of certain generally accepted, although to some extent inconsistent, principles:

1. Each of us requires a place that we return to, and that we call *our home.* If this is true of individuals generally, it is even more true of children whose sense of security is far more tenuous. Prior to their parents' separation, they had such a recognizable place. It was called their home. One of their parents can establish a new residence, and they can even come to feel comfortable there. But it is still not their home; nor does it have the associations of friends and community that will make it such.

2. The trauma and permanent injury that children experience with their parents' divorce is, of course, occasioned by the very fact of their parents' separation. But that fact alone will not necessarily determine the severity of that trauma or how successfully they will be able to deal with it. More often than not, this will be determined by other considerations, principally by how that separation is effectuated and, just as importantly, by the *relationship* that they will have with both of their parents (and that their parents will have with one another) following it. In other words, that separation must be balanced by the constancy of an ongoing, supportive relationship between the children and both of their parents, most *particularly the parent leaving* the children's home.

3. Children require a *continuity* of experience. They should not be subjected to abrupt, disruptive changes which will disturb this, at least until they have *completed high school.* Arrangements for their care should respect this.

4. Custodial arrangements should recognize the fact that there will be *life changes* in the future, particularly in the lives of the parents, and should anticipate them. Thus, arrangements should not be made that can only work under the existing state of facts, when there is no reasonable likelihood that those conditions will continue for any extended period of time following the couple's separation and divorce.

5. Arrangements for children must respect the fact that children will have *lives of their own.* The individual plans that they will increasingly make for themselves, which are age-appropriate, should and must be respected. Accordingly, arrangements should not be made that will only burden them with conflicts over their own needs and those of their parents.

The object of any arrangement made by separating and divorcing couples with respect to their children should honor *as many of these principles as is possible* under the circumstances. It can be taken as a truism that when either of the parents espouses *one* of those principles at the expense of all of the others, that parent is putting his or her own needs ahead of those of the children. Husbands and wives are people too, and their agreement should properly reflect their own needs, including their understandable need to maintain a close relationship with their children. However, they are *parents first and foremost*, and if sacrifices have to be made, it is they, and not their children, who should be expected to make them.

On occasion, though admittedly rarely, one of the parties, usually the husband, will attempt to solve the problem by suggesting that the children continue to live in the marital residence, with the parents alternating between that home and a small apartment which each of them occupies when the other is living with the children. In addition to its other supposed virtues, it is argued that it will not require the parents to maintain two complete, intact homes for the children, let alone for the children to alternate back and forth between those homes.

This arrangement, however, has a number of serious drawbacks, not the least of which is that it does not help the children accept the fact of their parents' separation and divorce because it does not seem complete to them. Their parents may not be living together, but they are still somewhat *playing house* together. Even more importantly, however, it is an arrangement that *cannot possibly last* for very long. In fact, it can only last until one of the parties becomes emotionally involved with a third party. (While the husband may be willing to move back and forth from his apartment to his and his former wife's home, his new girlfriend or wife will obviously not take so kindly to this arrangement. Nor will her children, or his for that matter.)

Thus, while perhaps an understandable arrangement when the youngest of the children has but nine months of his or her senior year of high school to complete, it is not an appropriate arrangement if it must continue beyond that, perhaps for years. It also has the decided disadvantage of affording neither of the parties very much privacy in their new lives. Since they both share the same accommodations, whether they are living with the children or not, they cannot help but feel that they are living in a fishbowl. Just as importantly, when each of them should be attempting to effectuate an emotional as well as a legal divorce, the constant reminder of the other party's presence wherever they turn can only tend to make this more difficult. In fact, these reminders can be extremely painful.

Few couples opt for this kind of a joint custodial arrangement. Rather, what is generally proposed is an arrangement whereby each of the parties will have his own home (one of those homes usually being the former marital residence) with the children alternating between the two homes on an agreed-upon basis. Unfortunately, there are certain logistic difficulties with any such arrangement. To begin with, the parties will need to maintain two relatively complete, intact homes, and few indeed are the couples who can afford to do this. Secondly, it is necessary that those homes be either within the same school district or, if they are not, that the party who does not live within the children's school district be able to arrange for them to get to and from school when they are with him. (An obvious exception to this is when the children live, for example, in an inner city and attend a private school that maintains bus transportation to both of the parents' homes.) That is why this "pure" type of joint custody, which sees the children spending equal periods of both work and free time with both of their parents, is so rarely seen in practice, despite articles in the popular press that might suggest otherwise.

While obviously not always the case, the fact remains that in more instances than not, when strict joint custody is being insisted upon, the arrangement being proposed has less to do with working out a "shared parenting" agreement than it does with complying with some philosophical concept of one of the parties. This is the case, for example, where one of the parties maintains that the children's time must not only be divided between them exactly equally in quantity, but also in quality, so that the equal division must extend to weekdays, weekends, birthdays, religious holidays, national holidays as well as school vacations and recesses. Nor will he permit such an arrangement to allow that he be separated from the children for more than two or three days at a time. Although the weeks and months of the year will have to be fractured and refractured to accomplish his insistence upon absolute equality, he steadfastly maintains that the plan is completely workable. In truth, however, it is not even easy to formulate the plan, let alone to live by it, and the children and each of the parties will be required to carry a copy of it in their back pockets at all times if they are ever to know where they are supposed to be at any given moment. Still the party in question insists that there is nothing complicated about the arrangement, let alone a burden on the children, to which they cannot easily adapt.

Whatever joint custody means, it does not mean this, and a parent who persists in his insistence upon it is more intent on establishing a *principle* in connection with his divorce than he is in working out an appropriate custodial arrangement that will meet his legitimate need to maintain a meaningful, ongoing relationship with his children. One possible technique to bring home this reality might be to suggest that he, rather than the children, do the moving that will be required to effectuate such an arrangement. After all, it is a lot easier to discount the inconvenience involved in a custodial arrangement when it is not *your* inconvenience. But if the dispute is not really *about* the children, but simply *over* them, which is so often the case in these instances, it is doubtful that any amount of rational argumentation will be sufficient. Fortunately, at least where mediation is sought on a voluntary basis, the mediator will very rarely be confronted with this situation.

As we have noted previously, a couple should be encouraged to decide the important issues concerning their children without regard to labels. Once such an agreement has been reached, however, if either or both of them feel more comfortable in attaching a particular label to that arrangement, whether that label be "joint custody," "shared parenting," or something else, there is absolutely nothing wrong in that. On the contrary, if the label will serve to help one of the parties to live with the arrangement, then it serves a useful purpose.

On occasion, the wife, with whom the children will principally reside, may feel threatened by the label because she worries that it may impair her right to continue to live with her children on an ongoing basis. If she agrees to "joint custody," she fears that her husband will later be able to use this as a means of securing sole custody, and taking the children from her.

Aside from the fact that this is a rather remote possibility—and certainly not the mental set of most people who seek mediation on a voluntary basis—the fact remains that no judge reading the agreement will be mislead by the label, or have any doubt as to who really has custody of the children. For while laymen tend to think of joint custody as meaning one thing, and only one thing, and to misconstrue joint custody statutes in the process, courts dealing with the practical issues of joint custody have learned to make the very important distinction between "legal" custody (with whom the responsibility and decision-making powers lie) and "physical" custody (with whom the children make their primary residence), to understand that "joint" custody is not always joint as to both, and to recognize that fact when they see it.

DECISION MAKING

Not uncommonly, the party with whom the children will not primarily reside will attempt to reinforce his relationship with them by insisting that he share in all decisions affecting them. While it is certainly understandable that he would *wish* to do so, this simple request is not without its complications. Suppose that the agreement provides that all important decisions shall be made *jointly* by the parties. What if the parties disagree as to whether or not the decision in question is important? Suppose they even agree that it is an important decision, but cannot agree on how it is to be decided? When the parties were living together as a family, certain factors in their relationship served to decide these questions, for better or worse. Unfortunately, to a very great extent those *natural balances no longer exist*. They are not even able to successfully shout their way to a decision, if that is how it was handled in the past.

Fortunately, and common opinion to the contrary, there are *not* really very many important decisions that parents are required to make with respect to their children that *economic circumstances* do not make for them. (They go to sleep-away camp not because they agree or disagree that the children should have the benefit of this experience, but because one or both of the parents can afford to send them.) Unless the children attend private school—and this, too, is a question of economics—they rarely even decide what school their children will attend. In short, decisions that parents make with respect to their children are by and large the day-to-day decisions that they will have to make—what they will have for dinner, when they will go to sleep, with whom they will play, whether they will go to the movies, etc.—and these, quite obviously, will be made by the parent with whom the children are then staying.

While there is nothing wrong with providing in the agreement that parents will jointly make all of the important decisions affecting their children (or, as is sometimes the case, that the custodial or residential parent will consult with the other parent on all decisions of importance), and then to hope for the best, the far better procedure is to *anticipate in advance* what issues, if any, are likely to arise between the parties concerning their children, and to decide them as part of the mediation.

These issues generally concern whether the children will attend public or parochial school, whether they will be raised in any particular religion (if the parents are of different religions) or receive a certain prescribed religious instruction; where the parent with whom the children are living will reside; and whether that parent will have the right to have an "unrelated adult of the opposite sex" (a boyfriend or girlfriend), reside in the house with him or her.

In this regard, the mediator should follow the adage, never put off for tomorrow a problem that you can just as easily discuss and decide today. This does not necessarily mean that the mediator need inquire about all of these particular issues, and they will usually be brought up for discussion during the course of the mediation in one of a number of ways. One of the parties may already have the issue on his mind. Other possible issues—for example, the question of whether the wife will have the right to live in the parties' home with another man, or who will be responsible for the payment of orthodontic treatment—will be addressed when the question of the parties' marital residence and medical expenses is discussed. In other instances, the issue may be brought to the fore simply by a question posed by the mediator as to how decisions affecting the children will be made in the future. In each instance, when a question or potential question is raised, it should either be decided in advance or, if that is not possible, provision should be made as to how it will be decided if it arise in the future.

Unfortunately, every rule has its exception. Consider the following situation. A mediator is working with a young couple who have been married for four years and have a two-year-old daughter. The husband is Jewish and the wife Catholic and at the time of their marriage, although she did not convert to Judaism, the wife agreed that their children would be raised in the Jewish religion. That, of course, was a commitment that the wife made when she was contemplating her marriage, not her divorce, and when she assumed it would last forever. She is really Catholic, however, and the conditions under which that commitment was made no longer exist. Nor does she feel comfortable having to honor it in the future. She is young, and if she marries again she may well have other children. More importantly, in all likelihood her next husband will not be Jewish, which means that if she is forced to honor their original understanding, she will be forced to raise her children in different religions.

Although fleeting mention was made of the wife's previous commitments, neither of the parties has said any more about it. What should the mediator do? Should he, himself, place the issue on the table, or should he let sleeping dogs lie? To put it more forcefully, is it *responsible* for a mediator simply to ignore an issue that may later come back to haunt the parties?

It is not possible to give blanket answers to such questions, and in each instance the mediator will be required to assess the situation as best he can, and make a judgment call. When the issue first arose here, the mediator initially left it where he found it. He interpreted the fact that the husband had mentioned the wife's commitment as an indication that the question was on the husband's mind. However, having raised the question, and having gotten a noncommittal response from his wife, the husband then went no further. The mediator interpreted this in the following way.

Neither of the parties had really had an opportunity to sort out their feelings here. Thus, if the husband pressed forward with the issue, and threw his I.O.U. down on the table, he might only do so at the risk of causing them to come to an impasse. Also, it might only be an impasse they could avoid at a later date when they were able to deal with the problem in more concrete terms, rather than abstractly. Further, the husband was anxious to maintain a good relationship with his wife and sensed, and perhaps with legitimate cause, that the commitment she had freely given previously was not as easy for her to give at this time. Thus, rather than pressing the issue, the husband decided to take his chances.

Interpreting the fleeting exchange between the parties as he did, the mediator decided not to press the issue. If he was correct in concluding that the husband had decided that it might not be safe water for him to wade into, as anxious as he was to get to the other side, the mediator felt that he should respect that and not push the husband further than he had chosen to go on his own. Did that mean that the issue might not be brought up again and addressed during the mediation? That was, of course, possible, a prospect the mediator was not very happy about and would have liked to foreclose on if he could. However, it was also possible that he might yet find occasion to address it, further on in the mediation, when the parties had had more time to *acclimate themselves to the realities* of their divorce, and when such a discussion might not be as threatening.

As we have noted, when it is not currently feasible to resolve an issue, or to anticipate all of the issues that may arise in the future, the mediator should attempt to build in some procedure for dealing with these problems in the future, should they arise. Absent a provision for the parties to resort to some formal procedure (for example, binding arbitration), and even prior to invoking such, it makes sense to include in the agreement a provision that in the event of such a dispute, the parties will consult with a *designated person* (perhaps the mediator himself) in an attempt to resolve it. While this language is obviously only precatory, it nevertheless represents a gentlemen's agreement to *talk* rather than simply to *ignore* the issue. Further, it encourages the couple to *return* to a procedure that once before proved successful, or at least partially successful, for them.

SHIFTS IN CUSTODY

New and egalitarian attitudes toward custody often express themselves in different ways. The noncustodial parent (usually the husband) does not object that the children will presently remain with their mother; rather, he simply wishes to include a provision in the agreement permitting the children to opt to live with him when they reach a certain age, for example, after they reach their twelfth birthday.

On the face of it, there is little to object to in this request. After all, why shouldn't a boy, who will live with his mother for the next four to five years, also have the opportunity, at his option, to experience living with his father? Unfortunately, there are serious potential problems hidden beneath this simple request. One of the most baneful aspects of traditional adversarial divorce proceedings is the fact that children are invariably drawn into the struggle between their parents. To a very great extent, there are no real, substantial differences between the parties. Both are really fit parents and either could do a good enough job. Without any real distinctions between them, each senses that the key to the court's determination may well be the children's preferences. As a result, electioneering, politicking, and even subtle bribery become commonplace.

Another unfortunate aspect of traditional divorce proceedings is that they do not resolve the conflict between the parties. Rather, that conflict all too often extends well beyond their divorce, with *money and children usually the weapons*. One factor that aids the continuance of that conflict is the knowledge that if a parent can change a child's preference, even after the divorce, he may still be able to retrieve victory from defeat.

In point of fact, if one or more of the children wish to live with the other parent after a certain period of time, the reality is that it *will happen*; and there is very little today that can be done to prevent it. But that does not mean that it should be encouraged. It is not the shift in the living arrangements of the children that is necessarily undesirable. What is so undesirable is the *power* with which the children will so often be invested in order to effectuate such a shift. Children in our society have power enough as it is. It is age-appropriate that they should be able to exercise some of that power, and to express their individual interests and wants, particularly when they are going through the separation/individuation stage of their adolescence. But it takes a very delicate balancing act on the part of a parent to deal effectively with a child going through this difficult period of adjustment. It does not help the custodial or residential parent, nor the child for that matter, to have that balancing act skewed by the other parent, by additional power handed to the child and taken away from that parent. In such a situation, a mother can often stand paralyzed as her son challenges her authority at his father's prompting, afraid to exercise her authority for fear that her son will then accept his father's open invitation to come and live with him if the going gets rough. All too often, the son actively participates in this little demi-drama, having little if any awareness of the role he is really playing.

As was noted, this can all occur even *without* a clause in the parties' agreement giving the children this right. The changes that have taken place in our society over the last number of years have not left children unaffected, and it is difficult today to make a 13- or 14-year-old child (and sometimes even an 11- or 12-year-old child) live with a parent with whom he does not wish to live. Nevertheless, there is little purpose served in encouraging this, or making the child's power too explicit. On the contrary, the role of each of the parties as a parent should be encouraged and reinforced by the other, not just for their own individual benefits, but, and more important, for the benefit, in the form of security and stability, that it provides for the children.

VISITATION

The term "visitation," like the term "custody" has strongly negative connotations. Prisoners are taken into custody, and their relatives are given the opportunity to visit with them at stated intervals. Nothing disenfranchises a father more than to be told that he will have the right to "visit" with his children at set periods of time.

Rather than being asked when he would like to visit with his children, the parent with whom the children will not be primarily residing should be asked instead how and when he sees himself being able to spend time with them. The mediator should reinforce the fact that it is understood that he is going to continue to have an ongoing relationship with his children, and be an important influence in their lives, and that their job is simply to arrange time for him to be able to do that consonant with his work schedule and their own commitments.

In attempting to arrange for the noncustodial parent to spend time with his children, there are certain principles that should always be respected.

1. An arrangement should be avoided which will cause these "visitation rights" to become simply "entertainment rights." This occurs when, for example, a father is given the right to visit with his children from 10 A.M. Sunday morning until 6 P.M. on Sunday evening. What he has really been given is simply the privilege of entertaining them for eight hours. (As a general rule, what will distinguish visitation rights from entertainment rights is the ability to have the children overnight.)

2. The second rule is a corollary of the first and provides that, to the extent possible, the noncustodial parent's time with the children should duplicate, as closely as possible, the conditions under which he spent time with them when they lived together as a family. This is best accomplished by broad blocks of time on weekends, school holidays, and during the children's summer recess from school. (Since a parent can only spend time with his children when they are not in school, and when he himself is not working, visitation is by and large scheduled around the time when the children are not in school.)

3. Interspersed between these larger blocks of time should be shorter periods when the noncustodial parent will have an opportunity to see his children, if even only for a few hours. These shorter periods of time help to maintain continuity (and constancy) in the relationship. This is particularly important with younger children. Unlike the substantial blocks of time, it is not important that these periods will only allow for the noncustodial parent and the children to go out together for a quick bite to eat in the evening, as it is not intended that they will serve the same purpose as the more extended periods that he will spend with the children on other occasions.

(This is not to suggest that these shorter periods cannot include the right to have the children overnight; and if the parties live proximate to one another, and if the husband can arrange to get the children to school on the following morning, these opportunities can prove to be very valuable. They are particularly valuable if the parties have two or more children of disparate ages and sexes. If it is the husband's intention to have all of the children with him as a rule on weekends and school holidays, this can enable him to give each of them individual attention by exercising his weekday visitation with them one at a time, usually without any resentment on the part of any of them or inconvenience to the wife, as would be the case were the husband to exercise his visitation with the children individually on weekends, thus depriving the wife of the opportunity of having time off for herself.)

4. The arrangement should not be predicated simply on the couple's present circumstances, or on what is now possible. Rather, their agreement should spell out what would be the ideal arrangement in terms of the noncustodial parent's being able to spend time with his children, regardless of whether or not he will be able to avail himself of that full opportunity at the present time. (A husband may often balk at the suggestion that he should have the right to have the children with him for a period of four weeks during the summer, pointing out that he only gets a two-week summer vacation. While this is true, he may remarry in a year or two and then be in a position to have the children live with him for the four weeks, just as he has in the past, despite the fact that he may have to work for two of those weeks.)

5. The arrangement should respect the fact that the noncustodial parent will be building a new life for himself, and will need time for that purpose. Accordingly, an arrangement that permits him (morally requires him) to visit with his children every weekend may prove to be a burden as well as a privilege, and may create unnecessary conflicts.

6. The arrangement must respect the fact that the custodial parent needs time off too. Our awareness of the problems confronted by the noncustodial parent's being unable to live with his children often blinds us to the burden (mixed with the blessing) on the custodial parent, particularly when, as is so often the case in divorce, she is required to work outside of the home. Having a full-time job and raising children without the benefit of a second pair of hands is hard work. In fact, in many instances it is such an overwhelm-

ing responsibility that the custodial parent ends up being deprived of much of the joy in raising her children. The custodial parent needs a breather, and the only time that she will get it is when her husband takes responsibility for the care of their children.

Perhaps the most ideal arrangement within the conventional format of the children maintaining their primary residence with one of their parents is a situation in which the noncustodial parent has the children with him *every other weekend* (ideally, from Friday evening before dinner until Sunday evening after dinner, or perhaps even Monday morning) and *also* has the opportunity to see the children one or two nights a week for dinner—with perhaps the opportunity to have the children stay overnight at his home on one of those evenings.

For some couples, on the other hand, and particularly where the children are very young or where there will be little meaningful opportunity to spend time with them during the week, every other weekend may seem too infrequent. If that is the case, they can employ a variant of this that will still serve most of the principles involved. This involves a four-week visitation cycle. On the first, the children are with the noncustodial parent for the entire weekend, and on the second they are with the custodial parent for the entire weekend. On weekend number three the noncustodial parent has the children from Friday evening until Saturday evening or Sunday morning, and on the fourth he has them from Saturday night or Sunday morning until Sunday evening or Monday morning. The effect of this arrangement is to permit each of the parties to be with the children for a substantial period of time on three out of four weekends and, at the same time, also to have some time off on three out of four weekends.

For some couples, nothing short of visitation every weekend will suffice. Even with couples who prefer this arrangement, however, variation can still be the rule, with the noncustodial parent having the children with him from Friday evening until either Saturday evening or Sunday morning one weekend, and from Saturday evening until either Sunday evening or Monday morning on the other. This kind of variation has the benefit of giving the noncustodial parent different kinds of experiences with the children and doesn't lock him into a schedule that may conflict with his own personal life.

There is another weekend variation that can often be utilized to resolve a dispute between the parties concerning joint custody. Although it may offend certain groups to say so, as we have noted elsewhere, disputes *over* children are not always disputes *about* children. For reasons not very hard to understand and to sympathize with, the husband has great difficulty with the fact that losing or giving up his marriage may also mean that he must lose or give up his children. This is expressed by him in the request that the parties have either joint legal or joint physical custody of their children. The wife hasn't the slightest intention of standing between her husband and their children, believes that he is a devoted father and is mindful of how important it is that there continue to be a strong relationship between him and the children. Nevertheless, she is very threatened by the idea of joint custody, particularly when it is cojoined with the suggestion that the time of the children during the week also be divided between the parties.

Unfortunately, and even though it will be far more difficult for the husband than he is willing to admit to reconcile his business and parental responsibilities during the week, the weekdays are very important to him. Why is this? Because if the husband is given the right to be with his children from Friday evening until Sunday evening, all that he feels that he has been given is the right to *visit* with his children. However, if he is given the right to be with them for the same length of time, from Monday evening to Wednesday evening, he now feels that he too has custody of them.

As we have noted, the wife is threatened by this request. Aside from the fact that she does not like the weekdays of the children to be broken up and, regardless of the possible advantages to her in the suggestion, she still feels that she has lost her children in an important sense. On occasion, particularly where these issues can be discussed openly with the parties, it may be possible to resolve the dispute over joint custody by starting the weekend one day earlier, on Thursday evening, and by ending it one day earlier, on Saturday evening or possibly Sunday morning. (This, of course, presupposes that the husband can arrange for them to get to school on Friday morning.) The wife may feel less threatened by this proposal. At the same time, it may satisfy the husband by giving him at least one weekday with the children, and satisfy them both by giving each of them a substantial period of time with the children on the weekends.

Having determined the time that the noncustodial parent will be able to spend with the children on weekends and during the week, the couple's attention should next be directed to holidays during the school year. As a rule, it is not necessary for the mediator to concern himself with isolated, one-day school holidays. If these occur during the week, they are generally not of concern to the noncustodial parent, since if he is required to work on the day in question, it is of no value to him anyway. If, on the other hand, they are national holidays, particularly those national holidays that have been assigned by law to the nearest Monday, it is a far better procedure to consider them to be part of the weekend and to be assigned to that party the children are to be with on the preceding day. Thus, if the noncustodial parent is to have the children for the full weekend in question, it is only logical that he should have the children on Monday as well, if that is a holiday, since this will afford him the opportunity of being able to take a long weekend away with them should he wish to.

The school holidays that are really at issue are the Thanksgiving school vacation, the Christmas school vacation, and the Easter school vacation. In some cases, the children may even have an additional school holiday, such as a February recess. These school holidays are important for a number of reasons. To begin with, they represent one of the few substantial periods of time during the year when the noncustodial parent can have the children live with him on a somewhat normal basis. Additionally, they represent an opportunity for the noncustodial parent (and the custodial parent as well) to vacation with the children away from home and, even if this is not something that is economically feasible at the present time, it is still possible that it may be in the future. Subject to the problem that the significance of Christmas has for many families, one way to deal with these vacations is simply to alternate them between the parties in successive years. This can be done by providing, for example, that the father will have the children with him during their Thanksgiving school recess in odd years and the mother in even years.

Instead of alternating the school holidays, some parents prefer to divide each of them between themselves. Thus, if there is a ten-day spring school vacation, the father will have the children with him for the first five days and the mother with her for the last five days. Particularly if it is not the intention of either of the parties to go away with the children, this is a very sensible way to handle the school vacations, as in those instances it is more than likely that neither one of the parents would want, or perhaps even be able to have, the children for more than half of the vacation time, particularly if they both work.

The only time that this arrangement creates a problem is when one of the parties would like to use the occasion of the children's recess from school to vacation away from home, and might find four or five days insufficient for that purpose, particularly if he intends to travel some distance to accomplish this. A way of handling this is to combine both of the previous arrangements. Thus, the agreement can provide that the parties will alternate the school holidays in successive years, but that if the parent who has the right to have the children for a particular school holiday does not intend to be away with the children during the time in question, then the holiday will be divided equally between them.

Christmas represents a special problem, and will have to be dealt with by the mediator on a case-by-case basis. As with Thanksgiving, it is perhaps best to start out by determining whether or not there has been any special arrangement the family has traditionally followed in celebrating this holiday. Very often the mediator will find that neither of the parties is anxious to disturb that arrangement, even though it may mean that one of them may be somewhat excluded in the future, as, for example, when it has been the custom for them to spend the day with the wife's family. More often than not, the mediator will be able to work out an accommodation by dividing Christmas Eve and Christmas Day. Thus, for example, the agreement can provide that the husband will have the children on Christmas Eve until eleven or twelve o'clock at night (or overnight until early Christmas morning), and that he will then return them to the wife who will have them for the balance of Christmas Day.

Sometimes, and particularly if one of the parties is strongly attached to Christmas as a family holiday, the parties may even agree that the other party, even on those years when the children are to be with him or her for the full holiday period, will postpone taking them until the day after Christmas, and the fact that the Christmas school recess always extends for at least one week beyond Christmas Day will often facilitate such an arrangement.

Lastly, there is the summer recess from school. Although this period of time potentially represents the greatest opportunity for the noncustodial parent to live with his children on a substantial basis, and most closely replicates the conditions under which they lived together when they were an intact family, a mediator will very often find little interest expressed by the noncustodial parent, other than perhaps a week or two, during this period.

To a certain extent, this is understandable. The noncustodial parent, usually the husband, is often in a period of transition. He may not even have a permanent place of his own at the present time, or his economic circumstances may be such that, even if he does, it is too small comfortably to accommodate the children for any extended period of time. Added to this, of course, is the fact that he works, and may only have a very limited vacation, perhaps as short as a week, during the summer. Be that as it may, it would be a mistake to predicate his right to have his children with him on those present circumstances. As we have noted, it is far better to anticipate the possibility that his circumstances may change in the future and afford him an opportunity to be with his children, and to have them with him on a more substantial basis.

The converse of this can also occur, however. In this instance, the husband insists on having the right to have the children with him for the entire summer, or perhaps for all but a very short portion of it, claiming that the children will be living with the wife throughout the year and that this will be the only time when he will really have the opportunity to have them live with him for any extended period. While this is undoubtedly true, it is not, nevertheless, determinative of the issue unless, as will sometimes be the case, the wife will not oppose the suggestion. Aside from the argument sometimes advanced by the wife—that the husband is taking all of the *quality* time, and that she will be left with only the drudgery—the fact remains that even though the wife will have the children with her for the entire time they are in school, she would also like to experience being with them during their free time as well.

Nor is it difficult to understand this. This is particularly so when the wife herself works for, as we have noted, no matter how meaningful it may be for the wife to have custody of the children (for their primary residence to be with her), the fact remains that the juggling act she will be required to take on in order to meet all of her responsibilities will drain much of the enjoyment she would otherwise derive from being with her children, particularly on weekdays. Ideally, the wife will recognize that, whatever her own problems, the fact that the children's primary residence is with her should entitle the husband to at least some preference during the time that the children are not required to attend school. Just as ideally, however, the husband will also recognize that the wife and the children should not be deprived of time with one another during these same periods as well.

On occasion, a discussion of the noncustodial parent's right to have the children with him during the summer may bring into question the children's summer activities. This is particularly true when they attend day camp or sleep-away camp. Before commenting upon this, it is best for the mediator first to get a sense of the couple's own attitude toward this. Even if it would substantially interfere with his ability to spend time with his children in the summer, the husband may quickly defer to the fact that his right should be subordinate to their opportunity to participate in that activity. If that is the case, the only problem then is to arrange for the children to be with him either before or after the activity in question, or both. If the parties are not of a like mind here, the question then becomes one of priorities. Is it more important for the children to be with the noncustodial parent or to participate in the activity in question? Further, does the period of time that the children will be with the noncustodial parent justify disrupting their plans, if that is the case, for the balance of the summer?

Fortunately, these issues are rarely presented if all that is involved is day camp. Children go to day camp not only because it is an enjoyable experience but also because it serves the needs of providing for their care during the summer when the custodial parent is at work and unable personally to supervise them. If the children are with the non-custodial parent, however, instead of being at camp, then it is no longer the custodial parent's problem, and the noncustodial parent will either himself have to enroll the children in day camp, if he cannot personally supervise their care, or make other suitable arrangements for them while they are with him. If the issue is sleep-away camp, or some other summer activity that involves a substantial period of time, the problem is not as easy. All that may remain of the summer is a very short period, perhaps little more than two weeks. Nevertheless, the wife, for example, is not willing to permit the husband to have all of it, complaining that if she does, she will not have the children with her for any portion of the summer. If they split the time between them, however, then the husband will only be able to have the children for a little more than a week.

Although the wife may not always be comfortable with this, one solution is to let the husband determine whether or not the children will participate in the activity in question, thereby transferring the problem to one between the husband and his children alone. In this case the agreement can provide, for example, that the husband will have the right to have the children with him for a period of four or five weeks during the summer, except that if they attend sleep-away camp, then for half of the remaining time. The husband will now have to decide whether he is willing to sacrifice his opportunity to be with his children during the summer for them to have the benefits of participating in this summer activity. Whatever he may decide, however, the wife has been removed as a target of any competitive feelings he may have in resolving this conflict, since she has nothing to say about his decision.

Spelling Out the Arrangement

Occasionally the parties will complain that it is not necessary to spell out the noncustodial parent's visitation in the agreement. They will argue that they have been able to work this out quite easily between themselves in the past and are sure they will be able to do so in the future too. Or they will say that the children are of such an age that it serves no useful purpose to attempt to do this, and that the noncustodial parent can simply make those arrangements directly with the children based upon their respective needs. While this may well be true, it is nevertheless the better policy to spell out the visitation in the agreement, at least to a certain extent. It is the hope of the mediator and the couple that they will never have to look to their agreement with respect to these issues and that they will be able to work them out between themselves as they arise. Nevertheless, questions may come up between the couple in the future that they cannot determine so easily. In those instances, they should have the benefit of their agreement to fall back upon. That is what it is there for—to prevent what are simply *differences of opinion* from developing into perhaps unresolvable *disputes*.

Similarly, and even though it is true that visitation schedules that can be applied to a 7- or 8-year-old child cannot be similarly applied to a child of 15 or 16, and that to a large extent the noncustodial parent will have to work these arrangements out directly with them (giving due consideration to the plans they may wish to make for themselves), that does not mean that the agreement should not establish a *format* within which the non-custodial parent and the children will attempt to make their plans. All that it means is that there may have to be more *variations* in that schedule than is the case with younger children.

There is another reason why it makes sense to have such a schedule, even in the case of children who are over 18 and are technically emancipated adults. A child should not be placed in a position, for example, where both parents are asking him to spend his spring recess from college with them. If the agreement provides that the noncustodial parent is to have this right in odd years, and the custodial parent to have the same right in even years, he will not be placed in this position. Similarly, there is something to be said, particularly for older children, in having the agreement define their obligation to the noncustodial parent. A 16-year-old child naturally has legitimate needs of his own. By the same token, he may feel some sense of guilt if he does not spend time with the noncustodial parent. Having the agreement provide that the noncustodial parent shall have the right to be with the child every other weekend on Saturday, for example, will provide the child with a criterion by which to judge whether or not he has fulfilled his responsibility, thereby avoiding any guilt he may feel as a result of the situation.

The schedule of visitation should also contain provision for appropriate *notice*. Common courtesy dictates that the noncustodial parent give appropriate notice to the custodial parent of his intentions so that she can make her plans accordingly. If, for example, the wife assumes that her husband will be visiting with their children on a particular weekend and she has plans of her own, it will not be necessary for her to make arrangements for someone to be with the children. If she does not find out until the very last minute that it is *not* his intention to be with his children, however, she may well be left in the lurch. Obviously, the amount of notice depends upon the period in question. If it is a Wednesday night visitation for dinner between the hours of 6 and 8 P.M., one day's notice, or perhaps even just a couple of hours' notice, may be sufficient, as it is unlikely that the wife will have made any plans contingent upon this visitation. On the other hand, if it is a four-week visitation during the summer, the wife will want and need notice well in advance so that she can make her own plans.

One final word must be mentioned in this regard. The husband is to see the children on the weekend, and in accordance with the provisions of the agreement has advised the wife that he will be picking the children up at approximately 6 o'clock. The husband is detained at work or is caught in traffic, and is unable to get there at the appointed time. These things do happen on occasion and in most instances the wife will understand it, even if it may pose some inconvenience. However, she will *not* understand, and will certainly not appreciate, the situation where she has no way of knowing when, if at all, the husband will arrive. It would therefore be a good idea for the mediator to lay down the rule that if the husband will be detained by more than fifteen minutes, he will call the wife to advise her so that she is not left to wait and wonder.

RELATIONS WITH THIRD PARTIES

On occasion, an issue may arise because one of the parties objects to the other's being with the children in the presence of a third party. Although it is an issue that can be raised by either the husband or the wife, it is usually raised differently by each of them, and for different reasons.

If it is raised by the wife, more often than not her objection will relate to the husband's present girlfriend. (Rarely will the wife ever raise an objection to a future girlfriend of the husband's.) The wife's objection here is a by-product of two different, although not necessarily unrelated, emotional issues. To begin with, and if the husband is already emotionally involved outside of the marriage when the couple come into mediation, it is usually he who has initiated the divorce, and it is usually the wife who does not want it. She cannot help but view this other woman as having been instrumental in their divorce, if not its very cause. Her hurt and anger, fueled by her feelings of loss and rejection, are such that the wife has made a personal issue of it between herself and this other woman. Those feelings will become focused and further intensified if the wife knows the woman in question, or at least something about her, which is usually the case. They will become aggravated if the wife views her as of a lower status—as would be the case if, for example, she were the husband's secretary or one of his employees. The wife does not like the idea of losing to this woman, and if she cannot get *even*, she would at least like to get *back* at her.

At times there is a secondary consideration that motivates the wife's objection. Even when her feelings are not so personalized and focused, she may still be threatened by the *picture* of her husband, this other woman, and her children. It is not necessarily that she fears that she will lose her children to her husband's new girlfriend, as that will certainly not be the case. Nevertheless, she still may resent her husband's life being so *complete*, while hers is still so shattered, and keeping this other woman out of the picture, so to speak, may be her way of striking back at him. Finally, she cannot have helped but tell herself a story about her husband and this other woman, and part of her must want to hold on to that story and to shelter it from attack. It is easier to do this if she can keep her children close to her and not exposed to evidence that might possibly call it into question, as would occur, for example, were her children to return from a weekend's visit with their father and report that they had been treated kindly by the woman in question and that they had all had a very good time together.

The mediator, to be sure, will probably see the situation very differently. Nevertheless, he is not easily going to persuade the wife or get her to see it other than she does. She does not wish to be shown that she is wrong. Rather, and since she may still wish to nurse her wounds, she wants support for the fact that she is right. Again, and from the mediator's point of view, this other woman is a fact of life, particularly if the husband should later marry her. Thus, he knows that it would be best if the wife could accept and learn to live with the fact of her existence. The wife is not ready to hear any of this, however. In fact, she may simply answer with the observation that while that may be true, they are not married yet.

While the husband can suffer the same feelings when it is the wife who is emotionally involved with someone outside of the marriage, and while he too may voice his objection to this other person, the objection will usually be expressed differently. Perhaps it is because the children will be living with his wife on a permanent basis, and he does not see them "going" to her as she sees them "going" to him. Perhaps it is because it is harder for men to acknowledge their hurt at the hands of another man than it is for women to acknowledge theirs at the hands of another woman, or because it is not as socially sanctioned for them to do so, just as it is not as socially sanctioned for men to cry as it is for women. Though they may on occasion express their feelings as vehemently as do their wives, they rarely complain about the fact that their children will be in the presence of their wife's boyfriend. Rather, they usually disguise their complaint, and set it on firmer ground, by employing a different line of defense. Thus, the husband's objection is not to his wife's being with her boyfriend in the presence of their children. It is to her boyfriend moving in to live with her and their children in his home.

The argument is usually a fairly effective one. By placing it where he has, the husband has not acknowledged that his wife's relationship with her boyfriend bothers him. He has even finessed, at least to some extent, the charge that he is trying to run his wife's life or tell her what she can or cannot do. She can do anything she wishes and see anyone she wants to, including her present boyfriend. She simply cannot move her boyfriend into their home. After all, the husband is forgoing the present enjoyment of the equity in his home for the benefit of his wife and children, not for the benefit of his wife's new boyfriend. For good measure, the husband will often also throw in the fact that he considers it inappropriate that his children should be exposed to their mother's relationship with her boyfriend in their own home and, with great moral authority, attempt to foreclose on the issue by insisting that he will not stand for it.

Nor is the husband's argument about his proprietary interest in his home necessarily a manufactured one. In point of fact, the husband will usually have great difficulty with the idea of another man moving into his home and enjoying its amenities, particularly if he has not paid for them. (It is for this reason that while a wife will rarely raise the question of her husband's future girlfriend, a wife's future boyfriend is usually as objectionable to the husband as her present one. In fact, this is true whether or not she has a boyfriend at the time at all.) As a result, the husband will usually insist that the home be sold should the wife remarry, or should she reside in the home with another man, unless his interest in the home is bought out at that time.

On occasion, the objectionable person is a relative or friend, and not a boyfriend or girlfriend. (A husband or a wife may also have an objection to the other's parents, but it is an objection that will rarely, if ever, be seriously raised, since it is not socially sanctioned to do so and since the husband or wife has learned to live with his or her objection.) Here, the complaint is usually grounded in the conduct of the party in question or the fact that he or she represents an *improper influence* on the children. This can be because he is addicted to drugs, engages in criminal activity, or otherwise comports himself in a way that renders his relationship with the children objectionable in the eyes of one of the parties. The other party, for his part, either denies the charge or insists, even if it is true, that the conduct in question never takes place in the children's presence. In most instances, it may be very difficult for the mediator to make an informed judgment in his own mind as to whether or not the conduct actually takes place or, if it does, whether the circumstances are such that it is injurious to the children. Even if he were able to do so, however, this does not mean that he will be able to resolve the dispute between the parties, as it may only be a mask for a conflict between them on a deeper level.

The problem of the relationship between either the husband or the wife and a third party can be one of the knottiest dilemmas with which a mediator is confronted. This is because it is almost impossible to separate the party's objection from the strong feelings that have given birth to it; and the argument that follows does not lead to any resolution. Also, the mediator can easily incur the displeasure of one of the parties—more often the wife than the husband—if he does not handle it very carefully.

The mediator would like to suggest that the husband and wife are both good parents, concerned with the well-being of their children, and that they should each rely on the others' good judgment; and leave it at that. (Unfortunately, however, this is not always as simple as that. On occasion the convenience of one of them is so compelling that they will not stop to think what effect their conduct will have upon their children or will simply rationalize it away with simplistic slogans.) And he would like to say that the remedy for the possible misconduct of one of the parties in this regard is not to line their agreement with straitjackets that inappropriately limit the freedom of movement of either of them, but with appropriate *action*, should conduct truly injurious to the children occur.

These arguments will usually prove ineffective, however. They are particularly futile when the complaint is about specific conduct of the offending party, not a general complaint about the party himself. (The wife does not complain that the husband's cousin is not *nice*. She complains that he is an alcoholic or a drug addict and that if the husband visits with the children in his cousin's presence, they will be exposed to these vices.) Here the wife is not complaining about what the third party may do in the future. She is complaining about what he has already done. If the husband acknowledges that the conduct has occurred, the mediator's job is made a lot easier. Unfortunately, that will usually not be the case, and the couple will engage in a factual dispute about which the mediator has no independent knowledge.

Without suggesting that this will always prove effective, one procedure that a mediator might employ is *exaggeration*, particularly if the party raising the objection is the wife and what she objects to is her husband's present girlfriend. The wife has objected to the children being with the husband in his girlfriend's presence. Rather than addressing this, the mediator can turn to the wife and say, "I know that you are not attempting to tell your husband how to live his life, and that your only concern is for the well-being of your children, and you have every right to be concerned. I agree with you. I do not think that it would be in the best interests of your children if they were to be with their father in his apartment for a weekend with his girlfriend there overnight. Nor would it be appropriate for him to go on vacation with your children under the same circumstances. I think that what we should do, therefore, is to put a provision in the agreement that will insure that this will not happen."

It is possible that the wife will in this way be able to obtain the satisfaction that she wants and needs, and that she will not press beyond this point. It is also possible that, having given in to her on the most serious problem, the wife may now hesitate to make an issue of the far less serious one—whether the husband will have the right to be with his children in the presence of his girlfriend on *other* occasions. Needless to say, this is not an intervention that a mediator can employ unless he has first made a judgment as to how the husband will view the suggestion, and whether he will consider that the mediator has helped him or hurt him. Nor is it one that a mediator should employ before he has explored his other options. Since it involves the expression of a judgment on the mediator's part, there are inherent dangers in its use. Thus, it should be invoked only as a *last resort*, and where there seems to be no other way to break the impasse.

As in so many instances during the mediation, the mediator is going to have to tiptoe here. As we have already said, as he proceeds through the mediation, the mediator will very consciously avoid engaging in extensive exploratory surgery to look for all of the hidden problems. Nor will he always put them on the table even when he finds them. He therefore proceeds with less than complete information. Therefore it is always dangerous for him to put his foot down too firmly in a given place. His forays must be tentative, and he must always be prepared to step back if he feels that he has gone too fast or too far.

In each instance what he is looking for, and what he is trying to determine, is what each of the parties' reactions is to an advance that he has made. He is trying to find a position that both of the parties will be able to accept. At each point, as he tentatively moves an inch forward or an inch either left or right, he will attempt to make an assessment of how acceptable that ground is for either or both of them. Based on these readings that he makes as he goes along, he will then determine where it is that he should or can go next. In either case, if he sets his foot down gently, and proceeds with a *question* rather than with a *statement*, he is less likely to cause offense if it turns out that he has inadvertently stepped in the wrong place.

Residence Restriction

Implicit in the noncustodial parent's right to be with and to spend time with his children is the understanding that he will be able to implement this. As a practical matter, that means that the children will live proximate to him, and not at some distant location that will render his rights, so carefully spelled out in the agreement, nugatory.

Even if the parties should neglect to raise the question, and even though it can often be one of the most difficult that the mediator will have to deal with in the mediation (the wife hasn't the slightest intention of moving anywhere, but feels very restricted by her husband's suggestion that she should be limited in terms of where she can live; the husband does not really believe that his wife would uproot their children, but what guarantee does he have that she will not feel differently in the future and how would he ever get to see his children if she did), it must be addressed. Ignoring it does not solve it; nor does it avoid it. It just puts it off. And because the problem will not occur unless one of the parties then already has a fixed intention to move, it will prove very intractable when it does arise, and may not be resolved short of court litigation.[1]

Not uncommonly, the couple will be unable to look at the problem in a practical light, and will instead view it as being one of *principle*, the wife maintaining that the husband is attempting to control her life, and he maintaining that she is trying to take his children from him. It is also a dispute that is laden with a great deal of potential emotional baggage. He may have difficulty separating the issue from the thought of her possible future husband and the influence that he will exert. She may have difficulty separating the issue from the fact that it was his decision to divorce that has left her where she is. And much heated energy can be expended here on a problem that may never arise at all, the couple nevertheless acting and talking as if a decision, which neither of them has made, is imminent. The mediator is not too comfortable either, because rather than let sleeping dogs lie, he himself has raised the problem. Nevertheless, and particularly in the mobile society in which we live today, it is a distinct possibility and must therefore be addressed.

If at all possible, it is best to eschew absolutes with respect to this issue—to avoid either *allowing* the wife to move wherever she wishes, for any reason, or to *prohibit* her from moving beyond a particular distance, regardless of the reason. A common compromise is to provide that the wife will not move beyond a stated distance unless, following her remarriage, her husband's new job or occupation will require him to move beyond that distance. Occasionally women object to this restriction, complaining that it is chauvinistic in that it gives recognition to the requirements of her present husband's occupation, and even her future husband's occupation, but not to her *own* occupation.

This is really not the case. If her present husband should move a thousand miles away, and thereby deprive himself of the ability to be with his children on a regular basis, he has no one to complain to but himself. Moreover, one would assume that in making such a decision, and in accepting a new position, he will take this inconvenience into account. It cannot be assumed, however, that his wife will take his inconvenience into account in the same way when she decides to move the same thousand miles away for her own benefit. We must also remember that we are not talking about the wife having a job or not having a job. We are talking about her having a job and her possibly having a better job—usually only a marginally better job. However, and for better or worse, that may have to be one of the compromises that she will have to make if she is going to have the right to have the children live with her. The burden has nothing to do with her sex. It is simply a *function of another desire* she has, namely, the privilege of having the children live with her rather than with their father.

If the situation is reversed, and if the husband is to have custody of the children, there is no reason the same residence restriction should not be imposed upon him. In actual fact, however, this will rarely ever be an issue when the children are to live with the husband. This is because in most instances the husband, unlike the wife, has roots (a business, profession, job) that tie him to his present place of residence in a way that his wife does not. As a result, there is little concern raised that the occupation of his future wife may disturb the wife's visitation as there is that the occupation of the wife's future husband may.

This is all very logical, and makes good sense. Unfortunately, and as the mediator will quickly learn, what is *logical to one person* may appear *illogical to another*. Besides, these are *not questions of reason*, to begin with. It is fine to say that a restriction on where the wife may live may have to be one of the compromises she will have to accept if she is to have the right to have her children live with her. Unfortunately, it may be a foregone conclusion that she will have custody of the children long before this issue is raised, and her husband may have neither the interest nor the ability to care for them permanently, let alone the serious desire of placing custody at issue. If that is the case, the argument loses much, if not all, of its force.

The discussion of this issue will also pose a problem for the mediator in another way. Moreover, it is a dilemma with which he will be faced time and time again throughout the mediation. On the one hand, it is not his business to *question how people feel*, or whether their feelings are *justified*, or even *consistent*. People are *not obligated to conform themselves* to our standards and judgments, even about what constitutes reasonable or unreasonable conduct. This is the way they *feel*, and that is as much a part of reality as is the table around which they are sitting.

Nevertheless, if the mediator is not able to change *some* of those feelings—to change the way one or both of them views the facts in question—the parties may be stuck at an impasse. The mediator must tread a delicate balance here, a balance made all the more precarious by the fact that in many instances it is his very acceptance of the person in question, including the legitimacy of feelings he may not necessarily share, that may ultimately afford that person the ability to let go of those feelings sufficiently to resolve the issue at hand.

Does that mean that the resolution that two different couples come to will not be the same in both cases? The answer is yes. Should that not offend the mediator's sense of justice, given that the same logic applies with equal force in both instances? The answer is no. The mediator is not attempting to help the couple come to a *correct* decision— whatever that means. He is helping them come to a decision in the *unique circumstances* that the facts of their lives and their individual feelings represent. It is thus not possible to check the results of that decision by comparing it with the conclusion reached by one or more other couples. In fact, it is not possible to check it at all. For although we have been trained to expect these determinations to conform to certain objective, independent yardsticks, as to what is fair or unfair, and to reject them as wanting when they do not, the mediator will have to learn to resist this all-too-easy temptation.

One of the anomalies here is that the discussions tend to reinforce the chauvinistic stereotype that sees the husband free to do as he wishes and the wife as restricted in the exercise of her legitimate desires. One way to attempt to avoid this problem is by reframing the issue. The issue is thus no longer whether the husband *or* the wife have the right to move beyond the stated distance. They *both* have this right. Rather, the question is whether either one of them will have the right should he or she so move to *take the children* with them. In short, is there an agreement that neither one of the parties will have the right to change the children's residence without the other's consent.

More often than not, the issue here will not be whether or not the wife can move with the children, but under what conditions she should have the right to move. While not always the case, this will generally concern the question of the wife's occupation, or that of her new husband. Why should the wife be permitted to move beyond the stated distance if her new husband's job requires it, and not if her own job requires it? Is there any justification for this? The answer is yes, for while the wife may be free to reject a new position some distance from her present home so that her former husband can maintain a relationship with his children, it may not be as easy for her to make the same decision when it comes to her new husband's job. More importantly, the decisions she makes with her new husband should be left, as much as possible, to them, without the additional burden on their relationship that a residence restriction upon her might entail. Not that this is ideal, or without problems. Nevertheless, it reflects the realities of the situation, and is an appropriate compromise on the husband's part.

Let us assume that the parties have agreed that the wife will live within a certain radius so as to enable the husband to have easy access to his children. What distance is appropriate? To a great extent, this should be determined by the realities of the situation. As a practical matter, and since he will need a base of operation from which to come and go, the husband will wish to visit with his children where he lives, and not where the wife lives. (She will want that also, as she does not want him to exercise his visitation in her home.) Accordingly, for him to visit with his children means first to go from his home to their home and back at the beginning of each visitation period and then to repeat this at the end. In order to understand the problem from the husband's standpoint, the distance between the two homes, both in time and in miles, has to be multiplied by four. As a practical matter, it is an undue burden upon the husband (who works all week) to have to travel more than an hour to pick up his children, and then another hour to bring them to his home. To extend his traveling time beyond this is to place barriers between him and his children. Accordingly, in most instances the appropriate restriction will be the distance that the husband can travel in an hour—usually not more than 40 or 50 miles.

Needless to say, the residence restriction upon the custodial parent should only obtain if the husband resides within a certain radius himself—usually 100 miles of the wife's present residence. If the couple lives in the New York metropolitan area, and the husband decides to move to Chicago, he really cannot complain that his wife then moves to Florida, or perhaps even to California, as it is not really any harder for him to visit them in either Florida or California than it would be had they continued to live in New York.

Finally, if it is anticipated that either the wife or the husband will move beyond a proximate distance from one another, it makes sense to make provision in their agreement as to what will be the noncustodial parent's rights to spend time with the children in that event. As a practical matter, if the parties live more than 100 miles from one another, weekday, and perhaps even weekend, visitation will be rendered meaningless. In that event, it is perhaps appropriate that the noncustodial parent should be given the opportunity to have the children with him or her on all major school holidays and for at least six weeks during their summer recess from school.

An ancillary but related issue concerns the question of transportation costs. Normally, the noncustodial parent is responsible for any expenses he has in visiting with his children, not only the expenses while they are with him, but also the expenses of getting them there. Under normal circumstances, however, this only involves the ordinary wear and tear on the noncustodial parent's automobile. If the custodial parent is to be permitted to move some distance, however, the cost of getting the children to and from the noncustodial parent will greatly increase. In fact, it can become a major expense item.

In such case, it is not uncommon for the couple's agreement to require the custodial parent to assume all, or at least a portion, of these expenses. While there may well be a disparity in the respective financial circumstances of the parties, if there is a support payment by the noncustodial parent to the custodial parent, in most instances the payment is at least in part a reflection of that disparity. Further, the additional cost which these transportation expenses represent have, in most instances, been incurred simply for the benefit of the custodial parent, and add nothing to the convenience of the noncustodial parent. Finally, and perhaps most importantly, it is far more appropriate to make the burden of these additional expenses a factor the custodial parent will have to weigh in deciding whether to make the move—just as he or she must weigh all the other factors implicit in the relocation—than to cast it upon the noncustodial parent who, by definition, has no say in the decision anyway.

GRANDPARENTS AND STEPPARENTS

To this point we have only concerned ourselves with the parties themselves, and their own future relationship with the children. What about the children's grandparents? And suppose that the husband in this case is the stepfather of the child or children in question, rather than their natural father.

In recent years, all states have passed legislation giving the court authority to grant grandparents visitation rights with their grandchildren, in much the same manner that they grant parents the right to visit with their children.[2] This legislation was brought about by the experience of many grandparents who found themselves caught in the middle of the disputes between their children and their children's spouses. In a number of instances, the grandparents even had to invoke their rights under these statutes against their own children as well.

Should this issue be of concern to the mediator? The answer is that it should not unless it is specifically raised by one of the parties, which will rarely be the case. If either of the parties is concerned about their parents' ability to maintain a relationship with their grandchildren, all that is necessary for them to do is to arrange for the children to be with their grandparents when *they* are with them. When the issue does arise, more likely than not it will have to do with the right, for example, of the husband's parents to see their grandchildren in the event of the husband's death. If this is of concern to the husband, there is absolutely no reason why provision cannot be included in the agreement to cover this. Sometimes the agreement will simply provide that, in the event of the husband's death, his parents will have the same rights to visit with the children that he did. More often than not, the grandparents will simply be given the right to see their grandchildren on weekends and perhaps for a week or two during the summer.

The problem of stepparents is more complicated, and in all likelihood it will become even more complicated in the future. Divorce has brought with it second marriages, and it has also brought with it the children of those marriages. Consider the following. The parties have been married for ten years. At the time of their marriage, the wife had a two-year-old child by her first husband. Following their marriage, the parties had a child of their own, who is now eight years of age. During all this time, the husband has been parent both to his child and to his stepchild, whose natural father has been all but absent from the scene. In reality, he has been the only father that his stepchild has known. He has tried very hard not to make any distinctions between his own child and his stepchild, and has treated them both equally. In fact, he has very strong feelings of attachment to his stepchild, as his stepchild has to him, and he would like to continue to visit with him following his and his wife's separation, just as he will visit with his own child.

It can be expected that this situation will arise with increasing frequency in the future, and courts have already been called upon to deal with it.[3] From the standpoint of the mediator, the problem should be dealt with in a practical way. If there is a strong bond between the stepchild and his stepfather, and particularly if he looks to his stepfather as his psychological father, there is no reason why an ongoing relationship should not be encouraged. After all, it was this attachment that caused the stepchild to look to the husband as his father in the first place, and there is little in the husband's separation from the stepchild's natural mother that will cause him to change that, any more than it will change for the child whom the husband and the wife had together. If their divorce is made to signal an abrupt change in that relationship, this can cause problems not only for the stepchild, but for everyone concerned. It can most certainly affect the relationship between the stepchild and his half brother or sister, since the stepchild will have to be conflicted over what he can only view as the preferential treatment accorded his sibling. Needless to say, the stepchild deserves better than this and, if at all possible, the mediator should attempt to get the wife to understand the complexity of the situation.

Obviously, if the stepchild has maintained an ongoing relationship with his natural father, which will more likely than not be the case with those couples who seek mediation on a voluntary basis today, the situation will be very different, and even more complicated. The stepchild's natural father may have learned to accommodate himself to the reality of the husband's presence, and may even have viewed him as a positive influence on his son. But that was when the husband and his former wife were married, and when the husband's relationship with his son did not interfere with his own. Now that they are separating and divorcing, however, all of that has changed. He may now even resent an ongoing relationship between the husband and his son and he certainly does not want it to get in the way of his own ability to see him. The wife may also have very different feelings in this case. She may well have some difficulty, and with good reason, in making arrangements that concern her former husband when he is not a party to them, and might well object to them.

On occasion, the problem is compounded by yet another factor—that the husband has adopted the stepchild as his own. Not uncommonly, this occurs when it is the couple's intention to have children of their own. The natural father has removed himself from the scene and the wife's child looks to her new husband to fill his shoes. The wife not only is pleased by this, and encourages it, but is concerned lest the husband should look less favorably upon her child then their own. She would therefore feel more comfortable if he adopted his stepchild and all of her children were therefore on the same legal footing.

The problem is that they may have only been married for but a short period at the time of their divorce and, while not necessarily wishing to acknowledge this at the time, the husband may not want the continued burden of an obligation that he assumed simply as a condition of his marriage. Yet having adopted the child, he is legally responsible for him. Nevertheless, such legal obligations do not tell the whole story, as the sad record of the failure of fathers to support their children following divorce all too clearly demonstrates.

These are but some of the many problems that reconstituted families may pose for mediators in the future. As a practical matter, and particularly if the husband has not adopted his stepchild, the issue may turn on whether or not he assumes responsibility for his support. Agreeing to continue to provide support for a child is a far more definite statement of responsibility than simply expressing the desire to continue to maintain a relationship with him. More importantly, it will be difficult, if not impossible, for the wife to accept one without the other. On the contrary, the husband's act of putting his money where his mouth is, so to speak, may be the very thing that will settle whatever reservations she may have had about an ongoing relationship between them.

MISCELLANEOUS CONSIDERATIONS

Two other issues that commonly arise are whether the provisions in the agreement for the husband to spend time with his children are rights or obligations, and whether he can exercise that opportunity with less than all of the children.

As was noted earlier, and aside from the genuine concern on the part of the wife that the husband maintain a strong relationship with their children, and provide them with the emotional support they need, there is her selfish (and understandable) motive in wanting time off. The wife does not get that relief if the husband fails to exercise his visitation, or if he exercises it but leaves her with one or more of the children. (In a real sense, to be left with one of the children is to be left with all of them.) Sometimes this is expressed by the wife's insistence that the husband be *obligated* to exercise his visitation rather than merely have that *right*.

In fairness, there is nothing illogical in insisting that being with one's children, like supporting them, is an obligation *as well as* a right. It is simply that it is a far harder obligation to enforce, and the attempt to do so sometimes creates more problems than it solves. On occasion, and in response to this, the wife may insist that if the husband does not exercise his visitation rights, that he be obligated to pay her the costs she incurs in having to hire someone to care for the children during the period when he should have visited with them. Without suggesting that this suggestion is inappropriate, such a provision does not solve the problem; it simply shifts the resentment from one parent to the other. Without question, the husband has a moral obligation to maintain his relationship with his children and, unforeseen circumstances excepted, to spend time with them as has been agreed upon between the parties. The best way to assure this—to the extent that it is going to be assured at all—is to foster and maintain an open relationship between the noncustodial parent and the children, and between the noncustodial parent and the custodial parent as well—not by building penalties into the agreement.

The situation is less than ideal for everyone. Understanding and support, rather than recriminations, are the best avenue of approach. There are parents who are not warm and responsive to their children's needs, and who do not have a good relationship with them, and their divorce will not change this. Perhaps even worse, there are parents who had a good relationship with their children prior to their separation who do not maintain it as they should once they are divorced. On the other hand, there are instances when the noncustodial parent actually develops a *stronger* relationship with his children *after* the separation than he had with them when they lived together as a family. These are all part of the reality with which the mediator will be confronted as he goes along.

Fortunately, most parents, and particularly parents who seek mediation on a voluntary basis, are concerned for their children, and have a good relationship with them. In fact, one of their most important concerns is to maintain that relationship. How the couple relate with one another is the best guarantee of this, and flowery words of good intentions in their agreement are no substitute.

The custodial parent may still feel that she has been left with the problem and may not like it. She may even insist that, should her husband fail to exercise his rights to be with their children, that he should be responsible to provide substitute care for them, or at least to reimburse her should she be required to do so. Although this is not a problem that will arise very often, mediators can expect to be faced with it with increasing frequency in the future. In the past, when a husband failed to exercise his visitation with his children, the inconvenience to the wife was usually minor. However, and as more and more women are shouldering occupations that carry the same responsibilities as their husband's, his failure to exercise visitation may now disrupt their careers as well. Even if the inconvenience occurs on a weekend, when the wife does not have business commitments, it will still interfere with free time that is as significant to her as his is to him.

In large measure, the answer to this problem will often depend upon how the couple view the time that they will each have with the children. If they both have demanding careers, and if their discussions have centered around the attempt to reconcile their obligations to their children with those commitments, the tenor of their discussions may have made it inappropriate for one of the parties to expect the other simply to take up the slack. If so, it would be completely in order for the party concerned about the problem to raise it as an issue, and to insist that the other party bear the burden of the problem which he has created.

On the other hand, if their roles are the more traditional ones, the issue may not be so pressing. Although the wife may work, her hours are more narrowly circumscribed. This is not to suggest that her convenience is not as much to be respected as her husband's, but that where the consequences of irregular visitation are perhaps less critical it may be best to leave the resolution to the give and take between the parties rather than to try to encode it in their agreement.

The second problem is also not without its difficulties. Without question, the rule should be that the husband will visit with all of the children. Whether this is spelled out in the couple's agreement or left to their good faith is more a question of diplomacy than of draftsmanship. Aside from the fact that the wife does not have time to herself if she is left with one of the children, there is the additional factor that the child left behind may feel slighted and perhaps even rejected. This is not to deny, however, that there are situations in which visiting with the children separately is warranted.

Suppose, for example, that the parties have a 12-year-old son and a 5-year-old daughter. There are activities (going to a ball game) that the husband would like to experience with his son that his daughter will not enjoy, and perhaps may even balk at. Or suppose that there are four children of disparate ages and sexes. The husband may feel that it is too much for him to have all four children in his small apartment for an entire weekend, or that he could greatly improve on the quality of their time together if he had the two youngest one weekend and the two eldest the next. There is legitimacy to these arguments. Thus, while visiting with the children separately should not be the rule, in these circumstances the parties should be encouraged to bend the rule, even at inconvenience to the custodial parent, to improve the quality of the time that the noncustodial parent spends with his children.

CHAPTER 15

MARITAL RESIDENCE

The custody of the children having been determined, the next question to be decided is that of the disposition of the parties' marital residence. Whether a one-family house, a condominium, or a cooperative apartment, the marital residence, if owned by the parties—which will generally be the case—can be one of the most difficult issues for the couple to resolve, since their home also represents their single largest asset.

As a rule, the party with whom the children will principally reside (usually the wife) will want to maintain the home for herself and the children rather than sell it. Nor is there any question that, if possible, this is most desirable. The parties' children are already going through a very difficult period of adjustment. To add to this the trauma of having to be uprooted from their home and community will only compound their problem. Accordingly, every effort should be made to permit them to continue to live in their home, at least until they have come to terms with their parents' separation and preferably until they have completed their schooling.

The importance for the children of continuing to live in their home of course depends on their ages. If a child is a junior in high school, and if the sale of the home would mean a move outside the school district, requiring him to finish in a new school, this will create a very serious disruption and may even spoil for him much of the enjoyment and value of his high school experience. And the very fact that he will complete high school in two years means that postponing the sale of the home until his graduation will not represent such a serious hardship for the parent whose money will remain tied up in the home until it is sold. Even if the home is too expensive for the parties to maintain indefinitely following their separation, if it is only necessary to do this for a relatively short time, they may be able to find a way.

If, on the other hand, the child is a preschooler, educational continuity is not relevant, nor are the close friendships that older children develop. In this case, not only would the sale of the marital residence (and the relocation of the child) not have such a disruptive effect, but it might even be appropriate. Thus, if it is very problematic whether the custodial parent will be able to maintain the home financially, and if it looks as if she may be forced to move anyway, it may be better to effectuate such a move immediately, and to establish a new home for the child that will perhaps be permanent, before strong school and peer attachments are formed.

By the same token, the burden on the party whose money will be tied up in the home until its sale may be inequitable if that sale has to be postponed, perhaps thirteen or fourteen years, until a four-year-old child graduates from high school. Again, if that equity represents the only asset of any real value that the couple has acquired during their marriage, its deferred use may mean that the party who leaves the home will be unable to buy another home for himself during this time. Certainly he will not have the benefit of that equity during the period following his separation that may well be the tightest for him financially.[1]

These are the extreme examples and easiest to determine. Those that fall in the middle, however, may not be so simple, since they will present a more delicate and, therefore, more difficult balancing of equities. But when it is clearly in the children's best interests for them to remain in their home, in *most* instances the party with whom the children will *not* be living, usually the husband, *will* be willing to make the sacrifice necessary to permit them to do this; even if that means that he will not have the use of his money for some period of time.

When he is *not* willing, his refusal will usually have little to do with the balancing of these equities. Rather it will have to do with the fact that something is blinding him to his children's best interests. This is most commonly the case when it is the wife who wants the divorce and the husband does not. Here the husband is unable to see his children's well-being. All he can see is that he is going to have to bear the burden of a decision *he* did not make and does not want, while, at least from his standpoint, his wife will be left having her cake and able to eat it too. Because that seems unfair to him, he resists accepting it. If that is the case, the mediator may well have to put this fact on the table and address it if he is going to be able to resolve the issue.

CAN THE WIFE AFFORD TO LIVE IN THE HOME?

The discussion to this point has assumed that the wife will be able to afford to continue to live in the home. That, of course, is the threshold question. Tied to this is the question of what would be the comparable cost of other housing accommodations for her and the children. If the cost of maintaining the home is clearly beyond her means, it is no favor to the wife to let her continue to live there; and rather than wage a losing battle, the mediator must try to help her acknowledge the economic realities and accept the fact of its sale.

Even at this early point, the mediator should have been able to form a judgment in his own mind about this. The information he obtained from the parties during their initial consultation provided him with the basic facts concerning the cost of maintaining the home (principal, interest, and real estate taxes), as well as the family's income. He also knows the equity in the home in relationship to its total value and is probably also generally familiar with the cost of apartments in the area. (If he is not, he could easily have made a call to a real estate broker in the meantime, and obtained this information.) He thus already has a handle on what is realistic under the circumstances.

It has been a traditional rule of thumb that a family should not spend more than 25% of its spendable income on housing. If the parties live in an apartment, that would mean rent and electricity. If they live in a private home, that would mean the principal and interest on their mortgage, real estate taxes, home owner's insurance, fuel, electricity, and ordinary household repairs. With the increased costs of housing, energy and finance charges,[2] this figure has been pushed up considerably, and 30 to 33⅓% is probably still considered acceptable today, particularly if the parties own their own home, have the advantage of being able to deduct mortgage interest payments and real estate taxes for income tax purposes, and thus have a larger spendable income in relation to their gross income.

In the case of separated parties, however, this rule has to be modified even further, and it is not uncommon to find the parent with whom the children primarily reside spending 40 to 45% of her spendable income to maintain her home.[3] While not *desirable*, it is nevertheless probably necessary and acceptable, as the percentage increase simply represents a cutback in less essential areas. Occasionally, the parent (usually the wife) with whom the children are to reside will try to hold onto the home even when to do so will require an allocation of 50% or more of her income. This is obviously dangerous since it will leave the wife house-poor and condemn her to a situation in which the quality of her life and that of her children will be seriously compromised in order to stay in the home, with the consequential residual emotional fallout (resentment) that is inevitably its price. Again, it must be the mediator's job to act as a reality principle in these instances.

THE COST OF COMPARATIVE HOUSING

Related to the question of whether or not the parent living with the children will be able to afford to continue to live in the home is the question of the cost of other comparable housing. If the home was bought many years ago, and if the mortgage payment is relatively low, the cost of maintaining the home as the children's residence (even including the cost of insurance, fuel, electricity, etc.) may actually be *less* than the cost of renting an apartment. And, of course, the accommodations in the parties' home are usually more commodious than any apartment could possibly be. On the other hand, and particularly if the home was bought more recently, the rent for an acceptable (but by no means comparable) apartment may be substantially less. This may suggest that it would make more sense from a financial standpoint to sell the home and rent an apartment.

This comparison is complicated by the fact that the tax deductions on the home take on a different appearance when the couple was living together as a family and when they are separated and divorced. One reason why most couples can afford to own and maintain a home is that they are able to *deduct* probably two-thirds of the expense of maintaining it (representing mortgage interest and real estate taxes) for income tax purposes. And since they are usually in a relatively high income tax bracket (at least with the last earned dollars of income), that means a substantial tax savings. When a couple separates and divorces, however, there is a change, at least initially, in their respective financial pictures, and the deductions for the parties' home are usually taken by the party with the lower income. This means that the same dollar payment will result in less of a tax savings than it did previously.[4]

Even these considerations cannot lead to a conclusion without considering an additional factor—the amount of the equity in the home in relation to its total value. Till now, the couple has been deprived of the use of the money tied up in their home except to the extent that it has enhanced the quality of their life by permitting them the pleasure of living there. In the past this was not a serious consideration, however, since, besides enjoying the standard of living that ownership of their home afforded them, tying up that equity represented a form of *forced savings*. In fact, from many standpoints it was an astute form of financial planning, particularly given the fact that, under the law prior to 1986, the profit derived upon the sale of the home would come to the parties in the form of a capital appreciation (with income taxes paid at capital gains rates) rather than as ordinary income, which would be the case had the equity been deposited in a certificate of deposit, for example.[5] Beyond this, and if the parties did not sell the home until one or the other was 55 years of age, $125,000 of that profit could be completely sheltered from tax pursuant to the provisions of the Internal Revenue Code.[6]

The question, of course, is whether the couple can now afford the luxury of these forced savings. If the equity in the home is small, and if freeing it would thus not produce a source of any real income for either of the parties (or permit them to buy separate, less expensive homes), the sale of the marital residence would not be justified on that account, and it would be far better to maintain it for their children. On the other hand, if there is a very substantial equity in the home, that fact cannot be ignored, and the family may well not be able to afford to postpone the use of these savings for some time in the future. *This is the future*, and they are needed now.

Generally speaking, the most difficult time a family will face financially is immediately following their separation. While events could unexpectedly occur in the future that may worsen their situation, it is appropriate to assume that this will not be the case, and that their circumstances will *improve*. Where they need help is *now*, since all their efforts will be directed toward improving their respective circumstances in the future. It is now that the wife is without adequate employment and forced to go back to school to prepare herself for the future. It is now that the wife is forced to go back into the labor market although she does not have the skills to earn any real money. It is now that the husband must find an apartment for himself, with the heavy financial burden that this involves. It is now that the wife is faced with the very heavy baby-sitting costs involved in her attempting to augment the family's income. In time, the circumstances of each of the parties may improve to lessen these burdens. Similarly, in time each of them may become involved in new relationships that will enable them to share those burdens with someone else.

All these factors have to be weighed in making the decision whether it is feasible or practical to attempt to maintain the marital residence. Of course it would be *better* to maintain the home for the children. But when the equity is substantial, a comparison of the costs in maintaining it (including the consequential sacrifices that may have to be made in other areas to do so) with how the economic burdens of divorce might be eased if that equity were available for that purpose, may *still* lead to the conclusion that a sale is in order.[7]

How Long?

If it is agreed that the wife, for example, will have the right to occupy the home for a period of time, the next question is, for how long? The wife, of course, would like to have the right to live in the home for as long as *possible*, and from her standpoint the perfect agreement would be one that would leave the sale of the home completely within her discretion. It is not that she really wishes to live in the home forever, or has even given any serious thought to this. It is simply that she feels threatened by the thought of being forced to relocate, and the further off that she can put it, the more comfortable she will feel. Her husband, on the other hand, looks at it very differently. The home probably represents their most substantial asset, certainly their most substantial liquid asset. If he is ever to buy another home for himself, it will only be possible if he is able to obtain his share of the equity in his present home; and if his wife is permitted to live there indefinitely, or even for an extended period, he may never have the use of these monies for that purpose. In short, the equity in the home is of no practical value to him so long as the wife is permitted to live there.

These conflicting attitudes will be expressed in the disagreement the parties will very often have as to when the home is to be sold. From the husband's standpoint, he is agreeing to permit the wife to remain in the home, not for *her* benefit, but for the benefit of their children. Accordingly, he will want the home to be sold as soon as it is no longer justified in terms of their benefit. This will usually be when the youngest child graduates from high school. In most instances, and particularly if this event is perhaps seven or eight years off, the wife will have no objection to this suggestion. At other times, however, and particularly when this will occur in a much shorter period of time, she may feel very threatened by it. This she will often express by the request that she be permitted to continue to live in the home until the youngest child is 21 or completes college, which-ever is later.

In truth, there is a big difference between selling the home when a child is in high school and when he is in college. When a child graduates from high school, and whether he goes on to college, enrolls in a trade school or simply goes out to work, the tightly knit relationships he maintained in high school tend to begin to come apart as his friends go in their different directions and new relationships are formed. Neither the past relationships that he still has, nor the new ones that he is forming, will be greatly affected by the sale of his home. While it most certainly will represent a change in his life, it is not the disruptive change it would be if the home were sold while he was still in high school.

There is thus force to the husband's argument that the detriment to him in continu-ing to have his equity tied up in the home is not offset by the benefit to the children after this point. This is particularly true given that we are talking about a detriment principally to only the youngest child, the older children having already not only graduated from high school but perhaps even from college. If a compromise is required, it can perhaps be based on the question whether the children attend college following their graduation from high school and where that college is located. If a child attends a local college, and is going to live at home, perhaps the sale can be postponed until his graduation. On the other hand, if he lives at college during his attendance, there is really very little necessity for the wife to maintain the home as a place for him simply on holidays and during his summer vacation, and though it might be a convenience, it is not such as to justify keeping the husband's money tied up in the home to serve that end.

The Wife's New Husband or Boyfriend

It has been agreed that the wife will have the right to continue to live in the home until all the children have graduated from high school. How will that right be affected by the fact that the wife may remarry prior to that time, or by the fact that she may live in the home with her new boyfriend?

From a logical standpoint, neither of these facts should affect her right to continue to live in the home. After all, the husband has agreed to permit her to do so, not for her benefit, but for the benefit of their children, and that benefit is not altered or diminished to any extent by the wife's remarriage or by the fact that she is now living in the home with another man. Nevertheless, the husband will usually bridle at this suggestion. Even if it was he who wanted the divorce in the first place, it is difficult for him to see himself replaced by someone else. To ask him to pay for it on top of that may just be too much for him. Thus, it will be his position that if the wife and her new husband wish to continue to live in the home, they should be obligated to buy out his interest; otherwise it should be sold. In most instances, and because there are often unstated but nevertheless generally accepted norms about these matters, the wife will usually agree that she should not have the right to continue to live in the home past her remarriage, at least without paying the husband for his equity.

On occasion, however, the wife may take exception to this and may view the husband's suggestion as an infringement of her right to go about her business, and to make a new life for herself, and as an attempt by him to limit her, or even control her, in this regard. While it may appear that way to the wife, the fact is that the parties *will, of necessity, continue to exert control over one another,* and to affect each other's lives. This is not by design, but simply by circumstances. If the home were sold today, and the proceeds divided between the parties, each could go his or her own way without interference from the other. That is not going to be the case, however. Rather, and primarily at the wife's request, and whether or not primarily for her benefit, nevertheless still to her advantage, she is going to have the right to continue to live in the home, at least for a period of time. If that is the case, the parties will still be somewhat wedded to one another, and it is as pointless as it is unrealistic for the wife to complain about this. On the contrary, what has to be done in each instance is to weigh the equities as between the parties and to strike an appropriate balance. In doing this, the mediator should eschew the use of these kinds of emotional labels. They settle nothing and only tend to cement already fixed positions. Instead, the problem should be looked at from a practical standpoint.

The problem at the present time is that the wife cannot buy out the husband's interest in the home, even if she wished to, since she does not have the funds necessary for that purpose. Nor does she have the credit to go to a bank and refinance the mortgage to get those funds. Even if she did, she would in all likelihood only solve one problem by creating a bigger one, since she probably would not be able to afford the increased mortgage payment such refinancing would entail. Her remarriage, however, may well change all of this. The wife and her new husband's combined incomes may not only be sufficient to secure such a mortgage loan but, and just as importantly, also be sufficient to repay it. If so, there is no reason the burden should not be where the benefit is, and the wife, along with her new husband, required to buy out the husband's equity.

The wife does not object to this, at least in principle. However, she says that she does not want to have to buy her husband's equity out, or have to suffer the penalty of selling the home, simply because she remarries. She only wants to have to do this if she and her new husband are "financially able" to afford to do so. But when will the wife and her new husband be financially able to do this? The husband does not feel secure in simply agreeing to permit the wife to continue to live in the home following her remarriage unless her new husband is financially able to buy him out, for there may well be disagreement between the parties as to whether he is. Without doubt, to leave the parties' understanding at this will only leave them with a problem, and perhaps even a lawsuit. Accordingly, the issue should be determined at the present time, as arbitrary as such a determination may be.

As a practical matter, and although it is not without its problems, the best way to do this is to base the question of financial ability on the new husband's income, or the combined incomes of the wife and her new husband. Thus, their agreement can provide that if his (or their) income is not in excess of a stated amount (or a certain percentage of the then value of the home), the wife will not have an obligation to buy the husband's equity out. If it is, however, then she will have such an obligation. If this approach is applied, then, in determining her new husband's income, it is appropriate to subtract from it the amount of any payments he will be obligated to make to *his* former spouse. Similarly, if the wife's income is to be considered, it is appropriate to add to it any payments the husband will continue to be obligated to make to her following her remarriage, even if they are only for child support.

Suppose the wife will not be required to buy out the husband's equity upon her remarriage. Will she then have an obligation to make any payment to the husband on account until it is sold? The wife's new husband will be given the benefit of the parties' home by reason of his marriage to the wife. And it has to be assumed that this will represent a savings to him in not being required to pay rent elsewhere. Until her remarriage, the husband could not ask the wife to pay him for the privilege of living in their home, as her finances did not permit such payment. Is it inappropriate that he not be paid something, however, now that she has remarried—that he not have some present benefit from the equity he still has tied up in the home? While the mediator may not necessarily want to raise this issue himself, he may consider putting it on the table as a way of breaking an impasse over the husband's insistence on the sale of the home should the wife remarry, and her equally strong resistance to this idea.

An even more difficult question is whether or not the wife will be required to sell the home should she permit her new boyfriend to live in it (or whether she will be permitted to have her boyfriend live there at all for that matter). The husband may feel strongly, and perhaps even more strongly than he did about her remarriage, that the home should be sold in this event, for in a strange way the wife may be better sheltered from her husband's feelings toward her new emotional involvement if it is protected by the respect traditionally accorded those feelings when they are sanctified by the act of marriage than when they lead simply to shared living arrangements. From the wife's standpoint, unfortunately, these shared living arrangements do not provide her with the same financial security as her remarriage does. She cannot go to a bank with her new boyfriend and refinance the mortgage on her home based on their living arrangements, as she could with her new husband. Moreover, and almost by definition, her new living arrangements probably do not represent the same kind of commitment or, therefore, bespeak the same kind of permanency, that a decision to marry would entail. In fact, from her standpoint it is just such a condition that will place a real restriction upon her, as it may well prevent her from testing out that new relationship, as she would like to, before making such a commitment.

Even if the wife is willing to agree to this, as she often will be, the matter is not at an end. Rather, the mediator is still left with a conundrum. We know what we mean when we talk about the wife's remarriage. But what does it mean to say that the home will be sold if the wife "lives" in it with her new boyfriend? It may be clear what that means if the wife's boyfriend gives up his own apartment, moves into the home with all of his belongings, and takes his meals and sleeps there seven days a week, 52 weeks a year. That is certainly *living* in the home, just as the mere fact that he has a Saturday night dinner with the wife in the home, perhaps staying until 2 A.M., is *not*. But what about all of the possibilities in between? Is the wife to suffer the heavy penalty of being required to sell the home simply because she permits her boyfriend to spend the night at the home on occasion, or perhaps even for a weekend?

At times, the couple will attempt to solve the problem in an apparently rational way by saying that the wife's boyfriend will be deemed to live in the home if he sleeps in the home for so many nights or more in any week, or for a period of so many consecutive weeks or months. Unfortunately, these attempted compromises often precipitate very trivial discussions, with the husband maintaining that the wife will purposely have her boyfriend sleep out of the home every so often just to avoid the claim that he lives there on a permanent basis. Worse yet, almost any definition will leave the parties with a potentially serious problem.

How will the husband go about proving that the wife's new boyfriend is actually living there, other than by calling their children as witnesses—hardly a desirable recourse? For unless he hires a detective to watch the house 24 hours a day, seven days a week, 52 weeks a year (or for whatever prescribed period will be necessary), it will simply be his word against the wife's. This is not an attractive solution. Also, the husband will often say, and perhaps even believe, that the wife will purposely live in the home with her boyfriend, rather than *marry* him, just to avoid the penalty of having to sell the home upon her remarriage. The whole situation breeds distrust and stirs up emotional issues for both the husband and the wife.

When this question is first raised, the wife may complain that it is unfair that the husband has the right to live with his girlfriend wherever he may wish, but that she does not have the same right to live with her boyfriend as she wishes. The husband, of course, will answer that this is not true. He cannot live with his girlfriend wherever he wishes. He cannot live with her in their home, as the wife is asking to do with her new boyfriend. This may be met by the wife with the observation that this restriction upon the husband is not really a restriction at all, since it does not prevent him from living with his girlfriend, but only from living with her in their home. As a practical matter, however, the restriction the husband wishes to impose upon her will mean that she will not be able to live with her boyfriend at all, as she must live in the home with their children. And, of course, the argument can go on and on.

Ideally, it would be better if the wife's right to live in the home were not affected by the absence or presence of her boyfriend. To be sure, there may be women who will not marry their boyfriends in order to avoid the penalty of being required to sell their homes. But that will be the exception, and although that fact may well cause a postponement of an intended marriage, the decision to marry or not to marry is usually based on far stronger considerations. Furthermore, within appropriate limits (for example, the husband might reasonably object to the wife's suggestion that she should be permitted to live in the home with her new boyfriend for five years before being required to make a decision as to whether or not she will marry him), the wife should be left free to make her decision based upon those more relevant considerations without the pressure imposed upon her by the penalty of this condition.

If the husband is adamant, and if the wife's right to continue to live in the home until the children have graduated from high school (or college) can only be secured under these conditions, it would be a mistake to hold up an agreement on that account. Obviously the mediator wants to resolve all of the possible issues so as to avoid future potential disputes between the parties. But if the decision comes down to choosing between a possible problem in the future and an irreconcilable one now, there can be no real choice.

Besides, even if the wife may have to accept this condition as the price for concluding an agreement, at least it will be she who, in the final analysis, will have control over her own fate here. It may be a great inconvenience, and perhaps even unfair, to the wife to be required to sell the home should she permit her new boyfriend to establish his residence there; but she does, nevertheless, have the ability to prevent that result if she wishes by not permitting him to do so.

Suppose that the parties come to an absolute impasse here, the wife insisting that she should have the right to live in the home with anyone she wishes and the husband insisting just as strongly that she should not. Should the mediator throw up his hands and announce that the mediation is at an end? Suppose further that the husband says that it is really pointless to proceed if this issue cannot be resolved? If this should occur, the mediator should simply take a sheet of paper and, as if this were standard procedure in all mediations, put the heading "Open Questions" at the top and make note of the issue, advising the couple that they will come back to *it*, and whatever other open questions there may be, at a later point, at the *end* of the mediation. This procedure should be followed for every such issue, except perhaps the issue of custody itself.

What assurance does the mediator have that he will be able to deal with these issues any more successfully at *that* time? In truth, he has none. Nevertheless, he is relying on certain assumptions that justify this procedure. The first tells him that the couple has an investment in coming to an agreement, and getting on with their lives, one that becomes even greater as they put more of their time and money into the mediation. Secondly, if the mediator postpones further discussion of this issue at this point, it is not simply because the couple have come to an impasse. It is, first, because too much emotionality has become encrusted around that issue and, second, because there is really nothing further to say. If it is taken up later in the mediation, however, some of this emotionality may have dissipated and it may then be possible to discuss it more profitably. Further, if there are to be compromises, in the form of trade-offs, made to reach a settlement, then it is perhaps best for the mediator to wait to see what he has to work with here, and deferring the issue will permit him to do that. Finally, and even though they are the same hard issues, they may well take on a slightly different appearance when, at the end of the mediation, they represent the one or two last issues that stand between the couple and an agreement, rather than, as they now are, simply *issues* (often of principle) that they are stuck on.

Before leaving the question of how the mediator will deal with an impasse such as this, or with other disagreements that may arise during the course of the mediation for that matter, a final observation might be made. It is on these occasions that the skill, ingenuity, imagination, and experience of the mediator will have to be brought to bear if the deadlock is to be broken, or a way through the impasse found. Nevertheless, even the confidence of an experienced mediator can at times be undercut in situations such as this when, by implication, both of the parties look to him for an answer that he does not have and, therefore, cannot give. If he is inexperienced, there may also be a tendency on his part to rush in and attempt to solve the problem, particularly if the disagreement between the couple is expressing itself in heated language or tension is building.

We would counsel a very different approach. To begin with, if he is secure in himself and in his ability, the mediator knows that the mere fact of his presence will in most instances act as a governor on the degree of emotionality that will be ventilated, and that, if it is not, that he can always step in at a later point to set limits should it be necessary. There is no reason, therefore, for him to rush in at the first sign of trouble. Secondly, he would like to see where the couple will come out on their own, without his intervention. It is possible that the intense feelings expressed are simply part of the necessary struggle that they must go through in order to reach a level that they can both accept. If that is the case, it is better to ride it out. Even if it proves unsuccessful, however, the mediator may still learn something in the process that may be of help to him.

There is another perhaps even more important reason for the mediator to exercise restraint. The mediator should always proceed on the principle that you should never attempt to solve another person's problem *for* him. Rather, what you must always do is bring home to him the fact that it is *he* who has a problem. The mediator is there to help the couple, and he genuinely wants to do so. But this is not to say that he has answers for all of life's problems, or that they can expect him to.

How does this understanding help the mediator? It clarifies his function in this instance, which, again, is to act as a reality principle. We act realistically, after all, because we are condemned to live in reality and to rub our noses in it everyday. If the mediator is to be successful in helping the couple conclude an agreement between themselves he will have to underscore that reality. He will not accomplish this by allowing the couple to make *their* problem *his* problem. He will do it, instead, by reinforcing the reality that it is ultimately theirs. In doing this, he pits their need and desire to get through the mediation, and to conclude an agreement, against the emotional resistance standing between them and an agreement.

He also relies on another understanding, and that is that in mediation, as in life itself, *doing nothing is sometimes doing something.* If the mediator is going to be successful at his craft, he will have to learn when to act and when to intervene. But he will also have to learn when to wait, and to watch what happens when he does.

THE RIGHT TO RENT THE HOME

As with the question of the wife's right to permit her new boyfriend to live in the home, the question of the wife's right to *rent* all or a portion of the home should also not be left to speculation and possible future dispute. The husband is permitting the wife to continue to live in the home principally for the benefit of his children. If, without either his prior knowledge or his consent, the wife rents portions of the home to strangers, the husband may later feel that his children are being inconvenienced in a way that he had not intended, and that she has violated the spirit if not the letter of their agreement. The purpose of resolving this issue now is to avoid this.

The question is rarely, if ever, whether the wife will have the right to rent the entire home. On the contrary, the sale of the home is purposely being postponed so that she, and usually the children, will continue to have the right to live there. Rather, the issue will be whether or not she should have the right to rent one or more rooms in the home. In fact, in some instances it is only by renting a room that the wife will be able to afford to maintain it for herself and the parties' children. (At times, the parties will even agree to making certain improvements to the home prior to signing their agreement just for this purpose.) In other instances, however, and particularly where the couple are more afflu- ent, the husband may take exception to this. This is because he feels that having a boarder in the home might be difficult for his children, or affect the quality of the life that he is trying to secure for them by permitting his wife to continue to live there.

The agreement should not only specifically provide that the wife either will or will not have such a right, but should go further in specifying whether or not she will be permitted to rent one room or two rooms, just the basement, or some other portion of the house, and so on. Again, the husband may have agreed to allow the wife to rent a portion of the home on one assumption (which the wife may have well shared at the time) and the wife may later act on another. It is far better to make all of this explicit.

As important as is the question of whether the wife will be permitted to rent a portion of the home is the question of who will be entitled to keep the rent paid by the tenant. It will not do for the wife to rent a room in the home to help herself out financially only to later find that the husband, as co-owner of the home, lays claim to half of the rent. This should therefore be determined in advance and spelled out in their agreement.

The Option to Buy the Home

Up until this point, we have talked about the wife's (or the husband's) right to live in the home being affected by certain considerations (the children's graduating from high school or college, the wife's remarriage, and so on) and the requirement that the house will be sold when or if any of these events occur. As a practical matter, however, the person who is not living in the home does not look to these events as the occasion for the sale of the home; he looks to them as the occasion of his recouping the money he has invested in it. He has been willing to suffer having his equity tied up in the home for a certain period of time for the benefit of his children. Now that any one of those events has occurred, he would like to have the use of that equity for his own purposes. In most instances, it will require the sale of the home to accomplish this. However, if the party living in the home (the wife, for example) can accomplish this by some other means, she should certainly have the right to do so. This can be done by giving her a first option to buy the home upon the occurrence of any of those events, rather than requiring its sale. It is possible that she will not be in any better position to do this then than she is now. Nevertheless, she should be given that option, as it is also *possible* that she may be.

Sometimes, when the question of an option to purchase the home is raised, the husband, for example, who will not be living in the home, will claim that *he* should have the first option, arguing that he had really always loved the home more and that he wants to maintain it as his future residence. There is rarely merit to the husband's argument, and almost without exception the wife should have the first option. It has already been determined that the wife will have the right to continue to live in the home. The home is being sold not because it has been agreed that the husband should now also have an opportunity to live in the home, but only because it has been agreed that he should now receive his equity in it. If the price to accomplish this has to be the inconvenience which the wife will suffer by reason of its sale, it has been agreed that the benefit to the husband outweighs that inconvenience. On the other hand, if it can be accomplished *without* a sale, there is no reason she should be required to suffer that inconvenience. Thus, if the wife wishes to maintain the continuity of her living arrangements, and can obtain for the husband the benefit he expects without the sale of the home, then she should be permitted to do so.

One way possibly to placate the husband is to agree to give him a cross-option to purchase the home in the event that the wife does not exercise her option to purchase it. Again, however, this should be a *second* option, and not a first. Nor should the mediator be concerned that he has been unfair to the husband by subordinating his rights to the wife's. In most instances, the right is only a vacuous one, whether he is given a first option or a second option. In all likelihood, and long before the time arrives, the husband will have already made new plans for himself, for unless the sale of the home has been set for a specific date in the proximate future, he cannot in effect tread water with his life, waiting for the time to come. Thus, the overwhelming odds are that he will either not want to move back into the home when it is to be sold, or that it will be impractical for him to do so even if he does. The question of his having the option to buy the home is therefore only an emotional one, having more to do with his ambivalence at leaving it than with the desire or practicality of his later returning to it.

The Sale of the Home

If it is agreed that one of the parties will have the right to continue to live in the home presently, it is not sufficient simply to agree that the home will be sold at a particular future date, and that the proceeds will then be divided between the parties by a certain formula. Although of no great consequence, the parties' agreement should, nevertheless, also provide for the *procedures* that will be employed in selling the home to avoid any dispute in the future.

It must be remembered that there may well be a conflict of interests between the parties at that time. One of the parties may wish to sell the home as quickly as possible, and the other party not at all. They may disagree as to the selling price, one wanting to sell it for whatever it will bring and the other wishing to hold out for the best possible price. They may even disagree as to whether the home should be sold privately or through a broker. It is the mediator's job to *anticipate* these possible problems and to *resolve them in advance*.

In large measure, disputes between separated and divorced couples are simply questions their agreements didn't answer. In most instances, and when the time comes, the parties will be able to sit down together and decide these questions. If they cannot, however, they should be able to turn to their agreement and find the answers. Suppose they cannot agree on the selling price? To be sure, their agreement cannot now provide what that selling price should be five or perhaps ten years from now. But it most certainly can provide for a procedure to be followed to establish that selling price (for example, that the selling price will be determined by a real estate appraiser selected by the president of the local real estate board) if they cannot then agree on it.

Similarly, such questions as whether the home will be sold privately or through a broker, what will happen if they fail to receive an offer equal to the selling price within a reasonable period of time, and so on, can and should be determined at the present time and be included in their agreement. Remember, it is not so important what procedure the parties decide to employ; what is important is that they decide upon a set of procedures that they will employ if they cannot then agree with one another.

MAINTENANCE AND CARRYING CHARGES

As a general rule (and with the exception of such items as life insurance, medical insurance, college education expenses, nursery school tuition, parochial school tuition, summer camp, and orthodontic treatment), it is not a good idea to have the agreement provide that the person who will be making payments to the other, either for his or her support or for that of their children, be required to pay the cost of specific living expenses. Rather, the agreement should provide, for example, that the husband will make *a certain stated payment* to the wife and that it will be her obligation to pay for her necessary living expenses *from that sum*.

There are a number of reasons for this. The first is that requiring the husband to assume certain expenses, rather than to pay a specified amount, can create future conflict between the parties. If, for example, the husband is obligated to pay the telephone bill, and the bill is 10 or 20 dollars more in a particular month than it was previously, that may cause friction between the parties. At the very least, either the wife may feel obligated to account for herself or the husband may feel put upon. At its worst, there may well be words between the parties that will tend to reopen old wounds that had begun to heal. Secondly, it leaves the husband in a somewhat vulnerable position. Whether it be a telephone bill, heating bill, or an electric bill, there is still always the possibility of mischief should an angry wife wish to find a way to get back at her former husband who is required, by the terms of their agreement, to pay it. Thirdly, rather than knowing in advance just what his obligation is, and therefore what will be left for him, the husband in each instance is required to wait to find out what his obligation will be for the month in question.

Finally, and most importantly, it keeps each of the parties wedded to one another, and in on one another's pots, more than is necessary and more than they will want. While it is not possible for a couple to be completely divorced, particularly if there are children between them, given the payments that will have to be made by one of them to the other, they should have an agreement that will not leave them married to one another any more than is necessary. A divorced wife does not want her former husband to know how much she spends on certain items, and she certainly does not want to have to explain or *justify* those expenditures. Yet that is always the risk when an agreement provides for the husband to be directly responsible for the payment of certain bills.

In keeping with this principle, the couple's agreement should provide that the party who is to continue to live in the home should be responsible for the payment of all of the maintenance and carrying charges. This includes not only the amount due to the bank with respect to the principal and interest on the mortgage, and on account of the real estate taxes, but fuel, electricity, water, and other utilities, insurance on the home, garbage collection, and repairs as well.

There are two possible exceptions to this general rule. The first concerns the cost of structural repairs to the home and the second concerns expenses incurred to prepare the home for sale. The theory here is that these expenses tend to maintain or improve the value of the home, the benefit of which the party who is not living in the home will continue to share. Certainly this is true with respect to decorative improvements that are made to prepare the home for sale, as it is unlikely that the party living in the home would have incurred such expenses for any other reason. (To ensure that the expenses were incurred for that purpose, it is simply necessary to provide that no such repair or improvement will be deemed to have been made for that purpose if it was made earlier than a certain date prior to that when the home is required to be placed on the market for sale.)

While, by parity of reason, there is good cause to suggest that the party not living in the home should share equally in the cost of structural repairs, there are two problems. First, even if it is assumed, for the sake of argument, that putting a new roof on the home tends to maintain its value (and the other party's interest in that value), that is not necessarily the case if ten or fifteen years have passed between the time that the roof is replaced and the time that the home is put on the market for sale. The addition of the new roof may have maintained the home's value, and some of that maintained value may still exist; but the person living in the home certainly had the more substantial benefit of that improvement. Secondly, and although there may not be any argument that a roof is a structural repair, there may be repairs made to the home that are not so easily categorized.

With respect to the first of these problems, it is possible to deal with it by providing, for example, that if the husband is obligated to contribute to the cost of any structural repair, he will be reimbursed at the time of the sale, from the wife's share of the proceeds, for his contribution to any repair made more than a certain number of years prior to the time that the home is placed on the market for sale. (Rather than using an arbitrary cutoff date, it is also possible to reimburse the husband on a sliding scale, for example, 10% of his contribution if the repair was made more than a year ago, 20% of his contribution if the repair was made more than two years ago, etc.) In each instance the principle is the same, namely, to have the payment reflect the fact that although denominated a "structural repair," in point of fact it was the wife, and not the husband, who derived most of the benefit from it.

With respect to the second problem, namely, what *constitutes* a structural repair, it is far better to avoid it altogether by arbitrarily defining a structural repair to be any in excess of a stated dollar amount (for example, $200, $300, etc.). The point is that built into the wife's expectations is the fact that there will be certain ordinary repairs that will be required to be made to the home while she lives there, and they should be paid for by her either from her own earnings or from the support payments she receives from her husband. On the other hand, she does not expect, nor is she prepared for, extraordinary expenses in connection with the maintenance of the home, and it may be more appropriate that their cost be divided between the parties. In this respect, however, it is important that their agreement be clear that what they are talking about are *repairs* and not additions or improvements. It is equally important to make clear how they will treat *replacements*, such as a new refrigerator.

One final note is in order. While the husband's concern here is real, in the sense that he does not want to be unexpectedly called upon to contribute towards an expense for maintaining the home for which he is no more prepared, and is perhaps no more able to meet, than the wife, as a practical matter his fear is really unfounded. Given what will be the wife's own financial circumstances in most instances, there is very little danger that she will voluntarily make any repair to the home that is not absolutely necessary. In fact, the husband would have a far greater right to complain that she will not keep up the value of the home by maintaining it in a proper state of repair, than that she may be profligate in expenditures to improve it for her own convenience. Finally, if the wife is to have the right to rent a portion of the home, or to live there with her boyfriend or new husband, then, and particularly if the husband is not to share in that rent, or receive any payment from the wife's boyfriend or new husband, the agreement can provide that these repairs will at such a point become the wife's full responsibility.

Occasionally, the question of capital expenditures to the home will come up in another way, with the party who is to have the right to continue to live there insisting that if he or she makes any additions or improvements to the home (an in-ground pool, an extension, etc.) that they should be reimbursed from the proceeds of the sale for the amount that they have expended for that purpose. There is one major problem with this suggestion, and that is that the value of the home will rarely, if ever, be enhanced by the amount of that addition or improvement. That means that if the other party agrees to this suggestion, he or she will end up contributing to the cost of something that the other party, and the other party alone, enjoyed. One solution is to provide that the reimbursement will be limited to the amount by which the improvement has added to the value of the home at the time of its sale, as determined by an appraiser.

As a practical matter again, it is highly unlikely that the party making the suggestion will ever really be in a position to make significant additions or improvements to the home, and in most instances the issue is really only an emotional one. Be that as it may, it must be kept in mind that the object is to enable the party who is to continue to live in the home to maintain his or her *present standard of living*, not to *improve* it, and if it comes down to a choice between using these extra monies to improve the standard of living of the party living in the home or beginning to get the other party the use of some of the money that he has tied up in it, then, all things being equal, the equities have to be in favor of the latter.

Finally, on occasion, the party who is to continue to live in the home (the wife, for example) will ask to freeze the husband's equity—to have the agreement provide that upon the sale of the home the husband will (only) receive a predetermined, fixed amount, regardless of what the increased value of the home may then be. This argument is advanced either because it makes the wife feel more secure, or because, being the party who will be taking care of the home, she feels that she should be the one to benefit from any appreciation in its value. At first blush this may seem unfair, particularly if the amount to be paid does not bear interest. Nevertheless, and whether because he views his future prospects to be better than hers or for some other reason, the husband may agree to this, and it should not offend the mediator if he does.

If the amount in question will bear interest, particularly a good rate of interest, the husband may actually consider the arrangement to be to his advantage, as he will thereby avoid seeing the appreciation in his equity in the home offset by the fact that the wife is not able to properly maintain its value. And, in the vast majority of the cases, that is exactly what will happen following their divorce, since if there is not enough money—as there never is—the first place the budget will be trimmed will be in the area of household maintenance.

This brings us to one final consideration. If one of the parties (usually the husband) has agreed that the other will continue to have the right to live in the home, he may express a concern that she may not properly maintain it and that his equity will be jeopardized on that account. Nor can it be suggested that this is not a *real* concern. On the contrary, as we have said, it is extremely unlikely that the wife, following the parties' separation and divorce, will be able to maintain the home in the same condition that the two of them did prior to their separation or divorce. Unfortunately, the remedy for this is not the inclusion of a provision in the agreement requiring the wife to do this, or to penalize her in some way if she does not. The circumstances of the parties will not permit either of them to invest in the upkeep of the home following their separation or divorce to the same extent that they did before it. In permitting his wife and children to continue to live in the home rather than demanding its present sale, the husband will be making an understandable sacrifice, and included in that sacrifice will have to be the fact that his home may well not be maintained as he would like, or as it should be.

DIVISION OF THE PROCEEDS

If the home will not be gifted by one of the parties to the other, or if one of the parties will not purchase the other's interest in the home (that is, if they will continue to own the home jointly), an issue they will be required to decide is how the proceeds of the sale will be distributed between them upon its sale. In most instances, couples will quickly agree to an equal division of the proceeds. This is not difficult to justify or understand. In many ways there are few items of property that are more reflective of the partnership aspect of marriage than the parties' home, and even in situations where almost all of the assets are held by the husband in his name alone, the parties' marital residence will still usually be held in both of their names.

To be sure, there may be instances when such an equal division is inappropriate. For example, one would be where, in a marriage of short duration, the parents of one of the parties contributed substantially all of the down payment at the time the home was purchased. Another would be where, in a second marriage, the home was purchased principally with the funds derived by one of the parties from the sale of a home that he or she owned prior to their marriage. However, even these disparities in the initial contributions of the parties to the purchase price of the home will become less and less significant the longer the parties are married. In a marriage of 25 or 30 years, for example, they may become largely irrelevant.

Another issue touching upon the disposition of the proceeds of the sale is the question of whether or not the person who will continue to live in the home until its sale, and make the mortgage payments, will be entitled to receive a credit for any reduction in the principal of the mortgage between the time of the signing of the agreement and the sale of the home. A portion of the payment made by the party living in the home to the bank holding the mortgage will go to reduce the principal balance of the mortgage (will pay off part of the debt). Over a number of years, particularly if the couple has already owned the home for 10 or 15 years, that principal reduction can be considerable. Should the person who will continue to live in the home be entitled to that credit?

In large measure, the answer here should depend upon who actually made the mortgage payments. If the wife works and earns a substantial income in relationship to the husband, and the payments that she receives are really for the support of the children (regardless of how it is denominated), then she may be correct in saying that it will be *her* earnings that accounted for the reduction in the principal of the mortgage. On the other hand, if the wife earns nothing or very little, and if all or substantially all of her income is derived from payments she receives from the husband, then in actuality it is he, rather than she, who will be making the mortgage payments. (Nor is this affected by the fact they are made from payments denominated as alimony or maintenance rather than as child support.) This is not to say that in this latter situation the husband should be given credit for the reduction in the mortgage. It is simply to argue against the idea that the wife should alone receive such a credit.

MISCELLANEOUS CONSIDERATIONS

There are certain other questions to be resolved in the parties' agreement. To begin with, it should be clear who, between the parties, will have the right to claim the home for tax purposes. Even though the party making the payment may only have an undivided interest in the home, if he pays the entire mortgage payment and real estate taxes, he will be entitled to the entire deduction.[8] Nevertheless, and so as to avoid any dispute between the parties (as where, for example, the wife makes the payments with monies given to her by the husband), the agreement should be clear on this point.

In certain instances, the husband may want the deduction and may therefore propose that he, rather than the wife, will make the mortgage payments. This will occur, for example, where the wife's income is such that it is not appropriate that there be a payment by the husband to her for her support. Nevertheless, since the level of support being considered for the children is considerable, the husband would like to be able to deduct all, or at least a portion of, the payments to be made by him to the wife. Providing that he will make the mortgage payments directly is a way of accomplishing this.[9]

To be sure, the wife may complain that she is now losing the right to take this deduction, as would have been the case had all of the husband's payments to her been denominated as child support (which she would then receive tax-free) and had she then made the mortgage payments herself. Be that as it may, the suggestion is usually made by the husband as a means of providing the wife with a larger child support payment than he would otherwise be able to make if the payments had to be made totally with after-tax dollars. If that is the case, there may not be merit in the wife's argument. Secondly, there is usually an advantage to the wife in this arrangement, given the fact that real estate taxes generally increase every year, so that the arrangement suggested by the husband will usually cast the burden of these increased payments on his shoulders, rather than on the wife's.

Occasionally, a husband will agree to continue to permit his wife to live in their home but will insist upon the right to borrow on his equity prior to its sale. He will, of course, agree to be responsible to repay the mortgage loan payments as and when they become due. On the face of it, this is a very reasonable request. Nevertheless, it is not without its complications. Nor is the problem in the fact that the wife will be required to join with the husband in obtaining that loan, or because it is to be secured by a mortgage on the home which is in both of their names.

Rather, it derives from the fact that the penalty that will be exacted in the event of the husband's default will not be borne equally by the parties. To be sure, if the husband should default and the lending institution is required to look to the home for the satisfaction of the indebtedness, his equity in the home will be diminished to the extent of that indebtedness. But it has already been diminished to that extent, so he is no worse off by reason of that fact. The wife, on the other hand, will either have to come up with the payment or payments due by the husband (and perhaps the entire principal balance of the indebtedness) or see her home sold out from under her. She may thus have cause to object to this suggestion, as reasonable and understandable as it may seem.

Does this mean that it is always inappropriate for the agreement to grant this right to the husband? We have not said that. The fact that there is a potential risk to the wife does not necessarily mean that it would be *wrong* to include such a provision, even if it is a risk that an adversarial lawyer, representing strictly the wife's interests, might strongly object to. In the adversarial world, that is always the basis of an attorney's objection—either that it does not favor his client or that it exposes his client to some risk.

In the real world, however, where mediation takes place, *exposure to risk is not a sufficient objection.* Rather, it is whether or not it is *appropriate to assume that risk under the circumstances.* It may well be that the husband's request is both understandable and appropriate in the given instance. And it may well be that the wife should assume this risk and rely on her husband's good faith that he will not put her in such a position by defaulting on his obligation.

If such an agreement is contemplated, there is a way of providing the wife with a little greater security, although admittedly not *much* greater security, when the occasion for the husband's default is his inability to make the payments in question rather than simply his unwillingness. The agreement can provide that the husband will not have the right to borrow on his equity in the home unless it is his intention to apply the proceeds of the loan toward the purchase of new living accommodations for himself. The agreement can then further provide that, as security for his obligation to make the mortgage payments, he will give the wife a *second mortgage* on the property in question which will contain a provision that a default by the husband in any of the payments required to be made by him on the loan obtained by the parties for the husband's benefit will constitute a default, as well, on the second mortgage given by the husband to the wife on the new living accommodations acquired by him.

The result is that the penalty that will be exacted in the event of the husband's default will now be one that will be borne equally by the parties. That being the case, it will no longer be possible for the husband to make the payments for the mortgage affecting his own living accommodations and ignore those due on the mortgage affecting the wife's.

By parity of reasoning, the husband may be concerned should the wife fail to make a payment due with respect to the mortgage. His equity is tied up in the home and he does not wish to see it diminished by having the home sold at a foreclosure sale. He may thus wish to have the right, should the wife default in making the mortgage payment, to make it on her behalf and to deduct the amount so paid from the next payment or payments due by him to her. There is nothing inappropriate in this request. Nor is there any detriment to the wife. If she cannot afford to continue to live in the home, then she should agree to sell it. However, she does not have the right to live there and not make the mortgage payments, thereby jeopardizing the husband's interest in the home.

RENTED PROPERTY

If the marital residence, whether it is a one- or two-family home or simply an apartment, is rented by the parties rather than owned by them, the situation is very much simpler. Here, the principal question is who will have the right to continue to live in the former marital residence which, if there are children, will usually be the person with whom the children will continue to maintain their primary residence. In contrast to the situation where the parties own the marital residence, it is not necessary for the mediator to concern himself with how long the party who will remain there will have the right to continue to occupy it, as their lease agreement with their landlord, and not any private understanding which they may have, will determine that.

In most instances, the circumstances—the fact that it was the husband who wanted the divorce and who moved out of the marital residence, or the fact that the wife moved with the parties' infant son to the home of her parents—will tend to resolve the question as to which of the parties will continue to occupy the home. Occasionally, and particularly if the parties are a young, childless couple, and whether for emotional reasons or simply for convenience, they may both wish to have the right to continue to occupy it. Suppose all other avenues that the mediator has explored in an attempt to resolve this issue prove unsuccessful. What should he do at that point? Would it be appropriate for him to suggest that they flip a coin to decide it? If the circumstances and the merits have not served to effectuate a resolution of the issue, then, without necessarily suggesting that the mediator intends the issue to be so resolved, if handled properly, introducing the use of a coin, can well serve as a reality principle.

First, it may convey to the parties the fact that if they are unable to resolve the issue by the application of more relevant considerations, then they may well pay the price of having it determined on an arbitrary basis such as this, or by a court. Secondly, it will underscore the fact that it is not only an issue that must be decided, but also, and more importantly, that after a certain point it is more important *that* it be decided than *how* it is decided.

Having determined who will have the right to continue to live in the home, there are only one or two other issues to be determined. The first concerns the security deposit given by the parties to the landlord at the commencement of the lease. If one of the parties is going to assign his or her interest in that security deposit to the other, or is to be paid a sum of money for doing this, their agreement should so provide, and a letter sent to the landlord signed by the party in question so advising him. Similarly, if it will be divided between the parties at the expiration of the present lease (or any renewal of the lease) that too should be set forth in their agreement.

Finally, there is the question of the right of the party who will continue to occupy the home to assign or sublet the lease agreement or to renew the lease in the joint names of the parties. For example, if the wife is to continue to live in the apartment with the parties' children, it may well be her desire and intention to renew the lease at its expiration. If that is the case, she may want the husband to join with her in executing the new lease should the landlord be reluctant to rely on the security of her signature alone. Nor is there any reason the husband should not agree to execute such a new lease as an accommodation to the wife. He certainly is concerned that his children have an appropriate place to live, and perhaps even that they be able to continue to live in their present home; and this consideration should be sufficient to offset whatever potential risk there may be in the fact that his credit is being extended by joining with the wife in signing a new lease. Again, and as with the situation where the wife is obligated to make a mortgage payment in the name of both of the parties, there are ways of adequately securing the husband.

If the marital residence is an apartment, and although the couple will not generally view it as an asset having value, it may have *potential* value. This would be the case, for example, if the couple had a very favorable lease that could be assigned, or if the building in which the apartment is located later becomes a cooperative apartment, with the tenants in the building having the right to purchase the apartment at a price considerably lower (an insider's price) than the apartment would be worth on the open market. Unless provision is made in the couple's agreement, there may later be a dispute between the parties as to who should rightfully be entitled to these benefits. Accordingly, these questions should be addressed at the present time.

CHAPTER 16

ASSETS AND LIABILITIES

To this point, the mediator has not directly addressed the question of the couple's assets and liabilities. Reference may have been made by the parties or the mediator to certain of these issues in one of the previous sessions. For example, the discussions dealing with the disposition of their home had to include the question of the distribution of the proceeds on its sale, if and when it was to be sold. Similarly, a discussion of the sale of the couple's home, particularly if the home is presently to be sold, will often include the fact that the rather substantial debts that they have will be satisfied from the proceeds of that sale. By and large, however, the discussion of these matters has only been tangential to other concerns. However, it is now time to address some of these questions directly.

The couple's assets fall into three categories. In the first are the furniture and other items of personalty that they have used in and about their home, and in their everyday lives, including their automobiles and perhaps even a boat that one of them owns. The second category consists of savings and checking accounts, stocks and bonds, mutual funds, and real property other than their home, which has already been disposed of. The third category consists of that broad group of assets that has generally come into consideration by reason of the modern equitable distribution statutes that have been enacted in some 41 states and the District of Columbia.[1] These include retirement benefits, business interests, the value of professional practices, royalties, etc.

Prior to the present meeting, the mediator has reminded the parties that he would like them to complete the financial data sheets he has given them, and he may even have reviewed this information in a cursory manner. It is now time to complete this, and if the parties have not done this on their own, the mediator should take the time to go over the financial data sheet with them, filling in the information that they have available, and having them make note of the information they have yet to obtain.

As a general rule, the mediator will discuss one topic from beginning to end before moving on to the next. The question of the disposition of the parties' assets, and perhaps even the responsibility for their debts, represents an exception to this. In fact, the mediator is not turning his attention to their assets and liabilities because he necessarily intends to resolve the question of their disposition at this time. Rather, he wishes to review their assets and liabilities in order to decide where he wants to go from here, and particularly because the question of how the assets will be divided and what interest each of the parties will have in them may directly bear on the other issues they must discuss, most particularly the issue of support.

Again, the mediator may already have received a preview of how those issues will be resolved. For example, if the husband has agreed to deed his interest in their home to the wife, the mediator may have already learned that this was in consideration of the fact that she was not going to make any claim on his business or professional practice. It is now time to add the balance of the pieces of the puzzle so that he will have a more complete picture.

If the mediator finds that the couple's assets, again apart from the equity in their home, are not substantial, and particularly if it is clear that their disposition will not affect the issue of support, there is no reason their division cannot be discussed to a conclusion at this point, and that would be the better practice. The one exception is the disposition of the household furnishings, furniture, and other items of personal property in their home. In most instances it is better to finesse a discussion of these items at this point, and to defer it to the end of the mediation, where it should be there discussed as a matter of housekeeping.

This can be accomplished by simply suggesting to the party who wishes to remove any items of personalty from the home that he make a list of them in the meantime. On the other hand, and particularly if the parties' assets are substantial, the mediator may wish to address only certain of them at the present time, and to defer a discussion of the rest until the issue of support is addressed. This will particularly be the case if some of those assets are intangible, such as a husband's professional practice, or where they are not liquid, such as his business or pension.

BANK ACCOUNTS, STOCKS, AND OTHER PERSONAL PROPERTY

The first category of personal property consists of savings and checking accounts, stocks and bonds, mutual funds, automobiles, boats, and the other liquid assets that one or the other of the parties owns. It may also include a second home or a vacant parcel of land. As a general rule, these assets should be disposed of prior to a discussion of the question of support and maintenance.

In most instances, a couple will tend to view assets such as these as joint assets, regardless of whose name the property is in, and will generally agree to divide them equally. An obvious exception to this would be, for example, stock that the wife inherited from her parents, or that was gifted to her by her parents during their lifetime.

While a bank account is simply money, some assets have a sentimental as well as a financial value. In fact, the emotional attachment to the property may have little to do with its intrinsic worth. This is often the case, for example, with the couple's china and silverware, and with the wife's jewelry. It is also often the case with the husband's boat, stereo equipment, and sometimes an extra automobile that he owns. In these instances, a practical, commonsense approach should be employed.

If particular assets were never viewed as investments, or in strictly dollar terms, during the parties' marriage, it is not necessary to convert them to a dollar value now simply because they have decided to divorce. If the wife attaches sentimental value to her silverware and china, there is no reason she should not be permitted to keep it, even though it has greater monetary value than her husband's motorcycle. In many instances there is no reason that she should not be permitted to keep it even if he does not own a motorcycle at all—even if there is no other property the husband will keep for himself to offset it. It is as unnecessary as it is unbecoming for a couple to sit down and attempt to place a value on every item of costume jewelry that the husband may have purchased for his wife during their marriage, even though it may amount to $2,000 or $3,000 in value. By the same token, it is of little significance that the car the wife will retain is a year older than her husband's. Nor is it necessary to make an adjustment in their values at some other time to compensate for this fact.

What is said about small differences does not, of course, hold true if the assets in question have real value. If a couple had purchased $30,000 worth of stocks and bonds, they would have considered that to be an investment. If they took the same $30,000 and instead bought a series of Picasso prints, those prints should be considered no less of an investment simply because they are hanging on their living room wall rather than sitting in a safe deposit box. Similarly, if the jewelry that the wife owns has a resale value of $30,000 or $40,000, it may or may not make sense to dismiss it from consideration as nothing more nor less than her costume jewelry, depending upon the circumstances. (If the parties are worth several million dollars, it may make sense to so dismiss it. If their circumstances are far more modest, and particularly if the jewelry has substantial resale value, it might not be appropriate to do so.)

Again, in each instance common sense must be applied. If the husband has just purchased a new automobile for himself that is worth $15,000, and his wife is driving a nine-year-old car having a resale value of no more than $500, it will not do to say that they have each come away with a car and leave it at that. An appropriate adjustment may well be in order. On the other hand, the mere fact that the car that one of them drives is newer or older than the other should not necessarily concern the mediator, particularly if it does not concern *them*.

One area of dispute that may erupt is where inherited money, or money that one of the parties received as a gift, has been commingled with other monies that are in the joint names of the parties, or was used to purchase property that was then put in both of their names.[2] This commonly arises, for example, when the couple's home was purchased with monies that one of them received from their parents. It can also occur when one of the parties inherits money that is then used to purchase securities that are placed in their joint names. Here again, common sense must be employed. If a couple has been married for 35 years, their lives and their histories are so intertwined with one another that it simply does not make sense to attempt to go back and separate the various strands to their places of origin. Thus, after 35 years of marriage, it should make little difference whether the initial contribution to purchase their home came from the wife's or the husband's family, and it would be naive indeed to believe that one could attempt to do equity between them at the present time by going back to these points of origin.

Nevertheless, there will still be those who will have some difficulty with this. For them, and particularly if the monies in question came from the wife or the wife's family, all that they will be able to see is the inequity in the fact that the wife will not have returned to her the money she originally invested in the house (let alone a fair rate of interest on that money) before the proceeds of the sale are divided between the parties. This inequity is compounded by the thought that but for the monies that the wife brought to the marriage (or received by way of gift during it) the couple may well not have been able to purchase the home in the first place. The husband has not only had the benefit of the wife's money during their marriage, but to add insult to injury he now also wants to share in it on their divorce.

But what of the disparate financial contributions each of the parties has made toward the maintenance of the home during the marriage, the husband in this case paying all of the costs and the wife none? If he is not entitled to more of the proceeds upon its sale on that account, doesn't his greater contribution at least cancel out the fact of the wife's initial investment and make an equal division equitable? Yes—except for one thing. The critics of this line of thinking would argue that the law in most jurisdictions holds that the contributions that each of the parties made during the marriage are to be considered equal. Thus, if the husband made a greater monetary contribution than the wife, it is presumed that she made a greater contribution in some other area, perhaps as a home-maker, to equalize it.

To be sure, this legal presumption may well make a lot of sense. More importantly, and in terms of the administration of our legal system, it may be a practical necessity. If the rule were otherwise, the dissolution of a marriage partnership would turn a couple's divorce into an accounting procedure, with each required to document all their direct and indirect contributions to the marriage. And, if that were the case, given the probabilities that any particular marriage will end in divorce, attorneys would probably be under an obligation to instruct future husbands and wives in the records they should keep during their marriage (how many dishes they washed, how many containers of garbage they took out, how many messages they took for one another, how many diapers they changed, etc.), just as businessmen are routinely counseled by their accountants as to the records they should keep, for future income tax purposes, of the business expenses they have paid in connection with their businesses. (Unlike businessmen, however, they will also have to be counseled to keep these records in a very safe place—perhaps in a private vault box— so that their spouses do not get their hands on them and destroy them should the question of divorce arise.)

It may be necessary to employ the presumption that marital contributions are equal. In many instances it may even be appropriate that we do so. But this is not to say that we should forget that it is but a legal fiction or, worse, that we should ever take it literally. Nor should we forget that it is a fiction that often flies in the face of common sense. Consider the following. Although the law has not said this in so many words, the presumption that the contributions that each of the parties made during the marriage were equal necessarily leads to the conclusion that the contributions they each brought to the marriage were also equal.

Suppose, for example, that the husband was a surgeon at the time of their marriage, and earned $200,000 a year. Suppose also that the wife was a schoolteacher, earning $30,000. It may well be that the contributions they will later make to the marriage will be equivalent in value. But does it follow from this that the contributions they each bring to the marriage are also equal?

Although this flies in the face of common sense, the presumption adopted by the law leads to no other conclusion. For although it would seem that the husband in this instance is making (bringing) a greater contribution to the marriage (at least in financial terms), as soon as they become married the presumption of equal marital contributions automatically credits the wife with some other contribution that offsets the additional $170,000 in income that the husband earns and, in effect, annuls it.

Suppose, instead, that the wife had married an accountant earning $45,000 a year. The application of the law's presumption in that instance would also give her a credit to offset the additional income that her husband earned. In this case, however, that credit would be $15,000. In short, the logical conclusion that follows from the presumption of equal contributions is that the very same qualities that the wife brings to her marriage are worth $170,000 in one instance, but only $15,000 in another. By parity of reason, if the wife had married the surgeon and her twin sister the accountant, and if they had both applied themselves to their marriage with equal effort, the effort of this wife would be deemed worth far more than her sister's, and she would therefore receive far more in the way of equitable distribution upon her divorce.

In other words, the presumption of equal contributions leads to the absurd result that the value of a person's contribution is dependent, not on their own worth, but on the worth of who they marry and, therefore, to the equally absurd result that the effort of the same person is worth different amounts in different marriages.

Fictions aside, the contributions two people make (bring) to a marriage are not identical, or of equal value. Nor are the contributions they make during their marriage. In fact, the greater the contribution that one of the parties brings to the marriage, the less may well be the contribution that the other will have to make during the marriage. If the wife in this case had married the accountant instead of the surgeon, she would probably have been required to continue to work, perhaps even after she had had children, and would thereby have had to shoulder the burden of being a breadwinner as well as a homemaker. Because of the financial contribution that her husband makes to the marriage, however, she will not be required to work, certainly not after they have children, and will have the luxury of truly enjoying her role as a mother and wife in a way she would not have been able to had she only married the accountant. In fact, and due to her husband's very large income, she will be able to afford help with many of the more routine aspects of homemaking (a housekeeper or cleaning lady, baby-sitters, etc.), thereby further lightening her burden and, therefore, the contribution she will have to make to the marriage.

The simple truth is that the resources two people bring to their marriage (and, perforce, the contributions they make to it) are *not* the same or necessarily equivalent. Thus, and particularly in marriages of long duration, if we wish to insist on the presumption of equal contributions during the couple's marriage, we are going to have to ignore the disparity of their different resources (contributions) at the time of their marriage. To put it another way, if it does not offend us that the husband brought a far greater earning power to the marriage than his wife, why should it offend us that she brought a $50,000 gift from her parents, or even the possibility of a large inheritance from her parents for that matter?

If we are going to accept the view, at least in first marriages of long duration, that marriage is to be treated as a total partnership, and indulge in the fiction of equal contributions, then we are also going to have to indulge in the fiction that neither one brought more to the marriage than the other—that neither one considered that they were doing the other a favor in marrying him or her. And we certainly cannot single out one of those resources—in this case the gift of $50,000 which the wife received from her parents—as deserving of separate treatment.

Should our thinking be affected by the fact that instead of putting the house in their joint names, the wife had used her gift (or inheritance) to purchase a home in her own name alone—that she was careful to assure that the gift remained her separate property? After all, the medical practice that her husband had when they met did not become half hers by reason of their marriage and it will remain his alone after their divorce. Why should it be any different with her $50,000?

The answer here may again depend upon the length of the marriage, not the arbitrary character of the legal fictions that the law employs to resolve these issues. The longer the couple are married, the less relevant these distinctions are. Thus, in marriages of long duration, the relevant question is not *how they started out*, but *how they will be left*. In most instances, the law too recognizes this, at least within the limits of the legal fictions it employs. Thus, while the court may not be able to give the wife a direct interest in her husband's medical practice, it may be able to do so indirectly by requiring her husband to share his future income from it with her in the form of alimony.

What is true of a 35-year marriage is not true of a five-year marriage, however, and, as our modern divorce laws have come to recognize, divorce means different things in the life of a couple who have been married for but a short time and in the life of a couple who have lived together literally their entire adult lives.

In marriages of short duration, the object should be to try to return the couple as nearly as possible to where they were at the time of their marriage. Thus, if the wife's father contributed $50,000 of the consideration that was used to purchase the parties' home, and they have been married for but a relatively short period of time, there is great merit in the wife's contention that it is appropriate that the money be returned to her father. Nor should the question hinge on whether or not the $50,000 was a gift or a loan or, if a gift, whether it was made to the wife alone or to the husband and the wife jointly, regardless of the fact that the law might well hinge its decision on just these kinds of distinctions.

The wife's father should not be faulted for acting as a father and a father-in-law rather than as a lawyer. Nor is it appropriate to apply criteria (even if they be legal criteria) at the time of the couple's divorce that they did not apply (and would probably have considered inappropriate to apply) at the time of their marriage.

The fact remains that the wife's father would not have made the gift of $50,000 but for the fact of his daughter's marriage and but for the fact that his daughter and her husband wished to purchase a home for themselves. It would have been inappropriate of him to have attached, as a condition to that gift, a promise from his daughter and her husband that if they were divorced within a certain period of time that his gift would be returned to him. Similarly, it would be just as inappropriate for the parties, and in this case the husband, now to object to its return simply because there had not been such an explicit condition.

Sometimes a husband will resist returning the money advanced by the wife's father, even if it was clearly a loan and documented as such, because he believes that the wife's father will either simply forgive the loan or, if it is repaid, turn around and return it to his daughter. This is irrelevant. The fact that the father, as between himself and his daughter, may wish to forgive that indebtedness does not mean that the husband, as between himself and the wife's father, should not repay it. One issue has nothing to do with the other.

BUSINESS INTERESTS

The second class of property consists of the business or professional practice owned by the husband or wife, retirement benefits they will receive as an incident to their employment, and perhaps even royalties on a book one of them has written. As a general rule, a discussion of these assets should be deferred until the question of support and maintenance is addressed. In fact, in many instances, it will be best to resolve the question of support before these assets are discussed at all. In other cases, however, it will not be possible to settle the question of support until there is first some agreement on these questions. In this regard, the mediator will always be left with somewhat of a chicken and an egg problem here. The two are obviously related, and in each instance he will have to determine whether they should be taken up separately and, if not, in what order.

Certain practical and theoretical concerns can make a discussion of these issues one of the most difficult in mediation. As has been noted, the modern conception of marriage embodied in our divorce laws holds that marriage is to be treated as a total partnership, both economically as well as emotionally. In short, and for partnership purposes, a husband and a wife are supposed to be considered one. Unfortunately, there are some very difficult problems with this legal conceptualization, not the least of which is that it flies in the face of our common sense. The parties were separate individuals before they married, they will be separate individuals when their marriage ends, and, legal fictions notwithstanding, they were still separate individuals during their marriage.

The second difficulty springs from the first. It is not difficult for a couple to view their children as issue whom they had together and raised together, despite the fact that the wife usually made a greater direct personal contribution toward those partnership efforts. And it is not difficult for a couple to view the home that they bought, that they have maintained, and that they had lived in, as something that they built together, despite the fact that the husband usually made a greater direct financial contribution toward those partnership efforts. It is not so easy, however, for them to view their other individual efforts in the same manner; and in many instances the law's insistence that these individual efforts constitute joint and equal partnership efforts becomes strained to the point of doing violence to our credulity. This is particularly so when the law insists that the benefits of those past individual efforts be apportioned between the parties, and that they both share in them, so that one of them does not leave the marriage on a more secure footing than the other.

Consider the following example. A husband and wife, of unequal ability, are both enrolled in the same law school. The husband's average is 95, and his job prospects are very encouraging. His wife, on the other hand, has an average of only 75, and she cannot expect to obtain a job that will pay anywhere near that which her husband will receive. Just prior to their graduation, they decide to divorce. Would it be equitable for a court to direct their law school to change their grades, and either to average them so that they both had 85 averages, or at least to modify the gap between them so that they could go forth, if not with equal opportunities, at least not with such disproportionate ones? Few, indeed, will be those who would suggest that this would be appropriate. But is it any more appropriate to attempt to correct the disparity in their future prospects by requiring the husband to pay the wife one-half of the difference between their respective salaries, or even a portion of his own, just because they were married while he was in law school? Again, the question is a rhetorical one.

Let us advance the argument one step further. Suppose that the couple had not divorced following their graduation from law school. Instead, they had each gone out into private practice. Some ten years later, when they now divorce, they each have established practices. However, the wife has been far more successful than her husband and earns twice as much as he does. As a result, her professional practice is far more valuable than his. Would it be equitable for a court to direct the wife to pay her husband one-half of the difference in the value of their respective practices? Again, if they are deemed to have made the same contributions to their marriage, shouldn't they then leave on an equal footing, instead of one having a practice that is worth two or three times the other's? Again, the question is a rhetorical one, or at least should be.

Let us take the argument still another step. The husband and the wife are again both practicing attorneys, except that the wife is employed in the legal department of a large corporation and the husband is in private practice for himself. The wife's job is obviously not a marital asset. Nevertheless, the husband's private practice is. Does it follow from this that he should have to share its value with her, and would it offend us if he did not? Certainly, if the wife has a job today, while her husband has a private practice, simply because either her career goals or her interests were different from his, and not because the demands of her duties as a wife or mother placed a limit on them, we would hope that it would not offend anyone if she did not receive any interest in it.

The purpose of the legal fictions created by the various equitable distributions statutes was not to annul individual differences, or to insult our common sense, though in many instances the literal application of those fictions would do just that. It was to *rectify inequities* that resulted from *changes in position* that people made as a result of, or in reliance upon, their marriage. The wife in the above example would not have been a better or worse law student had she not married her husband, and she certainly did not change her career goals because of the responsibilities that her marriage required her to assume. Nor would they have been more or less successful practitioners, or pursued different career goals. In short, whatever differences exist between the parties at the time of their divorce had nothing to do with their marriage.

These, of course, are the easy cases. The hard ones are those in which the position of one of the parties (usually the wife) in relationship to the other cannot be explained simply in terms of differences in ability. She may have been more able than her husband when they got married. Nevertheless, her role in that relationship *precluded* many of the activities that would have enabled her to *use and develop those abilities*. It will not do to say that she too could have done the things that her husband has done. Those were not *society's expectations of her*, nor, therefore, the expectations she had for herself. They may not have even been the expectations that her husband had of her, and it might well have disturbed his concept of the order of things had she behaved other than as was expected of her.

That was fine while they were married. Now that they are divorcing, however, she is left at a considerable and, worse, irreparable disadvantage in relationship to her husband. She does not see the tremendous individual effort that has been expended by her husband in building his career, his profession, or his business. All that she can see is the irrefutable fact that his life is forever assured by the success that he has won, a success which she expected to share but which now will never be hers. And she cannot help but think that there is something terribly inequitable in that.

To be sure, we are talking principally of those women caught in the societal crease between the world that was and is no more, and the world that is coming but is not yet here. These are the women who married in the 1950s, the 1960s, and perhaps even in the early 1970s. It cannot be said of them that they were sufficiently forewarned, and that if they find themselves in a position of inequity, they have only themselves to blame. That would be nonsense. For these women, the *rules were changed in the middle of the game*, and they can rightfully complain about the inequity of this and where that has left them.

But what about women who marry today, or have married in the last 15 years? For better or worse, these women will be charged with a new responsibility and increasingly forced to accept the reality that divorce will not be deemed the occasion to correct whatever inequities exist between husbands and wives, except to a very limited extent. Thus, even though working mothers labor under a far greater disability than do working fathers, and as unfair as that may be, they will simply be required to add the additional burden of being able to support themselves properly in the event of their divorce as one of the obligations they assume in marrying.

Is it fair that women should labor under a greater disability than men? No: but then when was it ever suggested that the lives that are given to us, and that we lead, are necessarily fair? Is it any more fair that the careers and lives of men have been interrupted, and sometimes ended, by their being drafted into military service while women were exempted? And would it make sense for men to complain that since we now believe that our laws should be gender-neutral, that it is unfair that our societal expectations still prevent us from enacting legislation that require men and women to be drafted equally?

Or would it make sense for men to complain that either due to biology or because of the tasks that have traditionally been assigned to them, their wives have a greater life expectancy than they do? Again the question is a rhetorical one. Divorce, like life itself, is not fair to either of the parties; it is just *unfair to them in different ways*. While we should most certainly *try to narrow those inequities*, it is naive to believe that we will eliminate them, particularly by legislative changes in our divorce laws. Again, one of the worst aspects of traditional adversarial divorce proceedings has been its implicit suggestion that there is *justice in divorce*, and that its purpose is to secure it. Divorce mediation must not mimic this mistake. For justice to emerge, the parties are going to have to have a *shared view of what is fair and just*. By definition, however, they will not. In fact, they will have very different views. Nor is a mediator going to change that. If that is the case, it will do no good to suggest to a couple that there will be justice in their agreement. Rather, it is a mediator's job to help them accept it even though, from their standpoint, there will not.

Whether fair or unfair, the fact remains that the by-products of individual effort will never be distributed equally or even equitably, regardless of the labels the law may attach to them. In each case, the court's attitude, and the attitude of the party whose individual effort is involved, will depend upon how the asset in question is viewed. Suppose a couple has $50,000 in savings that were derived from the husband's law practice. These savings will simply be viewed as "money in the bank," despite the fact that they were derived from individual effort. In all probability, therefore, they will be divided equally between the parties.

When we consider the husband's law practice, however, and place a value upon it in terms of what it will enable the husband to earn in the future, it no longer looks like *money in the bank*. Rather, it looks much more like *individual effort*. As a result, the wife will never be awarded one-half of its value by the court. (Another reason for this is that the future individual effort will be that of the husband alone. In the past there was the fiction of marital effort that give the wife an interest in the $50,000 from the husband's practice that went into their savings, but that same fiction says that all future efforts that will be expended to realize the value of his practice will be those of the husband alone.)

Suppose, instead, that the husband owned a business that had assets of $500,000 (consisting of the equity in the building the company owns, its fixtures and equipment, etc.), and that, based upon future earnings, it could be sold for $1,500,000. Here you have a hybrid. If a court heard evidence of the value of the company's building, fixtures, and equipment, it would tend to view them as fixed assets (though not quite money in the bank). The worth of the business based upon future earnings, however, would appear more like individual effort, though not quite like the individual effort of a lawyer or a doctor in his private practice. In short, and regardless of whatever logical distinctions there may or may not be, all marital property will not be viewed or treated in the same way.

Another factor that compounds this problem is the question of where the money will come from to satisfy the husband's or the wife's interest in this marital property. Again, if the marital property is a bank account or mutual funds there is no problem. All that has to be done is to divide the property between the parties. But suppose it is the husband's interest in his law practice or medical practice that is at issue? He might have the financial wherewithal to pay a portion of its value to his wife if he were selling it, but he is not. To be sure, where there are other marital assets of substantial value, there can be a trade-off, with the wife receiving a larger share of these assets, and perhaps all of them, in exchange for a release by her of any interest that she may have in her husband's practice arising out of their marriage.

(This will commonly happen when they own a home, the husband deeding his interest in the home to the wife for her release of her interest in his business.) If that is not possible, however, all that is left is for the husband to make payment to the wife in installments, over an extended period of time. It must be recognized, however, that these payments are not being made from capital (though they are ostensibly payments in satisfaction of the wife's interest in a capital asset) but rather from the husband's income.

In short, calling the husband's law practice a marital asset in which his wife has an interest does not increase the husband's *ability* to make payments to his wife; it simply increases his *obligation* to do so. But if, instead of being given an interest in the value of his law practice, the wife is awarded support in the future based upon the fact that at the time of their divorce her husband has been left a lawyer and she simply a former homemaker, and if the payments that the husband makes to the wife are derived from his income as a lawyer, hasn't the wife really shared in the benefit of that practice?

This brings us to the last complicating factor. The wife is entitled to receive an interest in the marital property because her partnership efforts directly or indirectly contributed to them. Thus, if at the end of their marriage the parties have assets worth $100,000, then upon the dissolution of their partnership, those assets should be divided between them. In effect, the wife is being paid for the past services she rendered to the partnership. But if she is being paid for the past services she rendered to the partnership, why is she also being given future support? Isn't that paying her twice?

She is given support for two reasons. First, because few couples have sufficient marital assets to compensate the wife for her past efforts. Second, and more importantly, because the respective roles of the parties during their marriage have left the wife at a distinct disadvantage relative to her husband in terms of her ability to support herself in the future.

Unfortunately, it will take some time yet before the question of the division of marital assets that involve individual effort is finally resolved. The problem at the present time is that it is not possible to view this question in an unbiased manner for the reason that, in the overwhelming majority of instances, the marital assets in question involve the individual efforts of the husband. The issue has thus become clouded by the inequities that women feel generally in relationship to their husbands at the time of their divorce.

In fact, it will not be until more of those marital assets involve the individual effort of women that we will be able to separate the question of this individual effort from the question of gender. The time is coming, however, and as mediators will learn in their practices, particularly as they are dealing with women under the age of 40, that change is already on its way.

APPRECIATED PROPERTY

What if a husband owned a small business and a hundred shares of IBM stock at the time that the parties were married? The business has grown into a big business and the IBM stock has tripled in value. Does the wife have any interest in these assets? True, property that was owned at the time of the parties' marriage, like property inherited during a marriage, is generally considered separate property in which the other party has no interest.[3] But what if that property has changed substantially during the couple's marriage? Here the husband's business, represented by 100 shares of ABC Corp. owned by the husband, consisted of one drugstore at the time of their marriage. The husband still only owns the same 100 shares of ABC Corp., but that business has grown to some 15 stores in the intervening years.

Some courts have taken the position that the appreciation in the value of separate property will be considered marital property if it was active rather than passive appreciation (if it was due to the direct or indirect efforts of either of the parties).[4] In other words, the husband's business, and the value of his shares of stock in ABC Corp., increased in value because of the efforts he put into that business. The husband's shares of IBM stock, on the other hand, appreciated in value because of the efforts of the officers and directors of IBM, not because of *his* efforts. In other words, that is passive appreciation, and since it is his marital effort, and not the efforts of the officers and directors of IBM that the wife is considered to be entitled to share in, the appreciation in value of the shares of IBM stock is not generally considered a marital asset in which the wife has an interest.

There is a hybrid situation that must also be discussed. This concerns separate property that one of the parties owned at the time of their marriage that stays the same, but changes nevertheless. At the time of the parties' marriage, the husband owned a stock portfolio worth approximately $200,000 that was in his individual name. Over the years of the marriage he has bought and sold shares on a regular basis, always reinvesting the proceeds of those sales in other stock also taken in his name. Never were the profits from the sales of these shares commingled with other assets that the parties owned. Similarly, absolutely no money that was acquired by either the husband or the wife during the marriage from any other source was ever employed to purchase stock that was or is now part of the stock portfolio. The stock portfolio, now made up of entirely different shares of stock than was owned by the husband at the time of the parties' marriage, is now worth $500,000. Does the wife have any interest in that appreciation?

Again, the appreciation in the value of the various shares of stock owned by the husband was a result, not of the husband's efforts, but of the efforts of the officers and directors of the corporations involved. Nevertheless, the husband did expend his own effort during the marriage (marital effort) in managing his stock portfolio and, perhaps more importantly, in making the important decisions involved in deciding to buy or sell the shares in question. Is this marital effort really any different from the marital effort that the husband might have expended in the management of his business? To put it another way, how *much* effort must a party devote to the management of his separate property for that effort to be viewed as marital effort? After all, even if the husband's stock portfolio consisted of the very same shares of stock at the time of the couple's divorce that he owned at the time of their marriage, and he had not bought or sold a single share, there was still some effort exerted on his part during the marriage in keeping records of dividends, or statements from his broker, etc. Unfortunately, the legal fictions of active and passive appreciation collide with one another here and do not provide an easy answer.

PENSIONS

Retirement benefits are considered property in which each of the parties has an interest arising out of their marriage.[5] As a general rule, only property that was acquired during the marriage is considered marital property (property that the court has the power to distribute at the time of a couple's divorce). The acquisition of most property (for example, a home, stocks and bonds, etc.) does not pose a problem here, as the home was acquired (title was taken) at one point in time. Pension benefits, however, are a little different. They are more analogous to a plan that permits the employee to purchase shares of stock in the corporation each year based upon his salary. At the time of his retirement, he may own 100 shares of the corporation's stock, but he did not acquire title to all of those shares at the same time. Some of the shares he purchased prior to his marriage, some during his marriage and the balance of the shares he purchased following his divorce.

The threshold question faced by a court in distributing pension benefits is to determine what portion of those benefits (in our analogy, what portion of those shares of stock) constitute marital property. The answer generally given has been that it was those benefits that were acquired by the employed spouse during the period of the parties' marriage. Thus, if the husband had worked at his present place of employment for 5 years prior to the parties' marriage, if he had continued to work there for the 20 years that they were married, and if he works there five more years following their divorce before he retires, two-thirds of those benefits will be deemed marital property in which the wife has an interest.[6]

The only problem is that, unless the husband is already receiving his pension benefits or will begin to receive them momentarily, it is not possible to know how many more years he will work at his present place of employment following his divorce (it is not possible to presently calculate what portion of the total benefits constitute marital property.) As a result, some courts have devised a formula that provides that the wife (in this example) will receive a certain portion of a fraction of these benefits in which the numerator is the total number of months that the husband has been employed at his present place of employment during the period of the parties' marriage, and the denominator will be the total number of months that the husband will have been employed at his present place of employment at the time of his retirement.[7]

The problem with pension benefits is not whether the nonemployed spouse has an interest in those benefits. That is generally established by the law of the state in which the parties live. Nor is it generally the problem of determining what the value of those benefits is.[8] All that is necessary is to assign the nonemployed spouse (for example, the wife) a portion of the benefits that her husband will receive when he receives them. Nor is there a problem in terms of how the husband will satisfy the wife's interest in this martial asset. Since he will not get the benefit of his pension for many years to come, it does not offend our sense of justice that the wife, too, will have to wait those same number of years before she will receive her share of these benefits.

The problems are more difficult. To begin with, the mediator may be faced with a psychological problem. Not infrequently it is very hard for a husband to view his pension as a marital asset. Although he realizes that his pension has value, and although he will acknowledge that his wife may have an interest in it under the law, it still bothers him that he will have to share it with her. This is what he has worked for all his life, and this is what he expects to be able to live on when he retires. In fact, but for his pension he may not be able to retire at all. To take his pension from him is therefore akin to taking away his birthright.

The second problem is a practical one. Although the logic of our modern divorce law says that it is inequitable that a husband should be able to retire in his old age, but that his wife should not, dividing the husband's pension between them does not necessarily correct this inequity. Rather, what it may mean is that neither one of them will ever be able to retire. Pensions alone do not always permit people to retire well. All too often they only permit people to retire barely, and then only if they have social security benefits or other income to supplement their pension benefits.[9] To take those benefits and divide them between the parties—no matter how fair that may be—may simply mean that they will now both have to continue to work.

The third problem is the most formidable. This problem derives from the fact that to give one of the parties an interest in the other's pension may, on occasion, be as unfair as to award them no interest at all. In most instances, we are not talking about a situation where the husband, for example, is already receiving his pension benefits, or where he will receive them shortly. Those are the easy cases. Rather, we are talking about the situation where he will not receive them for many years to come. Nevertheless, we are being asked to make a present decision about the distribution of those pension benefits which, almost by definition, completely ignores all of the events that will occur between now and then, let alone what the circumstances of the respective parties will be at that time.

Nor is it an answer to this to say that all that we are attempting to do is to make a determination based upon the past equities, or even based upon the present circumstances of their lives, for that matter. The fact remains that we are still making judgments about the future without having available to us all of the appropriate information that we would need for that purpose.

As we have pointed out previously, one of the gross inequities of our previous divorce laws was that if a wife remarried within a few years of her divorce, in many instances that meant that she received literally nothing for her contribution to the marriage, particularly if there were few joint assets and her only recompense was the alimony that was awarded to her on her divorce, but which she then lost with her remarriage. On the other hand, one of the inequities of our modern divorce laws—and this is particularly true when it comes to pension benefits—is that a court is powerless to change a result that may appear to be *equitable today* but may prove to be *inequitable tomorrow*.[10]

Suppose, for instance, that a court awards support to a wife and changed circumstances suggest that the award should either be increased or decreased. In most instances the court can correct this inequity since it continues to have the power to modify its previous determination. Nor will it be an objection to this to say that in doing this the court is introducing considerations that occurred following the parties' divorce, when the support award was supposed to be predicated upon the factors arising during their marriage. Suppose instead, however, that the court has divided a joint savings account between the parties and that the husband, shortly after the parties' divorce, is required to exhaust his share in an illness that he suffers. Can he go back and, based upon the inequity that his wife should be left with so much and he with so little, which was obviously not the court's original intention, ask the court to give him a share of the account previously awarded to his wife that is still in her possession?

The answer is no. The savings account was marital property, and since the court has already divided it, and distributed it between the parties, the court has no power to take back that which it has previously given.[11] Nor, as a general rule, should it be otherwise. To a great extent, divorce means, and must mean, that the parties are each given what is considered appropriate provisions, and sent on their way. In the past, if what was given to either of them was wanting, they each had a right to look to the other, and it was only appropriate that they did so. From this point forward, however, they must each proceed on their own account. To be sure, this may result in inequities on occasion. But the possibility of these inequities is generally offset by the benefit that occurs in not permitting them continually to look back and compare how they are doing in comparison with one another. For that too is what divorce is about.

Unfortunately, the inequities that can result from the present distribution of benefits that will not be received for some time to come are great indeed. Suppose, in the intervening years, the wife goes back to work and receives her own pension, perhaps even equal to or better than the husband's. Does it make sense to suggest that the wife should be entitled to keep her entire pension, just because she happened to have earned it at a time when the parties were not married, but that the husband should be obligated to share his pension with her, just because he happened to earn a portion of it while they were? In short, does it make sense to suggest that, in their old age, the wife will have her entire pension and perhaps a third of her husband's as well?

As we have noted previously, the fact that effort was expended during the period of the parties' marriage can be as *irrelevant* to the determination of what is equitable as it can be *relevant*. Suppose that the wife does not go back to work but that she instead remarries and that at the time of her former husband's retirement she is being properly supported by her then husband. To be sure, she has "earned" an interest in her former husband's pension based upon their marriage. But as between the two of them, does she really need it?

Mediation lends itself to the resolution of certain of these problems in a more constructive manner than do traditional adversarial divorce proceedings. For example, it is sometimes not too difficult to demonstrate to a couple that the allocation of the husband's pension benefits should perhaps be based upon need and that, for example, if the wife is still working at the time of her husband's retirement, that their agreement can provide that she will not receive any portion of those benefits so long as she is employed, or provide that she will not receive those benefits if she will receive pension benefits of her own equal to, for example, two-thirds of those of her former husband. It is even possible for their agreement to provide that she will not receive those benefits if she is remarried at that time.[12]

There is also another way of handling these pension benefits. People attach different emotional tags or values to various items of property. The husband may simply not view his equity in his home in the same manner that he views his interest in his pension. On occasion, he will be willing either to forgo his interest in that equity or, perhaps, to forgo a portion of it.

Suppose, for example, it is determined that the present value of the husband's pension is $150,000 and that it is agreed that the wife has a one-half interest in that value. Suppose also that the equity in their home is also $150,000 and that it is agreed that the wife's interest in that equity is also one-half. Perhaps the husband can deed his interest in the party's home to the wife in exchange for a release of her interest in his pension.

There is a problem, however. In most instances, the parties will not know the present value of the husband's pension. All that the husband receives from the plan administrator is a yearly statement indicating the projected monthly or yearly payment that will be made to him at a stated age or ages based upon his present salary, together with a statement of the amount that he has contributed to the plan (if it is that type of plan) and the death benefit that will be paid should he die before reaching the age of retirement (if the plan in question includes such a death benefit). However, it does not include a statement of the pension's present value, and this can only be determined by a skilled pension evaluator.

This poses a problem for the couple, and perhaps even for the mediator. How do they know whether or not it is appropriate to exchange the husband's present equity in the marital residence for the wife's future interest in the husband's pension? Worse yet for the mediator is the question of whether or not it would be responsible for him to permit them to do this unless they made that decision on a more informed basis. In short, isn't it necessary to employ a pension evaluator to provide the parties with the present value of the husband's pension?

On the face of it, the answer would appear obvious. Nevertheless, a word of caution is in order. In an important sense the value the pension evaluator will assign to the husband's pension is not a *real* value, even though it may be an *accurate* one. To begin with, it is not real in the sense that the equity in the parties' home is real. The husband cannot sell his pension and he cannot reduce it to present dollars, as the wife can do with her home. It simply represents the discounted (present) value of the husband's future benefits. This value is not a real value for yet another reason. The pension evaluator cannot possibly know what the husband's future benefits will actually be, for he does not know whether the husband will even live to retirement age, let alone how many months or years he will live to receive those benefits if he does. All that he can do is make certain *assumptions* about the husband, based upon actuarial tables, and then calculate the value of those benefits on the basis of those assumptions.

Thus, given the husband's present age, the pension evaluator may project that the husband will live to be 74 years 6 months of age, based upon present actuarial tables.

However, there is nothing to say that those tables may not change in the future, as they most certainly have in the past. Even if they do not change, however, this is not to suggest that the husband will actually live to be 74 years and 6 months. In fact, his chances of actually dying at that time are probably no greater than one in a hundred.

Thus, and since a pension evaluator can only make his projections by adding one assumption upon another, though the determination he comes to may be both responsible and accurate, it is still, nevertheless, a fiction. Unfortunately, however, the parties will not believe that, or accept it as such. If the pension evaluator comes back and advises them that the present value of the husband's pension is $100,000, then they will tend to treat this number as if it were money in the bank, and there will be very little that the mediator will be able to do to get them to view it otherwise.

This brings up the second problem. Without question, the value assigned to the husband's pension by the pension evaluator will be either more or less than the equity in their home, probably by several thousand dollars. Let us suppose, for example, that the value assigned to the husband's pension is $30,000 more than the equity in their home. On the assumption that the parties were going to share equally in both of these assets, this would mean that the husband would have to pay the wife the sum of $15,000 for a release of her interest in his pension benefits.

Unfortunately, the husband will probably bridle at this, as it will be very difficult for him to see why he should deed his interest in his home to his wife and then have to pay her $15,000 for the privilege. Even if there are other assets available, such as joint savings accounts or a money market fund, that the husband could assign to the wife in satisfaction of his obligation, he will still not appreciate the suggestion. On the contrary, it may only make it worse, for all that he will be able to see is that his wife has not only been left with their home, but all, or almost all, of their liquid assets as well.

Suppose the situation is reversed, and it turns out that the present value of the husband's pension is $30,000 less than the equity in the parties' home. It is the same problem, but perhaps worse. In agreeing to the proposal, the wife expected her husband to give her their home, not to have to pay for it, and having to pay for it will bother her as much or more than paying for his pension will bother the husband. It may well be that a mediator can demonstrate to the wife that the equity in the home that she will keep is equal to the present value of her husband's pension, plus the money in their joint savings accounts. However, this will still leave the money in those joint savings accounts in her husband's hands, and this will still leave her with little, if any, money in the bank, and feeling very insecure. This being so, it will be very hard for her to view the proposed exchange as being fair.

Another, equally serious problem arises in attempting to reduce the husband's pension benefits to a present dollar value, as that value cannot help but irrevocably alter their view of the considerations that led each of them to consider the exchange in the first place. While the economic benefits associated with each of these assets was undoubtedly a factor in each of the parties' decisions, it was by no means the *only* factor, or even the most important one. Quite the contrary, more often than not there were other considerations that were equally important, even though it is not possible to measure them in monetary terms.

The wife's interest in owning her home outright is not simply based on the dollars that the equity in that home represents. It is based primarily on her desire to own it. The parties' marital residence is not simply an economic asset. It is the wife's home and part of the very structure of her life. That being so, it is very discomfiting to her to have to live under the terms of an agreement that will force her to have to sell it at various points in time, regardless of how appropriate that may well be on a rational basis. She would be far happier having the security of knowing that she will not have to do this. It may well be that the benefits to the parties' children in maintaining that home after the youngest graduates from high school in three years is not sufficient to justify the husband's being deprived of the substantial equity that he has tied up in the home; but the wife would still feel more comfortable not having that decision forced upon her. In fact, it was primarily emotional considerations such as this—which in the final analysis account for most of the important decisions that we make in our lives—that originally accounted for the wife's desire to exchange her interest in her husband's pension for a deed to the home.

The same is true of the husband. To be sure, he may tend to view the pension and the home in more purely monetary terms than will his wife since, not being the one who will continue to live in the home with the children, it has already lost much of its primary emotional meaning for him. But, and somewhat ironically, it is the very fact that the home and his pension have been reduced simply to economic assets that now adds emotional fuel to his desire to effectuate an exchange of them.

Psychologically, the husband has a need and a desire to put the past behind him. He wants to go on and build a new life for himself with a clean slate. To be sure, he knows that he cannot completely do this, as of necessity he leaves with continuing obligations to his children and perhaps to his wife as well. But he would like to be able to look to a point in the future when those obligations will come to an end, and he will finally be free, rather than have them pursue him to the very day of his death. Not infrequently, the husband's pension tends to represent this, often for the very reason that it is a benefit that he will not actually receive for many years to come. Because of this, he tends to view the wife's continuing interest in that pension as a *permanent mortgage on his life*. Nor is it any answer to point out to the husband that he will continue to retain his interest in the parties' marital residence, and that he will eventually receive half of its equity. So will his wife, but she will also have the *use* of it now, which he will not.

To make matters worse, when the husband does finally receive his one-half interest in the home, this is not to say that he will now be able to buy a home of his own. After all, he will not then have the benefit of his wife's one-half interest in their home as she now has his. He will not even have the benefit of his own one-half interest. Since it is not his principal residence at the time of its sale, he will lose the privilege to roll over the proceeds that he receives into a new principal residence without first having to pay tax on the profit that he derives from its sale.[13] Worse yet, when he finally does receive that equity, by definition it will be at a time when the children have graduated from high school, and perhaps even from college, and when owning a home will probably be less important to the husband. In the meantime, he will be forced to live in accommodations that are clearly inadequate. It is for these reasons that he has agreed to exchange his interest in that home for his wife's interest in his pension.[14]

Before permitting the parties to agree to this exchange, however, and in an effort to be responsible, the mediator has decided to have the home evaluated by a real estate appraiser, and the present value of the husband's pension determined by a pension evaluator, and has been advised that there is a $30,000 difference in the values ascribed to each of these assets.

Suppose it is the pension that is found to be worth $30,000 more. Since, in all likelihood, the wife will be given the right to continue to live in the home even if such an exchange is not effectuated, this will tend to cause her to discount the value to herself in such an exchange. It will also make it more difficult for her to see that the values assigned to the home and the pension do not reflect the fact that the asset that she will receive in the exchange has a present value, besides its economic value, while the asset that her husband will receive does not.

Nor will the wife be able to place any value on the fact that, should she sell the home, she will have the use of the money represented by its equity for these many years while, in terms of the husband's pension, he will not. As we have said, once a value is assigned to the husband's pension, the wife will tend to view it as money in the bank. Thus, and almost as night follows day, to place a present value on the husband's pension in order to assure that the exchange is fair is simply to decree that there will not be any exchange at all.

But would it not be absolutely irresponsible for a mediator to permit the parties to agree upon the exchange without such an evaluation—to agree upon the exchange unless they both knew what they were exchanging? Not necessarily. It would only be irresponsible if, first, a fair exchange necessarily meant an exchange of equal dollar value and, second, if the determination made by the pension evaluator represented the real value of the husband's pension. However, it is not irresponsible if neither of these assumptions is correct—which they are not.

Obviously, if a mediator is confronted with a situation where the husband has only been employed by his present employer for a period of two years (with the only pension rights that he has being based upon these two years of employment) and the equity in the parties' home is $200,000, he will feel very uncomfortable about an exchange of one asset for the other, even if he does not believe that the what is being exchanged must have equivalent dollar values for the exchange to be appropriate. By parity of reasoning, he will have the same difficulty if the husband has been employed in his present position for 30 years, accruing pension benefits throughout this period of time, and the equity in the parties home is only $50,000. But that does not mean that he should feel the same way in those cases that fall in the middle of these extremes. Nor does it mean that he cannot satisfy himself as to the appropriateness of the exchange without a determination of the present value of the husband's pension benefits.

How can he do this? Principally by looking at the value of the equity in the parties' home. In most instances, the party with the pension will be the larger wage earner. In fact, the problem has arisen in the first place because the wife does not have a pension of her own. Nor is it likely that she will have one in the future. Rather, it is the equity in her home which she hopes will constitute her future pension. If that is the case, the question that the mediator should concern himself with is not whether or not the equity in the parties home is equal to the present value of the husband's pension (which by definition he does not know) but whether or not it will be sufficient, or reasonably sufficient, to provide her with support—a pension of her own—upon her retirement.

The home is presently worth $200,000 and has an equity of $150,000. The question then is whether or not the monies that will be left to the wife will be sufficient to provide her with such a pension. More importantly, the question is whether the equity in her home is sufficient to provide her with a pension comparable to her husband's projected pension benefits. If they are, and if the parties are satisfied with the exchange, it should be of no concern to the mediator that neither he nor either of them knows the present value of the husband's pension.

How can the mediator make this determination? One way, (though not necessarily the only way) would be to find out what kind of an annuity the wife would be able to purchase were she to sell her home today, pay the taxes that would be due, and invest the proceeds of the sale, first, in an annuity payable to her husband over the duration of his life, commencing at the age in which he would normally retire, and, second, in an annuity payable to *her*, for the duration of *her* life, commencing at the age that *she* would normally retire.

Why is it necessary to have both of these answers? In a certain sense, it is not. After all, if the question is whether or not the home is equal to the husband's pension, then the only question should be what kind of an annuity would the husband be able to buy with the proceeds from the sale of the home, and how would that annuity compare with the benefits that he will receive under his pension. Unfortunately, however, that will tell the wife little about what kind of an annuity she will be able to buy on her own life with the same monies.

Does this mean that the exercise is a pointless one? Absolutely not. While the initial inquiry may have been whether or not the exchange of the parties' home for the husband's pension was a fair one, in many ways that is an impossible, and perhaps even pointless, question. What the mediator will accomplish by asking the question he has will be to change the question into a more appropriate one.

The wife is not hesitating because she does not wish to exchange the husband's interest in their home for her interest in his pension. She is hesitating because she is not sure whether the exchange is fair. In short, her problem is that she feels that she is comparing apples with oranges, and that she may be getting shortchanged in the process. If the mediator can demonstrate that her apples (her home) can also be viewed as oranges (a potential retirement fund), he may be able to remove the impediment in the wife's way and give her the ability to do what she would really like to do in the first place.

Suppose the mediator concludes that the equity in the parties' home will not be sufficient to provide the wife with an annuity of her own equal to her husband's pension. Does that mean that an exchange of that equity for her interest in her husband's pension is inappropriate? Not necessarily. Again, it must be remembered that the comparison really is between apples and oranges, and that if the mediator was attempting to determine what kind of an annuity the wife could purchase with the equity in her home, it was simply for the purpose of making a comparison between those apples and oranges less difficult.

What that comparison ignores, however, are all of the factors that can, and properly should, be considered in making the determination. Again, the concept of marital property is simply a means of doing equity between the parties. It is not to be confused with equity between the parties, however. Thus, if both of the parties would really like to make the exchange, it is no less appropriate simply because that exchange would not be the one reached by the strict application of equitable distribution principles. *The parties and the court are not trying to do the same thing.* There is no reason, therefore, why they should have come to the same result.

One last point must be mentioned in connection with pension benefits. Pension benefits come in three forms: (a) a lump-sum payment made at the time of the wage-earner's retirement, (b) a fixed payment made during the wage-earner's life, or (c) a fixed payment, at a reduced amount, made during the wage-earner's life and then, after his death, a continuing fixed payment to his surviving spouse.[15] Whether or not the wife will have any interest in the husband's pension during his life, serious thought should be given to whether or not she will have an interest in his pension following his death. In other words, serious thought should be given to whether the agreement will contain provision requiring the husband to choose that option that will provide such benefits to the wife.[16]

(In this case, the wife will be entitled to such benefits despite the fact that she will not be his wife at the time of his death, and even though he may have another wife at that time.) The reduced payments that the husband will receive during his lifetime in consideration for the payments being made to his surviving spouse following his death are not that large, and this provision thus represents a very substantial and important benefit to the wife.

At times, a husband will have no objection to the fact that his wife will share in his pension during his lifetime. What he objects to, however, is her insistence that he choose that option that will provide her with benefits following his death. Here the husband's objection is not that he wishes to name his future wife as the beneficiary of those survivorship benefits instead of his present wife. Rather, his objection is that if he should choose that option, it will mean a reduced payment to him during his lifetime. Thus, if the husband would be entitled to receive $2,200 per month in retirement benefits were he to choose an option that provided those benefits only during his own life, they may be reduced, for example, to $1,800 per month should he choose that option that will provide survivor benefits to his wife.

The husband has a very good argument here. While it might be appropriate for him to share those retirement benefits equally with his wife—for each of them to receive $1,100 a month following his retirement—if he elects that option that will provide survivorship benefits for his wife, he will not only receive $200 less per month than he otherwise would but, worse, he will receive less than half of those benefits. After all, although his wife will also receive $200 less per month during his lifetime, she will be entitled to receive the full survivor's benefits following his death. In short, she will receive greater benefits from her husband's pension than will he.

In many instances, there is an easy way to solve this problem. This can be done by providing that the husband will select that option that will provide survivorship benefits to his wife but that during his lifetime he will receive the same amount from those retirement benefits that he would have had he selected the option that would have only provided benefits during his lifetime. (In this case, the husband will receive $1,100 of the total $1,800 monthly payment—the same $1,100 that he would have received had he not selected the option providing for survivorship benefits—and his wife will receive $700). In this way the husband will be no worse off by reason of the fact that he has selected the option that will provide survivorship benefits for his wife, and she will have the security of receiving those benefits after his death for the rest of her life.[17]

Does this make sense as far as the wife is concerned? The answer is that it probably makes a great deal of sense. The wife is probably younger than her husband. Her life expectancy is also probably greater. In fact, given her age and her life expectancy, she should probably live at least 5 to 10 years longer than her husband. More importantly, she is not really concerned about receiving an interest in her husband's retirement benefits during her productive years, while she can work. Not having a pension of her own, she is more concerned about receiving those retirement benefits after she is no longer able to work. Most importantly, she does not want to lose those benefits simply because her husband should die. And even though she may receive less while he is alive, the security that this trade-off will provide her may well be worth it to her.

HOUSEHOLD FURNITURE AND FURNISHINGS

As we stated at the outset, the question of the division of the couple's personal property should generally be the last topic to be taken up. Very often items having no great monetary value nevertheless have a great deal of emotional valence attached to them, and if the question of the division of these items is taken up too early, the heat that this discussion may generate can actually ballast any chance of an agreement between the parties.

On the other hand, when almost everything else has been put in place, and an agreement now hinges on the disposition of simply two or three items of personal property, there is a far greater likelihood that the parties will negotiate their way around this difficulty rather than allow it to destroy the possibility of an agreement.

As a general rule, it is not a good idea to have the parties make a list of all of the furniture and household furnishings in question. It is much better to start out by determining which of the parties will, by the nature of the circumstances, end up with the greater proportion of those household furnishings (usually the party retaining custody of the children or the party remaining in the marital residence) and to then have the other party prepare a list of the household furnishings he wishes to take with him. Even if the parties are childless, and simply live in an apartment, it is better to fall back on the presumption that the wife will be left with the larger portion of the household furnishings and ask the husband to prepare a list of what he wants, if that will work. (This presumption does not always operate where the parties are childless and have been married but a short time; and it of course tends to operate in the opposite direction if the parties are already separated and it is the wife, rather than the husband, who left the marital residence.)

There are situations, however, where lists may be necessary. The first is whether you have a young couple, without children, living in an apartment and there is really not a great deal to divide. They may insist upon an almost equal division of what they have, and the preparation of a list in this instance may be in order. The second instance is where the party who is supposed to prepare a list of what he would like to take from the home prepares such a lengthy list that the other party complains that it is more than has been left to her. It may then be necessary for her to support this contention by preparing a list of her own of what will be left. Finally, in some instances the mediator will find parties who have a great many small paintings and objets d'art that again, although of no great intrinsic value, nevertheless have value to them. The departing party may not dispute the division of beds and everyday silverware, but he may insist on an equal division of these nonutilitarian items. The only way that this can be accomplished is by preparing a list. If there are a large number of items in dispute (particularly if they are objets d'art, paintings, etc.), one procedure that can be followed is to allow the parties to alternately pick the items from the list. (When they are through, each party will usually find that he or she did not get certain things that they wanted. If that is the case, they can then barter with one another to correct the situation.) This procedure can work very effectively.

However, it is important to keep careful track of the items on the list that each of the parties has selected, and after the selections have been made, and the bartering back and forth completed, to be sure that the master list clearly designates which of the parties is to get each of the items in question. The list should then be either signed or initialed by the parties so that there is no dispute later as to who is entitled to what.

Generally, the departing party will not try to take much with him. Often he will take literally nothing, except his clothing and personal effects, although it is common for husbands to make claim to the color TV and to the stereo, just as it is common for the wife immediately to look to the good china and silverware as her special property. Nevertheless, the husband may at times look to some of the furniture in the house for the purpose of furnishing his new apartment and may contend that he is simply without the funds to purchase furniture on his own. While the wife may understandably be upset by this suggestion, and the thought of having gaping holes in her furnished home (particularly if the furniture he is laying claim to sits in the middle of her living room or den), it may, nevertheless, be an indignity she will have to suffer if his claim is justified by the economic circumstances.

(If he has not already done so, it would be a good idea to have the husband look for a new place for himself so that he will see just what it is that he will actually *need*. It may turn out that he decides to take a furnished room and thus does not need all of the furniture that he now thinks he will. Moreover, the fact that the husband does not take the furniture now, but allows his wife to use it, does not mean that it cannot nevertheless remain his, or that he cannot later remove it when the house is sold).

Sometimes a husband will insist upon an absolute equal division of all of the furniture and household furnishings, even when his wife will continue to live in the marital residence with the children. This, of course, is unrealistic. If the wife is to have custody of the children she is not only entitled to all of their furniture and belongings, but she even has a greater claim to such things as the kitchen table and chairs for the reason that there are more people in her household who will have need of them.

If at all possible (and this is true whether the parties are working from a list or not), the division of the personal property should be left to the parties themselves as much as possible, and a mediator should only enter the picture to discuss those items that remain in dispute. In fact, he should agree to discuss even these limited items only as a very last resort. In private practice, matrimonial lawyers constantly tell people that they cannot decide the question of their pots and pans (and, in effect, will not be bothered by it). It is their way of refusing to give the significance to these items that the parties do, and subtly undermining the importance that they attach to them. It is only when the agreement is entirely concluded, and its signature hinges on the disposition of only a lamp and an easy chair, that they will enter the discussion—and then usually just to point out how ridiculous it is to permit these items to stand in the way of an agreement between them.

CHILDREN'S ASSETS

On occasion, a mediator will be confronted with assets that are owned not by the parties but by their children. Not uncommonly, they are held in the name of one of the parties under the Uniform Gift to Minors Act enacted by the state in which the parties live. If this is the case, there should be a clear understanding between the parties as to whether or not the party who is holding the money will have the right to spend any portion of it, even for the child's benefit, and if so, under what conditions. For example, it should be clear whether that party will have the right to apply these funds toward the child's college education expenses and, if both of the parties have an obligation to pay for those expenses, whether that payment will go in reduction of both of their obligations.

On other occasions, one of the parties may have an account in his own name that bears the designation "in trust for" one of their children. Parents often hold money that their children receive as gifts in this form. In other instances, this is really their own money, and they have simply put this designation on the account to indicate to whom the account will go in the event of their death. Again, it should be clear whether or not this money actually belongs to the parties' children and, if so, how it will be treated.

Debts

Debts generally fall into two categories. In the first, there are those long-standing obligations that the parties have in connection with the purchase of specific items of real or personal property. These would include the mortgage on their home, a home improvement loan, and even the auto loan that was taken to finance the purchase of their car. As a general rule, these are not considered to be debts, any more than the rent that a couple pays on their apartment would be considered to be a debt. Rather, it is simply an obligation that goes with the benefit, and in most instances the party who will retain the benefit will also retain the obligation to satisfy the loan against it.

The second class of debts consists of all of the other obligations the parties have. Invariably, these include charges made on one of the parties' American Express Card, Visa Card, or MasterCard. They also will usually include obligations to department stores and physicians and dentists. On occasion, there may even be debts owed to family members.

As a practical matter, if these debts are very considerable, they will usually be discussed in connection with the disposition of the parties' home because not uncommonly, and in an effort to start on a clean slate, the parties may decide to sell their home and satisfy these debts at the time of their divorce. As much as they would like to avoid this, the debt service charges on these various obligations is so large that unless they are satisfied, there will simply not be enough money left from their income to pay for their living expenses, which have now been increased by reason of their divorce. When these debts are not unduly large, one of the parties, usually the husband, will agree to assume them. Or, the parties may use one of their savings accounts, or certain of their stocks, for that purpose. (Not uncommonly, one of the parties will agree to assume certain of these debts in exchange for being permitted to keep certain of their assets.) In any event, each of these debts must be specifically assumed by one or both of the parties and their obligations carefully delineated in their agreement.

As a practical matter, it is best to attempt to satisfy these obligations at the outset, when that is possible. To begin with, it would be far better for each of the parties to be able to start out with a clean slate, and not to have to worry about these outstanding obligations, with the very considerable interest they usually bear. Secondly, the obligation to satisfy these debts at a future date can have a distorting effect upon the discussion of support. If the husband, for example, is obligated to make payments of $300 per month in satisfaction of these preexisting debts, that will obviously affect his ability to make payment to his wife for her support and that of their children. It will also cause her to complain that he has built this debt service obligation into his budget so as to reduce his ability to make support payments to her, despite the fact that it will not be an ongoing obligation for the rest of his life.

To avoid this, and to provide each of the parties with a more secure footing from which to start, it would be far better to satisfy all of these debts at the outset, if that is possible. Unfortunately, that will not always be the case. In these instances, the answer may even have to be to delay the couple's actual physical separation for a period of time to enable them to satisfy, or at least substantially reduce, these outstanding obligations.

Finally, the financial contributions that the parties made individually toward their living expenses during their marriage should not have any effect on the outcome. Implicit in the couple's marriage was the recognition that although each of them would be contributing to the relationship, their respective contributions would be of a different kind. It is inappropriate, therefore, now that they are separating, for one of them to complain that in strictly financial terms his contribution was larger, or to urge that he, and he alone, was responsible, for example, for the financial maintenance of the home. Even when the couple is childless, and both worked, their respective contributions to the payment of their living expenses should be ignored. It may well be that the husband earned twice as much as the wife and therefore contributed twice as much financially to the upkeep of their home. The wife's contribution to the marriage was not, therefore, any less equal. More importantly, even in childless marriages, it would be wrong to judge contributions strictly in financial terms and, in doing so, thereby build into their marriage a disparity in contributions.

In short, it would be error, in an *attempt to do equity* between the parties at the time of their divorce, to *do violence* to what should be our *proper attitude* toward the parties during their marriage. Quite the contrary, there must be an appropriate balancing of our concern to *support the social constructs* that make marriage possible with the nevertheless *inconsistent realities* that we are forced to face given the fact of divorce.

CHAPTER 17

SUPPORT AND MAINTENANCE— PRELIMINARY CONSIDERATIONS

The next issue the mediator will generally address is that of support. Before undertaking a discussion of this subject, however, it is perhaps appropriate to address certain threshold questions that the mediator will have to answer. These have to do with the use of budgets in arriving at the appropriate support payment to be made by one of the parties, usually the husband, to the other; the use of support schedules or formulas in determining that amount; and the question of a temporary support agreement between the parties.

THE USE (AND MISUSE) OF BUDGETS

It is standard practice for mediators to ask each of the parties to prepare budgets for themselves. Not uncommonly, they are each given forms at the conclusion of their first meeting for that purpose. Just as commonly, the next session (and often the next several sessions) are used to go over these budgets, as well as to compile and review all the other financial information they have been asked to assemble. This is usually done as a matter of course because it is considered a businesslike approach to mediation, in much the same way that an adversarial attorney would start out to assemble this information before beginning his negotiations with his opposing counsel.

Unfortunately, the summary use of budgets in mediation, as well as the procedure of using the first several sessions to review this information, has not been given the consideration it should. Rather, it has simply been assumed that this is the appropriate procedure, and the only appropriate procedure, to follow. In point of fact, however, and rather than being a responsible approach to the problem as it is thought to be, it is but another example of the tendency to view mediation as a procedure that simply duplicates, albeit in a far more constructive manner, traditional divorce proceedings, without questioning the essential differences between the two. As a result, procedures that have a certain function in adversarial divorce proceedings are carried over into mediation without any real understanding of that function or how they advance or hinder the purposes of the mediation.

While it obviously serves a useful purpose, a budget is, nevertheless, an adversarial weapon. Traditionally, it has been used by the wife's attorney to demonstrate to the court how great her needs are, and to justify, based upon the previous standard of living of the parties, an award greater than that which the husband is willing to pay. (It is also intended to try to counter, to the extent possible, the fact that the court will not divide the husband's income by the number of mouths that have to be fed, and then assign each family member an equal share, but will instead assign the husband the lion's share.) He in turn prepares his own budget, also as an adversarial weapon, to demonstrate his inability to meet his wife's demands. In short, these are weapons used in the game of attempting to get as much as you can and give as little as you have to.

Transposed into the setting of mediation, this summary use of budgets has a counterproductive effect. To begin with, to tell a wife that it is important that she prepare a budget of her necessary needs is implicitly to suggest to her that one of the intended purposes of mediation is to determine those needs and then to fulfill them. To do this, however, is to send her off with false expectations. With minor exception, her budget will contain all of the previous living expenses of the parties. This, however, was when they were living together as a family. Her husband now has his own home to maintain, and his own separate living expenses, and it will simply not be possible for the mediator to meet the expectations he has created.

Secondly, to send the couple off with this "homework" (and the other homework mediators invariably assign to the couple), leaves the mediator with a dilemma. If he then ignores this material at the next session, and goes on to other matters, each of the parties, and particularly the wife, will feel annoyed that they were asked to take all the time this required (usually in a relatively short period) only to have the mediator ignore it.

If, on the other hand, the mediator uses the next session, and often the next two sessions, to go over all this material, he commits an equally serious error. To begin with, he is underscoring the areas of *conflict* between the parties—their differing views of what is appropriate for each of them to give and get—rather than areas of greater mutuality, such as their children. More importantly, his attention to these clerical, businesslike matters only tends to ignore what is far more important, namely, the emotions that underlie all of the issues that are on the table. Instead of allowing some of this emotionality to express itself, so that it can be addressed if it is appropriate to do that, these feelings become bottled up while the mediator and the parties direct their attention to questions of housekeeping.

There is a third and perhaps even more fundamental problem. More importantly, the procedures that mediators routinely employ in the use of budgets tends to obfuscate this problem. There are three questions that the mediator and the couple must answer in each instance. They are: whether the party with the larger of the two incomes should make a payment to the other party for his or her support or that of their children; how much that payment should be; and how long it should continue. In their zeal to be responsible, and to incorporate into their practice procedures that they believe will assure a proper result, mediators have failed to realize that the parties' budgets do not and cannot provide the answers to these questions.

Consider the following. A couple have been married for eleven years, and have one child, age nine. The husband earns $45,000 a year and the wife $30,000. In reviewing their respective budgets, the mediator finds that the carrying charges with respect to the parties' marital residence (mortgage payments, real estate taxes, utilities, insurance, etc.) are approximately $1,450 a month and that the husband's projected rent is $800 per month. He also finds that the wife's overall necessary expenses to maintain herself and her child in their home exceed by $250 per week, or approximately $13,000 per year, her after-tax income from employment.

What has the mediator learned from a review of these budgets? Have they told him whether or not the husband has an obligation for the support of his wife, as distinct from an obligation for the support of their child, and if so, how long that obligation should continue? Obviously not, as the determination of those questions has more to do with the length of the parties' marriage and the amount of the wife's income in relationship to that of her husband than it does with their respective needs as reflected in their budgets. Has it even told the mediator the amount that the husband should provide to the wife for the support of their child? Again, the answer is no, since that obligation is primarily based upon the husband's income in relationship to his wife's and not on the gap between her needs, as expressed in her budget, and her own ability to meet those needs.

Thus, as the husband here could not expect to be obligated to pay only $25 a week for the support of his child simply because his wife was able to pay for all of her and their child's expenses from her own income, except for that amount; nor can the husband here be expected to pay child support of $250 per week simply because those needs exceed her ability by that amount. The question that the mediator and the couple are really trying to answer is how much support the party with the larger of the two incomes should pay to the other party, and contrary to common assumptions, their *respective budgets do not hold the answer* to that question.

There is a further problem with this use of budgets, related to the last one. To invite a discussion of these budgets is simply to invite an attack upon them. The husband cannot possibly write out a blank check to cover all of the wife's expenses. Rather than simply saying this, and not wishing either to acknowledge or underscore the fact that he will be left far better off, at least on a per capita basis, than will his wife and children,[1] he attempts to justify a smaller payment by attacking various items in her budget.

Does she need to spend as much as she claims for clothing? Is it necessary that she continue to spend the same money she previously has for her therapy, or to continue her cable television subscription for that matter? Isn't the amount that she has listed for the telephone excessive, particularly given the fact that he will no longer be living in the home? Does she really believe that she will be able to spend as much as she has listed for entertainment, or that she must continue to have someone take care of the lawn? Discussions of this nature are counterproductive. Aside from the fact that they go nowhere, and reach no definitive conclusion, they simply *exacerbate the preexisting feelings* of hurt and anger. In short, they can take the mediator down a blind alley in which the mediation can get lost.

There is yet another and, in a certain sense, even more serious problem with this procedure, and that is that in employing budgets as they do, mediators are being *dishonest* both with themselves and with the parties. Why has the mediator given each of the parties a budget and sent them off to complete it? And why, once they have done that, will he then review each of their budgets with them? The answer that the mediator will give is that this is a responsible procedure, first, to determine what their respective needs are and then to assure that their needs, particularly those of the dependent wife and children, are met. Unfortunately—and this is where the dishonesty comes in—the procedures mediators then employ in connection with these budgets do none of these.

Let us suppose, for example, that before reviewing each of their budgets, the mediator had already come to an independent determination of their combined needs. Suppose further that regardless of what their budgets then showed, that after he reviewed them he always found that their combined needs equaled exactly the amount that he had previously determined them to be, before he had ever seen their budgets. To what extent would we be willing to accept his claim that he had determined their needs based upon a review of their budgets? In fact, if that were the case, wouldn't we feel that there had been some sleight of hand employed by him? Needless to say, these questions are rhetorical ones, as we would view with deep suspicion the budgetary legerdemain that the mediator had employed.

And yet, this is exactly what mediators do, although they are not generally aware of it. The ultimate reality, and therefore the bottom line, is what each of the parties presently earns or is capable of earning. Nor do the needs of the parties, as expressed in their respective budgets, alter this. Thus, the religious invocation of the parties' budgets does not guarantee that their respective needs will be met. In fact, their introduction does not even then lead to a search for the extra dollars that are missing. On the contrary—and this again is where the dishonesty in the present use of budgets comes in—it simply leads to an exercise wherein the mediator and the parties then trim those budgets down to meet the dollars available. In short, the mediator has not met either of the parties' needs, as he has suggested to them that he would; he has simply cut them back and redefined them. To make matters worse, he has probably wasted one or two sessions, and much unnecessary heat and energy, in the process.

This brings us to the final problem. The standard practice employed by mediators today in using budgets often *focuses the question in the wrong place*. As we have noted, implicit in the direction made to the wife that she prepare a budget of her necessary needs is the suggestion that the mediator's efforts will then be directed to meeting those needs. Not infrequently, however, the critical issue in the mediation is not what it will cost the wife to continue to live with the parties' child in their marital residence, but whether or not she can realistically afford to do so. Again, it is the *available dollars, not* the parties' respective *budgets*, that holds the answer to this question. However, starting out with these budgets, as mediators invariably do, all too often only tends to obfuscate this critical distinction.

But how can the mediator begin the couple's mediation without having all of this information at hand? Very easily. He can simply proceed to discuss those issues that are less dependent on this information, particularly the question of the children and their marital residence. Aside from permitting him to finesse these issues for the time being (and the question of support, which these budgets invite, can be one of the most difficult issues of all), they also permit him and the couple to concentrate on those areas where their common interests are the greatest. And it is of course these areas of commonality— whether it be their common interest in their children or simply their common interest in concluding the issues between themselves—that the mediator wishes to reinforce. Just as importantly, and as we have noted previously, it allows some of the emotionality that may exist to express itself and gives the mediator an opportunity to address it.[2]

Is this to suggest that budgets are unimportant in mediation? Obviously not. It is simply to suggest that by indiscriminately throwing them on the table at the outset, as mediators have been taught to do, they *misuse budgets*, for the wrong purpose and at the wrong time. And, they thereby lose the opportunity to use them for their own purposes, and at the right time. What do we mean by this? To make our point, we will invoke an analogy, and will suggest that the prevailing use of budgets in mediation sees the mediator as the conductor of an orchestra, whereas we see his role as more akin to that of the manager of a baseball team.

For the conductor of an orchestra, each of the instrumentalists has his assigned part and has been given his script (sheet music) which he will strictly follow. More importantly, each of the performers is at all times under his immediate direction, and it is he who leads them through their respective performances. Further, as he would not expect the performance to proceed smoothly if each of the players did not have their music in front of them, nor would he expect the mediation to proceed properly unless each of the parties had their budgets before them. Mediators who conduct themselves in this manner will insist that although the parties may control their agreement, the mediator controls the mediation and how it will proceed.

Mediators who view their role as more akin to that of the manager of a baseball team proceed very differently. The manager–mediator knows that the game has a life of its own. Though he has carefully coached his players and can obviously guide their play, he cannot control it, anymore than he can the game. Thus, he simply sends the players out onto the field and lets them go about their business. Nor does he ever attempt to take over the play. Rather, he only steps in to make corrective adjustments or substitutions when the play is not going well and to make suggestions as to how they can improve it. If the players are doing reasonably well, he may have very little to say at all, and will simply sit on the bench and observe the game from a distance. The parties do not need him when they are doing well on their own. They only need him when they are having difficulty. Nor does he rush out onto the field to direct the play at the first sign of trouble. More often than not, he will instead wait to see whether they are able to correct the problem on their own before he will intercede.

After all, his job is not to sit down and make an agreement for them. His job is to see where they are in agreement and to help them where they are not. (Mediators, ignoring this, have on occasion become so immersed in preparing and going over these budgets that they have not even stopped to find out whether this was one of the issues in dispute between the couple. Sometimes it is only after they have spent a great deal of time going over the budgets with the parties that they have first learned that they had already agreed upon the amount of support.)

At any given point something will take place in the mediation that will either advance it or impede it. If difficulties arise, the mediator must of course intervene to deal with these, and he obviously brings with him a great deal of experience and skill to assist him in directing the play to a successful conclusion. He also has a complement of tools he can call upon for that purpose. One of these tools is the budget he has asked each of the parties to prepare. But he does not employ this tool automatically, or, necessarily, in every instance. On the contrary, he will first make a judgment as to whether the use of the budget will help him to address the issue successfully, and whether it should be employed at this time.

Let us suppose, for example, that the wife is desirous of continuing to live in the home with the children. Unfortunately, the home was purchased recently, and the mortgage payment, together with the real estate taxes, is prohibitively high, and there is simply no realistic way in which she will be able to do this, no matter how advantageous it might be. Obviously, part of the mediator's job is to *bring home this reality*, and to get the wife to accept the fact that one of the incidents of her and her husband's divorce is that it will *not* be possible for her to continue to live in the home. Here the mediator views the wife's budget as such a reality principle. Asking the wife whether or not she has completed her budget, the mediator takes a look at it and points out her dilemma. If she is to stay in the house, her husband will have to give her 75% of his spendable dollars in order for her to pay her bills, which is unrealistic. If he gives her what he can afford, however, she will in turn have to spend perhaps 60 or 65% of her spendable dollars simply on housing, which is just as unrealistic.

In the reverse situation, the wife uses her budget as a weapon. Two months before, her husband announced his intention to separate from her, and she learned that he was seeing another woman. Before he "walked out on" her, somewhat overcome with guilt, he assured her that nothing would change for her and their two children. Hurt and angry, she intends to keep him to his word and produces a budget of her needs. While attempting to demonstrate how realistic she has been, and the sacrifices she has made in eliminating from her budget certain expenditures previously made by the parties, she has, nonetheless, presented her husband with a bill that will leave him with virtually nothing. The mediator could engage the wife in a discussion of each of the items in her budget to determine just how justified they are; but he knows that this budget may be as much an expression of her hurt and anger, and perhaps even her fear of being on her own, as it is a realistic balancing of their respective needs. He realizes, therefore, that any such discussion would be counterproductive.

Instead, he does not question any of the items in her budget, but simply meets her with the observation that her husband is not prepared to pay her that amount of money. Or he turns to her and, using her own budget, comments that if each of these items are as necessary as she suggests, there is simply not going to be enough money to meet her needs without tapping into the equity in their home, and that, of course, would require its sale. (Here, the mediator is playing out the strategy that in mediation, as in therapy, you never solve another person's problem for them. On the contrary, it is the mediator's job to bring home to the party that it is the party who has the problem, rather than allowing him to make it the mediator's).

From the standpoint of the mediator, the budget is always used as a reality principle. In this particular instance, the legitimate needs of the parties simply exceed, by some distance, the income available to them. Rather than using their respective budgets to solve this problem, which, of course, they cannot, the mediator instead uses the budgets as a means to bring home this reality. The husband and the wife have been locked in a debate as to whether or not the wife is able to work and how much she would earn if she did, or, if she is already working part-time, whether she could work on a full-time basis. The mediator could step into that debate, but he knows better. It is not a debate likely to lead to any real conclusion, and he knows that he will probably only get lost in it.

More importantly, it is probably only a mask for a dispute on a deeper level. Turning to the wife's budget, he sympathetically points out to her the reality that if it is not possible to add additional dollars to the pot then, *as legitimate as her needs are, they will not be able to be met*. It is not for him to say whether she is or is not able to earn more than she does now, and he cannot know that. Nevertheless, he can see that either additional monies will have to be found or that a reevaluation of her expenditures will have to be made.

In another instance, the husband takes an extremely unrealistic position in terms of what it is that he is willing to provide for his wife and children. Rather than engaging in a philosophical discussion with the husband as to how much or how little he *ought* to be required to provide for them, the mediator instead takes out the wife's budget and, turning to the husband, asks him how he proposes that his wife and children will meet their necessary expenses on the amount he is proposing. Here, the mediator is shifting the problem from the wife back to the husband, where he believes it properly belongs. More importantly, he is suggesting to the husband that the mediation will not proceed to a successful conclusion unless he addresses that problem in a responsible manner. [3]

What then is the best procedure for the mediator to follow in using budgets? What we are suggesting is that the *best procedure is not to have a set procedure*, and certainly not an inflexible one. While it is perfectly appropriate to provide couples with budgets, it should not be given as a homework assignment. It is sufficient to advise them that many couples who are going through the process of separating and divorcing find it *useful* to make a budget for themselves of what their future expenses will be and that if they would like to do that, the mediator has provided them with a form for that purpose. However, having done that, it is not necessary to refer to those budgets again unless there is reason to do so.

Why is it that mediators have not generally followed this procedure and why instead have they been so slavishly bound to the summary use of budgets? There are two reasons for this. The first is that mediators have considered this simply responsible conduct—a way of incorporating into mediation practice procedures thought to be employed by attorneys in more traditional adversarial divorce proceedings. Mediators, after all, are anxious to assure that the agreement concluded by the parties will be fair, despite the absence of the procedures employed by adversarial attorneys that are supposedly designed to assure this. Quite understandably, they have felt that they could achieve this by assuring that the agreement properly provided for the needs of each of the parties and their children, as was expressed in their budgets.

The second reason is not as obvious. In fact, it is one that mediators themselves have generally not recognized or acknowledged. And that is that in attempting to solve the problem of how much support should be paid by the husband to the wife, they are themselves as much dependent upon the answer that an analysis of the parties' respective budgets is intended to provide as are the parties themselves. Thus, if the mediator is confronted with a husband who is employed and earns $45,000 a year, and with a wife who is a homemaker for the parties and their two infant children, the mediator simply has no idea how much support the husband should provide for his wife and children—what amount would be "fair" for him to pay—and he has unquestionably assumed that the answer to that question lies in the analysis of the parties' respective budgets. In addition, he labors under the mistaken belief that in doing this he is simply following the same procedures that adversarial lawyers employ in answering this same question.

But isn't that exactly what adversarial lawyers do? The answer is no. If the wife in this instance consulted an adversarial attorney, he would be quite capable of determining the amount of support that it would be realistic for him to ask on the wife's behalf without ever once taking a look at her needs as expressed in her budget, based simply upon his judgment as to her husband's ability to provide that support. Moreover, the attorney representing the husband would be able to do the same. While, to be sure, the wife's attorney may have her prepare a budget of her necessary needs, that would not be for the purpose of determining how much he will ask that the husband pay to her for herself and their children but, and as has been noted previously, simply for the purpose of *justifying* it. In short, the summary use of budgets in mediation is *not a responsible way of replicating procedures employed in traditional divorce proceedings*, but simply a misunderstanding of those procedures and, more particularly, how budgets are employed in them.

Why is it that budgets are not used by adversarial attorneys, and wouldn't it be more responsible of them if they did? After all, the fact that adversarial attorneys are willing to make these judgments without the use of budgets does not mean that mediators should. The answer to this question is rather complex. To begin with, and as we have previously noted, while the preparation of a budget by each of the parties will *demonstrate what the problem is, it will not solve that problem*. All that the two budgets will reveal is that there is not enough money to go around—that the needs of the parties as expressed in their budgets exceed their available income.

The real question, however, is not how *much* each of the parties needs but *how* the available dollars should be divided between them. Again, and contrary to the conventional wisdom in mediation circles today, the two budgets do not provide an answer to this question. In fact, different mediators, working with the same couple, and employing the same budgets, may come away with very different answers. These budgets, therefore, are simply a means of attempting to deal with the problem—in therapeutic terms, a strategy or intervention. But they are not the only means, let alone a necessarily better or more responsible one, and it is only because, in employing this intervention, mediators talk in terms of "needs," that they have the *illusion* that they are.

There is a second and perhaps more fundamental reason that budgets are not summarily employed by adversarial lawyers. Budgets tend to emphasize *need* as the appropriate yardstick to be employed in solving the problem. Adversarial attorneys, however, tend to use another criterion, based upon a different view of the problem. From their standpoint, the proper measure is not how much it is that the wife and children need, but rather how much it is that the husband is *able* (and willing) to pay her.

Why is this? For the simple reason that if the husband is not able to maintain some reasonable life for himself with the money that will be left to him, then, as experience has shown, there will not be sufficient *motivation* for him to stay around and exert the necessary effort to earn the money; or, as is far more commonly the case, to make the payment even when he does. Thus, adversarial lawyers have learned to look to the ability of the person making the payment, and not to the needs of the person receiving it, as the more appropriate gauge. Moreover, and based upon their experience—and not on an analysis of either of the parties' budgets, as is commonly assumed—they have developed a rough sense of what that ability is.[4]

As we have argued previously, though mediation considers itself to be an alternative to traditional adversarial divorce proceedings, it has nevertheless borrowed heavily from that practice. As we have also argued, it has often done this without any real understanding of how those practices serve adversarial ends; let alone an awareness of how inconsistent they are with mediation's own purposes. The use of budgets in mediation is a good example of this. Paradoxically, this is *one* area in which mediators will have to borrow from the adversarial understanding if they are ever going to break their dependence upon budgets and free mediation practice from the slavish use of them. Thus, instead of using the couple's respective budgets to arrive at a starting point as to the appropriate level of support, mediators are going to have to learn to make those judgments independent of those budgets, based upon the respective abilities of each of the parties, and then, if necessary, to make such adjustments as are required based upon the needs of the parties expressed in those budgets.

Does this mean that a mediator can conclude an agreement for a couple without ever having reviewed their budgets? Absolutely. As unpleasant as it may be to accept, the fact remains that the ultimate reality is the available dollars, not the needs of the parties as expressed in their respective budgets, and it is this reality that the mediator must bring home to them. All that the mediator can do is *divide the pie*, not guarantee that each of the parties will have *enough to eat*.

Again, the reality is that there is never enough money to go around. It is like being given a tablecloth that is too small for the table. If you pull it down so that it completely covers one end of the table, the other end is left uncovered. All that you can do is spread it around so that each portion of the table is somewhat protected, and no portion of the table is left more exposed than another. It is this reality, rather than the false expectations engendered by the unthinking use of budgets, that it is the mediator's obligation to convey.

Again, this does not mean that budgets serve *no* useful purpose, as they obviously do. It simply means that budgets should not dictate the manner in which mediation is conducted, and that, on the contrary, it is the goals that mediation sets for itself that should determine when and how they will be used. Most importantly, it means that a budget is simply a tool in the mediator's arsenal to be used as a strategy or intervention where appropriate, not a procedure that must be employed as a responsible means of arriving at a correct level of support, let alone one that will guarantee such a correct level.

There is one final point to be made. Let us assume that it would be appropriate, or perhaps even necessary, for the mediator to have the wife complete a budget for herself in a particular instance. Even here, we would still take exception to the procedures normally employed by mediators for that purpose. In directing the wife to prepare such a budget, the mediator must always keep in mind that he does not want or intend to then review this budget as if it were a supermarket receipt listing all of the purchased items, with the total cost at the bottom. Rather, it will be his intention to employ that budget as a tool. If that is the case, he does not want to permit the wife to prepare a budget that can lead to one conclusion, and only one conclusion, for if he does this, he will not leave himself with any running room. Rather, he will simply have given the wife license to prepare a straitjacket for him that he will then have to attempt to get out of.

How then should the mediator instruct the wife? He should tell the wife that he wants her to prepare two budgets. The first budget—which is the budget she would no doubt have prepared if left to her own devices—is to contain a list of her expenses based upon her experience when she, her husband, and their children were living together as an intact family. Having done that, however, he then wants her to prepare a second budget. He knows that she would like to continue to live in the home with her children and he is trying to determine how (but perhaps really *whether*) she will be able to do that.

He therefore wants her to assume that she has just been informed that her husband has passed away unexpectedly and, worse, that all of the policies of insurance on his life have lapsed. Her husband's family has indicated to her that they would like to help her if they can. However, before committing themselves, they would like to know the very least amount that she will need from them if she is to be able to continue to live in the home with the children. The mediator should assure the wife that it is not his intention to suggest that this second budget will be used to determine the amount of support that she will receive from her husband, as he knows that she cannot possibly live on that amount. Nevertheless, it is very important that she prepare this "bare-bones" budget, as he has found from experience that it will be very helpful in answering many of the questions they will have to address, including even whether or not she will be able to afford to continue to live in the home and what extra money she will need for that purpose.

What the mediator has done here is to give himself a much wider latitude than a single budget will permit. More importantly, by not allowing the wife to present him with but one budget, he will also prevent her from being able simply to throw the problem in his lap to solve. On the contrary, it will enable him to throw it right back in hers, where he wants it to be.

Secondly, rather than putting the husband, or perhaps even himself, in the position of having to pare down her first budget, or take exception to it, by having her prepare a second, bare-bones budget, the mediator has made the wife do this *herself*. Thus, rather than getting lost in a discussion of whether or not the amount which she originally listed for the cost of telephone service is negotiable, and can be reduced, he has forced her to concede in advance that it is. Furthermore, she must either do this or suffer the penalty of not having done what she was instructed to do.

Quite obviously, the wife and her children cannot be expected to live on the second, bare-bones budget. Nor, however, can the husband afford to maintain them on the basis of their previous standard of living, as is expressed in the wife's first budget. But the mediator did not have her prepare either of these budgets for that purpose. Rather, he is now in a position to sit down, free of the restraints that *either* of these budgets might impose, to prepare his own budget—a third budget—for the wife. More importantly, and unlike either of the other two budgets, it is one that may well help to solve the problem.

The Use of Support Formulas

It has been suggested throughout that the mediator should *not* have a fixed, preset procedure by which he conducts mediation. This is based on the principle that the flow should be *from* the couple *to* the mediator, and not the other way around, and that in intervening in the lives of other people, even a couple in the process of a divorce, one should always keep a respectful distance and only participate when one is asked. It is also based on the principle that the mediator will know better where he is needed, and where he can be of help, if he simply observes the flow from the sidelines, rather than attempting to take control.

It must, nevertheless, be acknowledged that, at least to a certain extent, the question of the appropriate level of support must be an exception to this. Whether a couple should sell their home at the present time or agree that the wife shall have the right to continue to live there for a period of time if she is able to is not a question that necessarily has a right or wrong answer. Thus, while a mediator may have his own personal view of what would be appropriate under the circumstances, if the couple decide to the contrary, they have not reached the *wrong* decision. In a very fundamental sense, there *is* no right or wrong decision. More accurately, the right decision for this particular couple is the decision that they *agree* upon.

The problem is not so simple with the question of support, however. The couple's difficulty is that they really do not know, and cannot know, what would be an appropriate support payment. Nor can it be said that the appropriate support payment is whatever payment they agree upon, as would be the case, for example, with respect to the disposition of their marital residence. On the contrary, they agree upon the yardstick to be applied, and that gauge is that the payment in question should be one that provides for an appropriate sharing of the benefits as well as an appropriate assumption of the risks. Their problem, however, is that they do not know, and in a real sense cannot know, how that measure should properly be applied. As a result, they could be left with an endless debate, leading nowhere.

Where does this leave the mediator? Although he knows that there cannot possibly be one and only one correct answer to this question, he also knows that if he is going to be of any assistance to them then he is going to have to make a judgment in his own mind as to what is appropriate or inappropriate under the circumstances. If he does this, then, and if either or both of the parties stray too far from the mark, he knows that it is his job to direct them a little closer to it.

As we have noted previously, and at least initially, it is not necessary first to determine each of the parties' needs before making this judgment. On the contrary, it can be made quite apart from those needs, based simply on their respective financial circumstances. While there are admittedly no formulas that can or should be applied in a procrustean fashion to make such a judgment, and while there will be almost as many answers to the question as there will be those who are asked it, it would be helpful, nevertheless, if mediators had some *guidelines* they could employ to assist them in this respect. With that in mind, the next chapter includes three separate sets of guidelines that should assist mediators in making a threshold determination as to whether support is justified and, if it is, how much the payment should be and how long it should continue. Based on these guidelines, and before the question of support is addressed, the mediator should make his own determination as to each of these questions. If he has done that, and once the discussion proceeds, he will then know what his job is and where he has to lead the discussions.

Should the mediator provide the couple with these guidelines as part of the information that he gives them before they undertake their mediation? The mediator must be very careful here. To begin with, these are simply our subjective judgments. While they are based on years of experience dealing with the question of what would or would not be an appropriate payment to be made by one party to the other for his or her support and for the support of their children, this is not to say that there may not well be other persons, possessing equal experience, who might come to a different conclusion, or perhaps even take issue with these guidelines.

There is a second problem. If the mediator were to provide the couple with these guidelines, his purpose would be to help them in their discussions. However, and to the very extent that those guidelines tend to lead them to a definite conclusion, they also tend to foreclose on such a discussion, and to result in decisions that are made, not on the basis of the needs of the respective parties, but instead on procrustean formulas. Furthermore, they may cause one of the parties inappropriately to question what he would otherwise simply do.

For example, and based on the circumstances, the wife has requested support for a period of seven years and the husband is inclined to provide support for that length of time. However, the guidelines in question suggest that the appropriate length of support should be for four or five years. To introduce them would only be to introduce a counterproductive consideration that will unnecessarily confuse the issue for the husband.

There is yet a further danger in the use of these guidelines. Almost invariably, they will vary from the expectations of one of the parties. Thus, to lay these guidelines down as if they necessarily represent what is fair or appropriate may simply be abruptly to throw cold water on those expectations. And since that cold water will seem to have come from the hands of the mediator, whatever feelings are engendered in the process may well be directed at him. The disappointed person may even feel that the formula represents the mediator's own opinion, or worse, his own particular bias.

To be sure, the mediator may well have the same job to do at a later point, in terms of bringing the expectations of one of the parties into line with the realities of the situation. However, he will want to do this subtly, and a bit at a time, rather than in such a broadside fashion. Thus, and in addressing the question of support, it is recommended that the mediator keep all of this information to himself, at least initially, and that he simply start out the discussion with the question, "Have (either of) you given any thought to the question of support?"

On occasion, when the subject of support is brought up, both of the parties may stare at the mediator with blank expressions, having no ideas on the subject whatsoever, and not knowing where to begin. In other instances, the mediator will find that the couple has already undertaken a discussion of the question but has come to an impasse, the husband proposing one figure and the wife another. In yet other situations, the mediator will find that the couple has already resolved the issue between themselves. Whatever the case, the answer that the mediator is given to his introductory question will tell him where they are and how he can help them.

Suppose that the couple turn to the mediator and ask him what he thinks is "fair." If this question is posed at the very outset, the mediator should decline to answer it, for it is almost impossible for him to do so without disappointing, and perhaps even offending, one of the parties. Let us suppose, however, that the question is put to him after he and the parties have discussed the issue for some period of time. Should he then give them an answer to their question? The mediator may well have no problem, in terms of his experience, in suggesting an appropriate amount, assuming that the setting is such that he will be able to do that without either of the parties feeling that he is being partial in offering that figure.

The more difficult problem for the mediator, however, is that very often implicit in the question is the request that the mediator tell the couple what a court of law would direct (say is fair) under the circumstances. For obvious reasons—not the least of which is that the mediator may not be a lawyer, and therefore not permitted to give such an answer, or that he may be a lawyer, but still not feel that he can give one—the mediator does not wish to answer the question. Nevertheless, the parties feel very much at a loss. Can't the mediator help them out somehow? Isn't there some *formula* that the court uses to make such a determination?

The mediator's job at this point is to perform a very delicate balancing act. On the one hand, he wants to undercut the couple's mistaken assumption that there are simple legal answers to these complex problems, and to persuade them instead to deal with the question in terms of the realities of their separate needs and their respective abilities to meet those needs. (At the same time, and on occasion, he may also want to reinforce the reality that if they want to know exactly what a court would do, they are going to have to pay the penalty of going to court to find out.) On the other hand, it is not his wish just to frustrate them, or to give them the impression that he is not trying to be of help, by leaving them in the dark. Moreover, he knows that, as realistic as it may be for them to attempt to answer this question in terms of their respective needs and abilities, looking at those needs and abilities alone will not provide a necessary answer. Thus, he recognizes the difficulty they are having in trying to determine what is "fair," and would like to help them if he can.

In most instances, and when the parties are struggling with the question, the mediator will attempt to direct the flow of their discussions to a place that he considers to be appropriate, based upon his own evaluation of the situation, and the financial abilities of each of the parties. If his efforts in that respect prove unsuccessful, however, he may then decide to resort to a formula and use it as an intervention. After all, the purpose of mediation is not to have endless discussions that go nowhere and settle nothing. Rather, it is to help the couple conclude an agreement. If they have been unable to do this, then, and as subjective as these formulas may be, they will at least serve the purpose of possibly helping the couple to reach such an agreement.

We have already commented on the fact that formulas or guidelines can be employed when neither of the parties has any real idea of what is appropriate, and they are therefore both groping in the dark. They can also be used when the parties have very different and divergent opinions as to what is appropriate. Not uncommonly, the parties will come to the discussions with very fixed ideas. The wife has consulted with several attorneys who have advised her that she is entitled to receive support from her husband for at least ten to eleven years, while the husband has consulted with several attorneys who have told him that he is not obligated to provide her with support for more than four or five. Similarly, she has been told that she should receive support of $350 a week, while he has been advised that he is not obligated to provide her with more than $200 per week.

In a situation such as this, and after asking the couple how they propose to resolve this difference of opinion, the mediator might mention that he has in his possession a set of guidelines that has been prepared by a very experienced matrimonial lawyer and that if they would both like him to do so, but only if they would both like him to do so, he will provide them with copies of these guidelines and, based upon them, determine what the appropriate amount and duration of support should be.

There is another very effective intervention that can be used here. The mediator points out to the couple that they have been left with a problem in that they have received very different opinions from their respective attorneys. Unfortunately, and if a way cannot be found to bridge that difference, they are going to be forced to go to court and have a judge resolve it. Since a judge is simply an attorney who wears black robes, his opinion is really no better than that of any other similarly qualified attorney, *except* that it will be *binding* upon the parties.

Rather than spending the considerable time, money, and effort that would be involved in obtaining an opinion from a judge, only then to be bound by it even if they are not happy with it, wouldn't it make a lot more sense to get such an opinion informally, from a qualified matrimonial attorney? The mediator happens to know a matrimonial attorney, who is both very qualified and very fair, who, he is sure, would be willing to help them. If the parties wish, they can each prepare a statement of the factors that they feel should be considered in making the determination, including any statement they would like to make in answer to that prepared by the other party; and he will present them to the attorney in question for his opinion. In this way they will get a quick, inexpensive answer to their question.

The mediator should not be surprised if one or both of the parties hesitates in accepting this suggestion. (If the intervention is to be effective, he will have to underscore that hesitancy.) Why are they a little nervous about posing this question to an independent matrimonial attorney, as the mediator has suggested? After all, isn't this the same question that they each posed to the attorneys whom they consulted with separately?

The difference, of course, is that they each felt on safe ground there, as neither expected to be given an answer that he did not wish to hear. After all, we retain lawyers to support our positions, and to tell us what we *want* to hear, not to be told the unpleasant truth. And that, of course, is exactly what each of them is afraid that the attorney selected by the mediator will tell them. Unfortunately, that too is what the judge, who, after all, is also simply an independent observer, will tell them. The parties therefore have a choice. They can continue to listen to the comforting advice that they have each been given by their attorneys. If they do this, however, the price that they will pay will be that they will be left without an agreement. Or, and recognizing how pointless all of this is, and where it inevitably leads, they can attempt to solve the problem by seeking independent counsel.

At times, guidelines can serve another purpose. In a particular instance, the wife has asked for support for herself equal to almost 50% of her husband's income. Based on other occurrences that have taken place during the mediation, the mediator has concluded that the wife's request is predicated more on the fact that she knows that her husband will not agree to this amount than it is on her expectation that she will actually receive it. Although she has loudly proclaimed on many occasions that all that she wants is to get done with the matter and get a divorce, the mediator has become convinced that while that may well be true on one level, on another level she is very afraid to let go of the marriage. Thus, by repeatedly insisting upon the fact that she wants to get done with the matter and at the same time throwing a roadblock in the way, she is able to have it both ways.

The mediator would like to address the wife's fears. Unfortunately, and as he has seen on other occasions, she has directed at him many of the feelings engendered by her conflict. He thus suspects he may get little thanks for his efforts. Nor will he be successful in getting the wife to acknowledge the fact that this is what she is doing. In such a situation, it is possible that the use of these guidelines may force the wife better to accept the reality that she can either insist upon 50% of her husband's income and not have a divorce, or accept a more realistic level of support and get a divorce. Just as importantly, it may force her to accept the fact that she cannot continue to make this someone *else*'s problem, rather than her own.

Before leaving the question of support guidelines, there is one other issue that must be addressed, and that is what the mediator should do when the parties themselves come into the mediation armed with formulas or, for that matter, simply with expressions of opinion given them by others, that are not grounded in any formula. ("I know a man whose circumstances are the same as mine who is only paying . . .") While, initially, the case law of many states held that child support could not be determined by the use of a formula, support guidelines were later adopted in several states and local areas either by legislation, court decision, court rule, or other means.

Until now, however, this has not been a substantial problem. To begin with, these guidelines have generally been employed on a more or less local basis. Secondly, the fact that they were *guidelines*, and guidelines only, was reinforced by the fact that the ones that were used in one locality were not necessarily identical to those used in another. Thus, support guidelines have not generally been a significant factor in the negotiation of private agreements between husbands and wives, either as a help or as a hindrance.

There is no question but that the use of formulas, at least in determining child support payments, will become much more of a factor in the future, however. In an effort to improve the collection of child support payments, Congress passed the Child Support Enforcement Amendments of 1984.[5] This law is known mainly for the fact that the states were required to establish a system under which court- or agency-ordered payments could be withheld from the wages or other income of a parent who was delinquent in making them.

What is less known, however, is that in an attempt to implement the collection of child support payments, the law required each of the states to develop guidelines setting forth the amount of child support that should be awarded. Although the law does not require that these guidelines be binding, they must, nevertheless, be made available to all judges and other officials who are charged with the responsibility of fixing support for children.

It has been suggested that these guidelines will have a substantial impact on matrimonial practice. For the same reason, they may also have a substantial impact upon divorce mediation. To begin with, they will bear the imprimatur, not of some local family or domestic relations court, but of the state itself. Secondly, and perhaps even more importantly, there may not only be greater harmony in the decisions of different courts within the state, but there may also be far greater harmony between the decisions of courts in the various states. This is because one of the purposes of these guidelines, at least as far as Congress was concerned, was to attempt to minimize, if not eliminate, the tremendous disparity in child support payments from state to state. The result is that these guidelines may begin to represent what is and what is not considered to be appropriate child support, not only in a court of law, but even in mediation.

To begin with, and whether they are binding upon a judge or not, it can be expected that they will increasingly be utilized by the courts. A judge, after all, really does not know, any more than a mediator does, what an appropriate support payment is or is not, even though, based on the fact that he has made so many decisions before, he may *think* that he does. Support guidelines therefore solve a problem for a judge in that they give him a ready answer and, just as importantly, one that is easy for him to justify and just as hard for others to take exception to. There will therefore be a natural tendency, particularly for newly appointed or elected judges, to fall back upon these guidelines. Furthermore, there will be good reason for them to do so, as they will tend to encourage more uniformity in the decisions of different judges. In fact, one of the shortcomings of our present system has been the fact that the amount of support ordered by two different judges can differ markedly, even when those judges sit, not in different states, but in the very same courthouse.

What does this mean for a mediator? To a certain extent, these guidelines may make a mediator's job easier, just as they will the job of a judge. In that respect, these guidelines may well represent a benefit. After all, if one of the purposes of any procedure to which a couple may resort is to get them to an agreement, and to do that quickly, then these guidelines will certainly tend to serve that purpose. More importantly, if a wife is forced to accept child support of only $60 a week, or a husband is forced to give that amount, because that is what the guidelines prescribe, it is far more likely that they will each be able to do this, and do it without ongoing residual negative feelings, than if they had been forced to do so simply because the *other party* had insisted upon the payment in question.

That is on the benefit side. However, those guidelines can also be a detriment. The person who will put those guidelines on the table will do so because they will tend to support the position he or she is taking. In fact, one of the reasons that he will put them on the table will be to foreclose on the other party. Unfortunately, the mediator may find himself foreclosed upon as well. The mediator has purposely avoided the use of these kinds of procrustean formulas, and has instead attempted to have the parties deal with the problem in terms of their respective needs and abilities. This was not too difficult to do in a world where these guidelines did not exist. But one of the parties has now thrown down the gauntlet of these guidelines, and in doing so he may have effectively changed the relevant standard. Worse yet, he may have terminated the discussion.

Suppose, for example, it is the husband who has thrown the guidelines down on the table. What is the wife to do? After all, it was one thing for her to reject an offer made by her husband in mediation because she believed that she could do better in court, whether she held that belief for good reason, bad reason, or no reason. However, in throwing those guidelines down on the table, her husband is now suggesting, and perhaps very persuasively, that she will *not*. This can present a real dilemma for a mediator. Nor are there any easy answers to it. After all, while these guidelines may only be legal fictions, the more *consistently* they are applied the *less* fictitious they will appear, or, for that matter, actually *be*. Quite the contrary, they will become very much *a part of the reality* with which the mediator will have to deal.

There is a related problem with which a mediator may find himself confronted on occasion. The husband does not come in with a set of guidelines that he throws down on the table. Rather, he comes in with a story of a man whom he knows, whose financial circumstances are equal to, if not better than, his own, who is not required to pay the amount of support that his wife is demanding, and he throws this out, much as he might throw down a set of guidelines, to end the debate and resolve the dispute in his favor.

The mediator will have a difficult problem here, particularly if he privately feels that the amount the wife has requested is fair and reasonable under the circumstances. The husband holds the trump cards and the mediator none at all. The mediator does not know what this other person's circumstances really are, let alone whether they are the same as the husband's. He doesn't even have the actual agreement or court order establishing this other person's obligation in front of him. Nor does he know whether this other person described his circumstances accurately, or whether the husband heard them accurately for that matter. Finally, he doesn't even know whether or not this person was the one person in a hundred whom the husband spoke to who represented the exception to the rule.

Nor would it make any sense for the mediator to attempt to engage the husband on any of these questions. The husband did not come in to reason rationally. He came in to make a point, and the mediator would be making a great mistake were he to attempt to argue with him. He will get nowhere, will prove nothing, and will only find himself in a situation where he has provoked a personal confrontation between himself and the husband.

What should the mediator do in a situation such as this? What the husband has done is to hand the problem to the mediator. He has come in, with all the facts stacked in his favor, and asked the mediator to solve the riddle of why he should have to pay more than another husband, in similar circumstances, is required to pay. The mediator must *not accept* the problem, however. Rather, he should return it to the husband. How can the mediator do this? By turning to the husband and saying, "Frankly, I do not understand why the gentlemen in question does not pay more child support than he does. There may be very good reasons for it; I really do not know. It is very hard for me to understand this, however. Let me show you the guidelines that have been promulgated by the Office of Court Administration, and which are used by every judge in this state. As you can see for yourself, those guidelines clearly indicate what the minimum payment for someone in your financial circumstances should be. . . ."

Now it is the *husband* who has the problem, not the mediator. Better yet, and although the mediator may have been the one who has handed him the problem, he isn't the one who has given it to him. Rather, it was given to him by the Office of Court Administration. To make it a little easier for the husband to swallow the pill, the mediator can then add, "I know that you feel the payment that your wife is asking is high. As you can see, however, that seems to be what husbands in your circumstances *are* required to pay."

Temporary Support Agreements

We have recommended that the mediator should not address the issue of support until certain other issues have been resolved, and certainly not at the outset of the mediation. This is at a variance with the procedure followed by many mediators. In fact, one of the very first issues that they will address with the couple will be that of support. The reason for this is that although mediators may be prepared to leave the final disposition of that issue to a later point in the mediation, they consider it one of their threshold duties to be to assist the couple to work out an *interim financial arrangement* until the issue of support is later addressed more formally and a final agreement concluded between them. In fact, those mediators who follow this procedure would consider it irresponsible to do otherwise. Again we will take exception to this and will argue that the practice is as unnecessary as it is misguided.

Why is it unnecessary? For the simple reason that it will literally never become an issue but for the fact that the mediator has made it one.[6] As any mediator who makes it a practice simply to ignore the question will verify, the issue of how the couple's expenses will be paid during the course of the mediation will almost never become a problem or, therefore, have to be dealt with by the mediator. To be sure, if the mediator himself raises the question of how these expenses are to be paid, and, more particularly, which of them the husband will pay directly and how much he will give to the wife so that she can pay for the rest, it will then have to be addressed and answered. But if he doesn't, then it won't. It is almost as simple as that.

But what is necessarily wrong with the mediator's raising the issue? Many things, not the least of which is that the mediator and the couple will begin the mediation addressing the wrong issues and, since most mediators feel that they cannot discuss the issue of support unless and until the couple have each first completed their budgets, they may well spend two and perhaps three sessions in the process.

But the real objection to the procedure is that it once again mistakenly assumes that proper mediation practice is one that duplicates what adversarial lawyers do, with the result, once again, that practices that are employed in adversarial proceedings are carried over into mediation practice without any consideration, let alone understanding, of what their place in those adversarial proceedings is and how consistent or inconsistent they are with mediation practice.

To be sure, one of the very first issues that an adversarial lawyer will have to address is the question, if he is the husband's attorney, of how much support his client should voluntarily give during the pendency of the proceedings and, if he is the wife's attorney, how little she should willingly accept before making an application to the court for that purpose. The issue is raised at the outset because it has both a practical and strategic importance. Its practical importance stems from the fact that, the nature of adversarial proceedings being what they are, it may well be many months, and perhaps a year or more, before the issues are finally resolved, either by an agreement between the parties or by the court.

Given the nature of adversarial proceedings, it would be unrealistic to expect that these matters will simply take care of themselves. On the contrary, and in a world where each of the parties will all too often deal with a problem simply by resorting to self-help, the wife cannot help but worry whether or not her husband will unilaterally reduce her support payments, as he cannot help but worry whether or not she may attempt to help herself to whatever she wants by charging things on his credit. The result is that insecurity, and sometimes fear, becomes an almost inevitable by-product of the couple's physical separation, and sometimes simply their decision to separate and divorce, particularly when that is coupled with the entry of lawyers into the picture. It is this that causes each of the parties to feel that this is an issue that must be resolved at the very outset.

There is another, and perhaps even more important, reason that the issue of temporary support becomes critical in adversarial proceedings. Adversarial proceedings are characterized by *positioning* on the part of both of the parties, as each is concerned with how his or her position, and the appearance that position creates, will affect the final outcome. Suppose, for example, that the husband were to act in a responsible manner and continue to pay all of the previous household expenses, even if that meant that he had to allocate 75% of his spendable income for that purpose. Can he rely upon the fact that the court will understand that, to keep his own expenses to a minimum during this period of time so that he could afford to do this, he purposely lived with his parents rather then taking an apartment of his own?

Or will he be prejudiced by the fact that he has made such large payments in the interim by the court's concluding that his wife really needs this amount of support or, worse, that he can afford to pay it? In an adversarial world, where a wife so often questions the amount of her husband's purported income, claiming that some of his earnings are hidden and have gone unreported, there is always the danger that the husband may find himself being punished for the fact that he has acted responsibly. As a result, husbands are routinely admonished by their attorneys that they must be careful not to "set a precedent."

The husband's attorney may go even further. He may want the husband purposely to reduce the support payments he is making to his wife to establish a "reverse precedent." After all, if the husband sharply reduces the payments that he is making to his wife, but she nevertheless accepts the payments, when the case gets to court, the husband's attorney may well be able to argue that the best proof that the wife does not require as much as she claims is the fact that she has been able to live on less. Moreover, since most women would rather get by on less than they need, than to go into debt in order to continue to live as they should, this may add support to the husband's attorney's argument. Faced with this predicament, what will the wife's attorney tell her to do? He may tell her to borrow money from her parents—which she will either actually use or not use—to demonstrate the fact that the payments her husband has made to her were inadequate.

Not infrequently, this positioning by each of the parties takes a different form. In the background, there is always the question of whether or not it would be better for the husband or the wife were they to let the court fix the amount of interim support rather than simply leave the situation as it is. Although courts routinely announce that temporary orders of support will have no bearing on the judge's final determination, there are many attorneys who do not believe this, and often with good reason. On the contrary, and since there is really no necessary logic to the amount that a court will or should award, and since judges, like other people, often look for an easy way out, there is always the possibility that the judge who finally tries the case may simply adopt the temporary order as his permanent order. In those jurisdictions where a particular judge is assigned to the case at the very outset, and then handles it from beginning to end, there is an even greater likelihood that this will happen. Furthermore, the fact that the husband has made all of the payments directed by the court may be taken as proof that he is *able* to make them, just as the fact that the wife has been able to support herself on the amount that she has received may be taken as proof that she does *not* need more.

Each of the parties, therefore, views a temporary order of the court as a potential strategy in the contest. If the husband's attorney feels that it may be to his client's advantage to have the court direct the interim payment, rather than have his client make it voluntarily, he may force the wife's attorney to bring on the motion by reducing the support payments to her. Similarly, if the wife feels that such an order may be to her advantage, she may initiate the motion herself. Unfortunately, positioning being so important in adversarial proceedings, the parties normally do not rest content at that point, and once the court has issued its temporary order, each very often engages in further jockeying in relation to that order.

Is this to suggest that an attempt to arrive at a temporary agreement as to support in mediation will result in the same gamesmanship? Obviously not. But that does not mean that the issue may not be affected by at least some of the same considerations. The parties cannot help but feel that the present discussions are but a preview of those they will later hold on the same subject. Nor can they completely discount the effect that any temporary arrangement they may work out will have on those later discussions. More importantly, however, and even if this will not be the case, in the vast majority of instances, there is simply no necessity, and therefore no reason, to raise it as a threshold question. On the contrary, in almost every instance the couple will work this out very nicely on their own without the mediator's assistance.

Let us consider this more specifically. The couples a mediator sees will fall into three categories. On the one hand, there will be those couples who are still living together and who will probably continue to live together until an agreement is concluded. On the other, there will be those couples who have already been separated for some time, perhaps as long as six months or a year, by the time they come into mediation. Finally, there will be a third group, which will consist of those couples who have just recently separated or who are just about to separate. The first group has no need for an interim agreement, as there is no reason they should not continue to handle their affairs during the mediation just as they have in the past, which is exactly what they will do. Since nothing in their living arrangements is going to change, there is no reason their financial arrangements should change either.

Nor will there be any difficulty with the second group either. For some time now there has been a modus operandi that has been utilized and accepted by the parties. Perhaps they have discussed the amount of the payments between themselves. Perhaps the husband has simply decided on his own what he will give to his wife. Whatever the case, payments have been made and accepted. Perhaps they are excessive; perhaps they are inadequate. It really doesn't matter. Nor is it necessary to adjust the amount of those payments at the present time. After all, the purpose of a temporary agreement is not to determine the ultimate level of support. It is simply to arrive at a figure that the parties can accept for the time being. Since they already have such a figure, there is no need to change it.

The husband may claim that the payments are too great or the wife that they are too little. In either case, and unless the mediator is convinced that there would be a terrible hardship to one of the parties were the payments to continue, even for the short period of time that the mediation will take, he should finesse the issue by advising them that this is one of the issues that they will address during the course of the mediation, but at a somewhat later point.

The third group represents a potential problem, in the sense that they will have to make an accommodation to this new situation. But this does not mean that they will not be able to work out that accommodation on their own, without the mediator's intervention; in most cases, they will. In leaving this up to them, the mediator follows the same rule that he employs throughout the mediation: he views the problem as the couple's problem, not *his* problem. Secondly, he does not consider it his job to rush in just because he sees that the couple have a problem, let alone a potential problem. Rather, he waits quietly on the sidelines until he sees that they are having difficulty with it or until they ask him for help. Most importantly of all, however, even when he does intervene, he does not consider that it is his function to *solve* their problem. Rather, it is to *establish the conditions that will enable* them to solve it on their own.

Sometimes that means defining the problem more clearly. Sometimes it means giving them some ideas to work with. Sometimes it means brushing aside some of the impediments that stand between them and its resolution. Sometimes it means providing them with a better setting in which to address it. And sometimes it means more. But his first inclination is always to leave it with them and to see what they will do with it on their own.

In fact, and following that understanding, he himself will place an issue on the table for discussion in only one of two instances. The first is when he feels, as a matter of professional responsibility, that the issue is one the couple should address and resolve during the course of their mediation and he is afraid that, if he does not call it to their attention, they may not raise it on their own. The second is when the couple advise him that they are locked in dispute over an issue they cannot resolve.

Suppose that the wife really is concerned as to how her expenses are going to be paid, and does not feel confident that she and her husband will be able to work this out or, to be more precise, that she can rely upon the fact that he will make appropriate provision for her on his own. She and her husband are presently living together and there is no problem yet. But he is planning to move at the end of the month and she is very concerned as to what will happen when he does. Should the mediator then put the question of temporary support on the table and address it? Absolutely not. The fact that the wife is concerned does not mean that she has any *real cause* to be concerned. Nor does it mean that if it becomes an issue, that they may not be able to resolve it on their own and seek their own level, so to speak. In short, there is no reason for the mediator to anticipate the problem. On the contrary, he should wait to see whether or not it actually becomes one.

Is this to suggest that when the wife raises the issue with the mediator that he should explain to her the axioms on which he is proceeding? No more than he should tell her that this is something that she and her husband should discuss between themselves. The wife is expressing legitimate fears, and the mediator has an obligation to address them. But that does not mean that the appropriate way to do this is to place the issue of temporary support on the table.

What *should* he do, then? The mediator should turn to the wife and tell her that although he *understands* her concern, that her fears are nevertheless misplaced. There is no question but that husbands who leave their wives, particularly those who resort to adversarial proceedings, often neglect their obligations and provide them with grossly inadequate support. But that is not what happens in mediation. In fact, and although this is the common experience of wives in adversarial proceedings, not once in the many years that he has conducted mediation has he ever had a wife come to him and present him with a notice from a utility company threatening termination of services or a letter from a bank threatening a foreclosure action.

This simply does not happen in mediation. Couples who come into mediation most certainly have their differences; but they are not irresponsible. After all, if her husband had simply wanted to play games with her he would have gone out and hired an attorney, not have come into the mediation with her as he has. He does not want to see his children put out on the street any more than she does, and if he moves out, he will not do so unless and until he has made appropriate arrangements to take care of them in the interim.

What the mediator intends to accomplish by this are two things. Firstly, of course, he wishes to reassure the wife, and to assuage her fears. More importantly, however, and in a message sent to the wife, but really addressed to the husband, he wants to set forth what is considered appropriate and inappropriate conduct in mediation. In doing this, the mediator has now left the husband with a choice and a dilemma. He is either going to have to accept what the mediator has told him he expects of him, or he will have to speak up and take exception to it.

There is another message that the mediator can convey, and a reality that he can reinforce, at this point. Moreover, it is one that will be particularly effective where it is the husband who wants the divorce and, therefore, to get on with the matter. There may well be real problems that will arise and that will have to be addressed during the course of the mediation, and he will deal with them if they do. Nevertheless, he really does not believe that the husband wants to come to these meetings every week simply to be confronted by his wife with these transitional problems. Nor does he believe that he wants to take up their valuable time together to discuss them, when, if they can use that time more profitably and can conclude an agreement, they will no longer be issues. He is really far too intelligent to waste his time in this manner. Again, what the mediator has done here is to point out to the husband what his problem is and to underscore it for him.

If a mediator follows this procedure, he will find that the question of a temporary agreement will almost never be raised as a serious issue. But what if it is? Suppose that either the husband or the wife insists that the matter of how they are going to handle their finances during the mediation be discussed at the outset? Does that mean that the mediator should then immediately pull out the couple's respective budgets and address the problem in that fashion? Again, the answer is no. On the contrary, he must use the occasion to emphasize what will be his attitude throughout the mediation, namely, that they are faced with a common problem that they must solve together.

What is the problem here? It is that if the husband moves out of the home and takes his own apartment, there simply will not be sufficient funds available to meet both his expenses and the expenses of his wife and children, even on a minimal basis. What the mediator must do, therefore, is to get the couple to solve that problem before the husband moves. Perhaps the problem is that the wife will not be able to make it unless she can first find a tenant to rent one of the bedrooms. Perhaps there is some work that has to be done in the basement to complete it as a separate apartment so that the wife can rent it. Perhaps the wife is engaged in a course of study to prepare her for employment, and will not complete it for another three or four months. Perhaps the wife simply needs time to get herself a job. Maybe it will take another couple of months before the home can be put on the market for sale. Perhaps the wife will not be able to work unless the parties purchase a second car for her use.

Whatever the delaying factor is, the mediator must underscore the reality that it is a *real* problem, that it is *their* problem, and that it must be responsibly addressed before either of them goes running off on his own. If these were adversarial proceedings, the husband would simply *act* (in this case, leave) and the parties would then each attempt to address whatever problems they have been left with. That is not what is done in mediation, however. People simply do not resort to self-help and then leave the other person with the problem. On the contrary, *the problem comes first*.

CHAPTER 18

Support and Maintenance—
When, How Much,
and How Long?

While other issues may sometimes generate more emotional heat and energy, the question of support is perhaps the most *complex* with which the mediator will have to deal. By definition, the problem of support is compounded by the fact that a couple who, in most instances, barely had enough, will now have to attempt to make it on less than enough. The fact of their separation and divorce means that one of the parties, usually the husband, must establish a separate place to live, and if he is to meet the expenses of that second home, money that was used in the past to maintain the parties' standard of living will have to be diverted for that purpose. To talk, therefore, about maintaining the wife's and the children's previous standard of living, as the law traditionally has done, is ridiculous, and even insulting, as the law has never provided them with the funds necessary for that purpose.

Mediators must not mislead the parties in the same fashion. One of the elements that mediation borrows from the mental health profession is the principle of reality. In the context of separation and divorce, that means that a couple must be made to realize that the money available to them will have to be spread thinner, and that the previous standard of living that they enjoyed will, of necessity, have to be diminished.

There is an additional reality that compounds this problem, and that is that the dollars available to the couple and their children will not be divided and allocated between them on a per capita basis. Thus, if a husband and wife have two children and $28,000 of spendable income which is all earned by the husband, the wife will not receive three-quarters of that amount, or $21,000, for herself and the two children, and the husband only $7,000. On the contrary, those available dollars will in most instances be divided between them almost equally.

Women's rights advocates have pointed to this fact and argued that it proves that women and children suffer more than men in divorce. In fact, they have gone further and suggested that whereas divorced women and their children suffer an immediate 73 percent decrease in their standard of living, the standard of living of their husband's increases by 42 percent.[1] These kinds of polemics add nothing of any value, and the statistics upon which they are based are both inaccurate and irresponsible. They are based on the fallacious assumption that, in the example given, the husband, the wife, and the two children, each lived on $7,000 a year prior to their separation. Since the husband will now have more than $7,000, and the wife and two children less than $21,000, it is concluded that the standard of living of one of them has improved while the standard of living of the others has worsened. But it will be very hard to persuade a husband, who has left his home, his family, and his community, and who is now living in an efficiency or perhaps one-bedroom apartment, that he is so much better off as a result of his divorce. It will be hard simply because it is not true, and statements such as these, drawn from studies that supposedly demonstrate their accuracy, only call to mind Disraeli's dictum that there are three kinds of lies—lies, damn lies, and statistics.

Whether fair or unfair, there are certain practical realities which lead to this unequal allocation of dollars. To begin with, the husband simply cannot maintain himself on one-third of what it costs the wife to maintain herself and their two children. Thus, the fact that it may cost the wife $900 a month to maintain the parties' marital residence for herself and their two children does not mean that the husband will be able to find a place for himself for $300 a month. On the contrary, he may be forced to spend half as much or more as it costs the wife, and then only to end up with a one-room apartment; and the same is true with most of his other expenses. In short, and polemics aside, it costs the husband more to live alone than it did for him to live with his wife and children.

Then, too, there are certain political realities. The husband has worked many years to get where he is, and contrary to a great deal of current romanticizing about the satisfaction and rewards of work, for many men it has been a struggle, and a path strewn with as many defeats and denied expectations as it has with victories. Not without reason, he expects to have the satisfaction of his achievement, and that satisfaction is measured in financial terms and in the standard of living that the money he earns affords him. Without question, the fact of his and his wife's separation and divorce means that much of that reward will be denied him.

If it is *all* denied him, however, and if he is not permitted to enjoy enough of the benefits of the success that he has won, and that he will earn by his efforts in the future, his attitude will be very different. If that is the case—if he comes to feel that he is only working for his former wife, or even only for his children—he may well become resentful. And his wife will have to live with that anger and resentment. One can talk of legal or moral obligations all one wants. The fact remains that a husband will continue to make the payments, and will only continue to make the payments, so long as he does not come to believe that the only purpose in his working is to *provide for everyone other than himself.*

Nor does this have anything to do with sex, as is sometimes assumed. Professionals who work in this area, and who are increasingly confronted with the situation where it is the wife's earnings or business, and not the husband's, that is at issue, have come to learn that women can think, act, and talk exactly like men when they are in men's shoes. If one needs an object lesson here, all that is necessary is to wait until the situation arises where the children will continue to live in the home with their father, rather than with their mother, and the issue is now how much child support the wife will have to pay to him, or where it is the wife's business or pension that is in issue, and not the husband's. In short, it is not a function of sex. It is a function of *position*, and of the fact that none of us wants to give up too much of what we have, particularly if we have had to work for it.

PROBLEM SOLVING

As we have noted previously, the mediator should emphasize the fact that the problem that the couple are here to discuss is a common problem. Nowhere is that more true than with the question of support. Nor is that problem one of simply dividing the available dollars—although those available dollars are, ultimately, the reality with which the couple must deal. Rather, it is the problem of seeing how the husband, on the one hand, and the wife and children, on the other, are each going to have enough dollars to be able to live adequately following the parties' separation and divorce. In many instances, and since the available dollars are simply not sufficient for that purpose, it is also the problem of how to *increase* those dollars. In fact, this may be the first problem that the mediator and the couple will be required to address.

Mediation provides a perfect context for the couple to address this question constructively, because it does not view this as the *wife's* problem or the *husband's* problem. That means that the problem will not be solved for *one* of the parties unless it is solved for the *other* as well, and the mediator must continually underscore this fact. In traditional adversarial divorce proceedings, where the object and only object is simply to get as much of the pie as one can, the attitude is exactly the opposite.

Moreover, since one's claim to a larger portion of the pie is predicated upon one's disability, and not upon one's ability, each of the parties goes to great lengths to try to demonstrate that his circumstances are worse than they really are. Thus, husbands who are in business for themselves traditionally have their worst year at the time of their divorce. Those who are employed feign the same disability, and expected raises and promotions suddenly become threatened or disappear altogether. As for their wives, they present their ability to derive income from employment as minimal at best, and they are universally admonished not to accept employment, and thereby acknowledge their ability to earn money, during the course of the proceedings.

As we have noted, these attitudes are derivative of the context in which traditional adversarial divorce proceedings take place. Since this is not the context in which mediation takes place, the mediator should not assume that he will be confronted with this same kind of positioning, and he rarely will be. Moreover, he should reinforce the inappropriateness of this attitude by the manner in which he approaches the problem posed by the question of support, which is to fashion an agreement that will meet the needs of both of the parties as well as their children. Again, this must be presented as a *common* problem in the sense that the agreement must look to *protect each* of them, and no one of them at the expense of the other.

At times it is obvious from the outset that sufficient funds are simply not available. In that case it is the mediator's job to explore with the couple how additional monies can be found. In the normal situation, the focus of attention will be upon the wife, who is presently not working. In all probability, she is not working because the parties still have young children and by common agreement decided that she would remain at home with them at least until they were older. Without questioning the reasoning that led to this conclusion, the fact remains that the circumstances that permitted it no longer exist. Nor does it make any difference whose decision it was to separate and divorce. For better or for worse, and while acknowledging the added burden that this will place upon the parties' children, who will now feel additionally estranged in not only losing their father on a day-to-day basis but in losing the constancy of their mother's care as well, there is simply no choice. Without the additional income that the wife's employment will produce, there is no way in which even the most basic needs of the children can be met.

Thus, while the wife's return to work is usually postponed in traditional adversarial divorce proceedings until after the matter is concluded, in mediation her return to work may be a *precondition* to its conclusion. In fact, the parties and the mediator may devote a great deal of time to implementing a plan that will enable the wife to obtain gainful employment, and, if necessary, to first get the necessary training or education she will require for that purpose. As we have noted previously, and unlike traditional divorce proceedings, where the husband simply separates form his wife and children and leaves them with the problem, in mediation his departure may be postponed in order to keep the combined living expenses down until the wife has found employment or completed the necessary course of study that is its precondition. In short, mediation is a process that attempts to address the problems that have been created by the couple's divorce, and not one that simply leaves each of them with that problem.

Is Maintenance and Support Justified?

The issue of support poses three questions that must be determined in each instance. They are (1) is a payment of maintenance or child support justified, (2) if it is, how much should that payment be, and (3) how long should that payment continue?

Before he undertakes a discussion of any of these questions, however, it would be a good idea for the mediator to make some informal judgments on his own. It is not the mediator's job to see to it that a couple concludes an agreement between themselves that conforms to some preconceived notion on his part as to what would or would not be appropriate. Nevertheless, having had more experience at this than the couple, the mediator should be able to form some judgment as to what he thinks is appropriate. More importantly, in many instances the mediation will not be able to proceed to a successful conclusion unless he does this.

It must be remembered that in a certain sense these questions are really unanswerable. For example, it is one thing to say that a certain level of support is appropriate or inappropriate, for there is at least the yardstick of the parties' *needs* to compare it with. But what yardstick do you use in determining how long the payments should be made? To make that judgment you must first decide what obligation the fact of the couple's marriage places upon the financially more secure partner—which is often difficult—and what the respective circumstances of each of the parties will be at a given point in the future—which is almost impossible.

With this in mind, we have prepared a list of guidelines that may be helpful to the mediator. A word of caution is in order, however. These guidelines are not to be taken as graven in stone, and they are certainly not to be taken as representing what is fair or appropriate, let alone what a court would or would not do. Rather, they are simply working rules of thumb that may be helpful in determining when a payment by one party to the other, either for the other party's support or that of their children, is justified. It must be remembered, however, that these guidelines only indicate whether support is called for, not what the amount of that support should be. Furthermore, they only indicate whether support is justified in terms of the respective earnings of the parties and not, in the case of support for the parties themselves, in terms of the length of their marriage. Those factors will be considered at a later point.

In applying these guidelines, *gross income*, rather than net income or take-home pay, should always be employed. While, in most instances, that means gross income from employment, there may be situations in which either or both of the parties has substantial income from investments. If that is the case, the income from those investments should be considered as well, to the same extent as it would be were it derived from employment.

These guidelines are as follows[2]:

1. If the parties have children who require support, and if the parent with whom the children will primarily reside earns at least 35% of the amount that the other parent earns, then the parent with whom the children will reside will not receive support from the other parent for himself or herself. In that instance, the other parent will only have an obligation to make payments for the support of the children.

Thus, if the wife earns $10,500 (and the children will live with her), and the husband earns $30,000, the wife will be deemed capable of providing for her own support in relation to the husband's earnings, and the husband will only be required to provide child support. (This is not to suggest that this wife is really capable of supporting herself if she earns 35% of what the husband earns. It is merely to say that the husband's income is not enough in relationship to the wife's to justify both a child support and spousal support payment.[3])

However, if the wife earns less than 50% of the husband, then, in relation to the husband's earnings, she will not be deemed capable of contributing toward the support of the children, and that obligation will be the husband's alone. (Again, this is not to say that this husband is really capable of bearing the child support obligation alone. It is simply to say that unless her income is at least 50% of his, the wife cannot afford to share that responsibility with him to the extent of reducing his child support obligation to her.)

2. If the parties have children who require support, and if the parent with whom the children will primarily reside earns more than half of the amount that the other parent earns, then the parent with whom the children will reside should be required to assume some portion of the support of the children. Thus, if the wife earns $30,000 (and the children will live with her), and the husband earns $40,000, the wife's earnings (again, in relation to the husband's earnings) are more than sufficient for her own needs. In that instance, a portion of the amount that the wife earns in excess of half of the amount that the husband earns is available for the support of the children.

In other words, though it is still justified that the husband should have an obligation to the wife for the support of their children, that obligation is less than it would have been had the wife earned only $20,000, or half of the amount the husband earned. (While it may seem inconsistent that although the husband has no obligation to the wife for her support if she earns at least 40 percent of what he earns, that she has no obligation to contribute toward the support of the children—that he gets no reduction in his child support payments—unless she earns at least half of what he earns, that is not so. In each instance the question always is who should get the benefit of any additional dollars available, and to what extent. The judgment here is that if the wife earns only 40% of what the husband earns, and is therefore only receiving child support from the husband, as between the two of them her need is the greater, and, at least until she earns at least 50% of what he earns, she should get the benefit of those additional dollars.)

3. If the parties have children who require support, and if both parties have equal (or nearly equal) incomes, the support obligation for the children should be divided equally between them. However, in that case the amount of support that has been allocated to a child should be increased by between 33⅓% and 50%. Thus, if, based upon the husband's income alone, it would have been appropriate for him to pay to the wife $60 per week for the support of a child had the wife's income not been more than 50% of his—if the wife had no obligation to contribute toward the support of the child—if her income is equal to his, the husband should then be obligated to pay her one-half of between $80 and $90 (or between $40 and $45), rather than one-half of $60 (or $30).

The reason for this is twofold. To begin with, the amount that the husband would have been required to pay to the wife for the support of the child, had the wife's income not been equal to his, would not really have been sufficient to provide for the support of the child. Secondly, the very fact that he can now share the cost of supporting the child with the wife improves his financial ability and enables him to make a slightly larger payment.

4. If the parties have children who require support, and if the parent with whom the children will primarily reside earns more than the other party but less than twice as much as the other party, then the other party should still be required to make some payment for the support of the children. In that instance, a portion of the amount that the other party earns in excess of 50 percent of the amount that the parent with whom the children will reside earns is available for support of the children.

5. If the parties have children who require support, and if the parent with whom the children will primarily reside earns at least twice as much as the other party, then the other party should not have any obligation to make payment to the party with whom the children will reside for their support. Thus, if the wife earns $40,000 (and the children will live with her) and the husband earns $20,000, the husband should not have any obligation to her for the support of their children. Again, in relation to the wife's income, the husband's income is only sufficient to provide for his own needs, and he should not be required to pay her child support.

While, at first blush, it may offend us that a parent should have no financial obligation to support his children, it should not. If we are going to agree that each of the parent's obligations is to be predicated upon their ability vis-à-vis one another, then we should not be offended if such an obligation is not imposed when there is no such ability.

For example, would we be offended if this situation were reversed—with the children living with the husband who earned $40,000 rather than with the wife who earned $20,000—if she were not called upon to make payment to him for their support? We shouldn't be, since in relation to the husband, the wife's income is only sufficient for her own needs. (Rarely will a mediator be faced with the question of whether or not a wife with whom the children will reside should have an obligation to the husband for his support, even if her income greatly exceeds his. To begin with, this fact pattern will rarely occur. Secondly, the fact that the wife's income greatly exceeds the husband's does not necessarily mean that she has enough to meet all of the children's expenses as well as her own. Thus, and particularly if the wife is willing to shoulder the burden of the children's support without contribution from the husband, then, and barring special circumstances, she should not be given the additional burden of contributing toward the husband's living expenses as well. Thirdly, if the husband is not burdened with the responsibility of providing for the support of the children, and is only obligated to look after himself, it will generally be felt that he should be able to do so, and that if he is not, then, and again barring special circumstances, it is not the wife's obligation to help him. There will be few who will have any difficulty with this. However—and although the logic would appear to be as strong in the reverse situation—there will still be many who will have difficulty accepting this if it is the *wife* who has the smaller of the two incomes and it is the husband with whom the children will primarily reside.)

6. If the parties have children who require support, and if the parent with whom the children will primarily reside does not work (and cannot work), or works but earns (or is only capable of earning) less than 35% of the amount earned by the other party, then the other party should be responsible to provide support both for that party and their children. Thus, if the wife earns $7,000 and the husband $40,000, and the children will live with the wife, then the husband should have an obligation both for her support and for the support of their children.

7. If the couple has been married for less than 8 years and do not have children, again barring special circumstances, neither party should have any obligation for the support of the other, regardless of the disparity in their respective incomes.

8. If the couple has been married for more than 8 years but for less than 15 years and do not have children, and if one of the parties does not work (and is not capable of working), or works and earns (or is only capable of earning) less than 33⅓% of the amount earned by the other party, then the party earning the smaller amount should receive support from the other party. If they have been married more than 15 years but for less than 25 years, the figure 33⅓% should be raised to 40%. If they have been married for more than 25 years, the figure 33⅓% should be raised to 45%, except that if one of the parties is 50 years of age or older, it should be raised to 50%.

9. If the couple has grown children whom they are no longer obligated to support, and if one of the parties does not work (and is not capable of working), or works and earns (or is only capable of earning) less than 40% of the amount earned by the other party, the party earning the smaller amount should receive support from the other party. (If, however, it is the wife who earns less, the operable amount will increase from 40% to 45%). Thus, if the husband earns $60,000 and the wife less than $24,000, the husband should be obligated to provide support for the wife. Again, a payment is required of the husband, not because their incomes are unequal, but because the disparity in their incomes is such that it cannot be said that the wife can reasonably provide for herself on her own in relation to the husband's ability to provide for himself. It is also required because it is assumed, in this instance, that since the wife was required to devote her energies to raising the parties' children and providing a home for her husband, she lost some of the opportunity which she might otherwise have had to improve her position in the market place.

While it may at first seem inappropriate that one of the parties should have to earn at least twice the amount that the other party earns for him or her to be obligated to support the other party, it must be kept in mind that a support payment is not occasioned only because the parties earn different amounts. Nor is it intended to annul those differences. It is only intended to reduce them when they are too great. It must also be kept in mind that the disparity in the incomes of the two parties is not as great as it may at first appear since the income of the higher wage earner will be substantially reduced by the taxes that he will pay, usually at a higher rate, on the amount that he earns in excess of the earnings of the lower wage earner.)

10. If, in the above example, the couple has been married for more than 25 years, then the party with the smaller income will be entitled to support if he or she earns less than 50 percent of the amount earned by the other party. However, in this case the party who earns the smaller amount will also have to be 45 years of age or older, if it is the wife, and 50 years of age or older, if it is the husband, in order for the operable amount to increase from 40 or 45% to 50%. In other words, if the couple have been married for 25 years and the wife is 44 years of age, she will not be entitled to support, even if she does not earn 50% of what her husband earns, provided she earns at least 45% of what he earns. However, if she is 52 years old, she will.

CASH INCOME

A recurring problem in traditional adversarial divorce proceedings, particularly where one of the parties is self-employed, is the question of cash income. Again, the adversarial context of those proceedings tends to magnify the problem and make it bigger than life. The issue is generally first raised by the wife's attorney, very often in papers submitted to the court in support of an application made on her behalf either for counsel fees, temporary maintenance, or child support. For various reasons (perhaps because the wife really does not know the full extent of the husband's cash income, perhaps to apply pressure to him in the form of the possible threat of the IRS, or perhaps simply because adversarial proceedings lend themselves so much to exaggeration), the amount of cash is usually inflated in the wife's papers. Thus, instead of suggesting to the court that the husband's cash income is about $20,000 a year, as was indicated by the wife to her attorney, the court is informed that it is between $30,000 and $40,000 a year.

In addition to the inherent problem that he has in discussing, let alone acknowledging, the presence of cash income that went unreported on his return, the husband is now faced with an additional dilemma. Given this exaggeration, if he were to acknowledge that there was cash income, the court might possibly accept the wife's estimate of the amount of that income. Accordingly, the papers prepared by the husband's attorney, in response to the wife's claim, strenuously deny the existence of any cash at all. In fact, it is not uncommon for the case to proceed to trial in this bizarre posture, with the wife steadfastly insisting that there is substantial unreported cash income which the husband, just as steadfastly, denies exists at all.

Critics of mediation, particularly matrimonial attorneys, have pointed to this problem as representing a flaw in mediation practice. Thus, if one of the parties is in business for himself, and receives income in cash, they insist that there is a very serious problem of disclosure. Moreover, it is a problem that the mediator—who obviously has no independent knowledge of the parties' finances, and is not in a position to conduct the necessary discovery proceedings—cannot properly deal with. On the contrary, it is only the safeguards afforded by adversarial proceedings that can properly protect the other party in this situation.

In actual fact, the problem of cash income in divorce mediation has been very much exaggerated. To begin with, implicit in the criticism is the suggestion that this is a

problem that traditional adversarial proceedings, and the supposed safeguards they provide, solve. Nothing, however, could be further from the truth. While, to be sure,
adversarial matrimonial attorneys have elaborate pretrial discovery procedures available to
them in aid of their attempt to obtain a picture of the husband's real financial circumstances, no responsible matrimonial attorney would ever suggest that those procedures
guarantee that a true and accurate picture will emerge.

More importantly, the wife's attorney will not be able to *prove* the existence of this
cash income by means of these discovery proceedings, or from an investigation of the
husband or his books and records, as this will prove nothing. (By definition, the husband
is not going to acknowledge the existence of this cash, and quite obviously, there are no
business records of it.) Rather, he attempts to prove it through the wife herself, who
provides him with a list of past living expenses that demonstrate that the parties spent more
than the husband claims that he earned, a fact that the wife can just as easily assert in
mediation.

Thus, and contrary to the mythology of adversarial proceedings, it is simply not
possible, except in the very rarest of cases, to prove the exact extent of the husband's
unreported cash income, and all attempts always run the risk of either appearing as gross
exaggerations, deserving little credibility, or of falling far short of the mark. To make
matters worse, the very nature of traditional adversarial divorce proceedings is such as to
make this cash income more of a problem than it otherwise would be, for, and as we have
noted previously, those proceedings tend to encourage the husband to hide as much as he
can and thereby to force upon the wife the burden of trying to uncover it.

Fortunately, and whether adversarial attorneys wish to believe it or not, this problem
rarely occurs in divorce mediation. In fact, this is yet another example of the phenomenon, which we have noted previously, that certain practices, which are almost the
bread and butter of a matrimonial attorney's practice, simply do not occur, let alone
become a problem, in mediation. The very fact that the discussions take place in the kind
of setting in which mediation occurs tends to promote a more open and honest airing of
these matters. In fact, the mediator will find that the question of cash income is usually
talked about in mediation almost as casually as is any other topic brought up for discussion. He will also find that in most instances the other party (usually the wife) is fully
conversant not only with the fact of this cash but also with the approximate amount of it.
In short, there is little evidence to suggest that the elaborate pretrial procedures of the law
are a more effective guarantee that full disclosure will be made than is the context in
which mediation occurs.

In this regard, the mediator will be confronted with one of three possible situations.
In the first, and in response to the mediator's inquiry, the wife will advise him that she is
not only aware that her husband has cash income, but also that she knows the exact extent
of it. In the second, the wife also says that she knows that her husband earns cash income
but that she does not know the extent of it. However, she advises the mediator that she
believes her husband to be honest, and trusts him, and that if he says that this cash
income is a certain amount, she will accept that. In the last situation, the wife informs the
mediator that although she knows or believes that her husband has cash income, she is
not only ignorant of the extent of it, but also does not trust him and would therefore not
accept his representation as to the amount of it, even if he were to acknowledge it.

There is no reason that the first two of these three situations should represent a
problem for the mediator. To be sure, the wife may be wrong when she says that she

knows what her husband's cash income is, and she may also be wrong when she says that she can trust him. Nevertheless, most people really do know their husbands and wives, and in the vast majority of instances their judgments in this respect will be correct, and should be accepted as such.

But what about those instances in which it is not correct? Shouldn't they be of concern to a mediator? While the critics of mediation would suggest that they should be, and that this is one of the serious risks of mediation, the answer still is no. As we have previously noted, mediation and traditional adversarial divorce proceedings take place in very different contexts. Those different contexts affect what is considered to be appropriate or inappropriate conduct on the part of each of the parties. This in turn provides each of the parties with different opportunities and exposes them to different risks.

Thus, given the context in which adversarial divorce proceedings take place, the wife's attorney is always forced to view the husband with suspicion. If the husband is in business for himself, the wife's attorney almost always proceeds on the assumption that the husband has cash income that has gone unreported, even if this is not true. Her attorney may even believe that the husband has unreported cash income when he is not in business for himself, particularly if he has a position of importance in a relatively small, privately owned company.

Furthermore, the wife's attorney does not believe that he can accept any statement that the husband might make concerning the presence or absence of any such unreported income, or the amount of it, and given the context in which traditional adversarial divorce proceedings take place, and the suspicion with which the wife's attorney views the husband, he is probably justified in that opinion. For traditional adversarial divorce proceedings would so penalize a husband who is honest that, like the self-fulfilling prophecy, in assuming that he is dishonest it invariably makes a liar of him. The wife's attorney now has a problem, however, for in having created a context that rewards the husband if he is a liar and penalizes him if he tells the truth, he cannot now take a chance, and risk believing him.

Given this fact, the husband is subjected to the requirement of extensive pretrial discovery proceedings in an effort to determine the exact extent of his income. In fact, these procedures are so routinely employed, and have become so much a part of the fabric of traditional adversarial divorce proceedings, that divorce lawyers have lost their ability to see them as simply one of the prices that a couple pays for resolving their disputes in this manner. In short, these extensive pretrial discovery proceedings are not one of the benefits of adversarial divorce proceedings; rather, and given the context in which those proceedings take place, they are simply one of its necessities.

There is a high price to these proceedings, however. They are extremely costly, inconvenient, and time-consuming, and they only tend to exacerbate the resentments that make a resolution of the issues between the couple so difficult. Thus, they have become one of the costs (risks) to the parties in attempting to resolve these questions by means of traditional adversarial divorce proceedings. The point is that even if there is a risk to the wife in her assuming that she can rely on the trust that she has in her husband, that does not mean that it is not a risk worth taking. The question is not whether there is a risk—there is a risk no matter *what* she does—but whether it is a *legitimate* risk. After all, that is the same question that she will have to ask herself if she turns to adversarial divorce proceedings.

Before proceeding to discuss the third possibility, however, there is one further point that must be made. On occasion, a wife will advise the mediator right from the outset that she does not believe that she can trust her husband or, therefore, the mediation process. This is most likely to occur when it is her husband who seeks the divorce over her strong objection. Often the mediator will be somewhat baffled by the intensity of the wife's apparent distrust, either because there is little in the husband's financial circumstances that would permit him to hide anything or because, even if that is not the case, there is little about him that suggests that he would.

A mediator with an alert eye and ear will often note something here, however, and that is that the wife and he are talking about trust in two very different ways. It is not that the wife really does not trust her husband. In fact, if the mediator were to probe her objective attitudes toward him, he would probably find that she believes him to be a very straightforward, responsible person. It is just that after "what he has done to her," she can no longer trust him. In other words, she and the mediator are talking at cross-purposes. He is concerned with whether or not the wife feels that her husband will be forthright as to his financial circumstances. The wife, however, cannot even get to this point, for she is still so overwhelmed by her loss and by her sense of betrayal, that the very cornerstone of her faith in her husband has been blasted. As a result, she can no longer trust him at all. When this is the case, the mediator will generally learn this long before the issue of support is raised. In fact, it will probably come out in the very early stages of the mediation. If that is so, the mediator will have to address this issue with the wife carefully, and slowly. Moreover, it would be best for him to do this apart from the question of support, and before it is specifically addressed.

Let us suppose, now, that the mediator is confronted with the third situation. The wife not only maintains that she is ignorant of her husband's finances, but worse, that she does not trust him and would not believe anything he says. The husband may be telling the unvarnished truth. Nevertheless, the mediator has a problem, for the wife has put him on notice that she views herself as proceeding at an unfair disadvantage. Moreover, the mediator here cannot say with any sense of assurance that when the wife is talking about her distrust of her husband that she is talking about anything other than the veracity of his representations as to his financial circumstances.

Is the mediator under an obligation to decline to proceed with the mediation at this point? On the face of it, it might seem that he is; but that is not necessarily so. Thus, and before he makes any such decision, he should first ask the husband whether or not he would be willing to have himself examined under oath by an attorney selected by the wife, and his records inspected by an accountant of her choice, in the same manner that he would be examined were the parties each to employ adversarial proceedings. If the husband agrees to this, the mediator should have no compunction about proceeding with the mediation. To be sure, the husband may be an inveterate (and very clever) liar, and it may very well be that the discovery proceedings employed by the wife's attorney and her accountant will fail to produce all of his income. However, this is not a function of the fact that the parties have chosen mediation, since the wife has now had the advantage of the same safeguards that traditional divorce proceedings are supposed to provide her. Rather, it is a function of her husband's dishonesty, against which even those safeguards were unable to protect her.

But shouldn't a mediator be concerned that the wife has failed to discover all of her husband's unreported income, and is therefore proceeding at a disadvantage? Absolutely not. Let us suppose that the wife had retained an adversarial lawyer to represent her.

Would he be unwilling to proceed with the case simply because he was not convinced that his pretrial discovery proceedings had succeeded in uncovering all of the husband's unreported income? Obviously not. In fact, these are exactly the conditions under which he ends up proceeding in most instances where the husband has cash income. It may not be fair that the wife should be forced to proceed at such a disadvantage, but if the wife is going to suffer this disability, it is still better that she suffer it in a mediated settlement rather than a settlement arrived at through traditional adversarial procedures.

There is one final question that must be addressed. If financial discovery proceedings conducted by an attorney (and accountant) would tend to act as a safeguard against the risk of a husband's failing to disclose unreported income, wouldn't it be a good idea to subject the husband to this kind of a financial examination in every instance? In fact, wouldn't this be a responsible way to take some of the risk out of mediation and thereby improve it? While, at first blush, it would seem that it would be, the answer nevertheless is no. *Mediators should not be misled by their critics.* For better or for worse, the parties cannot have the best of both possible worlds, and that is because those worlds are inconsistent. Every time one of the parties attempts to avail himself of certain of the benefits of traditional adversarial proceedings, he undermines certain of the benefits of mediation. In fact, placing the couple in an adversarial setting may actually destroy the very preconditions that enable mediation to succeed in the first place, and the benefits of mediation are simply too great to run that risk.

But isn't that just what the mediator did when he suggested to the husband that he permit his wife's attorney and accountant to examine him and his books and records? The answer is no. There was no such risk in that instance for, if the husband had not consented to allow the wife to examine his books and records, and thereby given her the assurance she needed, she would not have consented to participate in the mediation in the first place, and the parties would have been forced to resort to traditional adversarial divorce proceedings anyway.

Suppose that the husband declines to permit the wife's attorney and accountant to examine his books and records. What should the mediator do then? In actual fact, this situation will rarely, if ever, occur. The admonitions of certain of the critics of divorce mediation notwithstanding, husbands who wish to play financial games with their wives look to adversarial divorce proceedings, and not to mediation, for that purpose. Nor do they attempt to lure their wives into mediation so that they will be able to do this, as is so often thought to be the case. Even if that were so, however, rare indeed will be the day when a wife will permit herself to be placed in this position.

Let us suppose, nevertheless, that the husband in this instance will not agree to permit his wife to conduct the examination. Let us even suppose that it is not because he really has anything to hide. On the contrary, his refusal stems simply from the fact that he is insulted by his wife's suggestion. Be that as it may, the mediator is left in a dilemma. Even if he were to be convinced that the wife would still be far better off to deal with her husband in mediation rather than in adversarial proceedings—and we are not suggesting that the mediator would or should be so convinced—he will still have a serious problem.

The mediator cannot simply concern himself with the parties themselves, or, in this case, the wife. On the contrary, he must also assure himself that he has *protected the mediation process* as well. How will it look if the mediator has permitted the wife to proceed under these circumstances, and in the face of her repeated expressions of fear and concern for her own protection? And what kind of an agreement would the mediator leave the parties with if he were to disregard this and proceed with the mediation? Regardless of the reason for the husband's refusal to open his books and records to his wife, in so refusing he has thrown his gauntlet down at the feet of the mediator, and the mediator cannot ignore it. Rather, he must decline to proceed with the mediation.

There is one final question that must be addressed here, and that is whether or not the mediator should feel uncomfortable at the fact that the parties are openly discussing income with him that they have failed to report on their tax returns? For that matter, should he not feel uncomfortable in the fact that he is joining them in those discussions? The answer is no. The fact that the couple has failed to report all of their income should be of no concern to the mediator, any more than it would be of concern to matrimonial attorneys or, one may be surprised to find out, to judges who routinely try matrimonial cases and hear evidence concerning this cash income.

It is not a mediator's job, any more than it is the job of a therapist, to step in and pass judgment when he hears of conduct of which he does not approve, even if that conduct is immoral and perhaps illegal. With rare exception—such as when a therapist learns that a parent has been guilty of physical abuse to his child—the law does not require us to be our brother's keeper. Nor should we be. The mediator did not tell the couple not to report this income. Nor has he suggested to them that they should not report it in the future. He is simply engaged in a discussion as to the level of payments that should be made by the husband given the fact that he receives income that, as a practical matter, he has not and probably will not report. In fact, the situation is not very different from what would have been the case had this information been elicited in court, and the judge had ordered the husband to make support payments at an increased level because he was convinced that he received income that has gone unreported.

INDIRECT INCOME

Analogous to the problem of unreported cash income is the problem of living expenses paid for by the husband through his business. Here the question is not whether this indirect income exists, though, in adversarial proceedings, the extent of that indirect income is also often an issue. Rather, the question is how it should be treated. The husband's business provides him with an automobile. It also pays for the insurance on that automobile as well as the cost of running it—repairs, gas, oil, replacements. The business supplies him with the benefit of medical and hospital insurance, as well as life insurance, and pays the premiums on those policies. It also provides him with credit cards that he uses freely for personal expenses, particularly for travel and entertainment with his family. And, of course, these indirect benefits can be more extensive, and can include the payment of telephone bills, electric bills, fuel bills, household repairs, gardeners, house-keepers, country club dues, marina fees, and much more.

Lawyers in traditional adversarial divorce proceedings have always had some diffi-culty in dealing with these indirect payments (fringe benefits). Unlike negligence lawyers, who are almost always either plaintiffs' attorneys or defendants' attorneys, most matri-monial lawyers represent both husbands and wives. As a result, they do not tend to develop quite the same mindset as do attorneys who only represent one class of litigants. Thus, and even though a matrimonial attorney can quickly and easily change the set of glasses that he uses in viewing the problem from the wife's standpoint to those that he uses in viewing the problem from the husband's standpoint, there cannot help but be a certain carryover in attitude from one class of cases to the other. The attitude of matrimonial attorneys toward these indirect payments represents one of those instances.

What is that attitude? Simply that matrimonial attorneys do not view the indirect income a husband receives in the same way that they view unreported cash income. Thus, if the husband had an income of $70,000 "on the books," and unreported cash income of $10,000, he would be viewed as having an income of $80,000. In fact, he might be viewed as even having a greater income, since he would have to earn substantially more than $80,000 in order to be left with the same spendable dollars. However, if he had the same salary of $70,000 and if his business paid for $10,000 of his living expenses, he will be viewed as having an income of only $70,000, but as also having the benefit of $10,000 worth of expenses paid for by his business. In other words, and although the wife's lawyer would make a mental note that the husband had $10,000 of expenses paid for through his business, that additional $10,000 would not be viewed as having the same value as it would were it cash income.

The point is that expenses paid for through the husband's business never seem to be charged to the husband in an amount equal to the cost to his business. In fact, and unless they are extensive, they do not generally affect the husband's support obligation very much at all. Thus, if all that the business pays for is the husband's medical and life insurance, no mention of this will be made at all by the wife's attorney, and, if it is, it will be greeted by the husband's attorney with merely a shrug of the shoulders. Even when those payments extend to the husband's automobile, and are therefore really significant, the cost is not usually directly added to the husband's income. Rather, in pressing for a liberal (though not necessarily greater) payment for the wife, the wife's attorney will simply point out the fact that the husband, after all, does have this benefit.

It is unlikely that mediators will be able to deal more effectively with this indirect income than are adversarial attorneys. It is simply very hard to get a husband to accept the fact that this is real income to him, and, even more importantly, that he should pay more to his wife on that account. From his standpoint, he still only has the same $70,000 in pretax dollars to share with her, and he does not see why he should receive less of it on that account.

Without attempting to justify the husband's position, it would perhaps be helpful to understand it. The husband has no doubt worked very hard to get where he is, and if he is good at what he does, he may not even get paid what he is worth. What has been denied him in direct compensation is often made up to him indirectly. He has been made assistant vice president and been given a windowed office. Or he has been given a company car and been told by his boss that he can charge $200 a month on his American Express card for his personal use. Or, if he is self-employed, he provides himself with these same things. In either event, he does not view any of this as additional income. It is just one of the fringe benefits—like the title of assistant vice president—that he gets as an incident to his employment.

It is hard at times to explain this curious phenomenon. After all, what is the difference between the husband's receiving unreported cash income of $5,000, and having his business rent him an automobile and pay his expenses in connection with its use, also at a cost of $5,000? Perhaps it is the fact that the husband would be free to use the $5,000 of cash income in any way that he wished, whereas in the other case he is bound to receive those benefits in a given way. Perhaps it is also because these benefits are not paid in cash. If, for example, the husband has after-tax dollars of $40,000, $10,000 of which is unreported cash, and he divides that equally with his wife (and children), they will each have $20,000 in spendable (cash) dollars. On the other hand, if the husband has this same $40,000 (consisting, in this case, of $30,000 after-tax income and $10,000 of expenses paid for by his business) and he gives his wife the same $20,000, he will be left with only $10,000 (cash) income. To be sure, he will still have the other $10,000 of expenses paid for by his business. But he will simply not see that he has been left with the same dollars as his wife.

The other reason that it is difficult for a husband to view these benefits in direct dollar terms is the fact that he probably would not have bought them if he had had to pay for them himself. To be sure, the husband drives a Cadillac that is rented through his business at a cost of $450 a month. And he and his wife go to dinner on Saturday night and spend $60 or $70 that he charges on his American Express card that is paid for by his business. But he only drives a Cadillac and spends $60 or $70 on dinner because he does not pay for it. If he did, he would drive a different car and eat out far less often. In other words, the Cadillac (rather than the Chevrolet that he could afford on his own) is given to him as a reward and as an incentive, as are his larger office and title, and it is very hard for him to see them as separate and apart from his job. The salary goes to support him and his family. The fringe benefits are his reward.

Having acknowledged that, however, it is still a fact that they do, nevertheless, represent real benefits and whether or not the husband is provided with a Cadillac, or only the Chevrolet that he could afford on his own, in either event he is relieved of the financial responsibility of providing them for himself. In addition, whereas in the past the wife, by the mere fact of her marriage to the husband, could share in those benefits, she will now be deprived of them by their divorce. Particularly when they are substantial in nature, they must be taken into account in determining the parties' respective abilities.

In the example given above, it was suggested that it may not be too hard to understand the husband's attitude toward these fringe benefits, considering how hard he has worked to get where he is and perhaps even the fact that, at least from his standpoint, he may be worth far more than he is being paid. On occasion, however, the mediator may be confronted with the exact opposite situation. The husband may or may not have worked very hard to get where he is. But he is paid far more than he is worth. The husband is employed, or is a partner, in a large brokerage firm, and earns in excess of $300,000, $400,000, or perhaps $500,000 a year. In addition, he has very extensive travel and entertainment expenses, most of which are for his personal benefit, that he is able to write off on his business. The business may even pay for his apartment, or other of his living expenses. Certainly this indirect compensation cannot be ignored.

Paradoxically, and even though those fringe benefits may be far more extensive, they will probably be less relevant here than they were in the previous example. In most instances, a husband cannot afford to pay for all of the previous living expenses of his wife and children. That is why these indirect benefits become such an issue. Where a husband earns a very substantial income, however, even apart from these indirect benefits, he may well be in a position to pay his wife exactly what she needs. She has made a budget of her present living expenses, which total $84,000 a year in after-tax dollars, and her husband is prepared to write her out a check for this amount. But is it fair that the wife and three children will be left with only $84,000 a year when the husband will be left with an amount far in excess of that?

It may *not* be fair—whatever that means—but it also really does not make any difference. The wife and children will be able to live in the future almost exactly as they have in the past, and the husband has even protected the dollars he will pay her with a cost-of-living increase. Presumably, she has also received an equitable distribution of their marital property. She and her children really have everything that they need, and if that is so, the wife has no right to complain and little reason to. The fact that her husband's efforts will leave him with more than he needs, in relation to her, is really irrelevant and should not concern the mediator. Quite the contrary, and rather than viewing her own situation in relation to her husband's with disfavor, the mediator should help her appreciate just how fortunate she is, in relation to other divorced women, even divorced women within her own social circle, in being left as secure as she will be in her divorce.[4]

Overtime Pay and Bonuses

Not uncommonly, the mediator will be confronted with a situation where the husband's base pay is \$25,000 but his earnings in the previous year were \$34,000, the difference representing overtime pay. On which of these two figures should the husband's obligation be predicated?

Although not in a completely analogous sense, blue-collar and white-collar workers sometimes tend to view overtime pay the way executives and self-employed persons view indirect compensation. In short, they do not believe that their obligation should be based upon anything other than their base pay. The husband's rationale, of course, is a little different here. On the one hand, he will argue that his overtime pay is subject to fluctuation and is not guaranteed. On the other hand, he may sometimes argue that he is not obligated to work the long hours that he does to earn this extra money, that it has been a strain upon him, and that with the additional pressures his divorce has created, he does not wish to have to work as hard in the future as he has in the past.

Fortunately, and as was the case with cash income, the mediator will find that there is nowhere near the exaggeration here as there is in adversarial divorce proceedings, which are always attendant with reliable rumors that all overtime work is going to be terminated shortly, or severely restricted. On the contrary, husbands tend to be far more candid about the prospects of continued overtime work.

On occasion, this same anomaly may present itself in a different form. The husband is a schoolteacher, and tutors students in his free time after school. During the summer months, when he is not required to work, it has been his habit to work in a summer camp to earn additional income. At other times, and even when the husband has a full-time job throughout the year, he may earn additional money through part-time employment. Should the wife be entitled to share in this additional income? While a man is obviously obligated to work to support his family, is he obligated to have to work two jobs to do it? And if he is willing to take on a second job and work more than he has to, shouldn't he be entitled to the benefit of those additional efforts without having to share them with his wife?

In each of these cases a pragmatic approach should be taken. In most instances, that means that the mediator should take the parties where he finds them. If the husband, who is a schoolteacher, traditionally tutored students during the year and took employment for one month during the summer in a program run by the school, then that is who the husband is, and there is no reason that he should be treated or viewed differently simply because he and his wife are divorcing.

Many jobs have overtime routinely built into them, and many unions bargain for shorter work weeks, not because they want or expect union members to work shorter hours, but simply because they wish to be compensated at overtime rates for a greater portion of the hours that they do work. If that is the case, why is this any different from the situation of an attorney or executive who works a 50-hour week rather than a 40-hour week as part of his job? On the other hand, if the husband's overtime pay in the last two years was unusual, and born of special circumstances that are not expected to continue, or if the husband had not normally worked a second job and had only taken it to meet certain unexpected financial needs that arose, it would be unfair to charge him with the responsibility of working those additional hours forever simply because he was found to be working them at the time of the parties' divorce. Again, the mediator will have to view this pragmatically.

Suppose that it is not clear whether this overtime pay or additional income will continue on a recurring basis or will instead be short-lived. How can the couple arrive at an appropriate level of support without knowing this, particularly if this additional income is fairly substantial? One way is to predicate the support payment on the husband's total income at the present time, and to reduce it if he should no longer earn this additional income in the future.

Conversely, the support payments can instead be predicated on the husband's base pay from his principal job, and the agreement can then provide for an increase in those payments should he still enjoy this additional income in the future. This will not only better guarantee an equitable result but, and perhaps more importantly, will enable the mediator to finesse the question of whether or not the husband will actually receive this additional income in the future.

Analogous to overtime pay that a blue-collar worker earns is the bonus the executive sometimes receives. Again, and particularly where the bonus is small in relation to the husband's salary, he may tend to view it as a fringe benefit that should not be included in determining his income for the purpose of setting his support obligation. He may even argue that, as with overtime pay, it is not something that is guaranteed to him, that he has not always received it in the past, and that he is not certain that he will receive it in the future.

Again, a pragmatic approach should be taken by the mediator. If the husband earns $60,000 a year and in the past five years has twice received small bonuses of $2,000 or $3,000, based upon a percentage of the earnings of the company, it is not necessary for the mediator to concern himself with these additional earnings, any more than he would had they represented nonrecurring overtime pay.

On the other hand, if the husband is in an industry where his salary represents only a portion of his real income, and he has historically received a substantial bonus each year, equal, for example, to perhaps half of his $60,000 salary, then he really earns $90,000 a year, and his bonus simply represents a different method of payment with respect to a third of his salary. Again, if the husband is really concerned that he may not always continue to receive a bonus in this amount—and that can be a legitimate concern in many industries—the way for the mediator to handle this is not to exclude the bonus from consideration, but to build into the agreement a provision that will reduce the husband's support payments should his income, including his bonus, fall below a fixed amount.

The Amount of Support and Maintenance

Up until this point, we have been concerned with whether or not a payment from one party to the other, either as maintenance or as child support, is justified, and the question of what income of each of the parties should be considered in determining this. Let us now assume that it has been determined that a support payment is justified. That being the case, it is then necessary to determine what that payment should be.

As we have noted previously, it would help the mediator if he could form some opinion in his own mind before the discussions proceed. Again, his attempts to do this are fraught with problems. To begin with, there are no hard-and-fast rules as to what is fair or appropriate, and husbands and wives can certainly not be expected to have similar views on the subject. Also, even though those views have in large measure been determined against the background of what a court would or would not award, it is not possible to know this for sure, and even the experienced attorneys representing the husband and the wife will have different opinions on the matter. Moreover, these judgments are not consistent from state to state. They are not even consistent within the same state. [5]

With this understanding, the following guidelines are proposed as aids in helping the mediator make that determination. In applying these guidelines it must again be remembered that although they refer to earned income alone, investment income must be included as well.

A final note is in order. From the standpoint of traditional adversarial practice, a husband's attorney would probably view these guidelines as being on the high side of the husband's obligation. That should mean that, from the standpoint of the wife's attorney, and whether either he or the wife thought that the proposed payment was fair from a philosophical standpoint, he would generally recommend that the wife accept a payment predicated upon these guidelines. Given the nature of adversarial proceedings, however, that will not necessarily be the case. Rather, a wife's attorney might well view them as being on the low side of the wife's entitlement. In the absence of agreement between attorneys for husbands and wives, mediators will have to do the best they can. Ironically, rather than invalidating the usefulness of these guidelines, their disagreement, particularly if it is as we suggest, may tend to do just the opposite.

To the extent that these guidelines refer to after-tax dollars, the mediator should make his own calculations as to what those after-tax (take-home) dollars are, rather than accepting the figures given to him by the parties themselves, or even taking them off their pay slips, as there may well be deductions on those pay slips that should not properly be considered in determining their take-home pay. In this regard, and with rare exception, the mediator should only credit the wage earner with the involuntary deductions that have been taken from his pay—withholding taxes, F.I.C.A., union dues, and so on. (Very often, employees have savings plans or stock purchase plans that they have automatically deducted from their salary. On other occasions, they may have deductions taken for credit union loans or for the repayment of other obligations. These are payments that should be made by the party from the income left to him to meet his own personal expenses. They should not normally be deducted from his salary to arrive at his take-home pay for the purpose of determining his support obligation to the other party and their children.)

Admittedly, it is not possible to determine a person's actual after-tax income on this basis, particularly if he will have an obligation to his spouse for her support. The reason for this is that since the amount of that support will represent an additional deduction to the husband, it will cause a reduction in his taxes, and will therefore increase his after-tax income. Nevertheless, for the purposes of these guidelines, this factor should be ignored. Without pretending that these guidelines precisely reflect this fact, they have been established, nevertheless, with that understanding.

These guidelines are as follows:

1. If the couple has two children who require support and whose primary residence will be with the wife, and if the wife does not and cannot work, she should receive 50% of the husband's spendable income (take-home pay) for herself and the two children. Thus, if the husband earns $28,000 and if his take-home pay, after all involuntary deductions, is $20,000, she should receive $10,000. While the amount of the payment will increase or decrease if the parties have more or less than two children, that deviation should be marginal. Thus, the wife will not receive $13,333 (or a third more) because they have three children. Nor will she receive $6,666.66 (or a third less) because they only have one. Further, the decrease and increase will not necessarily be the same. Thus, if the parties only have one child, the support payment should equal 45% of the husband's take-home pay. If they have three, it should equal 55%. In no event should it exceed 60%, regardless of the number of children that the couple have.

2. If the couple has two children who require support and whose primary residence will be with the wife, and if the wife works (or is capable of working), and earns (or is capable of earning) less than 35% of what the husband earns, she should receive between 35% and 45% of the husband's spendable income (take-home pay) for herself and their two children. If the parties only have one child, she should receive between 30% and 40% of the husband's spendable income. If they have three or more children, she should receive between 40% and 50% of the husband's spendable income. In no event should she receive more than 50% of the husband's spendable income, regardless of the number of children they have. (Whether the wife will receive the higher or the lower amount will depend in each instance upon how much less than 35% of the husband's income she earns.)

3. If the couple has two children who require support and whose primary residence will be with the wife, and if the husband is not obligated for the support of the wife, but is alone obligated for the support of the children—the wife's gross income is no less than 35% and no more than 50% of the husband's gross income—the wife should receive child support equal to between 25% and 30% of the husband's spendable income (take-home pay). If the parties only have one child, she should receive between 20% and 25% of the husband's spendable income and if they have three or more children, between 35% and 40% of the husband's spendable income. In no event should she receive more than 40% of the husband's spendable income, regardless of the number of children they have.

4. If, in the above example, the wife's gross income is more than 50% of the husband's gross income, but less than the husband's gross income, the wife should receive a fraction of the amount of child support that she would have received in guideline number 3 in which the numerator is half of the husband's gross income and the denominator is the numerator plus the amount of the wife's gross income in excess of the numerator. Thus, if the wife's gross income is $25,000 and the husband's gross income is $40,000, the numerator will be $20,000 and the denominator $25,000, or 20 and 25, respectively. Since the wife will, in effect, be deemed to have $5,000 to contribute to the support of the children and the husband $20,000, for a total of $25,000, he will be obligated to pay to her $20/25$, or 80%, of the amount that he would have been required to

pay to her under guideline number 3, if she had no obligation to contribute to the support of the children.

5. If, in the above example, the gross incomes of the husband and the wife are equal (or nearly equal), their respective obligations for the support of the children will also be equal, and the wife should receive 50% of the total child support obligation for the children. However, it must be remembered that as the wife's gross income approaches the husband's gross income, the original child support obligation (the payment that the husband would have been required to make to the wife for the support of the children under guideline number 3 if her income was no more than 50% of his) has to be increased to reflect their combined increased ability to provide for the support of the children. Thus, the child support payment that the husband would have been obligated to make to the wife under guideline number 3 should be increased by between one-third and one-half, and the husband should be obligated to pay to the wife 50% of that increased amount.

6. If, in the above example, the wife's income is greater than the husband's income, and the children will reside primarily with her, then the base that should be used to determine the husband's child support obligation should be half of the wife's gross income rather than half of the husband's gross income, and the dollars available for the support of the children should be deemed to be the combined incomes of the parties in excess of that amount. The husband's obligation should then be a fraction in which his gross income above that base is the numerator and the denominator is the numerator plus the amount of the wife's gross income in excess of the numerator. (Thus, if the husband's gross income is $25,000 and the wife's gross income is $40,000, then the husband should pay to the wife ⅝, or 20%, of the amount that he would have been required to pay in child support under guideline number 3.)

There is one final calculation that should be made. It will be remembered that under guideline number 5, when the couple's incomes were equal, the husband's original child support obligation under guideline number 3 was increased by between one-third and one-half, and he was obligated to pay 50% of that increased amount to the wife. When the wife's gross income begins to approach twice the husband's gross income, however, that increased amount must be reduced again. When the wife's gross income is twice that of the husband's, he should have no obligation to her for the support of the children.

7. If the couple has no children who require support, and if the wife does not and cannot work, she should receive one-third of the husband's gross income. Thus, if the husband's gross income is $30,000 she should receive maintenance of $10,000. (Again, while it might seem unfair, particularly in a marriage of long duration, that a husband will be left with twice the amount that his wife will, this is not the case. Firstly, he will not be left with twice as much, as the income taxes he will pay on his additional income will significantly reduce that difference. Secondly, he is obligated to pay the costs involved in working—transportation, additional clothing, lunches, etc.—which can be very considerable. Finally, and as a general rule, there should be more benefit, as there is more effort, in working than in not working. In fact it would be unfair if it were any other way.)

8. If the couple has no children who require support and the wife works (or is capable of working) but earns (or is capable of earning) no more than 25% of what the husband earns, she should receive 25% of the husband's gross income or 33⅓% of the husband's gross income less 50% of her own, whichever is greater. (Thus, if the wife earns or is capable of earning $6,000 and the husband's gross income is $30,000, she should receive maintenance of $7,500. However, if the wife earns or is capable of earning only $3,000, then instead of receiving maintenance of $7,500—which would leave her with a total

income of $10,500, she should receive maintenance of $8,500—33⅓% of the husband's gross income less 50% of her own—which would leave her with a total income of $11,500.) However, if the parties have been married for 25 years, and if the wife is at least 50 years of age, then she should receive 33⅓% of the husband's income less 25% of her own rather than less 50%.

9. If the couple has no children who require support and the wife earns (or is capable of earning) an amount greater than 25% but less than 50% of the husband's gross income, the wife should receive maintenance in an amount equal to 40% of the combined incomes of the parties less her own income. (Thus, if the wife earns $20,000 and the husband $70,000, the wife should receive maintenance of $16,000—40% of $90,000, or $36,000, less $20,000.) However, if the couple has either been married for 20 years or more and have had children, and the wife is 45 years of age or older, or, and regardless of whether or not they have had children, they have been married for 25 years or more and the wife is 50 years of age or older, the 40% should be increased to 42½%.

ALLOCATION OF SUPPORT PAYMENTS

In addition to determining the total payment that will be made, in this case by a husband to a wife for her support and that of their two children, it is also necessary to allocate that payment—to designate how much of the payment will be considered as maintenance for the wife and how much as support for the children. The reason for this is that there are very different tax consequences in the two payments from both the husband's and the wife's standpoint. Generally, a payment made by a husband to a wife for her support must be reported as income by the wife on her income tax return. Similarly, the husband may deduct the amount of that payment on his income tax return. In other words, the payment made by the husband to the wife is a pretax payment, which means that he makes the payment without having to pay tax on the income he used for that purpose. By the same token, the wife is required to report the payment for income tax purposes, and to pay tax on it. Payments made by the husband to the wife for the support of the children, on the other hand, are after-tax payments. That means that the wife is not required to report the payment as income on her tax return and the husband may not deduct it on his.[6]

As a general rule, the allocation should be weighted in favor of the maintenance payment.[7] The simple reason for this is that the very fact that the husband is making a payment to the wife for her support (rather than a payment simply for the support of the children) means that the wife earns less than the husband and is probably in a lower tax bracket.[8] This in turn means that there will be less dollars taxed on every dollar of the husband's income that is shifted from his return to hers. If, on the other hand, as is the case with payments allocated as child support, the husband must first pay the tax on his income before making the payment to the wife, he cannot afford to make as large a payment, and the amount that the wife will receive will therefore be less.

As a general rule, and if the parties have two children, the payment should be allocated 60% as maintenance for the wife and 40% as support for the children. Thus, if the husband is to pay $200 per week to the wife, $120 should be allocated as maintenance for the wife and $80 as support for the two children. This allocation assumes that the wife does not work (and does not have other taxable income) and that the husband alone is obligated for her support. If the wife works, and the $200 per week payment that the husband would otherwise make to her is reduced by reason of that fact, such reduction should be taken from the amount that would have been allocated as maintenance. Thus, in the above example, if the total payment that the husband is obligated to pay to the wife, both for her support and for the support of the children, is $150 per week rather than $200 per week, based upon the wife's income, then $70 of the amount should be allocated as maintenance for the wife and $80 for support of the two children.

If there are more or fewer children, the allocation will obviously have to be changed. It is suggested that with one child the payment be allocated two-thirds for the wife and one-third for the child and that with three children it be allocated 50% for the wife and 50% for the children. Regardless of the number of children, in no event should more than 60% of the payment be allocated as child support.

While, on the face of it, it would seem that a mediator will never be faced with an allocation problem where only child support is in issue, that is not always the case. Sometimes the wife will receive no support for herself, not because she earns an amount comparable to the husband, but simply because she earns an amount that, in relationship to his own earnings, does not quite justify a payment to her. While a mediator might think that this should simplify the problem in that the husband will now only have a child support obligation to pay, that may not necessarily be the case.

Why is that? Because the husband may be thinking of a support payment for the child at the same level as would have been the case had he been required to pay $200 per week to his wife, allocated $125 as maintenance or alimony and $75 as child support, were she not able to work and were he obligated for the support of both his wife and his child. If he is not obligated to contribute to his wife's support, he may feel that he should only be required to pay her the same $75 per week for the support of their child. To the wife, however, that support payment, standing alone, may appear very insufficient. She feels that the proper level of support should be $100 per week. Sometimes, it may be possible to bridge this gap by suggesting that the husband make the $100 payment but that $25 of that amount be allocated as alimony. To be sure, the wife will receive somewhat less than $100 in spendable dollars, but, and particularly if she is to continue to live in the home and to take the deductions for real estate taxes and mortgage interest payments, she may not end up with very much less. Similarly, and although the husband will have to pay more, he may be willing to accept the additional payment if it is structured in this manner.[9]

To be sure, and since it is denominated as alimony, the additional $25 will end upon the wife's remarriage, which would not have been the case had it been denominated as child support. Nevertheless, the husband may be willing to have the agreement provide that the child support payment will increase upon the wife's remarriage from $75 to $100, or perhaps to some number in between those two. Even if that is not the case, however, it may be of little practical consequence. The wife's problem is now, not when she remarries, and it may not even be so inappropriate for her to assume the burden of that additional $25 at that time, as the fact of her remarriage may permit her to use more of her own earnings for the support of her child than she is now able to.[10]

THE EFFECT OF THE DISTRIBUTION OF MARITAL PROPERTY UPON SUPPORT

Up to this point, no consideration has been given to what effect, if any, the property distributed to the wife at the time of the divorce (or her own separate property) will have upon the amount of maintenance that is to be paid to her by her husband.[11] It is now necessary to add this factor to the consideration.

As was previously noted, the modern view of marriage as being an economic as well as an emotional partnership has meant that all of the assets acquired in the course of the marriage will be distributed between the parties at the time of their divorce. In a certain sense, the distribution of a portion of the marital property to the wife represents payment to the wife for her contribution to the partnership over the years of the marriage. But if the wife is to receive assets having a value of $300,000 or $400,000 upon her divorce, isn't that sum of money, together with the support that the husband provided her during the course of their marriage, just and fair compensation for her contribution, in terms of past efforts, to that marriage? And if it is just and fair compensation, why does her husband owe her more? In other words, why should he be required to pay her ongoing support as well?

That, of course, is how the husband may view it. But there is also another side to the coin. Even if the property distributed to the wife is just compensation for her contribution to the marriage, the husband has also received compensation in kind, and perhaps even more, as in most instances he will also receive 50% or more of the marital assets. Thus, not only has he received as much compensation as the wife for his past efforts toward the marriage, but he has also been left with a very substantial income that the wife does not presently enjoy and, in all likelihood, will never earn.

On the face of it, the second argument would seem to have the greater force. The one exception to this would be the instance in which the wife's assets are liquid, e.g., the proceeds of the sale of the home, stocks and bonds, savings accounts, etc., while the assets that the husband is left with are represented by the value of his business, professional practice, etc.—assets that permit him to earn a living, but that do not throw off income aside from those earnings. If the husband and the wife are each to be left with assets that will be income-producing, and if, in addition to this, the husband will have a substantial income from employment that the wife does not enjoy, it would seem that the respective positions of the parties in relationship to one another are inequitable, and that the amount distributed to the wife as marital property should not normally affect her entitlement to support.

Be that as it may, as a practical matter, the value of the property distributed to the wife at the time of the couple's divorce does weigh heavily, not only as to whether or not the wife will receive support, but also as to the amount and duration of that support. There are two reasons for this. The first stems from the fact that the law has increasingly looked to maintenance as being rehabilitative. Thus, if the wife will be left with $400,000 in liquid assets, and if those assets, properly invested, will provide her with an income of $30,000 to $40,000 per year, the law will tend to view her income from investments as equivalent to income she would receive from employment and therefore to deem the wife rehabilitated.

The second reason is a bit more complicated. In the past, support was awarded to the wife not simply because of a disparity between her and her husband's incomes, but because her income was not sufficient to support her on a reasonable basis. However, if the wife will receive a very large distributive award, and if the income that she will derive from those assets, together with the income she receives from her own employment, will be reasonably sufficient to meet her needs, she may receive little, if any, support.

Thus, as an example, if the wife receives the proceeds of the home and other assets that have a combined value of $400,000, and earns $20,000 a year as a social worker, and her husband will retain assets, including his law practice and IRA accounts, that also have a value of $400,000, and will earn $80,000 or $90,000 a year as an attorney, a court will not necessarily, on that account, also direct him to provide her with support and, if they do so, the amount and duration of that support will be relatively small. The reason for this is that although the husband's earnings may be four or more times that of his wife, her own assets are nevertheless sufficient to support her on a reasonable basis.[12]

Even when the amount distributed to the wife, supplemented by her own earnings, will not be sufficient to provide for her support, it may still affect the amount of that support. While this would obviously not be the case if the couple's total assets are $60,000, which, if they were divided in half, will leave the wife with only $30,000, it will be the case if those assets are even $150,000, $75,000 of which will go to the wife. Again, the threshold question is whether or not the wife will be left with enough money reasonably to support herself: not the disparity in the respective incomes of the parties.

As a particular matter, the income the wife will derive from investing the monies that she will receive by way of equitable distribution should be viewed as additional income from employment. Thus, if the wife earns $10,000 and the husband $30,000, and if they can each be expected to derive $7,500 of income per year from the $75,000 of liquid marital property that will be left to each of them, the wife should be viewed as earning $17,500 and the husband $37,500, and the maintenance and child support to be paid by the husband to the wife based on the appropriate guidelines should then be predicated upon those figures.

In applying those guidelines, however, it is important to remember that when the wife's total earnings reach the point where she will be able to reasonably support herself on her own, then the fact that her husband's earnings are significantly more than hers becomes increasingly irrelevant, unless, perhaps, when they have been married a long time and his income is more than twice hers. Secondly, the potential earnings the wife could derive from the property distributed to her should not be considered where, for example, the monies in question represent the proceeds of the sale of the parties' marital residence and the wife intends to reinvest these monies in a new home for herself.

THE EFFECT OF SEPARATE PROPERTY UPON SUPPORT

The previous discussion concerned the effect that the distribution of marital property will have upon either of the parties' obligation to provide support to the other. The same principles apply with respect to each of the parties' *separate* property.[13] In other words, the fact that the wife will be left with $250,000 of inherited money rather than $250,000 of distributed marital property should not change the effect that this property will have upon either the *appropriateness* of an award of support or the *amount* of that award.

Wouldn't that be to penalize the wife, however? Let us assume that the husband earns $35,000 and that the parties have been married for 24 years. Let us further assume that the wife has not been employed outside the home in all of that time, but has instead devoted her efforts to raising a family and maintaining a home for her husband. Let us finally assume that the wife cannot be "rehabilitated" in any meaningful sense, and that although she can work, her earnings from her employment will never be sufficient, on their own, to support her in any meaningful way. Is it fair, simply because she had the good fortune to inherit this money from her parents, that she should not be compensated for the contribution she made to the marriage over these many years and, if there are not substantial marital assets to provide that compensation, that she should not receive that compensation in the form of support from her husband?

While the question may appear simple, the answer unfortunately is not. It will not do—and this is what makes the whole question of maintenance so complex—to attempt to answer these questions by taking sound legal principles and then playing them out to their logical conclusions. Ultimately, it is the result that counts, and not the logic or reasoning that got us to that result. If we start with certain fixed principles (our assumptions as to what is fair and appropriate) and apply them in a logical manner to the facts of the particular case, it is because we believe that doing this will guarantee that we will arrive at the correct conclusion. However, if we do not like the conclusion to which that logic and reason has led us, then we must reject it. Once again it is where we end up, and not how we got there, that counts.

While the law may in theory make sharp distinctions between separate property and marital property, these distinctions should not be taken too literally, for, if they are, the parties may be left in very inequitable positions. Take the following example. A husband and wife have been married for 30 years. Their children are all grown and they both work, earning approximately the same salaries. Their one substantial asset is the home they own, which has an equity of $150,000. How should the proceeds of the home be divided between them? Without question, there will be few who will feel that it should be divided other than equally. But suppose now that the husband also has $750,000 worth of stock that he recently inherited from his parents, and that the wife has no separate property of her own. Would it offend our sense of justice if the wife were to receive the entire equity in the home, or at least more than 50%? But if this were to happen, wouldn't the wife have indirectly shared in her husband's separate property?[14]

Let us consider another example. Again the couple have been married for 30 years and own a home with an equity of $150,000. In this case, however, the wife earns only $15,000 a year while her husband earns $75,000. Based upon the length of the marriage and the disparity in their respective incomes, one would expect that the husband would be required to provide support for his wife. Here, however, and instead of the husband having separate property that he has inherited, it is the wife who has come into an inheritance, this time of approximately $500,000, which is her separate property. Will the wife's separate property affect the husband's obligation to her for her support? Without question it will. But if the husband's obligation for the support of his wife has been reduced by reason of her separate property, has he not indirectly benefited from it? There is no question that he has. It makes no difference, nevertheless.

We cannot take our conceptualizations too literally. They are simply convenient devices that we employ because in most instances they lead to a result that is *generally* appropriate, given the attitudes that we hold about the responsibilities that husbands and wives owe one another by reason of their marriage. But they do not do this in every instance. Quite the contrary, and as we noted previously in the discussion of the distribution of the couple's assets, after 30 or 40 years of marriage the line between separate property and marital property can get a bit blurred, just as the distinction between the two can become somewhat irrelevant. Nor should that bother us. There is nothing sacrosanct about the notions of separate property and marital property, and if their strict application will leave the parties in inequitable positions relative to one another, there is no reason that they should be applied.

DURATION OF SUPPORT

Once the amount of support has been determined, it is next necessary to determine the duration of that support. Sometimes it is not possible to separate these two questions, however. While this is not generally true of support payments that will be made by one of the parties to the other for their children, when it comes to payments to be made, for example, by the husband to the wife for her own support, the amount of that support may be directly affected by its duration. In other words, while a husband may be willing to agree to pay his wife $100 a week for her support if that support will terminate in five years, he may, nevertheless, be unwilling to pay that same amount if it will continue for ten.

On the face of it, it would seem that the question of the duration of child support should not be a significant issue, since it is generally regulated by state law. Thus, for example, while the appropriate state statute may give the court a great deal of discretion in fixing the length of the wife's support, no such latitude is generally given with respect to child support. In other words, if the law of a particular state provides that a parent is obligated to support his or her child until that child attains age 21, then (and excepting only some intervening event such as the marriage of the child) all parents are obligated to support all children until that age.[15]

Notwithstanding this, the issue of the duration of child support may still come up in mediation in certain instances. The first will be occasioned by the fact that many people have a misconception as to their obligation in this regard. They know, for example, that a child becomes an adult under the law at eighteen for the purposes of voting, inheriting property, and marrying without their consent. Not uncommonly, however, they believe that this act of emancipation relieves them of the obligation to support that child as well. This is not necessarily the case.[16]

The second reason that the issue will arise is because, in making a general rule that applies to all parents, with respect to all children, the law provides a rule that, on occasion, is unrealistic in terms of a particular child. This most commonly occurs when the child pursues a college education, for while the law may provide that a child should be capable of supporting himself by the time that he is eighteen or twenty-one, and that a parent should therefore have no further obligation for his support beyond that date, as a practical reality that is not always the case. In order properly to prepare himself for future employment, the child has enrolled in college and will not graduate before he is twenty-one and a half or perhaps twenty-two and a half. To penalize a child who is responsibly engaged in the process of furthering his education in this manner, by cutting off his support at eighteen or twenty-one, simply because the law in the particular jurisdiction limits the parent's obligation to that age, makes no sense. In fact, one of the benefits of a negotiated agreement—and this is true whether the agreement is negotiated through mediation or in traditional divorce proceedings—is that it can more accurately reflect the realities of the particular situation, rather than having the duration of support be dependent upon an arbitrary, and in this case irrelevant, yardstick.

The obligation of the parent who is required to provide child support payments should thus always be elastic in nature. While it may end, as a matter of course, when the child becomes twenty-one, it should end earlier if some intervening event warrants it. This would occur, for example, if a child were to marry, were to graduate from high school and obtain full-time employment, were to enter the military service or were to live with the parent obligated to provide support rather than with the other parent. On the other hand, it should extend beyond the age of 21 if, for example, the child has not completed his college education by that date.

Occasionally, the parent obligated to make the support payments will be concerned that in agreeing to this he may find himself obligated to support the child until he is 35 years of age. While this is, in all likelihood, an exaggerated and unrealistic concern, it can easily be met by simply providing that the obligation to support the child will only continue past the age of 21 if the child is enrolled as a full-time college student on a normally continuous basis, and by further providing that, in any event, the obligation will terminate, for example, when the child attains the age of 23 years, regardless of whether or not he has completed his college education. (This does not mean that when the child becomes 23 that the father may not still be willing to provide support for the child, should he deem it appropriate, but only that he will not be contractually obligated to.)

The question of the duration of spousal support, usually the support paid by the husband to the wife, is a far more complicated matter. In the past, and consonant with the idea that marriages were intended to last forever, and that the obligations assumed in marriage were therefore permanent, a husband was obligated to support his wife indefinitely. In other words, barring his wife's remarriage, alimony payments continued until either the husband's or the wife's death.

The shift from traditional to companionate marriages,[17] the tremendous increase in the number of married women in the labor market,[18] as well as the rapid increase in the divorce rate which occurred in the early 1960s,[19] forced society to rethink the entire question of marriage. While no aspect of contemporary marriage has gone untouched, the principal attention has been given to the question of the disposition of the assets acquired by the parties during their marriage and the obligation for support that one of the parties (usually the husband) should have to the other following that marriage.

As has been noted previously, present day law generally treats marriage as a business partnership, with the assets acquired during the marriage (other than by gift or inheritance) representing partnership assets. Based upon this conceptualization, divorce is viewed as the dissolution of that business partnership and the occasion for the allocation and distribution of the partnership assets among the partners. Most importantly (and it is this that distinguishes the present law from the law that it replaced), *title* is no longer a factor in determining how that distribution is to be effectuated. It is the fact that the property was acquired during the marriage, rather than the manner in which title to the property was taken, that is alone deemed relevant.

In terms of spousal support, this rethinking has principally affected the question of the duration of that support. In undertaking this rethinking, however, the law has found itself on the horns of a dilemma. The realities of modern marriage simply do not justify requiring a husband, for example, to support his wife forever simply by reason of the historic fact of their past marriage. Nor can a wife be heard to complain that she has changed her position (given up gainful employment, devoted her efforts to providing a home and raising a family, etc.) by reason of that marriage as justification for permanent support. Thus, given the prevalence of divorce in our society, each party to a marriage today is charged with the knowledge that their marriage may end in divorce, and that they may be inconvenienced in the process, and in entering into a marriage they each assume that risk and cannot later be heard to complain.

On the other hand, however, there is the reality that the husband and the wife did not both necessarily change their positions in the same way, or to the same extent, as a result of their marriage, and that, at least from a financial standpoint, one may well be left at a distinct disadvantage vis-à-vis the other following their divorce. This most commonly occurs when the wife either gave up her employment or stopped her educational pursuit in order to have children and raise a family. Thus, while it may make sense to talk about assumptions of risk in marriage, one simply cannot ignore the fact that those *risks fall unevenly*, and therefore unfairly, and that more often than not the party who continues to pursue his career (usually the husband) has not been adversely affected by the fact of the marriage, and may actually have benefited by it, while the other party has not.

The dilemma posed by these competing principles has been resolved by viewing spousal support as being basically "rehabilitative" in nature. This also conforms with our present feeling that spousal support should not be punitive in nature, which is reflected in the fact that it is increasingly referred to as maintenance rather than as alimony. Accordingly, a wife is not entitled to support simply by virtue of the fact that she was married to her husband; she is entitled to support because she has been left at an *economic disadvantage relative to her husband by reason of her marriage*, and needs his support to enable her to reestablish herself in the working world.

The concept of rehabilitative maintenance is not without its problems, however. Foremost among these is the simple reality that in most instances the support payment that will be made by the husband to the wife is not and cannot be rehabilitative in any meaningful sense. For the wife to be given the advantage that her husband has, and that she has lost, would mean to give her the education or technical training, and the *experience* that goes with it, that he possesses and that she does not have. And if rehabilitative maintenance means anything, it should mean to provide the wife with the funds necessary for that purpose.

The maintenance payments that the husband makes to the wife do not provide this. All those payments do is provide her with support, and inadequate support at that, for a short period of time. Secondly, and just as importantly, it is simply not possible to make up to the wife the *time* that has been lost; and no payment to her by the husband can pretend to do that. Rehabilitative maintenance is thus not really rehabilitative at all, and it is mockery to suggest that the wife, with the benefit of that payment, will be left where she would have been had she not married. Rehabilitative maintenance, or more accurately, limited support, is simply the *compromise* that has been worked out between these two conflicting principles, not a solution to the problem.

Superimposed on these two principles, and the compromise that has been effectuated to accommodate them, is yet a third factor—the duration of the marriage. For while it may make no sense to impose a lifetime support obligation on a husband who has been married for only three years, to a woman who is now 24 years of age and requires no rehabilitation, it is equally inappropriate to suggest that a husband who has been married for 32 years, to a wife who is now 56 years of age, and who will never be rehabilitated in any sense of the word, should not have a permanent support obligation. These are the easy cases, however. The hard ones are all those in the middle.

Unfortunately, logic will not help here. Permanent support was not awarded to a wife in the past because of any necessary *logic*; it was awarded, at least initially, because a husband's support obligation was deemed to be a permanent one. Similarly, if permanent support is not awarded today to a 45 year-old who has been married for 25 years, again it is not because it would offend any necessary logic to do so. Rather, it is because the prevailing climate of opinion today is that a 45 year-old woman—even one who has been married for 25 years—is not entitled to support from her husband for the rest of her life simply because she was married to him. In short, there is no right or wrong here. It is simply a question of what people, at any given time, *expect*, and are therefore willing to accept.

Sometimes, when there are children, their presence will provide the needed yardstick. By definition, and if the children's primary residence will be with the wife, it will be necessary for her to maintain a home for them at least until the youngest child graduates from high school. Regardless of the philosophical merits of all the competing arguments, the fact remains that she will need funds sufficient for that purpose until that event occurs. In many instances, that reality can be used to define the duration of the wife's support as well. [20]

There is often another consideration that makes this occurrence an appropriate occasion to terminate the wife's support, and that is that the parties' home will usually be sold when this event occurs. This, in turn, means that the wife will now have her share of the equity in the home available for her use. In many instances, the income she will be able to derive from the proceeds may closely approximate, and perhaps even exceed, the support payment that she will lose at that time.

Again, there is no definitive formula that can be used to aid a mediator in determining the appropriate period of support. Nevertheless, it might be helpful to consider, at least as a starting point, the following considerations.

1. If the parties have been married for less than eight years and do not have children, then, and barring special circumstances, support for any period, in any amount, is not warranted. This is true even if the disparity in their respective incomes would, of itself, justify a support payment.

2. If the parties have been married for more than eight years but for less than fifteen years and do not have children, and if a support payment is warranted—if the disparity in the parties' incomes is such that a payment from one to the other is justified—the support payment should be for between one and three years.

3. If the parties have been married more than 15 years but for less than 20 years and do not have children, and if a support payment is warranted, the support payment should be for between three and four years. However, if the party with the smaller income is 45 years of age or older, the payment should be for a period of four to five years.

4. If the parties have been married for more than 20 years but for less than 25 years and do not have children, and if a support payment is warranted, the support payment should be for between four and five years. However, if the party with the smaller income is 50 years of age or older, the payment should be for a period equal to between one-quarter to one-third the duration of the marriage.

5. If the parties have been married for 25 years or more and do not have children, and if a support payment is warranted, the payments should be for a period of between five and six years. However, if the party with the smaller income is 50 years of age or older, the

payment should be for a period equal to between one-third and one-half the duration of the marriage.

6. If the parties have children but have been married for less than five years, and if a support payment is warranted, the payment should continue until the youngest child enters school on a full-time basis. If they have been married for between five and ten years, it should continue for one to three years, or until the youngest child enters school on a full-time basis, whichever is longer. If they have been married for between ten and 20 years, it should continue for three to five years, or until the youngest child enters school on a full-time basis, whichever is longer, except that if the wife is 40 years of age or older, the payment should continue for a period equal to between one-quarter and one-third the duration of the marriage.

7. If the parties have children and have been married for more than 20 years but less than 25 years, and if a support payment is warranted, the payments should continue for five to seven years. However, if the party receiving the payment is 45 years of age or older, the payment should continue for a period equal to between one-third and one-half the length of the marriage.

8. If the parties have children and have been married for more than 25 years, and if a support payment is warranted, the payments should continue for a period equal to one-half the duration of the marriage. However, if the party receiving the payment is 50 years of age or older, the payment should not be limited other than by the remarriage of the party receiving the payment, or the death of either party.

To a certain extent, and this is particularly true of short marriages, the object is to attempt to *restore* each of the parties, as closely as is possible, to their *condition* when they married; not to bridge the distance between them after their divorce. Suppose, for example, that when the parties married five years ago the wife was earning $15,000 and her husband $25,000. Suppose that at the present time she is earning $20,000 and he is earning $45,000. Is that not where each of them would have been had they not married?

In other words, is the disparity in their present incomes *a function of their marriage* (the wife did not give up her job or stay home to raise children) or simply *a function of the fact that they were different people,* possessed of different skills and abilities, when they married, as they now are when they are divorcing? And is there anything in their marriage that should cause their divorce agreement to be the occasion to correct that disparity? The answer is no. Even if we were to assume that they were of equal ability, and the husband's preferential status stems from the fact that society rewards men, in terms of higher pay, more than it does women, is their divorce an appropriate occasion to attempt to correct this injustice? Again the answer is no. The purpose of their divorce is to attempt to correct the *imbalances born of their marriage, not to correct all of the ills of society.*

LIVING WITH ANOTHER MAN

Tied to the question of the duration of the husband's obligation for the support of the wife is the question of whether or not that obligation should be affected by the fact that the wife subsequently lives with another man. The husband agrees that he has an obligation to support his wife, and even agrees that that obligation should continue, during his life, until she remarries. Nevertheless, he insists that his obligation should terminate if she lives with another man. In a different form, this is the same question that was raised in the discussion dealing with the parties' marital residence, in considering what effect the wife's living with another man would have upon her right to continue to occupy the marital residence. However, while the concern then was with the wife's living with another man in the marital residence, here the concern is not limited to where that relationship is maintained.

The difficulty here is in attempting to apply practical considerations to what is basically an emotional issue. From the husband's standpoint, the objection is raised as if his very masculinity is called into question by the suggestion that he should still have to support his wife when she is living with her boyfriend; and quite commonly his feelings in this regard are in no way diminished by the fact that it was he who initiated the divorce and left her. They may not even be diminished by the fact that he, himself, is now living with another woman. He simply does not see why that responsibility should be his rather than her new boyfriend's.

From the wife's standpoint, however, the issue is a more practical one. To be sure, she may view her husband's objection as simply an attempt on his part to continue to control her life, and that may exasperate her. But she is far more concerned with the practical limitations that the husband's insistence will place upon her ability to build a new life for herself, and with the consequences of the penalty being exacted by her husband based upon her future conduct.

In dealing with this issue—and without suggesting that these stratagems will necessarily be sufficient to cut through the emotional resistance that he will meet—it will be helpful for the mediator to keep in mind the considerations implicit in a provision for the support of the wife and in the limitations placed upon its duration. Support is provided not out of principle, and most courts today are long past the point of viewing such support as a penalty, based upon the misconduct of the husband, or a reward, based upon the innocence of the wife. Rather, it is born of the reality that in most instances society, and the responsibilities placed on each of the parties in their marriage, has left the husband in a far better position as a wage earner than it has the wife. Nor does the fact that the wife may subsequently live with another man change this.

The question, therefore, is what should be the nature of that obligation, and how long should it continue? As the law (somewhat arbitrarily) imposed that obligation at the time of the parties' marriage, it also (and again somewhat arbitrarily) terminates it with the wife's remarriage. In between those events, however, and barring the husband's own death, it has traditionally recognized but one event that would end a husband's obligation for his wife's support, and that was where the wife lived with another man and, sometimes, held herself out as his wife.[21] This provision of the law only applied to the court's own decree, however. It had no application to private agreements—separation and property settlement agreements—that the parties voluntarily entered into, unless those agreements specifically incorporated such a limitation. It is just such a limitation that the husband is now suggesting.

In principle, a husband is obligated to provide for his wife's future support because of the contribution that she made in the past toward their joint lives. (The disparity in their circumstances may be what triggers the obligation, but it is the wife's *past* efforts that serve as its basis.) This is the same rationale that justifies the wife's sharing in a portion of the assets in the husband's name accumulated during their marriage. If that is the case, however, why should her entitlement be dependent upon her *future* conduct? Certainly no one would suggest that she should lose her share of the marital assets that were distributed to her on her divorce should she later live with another man. Nevertheless, cohabitation has increasingly come to be accepted as an event limiting the husband's obligation for spousal support in agreements negotiated between husbands and wives. The one exception to this is in marriages of very long duration, where the wife is in her mid-fifties or older. In this situation, husbands generally do not feel as comfortable, at least at the present time, in suggesting this limitation.

Unfortunately, the concept is even more difficult to define than it is for women to accept, and even the most experienced matrimonial lawyers have been unable to arrive at an acceptable definition. Certainly, it is implicit in the fact of the parties' separation that they will each attempt to build new lives for themselves, which includes developing intimate relationships with others.

Moreover, given the present mores of our society, and the age and position of the parties, it cannot be suggested that it was not contemplated, or that there is anything improper in the fact, that the wife may spend the night at the home of her new boyfriend or even vacation with him. Nor can it be maintained that her right to support should be forfeited in that event. Nevertheless, even granting that, if the wife should thereafter live with a man for a continuous period of six years, and on the same basis that they would live together if they were husband and wife, why is that fact not as relevant in terms of judging the husband's continuing obligation to her for support as would be the fact of her remarriage?

Again, these are the easy cases. It is the ones in the middle that are more difficult. The wife's new boyfriend pays for none of the wife's living expenses and in fact maintains his own apartment. However, they spend one or two nights, and almost every weekend, together (either at her home or at his apartment) and have taken numerous short trips and an occasional vacation together. Are the wife and her new boyfriend living together, and is their relationship such that the husband's obligation for her support should terminate? There is no answer.

Occasionally lawyers attempt to solve the problem by giving the term "living to-gether" a precise definition. For example, they may provide that they are living together if the wife and her new boyfriend share a home together for a period of two continuous months. But what if her boyfriend moves out for a week, or even a day, during this two-month period? And, as was noted in another context, how does the husband sustain his burden of proof to establish the fact of the boyfriend's continued presence short of hiring a round-the-clock detective to maintain a surveillance of his wife?

Needless to say, the question of whether or not the wife's support will terminate if she lives with another man is a most difficult one. If possible it should be avoided. At times, however, it cannot be, because of the husband's insistence. In those instances a mediator will simply have to do the best that he can. At a minimum, perhaps he can get them to agree that should there ever be litigation over this issue in the future, that neither of them will call the children as witnesses, or introduce into evidence any writing of theirs.

ESCALATION

Not uncommonly, the wife may request that the agreement contain provision for an escalation in the support payments, either for herself or for the parties' infant children, based upon one of two considerations. Firstly, it may be based simply on the fact of the ever-increasing cost of living, as without such a provision the wife may feel that the dollar payment that the husband is required to make will be an ever-diminishing one. Secondly, the custodial parent has only accepted the support payment provided for in the agreement based upon the husband's present income; and if that income had been greater than it is, she would have expected a greater amount. Particularly if the parties have been married for but a short time, the children are still young, and it is legitimate to expect that the husband's income will increase substantially in the near future, it is understandable that the wife will want to share in that increase, or look to it to ease the financial burdens she will be assuming, just as would have been the case had they remained married.

The question of an escalation clause in a separation agreement can be one of the most difficult ones that a mediator will have to handle; and even in private practice attorneys attempt to skirt the issue whenever possible. Husbands' attorneys do not raise the question (and hope that it will not be raised) for obvious reasons. No matter how responsible a husband may be, and no matter how willing he is to do the right thing by his family, he cannot help but view his continuing obligation to his first family as somewhat of a lien upon his life. For most men, their divorce means that with one swift stroke they will be reduced to a standard of living no better, and probably worse, than that which they and their wife enjoyed when they first started their life together. Little wonder then, even if they are willing to make responsible provisions for their family, that they wish to preserve the possibility of reclaiming the life that they are losing. From their point of view, this is only possible by a future improvement in their circumstances. It is not hard to understand, therefore, their reluctance to share any portion of that improvement with their present wife.

The wife's attorney is almost as reluctant to raise the question of an escalation clause, as much as he would obviously like to see it in the agreement. If he suggests it to the wife, or even if he simply encourages her own suggestion to that effect, it may be impossible for him later to persuade her to accept an agreement *without* such a provision. And yet, to insist upon such a provision may well be to jeopardize the possibility of any agreement between the parties at all.

In the past, attorneys have ultimately fallen back upon the reality that a husband is generally not obligated to make provision for his wife and children other than based upon his *present* circumstances, that a court does not generally have the power to write in such an escalation clause before the event,[22] and that courts are not generally sympathetic to later applications to increase the level of the payments based upon a change in the cost of living alone.[23] Moreover, even when the application is predicated upon a change in the husband's financial circumstances, it is usually necessary to show that the change in his circumstances has been substantial.[24]

There are other good reasons for the exclusion of an escalation clause in the agreement. An agreement cannot pretend to effect anything other than a kind of "rough justice" between the parties. As a practical matter, the husband and the wife will not continue to be partners in each other's good fortune or misfortune. Henceforth, *each is on his own* and will have to make do with what he or she has been given. More importantly, and at least to the extent realistically possible, they should be made to do this, rather than encouraged, in the name of what is "fair" or "right," continually to look back at one another.

As justified as they may often be, the fact remains, nevertheless, that escalation clauses tend to leave each of the parties with a spoon in the other's pot, and afford each of them an opportunity to gauge just how well the other party is doing in relationship to themselves. To the extent that mediation hopes to help couples effectuate a *psychological* divorce, as well as a *legal* divorce, this is not helpful. Rather, they should be encouraged to *look to themselves*, rather than continually to look back at one another to make these comparisons.

Having said that, it must be acknowledged, nevertheless, that "rough justice" can at times be *injustice*. This is particularly true if the husband's income substantially increases following the parties' separation and the wife and children are still left with the same dollars that they had before, diminished in purchasing power by ever-increasing inflation. There can thus be no hard-and-fast rules here. Rather, the problem will have to be dealt with on a case-by-case basis, and in each instance there will have to be a delicate balancing of the equities.

Even if it is agreed to include an escalation clause in the agreement, a question still remains. On what will that escalation clause be based? While it is common to think in terms of an increase in the Consumer Price Index (CPI), an escalation clause based upon the CPI may be unrealistic if the husband's income does not increase at the same rate. One way to deal with this problem is to provide that the percentage increase will not exceed the increase in the husband's income. Thus, if the increase in the CPI is 8% in the year in question, but the increase in the husband's income is only 5%, the increase in the support payments will likewise be limited to 5%. The problem here, however, is that if in the following year the CPI increases by 5% and the husband's income by 8%, the support payments will again only increase by 5%. Thus, while this formula protects the husband if the increase in his income does not keep pace with the increase in the CPI, it does not protect the wife by making it up to her when the increase in his income exceeds the increase in the CPI. This, of course, can be corrected by a provision that makes the increases based upon the CPI cumulative, provided, again, that the cumulative amount does not exceed the cumulative increase in the husband's income.

Let us assume, for the sake of argument, that the husband has a job that provides for an increase in his salary exactly commensurate with the increase in the CPI. If that is the case, wouldn't it then be appropriate to use the CPI as a yardstick as to his future support obligation? The husband may not think so. He may argue that even if his salary increases at a rate equal to the CPI, it may still be unfair to him if his increase is in pretax dollars but he is obligated to pay an increase, commensurate with the CPI, in after-tax dollars. After all, to keep pace with an inflation rate of 10% per year, the salary of a husband in a 28% tax bracket would have to increase at the rate of almost 14% per year if the payment in question is a nondeductible child support payment.

Thus, he may insist that the increase in the support payments be a percentage of the increase in the CPI. Accordingly, if the husband is in a 28% tax bracket, and if the payments in question are child support payments, he may suggest that the agreement provide that those support payments will increase at a rate equal to 71.4% (10/14) of the increase in the CPI so as to factor into the support payments the fact that the husband will first have to pay taxes on the increased income that he receives. From the wife's standpoint, however, she has not been given the protection she expected. The CPI, after all, which is based upon the costs of goods and services, is geared to spendable dollars. If the wife only receives 71.4% of the increase in the CPI, she will then be left with less dollars in the future than she has now. Further, she could argue, with considerable merit, that the present child support payments have already been discounted for taxes, and that to give her only a percentage of the increase in the CPI, as the husband suggests, would be to discount them twice.

While it might seem that the answer to the problem is instead to relate the increase in the support payments to the increase in the husband's income, this too is not without its problems. To begin with, and even if the husband is willing to agree to an escalation clause, he usually does not want his former wife to be his future partner, and he is at best only willing to maintain her position, in terms of the CPI, not improve it in terms of his own future efforts and good fortune. A mediator might try to meet the husband's objection by suggesting that the increase be based upon his increased earnings, but limited to the increase in the CPI. In this case, if the husband's income increases by 12% but the CPI only by 8%, the wife's increase will be limited to 8%. However, the mediator is again left with the problem of how to deal, over a number of years, with the situation where the increase in the husband's income in some years exceeds the increase in the CPI, but in other years does not keep pace with it. While there are, admittedly, ways to deal with this problem, they create complex accounting procedures for the parties. While this may be necessary to do justice to the equities between them, it is nevertheless inconsistent with the equally important purpose of effectuating as much of a closure to their relationship as is possible under the circumstances. The answer to this problem must be carefully to balance these considerations in each instance.

One further problem must be mentioned. By definition, it is in just those instances when it is most common to think in terms of escalation clauses (for example, where the husband is affluent or is likely to be in the future) that the husband's income is most often difficult to ascertain and subject to the most concealment. Although the husband is dealing with the wife in an open, honest manner now, it cannot be assumed that he will be quite as forthright in the future. In fact, the very presence of an escalation clause, which penalizes him for what he views as his future individual efforts, acts as a deterrent to this.

Further, by basing the increase upon the husband's income, rather than upon objective figures published by the Department of Labor (the CPI), the husband is once again obligated to lay bare his future income tax returns, including not only his own income but perhaps even the income of his future wife, who will of course join with him in filing income tax returns. The husband does not want to have to share this information with his former wife, however, and with good reason. By divorcing his wife, he wants to get her and keep her out of his business, not perpetuate her involvement in it, as such continued involvement can only tend to create future conflict between them. If the wife finds that his income did not increase as much as she expected, she may become suspicious that he is hiding his true income from her. On the other hand, if she finds more than she expected (particularly about his new wife), she may become resentful of his good fortune in relationship to her own. Either way, they are still in each other's pots, and it is bound to create dissension, or at least perpetuate it, which is just as bad.

DEESCALATION

Deescalation does not generally refer to a decrease in the support payments based upon a decrease in the husband's income. Although theoretically a serious question, as a practical matter separation agreements generally do not contain provision for a decrease in support payments based upon a change in the husband's circumstances, though there is, of course, no reason that they cannot. (If his circumstances do, in fact, change for the worse, for all practical purposes the wife will be powerless to enforce his contractual obligation unless he has substantial assets to which she can look. Moreover, if their agreement is incorporated into their judgment of divorce, many courts have the power to modify their agreement, and therefore the husband's obligation, in such an event.[25]) Rather, it generally refers to a decrease in the support payments based upon an increase in the wife's own income.

The most common occasion for providing for a deescalation in the support payments is where the wife does not presently work, where the agreement is concluded on the assumption that the wife will not derive income from employment, and where the present provision for support would be unfair to the husband if she did. The other occasion is when, though it is anticipated that the wife will or *may* work in the future, it is impossible to predict with any degree of accuracy just how much she will earn or when she will earn it. The way to deal with these situations is simply to provide for a reduction in the support payments should the wife obtain future employment. However, the reduction should not be a dollar-for-dollar reduction. In other words, the wife's support should not be reduced by an amount equal to her earned income.

First of all, the reduction should reflect the fact that it costs the wife something to work (gasoline and car maintenance, baby-sitters, additional clothing, lunches away from home, and so on). Secondly, the wife will be required to pay income taxes on the money that she earns from employment, and although she will in all likelihood also be required to pay income taxes on the support payments that she received from the husband for herself, the deductions taken by her employer from her salary, which will also include withholdings for FICA and perhaps certain other involuntary deductions, will be larger than the bite that will be taken from her support payments. Finally, the wife should derive some *benefit* from working—which would not be the case if its *only* effect was to reduce the husband's obligation to her.

One method of handling this situation is to provide for a percentage reduction to the extent that the wife's income from employment exceeds a certain figure per year. If this method is employed, it should always be based upon her yearly income, and not simply upon her income over a shorter period of time. The reason for this is that though the wife's employment at a salary of $400 per week might well trigger a reduction in her support payments, if it turns out that she was only employed for four weeks during the year, that would probably not be the case.

If this method is employed, the agreement can provide, for example, that there will be a one-dollar reduction in the support payments for every two dollars of income that the wife earns in excess of $5,000 in any year. In that event, if the wife earns $10,000, her maintenance would be reduced by $2,500. In each instance the floor (the amount that the wife can earn without its affecting her support payments) should be determined based upon the husband's income. If the husband earns only $20,000, a floor of $7,000 may be too high. On the other hand, if he earns $75,000, it may be too low. As a rule of thumb, it is suggested that the floor should be equal to between 15 and 20% of the husband's present income.

Why is the floor based upon the husband's income rather than being a fixed amount (for example, $5,000) in each case? In fairness, this is a judgment call, and legitimate arguments can be mounted on both sides of the case. Our preference for a floor based upon a percentage of the husband's present income is predicated upon our view of the equities. The available dollars are not being apportioned between the parties as they are because that is necessarily *fair*. They are being apportioned as they are because it is *necessary*. That being the case, and while both of the parties need relief, the wife needs it *more*, particularly if there are children whose primary residence will be with her.

While, in one sense, a husband who earns $75,000 a year is in the same boat as a husband who only earns $20,000 a year, in the sense that he will pay to his wife the same percent of his spendable dollars, he is still better off in terms of absolute dollars. Thus, he can probably afford to postpone the relief that will come from a decrease in his support payments, based upon an increase in his wife's income, than can a husband who earns substantially less than he. She, by the same token, will need more of these additional dollars, particularly where there are children, to bridge the gap between their respective financial circumstances. This is particularly true if the husband's financial circumstances (income) are likely to improve in time.

If a mediator were to employ a fixed floor (for example, $5,000 a year), it is perhaps most appropriate in those situations where the agreement contains an escalation clause based upon the husband's future income. Here, the wife will receive additional support apart from her own efforts. That being the case, it is more appropriate that a greater portion of her increased income be shared with her husband, just as he will share his increased income with her. On the other hand, if he will be able to retain his increased earnings for himself—if the agreement does not contain an escalation clause—there is less occasion for the wife to share her increased income with him. This is not to say, however, that it is inappropriate to include provision for a decrease in the husband's payments, based upon the wife's future earnings, simply because the agreement does not contain an escalation clause, based upon his future earnings. (After all, it must be remembered that the primary consideration for a deescalation clause based upon the wife's future income is the fact that the present payment that the husband is making is specifically predicated upon the fact that the wife does not work or, if she does, that her income is only what it presently is.)

It is simply to say that the equities in each case will have to be viewed separately. Thus, it if is anticipated that there will be a substantial increase in the husband's income, and the agreement contains no provision for an escalation in the support payments, that fact may cancel out the appropriateness of a deescalation based on the wife's future earnings. (After all, the wife only accepted the support payments that she did based on her husband's present income, and because of her own earning potential.)

In discussing a deescalation clause based upon the wife's future income, it is important that the wife understand that she is not giving back to the husband as much as it may at first appear she is. Let us assume, for example, that a wife is to receive $20,000 per year in support from her husband and that their agreement provides that those support payments will be reduced by one dollar for every two that she earns in excess of $10,000. If the wife were to earn $30,000, there would thus be a $10,000 reduction in the support payments. This does not mean that the wife has suffered a loss of $10,000, however. Since her taxable income is $40,000, and since she has been pushed into a higher tax bracket on that account, if she had received the additional $10,000 in support from her husband, she would have been required to pay a very substantial portion of it in federal, state, and even local income taxes.

Thus, it may well be that her real loss was only $7,000. For the same reason, he is not now $10,000 richer. Quite the contrary, the very fact that he is making a payment to her at all means that he is in a higher income tax bracket, and he will therefore have to pay an even larger share of the $10,000 in income taxes. Accordingly, his actual income may only have increased by $6,500.

Should the reduction necessarily apply only to alimony? While, at first blush, it might seem that it should, the answer is nevertheless no. The husband is only paying the amount of child support that he is because the wife has little or no income of her own. However, if her income increases, and particularly if it becomes substantial in relation to his own, there is no reason that she should not shoulder at least a portion of that obligation too, just as she would have had she earned that amount at the time of their agreement.

As a practical matter, the mediator will not often be confronted with this situation. The issue will usually arise where the wife does not presently work, or works and earns very little, not where she has been employed at a substantial period of time. (If she is presently employed at a substantial salary, this will be factored in to determine the husband's present obligation and not, in the form of a deescalation clause, to determine his future one.) And it is in just those situations, where the wife did not pursue her education or vocational training further, or where she has been out of the labor market for some period of time, that she is least likely to earn a substantial income when she does return to work.

Suspension of Payments

Occasionally the question arises as to whether or not the child support payments should be suspended during the period of time that the children are with the husband. In general, the answer to this question should be no. Quite obviously, if the children, or any of them, should later come to *live* with the husband rather than with the wife, it is only appropriate that there be a suspension, or at least a sharp reduction, in the child support payments, as the husband is now directly responsible for their support and maintenance. (The couple's separation agreement will accomplish this by providing that a child will be deemed emancipated for the purposes of a husband's obligation for support if the child no longer permanently resides with the wife.) Nevertheless, it is best to discourage the suggestion that there should be a suspension of these payments during the husband's visitation with the children, even if that visitation extends over a period of a number of weeks during the children's summer recess from school.

To begin with, and although the agreement provides for weekly or monthly payments, if the husband is paying his former wife $100 per week for the support of their child, in a real sense it has been agreed that his contribution toward the support of that child will be $5,200 per year, taking into consideration the wife's total expenses for the child over the course of the year, as well as the fact that the child will be with the husband for certain periods of time. All that the agreement has really done has been to permit the husband to make the payment of $5,200 at the rate of $100 per week. If there is a suspension in those payments during the time that the child is with the husband, however, then the wife will not receive the full $5,200 that it has been determined she should get from him for the child's support.

Secondly, and although the husband's expenses will be somewhat increased when the child is visiting with him, that is not to say that the wife's expenses will be substantially reduced by reason of this fact. On the contrary, and with the exception of the child's food, and possibly his entertainment, her expenses will not be diminished at all. If there need be further reason, it can be found in the fact that in no instance does the husband ever pay to his wife the full cost of supporting their children, and that whatever the disparity in their respective circumstances, and no matter how generous the payment, it is *always* inadequate.

Reduction in Child Support

Court-ordered awards of child support generally direct the payment of a stated number of dollars for each of the children. This means that when a child is no longer entitled to support, the total payment is reduced by that amount. Thus, if the court directs a husband to pay $50 per week for each of his three children, for a total of $150 per week, when the husband is no longer obligated to support one of the children, the payments will automatically be reduced to $100 per week.

Unfortunately, the attitudes of each of the parties will all too often mirror what courts do or do not do, as if there were necessarily something right or appropriate in their determinations. Thus, the private agreements of separating husbands and wives tend to mirror this thinking. Nevertheless, and if at all possible, the mediator should attempt to discourage this kind of reduction. Why is this? For the simple reason that it does not do justice to the situation.

If, for example, the wife is to receive $200 per week for the support of the parties' two children, that portion of her expenses attributable to the children are not cut in half by reason of the fact that one child has now become 21 and has left her home. This, and the fact that the husband's ability to support the remaining child has increased by virtue of the fact that he is no longer obligated to support the older child, render such a reduction inappropriate. Accordingly, a 35 percent or 40 percent reduction, rather than a 50 percent reduction, would be more appropriate.

A similar question arises with respect to the wife's remarriage. The husband has agreed to pay the wife $200 a week for herself and the two children, and the payment has been allocated $120 as maintenance and $40 as support for each of the children. It does not follow, however, that upon her remarriage the husband's obligation should only be $80 per week for the support of the two children. To begin with, the wife's remarriage, and the fact that the husband is no longer obligated for her support, improves his financial situation and enables him to make a greater contribution toward the support of their children, which was never fully assumed by his payment of $40 per week in the first place. Just as importantly, the allocation of the $200 as being $120 in maintenance for the wife and $80 in support for the children was, by and large, simply a tax allocation.

In other words, 60% of the total award was allocated to the wife for the reason that the husband could not afford to pay her more after-tax dollars, and because he wished to shift some of the tax burden to the wife, who was in a much lower tax bracket. To suggest now that the allocation of $120 and $80 actually represented a determination as to the respective costs in supporting the wife and the children would therefore be inaccurate. Thus, and in this case, it would be appropriate to increase the support payment from $80 a week to perhaps $100 per week upon the wife's remarriage.

Suppose that the wife is working and earns an amount that does not justify a payment by the husband for her support and that the payment he makes to her is therefore simply for the support of their children. Should her marriage result in an increase in the husband's support obligation? Obviously not. Since the husband is not obligated to the wife for her support, there has been no change in the husband's financial circumstances by reason of her remarriage. Should it result in a *decrease* in the husband's support obligation? An argument could be made that it should, for whereas the wife was totally dependent upon her earnings for her own support in the past, she is now being partially supported by her new husband, or at least sharing her living expenses with him. If that is the case, she is now in a position to use a portion of her income to pay for the children's living expenses, and to share that cost with the husband, whereas she previously was not.

While there is obvious merit in this argument, it is nevertheless recommended that the wife's remarriage should not be used as an occasion to reassess the husband's obligation for child support. Here again the decision is made based upon a balancing of the equities. On the one hand, the mediator wants the couple's agreement, and their respective obligations to provide for the support of the children, to reflect their ability in terms of each of their financial circumstances. On the other hand, and again relying upon the principle of rough justice, he does not want to create a situation that brings with it more problems than it solves.

There are all kinds of life changes that could affect each of the parties' ability to provide for the support of their children, the husband's remarriage, in addition to the wife's remarriage, being but one of them. However, it is not possible to know in advance whether those events will actually *improve* their ability, and if so, to what extent, and it is of course possible that either of these events could render the parties *less* capable, rather than more capable, of contributing to the support of the children. (Suppose, for example, that the wife's remarriage results in her having a second child, and having to give up her previous employment.)

For obvious reasons, it is not recommended that the parties' agreement provide that their respective support obligations be reevaluated every time one of those myriad events occurs. Except in rare instances, the gain, in terms of exactitude, that will be effectuated by these adjustments will not justify the cost, in terms of the renewed ill will between the parties, that will in all likelihood have to be paid. The fact that the couple has attempted to conclude an agreement that is fair and appropriate at the present time does not mean that their agreement fails because it is not similarly fair and appropriate at every point in the future. In this regard, the mediator must always remember that the desire to leave the parties with an agreement that is fair must always be balanced against another objective— that of leaving them with an agreement that will tend to cause them to *look forward rather than back*. It is thus recommended that neither the husband's remarriage nor the wife's remarriage be viewed as an event causing an adjustment in the child support payments.

Stepchildren

As a general rule, the question of support for stepchildren is not generally an issue in a couple's separation or divorce. There are two reasons for this. The first is that though a stepparent may be obligated for the support of a stepchild during the marriage, he is not generally obligated for the support of that stepchild once the marriage ends.[26] Secondly, and particularly in marriages of short duration, the stepparent may not have an independent relationship with the stepchild, apart from his marriage to the stepchild's parent, and whatever relationship he has may well end in their divorce.

It is more than likely that these considerations and conditions may change in the future. To begin with, courts are increasingly imposing upon stepparents the obligation to provide for the support of their stepchildren following their divorce—particularly where the stepchild in question does not receive support from his other natural parent and the stepparent was aware of this fact when he married his present wife (or husband).[27]

Secondly, as the rate of divorce has increased, and the number of second marriages with it, and particularly where those second marriages have produced additional children, there is the likelihood of a far deeper relationship between the stepparent and the stepchild, who is now also the half brother or half sister of the stepparent's own children. Given this fact, it can be expected that this question may loom larger in the future than it has in the past, particularly in those situations where there is little if any contact between the stepchild and the natural parent with whom he does not live, and particularly where he has not and will not receive support from that parent.[28]

A word of caution is in order. We have mentioned the slow but noticeable change in attitude of the law toward the obligation of a stepparent toward his stepchildren following his divorce from the stepchild's natural parent. It must be kept in mind, however, that regardless of whether or not the stepparent has a legal obligation (as distinct from a moral obligation) to provide support for his stepchildren following his divorce under the law of the particular jurisdiction in question, once the stepparent has *agreed* to provide support for his stepchild following his divorce, and his obligation is incorporated into the parties' agreement, he now *has* such a legal obligation.[29] The fact that he may or may not have had such an obligation under the law of the jurisdiction in question will now be irrelevant. His obligation in that respect will be no different than any other obligation he has under the agreement, and he should understand this.

Joint Custody

The discussion of child support up to this point has assumed that the primary residence of the children will be with one rather than both of the parents. Suppose, however, that the couple's agreement provides for physical joint custody—for the children to live approximately half of the time with the wife and approximately half of the time with the husband. How should the question of child support be handled in this situation?

As a practical matter, the mediator will rarely come across this arrangement except where both of the parents work and earn relatively substantial incomes. In fact, if there is an increase in physical joint custody in the future, it will be occasioned more by this fact than by any of the philosophical arguments that have been advanced up until this point in its favor. Both of the parents want to work, and need to work, and neither one of them would be capable of assuming the full responsibility for both the care of their children and their obligations to work at the same time. In fact, the only way that they can meet the demands of their work is to share the responsibility for the care of their children.

The problem here is that both of the parents are going to be required to maintain complete, intact homes for their children. It might have been possible for the husband to have gotten by with a one-bedroom, or perhaps even an efficiency apartment, were the children only to have been staying overnight with him once a week. It is not possible for him to do this, however, if they are going to be living with him on a permanent basis. In fact, physical joint custody will not work if the accommodations in one party's home is so much less comfortable that the children will resist being there, and prefer instead to live in the home of the other party.

In short, one of the conditions that permitted the husband to be able to afford to make a payment to the wife for the support of their children, namely, the fact that he purposely kept his expenses for housing to a minimum, will no longer pertain. In addition, he will now be obligated to provide for the support of the children on a direct basis to a far greater extent than he would had they visited with him but once or twice a week.

Given these factors, and unless there is a very substantial difference in the respective financial circumstances of the parties, there will generally not be a payment by one of the parties to the other for the support of the children, and each will assume the obligation of providing for their support from their own respective incomes while they are with them. However, there is still an issue of child support that must be addressed. It is one thing for the husband and the wife to say that they will each pay for their own household expenses, and for the children while they are with them. But what about those expenses that are not specifically related to their individual households?

How, for example, will they handle the payment of the children's clothing, private school tuition, after school activities, household help, summer activities, etc.? The parties' agreement must specifically answer this question. In fact, it is a far more significant question when the parties will have physical joint custody of their children, since the very factors that permitted or necessitated this (that they both work, that neither can assume full responsibility for the care of their children and that they live proximate enough to one another so that their children can attend the same school from either of their homes), are also usually the very factors that will tend to increase the cost of these nondirect expenses.

How should the parties share these expenses? At first blush, it might seem appropriate that they share them in proportion to their respective incomes. Thus, if the wife earns $30,000 a year and her husband $50,000 a year, it might appear that she should pay three-eighths, and he five-eighths, of these expenses. This may be unfair to the wife, however. Her husband earns $20,000 more than she does. While this disparity in their incomes may not be sufficient to justify a support payment by him to her for the children to meet her costs in housing and feeding them, it is certainly not fair that she should have to shoulder almost half of these additional expenses, and he only a little more than half, given the fact that he has so many more extra dollars than she does. Does this mean that the husband should alone be obligated to pay for all of these additional expenses?

Not necessarily. While that might be appropriate if he earns $60,000 in relationship to the wife's $30,000, it might not be appropriate if he earns only $40,000 in relationship to her $30,000. After all, it must be remembered that in many instances these additional expenses will be very substantial and that they may even include private school tuition, particularly if, as is often the case where the parties have joint physical custody, they live in an inner city and are either not able to transport the children to and from the same public school or do not consider a public school appropriate for their children. Added to this problem is the fact that even if a particular distribution of the burdens of these additional expenses is appropriate at the present time, given what are now the respective circumstances of the parties, it may become inappropriate at a later date if their respective circumstances should change materially. Again, it is the very fact that the parties are both employed in substantial positions, which required or permitted physical joint custody in the first place, that makes this a real possibility.

How then should the parties share these additional expenses? It is suggested that they share them in proportion to their respective gross incomes above a base amount, and that this base amount be equal to two-thirds of the gross income of the party whose gross income is smaller. This formula is intended to avoid the problems that will be created with the use of either of the other two approaches, and to effectuate a compromise between them. Thus, and as we have already seen, if these additional expenses are assumed by the parties in proportion to their respective incomes, the party with the smaller income will be required to assume too large a portion of the obligation in relation to his or her ability vis-à-vis the other party. On the other hand, if we say that the earnings of the party with the smaller income are only sufficient for his or her own needs, and are not sufficient to bear the burden of these additional expenses as well, then they will all fall on the shoulders of the other party.

Applying this formula, if the gross income of the wife is $30,000 and the husband $50,000, then the base amount will be two-thirds of the wife's income, or $20,000. In that instance, the wife will be deemed to have $10,000 of income to contribute toward these additional expenses and the husband $30,000. They will then be obligated to contribute 25% and 75%, respectively, toward their cost. As a practical matter, their obligations should be predicated upon their incomes in the year immediately preceding the year in which these expenses are incurred, and each should be required to provide the other with proof of their incomes for the preceding calendar year by a certain date. While this may be unfair in the sense that there may well have been a change in their financial circumstances since that time, as a practical matter there may not be any other alternative. Thus, and while it might be fairer to base their obligations on their present incomes, many people simply do not know what they will earn in a particular year until the year is over.

Of course, if both of the parties are employed with fixed yearly salaries, without overtime pay, and there is little prospect that they will be employed on any other basis in the future, the mediator can use a more current yardstick. Nevertheless, there is still a potential inequity in using this approach since, after the calculations and payments for the year in question have been made, one of the parties could lose his position or otherwise suffer a substantial change in his circumstances before the year ends.

Having determined how they will share these additional expenses, there are still two other questions that must be addressed. The first is what additional expenses they will be obligated to assume and what dollar limit, if any, will be imposed upon these expenses? For example, the couple may agree that the children will be sent to private school and that they will be enrolled in an after-school program to care for them until the parents each return from work.

Nevertheless, it should be clear what dollars the couple are talking about. It may be that the wife will only have to contribute 25 percent of the cost of the children's private school, but if the combined cost for the two children is $12,000, the $3,000 that she will have to pay may still be more than she can afford. Accordingly, and so that there is no future misunderstanding between the parties, and unless the parties are both affluent, the mediator must address this question. In this respect, it is suggested that the agreement either provide for a cap on the cost of private school or, since those costs can increase with time, that it provide that the cost will not exceed what would be the cost had the children attended a particular school.

While this is sufficient with respect to those additional expenses, such as private school tuition or summer camp fees, the cost of which is set by others, it is not sufficient if the cost of these expenses is paid for directly by the parties themselves and is subject to their discretion. This, for example, is the case with clothing, baby-sitters and certain other exper.,es. If, for example, each of the parties will, on their own, be required to hire someone to care for the children after school, and before they return from work, the problem is relatively simple. By definition, they will each make their own arrangements for that purpose. But suppose that they are both to share the cost of those combined expenses. If that is the case, then it is necessary to place a limit on the number of hours, or the total dollars, that each of the parties will have a right to incur.

The same is true with the cost of the children's clothing. Even if the parties were to agree, for example, that they will spend $1,000 per year on the children's clothing, the combined amount of which will be shared by them in proportion to their respective incomes, they must still decide who will purchase that clothing. Suppose, for example, that they agree that they will each have the right to make expenditures up to a limit of $500. How will they guarantee that, in purchasing particular items of clothing, they may not find themselves working at cross-purposes?

To avoid this problem, and if at all possible, it is recommended that the same procedure be employed as would have been the case had the children's primary residence been with one of the parents, namely, that one of them, and only one of them, should have the right to buy the children's clothing. If this procedure is employed, it is also recommended that the party with the smaller income be the one responsible to purchase the clothing unless, for example, it has always been the custom of the other parent to make clothing purchases and that parent is better qualified to do so. The reason that the task is assigned to the party with the lower of the two incomes is that if either of the parties should have the desire, or feel the necessity, to buy an additional item or items of clothing for the children, the one with the larger income is in a better position to do this and bear the expenses involved.

Miscellaneous Considerations

As a general rule, the payment to be made by one of the parties (usually the husband) to the other for the support of the children is deemed to encompass all of their expenses. Accordingly, once the payment has been made, the husband's obligation for the support of his children is normally discharged and the obligation for their support now rests on the wife's shoulders. Whatever their needs may be, she will now have to look to those monies alone, as she has no right to ask, or he an obligation to give, anything more.

Because this is so, the wife will very commonly place other issues of support on the table. The payment that she is to receive from her husband is for the ordinary needs of the children, such as for food, clothing, and shelter, on a recurring basis. However, there has generally not been factored into those payments those expenses that do not occur on a weekly, monthly, or perhaps even a yearly basis, but that nevertheless arise over an extended period of time. Included within these might be orthodontic treatment, psychotherapy, unreimbursed medical expenses, the cost of summer camp or alternative summer activity, the cost of parochial or other private school, religious training and church or temple membership, college education expenses, tutors or other private instruction, and after-school or extracurricular activities.

As a general rule, the mediator need not concern himself with the question of medical or dental expenses, or with the cost of the children's college education, as those subjects will be specifically addressed at a later point in the mediation. However, and before the subject of support is concluded, these other questions will have to be addressed.

Again, the mediator should not take a preset attitude toward any of these expenses, let alone apply a standard procedure for dealing with them. Rather, he should in each instance first assess the situation in terms of the response of the other party (usually the husband) to the question raised (usually by the wife). If the husband feels inclined to make provision to pay for these expenses, either in whole or in part, it is then simply a matter of including provision for this in the agreement. If he does not, however, the mediator will have a thorny problem, and he will have to address it adroitly.

If the wife has been working from a budget, she may point to that budget to demonstrate that these items of expenses were not included in her thinking when she either asked for or accepted the payment that has been agreed upon. Unfortunately, that is not the issue. The payment that the husband has agreed to make to his wife has not been predicated upon her budget alone. On the contrary, it has been based on the husband's *ability*, and perhaps his own needs as expressed in his budget, and neither his ability nor his needs will change simply because these additional items were not considered or, therefore, included.

If the figure was not arrived at by resorting to their respective budgets, but represented instead simply a level of support that they were each willing to accept, the husband may contend that these expenses have already been considered, and his contribution toward them included in the payment he has agreed to make to his wife. This too is not the case. By definition, the agreed-upon level of support was *not* arrived at by reference to budgeted items or, therefore, the needs of the children. It represented simply a reflection of the husband's ability. There may be nothing wrong with the level of support on that account. But that is not to say that it encompassed a consideration of *these* expenses.

A discussion of these expenses can be complicated for yet another reason, and that is because they relate so *specifically* to the children. It is one thing for a husband to say that he cannot afford to pay his wife more than $75 a week for the support of their daughter. It is another thing for him to say that he will no longer pay for her piano lessons or to send her to day camp in the summer. To make matters worse, so many of the hurtful and baneful feelings that one or both of the parties is struggling with, that lie just beneath the surface, may erupt and become focused on these issues. Finally, it is a difficult issue because it violates our inherent belief that children should not have to pay for their parents' divorce, even though our common sense tells us that they do.

Whatever the problems, if these issues are placed on the table by one of the parties, they will have to be dealt with. That is particularly so since, if they are not, they will then simply become the obligation of but one of them, usually the one with whom the children presently reside. If it is not possible to resolve any of those issues at the present time, the mediator can perhaps finesse them by suggesting that the agreement provide that the husband will assume the obligation for these expenses, or at least a portion of them, in the future, if there is an improvement in his circumstances. This suggestion may be particularly effective if the agreement does not contain an escalation clause. Suppose, for example, that the husband earns $35,000 a year at the present time. The agreement could provide, for example, that if the husband's income should exceed $40,000, that he will then assume, or at least contribute to, the cost of the expense at issue. While this may not be an answer to the immediate problem, it may nevertheless serve as a solution to it.

One final question should be raised. Suppose that the husband, whether out of a misplaced sense of guilt or simply because of the pressure that the wife has put upon him, agrees to pay for certain of these expenses. Should the mediator be concerned that he may have done so even though he may not be able to afford to? This is not a question that mediators normally ask themselves. Nevertheless, it is a legitimate question, no less legitimate, in fact, than the question of whether or not a mediator should be concerned that the agreement does not contain provision for these expenses, and that they will therefore fall upon the wife, who may also not be able to afford them.

Nevertheless, the mediator should not concern himself with this question. As we have said repeatedly—and perhaps this is a point that can be made more effectively when it concerns a husband than when it concerns a wife—it is not a mediator's obligation, simply because a couple has come to him to help them deal with the problems which they have been left with as a result of the decision to separate and divorce, to take over their lives. Nor will it do, as we have again repeatedly admonished, for a mediator to justify this on the grounds that he is simply attempting to protect all of the parties and to assure that the agreement that they conclude is a fair one. An intrusion is *no less an intrusion because it is done for the best of reasons.*

More importantly, it is only justified when it is done for sufficient reasons, and the fact that a couple is separating and divorcing is not, of itself, such a sufficient reason. Nor is the fact that they may do it wrong if they are left to their own devices, or that one or both of the parties may be making a mistake. The mediator would not have questioned the husband's decision to provide his daughter with music lessons or to send her to summer camp if he had offered to do this while the parties were married. If that is the case, there is no reason that he should question it now simply because they are getting divorced.

Conclusion

As we have previously noted, the guidelines that have been enumerated throughout this chapter are that, and that alone. They do not represent inviolate standards or guarantee any necessary justice. In fact, it is not possible for a couple's divorce, or their divorce

TABLE 18-1. Alimony (Maintenance) and Child Support: The Three Basic Questions

1. WHEN—Is a Payment of Maintenance or Child Support Justified?

Maintenance (alimony) and child support[a]

Custodial parent's income in relation to noncustodial parent's income[b]	Noncustodial parent's support obligation
Less than 35%	Noncustodial parent has obligation to custodial parent both for maintenance and for child support.
35% to 50%	Noncustodial parent has obligation to custodial parent for child support only. (Although the custodial parent may also need support, the noncustodial parent's income is not sufficient to justify both child support and spousal support. Nor is the custodial parent's income enough to permit the custodial parent to share in the child support obligation.)
50% to 100%	Both parents are obligated to contribute (directly, in the case of the noncustodial parent, and indirectly, in the case of the custodial parent) toward child support in proportion to their incomes above 50% of noncustodial parent's income.[c]
Equal	Parents have an equal obligation for child support, except that the total child support obligation should be increased by between $1/3$ and $1/2$.[d]
100% to 200%	Both parents are obligated to contribute toward child support in proportion to their incomes above 50% of custodial parent's income. (Again, the total child support obligation should be increased by between $1/3$ and $1/2$.)
More than 200%	Noncustodial parent has no child support obligation to the custodial parent.

Maintenance (alimony),[e] where there are no children of the marriage

Length of marriage	Support obligation
Less than 8 years	No support obligation.
8–15 years	If one party's income is less than $33^1/3$% of the other party's income.
15–25 years	If one party's income is less than 40% of the other party's income.
More than 25 years	If one party's income is less than 45% of the other party's income. (This figure should be raised from 45% to 50% if the spouse who is to receive support is 50 years of age or older.

Where there are children of the marriage[f]

Length of marriage	Support obligation
Less than 25 years	If the wife's income is the smaller of the two, then if her income is less than 45% of the husband's. If the husband's income is the smaller of the two, then if his income is less than 40% of the wife's.

[a]This chart should be used where the parties have children whom they are obligated to support. The following chart should be used where the parties do not have children or, if they do, where they are no longer obligated for their support.
[b]All references are to gross income from all sources.
[c]Thus, if the husband earns $60,000 and the wife $40,000, and if the husband, based upon his income alone, would be required to pay $160 a week in child support, the husband will now pay three-quarters of that amount, or $120 a week.
[d]Thus, if the husband, based upon his income alone, would be required to pay $120 a week in child support if the wife had no obligation to contribute toward child support, the husband will now pay one-half, not of $120, but of between $160 and $180.
[e]Again, all references are to gross income from all sources.
[f]Here there are children of the marriage, but they are all over 21 or, if under 21, they do not require support. If they do require support, the first table should be used.

(continued)

TABLE 18-1 (*Continued*)

Where there are children of the marriage[f]

Length of marriage	Support obligation
25 years or more	If one party's income is less than 50% of the other's income and the party with the smaller income is at least 45 years of age, if the wife, and at least 50 years of age, if the husband. (If the wife is less than 45 years of age or the husband less than 50 years of age, support is still justified if the husband's income is less than 40% of the wife's or if the wife's income is less than 45% of the husband's.)

2. HOW MUCH SHOULD THAT PAYMENT BE?

Wife alone[g]

Circumstance	How much
Wife has no income	Wife should receive 33⅓% of husband's income.[h]
Wife has income but it is no more than 25% of husband's income	Wife should receive 25% of husband's income, or 33⅓% of husband's income less 50% of her own, whichever is greater. (If they have been married for 25 years or more, and if the wife is at least 50 years of age, she should receive 33⅓% of the husband's income less 25% of her own.)
Wife's income is between 25% and 50% of husband's income	Wife should receive an amount equal to 40% of their combined incomes less her own income. (If they have been married for 20 years and have children and the wife is at least 45 years old, or if they have been married for 25 years and the wife is at least 50 years old, she should receive 42½% of their combined incomes less her own.)

Children alone

Circumstance	How much
Wife's income is between 35% and 50% of husband's income.[i]	One child—20% to 25% of husband's net income.[j] Two children— 25% to 30% of husband's net income. Three or more children— 35% to 40% of husband's net income.
Wife's income is more than 50% but less than 100% of husband's income.	Total child support same as above but husband's obligation is a fraction of that amount in which the numerator is 50% of his gross income and the denominator is the numerator plus amount by which the wife's gross income exceeds the numerator.[k]
Wife's income is equal to husband's income	Total child support obligation should be increased by between 33⅓% and 50%. Husband's payment is 50% of that amount.[l]

---

[g]Although the reference here is to the wife, unless otherwise noted, she should have the same obligation to the husband as he would have to her.

[h]In discussing spousal support alone, all references to income are again to gross income from all sources.

[i]Again, unless otherwise noted, all references are to gross income from all sources.

[j]While the husband's support obligation is first based on his gross income in relationship to wife's, the amount of the husband's support obligation is a percentage of his spendable (after-tax) income, not a percentage of his gross income.

[k]If the wife's gross income is $25,000 and the husband's $40,000, the numerator would be $20,000 and the denominator would be $25,000 ($20,000 + $5,000). Thus, if the husband would have paid $150 a week had the wife's income been less than 50% of his, he will now pay 20/25 of that amount, or $120.

[l]Thus, if the husband, based upon his income alone, would be required to pay $120 a week in child support if the wife had no obligation to contribute toward child support, the husband will now pay one-half, not of $120, but of between $160 and $180.

TABLE 18-1 (*Continued*)

Children alone

Circumstance	How much
Wife's income is more than husband's but less than twice husband's income	Again, the child support obligation should be increased by between $33\frac{1}{3}\%$ and 50%. Husband's payment is a fraction of that amount in which the numerator is his income in excess of 50% of wife's income and the denominator is the numerator plus 50% of wife's income. [m]
Wife's income twice husband's income	Husband has no child support obligation.

Wife and children[n]

Circumstance	How much
Wife has no income and cannot work	One child—45% of husband's net income.[o] Two children—50% of husband's net income. Three or more children—55% to 60% of husband's net income.
Wife works but earns less than 35% of husband's income[p]	One child—30% to 40% of husband's net income. Two children—35% to 45% of husband's net income. Three or more children—40% to 50% of husband's net income.[q]
Wife works and earns more than 35% but less than 50% of husband's income	Here, technically, there will only be a child support payment. However, the normal child support payment should be increased by 40% and 60% should be allocated as maintenance.

Allocation of Payments[r]

Number of children	Alimony (maintenance)	Child support
1	$66\frac{2}{3}\%$	$33\frac{1}{3}\%$
2	60	40
3	50	50
4 or more	40	60

If the payment that the custodial parent would have received had he or she had no income is reduced because the custodial parent has income (or is capable of earning income), the reduction will be taken from the amount that would have been allocated as maintenance.

[m]Thus, if the husband's gross income is $30,000 and the wife's $40,000, the numerator would be $10,000 and the denominator would be $30,000 ($10,000 + $20,000).

[n]This assumes that the husband has an obligation to the wife both for her support and for the support of their children.

[o]While spousal support (alimony or maintenance) is usually calculated as a percentage of gross income, child support or, as here, spousal support and child support, is usually a percentage of net income, since a portion of the payment—the child support portion—will be in after-tax dollars. The percentage payments set forth here already have built into them the fact that a portion of the total payments will be deductible by the person making them, and reportable by the person receiving them, for income tax purposes.

[p]If the wife's gross income is more than 35% of the husband's gross income, the husband only has a child support obligation, which is determined by looking under the previous chart, entitled *Children Alone*.

[q]Whether the husband's obligation will be on the high side or the low side will depend, in each instance, on the amount of the wife's gross income. Thus, if the wife's gross income is close to 35% of the husband's, and they have one child, he should pay her 30% of his net income. If her gross income is 15% of his, however, he should pay her 40%.

[r]This allocation is primarily a tax allocation—it determines what portion of the payments the wife will have to declare as income and what portion she will receive tax-free—rather than a judgment as to the appropriate level of support either for her or the children. Thus, where her support payments may end (for example, upon her remarriage), the agreement should provide for a readjustment in the child support payments in conformity with the guidelines (*How Much*) for child support alone.

(*continued*)

TABLE 18-1 (*Continued*)

3. HOW LONG[s] SHOULD IT CONTINUE?

Where there are no children[t]

Length of marriage	Duration of spousal support[u]
Less than 8 years	None
8–15 years	Between 1 and 3 years.
15–20 years	Between 3 and 4 years. (However, if the wife is 45 years of age or older, then for a period of 4 to 5 years.)
20–25 years	For 4 to 5 years. (However, if the wife is 50 years or older, then for a period equal to one-quarter to one-third the length of the marriage.)
More than 25 years	For 5 to 6 years. (However, if the wife is 50 years of age or older, then for a period equal to one-third to one-half the length of the marriage.)

Where there are children[v]

Length of marriage	Duration of spousal support
Less than 5 years	Until youngest child enters school on a full-time basis.
5–10 years	For 1 to 3 years or until the youngest child enters school on a full-time basis, whichever is longer.
10–20 years	For 3 to 5 years or until the youngest child enters school on a full-time basis, whichever is longer. (However, if the wife is 40 years of age or older, then for a period equal to one-quarter to one-third the length of the marriage.)
20 to 25 years	For 5 to 7 years. (However, if the wife is 45 years of age or older, then for a period equal to one-third to one-half the length of the marriage.)
More than 25 years	For a period equal to one-half the length of the marriage. (However, if the wife is 50 years of age or older, then indefinitely—until death or remarriage.)

[s]These guidelines are meant to apply in the normal situation. Where there are special circumstances (such as the ill-health of the spouse receiving support) they can be varied. Thus, while the wife's ill health may not put the husband in a position greatly to increase the amount of support, it may cast upon him the obligation to pay it longer.

[t]This chart should be used to determine spousal support where there have been no children of the marriage.

[u]The obligation to provide support (*When*) is predicated upon the spouse's present employment status. That does not mean, however, that because the spouse is granted support for a period equal to one-third the length of the marriage, based upon the criteria used to determine that obligation (*When*), that he or she will necessarily receive support for this period of time. Thus, anticipating a possible change in the circumstances of the party receiving the payment, the agreement may contain a provision that the payments will terminate sooner should the income of the party receiving it reach a certain level before that date.

[v]This chart should be used to determine spousal support where there have been children of the marriage.

agreement, *ever to do justice* to either of them. If they come into the mediation with very different attitudes as to what is fair or unfair, then, and no matter how successful the mediator may have been in bridging the distance between them, they will also leave with different views as to how fair or unfair their agreement is.

Those groups who have campaigned for more equitable provisions for women in divorce have obviously been correct in suggesting that the treatment that was previously afforded women, when *title* rather than *equity* was the yardstick, was *in*equitable. Nevertheless, that does not mean that these groups have necessarily been happy with the application of more equitable principles.

Quite the contrary, it can be argued that women may have lost more in terms of support under equitable distribution than they have gained in terms of the division of marital property. This is particularly true where, as is so often the case, there is very little tangible property for the court to divide other than the parties' home, which in almost all instances is in both of their names, and would therefore have been shared equally by them in any event.

The major exception to this would be where the husband has pension benefits to which the wife is now entitled. While those pension benefits may well be substantial, it is very questionable whether most women might not be willing to forgo those benefits, which they may not receive for many years in any event, in exchange for the security of permanent support, even if, as a practical matter, that support may only terminate in but a few years if they remarry.

It would be wrong to assume, however, that this inequity can be or will be corrected in the parties' agreement. For better or for worse, no revision in the divorce law will ever be able to remedy the inequitable position in which women are left following their divorce. On the contrary, their inequitable position can only be corrected in the marketplace. That will only come from greater parity between husbands and wives in terms of incomes and occupations. By the same token, it will only come when women acknowledge that in the world in which we live today, being a wife and a homemaker is at best a very precarious occupation. It will also only come when they accept the very hard reality that they cannot expect to protect themselves from the risks of divorce by looking to their husbands alone and that, if they want that protection, they will increasingly have to look to their own resources for that purpose. This may not be fair, but it is the present-day reality.

Medical and Life Insurance

Up to this point the mediator has been concerned with those expenses that one or both of the parties will pay for. More accurately, he has been concerned with the apportionment of those expenses between the parties. There are certain expenses and certain risks, however, that neither of the parties can pay for or assume. On the contrary, they are so great that all that the parties can do is to insure themselves against the possibility of those expenses. Principal among these are the costs attendant to an extraordinary illness and the risk attendant to the death of one of the parties, principally the party obligated to make payment to the other for that party's support or for the support of their children.

Medical Insurance

With the cost of medical treatment what it is, there will be few people of any means who do not have policies of medical and hospital insurance, and this will certainly be the case with those couples who seek mediation on a voluntary basis today. Thus, the issue will not be whether or not one of the parties, usually the husband, will have medical and hospital insurance for his family's benefit, but whether or not he will have a continuing obligation to maintain it. Nor is there generally a real issue even as to this. Whether the husband receives the benefits of such insurance as an incident to his employment, either on a contributory or noncontributory basis, or whether he maintains his own private policies of insurance, there will literally never be any question but that he will continue to maintain that coverage. The question is simply the extent to which the wife and children will continue to benefit from that insurance.

As far as the children are concerned, there is again rarely, if ever, an issue. By definition, the husband now maintains a family plan that will generally include a child until December 31 of the year in which he or she reaches the age of 19 or, if the child should attend college, until the completion of college or the age of 23, whichever first occurs. Since neither the separation nor divorce of the parties will affect the fact that the children are still part of the husband's family, they will continue to receive the benefit of those policies.

This is not the case with the wife, however. She is only a member of the husband's family by virtue of her marriage to him, and upon her divorce she will automatically lose that status and, therefore, the benefit of his medical and hospital insurance. While the wife obviously can apply for insurance of her own, this can be costly and add yet an additional burden to an already tight financial situation.[1] The problem, unfortunately, is that the husband has little control over the situation. He can only give the wife what he has, and if what he has does not include her right to remain a beneficiary following their separation or divorce, then, short of underwriting the cost of a new policy for her, there is nothing that he can do. Sometimes, and given the understandable reluctance of the wife to be left without any insurance at all, this factor may even cause a delay in the timing of the parties' divorce. This is most often the case when the wife is preparing herself for employment, or will be employed at a not-too-distant point in the future, and wants to delay the divorce long enough so that she can be covered under the policies of insurance that she will receive incident to that employment.

While the question of medical insurance for the children is not generally an issue, there are still one or two questions that may have to be addressed. Suppose, for example, that the children are insured under policies of insurance that the husband receives incident to his employment. What will happen if the husband's employment is terminated? To be sure, he will, in all likelihood, again receive the benefits of such insurance when he is reemployed.

But suppose that there is a period of time between his present employment and his future employment? (This can be a difficult issue because although the children most definitely need the protection these policies afford, the very fact of the husband's unemployment may make it particularly difficult for him to be able to pay for it.) Or suppose that he gives up his employment to go into business for himself? In each instance the couple's agreement should provide whether or not he will have an obligation to purchase replacement policies of insurance for the children's benefit.

Sometimes the wife will be able to help out here. Thus, if the wife is herself employed at that time, and can cover the children under the policies of insurance that are made available to her incident to her employment, the husband can then be relieved of that obligation himself so long as she continues to receive the benefit of that insurance. The only question then is whether or not, if the wife is obligated to contribute toward the cost of such insurance, the husband will be obligated to reimburse her, either in part or in whole, for her contribution. In fact, the agreement can go further and provide that the husband will be relieved of his obligation to maintain insurance for the children's benefit any time that the wife is entitled to cover them under her own policies. In that case, the agreement should again provide what obligation the husband will have to the wife in that instance if there is a cost to her in including the children as beneficiaries under her own policies of insurance.

One last issue must be addressed, and that is the question of medical, hospital, and dental expenses that are not covered under the policies of insurance maintained by either or both of the parties. As we have noted previously, the weekly or monthly support payment to be made by the husband to the wife is intended to cover his contribution toward all of the normal recurring expenses of the children. But does that extend, as well, to unreimbursed medical and dental expenses? More importantly, and even if it does, are those expenses limited to what would be considered *normal* medical and dental expenses for the children, and not extraordinary ones? In short, who should bear the risk of these unanticipated expenses?

Typically, agreements will answer this in one of three ways. In the first instance, the husband will assume the cost of all unreimbursed medical and dental expenses. This is most often the case when the husband is affluent and enjoys a large income. In the second, the wife will be responsible for the children's normal unreimbursed medical and dental expenses (which may be defined as being, for example, up to $100 per child per year) and the husband will then be responsible for the balance. In the third, the unreimbursed expenses will be paid for by both of the parties, either equally or unequally. Again, this can either start with the very first dollar of unreimbursed expenses or with those dollars above a fixed amount.

It is important that the agreement address the question of these unreimbursed expenses. It must be remembered that the agreement fixes the *husband*'s obligation for the support of the parties' children, not the wife's obligation. What that means in practical terms is that once the husband has paid the wife everything that he is required to pay by the terms of their agreement, his legal obligation is fulfilled. If those payments are then insufficient for the purpose—and by definition they almost always will be—then they will have to be paid for by the wife. In other words, if the agreement is silent as to whose responsibility these unreimbursed medical and dental expenses are, then they are the wife's responsibility.[2]

Two items of medical and dental expense are very often treated separately. The first of these is orthodontic treatment for the children and the second is psychotherapy. Orthodontic treatment is treated separately for a number of reasons. Firstly, it is a large item of expense, usually costing several thousand dollars. Secondly, it is an expense that is paid for over a limited, specified period—usually two to three years—and thus cannot be built into the normal ongoing support payments for the children. Thirdly, and more importantly, it is generally either excluded or only partially covered even where the husband has a policy of dental insurance in addition to medical and hospital insurance. Thus, if the couple have young children, and it can reasonably be anticipated that they will need orthodontic treatment (and that they would have otherwise been provided with it) it is an issue that should be addressed.

The issue of psychotherapy for the children is an even more complicated one. To begin with, psychotherapy is very often an optional course of treatment. In other words, people do not usually go into psychotherapy because they wish to save their lives but simply because they wish to improve the quality of their lives. The second problem stems from the first. There are very few people indeed who could not benefit from psychotherapy, and certainly children who suffer the trauma of their parents' divorce squarely fall within that group. There can thus be a very legitimate difference of opinion as to whether or not the situation is such that psychotherapy is necessary under the circumstances. Furthermore, it is more than likely that the parties will disagree as to its necessity. Not only can it be anticipated that they may have different views as to the efficacy of psychotherapy in general, let alone to their children in particular, but it is even possible that their disagreement as to the advisability or necessity of treatment for their children may, in actual fact, simply be an extension of other unresolved conflicts between them.

Thirdly, there is the very considerable cost of psychotherapy. Most medical treatment does not vary that much from patient to patient. On the contrary, it falls within fairly uniform and standard limits. Such is not the case with psychotherapy. It may involve no more than several office visits. It can take place once a week. However, it can also take place several times a week over a period of three to four years. Moreover, there is a very considerable difference between the fees that different psychotherapists charge, given the fact that, and unlike medical and dental care generally, it is practiced by individuals having very different professional backgrounds and functioning in very different professional settings. Thus, treatment can range from a low of ten to fifteen dollars per session, when the child is seen by a social worker in a community mental health agency, to a high of $125 or more per session, when the same child is seen by a child psychologist or psychiatrist in private practice. Finally, these again are expenses that are generally either excluded by the parties' policies of insurance or, if that is not the case, limited to a fixed amount.

It therefore is better that the couple's agreement either specifically *exclude* or *include* psychotherapy as one of the unreimbursed expenses for which either or both of the parties will be responsible and, if it is included, that it provide whether or not there will be any limit placed upon the payment that the party who is responsible to contribute toward these costs is required to make. There are many ways to handle this. Thus, the agreement can provide that the treatment must be received at a community mental health agency or be provided by a specific therapist. It can provide that the obligation will be limited to a stated number of treatment sessions in a particular period of time or to a fixed dollar amount in the same period. And, of course, it can additionally provide for a total maximum obligation.

If at all possible, it would be preferable if a party's obligation for the cost of such treatment were not tied to his agreement as to the *necessity* for such treatment. In other words, it would be better to leave the decision as to whether or not the child needs treatment in the hands of the parent with whom the child primarily resides, and to protect the other parent, should that be necessary or appropriate, by limiting his financial obligation. To be sure, this may be inconsistent with the couple's agreement that all major decisions affecting the children will be made by them jointly, and this certainly would constitute such a major decision.

Nevertheless, agreeing as to whether or not a child requires psychotherapy may later pose a problem for them, particularly if tied to the resolution of that problem is the obligation of one of the parties to pay for it. If at all possible, and as much as it may do violence to the concept of joint parenting, it would be better if that decision rested in the hands of but one of the parents, usually the parent with whom the child will primarily reside, even though that solution admittedly generates problems as well. If that is not possible, then the next best thing would be to leave the decision, not in the hands of either or both of the parties, but in the hands of a third person (usually a psychotherapist) whose opinion they each respect.

Finally, there is the question of elective surgery, primarily cosmetic surgery. While it is highly questionable whether a court would impose upon a parent who has agreed to be responsible for all of the unreimbursed medical expenses of his child the burden of paying for strictly elective, cosmetic surgery, it is again better practice not to permit the issue to become a dispute that a court will be called upon to decide. Thus, it would be better to specifically exclude elective surgery. We are not talking here about plastic surgery that is required in connection with a serious accident or other disability. We are talking, instead, of the increased use of plastic surgery simply for cosmetic purposes. Whatever may be its value, it is both expensive and, like psychotherapy, all too often not covered by medical insurance. Nor is it a luxury that either party can normally afford to pay for at this point in time.

LIFE INSURANCE

As a general rule, a husband is only obligated to support his wife, and even his children, during his natural life.[3] That being the case, the provisions for support in the parties' separation agreement will usually terminate upon the husband's death. Accordingly, and to provide protection against this possibility—that the husband may die before his obligation to his children or to his wife has ended—it is common for the parties to provide in their separation agreement, as they have provided during the course of their marriage, that the husband will maintain insurance on his life that will name either the wife or the children as beneficiaries.

Unfortunately, although the logic of protecting the wife and children against the risk of the husband's death would appear to be the same as the logic that would protect them against unexpected medical illness, and while there are certain similarities in the problems of medical and life insurance, there are also some very marked differences. The similarities are twofold. The first is that, as a general rule, a husband will not be asked to do more in his divorce than he has done in his marriage. Thus, for example, and whether for good reason, bad reason, or no reason, if the husband did not see fit to maintain policies of dental insurance for his wife and children during their marriage, it will not be expected of him that he obtain the benefits of such insurance simply because he and his wife are separating or divorcing. Similarly, if the husband has only maintained $40,000 of life insurance on his life up until this point, he will not generally be asked to increase that amount now. Secondly, the husband will rarely question the necessity of continuing to maintain policies of insurance on his life, any more than he will question the need to maintain policies of medical and hospital insurance.

Those are the similarities. But there are also some marked differences. Firstly, and while obviously there are differences in the coverage that various policies of medical and hospital insurance provide, those differences are not as marked as the potential differences in the amount of coverage that different policies of life insurance can provide. Thus, a mediator can be confronted with two husbands of almost equal financial ability, one whose life is insured for $20,000 or $30,000 and the other whose life is insured for between $150,000 and $200,000. This is particularly true if the only policy that the first husband has is a policy of whole life insurance that he maintains privately; and if the one that the second husband has is a term policy that he receives incident to his employment.

The second major difference concerns the cost of such insurance. Understandably, husbands who are required to provide support for their wives and children look to cut back on certain of their other expenses if they can. It is not possible to do this with medical and hospital insurance, however. You either have it or you do not have it, and rarely, if ever, is that a real question. That is not the case with life insurance, however. It is possible to have the benefit of life insurance but still reduce the amount that one is required to pay for it. To do this, all that one must do is reduce the amount of coverage, and not uncommonly a husband will often seek to do this at the time of his separation and divorce. This will become an issue when the wife asks that he continue to maintain his existing policies of insurance and he objects to this and will only agree to maintain a lesser amount.

How much insurance should the husband maintain, assuming, for the sake of the argument, that he can afford to maintain the insurance that he should? The answer is really very simple. The amount that he should maintain is an amount that will guarantee to the wife and to his children that they will receive the same amount, by way of insurance, after his death, that they would have received by way of support had he lived.

Let us suppose that the children are twin boys aged six, that the husband has agreed to pay his wife the sum of $10,000 a year for their combined support until they graduate from high school at age 18, and has then agreed to pay for their college education expenses at a state university for four years, at a future projected cost of $10,000 each per year. His support obligation, therefore, is $10,000 in support for twelve years (or $120,000) and $20,000 in college expenses for four years (or $80,000) for a total of $200,000.

Does this mean that the husband must maintain insurance on his life that will provide a death benefit of at least $200,000? (Is that the amount that the wife will need to insure that she will have the necessary money to support the children through high school and to then send them to college?) The answer is no. Let us assume that the husband were to die the day after the execution of the agreement. His wife would now have the benefit of $200,000 of insurance. Let us also assume that she will be able to invest this money at a return of 5% after taxes. If that were the case, and without being required to touch any of the principal, she will be left with after-tax dollars equal to the support payments the husband would have been required to pay to her for the children had he remained alive. When they are 18, and ready to attend college, she will still have the same $200,000.

But, and assuming that the projected amount of $10,000 accurately reflects what will be the increased cost of college due to inflation or other factors, all that she will need for that purpose is $80,000. More importantly, she will still have the income on the principal of $200,000. To be sure, and since that income will be insufficient to meet all of those college expenses, she will have to invade the principal to a certain extent. Nevertheless, and when both of the children have completed college, she will probably still be left with approximately $140,000. In short, the husband could protect the payments that he is required to make to his wife with a policy of insurance providing for a death benefit of less than $200,000.

What amount should the husband provide in this instance? Assuming that the $10,000 per child per year accurately reflects the increased costs of college at that time, the amount that he should provide is an amount that will leave her with approximately $80,000 in principal at the time that the children are to enter college. To be sure, the wife will actually need somewhat less than that amount since, in the first year, for example, she will have the continued benefit of the interest that she will derive from the money she has put aside for the next three years, as she will have the benefit in the second and third years of the money she has not yet spent in the third and the fourth.

Nevertheless, anticipating the possibility of an increase in those college expenses beyond the projected amount, as well as the fact that the mediator may have based his decision on interest rates that may decline in the future, it is better to err on the side of caution. After all, while the object is not to tax the husband by requiring him to maintain insurance providing for a death benefit far greater than the wife will actually require, the critical issue is whether the husband is being asked to maintain $50,000 or $60,000 in insurance more than the wife needs, not whether he is being asked to maintain $5,000 or $10,000 more than she needs.

How should the mediator arrive at the amount of insurance that the husband should maintain? To be sure, he can calculate with some degree of accuracy what the husband's obligation will be in terms of fixed weekly or monthly payments, and perhaps even the cost of the children's college education. But how can he factor in the variables, such as the husband's obligation to contribute toward unreimbursed medical expenses or to the increased cost of living, if the parties' agreement so provides? And how can he be sure what rate of return the wife will be able to receive when she invests the proceeds of the insurance and, if that income is in taxable dollars, the amount of taxes that she will be required to pay on the money that she receives? The answer, of course, is that he cannot. All that he can do is *estimate* it.

We must remember that we are not talking about a husband whose total fixed payments, including college tuition, are $200,000, and who is prepared to maintain the existing policies of insurance on his life that provide for a death benefit of $200,000. We are talking about a husband who strongly complains that he cannot afford to maintain the level of insurance that he now does and who wants to reduce it drastically. What the mediator is therefore attempting to do is to find out whether or not the level of insurance which the husband is willing to maintain will be sufficient.

Let us suppose, in this example, that the husband offers to maintain insurance of $135,000. Let us assume further that, at least at the present time, the wife would be able to receive an income of 5% after taxes on this amount. Using a calculator, the mediator can quickly determine how much interest the wife will receive in the first year and, therefore, how much principal she will have to use in order to supplement it and get the $10,000 in support that it is assumed, by our example, she will need. The mediator now knows how much principal she will be left with in the second year. The mediator can then make the same calculations for the eleven remaining years. As Table 19-1 indicates, and based upon these assumptions, the wife will be left with approximately $83,000. Since this amount exceeds the projected college expenses that the children will have following their graduation from high school, even discounting the income that this amount will still generate while they are in college, the mediator can safely conclude that there is enough leeway built into the proposed figure to provide some protection against the contingencies that he cannot factor into his equation.

There is a second way to handle the problem, and that is to permit the husband to reduce the amount of insurance he will maintain as time goes by in exchange for his agreeing to provide greater protection at the present time. The discussion to this point has proceeded on the assumption that the husband will die the day after the agreement is signed. But suppose that he dies five years from now, and after he has already paid the wife $50,000 in child support. His future obligation is no longer the same as it is today. Since the wife's risk is therefore less, she does not need the same protection. Permitting the husband to reduce the level of insurance as time goes by may solve the problem for both of the parties.

On occasion, and particularly when the level of insurance to be maintained by the husband is relatively high and the children are still quite young, he may himself raise this suggestion. The premium payments may not be particularly onerous at the present time, but as the years go by, and particularly if he has insurance that is renewed every five years at substantially increased rates, they may well become such. Even if that were not the case, however, he is providing the insurance not as a matter of principle but as a matter of protection. The only question then should be whether the reduced death benefits that are being proposed will provide that protection.

TABLE 19-1. Calculation Showing Adequacy of Proposed Life Insurance

	Insurance proceeds		Interest		Capital depletion		Yearly expenditure
	$135,000 3,250	−	$6,750	+	$3,250	=	$10,000
1 −	131,750 3,413	−	6,587	+	3,413	=	10,000
2 −	128,337 3,583	−	6,417	+	3,583	=	10,000
3 −	124,754 3,762	−	6,238	+	3,762	=	10,000
4 −	120,992 3,950	−	6,050	+	3,950	=	10,000
5 −	117,042 4,148	−	5,852	+	4,148	=	10,000
6 −	112,894 4,355	−	5,645	+	4,355	=	10,000
7 −	108,539 4,573	−	5,427	+	4,573	=	10,000
8 −	103,966 4,802	−	5,198	+	4,802	=	10,000
9 −	99,164 5,042	−	4,958	+	5,042	=	10,000
10 −	94,122 5,294	−	4,706	+	5,294	=	10,000
11 −	88,828 5,559	−	4,441	+	5,559	=	10,000
12 −	$ 83,269—balance remaining for college						

Suppose that the present amount of insurance is inadequate. Does this mean that the wife is never justified in suggesting that the husband should increase it? Obviously, it does not. The question then is whether or not the husband will be willing or able to do in his divorce what he was not willing or able to do in his marriage. In most instances he will not. Nevertheless, it is always possible that he will.

Sometimes it is possible to provide greater protection without necessarily increasing the cost. In fact, it is sometimes even possible to do this and to save the husband money at the same time. This is the case when the policies of insurance which the husband presently maintains are policies of whole life insurance. Properly speaking, life insurance is not life insurance at all. It is death insurance. In other words, its purpose is not to protect the family against the risk that the wage earner will live beyond the time when his income is needed. It is to protect the family against the risk that he will die before that date. Viewed in that light, there is no reason to pay any more than is necessary to buy the amount of protection that the wage earner's family needs. Nor is there any reason to maintain the policy for a minute longer than there is a risk to the wage earner's family were he to die. (This would be like maintaining a homeowner's policy of insurance providing for $500,000 in fire insurance on a home only worth $200,000, or continuing to maintain the policy after the home has been sold).

Not all insurance is sold as death protection, however. Rather, it is also sold as an investment. Insurance such as this is generally called whole life insurance. It not only protects the wage earner against the risk that he will die before he attains the age of 65 years; it also protects him against the risk that he will survive to that age. In other words, it guarantees him that he will receive a stated sum of money at the age of 65, regardless of whether or not he dies by that date. Thus, while term insurance generally ends at age 65, and has absolutely no value to the insured (husband) at that point, a fully paid up policy of whole life insurance is like money in the bank.

Unfortunately, and except to the extent that whole life insurance represents a form of forced savings, it is the worst insurance to have. To begin with, it is many times as expensive as term insurance. As a result, since very few people can afford to maintain enough whole life insurance adequately to protect their family in the event of their death, the price that they pay for using insurance as forced savings is that they have left their families with inadequate death (life) insurance. To make matters worse, it is a very poor form of savings, and if the insurer's purpose had been to save for his old age, he would have done far better buying stock in the company rather than their insurance. When faced with this situation, a mediator may be able to solve the problem by having the husband inquire whether he can convert his present policies of whole life insurance into a policy of term insurance, but at a more appropriate level. Not uncommonly the mediator will be able to provide the wife the protection she needs in this way at no extra cost to the husband. On some occasions, it may even cost the husband less.

Suppose that the husband is either unable or unwilling to provide the necessary insurance. By the mediator's calculations, the appropriate amount of insurance should be $135,000; but the husband is only willing or able to maintain $100,000 of insurance. This does not mean that the wife is not given any protection. It only means that she is being given inadequate protection. More accurately, it only means that she is not being given the full protection that she needs for the first nine or ten years.[4]

To be sure, if the husband were to die today, the wife would need approximately $135,000 of insurance to properly protect her. But if he were to instead die nine years from today, the presently inadequate insurance would then become adequate. What the mediator should do in this case, therefore, is to resist the husband's suggestion that he should have the right to reduce the amount of the insurance that he will have an obligation to maintain prior to that date (the date when it will finally become adequate.)

Up to this point we have principally been concerned with policies of insurance that a husband maintains privately. But what about those policies of insurance that he receives incident to his employment? The problem here is that in most instances the husband will only receive the benefit of that insurance so long as he is employed in his present position. More importantly, these policies of insurance, which are commonly maintained at a level equal to 1, 2 or 3 times his salary, are often in an amount that the husband would be unable to duplicate on his own. What happens, then, if the husband should lose his present position, either voluntarily or involuntarily?

If he should secure other employment that will provide him with substitute policies of insurance, as will often be case, there will be no problem. But what if he doesn't? The problem here is that the husband will now have to add an item of expense to his budget that does not presently exist. Furthermore, the insurance that he received without cost incident to his employment may be far more than he can afford on his own. Understandably, therefore, he may resist this additional expense, and argue that he can only give the wife what he has. Or he may say that she will simply have to trust him to provide such insurance as he can afford. Sometimes he may say that he will provide this protection in his will. The mediator will simply have to do the best that he can here, even if that means getting the husband to agree that the wife will at least have the right to purchase these policies of insurance on his life on her own.

Till now we have talked principally of policies of insurance that will be maintained by the husband on his life for the benefit of his wife and children. What about a policy of insurance on the wife's life? If the children are to be in the husband's custody, and the wife is to make payments to him for their support, that would be clearly in order, as he would need the same protection in that event that *she* would need in the reverse situation. But suppose that this is not the case. Rather, the children's primary residence is to be with the wife and it is the husband who is to make child support payments to her. Does that mean that there is no need for a policy of insurance on the wife's life? The answer is no. To be sure, when the children come to live with him upon the wife's death, the husband will no longer be required to make child support payments and can apply those monies toward the children's benefit directly. However, just as the money that the husband paid to the wife was probably insufficient to meet all the expenses that she bore for the children, so too will they now be insufficient in his hands.

More importantly, particularly if the children are young, he may be required to bear the additional expense of a housekeeper, or at least a baby-sitter, to care for them while he is at work. If he had the benefit of the proceeds of insurance on the wife's life for that purpose, that might greatly ease his burden. Similarly, if, for example, it had been the parties' agreement that the wife would contribute toward a portion of the children's college education expenses, the policy of insurance on her life might guarantee that contribution in the event of her death.

Again, the question is not whether it would make sense for the wife to have a policy of insurance on her life even if, as will usually be the case, it is an amount less than the husband would be required to maintain. Rather, the question is whether or not she should be required to maintain such a policy of insurance if she does not already have one. In short, it is not a question of whether this is a risk against which it would be desirable to protect the husband. It is a question of whether or not it is a risk against which the parties can *afford* to protect him. This will rarely be a problem where the wife receives life insurance incident to her employment; nor will it often be, when the wife is not employed, or is employed but without life insurance, if she already maintains a private policy. Rather, the problem will arise when the wife does *not* presently maintain policies of insurance on her life.

In this latter situation, and even sometimes when private policies of insurance on the wife's life already exist, the issue will not be whether the wife will maintain, or continue to maintain, a policy. It will be who will have to pay the premiums. After all, it is not that the wife objects to having a policy of insurance on her life as a matter of principle. She simply does not want to have to pay for it, since it will never be of any benefit to her.

Again, the mediator should follow the general rule that with the exception of those expenses that the wife, for example, will incur in order to permit her to obtain employment, the parties' agreement should not require either of them to incur obligation for expenses *that are not presently part of their budget*. Thus, if the husband is concerned with this problem, rather than requiring the wife to maintain a policy of insurance on her life that she does not now have, their agreement should provide that the husband will have the right to obtain insurance on the wife's life at his expense should he so desire and that she will cooperate with him in this respect.

Having determined, for example, that the husband will maintain a policy of insurance on his life, and the amount of that insurance, there still remains one question: who will be the beneficiary? Without question, the wife has been the beneficiary of his insurance in the past, even if they have children. She may even still be the beneficiary of his insurance. Nevertheless, and now that they are divorcing, he may resist the idea that she should continue to be the beneficiary in the future. Nor will his objection necessarily have anything to do with the question of whether it was she, rather than he, who wanted the divorce.

What is it that concerns the husband? It is the wife's future husband. He fears that if she receives all of this money that, rather than being used for the benefit of his children, it will come into the hands of her new husband. In other words, what he fears (what he is threatened by) is the power of her new husband. Is this fear realistic? Probably not, but that, unfortunately, is not the issue. After all, up to this point the husband has been willing to name his wife as the beneficiary of this insurance without worrying about her future husband. If that is the case, why is he now worrying about it? Simply because he had never seriously considered his wife's remarriage before—this and the fact that his divorce has caused him to look at his wife differently, again even when it was he who initiated that divorce. In short, there may be no rational reason why the wife is any less qualified to be the beneficiary of his insurance now than she was before. Nevertheless, the husband *looks* at the situation differently—so differently, in fact, that he may not want to provide her with any insurance at all.

This will be expressed by the husband by his suggestion, and perhaps even his insistence, that the children, rather than his wife, be named as the beneficiaries of his insurance. If at all possible, the husband should be persuaded not to do this. If the purpose of the policy of insurance is to create a fund that will stand substitute for the support that the husband would have given to his wife for the benefit of their children had he lived, that purpose will only be served if the wife is able to utilize the proceeds of that insurance for their support.

However, and except in rare instances, this will not be easily accomplished if the children are minors and they are named as the beneficiaries. In such event, the proceeds of the insurance will come under the direct supervision of the court, which will insist that a guardian of the property be appointed to hold the proceeds for them. Even if that guardian is the wife, as in normal instances it will be, she will still be severely restricted in terms of her ability to use those proceeds for their intended purpose. Viewing these funds much as they would the settlement of a personal injury action, the court will insist that they be held for the children until they have reached their majority and will rarely, if ever, permit the wife to use the funds, or even the income from the funds, for their support, unless she is able to demonstrate that she is without her own funds for that purpose.

Instead, the court will insist that the money be deposited in interest-bearing savings accounts, certificates of deposit, or some other form of investment, there to accumulate until the children are of age. Furthermore, should the wife deem it necessary to use any of the monies for their benefit, she, and therefore they, will be subjected to the very time-consuming and expensive procedure of making application to the court for the purpose each and every time an invasion of the funds is required. In short, naming the children as the beneficiaries of the policies, as the husband insists, is simply to ordain that the wife may not have the full benefit of these monies to support the children during their minority as the husband had *himself* really intended when these policies were taken out.

When faced with this argument, the husband will sometimes suggest that he will place the proceeds in trust for the benefit of the children, perhaps under the provisions of his will, and name his brother, his mother, or some other friend or relative as the trustee. To demonstrate his good faith, he may even suggest a relative friendly to the wife, or offer to name her as co-trustee with the person he has designated.

The wife will generally resist this suggestion, as is understandable. While certainly a far better arrangement than to have the funds held under the supervision of the court—in the sense that the funds can now properly be applied for the support of the children without the necessity of time-consuming and costly applications to the court in each and every instance—the arrangement is still infantilizing to the wife, and she will understandably resent it. More importantly, the arrangement still requires the wife to obtain approval of, and therefore to account to, another person in order to obtain the necessary funds, and the husband's arguments to the contrary notwithstanding, it is simply inappropriate, as it is impractical, to impose this obligation upon her. Regardless of what may be the present relationship between the wife and the designated trustee, implicit in the possession of the money that will come under the trustee's supervision is a power that, almost by definition, has to affect that relationship to the wife's disadvantage.

In short, it is inappropriate to place upon the wife the onus of having to maintain a certain relationship with the person in question in order to assure that the funds are freely given, let alone to burden the wife's ability to obtain these monies with the onus of the trustee's possible negative attitude toward the wife's new boyfriend, husband, job, conduct, etc. Nor is this onus justified by the husband's desire to protect his children against his wife's mismanagement or misappropriation of the monies in question. Aside from the fact that this is a risk that the husband assumed when he made the wife the mother of his children, and when he previously named her the beneficiary of his insurance, the fact remains that it is still a far more acceptable risk than is the arrangement that the husband now suggests as its solution.

Suppose the husband will not back down from this position. Under no circumstances will he permit the wife to be the beneficiary of the insurance or even the trustee for the benefit of the children. He intends to name his brother, and that is that. When all else fails, the mediator should attempt to get the husband to agree that the agreement will contain a provision that will require the husband to include in the trust instrument a provision obligating the trustee (his brother) to pay to the wife from the proceeds of that insurance the same monies that the husband would have been obligated to pay to her but for his death.

Thus, even if the trustee should not be willing to invade the principal of the trust to provide the wife with additional monies for the support of the children, she will at least receive the same payments that the husband was directed to pay to her during his life pursuant to the terms of their agreement, without having to be dependent upon the largesse of the trustee for that purpose. While the wife may still feel some indignity in not being given the money outright, and while it is not hard to understand that, in a real sense she has no right to complain since she will receive everything that she is entitled to under the terms of their agreement and that, after all, is the only purpose that the insurance was intended to assure.

There is one last issue to be resolved: how long will the husband be obligated to maintain such insurance for his wife or for his children? Since the only purpose of the insurance is to protect the wife against the risk that the husband may die prior to the termination of his support obligation, when that obligation ends, and there is no longer any risk to protect, the husband should be relieved of his obligation. This may not mean that he will actually cancel the policies in question, or even that he will change the beneficiaries. It simply means that he will no longer be contractually obligated to name the wife, the children, or some other person on their behalf, as the beneficiary or beneficiaries of the policies should he decide to continue to maintain them.

On occasion, the wife may be unhappy with this suggestion. Regardless of the fact that the husband may no longer have an obligation to her for the support of their children, she may still ask, and perhaps insist, that the children remain as beneficiaries of the policies. What she is expressing, of course, is her fear that their divorce may result in her husband's building a new life for himself, and turning his back on his children in the process. Nor will it make any difference whether it is the husband or the wife herself who has requested the divorce.

If the husband has no objection to a provision in the agreement that will require him to maintain the policies of insurance in question indefinitely for the benefit of his children, there is obviously no problem with the wife's request. But what if the husband does object? Rarely will his objection be to the fact that he is being asked to maintain a certain level of insurance—the wife wanting the insurance that the husband will maintain for an indefinite period to be in the amount of $100,000, and the husband only wishing to maintain insurance of $50,000. Rather, his objection will be based upon principle. That being the case, it is not a dispute that will lend itself to compromise, with the couple splitting the difference down the middle and agreeing that the husband will maintain insurance of $75,000 for the children on an indefinite basis.

The equities here tend to be on the side of the husband. If the husband presently maintained $100,000 of term insurance, but only wished to name the children as the beneficiary of $50,000, reserving to himself the right to name his next wife or children as the beneficiary of the remaining $50,000, the wife would have every right to object. It may well be that the husband may remarry. It may well be that he will even have additional children. But that does not change the fact that *his primary obligation is to the children he already has*. It would be naive to suggest that they will not be affected, perhaps even financially, by any new life that the husband may build for himself and, whether the wife likes it or not, this will be a risk that they will have to bear when their father begins to build that new life.

But there is no reason that that risk should include the loss of the insurance on his life that he presently carries. The husband does not have the right to *reduce* his support obligation under the agreement simply because he decides to have other children. On the contrary, and before having those other children, he must take into consideration the fact that he already has that support obligation. And the insurance that he presently maintains on his life is part and parcel of that obligation.

When that support obligation ends, however, the situation is no longer the same.

The husband has fulfilled his legal obligation to these children, and whether he wishes to simply cancel the policies in question and use the premiums that he would otherwise pay to maintain them for his own pleasure, or whether he wishes to maintain them for the benefit of others to whom he is either legally or morally obligated, that is his business.

There is an additional problem with the wife's suggestion, and that is that it is unseemly. What is it in the mere fact of their divorce that gives the wife the right to protect her children from their father? Though she does not have the right, she may nevertheless feel that she has the need. Why is this? Because she fears that in leaving his children—and in letting them continue to live with her he is, in a sense, leaving them— he may also forget them. To be sure, this is a possibility, and one that has been all too common in the past with divorces that were hammered out in adversarial proceedings.

But this is not to say that this risk, or even the wife's fears, justify the infantilization that her request bespeaks. If there really is such a risk, in most instances the wife can protect her children just as well, if not better, by other means, and that is by assuring that her husband has every opportunity to maintain a meaningful relationship with them. While there are undoubtedly exceptions to every rule, the fact remains that in the majority of instances where a husband has turned his back on the children of his first marriage, his former wife has had more than just a small part in the proceedings. In fact— and this is the real crime—in many instances she has actually conspired to cause him to do just this.

But if it is inappropriate for a wife to protect her children against their father, why is it necessary that his support obligation be reduced to writing? In fact, why is it necessary for them to have an agreement at all? The answer is that it is necessary to have such an agreement, not to protect the children from their father, but to prevent a situation that would be injurious to all parties concerned. The wife cannot simply leave it to the husband to pay her such amount as he may feel is appropriate under the circumstances. Aside from the fact that she could not possibly budget her affairs on this basis, and that she would walk around in a perpetual state of insecurity, the absence of any agreement on this point can only be the occasion for constant disputes between the parties at every turn. Nothing could be more injurious to a healthy, ongoing relationship between the parties, or between the husband and his children, than this state of affairs.

For *everyone's* peace of mind, therefore, an agreement is essential. Where *does* one draw the line, then? It is not always easy. Nevertheless, there is a principle that can and should be observed in this respect. Whether the agreement should contain provision for the question in issue should depend upon whether or not it is *likely to be a source of dispute* between the parties that will end up having to be resolved by a court of law if it is not resolved in their agreement. Clearly the payment to be made by the husband for the support of their children is one of those questions. Just as clearly, that of whether or not he will name the children as the irrevocable beneficiaries on his policies of insurance, or as the heirs of his estate for that matter, is *not*.

CHAPTER 20

COLLEGE EDUCATION

In general, mediation attracts a more educated and more affluent group of people. This is the same group who have come to believe that the benefits of a college education are important and necessary for their children's future well-being. As such, it is an area of concern that they expect, and are willing, to discuss. In fact, given the setting in which the discussions between the couple take place, provision for college education expenses is more common in agreements concluded through mediation than it is in agreements concluded through traditional adversarial proceedings. This is particularly so when the children in question are not yet near college age.

While this subject must, of course, be raised when the children are of an age that such a decision will shortly be upon the parties, it is just as important to raise it even when they are not. To begin with, if at all possible, the couple should not be burdened with having this question postponed, and dealt with at a later time, when it can just as easily be dealt with now. Second, if no provision is made for their children's college education, then it may well become simply the obligation of the parent with whom the children are residing.

To be sure, that parent may have the right to apply to the court for an order requiring the other party to assume all or a portion of those college education expenses at the appropriate time. Nevertheless, and aside from the time, cost, and inconvenience (not to mention the potentially damaging psychological effects upon a child in having one of his parents make such an application against the other), courts, surprisingly, are not overly receptive to such applications. In some states, special circumstances must be demonstrated before any award will be made at all.[1]

The issue of the children's college education expenses is taken up separately for a second reason. It is not one of those items of expenses that are generally considered in determining the weekly or monthly payment that will be made, usually by the husband to the wife. That payment takes cognizance of the day-to-day expenses of the children. It does not, and generally cannot, include consideration for extraordinary expenses, particularly of the magnitude involved in the cost of college today. While it might seem prudent to include provision for the parties to allot a certain amount of their present budget for those future expenses, this is generally unrealistic. Most couples have not been able to do this when they were living together, and certainly will not be now that they are separating.

It is a commonplace to say that children should not be made to pay for their parents' divorce. (Not uncommonly, and particularly when that divorce is occasioned by the husband's decision over the wife's objection, she may subtly remind him of this.) The fact is, however, that they *do* pay for that divorce, not only emotionally, but also financially. Thus, when it comes to the children's college education, it may be that a child who had expected to attend a private school may well have to attend a public one, or that a child who had expected to go out of town to college may have to attend a school near his home. It will serve no useful purpose to make judgments, let alone perorations about this. All that one can do is make the best of it.

In each instance, while not necessarily prejudging the matter, the mediator must nevertheless make some tentative evaluation in his own mind as to what is possible before the issue is raised. Since college education expenses are generally one of the last items taken up in mediation, by the time that it is raised he should have more than enough information to do this.

By and large, couples will fall into three categories. In the first will be those couples sufficiently affluent that, despite their divorce, their children will still be able to enjoy whatever college education experience they would have had had they remained together. At the other extreme will be those families whose financial circumstances are so strained that it is simply foolhardy to pretend that any provision can be made for these expenses at all. The third category, which will be by far the largest, are the couples who will fall in the middle. They certainly intend to provide their children with a college education. Nevertheless, there will have to be limits upon their obligation to pay for it.

The problem of college education is complicated by the additional fact that, as with all child support payments, it is paid in after-tax dollars. Thus, we are talking not only about the money that has to be spent to underwrite these expenses but also about the taxes that will first have to be paid on the money earned for this purpose. Let us suppose, for example, that the couple in question has a combined family income of no more than $30,000 to $35,000 and that there is no real prospect of any material increase in their income. Based upon their earned income alone, this couple simply does not have the wherewithal to assume the obligation to provide their children with a college education. This does not mean that their children may not have the benefit of a college education; it only means that their parents will not be able to pay for it. They will have to apply for financial aid, work, and take out loans in order to put themselves through school. Does that mean that their parents will make no contribution at all? Not necessarily. In such a situation, it is appropriate for the parent who is providing support for the child to continue to do so while the child attends college.

Thus, while the husband may have looked to the child's graduation from high school as the occasion for relief from the burden of child support payments (the child being then able to go out and seek gainful employment), if the child is ambitious and industrious enough to find the means to pay for his college education expenses, then it is not too much to ask that the husband postpone the relief he expected and continue to make the regular payments for the child's support until he completes college. That, in effect, is his contribution to the child's college education—to continue to provide him with the basic support that he will need while he attends college.

Let us suppose that the combined family income is $50,000 or $60,000 a year. Here, and particularly if there is more than one child, the parties cannot afford to underwrite the entire cost of a private college education. To complicate matters, while the children may work or obtain student loans to defer a certain portion of those expenses, the family income may well be too high to qualify for very much financial aid. If that is the case, the larger of the two wage earners may agree to pay for the children's college education expenses, except to limit his obligation to a fixed dollar amount, or to an amount equal to what such an education would cost at a state university. This at least guarantees that the child will have an education and, in some states, a very good one. If their circumstances should turn out to be better than they had anticipated, then either or both of the parties, on a voluntary basis, can make up the difference between that amount and the amount that a private college education would cost, should they consider that to be important.

The Wife's Contribution

In agreements concluded in traditional adversarial divorce proceedings, the focus is usually upon the husband's responsibility for the children's college education expenses. In mediation, on the other hand, there is a greater emphasis upon the obligation that each of the parties will have, and it is not uncommon for that obligation to be apportioned between both of them.[2] This can be done on fixed percentages (for example, the husband agreeing to pay two-thirds of such expenses and the wife one-third) or the responsibility can instead be apportioned based upon what their respective incomes are at the time. If the latter approach is employed, it is very important to specify upon what income it will be based—whether from employment, from all sources, after-tax income, etc. It is also important to specify exactly what college education expenses the parties are talking about, and this is true whether or not they will be shared by them or simply paid by one of the parties alone.

Generally those expenses will include tuition, as well as room and board if the child will live at school. However, it must also be clear whether it will include books, university fees, transportation, an allowance, and perhaps even S.A.T. preparatory courses, testing fees, and college application fees. None of this should be left to conjecture, because even when these expenses are limited in amount, they can still be a source of future misunderstanding and friction between the parties.

Apportionment of a child's college education expenses might be very inappropriate, based simply on the fact that the parties are both parents of the children, when there is a gross inequity in their respective incomes. When that is not the case, however, there is nothing inappropriate in apportioning this responsibility, even on an equal basis. The cost of putting children through college today is extremely high. Even for families who enjoy a high standard of living, it still represents a tremendous financial burden. To meet these expenses, women have increasingly returned to work as their children began to approach college age, often completing a college or graduate degree better to prepare themselves for that purpose. If that was the reality when the couple was an intact family, it is even more a reality now that they have separated. Thus, placing a portion of the burden upon the wife (even upon a presently nonworking wife) is not necessarily inappropriate. It may simply be necessary if the children are to attend college—if she wants them to attend college.

There is another issue that will often arise that must be addressed. It has been agreed that the husband and the wife will share in the cost of the college education expenses based on their respective incomes. Suppose, however, that the wife, for example, following her remarriage, should terminate her employment, either because her new husband's circumstances are such that it is not necessary for her to work or because her commitments to her new marriage, and perhaps children of that marriage, preclude it.

This could be a very considerable problem. Although there is a disparity in their present incomes, the wife has acknowledged that she has an obligation to contribute to these expenses, at least in relationship to her ability *vis-à-vis* her husband. Moreover, and although the agreement has not said so in so many words, implicit in their understanding was the assumption that each of the parties would employ his and her best efforts, so as not to cast upon the other party an undue proportion of the burden of these expenses. That being the case, the wife would certainly complain were the husband to retire to Tahiti to take up painting or give up gainful employment because he married a woman who was so well-to-do that it was not necessary for him to continue to work. Does the husband have any less right to complain should the wife do the same?

Common sense, rather than logical consistency, will have to be the guide here. When the husband remarries and decides to have a new family, he is charged with the responsibility of taking into consideration *his obligation to his first family*. Nor will he be allowed to come back and seek a reduction in the child support payments that he is required to make for the children of this marriage based upon the fact that he is now required to support additional children. On the contrary, it would generally be held that this is something he had to consider before he had additional children.

By parity of reasoning, the wife should not be heard to complain that she cannot contribute toward the college education expenses of the children of the first marriage because she has been required to give up her employment to meet the demands of her new family. Rather, like her husband, this is something that she should have taken into consideration before she assumed those responsibilities.

While these two propositions may be logically consistent, that does not mean that the same obligation should be imposed upon the wife in that instance. More importantly, the appropriate result will be reached more by a balancing of the various equities than by any such consistency.

By definition, the fact of the parties' divorce meant the possibility of factors in the future that would not have arisen had the couple remained married. It also meant that, to a certain extent at least, each of the parties might have to bear some of the burden of these future occurrences. In each instance the question is the *extent* to which it is appropriate or inappropriate for them to have to do so.

Take the situation where the wife gives up employment simply because her new husband's financial situation is such that it is not necessary for her to work. In this instance, she has done this simply for her own convenience or for that of her new husband, or both. However, her convenience always has to balanced with the obligation that she has to the children of her first marriage. That being the case, there is nothing inappropriate in charging her with the continued responsibility of contributing to the cost of the children's college education expenses in that event. (In this instance, she could be attributed with the income that she earned during the last year of her employment, and the parties' proportionate responsibilities based upon each of their incomes at that time.)

But doesn't that mean that the wife's new husband will, in effect, be required to pay for a portion of those college education expenses? The answer is yes, but what difference does that make? Any time that someone marries another person, particularly another person who has responsibilities based upon a prior marriage, he assumes a state of facts not of his own creation, and obligations that are not rightfully his own. If he is not willing to do this, then he should not enter into the marriage in question. The new husband knows that his wife is required to work so as to make contribution toward the college education expenses of her children by her former marriage. If, either for his convenience or hers, he does not wish her to have to do that, then he must assume her obligation. Certainly, it would be inappropriate simply to throw it upon her former husband.

The situation is not the same, however, if the wife has ceased working in order to care for the children that have been born of her second marriage. While, to be sure, this also meets the wife's convenience, it is far a different convenience. In all likelihood, having children of that marriage is a far more intrinsic part of her relationship with her new husband, and far more important to that relationship, than is the situation where the wife has simply ceased working because she does not have to. Just as importantly, the sacrifices that the wife would have to make in working in each of these instances is not the same.

Fortunately, there are certain natural considerations that will aid the situation here, and minimize the conflicts between the first and second families. If the husband remarries and has additional children, they will by definition be younger than the children of his first marriage, and even though the husband will have the burden of feeding and clothing them at the same time, he will not usually have the burden of sending them to college at the same time. As far as the wife is concerned, it is most likely that her second marriage will result in additional children while she is still young and when, by definition, the children of her first marriage are also relatively young. What that means is that even if she is required to cease work in order to raise the children of her second marriage, she may well be able to return to work before the children of her first marriage are ready to attend college.

PROVISION FOR VERY YOUNG CHILDREN

There are times when it is very difficult to make appropriate provision for the payment of the children's college education expenses. One of these is when the children are very young. A couple has been married for seven years and has two small children, five and three. They are both college graduates, and certainly intend that their children will also have the benefit of a college education. But that is a long way off, and it is very hard to predict what their respective circumstances, let alone the cost of college, will be at that time. Because the husband is relatively young, his career is just starting and, unlike a man in his forties, it is less clear where he will end up. As for the wife, since she is presently not employed, it is even more difficult to predict just what her income will be at that time.

As in the situation where the children are close to college age, it is possible for the agreement simply to apportion these expenses between them, either in fixed rations or based upon their respective incomes at the time. However, there are problems with this, not the least of which is that, if the latter approach is used, their incomes alone may not be an appropriate yardstick of their relative abilities to meet those expenses. The husband and wife are young, and at least from a statistical standpoint, there is a very good chance that they will each remarry in the future. Either of them, and particularly the husband, may have additional children, which will further tax that income. With couples whose children are closer to college age, the variables that may change between the time of the signing of their agreement and their children's starting college are smaller. Thus, while recognizing that any present fixed arrangement may prove to be inequitable at the time, they may prefer to settle the question now and take their chances, so to speak, rather than leave it open and have to come back and address it in the future.

With other couples, however, particularly relatively young couples whose children are a long way from college, taking their chances may involve a very different assumption of risk. Thus, as much as they would like to avoid having to come back, they may feel that they have no other choice. There are simply *too many variables involved*, and too much time for them to play out. As a result, an arrangement arrived at now may prove very inequitable at the time that it is to be complied with.

In such a situation, it is not sufficient simply to provide that the matter will be discussed by the parties at the time and, if they are not able to reach an agreement, that it will then be mediated. Arrangements must be made not only for it to be discussed, but also for it to be decided. Thus, if the parties are not able to resolve it through mediation, then some alternative means of dispute resolution must be provided. Just as importantly, they must agree now on exactly what circumstances will be considered relevant for that determination, as otherwise they may just be left with an endless debate. Their agreement should *not leave them with an endless debate*; it should leave them with *a way to resolve it*.[3]

ABATEMENT IN SUPPORT PAYMENTS

A question that will commonly arise in connection with the children's college education expenses, particularly where the husband will be paying for all or most of them, is whether he will be entitled to a reduction in the child support payments while the children are in college.

The problem here is that the increased expenses of one of the parties and the reduced needs of the other do not necessarily balance out. Particularly if the children live at home while they attend college, there will be absolutely no reduction in the wife's expenses because they attend college. Even if they live at college, however, aside from their food and incidental expenses, her costs will remain much the same. In terms of need, therefore, the wife is *not* better off, or at least not much better off, because a child attends college.

In terms of ability, however, the husband is much worse off. On the same fixed income, he will now have to come up with extra dollars, sometimes substantial, in order to meet these expenses. To do that, and unless he is fortunate enough to be able to fund them from capital, there is going to have to be a tightening of his belt. In short, he cannot underwrite these expenses and continue to provide the wife with the same level of support that he previously did. She will have to underwrite indirectly a portion of those expenses by receiving less support from him and either suffer the loss or make it up elsewhere.

In making such an adjustment, two circumstances should be considered. The first is whether the child will be living at home while he attends college. As was noted earlier, if that is the case, there has been absolutely no diminution in the wife's needs. Similarly, and since the husband's obligation will be limited primarily to tuition, the extra burden cast upon him may not be that great, particularly if the child contributes something toward those expenses either in the way of loans or through work. If that is the case, it might not be appropriate for there to be any reduction in the husband's support obligation. If the child's attendance at college is still a few years off, and particularly if there will be no escalation in the support payments, these increased expenses that the husband will have to bear can perhaps come from his increased earnings at that time. If not, he may have to economize in other ares, or borrow the necessary funds, as might well have been the case had he and his wife not separated.

The second consideration is the amount that the husband is required to pay for these expenses. Thus, as an example, the parties' agreement could provide that if the husband's total costs in any calendar year do not exceed $2,500, there will be no reduction. However, if they exceed $2,500, but are less than $5,000, that the payments will then be reduced by 50%, but if they are more than $5,000, that the payments will be suspended altogether.

Having determined that there will be a reduction in the payments, it is next necessary to specify the period during which that reduction will be made. Will it be made throughout the entire calendar year? Or will it be made simply during the period of time that the child attends college? If the latter, it may be preferable somewhat arbitrarily to define the period as from the month of September through the month of May rather than attempting to calculate the exact number of days that the child is at college and at home (e.g., during the Christmas recess, over the summer, etc.).

This may be a rough form of justice, but sometimes simplicity is more important than absolute precision. On the other hand, one of the parties, usually the wife in this case, may prefer to use the exact number of days, claiming that the child will not actually be away at school for nine out of the twelve months, since he will be home on school vacations during this period. If it is not known what college the child will be attending—and, unless he has already been accepted at college or is already attending college, that will almost always be the case—it can be assumed that he will be at college for 210 days each year, including weekends. In other words, he will be at school for about 60% of the year.

GRADUATE SCHOOL

As a general rule, agreements concluded between divorcing couples do not make provision for their children's graduate school educations. To a certain extent, this is based upon convention. In traditional adversarial divorce proceedings, the negotiations between the parties always take place against the background of what a court will or will not do. If the court has the power to award the particular relief, the wife expects to receive it; if they do not, the husband does not expect to give it. While their agreement will, in many instances, vary from those strict expectations, they do, nevertheless, color their negotiations.

Graduate school education is simply not one of those items that a court directs a parent to provide for his or her children. Aside from the fact that the law has not yet reached the point of recognizing a graduate school education as a necessity—and it is only recently that courts have come to recognize a college education as necessary—the fact remains that courts are not in the habit, and in most instances not empowered, to direct parents to make provision for children who may be 23 or 24 years of age.

The other factor is simply one of economic reality. It may well be that the parties would *like* their children to have the benefit of a graduate school education. It may well also be that they would have underwritten the costs of graduate school for their children had they stayed together. And, of course, it is even possible that they may still underwrite those costs, either in whole or in part, despite their divorce. In most instances, however, the parties will simply have to look at the situation when it arises and deal with it then. The child will have at least been left with a college education, and even if his parents do not make provision beyond that, this is not to say that, armed with a college degree, he may not find the way to pursue his studies further on his own if that is important to him.

This is not to suggest that agreements never contain provision for one of the parties, or even both of them, to pay for the cost of their children's graduate school educations. If the parties are very well-to-do, and particularly if one or both of them has pursued graduate studies, the issue may be put on the table and provision made for it in their agreement.

Even when these conditions exist, however, there may well be some resistance, usually on the part of the husband, to include provision for graduate school expenses. A mediator must be careful here, as it is easy to misunderstand the husband's possible objection, which may have nothing at all to do with his payment of these expenses. Rather, he may well be objecting to the fact that in assuring that he will be a very good father to his children, the agreement may deprive him of the opportunity of being a father at all.

Of necessity, the fact of the couple's separation and divorce means that it is no longer possible simply to leave what the husband will do for his children in the future to his good intentions, as it has been in the past. Whether it offends him or not, that obligation will now have to be made specific, not because the wife does not necessarily trust her husband's good intentions, but because it is inappropriate and impractical that she should be left to have to *depend* upon them. But how far should that go? Unfortunately, the logic that has the parties reduce the husband's obligation to an agreement will not alone answer this. Rather, there must be a delicate balancing of the need to make appropriate provision for the children, including, if that must be the case, reducing what the husband would otherwise do for his children on a *voluntary* basis to a *legal* obligation, with the need to preserve to the husband the right to continue to be a father to his children, and voluntarily to make provision for them, even at the risk that he may not do so.

Thus, while it would be inappropriate for a mediator to fail to put on the table the question of whether or not the husband will be responsible for his children's medical expenses, it would be just as inappropriate for him to put on the table, for example, the question of whether or not he will be obligated to pay for his daughter's wedding and if so, to what extent. As a general rule, the line will tend to fall between college and graduate school expenses. Even though an argument could be made that both of these items of expense reflect elements of each of these considerations, at least at the present time college education expenses are considered to contain more of the former and graduate school expenses more of the latter.

Miscellaneous Considerations

Sometimes, even when parents expect to pay for the children's college education, they will still have their children take out college loans to help finance it. The purpose of this is to enable the parents to spread out the cost of their children's college education over a longer period of time. Where the children are close in age—and that is commonly the case—college education expenses tend to get bunched together. This is a convenient device to spread them out. However, if the agreement does not make clear that it is the parents' obligation to repay these loans, since they are in the children's names, they will have no legal obligation to do so. As a practical matter, the burden may then fall on one rather than both of the parents, although that may not have been their intention. On the other hand, if it is the intention of the parties that the children will be required to repay these loans, their agreement should specifically indicate that so as to avoid any future misunderstandings between them.

A second question concerns money belonging to the children. Not uncommonly, parents put away money for their children. Just as commonly, the children receive gifts from their grandparents or other relatives that are held by their parents for them. Will this money be used to defray their college education expenses? Will their parents' obligation to pay for these expenses only arise after all of these monies are first used for this purpose? These questions should be answered in the couple's agreement. If it is anticipated that these monies will be used to pay for these expenses, then their agreement should also contain provision that the parent who is holding the money in question shall not have the right to use those funds for any other purpose.

A third question concerns applications for financial aid. Suppose, for example, that the parties agree to divide the expenses between themselves equally. Suppose, also, that the wife applies for, and receives, financial aid for the child. Does that assistance reduce the obligation of the parties equally, or does the wife have the right to apply the entire amount toward her obligation? Although the answer to this question may be obvious, it is nevertheless better practice for the couple's agreement specifically to answer it.

Last, there is the question of the children's contribution toward those expenses through work. On the face of it, it would seem that it would be the better practice specifically to make provision for this in the parties' agreement. As a practical matter, however, this may be very difficult. What work will be available to the child, how much the child will earn, whether he will be employed only during the summer recess from school or during the school year as well—these are all questions that are very difficult to answer from a distance.

Nor, as a practical reality, is it always necessary. If the husband has agreed to assume the full cost of the children's college education at a private school, his circumstances are such that he probably does not intend or expect his children to work, or, if they do work, that they will have to apply this money toward their college education expenses. On the other hand, if they have agreed to share those expenses, or if the husband's obligation is limited to a fixed dollar amount, the question of a child's employment will, more often than not, tend to solve itself. After all, regardless of what their agreement may say, one or both of the parties will still be able to affect, to a large extent, the contribution that the child will be required to shoulder through employment.

CHAPTER 21
MEMORANDUM OF AGREEMENT

All of the discussions and the negotiations that have taken place during the course of the couple's mediation point to one thing—the separation agreement that each of the parties will execute. While this agreement will ultimately be prepared by an attorney (who usually has not participated directly in the mediation and may not even be known by the mediator), the mediator must, nevertheless, concern himself with the function of that agreement.

One of the purposes of divorce mediation is to leave the couple able to deal with one another effectively in the future, and if their mediation has been successful, they should be able to discuss and resolve matters between themselves without constant reference to their agreement. Nevertheless, what that agreement contains, and how it is written, is extremely important, as in large measure it will not only shape the formal aspects of the future relationship between the parties, but serve to avert unnecessary disputes between them as well.

In fact, it has been said that a dispute between a separated or divorced couple is simply a question that their agreement did not properly answer, for should the couple be unable to resolve an issue that arises in the future on their own, they should be able to fall back upon their agreement and find either an answer to the question or at least a procedure for dealing with it. Thus, a properly concluded and prepared agreement will meet three purposes: (1) define each of the parties' *future obligations* to one another; (2) anticipate those problems that may arise in the future and *determine in advance* the answers to those questions or, if it is not possible to give present answers to them, the *procedures* that will be employed in an attempt to resolve them; and (3) set forth in clear, definitive language the *terms* of the parties' agreement.

If an agreement fails to satisfy each of these three needs, it has, in a very material sense, failed the parties. Thus, if the agreement concluded by the mediator either fails to make provision for the question at hand or disposes of that question in such ambiguous language that it is not possible for the parties, or even their attorneys, to chart a clear answer from that agreement, then it will only serve to become a fresh battlefield for future disputes between them. If that is the case, wounds that have begun to heal will be reopened, litigation that has been avoided may have to be resorted to, and the emotional and financial burden implicit in such disputes will have to be shouldered anew.

Nor is it sufficient to leave these concerns to the attorney who will ultimately draw the agreement. In large measure, an attorney can only draw an agreement that is as good as the one that has been concluded by the mediator. Even if the attorney preparing the agreement should attempt to correct its deficiencies, he can only do this in part, as he cannot make an agreement for the couple when they have not come to one themselves.

It is very important, therefore, that mediators be aware of the kinds of agreements that tend to promote future problems and disputes between the parties. These are agreements that are not carefully thought out. These are agreements which tend to postpone until tomorrow problems that could just as easily be dealt with today. These are agreements that apply solutions that can only tend to create additional problems in the future. Worst of all, these are agreements that tend to rely on flowery words of good intention, in loosely drawn documents, to stand substitute for *real answers to real problems.* In short, these are agreements that leave the parties with the *illusion* of an agreement but not the *substance* of one.

Nor are mediators alone at fault in preparing such agreements. Lawyers are almost as guilty. However, that is not an answer, and it is still absolutely irresponsible for mediators to do this. If one of the goals of divorce mediation is to help separating and divorcing couples put their hurt and anger behind them, then it is irresponsible to conclude agreements that fail to do this.

Let us illustrate this with portions of two agreements, drawn in this instance by attorneys in a traditional setting, that were not carefully drawn. Both of the clauses in question concerned the wife's right to live in the marital residence for a period of time. The first of these agreements provided that "the wife shall have the right to live in the home for at least one year." The second agreement provided that "the wife shall have the right to live in the home with the children for three years, following which the home will be sold as soon as is practicable." In each instance, when the allotted time had expired, the respective husbands, who were looking to receive the equity they had tied up in the home, demanded its sale.

The first wife countered by saying that the agreement did not provide that she was to have the right to live in the home for "only one year," but rather, "for at least one year." The second wife countered by simply saying that to sell the home at the present time was not "practicable." In each instance it cost the women more money in attorney's fees to have a court define the terms "at least one year" and "practicable" than it had cost them to conclude the agreements. (The second of the two women, who was of very modest means, had to spend $7,000 to find out the answer to her question.) As if this price were not enough, in each instance the parties were forced to go back and do battle with one another, undoing, one would assume, much of the progress that had been made in the time since their agreements were signed.

In each of these examples, the parties were not required to address the question properly at the outset. Was the wife in the first instance to have the right to live in the home simply for one year or, under certain circumstances (not defined in the agreement), was her right to live in the home to be extended beyond that? Was the home in the second instance to be sold as soon as *possible*—that is, right away—or were the parties to look to other factors (again not defined in the agreement) to determine whether that was *practicable?* On the face of it, it is hard to believe that the parties really did *not* know what they meant and intended at the time. If that is the case, their present dispute stemmed simply from sloppy draftsmanship.

If lawyers are sometimes guilty of sloppy draftsmanship, mediators, unfortunately, are all too often guilty of sentimental thinking. This occurs, for example, when a mediator resolves every issue that may arise in the future with the simple provision that it will be disposed of by agreement between the parties and, failing that, by a return to mediation. Unfortunately, agreements concluded in mediation are rife with this kind of thinking. To make matters worse, it has often been justified by mediators with the suggestion that their agreement is supposed to be a "living document." A separation agreement is not supposed to be a living document, however, and if the couples whom we counsel were guilty, in the beginning, of overromanticizing their marriage, mediators should not now allow themselves to be guilty of overromanticizing their divorce.

Of course, one of the main goals of divorce mediation is to leave couples *better able to conduct necessary business* with one another *in the future* than traditional divorce proceedings leave them able to do. But this is only to leave them better able to do the business they *must,* not to condemn them to *have* to do such business together forever. In part, at least, the parties are where they are *because* of their inability to negotiate their differences. In divorcing, it is their hope not to correct this inability, but to *end* the occasion for it. Mediation does them no favor, therefore, by leaving them with an agreement the terms of which have to be forever renegotiated.

REVIEWING THE DRAFT AGREEMENT

As a general rule, a mediation is deemed concluded when the parties come to a tentative understanding and the mediator (if he is not a lawyer) prepares a summary of their understanding that the parties then take either to a single attorney, or to separate attorneys, to reduce to a legal agreement. From this point forward, the mediator generally considers his job done and the matter normally remains in the hands of the lawyers.

This is a mistake born, once again, of a misunderstanding of mediation and the role of the mediator. When the agreement is first prepared in draft form, the couple will then review it, in this case with the attorney whom they have retained for that purpose. From this point on, the mediation is now generally considered to be in its *legal* stage. As anyone who has reviewed a draft agreement with a couple knows, however, this meeting is actually only an extension of the mediation, not a different stage in mediation, let alone a procedure following it. Certain questions that had not been thought of will be raised. Portions of the agreements that have been concluded by the parties will now be questioned anew. In some instances, and because things appear differently in print than they did in their discussions, one or both of the parties will have second thoughts.

In short, this is not simply the occasion to review and explain to each of the parties what their agreement contains and its legal significance. Quite the contrary, the majority of the time will be spent in what amounts only to another mediation session. If that is the case, the mediator should be involved in the process. More importantly, the matter should not simply be left to one or more attorneys who have had nothing to do with the mediation up to this point, and who may not even have the necessary skills, let alone the necessary relationship with the parties, to mediate the issues that may arise.

The same is true of the completed agreement that is prepared for the parties' signatures after the draft agreement has been reviewed, revised, and put into final form. In most instances, if there are questions raised by either of the parties, they will be insignificant and of no material substance. If that is the case, they can be dealt with by the attorney handling the signing by simple interdelineations or other minor changes that can be initialed then and there by both of the parties.

On other occasions, however, what the attorney will be presented with are not really legal issues at all. The couple has come to an agreement by balancing numerous considerations. On the one hand, their upset (their fear, their hurt, their anger, and so on) has caused them to look to their agreement to accomplish certain purposes, some of which are unrealistic. It may have caused them, and may still cause them, to resist signing it and, thereby, to conclude it. On the other hand, there is the need to get on with the matter, to get it done and to put it behind them. At different points in time one or the other of these factors will gain the upper hand—the question is always in a state of balanced imbalance and it can shift one way or the other at any given moment. The person dealing with the couple—be he a mediator or an attorney—must always be sensitive to this fact. Nor must he be confused when that emotionality surfaces, no matter what its disguise.

Consider the following case. A couple who had been married for about eighteen years sought mediation, mainly at the request of the wife. While there were many positive qualities in the marriage, there were also many problems, not the least of which was the husband's dependence upon alcohol. Although the wife did not want her marriage to come to this conclusion, she realized that she had no other choice and, over her husband's strong objections, pushed on ahead. From her standpoint, and to accomplish this, she had had to make numerous emotional, and even financial, sacrifices.

The couple had gone over their draft agreement a few weeks earlier, had made some rather minor changes, and the agreement had then been put into final form and sent to them. In fact, it was now only necessary for them to come in and sign that agreement. When the couple arrived, however, the attorney, who had also conducted the mediation, noted that the wife's copy of her agreement was replete with numerous paper clips. This at first surprised him, since the couple was ostensibly there only for the purpose of executing their agreement. Purposely ignoring what he had observed, the attorney simply asked each of them whether they had any questions that they wished to ask before they signed their agreement. The wife quickly responded that she had quite a few, and that, following the mediator's suggestion, she had sought the services of an independent attorney to review the agreement with her. Asking her to turn to the first place in the agreement where she had a question, the attorney began to address them one by one.

After he had discussed the first two or three items with the wife, and noting that there was no substance to any of her concerns, most of which were picayune, he concluded that there was really something *else* at issue. Putting the agreement aside for the moment, he turned to the wife and said, "This is all very difficult for you, isn't it? I know that coming to the decision to divorce your husband and to end your marriage has not been an easy one, and that you have struggled a very long time to get to this point. I am sure that it must be very upsetting to have to come here and sign this agreement tonight."

At this point the wife reached for a handkerchief and applied it to her eyes. The attorney stopped, and after a short pause the wife looked up at him and said simply, "Let's get on with this." She then proceeded to remove each of the remaining paper clips from her agreement and turned to the signature page.

"Are you all right?" the attorney asked her. "Are there any other things in your agreement that you would like to go over before you sign it?"

"No," the wife replied. "Let us please sign it so that we can get it done."

Aside from the fact that an attorney, functioning strictly as an attorney, might not have understood that the objections that the wife was raising were not really what was at issue (and might not, therefore, have been able to help the wife), in handling this in a proper, businesslike manner, he may have only compounded the problem further by reinforcing the smokescreen that she had thrown up to mask what were her real misgivings, and what was really holding her back. If it is the couple's disappointment, their hurt, their fear and their anger that stand between them and an agreement, they are ever present and they must *always* be dealt with. Divorce mediation is of a piece and is not neatly separated into a mediation phase and a lawyering phase. On the contrary, it is all one.

MEMORANDUM OF AGREEMENT

The mediator's work will usually end in a document that has been given the name "memorandum of agreement," and it represents, in summary form, the understanding that has been concluded by the parties. In attempting to assist mediators in the preparation of this memorandum of agreement, we had a choice and also a dilemma. On the one hand, we could have included what we considered to be an appropriate memorandum of agreement, and at first blush this would have seemed the better procedure. On the other hand, we could have included an example of a memorandum of agreement that we consider to be inappropriate, and to have then indicated why. We have chosen to do the latter. There are two reasons for this.

First, and as true as it is paradoxical, a mediator will not learn as much from a good agreement as he will from a bad one. It is not always obvious just what is so good about a good agreement, let alone the problems that would have been created if it were not. The second reason is that our concern about the quality of the memoranda of agreements being prepared by mediators might not be taken as seriously if the reader had simply our own word to take for it. We felt it important, therefore, to illustrate our concern by using a real memorandum of agreement. The particular agreement that we have used is especially illustrative, because it cannot be excused with the suggestion that whatever infirmities may have existed in it would have been corrected by the drafting attorney, for in this instance it was the intention of the mediator, who was not an attorney, that the memorandum of agreement that he prepared for the parties was to represent their final agreement and to be signed by them. [1]

Except in minor instances, which are denoted by ellipses, we have reproduced the entire memorandum of agreement. For obvious reasons, all of the names and places have been changed. Rather than reproducing the entire memorandum of agreement, with our comments either footnoted or set forth at the end, we have followed the procedure of interrupting the memorandum from time to time to comment upon it. To distinguish it from our comments, the memorandum of agreement has been italicized.

Jane Smith (hereinafter referred to as the "Wife") and John Smith (hereinafter referred to as the "Husband") had made a decision to live separately and seek dissolution of their marriage relationship as a result of an irretrievable breakdown in that relationship. They both agreed to submit the issues of their dissolution to mediation conducted by Robert Brown.

The Husband and the Wife were married on November 10, 1967 in Glenwood, Pennsylvania. They executed their decision to separate on November 1, 1982. During their marriage they had two children, named Susan Smith, born June 20, 1974, and Peter Smith, born November 21, 1976 (hereinafter referred to as the "Children").

While it is common practice for attorneys to begin their agreements with recitals, the mediator should not do this with his memorandum, except perhaps for the perfunctory name, rank, and serial number type of information. The reason for this is that almost everything beyond this is unnecessary. To include more—and most of that "more" is usually flowery words of good intention—is simply to run the risk that it may be incorporated by the drafting attorney into the final agreement. Once there, there is then always the risk that these representations of good intention and propriety will have to be defended. Since they add nothing of substance, they should therefore be avoided.

The recitals suggest that the parties have already executed a prior agreement. This may have simply been a short, one-page document whereby, for example, the husband agreed to vacate the marital residence. As a general rule, it is not recommended that parties sign interim agreements as they go along. There are two reasons for this. Firstly, and although it cannot be avoided entirely, the mediator should not continually emphasize the legal aspect of what is taking place between them by the introduction of legal documents. Since he does not wish them to approach the problem in this way, he should not continually reinforce that point of view.

Secondly, and to expedite the mediation and the ability of each of the parties to entertain, and perhaps even tentatively accept, certain proposals, the mediator should reinforce the fact that the parties do not have an agreement as to *anything* unless they have an agreement as to *everything*. In fact, even *then* they do not have an agreement until it has been reduced to writing and signed by each of them. Having the parties sign interim agreements may well run interference with this understanding. It may even pose special problems should the mediation prove unsuccessful. In signing those interim agreements, did the parties intend that they were only to be binding if the mediation proved successful?

To be sure, life will go on and decisions will have to be made during the course of the mediation. And it is even possible that one or the other of the parties may change his position in a way that will affect the outcome of the mediation or, should mediation prove unsuccessful, their subsequent negotiations. Certainly that will be the case should one of the parties leave the marital residence, the mediation break down, and there is later a dispute as to custody that will have to be resolved by the court. Nor will it make much difference whether or not the party in question left unilaterally or by agreement with his or her spouse. Nevertheless, and consistent with the attitude that the mediator wishes to have prevail during the mediation, in most instances the mediator should simply ignore this.

There is a problem, given the circumstances that exist, that it is extremely difficult for the husband and the wife to live under the same roof with one another. If the parties feel that it will tend to relieve some of the tension, not only for themselves but also for their children, if the husband were to leave and find separate accommodations for himself, then they should seek their own level in that respect, and the mediator should not prejudice their ability to do this with his concern as to what future implications this may or may not have. The parties have a problem now, and they must deal with it now. Having done that, in most instances there is no necessity for them to document what they have done.

To be sure, if they were each to consult with separate attorneys, they would probably be given very different advice. But that does not mean that the rule that the mediator is following is wrong on that account. It simply means that they are each trying to do very different things. Divorce lawyers always look at their clients' positions, and are forever jockeying to improve them. As a result, their overriding concern with regard to the present problem is not how the proposed solution will affect it, but where it will leave their clients—whether it will improve or jeopardize their positions. This being so, if a divorce lawyer does not feel the need to apologize because he is willing to leave the problem unresolved rather than take the risk that its solution may prejudice his client, then a mediator should feel no need to apologize because he is willing to try to solve a problem that is a real problem today at the expense of what may only possibly be a problem in the future, particularly when his ability or inability to resolve that problem now may be the very factor that will most influence whether there will be a problem in the future at all.

The Wife and the Husband agree that they have each made full disclosure to the other concerning the nature and extent of their individual and joint marital assets. Both have cooperated in the evaluation of their personal property and their real estate which consists of their family home located in Ridersville, New York.

The Husband and the Wife have signed an agreement with Robert Brown and with each other to be fair and equitable throughout the mediation process. They have negotiated their agreement in nine hours of mediation conducted by a mediator affiliated with Family Mediation Service of Glenwood.[2]

There is absolutely no purpose served in having the agreement indicate how it was arrived at or how many hours it took. While the mediator may have felt that by stating that the couple took nine hours to negotiate their agreement he thereby demonstrated the thoroughness of their enterprise, there is no guarantee that it will be read as such by someone who may later seek to call into question what took place in the mediation. Quite the contrary, it may be argued that although the matters that the couple were required to resolve were extremely complicated, they and the mediator devoted but nine hours of time to them. In fact, and as this memorandum of agreement will clearly demonstrate, that time must have been insufficient given the fact that so many questions were left open.

Suppose, for example, that in a particular case, and since the parties' children were all adults and they themselves were both self-supporting, or simply because the parties had themselves resolved a great many of the issues before they met with the mediator, that the mediator had been able to conclude an agreement in but two or three hours. Would he want to recite this fact in their memorandum? Or may it only later be read to suggest that the matter was concluded hastily, and without proper forethought? As we have had occasion to note previously, the mediator must always protect the agreement that the parties will sign from later attack. It is no answer to say that the recitals contained in the memorandum of agreement will not be incorporated by the attorney who receives it into the final agreement that he will prepare. It is still a document that has been shown to the parties, and in all likelihood been approved by each of them, either verbally or in writing, before it was made the basis of their final agreement. It is thus one of the links in the chain that holds the agreement together, and, if it looks like a weak link, it may be the one that is later attacked by the person attempting to break it.

The purpose of this agreement is to provide for an amicable adjustment and settlement of all rights, obligations, interests, and financial matters existing between the Wife and the Husband arising out of their marital relationship. In order to settle all issues between the Husband and the Wife, including the division of property and debt settlement, spousal support, child support, and custody and visitation, they both agreed to the following provisions:

1. Separate Residence—The Husband and the Wife agree that they shall live separate and apart, and that each shall be free from the interference, authority and control, direct or indirect, of the other, as fully as though unmarried. The Husband and the Wife may both for his or her own separate benefits engage in any employment, business, or profession he or she may choose.

* * *

3. Custody and Visitation—As to the custody and care of the Children, the Husband and the Wife both agree as follows:

a. That each is a fit and proper person to have custody of the Children, but have decided that because the Wife will be more available and accessible to the Children, and because the Husband is currently faced with time constraints of a demanding career, that the Wife will have legal custody of the Children and they will reside with the Wife at the primary residence which she is currently seeking.

Since this is only a memorandum of agreement, the first paragraph should have simply stated that the parties agreed to the following provision. Again, and although the attorney drafting the agreement will include a clause dealing with "Separate Residence," there is no need for the mediator to do so. This is only a summary of what the parties agreed to, not their final agreement. Aside from the duplication of effort, by straying from the facts the mediator always increases the risk of saying more than is necessary or than he should.

With this in mind, and as a general rule, an agreement should contain *what* was decided by the parties, not *how* they came to that decision. If the agreement says that the wife was given custody because she does not work and because the husband does, what will happen if she later goes to work? The issue is not whether the court will change custody if that happens—they will not, certainly not on that basis alone—but whether it will give the husband the opportunity to argue that there should be such a change. The following is an example of how this clause could have read.

"The Husband and the Wife shall have joint custody of the Children and shall together be responsible for, and shall make, all of the major decisions affecting the Children's health, welfare, and education. Included in such decisions shall be the questions of medical, dental, surgical, or therapeutic treatment (except, in the case of an emergency, when it is not possible for the parties to consult with one another and agree upon the prescribed course of treatment); religious training and instruction; camps, trips, or vacations (other than those taken by either of the parties with the Children); schools, colleges, or courses of instruction; and organized recreational, athletic, or social activities.

The primary residence of the Children shall be with the Wife, who shall be responsible for, and shall have the right to make, all of the day-to-day decisions affecting the Children's health, welfare, and education while they are with her. The Husband shall have the same right while the Children are with him."

b. Both the Husband and the Wife will use their best efforts to foster respect, love, and affection of each child toward each parent, and that they shall cooperate fully in implementing a relationship which will give each child the maximum feeling of security that may be possible.

As a general rule, flowery words of good intention add nothing. While they can be excused, to a limited extent, when dealing with children, they should nevertheless be kept to a minimum. They should certainly never be permitted to stand substitute for what should have been substance in the agreement.

 c. The Husband and the Wife shall further cooperate fully in implementing a parental interaction schedule which will later be described to accommodate maximum contact with both parents and maintain contact with each child's friends and maintain continuity in schooling experience as much as possible.

 d. The Husband shall have liberal and open rights to visit and have the Children accompany him on daytime outings, overnight stays, at other residences, and extended trips and visits including vacations.

 e. The Husband and the Wife have also agreed that the Husband will have an extended time with the Children of one week during the summer designated as vacation which will be arranged one month in advance with the Wife so that it would be in the best interests of the Children taking into account their scheduled social activities.

 When dealing with young children such as these, who were six and eight at the time, there is no excuse for failing specifically to provide when the husband will have the right to spend time with them. Again, mediation seeks to leave the parties *able* to cooperate in the future, not *obligated* to do so. To put it another way, if they are left with such an obligation, it should be to cooperate to modify their arrangements as the circumstances require, not to have to make an agreement in each and every instance.

 This is a perfect example of the use of flowery words that say nothing. All that has been said is that arrangements will be made in the future to work out an agreement in keeping with certain considerations, all of which are in conflict with one another. To make matters worse, the mediator's use of words such as "cooperate" and "liberal and open" have blinded the parties to the reality of the situation and where they have been left—which is really with no agreement. (Even the one week in the summer, which is the only specific time allotted to the husband, is subject to future, ill-defined, considerations.) The following is an example of how this clause could have read.

 "The Husband shall have the right to exercise his partial custody with the Children as follows:

 "(a) The Husband shall have the right to be and spend time with the Children on alternate weekends commencing on Friday at 6:00 P.M. and ending on Sunday at 8:00 P.M. If the day preceding such weekend or the day following such weekend shall be a legal holiday or a day on which the Children are not required to attend school, then such weekend shall be deemed to include such preceding or following day. The Husband shall give the Wife at least three (3) days' prior oral notice of his intention to be and spend time with the Children on any such weekend.

 "(b) In addition, the Husband shall have the right to be and spend time with the Children one weekday evening (Monday through Thursday) each week between the hours of 6:00 P.M. and, overnight, until the commencement of school the following day or, if such following day shall not be a day on which the Children are required to attend school, then until 8:00 P.M. The Husband shall give the Wife at least one day's prior oral notice of his intention to be and spend time with the Children on any such weekday.

 "(c) In addition, the Husband shall have the right to spend time with the Children during the Children's winter (Christmas) and intersession school vacations in odd years and during the Children's spring (Easter) and Thanksgiving school vacations in even years. The Husband shall give the Wife at least thirty (30) days' prior oral notice of his intention to spend time with the Children on any such school vacation, which notice shall include the date on which such period shall commence and the date on which such period shall end.

"(d) In addition, the Husband shall have the right to be and spend time with the Children for one (1) week during the Children's summer recess from school. The Husband shall give the Wife oral notice of his intention to exercise any such right on or before June 1, which notice shall include the date on which such period shall commence and the date on which such period shall end. Notwithstanding anything hereinabove contained to the contrary, if any of the Children shall attend sleep-away camp, then the Husband shall exercise such right with respect to such child prior to the commencement of such camp, or following its conclusion.

"(e) Notwithstanding anything hereinabove contained to the contrary, in the event that the Husband shall not be away with the Children during their winter school vacation in odd years, then the Wife shall have the right to have the Children with her on Christmas day from 10:00 A.M. until 10:00 P.M., and on New Year's Day from 9:00 A.M. until 8:00 P.M., and in the event that the Wife shall not be away with the Children during their winter school vacation in even years, then the Husband shall have the right to have the Children with him on Christmas Day from 10:00 A.M. until 10:00 P.M., and on New Year's Day from 9:00 A.M. until 8:00 P.M."

f. The Husband and the Wife have agreed that if for any reason the Wife is temporarily unable to provide for the Children's needs, that the Children will temporarily reside with the Husband until the Wife is able to adequately provide for their care and well-being. This decision was reached by the Husband and the Wife, based on the understanding that there may be times and circumstances in the Wife's life as there are currently in the Husband's with his employment, that in the best interest of the Children the other parent may best serve as the primary care giver. These circumstances include both physical and mental health. The Husband and the Wife further agree that while the Children are in residence with the Husband that he will make all necessary decisions and provide for the care, education and maintenance of the Children. The Children will return to the Wife's residence and the Wife will resume her role of primary care giver when the Wife is able to again provide for their care and well-being, taking into consideration the best interests of the Children, their social activities and continuity of their schooling experience. This agreement may temporarily alter the amount of support payments while the Children are in residence with the Husband.

This long-winded clause adds nothing—except the opportunity for possible conflict and misunderstanding between the parties in the future. All that it says is that life is uncertain and that it is possible that things may occur in the future that may cause the parties to wish to alter their present agreement, or may even require them to do so. Worse yet, it gives the suggestion that these contingencies have been dealt with when they have not. What constitutes the wife's being "temporarily unable to provide for the children's needs?" How will we know that the wife is again "able to adequately provide for their care and well-being?" (From a drafting standpoint, using the word "needs" in the first instance and the words "care and well-being" in the second could suggest that a different standard is to be used to determine when they will leave the wife and when they will return, even though this was obviously not intended.)

The next sentence only compounds the problem. While this clause starts out by suggesting that the parties are talking about a change in custody based upon the wife's inability to take care of the children, it then (and perhaps unintentionally) shifts and suggests that the children may live with the husband in the future not because the wife is "unable to provide for the children's needs," but because it may be "in the best interests of the children" for the husband to be the primary care giver. If the first criteria is less than precise, and therefore open to debate, the second carries this fault to an extreme, a fact not helped by the next sentence, which only further compounds the confusion by suggesting that "these circumstances include both physical and mental health." The last sentence in this paragraph raises the problem one step further. Consider the words "may temporarily alter." Consider how many possibilities those words admit.

It could be said that this agreement suggests that the payments "may" be altered but not necessarily "will" be altered. It could be said that even if they will be altered that they will be altered for less than the full period that the children are with the husband. It could even be argued that the payments might be altered upward or downward. Even assuming, however, that the agreement had more clearly expressed the fact that the husband's support payments will be decreased during the period of time that the children are residing with him, it would still have added nothing but a potential problem unless the agreement also provided either how *much* that decrease would be or, if it could not do that, how it would be determined.

Finally, it is never appropriate to invoke the "best interests of the children" as a yardstick, since it is a yardstick that provides no measurement. Nor is it any the more defensible because it is the yardstick traditionally invoked by courts to justify their results. While this yardstick may be the one that a judge invokes to justify his decision, that is not to say that it is the one he applies to get to it.

* * *

i. It is the joint desire of both the Husband and the Wife to maintain mutual or joint decision-making regarding major changes in the life of either of the Children and they have agreed to consult one another, and jointly agree on all important matters which may arise. If, after negotiations, the Husband and the Wife are unable to arrive at a mutual decision, they have agreed to submit these parenting issues to formal mediation.

On the face of it, this clause seems a rather standard, straightforward provision. Consider, however, how much unintended and unnecessary possible confusion is engendered in all of this. Subdivision (a) of this article contains no provision that the wife is to have the right to make all of the day-to-day decisions affecting the children while they reside with her. Subdivision (f), however, provides that while the children are with the husband, he will not only make all of the day-to-day decisions but that "he will make all necessary decisions that provide for the care, education and maintenance of the children."

Now we are told that, regardless of where the children may reside, the couple "have agreed to consult with one another, and jointly agree on all important matters which may arise." On top of that, we have been given no indication of what constitutes an "important" matter. To be sure, even agreeing on what *are* the important decisions does not provide a mechanism for resolving them, and simply saying that they will be decided jointly by the parties, as we ourselves have done, may only leave the couple with a problem. Given the difficulty that one of the parties may have in feeling disenfranchised from his children, however, this may be one instance in which loose language such as this may be allowed because of the implications of giving that right completely to one of the parties.

j. As to the health insurance coverage of each of the Children, the Husband agrees that he will continue to provide health insurance for both of the Children. Their decision is based on the fact that the Husband receives family medical insurance coverage at no expense to him through his employment.

Does the fact that the couple's decision was based on the husband's receiving this insurance coverage as an incident to his employment mean that he does not have that obligation if he no longer receives the benefit of such insurance through employment? Suppose he leaves his job and goes into business for himself? Suppose he leaves this job and takes other employment that does not provide such coverage? Does his obligation end then? The agreement does not say. On the assumption that the husband will not be required to purchase this insurance on his own, the clause should read as follows:

"The Husband presently receives the benefits of certain policies of medical, hospital, and dental insurance as an incident to his employment. To the extent permitted by such policies of insurance, and until December 31 of the year in which a child shall attain the age of nineteen years (or, if a child shall attend college, then until such child shall complete college), the Husband shall maintain such child as a beneficiary of such policies of insurance so long as, and to the extent that, such policies of insurance are made available to the Husband as an incident to his employment. In the event that the Husband's present employment is terminated for any reason, the Husband's obligations hereunder shall end, except that such obligation shall thereafter extend to the benefits of any future medical, hospital, and dental insurance which the Husband shall receive or be entitled to as an incident to any future employment of the Husband."

k. The Husband and the Wife agree that each intends to help the Children with their college expenses to the best of their respective ability at the time of their attendance in college, if either of the Children chooses to enroll. In addition, the Husband has agreed to continue his purchase of U.S. Savings Bonds through his employment every six weeks to an amount of $391.00 per year. The Wife has also agreed to begin a savings account with money set aside each month for this purpose. Both the Husband and the Wife agree to increase the amount of this "set-aside" with increases in income.

This again is a perfect example of the attempt to use flowery words of good intention to stand substitute for substance. Aside from the husband's obligation to continue to purchase U.S. Savings Bonds of $391.00 per year (and even his obligation to apply those toward the college expenses of the children is left to inference), neither of the parties has any specific obligation whatsoever. (The agreement says that they "intend" to help their children, not that they "will.") Even if it were to be assumed, however, that this clause expresses more than just a moral obligation, it would be impossible to determine what specific obligation, if any, either of the parties has. What does it mean to say that they intend to help their children "to the best of their respective abilities?" Suppose one of the parties says that he would like to but can't? How much is the wife obligated to "set aside" each month? How much are either of the parties required to put away "with increases in income"? Having expressed their good intentions, the mediator has then closed the book on the subject.

Two approaches are available to a couple regarding the payment of college expenses for their children. Under one arrangement, the couple can agree now that each will pay for the children's college expenses, for example, in proportion to their respective incomes. The following clause provides this.

"The Husband and the Wife, respectively, each agree to pay and provide for the college education expenses of each of the Children in excess of such sum or sums that a child may receive, either by way of scholarship, loan, or endowment fund to defer the cost of such college education expenses, in proportion to their respective 'gross annual incomes.' For the purposes hereof, such college education expenses shall be deemed to include, but only include, tuition, room and board, university fees, books, and transportation to and from college four times each academic year.

"For the purposes of this Article, the term 'gross annual income' shall mean the Husband's or Wife's gross income of a character that constitutes gross income of a resident citizen of the United States for federal income tax purposes under the United States Internal Revenue Code and the regulations promulgated thereunder by the Secretary of the Treasury in force and effect from time to time, plus tax-exempt interest on all state and local obligations, except that there shall be excluded from the Husband's 'gross annual income' and included in the Wife's 'gross annual income' the amount of any payments made by the Husband to the Wife for her support and maintenance and for the support, maintenance, and education of the Children. At arriving at their respective 'gross annual incomes,' the Husband and Wife shall each be entitled to take all trade or business deductions of an employee, or a person carrying on a trade or business, permitted by either Section 62(1) or 62(2) of the Code and appropriate regulations."

Alternatively, the couple can decide that it is impractical and perhaps impossible to make a specific determination at this time as to the payment of these college expenses, given the age of the children and the uncertainty as to what the parties' respective incomes will be, or how costly college will be, ten or twelve years from now. They may therefore decide to defer the issue until the children are of college age and to then predicate their respective obligation's on their then financial circumstances and ability. If this latter procedure is employed, the parties' agreement must be very clear as to the following:

(1) what college education expenses are included.

(2) what procedure will be employed to resolve the issue if the parties cannot agree between themselves.

(3) what criteria will be employed and looked to to determine their respective financial circumstances and abilities. The following provision is an example of how these problems might be covered.

"The Husband and the Wife acknowledge that it is their intention and expectation that the Children shall have the benefit of a college education, and the failure of this agreement to make specific provision for the payment of the Children's college education expenses is occasioned simply by the fact that they do not know how much those expenses will be, to what extent it will be possible to meet such expenses by means of scholarships, loans, or contributions made by the Children from their part-time employment, or what their respective financial abilities to assume all or any part of such expenses will be.

"On or before October 1 of the year immediately preceding the year in which a child intends to start college, the parties will meet to discuss their respective financial obligations to meet such child's college education expenses, which expenses shall be deemed to include, but only include, tuition, room and board, university fees, books, and four (4) round trips to and from college.

"In the event that the parties shall fail to meet on or before October 1, or having met, shall fail to agree upon their respective obligations to pay such college education expenses by that date, then the question of the amount, if any, to be paid by either or both of the parties shall be settled by arbitration in accordance with the rules of the American Arbitration Association in Philadelphia, and judgment upon the award rendered by the arbitrator may be entered by either of the parties in any court having jurisdiction thereof. Nothing herein contained shall be deemed to confer upon the American Arbitration Association the right to make any other determination between the parties.

"In making its determination, and in assessing the respective financial obligations, if any, of either or both of the parties, the American Arbitration Association shall base such determination on the respective financial circumstances of each of the parties at the time in question except that, and unless there shall have been a material change in the financial circumstance of either of the parties, the respective financial circumstances of the parties in the calendar year immediately preceding the calendar year in which such matter is submitted for determination shall be considered as reflective of each of the parties' present financial circumstances.

"In determining the respective financial circumstances of each of the parties, the American Arbitration Association shall consider (a) the income which each of the parties derives from employment, or is capable of deriving from employment, (b) any other income which either of the parties may have from any other source, including, but not limited to, interest and dividend income, (c) the parties' respective assets (other than the equity in any home that either of them may own and use as their principal residence), (d) the contribution which each of the parties presently makes toward the support and maintenance of the Children, (e) the contribution which each of the parties is required to make to any household in which he or she is then living, (f) the contribution made, or capable of being made, by the then husband or wife of either of the parties to the support and maintenance of such party's household and living expenses, should they have remarried, which contribution shall be reflected by such other party's husband's or wife's income from employment or investments as well as the obligation which such party's husband or wife may have to any former spouse or spouses, or to the child or children of any former marriage."

1. *The Husband and the Wife agree to review arrangements as set forth above for custody and visitation under the following conditions: upon request by either the Husband or the Wife; if either the Husband or the Wife remarries; or if there are major life changes with either the Husband or the Wife or the Children. The Husband and the Wife agree that any changes in the custody and visitation will take into account the social and schooling needs of the Children as well as maintain maximum contact with each parent. If the Husband and the Wife are unable to negotiate and agree on changes, they both agree to submit the issues to formal mediation.*

While virtually all professionals agree that living arrangements for the children should be established on a long-term and settled basis, the mediator's enthusiasm, and his romanticized approach to the problem, have left the couple with an agreement simply for today. At any time, and virtually for any reason, either of the parties can request a change in the custodial arrangement. Not only that, but he has also suggested that certain life events—for example, either of the parties' remarriage—is an appropriate occasion to raise the question of the propriety of the present custodial arrangements. Worse yet, and having opened Pandora's box, the mediator has not given thought as to how then to close it. As with all of the other issues left open by the agreement, the parties will simply discuss them between themselves, and, if that fails, "submit the issues to formal mediation," which simply means to discuss it in a more structured setting. But what if mediation fails? Are the parties then simply left with the problem which the mediator has created? Apparently so.

4. Support and Maintenance—*As established in the prior section, the Wife will in all respects provide the primary care, educate and maintain and support the children properly and in such a manner as to provide them the best care, education, maintenance and support consistent with their needs as planned, discussed, problem-solved, and budgeted for by the Wife and the Husband.*

This sentence is unnecessary. It is simply the mediator's way of congratulating himself on the fact that he and the couple sat down and "problem-solved" (another romantic intrusion) the wife's and the children's needs based upon her budget. Since it is unlikely that all of the wife's budgetary needs were actually met, she may later take a look at this statement and find reason to view it, and perhaps the mediation itself, with dissatisfaction when she later concludes that it was untrue.

It has been mutually agreed that during the Husband's lifetime, he will make periodic payments for the Wife's support and maintenance and for the support, maintenance and education of the Children. The Husband agrees to pay to the Wife the sum of $438.00 every two weeks (26 pay periods per year) beginning December 1, 1982. This amount was agreed to based on the following:

a. The Husband and the Wife were married for 13 years.

b. During that time the Wife was employed full-time in the home as a homemaker, wife and mother and has had little opportunity for education, training and work experience. The Wife is currently unemployed and seeking work.

c. The Husband was employed professionally with a major airline during most of the marriage. He is currently employed as an executive with that airline with an annual gross income of $32,340.00.

d. Even though the Wife is unemployed and currently seeking either part-time or full-time employment that the sum agreed to has been established on a planned budgeted amount sufficient to sustain both the Wife's needs as well as the needs of the Children for the current time at her planned residence.

e. The amount of mutual debt (see Appendix I) and monthly payments being made by the Husband.

With very rare exception, the mediator should never set forth the *reasons* that led the parties to their ultimate agreement. The object is to *come* to an agreement, not to *justify* it. More importantly, by setting forth that justification, the mediator opens the result to possible attack when, at a later point, either or both of the parties questions the logic, as expressed in the agreement, that allegedly brought them to the result or, possibly, the factors that were not considered. If the result was achieved by a mathematical computation, where both parties assigned the same weight and the same significance to each of the figures, it would not be a problem. But with the factors here listed by the mediator, each of us, and each of the parties, can assign literally whatever weight we wish to them. Therefore, and since these factors do not prove, or even really justify, the result, they add nothing but potential trouble.[3]

Subdivision "d" is particularly troublesome. The husband is giving the wife $219 per week for her support and that of their two children, for a total of $11,388. It may well be that the husband cannot afford to give her more, based upon his current earnings. But that does not mean that the wife can really meet her legitimate needs, and those of the children, on this amount of money, and it is insulting to her to suggest, as that clause does, that she can. This is a perfect example of the misunderstanding and misuse of budgets. The mediator did not conclude an agreement that provided for a payment by the husband to meet "both the wife's needs as well as the needs of the children" as "established" by her budget. Quite the contrary, he pared down the items on her budget to an amount that the husband could afford to pay, and it is improper to suggest otherwise.

The amount and scheduled payment as agreed to by the Husband and the Wife in the above paragraph includes a child support payment of approximately $200.00 to $250.00 per payment. The Husband and the Wife agree that they will seek neutral tax advice to determine the actual breakdown of child support and alimony based upon their desire to minimize their tax consequences as a result of the dissolution.

To suggest that the husband will pay between $200 and $250 in child support every two weeks is simply to invite a dispute. In fact, it is hard to see how it can be avoided, since it is clearly better for the husband if the amount allocated as child support is $200 and clearly better for the wife if it is $250. (At a glance it would appear that the fact that the couple had agreed to the fixed amount of $438 every two weeks would save the situation by making the payment definite, but as can be seen here, it did not.)

Nor does it help to suggest that they will resolve the problem by seeking "neutral tax advice . . . based upon their desire to minimize their tax consequences. . . ." Once the couple has agreed to the fixed total amount, they cannot minimize their tax consequences. All that they can do is to determine whether the husband will bear the burden of the taxes, by allocating the child support payment as $250, or whether the wife will, by allocating it as $200. In any event, if the couple were going to seek such "neutral tax advice," they should have done so before the agreement was concluded, not afterwards. Again, the mediator has simply left open for the future a possible dispute that could have been, and should have been, resolved at the present time.

5. Adjustment to Support and Maintenance—*The agreed payment of support of $438.00 every two weeks may be adjusted by the following as agreed to by the Husband and the Wife:*

a. When either child reaches majority.

b. When either child marries or has permanent residence away from home.

c. If the Wife remarries or cohabits.

d. If the Wife and/or children experience increased or decreased needs.

e. If the Wife's income or resources should increase.

f. If the Husband's income or resources should increase or decrease.

g. Significant reduction of mutual debt.

h. If the children remain with the Husband at his residence and in his care as outlined in Section #3 Paragraph f for an extended time.

i. As well as adjustments for cost of living. The Husband and the Wife agree to renegotiate support payments if life changes as described should occur. If an impasse is reached, both the Husband and the Wife agree to mediate the issues in dispute.

While one would assume that this article is intended to evidence the fact that this is a "living agreement," designed to reflect the changing needs of the children, as well as the changing circumstances of the parties, it really only stands as evidence for the proposition that the parties have been left with no agreement at all. After having worked for nine hours to conclude an agreement, it turns out that they have only concluded an agreement for today. In fact, given the criteria enumerated by the mediator for possible future adjustments in the support payments, it is hard to imagine any change that might take place in the lives of either of the parties or their children—for example, their daughter enrolling in a dance class—that would not serve as such a basis. This is not to suggest that certain of these events could not and should not serve as the basis for an adjustment in support payments. It is simply to suggest that many of these matters could be dealt with now rather than simply put off for the future. After all, it will be no easier tomorrow—in fact, it will be harder—to agree on the amount of the reduction in the event of the wife's remarriage, or a child's reaching his or her majority, than it is today.

Secondly, there has been absolutely no procedure built into the agreement to resolve the issue should the negotiations between the parties, or mediation for that matter, fail. Finally, too many of the criteria are set forth in vague language that only invites possible future disputes between the parties, e.g., "cohabits" (does that include the wife's boyfriend staying overnight, or for a weekend?), "resources" (are those human, as well as financial?), "significant" (is that more than half or less than half?), "majority" (is that when a child is legally entitled to vote or when he is no longer legally entitled to support from his parents?).

If the agreement contains provision for an escalation clause that is to be triggered, for example, by an increase in the husband's income, then the agreement should specifically provide what increase in income will trigger that increased obligation and how much that obligation will be. The same is true if there is to be a de-escalation in the payments based, for example, upon the wife's future income from employment. In short, the agreement should indicate now how the couple will deal with each of these eventualities in the future. It is not sufficient simply to say that the payments will be "adjusted" if the "needs" of either the wife or children shall change. In fact, it is irresponsible to leave the matter like this.

The parties should be required to come back to renegotiate (re-mediate) their agreement only as a last resort. It must be kept in mind that the situation in the future will be far different than it is presently. At the present time there is a certain reality that tends to act as a governor upon the parties. That governor is principally the fact that if either of them feels that the agreement being concluded is too at variance with their expectations, based upon what they think a court will or will not do, then that party always has the ability to place the matter in the hands of a court, much as he might wish not to do so. The second factor is the underlying desire of the parties to get on with the matter and to get it done.

In large measure, neither of these factors will act as a governing force when the couple come back in the future to re-mediate their agreement. Suppose that the agreement provides, as it does here, that the support payments "may be adjusted by the following as agreed to by the husband and the wife. . . ." Suppose further that, and after the occurrence of one of those events, the parties go back to the mediator to renegotiate their agreement but are unable to agree on whether or not there should be such an adjustment and, if so, how much. Isn't what a court might or might not do a governor upon their discussions at this point? Absolutely not, because a court could not do anything at all. If the original mediation had fallen through, the court could have made an agreement for the parties. In other words, the court could have ordered the husband to pay his wife the sum of $450 every two weeks. But once the parties have come to an agreement, the court's hands are generally tied. They can enforce that agreement, and they can even interpret it for the parties. But they cannot make a new one for them.

There is thus no penalty on either the husband or the wife in refusing to acquiesce in the other's request, other than to incur the other party's displeasure. The agreement simply provided that should either of them so wish in the future, that they would talk to one another about a possible adjustment in the support payments. It may sound as if they agreed to more. But they really didn't. Furthermore, even if a court might feel that the language in the agreement was specific enough to permit it to modify the agreement, or that it had the statutory authority to do so in any event, it is much harder to predict whether the court would act here and, if it did, what that action would be, than it would be to predict what it would do had the parties been unable to come to any agreement at all. And the harder it is to predict what a court will do the less its possible determination will act as a governor on the parties' negotiations.

Nor will the need to get on with the matter act as a governor upon those discussions. They *have* gotten on with the matter, and have made new lives for themselves, and their inability to reach an accommodation on this issue at the present time will thus not prevent them from continuing with the business of their lives, as it might have originally. In short, these discussions simply do not have the teeth in them that their original discussions did.

Lastly, and as we have had occasion to comment upon previously, while it may be appropriate to provide for an adjustment in the support payments if there are major changes in the lives of either of the parties or their children, it is not appropriate to attempt to adjust those payments to reflect each and every change that may take place.

The support payments to be made by the husband to the wife should be expressed as follows:

"1. The Husband shall, during his natural life, and during any period in which the Husband is obligated for the support and maintenance of the Wife, as is hereinafter provided in paragraph "3," pay to the Wife, for her support and maintenance, the sum of $125 per week.

"2. The Husband shall, during his natural life, and until an emancipation event shall occur with respect to all of the Children, as that term is defined in Article "I," pay to the Wife, for the support, maintenance, and education of the Children, the sum of $100 per week; provided, however, that in the event that an emancipation event shall occur with respect to one of the Children, then the payments to be made by the Husband to the Wife, as hereinabove provided, shall thereafter be in the sum of $60 per week rather than $100 per week.

"3. The Husband shall be obligated for the support and maintenance of the Wife, as hereinabove provided, during his natural life, so long as he shall be married to her and she shall be alive or, in the event of their divorce, until she shall remarry or sooner die, except that, notwithstanding the foregoing, the Husband's obligation for the support and maintenance of the Wife shall terminate, in any event, and for all purposes, on December 31, 1990.

"4. The Husband acknowledges that the payments hereinabove provided in paragraph "2" for support, maintenance, and education of the Children have been agreed upon on the assumption that the Husband's "gross income from employment" does not, and will not, exceed the sum of $35,000. In the event that the Husband's "gross income from employment" shall exceed the sum of $35,000 in any year subsequent to 1983 in which the Husband is obligated to make payment to the Wife pursuant to paragraph "2," then the payments to be made by the Husband to the Wife in such year pursuant to paragraph "2" shall be increased by an amount that shall be calculated as follows: the present weekly payments to be made by the Husband to the Wife pursuant to paragraph "2" shall be multiplied by a fraction in which the numerator shall be the Husband's "gross income from employment" in the year in question and the denominator shall be $35,000. Thus, if the Husband's "gross income from employment" in any calendar year shall be $42,000, then the payments to be made by the Husband to the Wife pursuant to paragraph "2" shall be increased by $20, from $100 per week to $120 per week, except that if the Husband is only obligated to the wife for the support, maintenance, and education of one of the Children, then such payments shall be increased from $60 per week to $72 per week.

"5. On or before April 15 of each calendar year, commencing with the calendar year 1984, the Husband shall provide the Wife with a signed copy of the federal income tax return filed by the Husband for the preceding calendar year. The sums payable by the Husband to the Wife for such calendar year shall then be adjusted on the basis of the Husband's actual gross income from employment for such calendar year, and any excess monies payable by the Husband to the Wife shall be added, in equal amounts, to the next twenty (20) payments to be made by the Husband to the Wife following the Husband's submission to the Wife of such accounting; provided, however, that if the Husband is not then obligated to make payment to the Wife for the support, maintenance, and education of the Children, or any of them, or if his obligation to make such payment shall terminate prior to the expiration of said twenty (20) week period, then such adjustment, or the balance of such adjustment, as the case may be, shall be paid by the Husband to the Wife on or before May 1 following the termination of such calendar year for which such adjustment is being made, or upon the termination of the Husband's obligation to make payment to the Wife for the support, maintenance, and education of the Children, whichever shall last occur.

"6. (Define "gross income from employment".)

"7. Notwithstanding anything herein contained to the contrary, if there shall be any change in the status of the Wife or any of the Children which shall affect the amount which the Husband is obligated to pay to the Wife, or which will cause a termination of any such payment, as hereinabove provided, there shall be no adjustment or termination of the payment required to be made by the Husband during the week in which such change in status shall occur, and such adjustment or termination, as the case may be, shall be made, or shall take effect, as of the first day of the week immediately following the week in which such change shall occur."

6. Life Insurance—*The Husband currently represents and warrants that he is the owner of the following life insurance on his life issued by the life insurance companies listed below: John Hancock Mutual Life Insurance Company—death benefits $25,000. Connecticut General Life Insurance Company—$90,320.*

The Husband agrees to pay any premiums due on these policies required to continue the above-named insurance. Until November 21, 1998, when his youngest child reaches the age of 22, the Husband agrees that the life insurance policy shall name the Wife as the irrevocable beneficiary of the full death benefits except in the case of the Wife's death and thereafter the benefits shall be for the irrevocable benefit of the Children surviving until such time as the Husband would no longer be required to support the Children under the terms of this agreement.

The fact that it is appropriate to name the wife as the beneficiary during her lifetime does not mean that it is appropriate to name the children as the beneficiaries upon her death, particularly if they are infants. It is a far better practice to designate the trustee named in the husband's will as his beneficiary and to then have that will provide how those funds will be administered for the benefit of the children. Secondly, the agreement should provide, if that is the intention of the parties, that the husband will not have the right to borrow against any of these policies so as to reduce the death benefits payable upon his death.

7. *Real and Personal Property—The Husband and the Wife recognize their mutual debt of:*

Chemical Bank (Visa)	$2,212
Manufacturers (MasterCard)	1,732
American Express	472
Citibank (Checking Plus)	2,212
Sears	712
J.C. Penney	474
Macy's	271
Exxon	412
Dr. Bernard Jones	775
Dr. Milton Green	650
	$9,922

The Husband agrees to make regular payments as outlined in budget to maintain both his and the Wife's credit rating.

The budget appended to the agreement (which is not included) simply contains an item for debt service. Since that amount is not sufficient to pay the minimum amount due on each of these debts (when there is a minimum amount due) it is not clear what the amount of the Husband's payment should be. Nor does adding the word "regular" cure this defect. Does this clause permit the husband to apply the payments as he sees fit "to maintain both his and the wife's credit rating"? The agreement is not clear. Nor is it clear, except by inference, what the total payment is which the husband is to make each month. There is no reason why that should not be stated definitely, and there is every reason that it should.

The Husband and the Wife agree that upon their mutual decision to sell their marital residence that the balance on their mutual debt will be paid in full and the remaining balance of proceeds split between them 50/50.

The presence of this clause tends to reward the husband, and penalize the wife since, if the husband makes the smallest payments that he can in reduction of the debts in question, if any of those debts remain at the time of the sale of their home, the wife will be obligated to pay 50% of them. Again, this can only cause possible future disagreements between the parties.

The Husband and the Wife further agree that each will be responsible only for his or her own personal debt incurred since the time of this agreement dated September 28, 1982 and that neither the Husband nor the Wife will use any credit or charge account which would name or otherwise encumber the other party.

Actually, it is hard to understand what this means. By saying that each will "only" be responsible for their own personal debts incurred subsequent to September 28, 1982, the agreement implies that either they are not responsible for their own personal debts prior to that date or, since that makes no sense, that they may be obligated for one another's personal debts incurred prior to that date, though the agreement does not say how or in what manner.

The provisions with respect to the parties' debts could have been spelled out more simply as follows:

"1. The Husband and the Wife each represent to the other that they have not incurred any debt or liability whatsoever, whether for necessaries or otherwise, upon the credit of the other, or for which the other is or may be liable, and agree to save and hold the other free and harmless from and indemnified against, any and all debts, obligations, and liabilities of any kind or nature heretofore incurred by them, either for their benefit or for the benefit of any of the Children, whether for necessaries or otherwise.

"2. The Husband and Wife shall not and will not hereafter incur or cause to be incurred any debts or liabilities whatsoever, either for their own benefit or for the benefit of any of the Children, whether for necessaries or otherwise, upon the credit of the other party, or for which the other party is or may be liable, and shall and will hold the other party free and harmless from, and indemnified against, and will satisfy, all debts, liabilities, and obligations of every kind and nature whatsoever which may hereafter be incurred or contracted by him or her.

"3. There is excepted from the foregoing the debts set forth in the schedule of debts annexed hereto as Schedule "A," which said debts shall be assumed and paid by the Husband, who agrees to hold the Wife free and harmless from, and indemnified against, the same.

"4. Notwithstanding anything hereinabove or hereinafter contained to the contrary, the Husband shall be responsible for, and shall pay, all of the normal maintenance and carrying charges with respect to the Home incurred prior to the execution of this agreement."

The Husband and the Wife having made full disclosure of any and all checking and savings accounts, mutual stocks, bonds, and other investment securities, acknowledge that neither has any holdings solely or mutually and that all account balances reflect a zero balance at the time of this agreement. Both the Husband and the Wife warrant that neither has disposed of any jointly held monies or holding unbeknownst to the other party since September 28, 1982 without the knowledge and awareness of the other.

This statement should refer to a specific schedule, appended to the parties' agreement, which sets forth all of their income, assets, and liabilities. Such a statement is as follows:

"The Husband and Wife, respectively, each warrant and represent that the information contained on the Financial Data Sheet signed by each of them (a copy of which is attached to this agreement) setting forth their respective incomes, assets, and debts is true and accurate to the best of their knowledge. The Husband and Wife each further acknowledge that they are aware that the other party, in entering into this agreement, is relying upon the truth and accuracy of the representations made therein and, in particular, that the other party has no significant or material income or assets other than those set forth on those schedules and, further, that the other party has each of the debts, if any, listed therein."

As to their family home located in Ridersville, New York, the Husband and the Wife have mutually problem-solved and have mutually decided to rent this property for an approximate amount of $675.00 per month with a lease period lasting one year. This decision was made by both the Husband and the Wife based on:

a. The nature of the housing market on Long Island and the lengthy period of time often needed to sell a home.

b. The immediate need to reduce expenses in order to support two separate households.

c. The Wife's desire for she and the Children to take up separate residence away from her parent's home, where she and the Children currently reside, as soon as possible. The Husband and the Wife agree that prior to the end of the lease period (November 1, 1983) that they will renegotiate their decision to rent or sell based on their current financial situation and the nature of the housing market. The Husband and the Wife agree that if they are unable to mutually agree they will submit this issue to mediation.

Before commenting on this last paragraph, we would like to point out that the preceding five paragraphs have all been included under the rubric of real and personal property even though, as a practical matter, only the last paragraph deals with either real or personal property, except perhaps by inference. As a general rule, it would be better to break down the many items that are contained under this rubric into separate sections for easier reference.

As far as the disposition of the parties' marital residence is concerned, it is simply inappropriate to leave all of these decisions to future discussion, particularly where, as here, there is going to be a substantial distance between the parties. It is far better for the couple to make the best decision that they can *now*—for example, that the home will be rented for a year, following which it will be placed for sale. If this is done, the parties can, of course, both decide to delay the sale at that time. But if they are unable mutually to agree on the disposition of the house at the end of the year, they at least have an agreement. Here, if they cannot agree, the mediator has left them without one.

Upon the agreement to sell the family residence, seeking a fair market price, both the Husband and the Wife agree to dispose of any mutual debt and split the proceeds 50/50.

This is the only provision in the memorandum of agreement dealing with the sale of the parties' home. Furthermore, that provision assumes that they will be able to reach an agreement to sell it. Even if they do so agree, the problem is still not solved. Suppose they cannot agree upon the selling price. Suppose they cannot agree whether to sell the home privately or through a broker. Suppose they cannot agree upon any of the other issues incident to its sale. What are they to do then? The agreement leaves them without an answer.

Again, and except for the statement that the parties will split the proceeds 50/50, there is absolutely no provision in the agreement as to the payment of any other possible expenses incident to its sale. Suppose the husband decides that certain improvements should be made to the home in order to prepare it for sale. Who is to pay for them? Who is to pay for the attorney's fees or other closing costs incident to its sale, for that matter?

The sale of the marital residence is an event worthy of judicious planning. A more appropriate provision would be as follows:

"1. (Paragraph "1" provides that the Home is to be sold in the event of the occurrence of any one of a number of events, in accordance with the procedures set forth in paragraph "2," etc.).

"2. Within ten days following the date of the occurrence of any of the events set forth in paragraph "1" above, the parties shall meet or communicate with one another for the purpose of establishing a "Selling Price" for the Home. If the parties shall fail to meet or communicate with one another for such purpose or, having met or communicated with one another, shall fail to agree upon such Selling Price by such date, then either of the parties shall have the right to have the Home appraised by a licensed real estate appraiser selected by the President of the Long Island Real Estate Board, which appraisal shall be deemed the Selling Price for the Home, and binding upon the parties as such. The cost of such appraisal shall be paid for equally by the parties.

"3. As soon as the Selling Price for the Home has been determined, as provided in paragraph "2" above, the Home shall immediately be placed for sale and listed with each of the broker members of the Multiple Listing Service in the community in which the Home is located, through a Listing Broker selected by the Husband, upon written notice by the Husband to the Wife.

"4. The Listing Broker shall place the Home for sale at such higher "Asking Price" as the Listing Broker, in its sole determination, shall deem appropriate for the purpose of obtaining a purchaser at the Selling Price, and the decision of the Listing Broker as to such Asking Price shall, in the absence of an Asking Price agreed upon by the parties, be binding upon the parties.

"5. In the event that the parties shall not receive an offer to purchase the Home at a price equal to the Selling Price within sixty (60) days after the date on which the Home is listed for sale with the Multiple Listing Service, then the Home will be sold to the first person who shall offer to purchase the Home at a price at least equal to the highest price offered for the Home in said sixty (60) day period, except that in no event shall the Home be sold for an amount equal to less than ninety (90%) percent of the Selling Price in the absence of an agreement to such effect by the parties.

"6. Upon such sale there shall be deducted from the gross selling price, after the addition and subtraction of the requisite closing adjustments provided by the contract, (a) the amount paid in satisfaction of the First Mortgage, or the amount of the First Mortgage which the purchaser shall take subject to or assume, (b) the amount paid as brokerage commissions for bringing about such sale (but not in excess of the normal going rate of brokerage commissions in the community at the time of such sale), (c) the legal fees paid to the attorney selected to represent the parties in connection with the effectuation of such sale and (d) any transfer taxes, filing fees, or other recordation charges required to be paid by the sellers, and the balance then remaining from the gross selling price, after the deductions as hereinabove provided, shall then be divided between the Husband and the Wife as follows:

"(a) There shall first be paid and satisfied each of the debts set forth on Schedule "A," except that if either of the parties shall have satisfied any of such debts, either in whole or in part, that party shall first be reimbursed the amount so paid by him or her in satisfaction, or partial satisfaction, of such debt or debts.

"(b) The balance of the purchase price shall then be divided equally between the Husband and the Wife."

The Husband and the Wife are both aware that there may be tax consequences attached to their decision to rent and have mutually agreed to seek neutral tax advice regarding their decision.

The tax consequence in renting the marital residence is simply that the rent is deemed income for tax purposes. If the home is owned by both of the parties, one-half of that income will be attributable to each of them. Again, their agreement should provide how this will be handled rather than simply deferring the question.

In addition, the Husband and the Wife have mutually agreed to allow rental income to serve as income to the Husband, to be redistributed as support as described in Section #4. The Husband has included a minimal figure of $50.00 per month in his budget as expenses to be incurred in the maintenance and upkeep of their mutually held rental property. The Husband agrees to make all necessary improvements to maintain the present condition and value of their property.

This paragraph suggests many things but does not say any of them. If the husband is to have the right to keep the rental income, and is to be responsible to maintain the property, the agreement should simply say so. Adding that they have agreed to allow him to keep it "to be redistributed as support," or that they have "included a minimal figure of $50 per month" for maintenance, only adds to the confusion. That may have been part of the *thinking* that *led up* to their agreement, but it is *not* their *agreement*.

Suppose the cost of maintaining and keeping up the property exceeds $50 a month, or perhaps even the total rental income. Is the Husband obligated to make up the difference? It is one thing to say that the Husband will pay certain specific charges—real estate taxes, fuel, mortgage payments, etc. It is quite another thing to say that he will "make all necessary improvements to maintain the present condition and value of their property." Aside from being vague, and perhaps unrealistic, given their financial circumstances, it is only to invite dispute later on if he doesn't or can't.

The Husband agrees that he shall execute a last will and testament which will provide that the Wife will inherit his share of their mutually held property in Ridersville, New York in the event of his death and that the Wife shall similarly execute a last will and testament which will provide that the Husband shall inherit her interest in the same property. This provision of the agreement shall be in effect so long as the husband and the Wife mutually hold this property.

If the parties have come to an agreement that they each wish the other to have the home in the event that, at the time of their death, they are still married, the mediator should refer the couple to their advisory attorney to decide how that will be carried out. They might be told that simply transferring the home from whatever form in which it is presently held to themselves as joint tenants, with the right of survivorship, might be a far more efficient way of doing this. Since the deed would give each of them the right to inherit the property upon the other's death, the deed would not be dependent upon another instrument, in this case each of their last wills and testaments. The couple wants to hold their home as joint tenants, with the right of survivorship, to insure that title to the home will pass automatically, and by operation of law, at the moment one of them dies. The parties do not want the house to be probated under the deceased spouse's will. Probate is time-consuming and can be unnecessarily risky and costly.

As to the retirement benefits of the Husband, through his employment at American Airlines, information was requested and received August 27, 1982 (Appendix IV). As outlined in this document, if the Husband terminated employment 9/1/82 he would be *vested approximately $240 per month from the retirement plan to be payable at age 62. In addition, it was further stated that a reduced benefit of $110.00 per month was available at an early retirement age of 50. The Husband's contribution plus interest as of 9/1/82 was approximately $65.00 and to be withdrawn only at termination or retirement. The information provided was not deemed adequate by the mediator to facilitate the division of this marital property and further information is currently being sought in order to establish a present value which includes:*

1. The cost for the Wife should she choose to purchase the same benefit in an annuity. When this is procured, the Husband and the Wife will fairly and equitably divide this amount.

This is not an agreement; and it is irresponsible to leave the parties thinking that it is. Nor is the matter helped by suggesting that the amount will be divided "fairly and equitably." *What* will be divided fairly and equitably? The present value of the husband's pension or the cost to the wife in purchasing an annuity which will provide her with the same benefits? And *when* is it to be divided, at the present time or when the husband begins to receive his pension? Finally, how realistic is it to suggest that, given the additional expenses that the couple's separation involves, let alone the debt service for past debts, that they are going to be able to afford to go out and buy an annuity for the wife, or that the husband is going to be able to pay the wife one-half of the present value of a pension that he will not receive for many years to come?

As to the family automobile, which is a 1973 Volkswagen Beetle, the Husband and the Wife have mutually problem-solved their individual situations and negotiated that as of February 1, 1983, the Husband will sign all necessary documents in order to transfer full title and ownership of this car to the Wife. In addition, the Husband has agreed to make all necessary repairs and to maintain this car in optimum operating condition while it is in his use and prior to this transfer. The Husband agrees to deliver the car to the Wife's residence at this time. Upon the transfer of title on February 1, 1983, the Wife agrees to assume all future costs in repair, maintenance, and in procuring auto insurance. This decision was made based on the Husband's having easier access to public transportation and the Wife's need for personal mobility, the need to transport the Children to social outings, the Wife's greater need for grocery and other family shopping, and to support and encourage the Wife's seeking of gainful employment.

Again, while these factors may have influenced the couple's decision, it is only necessary for their agreement to state their decision, not how they reached it. The following clause will do that:

"The Husband and the Wife are presently the owners of a 1973 Volkswagen Beetle bearing New York registration number ABC-123. On February 1, 1983, the Husband shall assign and transfer to the Wife all of his right, title, and interest in and to said automobile. Simultaneously therewith, the Husband shall deliver the documents of title and registration to said automobile duly endorsed by the Husband for transfer to the Wife. Thenceforth, the Wife shall be solely liable for the use of said automobile, and the Wife shall record the transfer of ownership to said automobile within seven (7) business days of February 1, 1983."

As to the household effects remaining at the family residence in Ridersville, which includes household furnishings and appliances (See Appendix V), the Husband and the Wife have mutually problem-solved and negotiated that the Husband will conduct a sale *and sell all of the furniture and appliances (excluding appliances which are required by New York State Law for rental purposes) in an optimal way and that the proceeds in their entirety will be forwarded to the Wife. The Husband has also agreed to forward a payment of $200.00 in addition to the proceeds of the sale to the Wife. This agreement was made in consideration of the Wife and the Children and in an effort to contribute to the purchasing of other furniture and appliances needed to establish a new family residence for the Wife and the Children. This decision was reached by the Husband and the Wife after considering the value of the furniture and the appliances, and the cost of shipping, versus the cost of purchasing other furniture and appliances in the area of the Wife's residence.*

Under normal circumstances, it would be far better, if the wife were to receive the proceeds of the sale of the furniture, that she control that sale. Here, the parties were living at some distance from one another at the time, and that was impractical. She had no choice but to rely upon the good faith of her husband, which she may well have been justified in doing. There is nothing inappropriate in one of the parties relying upon the good faith of the other. It is only inappropriate for the agreement to *require* them to do this when it is not necessary. Again, saying that they have "mutually problem solved and negotiated" does not lend any more credibility to the result. Nor does the recitation of all of their reasons.

Any personal property, except as described above, all the clothing, jewelry and personal effects now in the possession of the Husband or the Wife shall continue to be the property of the holder. Articles which were left behind at the family residence such as silverware, kitchen utensils and linen will be shipped to the Wife by the Husband at no expense through use of transporting privileges provided by his employment at American Airlines.

8. Health Insurance Coverage and Medical Expenses—As to medical insurance coverage, the Husband will continue to provide for his own medical expenses and to maintain the current health insurance policy provided under the American Airlines Group Medical Plan.

The Husband agrees to continue coverage for the Wife under this same policy until a final decree of divorce has been entered. Thereafter, the Wife shall provide for her own health insurance coverage and any and all other medical and dental expenses.

The health insurance policy currently provided by the Husband's employer shall continue to provide coverage for the Children so long as they are eligible for enrollment under the Husband's policy.

In the event that at any time the policy referred to above can no longer be kept enforced by the payments of the premium thereon, the Husband shall pay the premium on a new policy or policies selected by him which provides substantially similar benefits.

The Husband and the Wife agree to divide any medical expenses not covered or in addition to that which is covered by the present health insurance coverage with 75 percent of these costs absorbed by the Husband and 25 percent to be absorbed by the Wife. This agreement may be renegotiated by the Husband and the Wife based on changes in income by either of them. If impasse is reached the Husband and the Wife agree to seek mediation of the issues.

It is not necessary to recite in the agreement what each of the parties is going to do for *themselves*. It is only necessary to recite what they are *obligated* to do for *one another* or for their *children*. Thus, it adds nothing to say that the husband will continue to provide for his own medical expenses or, for that matter, that the wife should provide for her own health insurance coverage after their divorce.

Although not significant in this instance, it is important to use the same terminology throughout. Lawyers call this "tracking" their language. Thus to talk about "medical insurance coverage" in one place and "health insurance coverage" in another, is to suggest that there is a difference. Employing the same designation in both places rules out any such possible interpretation.

The third paragraph of this section seems to suggest that the husband will maintain the policies of insurance for the children's benefit so long as he is able to. It could be argued, however, that this is simply a statement by the husband that it is his *opinion* that the children will continue to be covered under his present policy following his and his wife's separation and divorce, but that it is *not* an *obligation* on his part if that is *not* the case.

Paragraph four is no better. What it presumably means is that if the husband no longer receives the benefit of such policies of insurance, or if the children are no longer covered under those policies, that he will provide substitute insurance. But it *doesn't* say that. Instead, it talks about when the policy "can no longer be kept enforced by the payments of the premium thereon. . . ." But a policy can always be kept in force and effect by the payment of the premiums, if one is eligible to receive the benefits of that policy. It would be a lot simpler to avoid all of this confusion by *saying what is meant*.

The last paragraph is not without its problems either. Is the husband's agreement to pay for 75% of the unreimbursed expenses limited to those of the children, or does it extend to the wife as well? Again, this should not be left to conjecture. Suppose that one of the parties wishes to renegotiate the issue of this division but the mediator is unable to breach the impasse between them. Is the husband still obligated to pay 75% of the unreimbursed medical expenses and the wife 25%? Probably; but the whole tone of this and the many other similar provisions in the agreement make it less than clear.

Again, it is not necessary continually to insert into the agreement the fact that the parties have the right to change their agreement in the future if they wish to. That is *always* the case, whether the agreement so provides or not. That being so, the inclusion of these clauses leaves the suggestion that something *more* is *intended*. The problem is that the agreement doesn't indicate with any specificity what that something is. This paragraph is silent as to how long the husband's obligation to maintain these private policies of insurance for the children shall continue. Again, this should not be left to inference.

All that the mediator's memorandum should have said is the following:

"The Husband presently receives the benefit of certain policies of medical and hospital insurance in connection with his employment with American Airlines. He will continue to maintain the Wife as a beneficiary of such benefits, to the extent that he is able, so long as they are married. He will also maintain those benefits for the Children to the extent that he is permitted to do so, either with or without the payment of an additional premium. It is his understanding that they will be covered until December 31 of the year in which they reach their 19th birthday or, if they attend college, until they complete college or attain the age of 23 years, whichever first occurs. In the event that the Husband is no longer employed by American Airlines, or if for any other reason he does not continue to receive the benefits of this insurance, then, and unless the Children are covered under a policy issued to the Husband in connection with his new employment, he will purchase a private policy for their benefit. The Husband will be responsible for any premium payments due on any of these policies of insurance. In addition, he will also be responsible to pay for 75% of any and all medical or hospital expenses of the children that are not reimbursed by those policies of insurance. This shall not include dental expenses or psychotherapy. The Husband's obligation to maintain private policies of insurance for the Children shall terminate with respect to each child when his obligation to support that child shall terminate."

The final agreement to be executed by the parties should express the husband's obligation in the following language:

"1. The Husband presently receives the benefit of certain policies of hospital and medical insurance as an incident to his employment. To the extent permitted by such policies of insurance, and so long as the parties are married, the Husband shall maintain the Wife as a beneficiary of such policies of insurance so long as, and to the extent that, such policies of insurance are made available to the Husband as an incident to his employment. Similarly, to the extent permitted by such policies of insurance, and until December 31 of the year in which a child shall attain the age of nineteen years (or, if such child shall attend college, then until such child shall complete college), the Husband shall maintain such child as a beneficiary of such policies of insurance so long as, and to the extent that, such policies of insurance are made available to the Husband as an incident to his employment. In the event that the Husband's present employment is terminated for any reason, the Husband's obligations hereunder shall extend to the benefits of any future hospital and medical insurance which the Husband shall receive or be entitled to as an incident to any future employment of the Husband.

"2. Notwithstanding anything hereinabove contained in paragraph "1" to the contrary, in the event that the Husband shall no longer receive the benefit of such policies of insurance as an incident to his employment, then, and until an emancipation event shall occur with respect to a child, as that term is defined in Article "I," the Husband shall maintain comparable policies of medical and hospital insurance for the benefit of such child and shall pay any and all premium payments required to be paid in order to maintain the same.

"3. The Husband shall complete, execute, and submit, and shall cooperate with the Wife in the completion, execution, and submission, of any forms, instruments, or other documents that may be requested or required in connection with the receipt of any benefits due or payable under any of the aforesaid policies of insurance, and will pay and remit to the Wife, upon receipt, any and all benefits so received by him in connection with any illness, accident, hospitalization, or other treatment to the Wife or to any of the Children to the extent that payments have been made by the Wife on behalf or herself or any of the Children with respect to any such illness, accident, hospitalization or other treatment.

"4. Any and all medical and hospital expenses of the Children, or any of them, not covered by the aforesaid policies of medical and hospital insurance shall be paid for by the parties as follows: the Husband shall be responsible for, and shall pay, seventy-five (75%) percent of such unreimbursed expenses and the Wife shall be responsible for, and shall pay, twenty-five (25%) percent of such unreimbursed expenses. Notwithstanding the foregoing, the Husband's responsibility shall not extend to dental expenses or to psychotherapy, and if such expenses are incurred, they shall be the sole responsibility of the Wife."

In the event that either the Husband or the Wife dispute the terms of the agreements, seek to amend its provisions, or fail to uphold its requirements, then both the Husband and the Wife agree to seek mediation in an effort to resolve such differences voluntarily.

There is nothing inappropriate in having the agreement express the understanding that should a dispute arise between the parties in the future, that they agree to seek mediation in an effort to resolve it before resorting to litigation, even though the clause is not legally enforceable. It is just inappropriate to include it as many times as it has been included in this agreement. It should be mentioned once, preferably at the end of the agreement, in the article usually entitled "General Provisions," and not in connection with every specific substantive issue, such as support, medical expenses, etc. Finally, the clause should not talk in terms of the husband or the wife disputing "the terms of the agreement." It should simply refer to any future dispute between them concerning the agreement.

In the event that mediation fails to assist this couple in reaching an equitable agreement, either the Husband or the Wife may seek appropriate relief in a court of law and each agrees that this court shall be the Court of Common Pleas of Allegheny County, Family Division.

This is only to compound the error. This clause suggests, though it does not state, that if either of the parties is unhappy with the agreement or wishes to amend its provisions, and the parties are unable to resolve those differences in mediation, that they have conferred jurisdiction upon the court to make a new agreement for them. One would only hope not! Even if the couple could confer such jurisdiction on the court, what guidelines would the court use in determining their dispute? The parties have not said. If the parties are considering some specific remedy other than mediation, why not provide for binding arbitration in that event? It is certainly better than court litigation. The following clause may be used for that purpose.

"Any claim, dispute, or controversy arising out of or relating to this agreement, or a breach thereof, shall be settled by arbitration in accordance with the rules of the American Arbitration Association in Philadelphia, and judgment upon the award rendered by the arbitrators may be entered by either the husband or the wife in any Court having jurisdiction thereof; provided, however, that nothing herein contained shall be deemed to confer upon the American Arbitration Association the power to grant to either of the parties any right or rights not expressly provided by this agreement."

As to the pending divorce proceeding, the Husband and the Wife agree that the Wife shall petition and the Husband shall respond. The Husband and the Wife agree to share the costs of all legal fees, court costs and consultant fees such as tax accountants in the following manner:

a. The Wife has agreed to accept a reduced support payment in the amount of $467.00 for the month of October and the same amount for the month of November, to be paid October 1, 1982 and November 1, 1982, respectively, with the intent that the differences (approximately $500.00 per month) will be applied to those fees.

b. The Husband agrees to write all necessary checks in payment of mediation fees, legal fees, court costs and consultation fees.

The agreement should never provide *how* the couple will obtain a divorce, let alone that they agree that one of the parties shall be the petitioner or plaintiff and the other the respondent or defendant. The parties should simply *do* it, not *say* that they will do it. The law encourages marriage, not divorce, and there is a danger that a clause such as this may offend public policy.

While there is nothing wrong in having the wife accept a reduced support payment in exchange for the husband's assumption of certain responsibilities, it is better that that reduction be reflected in the article dealing with support, rather than here. There is always a potential problem if the parties cannot turn to a *specific place* and find everything that they have decided with respect to a subject. If they have to wade through the agreement to find it they may overlook it.

Finally, it is far better for the agreement to spell out what the various fees and costs are, for otherwise the husband has simply agreed to sign a blank check. To be sure, this is not always possible, as is the case with unreimbursed medical expenses, for example. But it should be here. At the very least, it should be indicated that his obligation will not exceed a certain amount.

The Husband and the Wife agree and understand that Robert Brown as mediator has acted as a neutral third party and each agrees to consult and independently retain their own attorney to review this memorandum of their agreement. The attorneys will analyze their property evaluation, negotiations, and overall intended settlement. The Husband and the Wife agree to obtain competent tax advice regarding the tax effect of their settlement, and each further agrees upon legal review, any recommendations for substantial change or restructuring of this agreement shall be referred back to mediation.

There is no point in having the parties agree that they will consult their own attorneys, and the memorandum should not contain any such understanding. What it should contain, if anything, is simply a statement to the effect that they both understand that it is their right to do this. Suppose either the husband or the wife do not consult with independent counsel. Have they breached their agreement? Worse yet, is it unenforceable for that reason? Why should any of this be left to speculation?

The memorandum is also silent as to how the final agreement will be prepared. Though it is not necessary that the memorandum so provide, it would still be better practice for the mediator and the couple to *discuss* this. The mediator does not even know *who* the two attorneys that the parties will consult will be, let alone necessarily know them. They in turn may view him as somewhat of an intruder in their work, and wish to have little if anything to do with him. That may only mean that the drafting stage may take on a life of its own, which the mediator wishes to avoid. It would make far more sense for the mediator to work out with the couple how all of this is to be accomplished, rather than simply leaving it to them or to the two attorneys.

For example, it could be agreed that the initial draft agreement will be prepared by the wife's attorney, who will then send it to the husband's attorney for either comment or language changes. If both of the attorneys are then satisfied with it, and if there are no substantive issues which have to be discussed or re-mediated, the couple will then sign it. If there are such questions, however, and rather than having the two attorneys negotiate them between themselves, they can agree to prepare a list of the open issues which will then be taken back to the mediator.

Obviously, from our standpoint, it would make far more sense if only *one* attorney, rather than two, was involved in the drafting process. Adversarial lawyers are adversarial lawyers. It is therefore very hard for them to draw *neutral* language agreements. On the contrary, they tend to draw agreements that favor their own clients. A single attorney, particularly one who has been involved in mediated agreements before, is far more likely to think in gender (husband and wife) neutral terms. If that is the case, the agreement will come out cleaner to begin with, and will not be subject to as many proposed language changes when, and if, the parties then take it to separate attorneys to review. If one attorney is used, their agreement should contain a provision somewhat as follows:

"1. The parties respectively acknowledge that this agreement has been prepared for them by John Harlan, Esq.; that he has represented neither of them individually, and that his services have been limited to assisting the two of them to conclude an agreement between themselves and in then reducing that agreement to writing. The parties further each acknowledge that John Harlan has answered any and all questions that they have had concerning this agreement, concerning the law of the State of New York and concerning any other matters arising out of their marriage relationship. Finally, the parties acknowledge that they each have been advised by John Harlan that they should consider whether they wish to seek independent advice by counsel of their own selection before signing this agreement and that they have had an adequate opportunity to do so.

"2. Each of the parties represents to the other that they have incurred no obligation to any other attorney in connection with the negotiation, preparation, and execution of this agreement, or any other matter arising out of their marital relationship, for which the other is or may be held liable, and each agrees to indemnify the other against, and to hold the other free and harmless from, any and all such obligations and liabilities.

"3. Each of the parties hereby waives any and all rights, if any, which he or she may have pursuant to Section 237 of the Domestic Relations Law, as amended from time to time, or pursuant to any other provision of law, to make application for counsel fees and/or expenses in connection with any action now pending between them, or in connection with any action which may be instituted by either of them against the other for a divorce, until the final entry of the judgment therein.

"4. The parties each represent and acknowledge that they have been provided, and have read, the provisions of Section 236, Part B, Subdivisions 1 and 5 of the Domestic Relations Law, wherein, among other things, is set forth the definitions of separate property and marital property, a married person's right to share in marital property and in the appreciation or increase of value of the other party's separate property to the extent that such appreciation or increase in value is due in part to his or her contributions or efforts, in the event of their divorce, and, more particularly, the factors to be considered by the Court in making a distribution or division of marital property or a distributive award to supplement, facilitate, or effectuate a distribution of marital property, and that the division of the parties' separate and marital property (whether in their individual names, joint names, or otherwise) as is in this agreement provided, has been made in light of the provisions of those Sections and with the intention that this agreement shall constitute an agreement for the disposition of the parties' property pursuant to Part B, Subdivision 3, of Section 236 of the Domestic Relations Law.

"5. The parties each represent and acknowledge that they have each been provided, and have read, both the provisions of Section 236, Part B, Subdivisions 1 and 6 of the Domestic Relations Law, wherein, among other things, is set forth the definition of maintenance, and a married person's right to temporary and permanent maintenance in such amount as justice requires, having regard for the standard of living of the parties established during the marriage, and, more particularly, the factors to be considered by the Court in making such an award, and the provisions of Section 5-311 of the General Obligations Law, wherein, among other things, is set forth the prohibition relieving a married person of the liability to support his or her spouse in such manner that he or she will become incapable of self-support and therefore likely to become a public charge, and the failure of this agreement to include or make provision for the support of the Wife by the Husband, or the Husband by the Wife, has been agreed upon by the parties in light of the provisions of those Sections and in light of the fact that each party is capable of providing for his and her own support, without danger of becoming a public charge, without contribution from the other."

Date: _____

_____   _____

Mediator   *Wife*

                                          _____

                                          Husband

Unless the mediator is an attorney, he should not draw the final agreement that the couple will sign. If he does, and particularly if, as here, he permits the couple to sign the agreement in front of him and witnesses their signatures, he runs the risk of being charged with practicing law without a license, which is a criminal offense in most jurisdictions.

Should the mediator have each of the parties sign, or even initial, the memorandum of agreement at all? There is really no reason why he should. The only reason that he would do this at all is as a means of having them acknowledge that the memorandum reflects their tentative understanding. But that is not the only way in which they can acknowledge this. It is not even the best way. Their acknowledgment derives from the fact that the parties have each had an opportunity to review the memorandum of agreement, to go over it with the mediator, and to make whatever corrections or changes they deemed appropriate. That is the important procedure, and all the rest is superfluous.

If the mediator feels more comfortable, for whatever reason, in having a couple sign or initial the memorandum, then it is very important that the memorandum contain a clause, right before the parties' signatures as follows:

"The husband and the wife are signing (initialing) this memorandum of agreement simply to acknowledge the fact that they have tentatively agreed that their separation agreement will contain the provisions set forth in this memorandum of agreement. However, it is the distinct understanding of the parties that this memorandum of agreement is not to be deemed a contract binding upon either of them, is to be totally without legal force and effect, and that neither of them will be obligated, or in any way bound, to any of the terms of this memorandum of agreement unless and until its terms are incorporated in the final agreement that is to be prepared for the parties' signature, and unless and until both of the parties have duly executed that agreement in the manner provided by law."

It is not necessary that the mediator and the couple discuss all of the terms that will ultimately be included in their final agreement, and many of these provisions, which are referred to as the "boilerplate clauses" in the agreement, can properly be left to the attorney who will draw the agreement. Nevertheless, there are one or two additional items that should properly be addressed by the mediator and not left to the drafting attorney.

Will the parties file joint income tax returns for the current year if they are still married on December 31, and who will be responsible for the payment of any taxes due? Suppose there is money found to be due on past joint tax returns filed by the parties. Whose responsibility will it be to pay those? Suppose one of the parties should default in his or her obligation under the terms of the agreement. Will the other party be responsible for the attorney's fees and expenses which that party incurs in attempting to enforce the terms of the agreement? Particularly if the parties do not intend to divorce immediately following the signing of their agreement, will they each continue to retain their right to claim an interest in the other's estate, or will they waive those rights?

These matters should be addressed and resolved before the mediation is concluded.

CHAPTER 22

INCOME TAXES

Agreements between husbands and wives incident to their separation or divorce are affected by numerous income tax considerations. Thus, if a mediator is intelligently to assist a couple to conclude an agreement between themselves that will give effect to their intentions, these income tax provisions will have to be kept in mind. While it is possible that a taxpayer may be subject to three separate income tax liabilities (for example, residents of New York City are subject to federal, state, and city income taxes) the following discussion will be limited to federal income taxes (see Table 22.1).

To begin with, a taxpayer's federal income tax liability is by far the most significant, since it is the largest. Secondly, where state and local income taxes are imposed, they very often closely mirror the provisions laid down by the Federal Internal Revenue Code. Lastly, it would be beyond the purpose of this chapter to discuss the tax codes of the various states.

ALIMONY OR MAINTENANCE

Generally speaking, payments made by one spouse to the other for his or her support (for example, a payment made by a husband to his wife or ex-wife for her support) are deductible by the person making the payment, and includible as income by the person receiving it, on their respective income tax returns. Thus, if by the terms of their agreement a husband is obligated to make payment to his wife (or ex-wife) for her support in the sum of $100 per week, and makes the payment each week and every week of the year, he will be entitled to take a deduction of $5,200 on his income tax return.[1] Similarly, his wife (or ex-wife) will be obligated to include that same amount on her income tax return, to the same extent as if she had earned the $5,200 through employment.[2] (While it used to be the law that if a husband deducted alimony payments on his income tax return he was deemed to have elected to itemize his deductions and therefore could not also take a standard deduction, he can now do both—that is, he can now both claim his alimony payments as a deduction and take the standard deduction as well).[3]

The Tax Reform Acts of 1984 and 1986 laid down certain new requirements in order for a payment to be treated as alimony (i.e., to entitle the person making the payment to deduct it and to require the person receiving it to report it). These requirements are as follows:

1. The payment made must be *in cash*.[4] If the payment is in cash, the fact that it is not made directly to the wife—for example, that it is made to a third party on her behalf—does not change the status of the payment.[5] Thus, if a husband, on behalf of his

Table 22-1. Federal Income Tax Rates[61]

Status	Taxable income	Tax payable
Married filing jointly	$0–$29,750	15%
	$29,750–$71,900	$4,462.50 + 28% above $29,750
	$71,900–$149,250	$16,264.50 + 33% above $71,900
	$149,250 +	28% of income above $149,250 + either (a) 28% of the value of the personal exemptions or (b) 5% of income above $149,250 whichever is less
Head of household	$0–$23,900	15%
	$23,900–$61,650	$3,585 + 28% above $23,900
	$61,650–$123,790	$14,155 + 33% above $61,650
	$123,790 +	28% of income above $123,790 + either (a) 28% of the value of the personal exemptions or (b) 5% of income above $123,790 whichever is less
Single taxpayers	$0–$17,850	15%
	$17,850–$43,150	$2,677.50 + 28% above $17,850
	$43,150–$89,560	$9,761.50 + 33% above $43,150
	$89,560 +	28% of income above $89,560 + either (a) 28% of the value of the personal exemptions or (b) 5% of income above $89,560 whichever is less
Married filing separately	$0–$14,875	15%
	$14,875–$35,950	$2,231.25 + 28% above $14,875
	$35,950–$113,300	$8,132.25 + 33% above $35,950
	$113,300 +	28% of income above $113,300 + either (a) 28% of the value of the personal exemptions or (b) 5% of income above $113,300 whichever is less

wife, pays the wife's rent or mortgage payment in cash or cash equivalent (check or postal money order), the husband is entitled to a deduction for the amount so paid and the wife is required to include that amount as income for tax purposes.

2. The payment must be a payment that is *required* to be made by the terms of a separation agreement or court order.[6] In other words, payments voluntarily made by one party to or for the other do not qualify. Thus, if the husband is required to pay his wife the sum of $100 per week (or $5,200 a year) by the terms of their separation agreement, and if he instead pays her $6,000 in that year, he will only be entitled to a deduction for the amount that he was required to pay her pursuant to the terms of the agreement, or $5,200.

3. There must be *no liability* on the part of the spouse obligated to make the payments to continue to make them *following the death* of the recipient spouse.[7] (Under the 1984 Act, it was not sufficient simply to rely on the fact that, under state law, support payments ended on the death of the recipient spouse. Rather, it was necessary that a decree or written agreement specifically so provide. This requirement has been eliminated by the 1986 Act.) In other words, if the agreement provides that the payments are to continue following the wife's death, and that they will only terminate upon the husband's

death or the wife's remarriage, no portion of the payments are either deductible by the husband or taxable to the wife.[8] (While the payments will not qualify as alimony if the agreement or court order requires that they be paid to the wife, or to her estate, following her death—that they are not to terminate upon her death—the same rule does not apply to her remarriage. Thus, payments made by a husband to his wife following her remarriage pursuant to the terms of their agreement will qualify as payments deductible by the husband and taxable to the wife to the same extent that they would have qualified prior to her remarriage. Again, the only requirement is that the payments must terminate upon the wife's death.)

4. If the parties are divorced or legally separated under a decree of separate maintenance, they *may not share the same household* at the time that the payments are made, unless one of them is in the process of moving and actually leaves within one month of the date of the payment in question.[9] Living separately in a home that the parties formerly shared cannot be deemed living in separate households. However, this rule does not apply to payments that are made pursuant to a written separation agreement.

5. The decree of divorce or separation, or the separation agreement, *cannot contain a provision* that the payments in question are *not to be includible* under the provisions of Section 71 of the Code and nondeductible under the provisions of Section 215.[10] Under prior law, a payment by one spouse to another was deemed includible and deductible not because it was designated by the parties as such, but by virtue of the fact that it met certain requirements (that they met the famous periodic payment test). If they met those conditions, then they were includible and deductible regardless whether or not the parties wish them to be. This has been changed under the 1984 Act. This means that the parties have far more latitude in determining in advance what tax treatment will be accorded the payments in question. While this has obvious beneficial consequences, there are also some problems as well.

In eliminating the requirement that payments be periodic or that they be made in discharge of any kind of obligation, the Code seems to characterize *any* payments made by one of the spouses to the other (other than those labeled as child support) as being includible as income for the party receiving the payments and deductible by the party making it. This may be true even if it can be demonstrated that the payments in question were made in discharge of a debt or other obligation owed by one of the parties to the other, or even if they were made in exchange for a transfer of property. Accordingly, unless the parties specifically intend that the payment in question be treated as an alimony payment (deductible by the party making the payment and includible by the party receiving it), the agreement should contain a provision *specifically exempting* the payment in question from such treatment.[11]

If all of the above requirements have been met, the payments will be deductible by the payor spouse and includible as gross income by the recipient spouse, regardless of the size of the payments made in any year and regardless of the length of time that the payments are to be made.[12]

Since married couples obviously negotiate their agreements in light of the income tax laws, it is not uncommon, particularly when the party who is required to make the payment is in a very high income tax bracket, for him to attempt to make the payments in pretax, rather than aftertax, dollars. He thus suggests that he will be willing to make the proposed payment to the wife *if*, and *only* if, he is able to add it (perhaps in an increased amount) to the alimony payments in the first three years. Since the Internal Revenue Service was not party to the negotiations that led up to the couple's agreement, they have no way of knowing whether or not the support payments contained in the agreement represent support alone or also include disguised property settlement payments. To prevent this "front-loading," the Code adopted the second of the two rules, the "recapture rule."[13] The recapture rule requires the spouse making the payment to include in his or her gross income (to recapture), and permits the spouse receiving the payment to deduct from his or her gross income, excess alimony payments made in the first and second postseparation years. (These payments are recaptured in the third postseparation year.)

Excess payments in the first postseparation year are defined as the amount in excess (if any) in the alimony paid in the first postseparation year over the total of (1) the average of the amount of alimony paid during the second postseparation year less the excess payments for such year and the amount of alimony paid during the third postseparation year, and (2) $15,000. Excess payments for the second postseparation year are defined as the amount (if any) of the alimony paid in the second postseparation year in excess of $15,000 plus the amount of alimony paid in the third post-separation year.[14]

A postseparation year is defined as any year in which a payment of alimony was made commencing with the year in which the agreement was signed.[15] Thus, if an agreement dated November 1, 1989 required the husband to make payment to the wife commencing as of December 1 that year, the year 1989 would be the *first* postseparation year. However, if by the terms of that agreement, payments were not to start until January 1, 1990, then the year 1990 would be the first postseparation year.

There are two important exceptions to the recapture rule. First, the rule does not apply to reductions resulting from the fact that the payments to be made (for example by a husband to his wife or former wife) are predicated upon the husband's income from a business, from property or from compensation from employment or self-employment.[16] Secondly, if the alimony payments cease before the end of the third postseparation year due to the death of either of the spouses, or due to the remarriage of the spouse receiving the payments, then the payments made in the year of such death or remarriage shall not be considered in determining whether or not the rule has been violated.[17]

It was noted previously that if the agreement provides that, instead of receiving a fixed dollar support payment, the wife will receive 30% of the husband's income from employment, the recapture rule does not apply, regardless of the fact that there are reductions in the payments within the first three postseparation years that would otherwise be in violation of the rule. This exception only applies, however, when the wife's support payments are predicated upon the husband's income, and his income alone. Suppose, instead, that they are also predicated upon the wife's own income. Here the agreement provides that the husband will pay the wife a fixed dollar payment. However, it also provides that that payment will be reduced in the event that the wife derives income from employment. The inclusion of this provision poses a possible recapture problem, as the exception only applies to the situation where the support payments are to fluctuate based upon the income of the party making the payment, not the party receiving it.

How is it possible to include such a provision and yet avoid violating the recapture rule? In this connection it must be remembered that the recapture rule is not violated by the inclusion in the agreement of a contingency that might cause a reduction in the payments in violation of the rule. It is only violated if the payments are actually reduced beyond the permissible limits. To prevent this from occurring, the agreement could provide that in no event would the reduction in the husband's payments, based upon the wife's earnings, exceed the permissible limit. In other words, the agreement can place a cap or ceiling on the reduction. It could even go further and provide that should the amount by which such payments would have otherwise been reduced exceed the permissible limits, such excess will be paid by the wife to the husband, as an alimony payment, in the fourth or succeeding postseparation years. Here the husband will get the full amount of the reduction agreed upon and all that will happen is that a portion of that reduction will be postponed beyond the proscribed period.

CHILD SUPPORT

Generally speaking, a payment made by one spouse to the other for the support of their child or children is not deductible for income tax purposes by the parent making the payment or includible as income by the parent receiving it; and this regardless of the fact that the child support payment is made to the parent (and not to the child) and can be spent by the parent for the support of the child as he or she sees fit. In other words, payments that are designated as child support payments are not considered alimony, even though those payments are made by the husband to the wife (or ex-wife), and the Code specifically excludes from alimony any payment so designated.[18]

Prior to the enactment of the 1984 Code, it was possible to disguise child support payments and have them treated as alimony in certain instances. Thus, if instead of paying his wife $100 per week for her support and $100 per week for the support of their two children, the couple's agreement provided that the husband would pay his wife $200 per week for their combined support, without indicating how much of the $200 was for the wife and how much was for the support of the children, the entire payment was considered alimony and the husband was entitled to $200 per week on his tax return. Similarly, and since it was considered alimony, the wife was required to include the entire $200 per week on hers. This payment was known as an "unallocated payment."

The use of an unallocated payment was very often an effective way to shift taxable income from a higher to a lower bracket (in this case from the higher bracket of the husband to the lower bracket of the wife), thereby saving the tax on the difference. It was particularly effective in those situations where the husband was a large wage earner, the wife was unemployed, and she and the children were to continue to remain in the former marital residence. The wife was in a very low tax bracket due to the fact that she had no earnings of her own. On top of that, she usually had fairly large tax deductions, as a result of the mortgage interest and real estate taxes that she paid in connection with the home. The husband, on the other hand, now had very few deductions that he could use to shelter his income from taxes, as he did not live in the home or make the payments in connection with its upkeep.

In addition, all of the payments that he made to the wife for the support of the children were after tax payments, which meant that if he were in an overall 40% tax bracket he would have to earn approximately $1.67 for every $1 in child support that he gave to the wife. The simple solution here was to designate the entire payment alimony (as an unallocated payment). Nor did it make any difference that it was really partially a child support payment, and that the husband expected a reduction in the payments when one or more of the children were emancipated, for the mere fact that the agreement provided that the unallocated payment would be reduced at stated intervals as each of the children became emancipated did not have the effect of labeling the amount so reduced a child support payment.[19]

The 1984 Code was specifically designed to prevent the use of such unallocated payments, and to overrule the decision of the Supreme Court of the United States that authorized it. Thus, to prevent a husband and a wife from attempting to mask child support payments as alimony or maintenance in the future, the Code provides that if payments to a spouse, which would otherwise be treated as alimony or maintenance for tax purposes, are to be reduced by the terms of their separation agreement (or by the terms of a court order) "on the happening of a contingency . . . relating to a child," the amount by which the payments are to be reduced will be treated as child support.[20]

The same result will occur if the payments are to be reduced "at a time which can clearly be associated with a contingency" relating to a child.[21] Thus, if a payment of $200 per week, denominated in the parties' agreement as alimony or maintenance, is to be reduced by the sum of $75 per week in the event of a child's death, marriage, or emancipation, or on a specific date which happens to be the child's 21st birthday, then $75 of the $200 payments to be made by the husband to the wife will be treated as child support and, therefore, will neither be deductible by the husband nor includible as income by the wife.

Suppose that the payments for child support are to terminate 9 months following the child's 21st birthday or upon her marriage, should she marry prior to that date. Suppose also, that the child does not marry before she reaches 21 years and 9 months, and that her marriage is therefore not the occasion for the termination of the payments. Payments are nevertheless in violation of the contingency test, for it is the fact that the contingency exists in the agreement, and not that it ever occurs, that is controlling. Thus, if the payment to be made by the husband to the wife is to be reduced by $75 per week in the event of the child's marriage, then $75 of the total payment will be considered as a child support payment that is nondeductible by the husband and nontaxable to the wife from the date of the inception of the agreement, regardless of the fact that the child never marries prior to the date that the payment would otherwise terminate.

The 1984 Code thus placed very severe limitations upon the use of what was formerly called an unallocated payment. Nevertheless, the Temporary Regulations promulgated by the Internal Revenue Service have provided taxpayers with some relief, and, therefore, some ability to shift child support payments from the higher bracket of the party making the payments to the lower bracket of the party receiving them. These provisions are generally known as "safe harbor" provisions.

As we have noted previously, if a payment that is to be made by the husband to the wife as alimony is to be reduced "at a time which can clearly be associated" with the happening of a contingency relating to a child of the husband, then the amount by which the payment is to be reduced will be treated as child support. (For the purposes of this rule, as with the rule relating to a reduction contingent on an event relating to a child, such as a child's marrying, the termination of the payment is also considered a reduction in the payment.) The Temporary Regulations provide two situations in which the payments that would otherwise qualify as alimony will be presumed to be reduced at a time clearly associated with the happening of a contingency relating to a child. The first situation is where the payments are to be reduced not more than six months before or not more than six months after the date on which a child will be either 18, 21, or the age at which a child reaches his majority under local law.[22]

The second is where the payments are to be reduced on two or more occasions that will occur not more than one year before or one year after a different child attains a specified age, which is the same age for each child, between the ages of 18 and 24 inclusive.[23] In all other situations, a reduction in the payments that would otherwise be treated as alimony will not be treated as being clearly associated with the happening of a contingency relating to a child.[24] In other words, if the agreement meets both of these two tests (if the payments are not to be reduced in violation of either of these two rules), then the reduced payments will be safe from attack and will not be treated as a child support payment.

The first of these ("the happening of a contingency . . . relating to a child") tests can be illustrated by the following example. Suppose that the parties have one child who is 10 years of age and who will graduate high school when he will be 18 years and 4 months of age. The husband would like to make a combined payment to the wife for her support and for the support of that child that will end (be reduced to zero) when the child graduates from high school. If the agreement were to provide that all of the payments by the husband to the wife were to terminate upon the child's graduation from high school, then the agreement would run afoul of the provision that the payments may not be reduced upon the happening of a contingency relating to a child, since the payments will end by the terms of the agreement when the child graduates from high school. As a result, the entire payment will be treated as child support, which means that the husband will not be entitled to deduct any portion of it for income tax purposes.

The second of these tests (a reduction "at a time which can clearly be associated with a contingency" relating to a child) can be illustrated by the following example. Suppose, instead, that the agreement provided that the payments were to end on a specified date (the date in this case being June 30 of the year in which the child is expected to graduate from high school). Here, since the agreement provides that the payments will terminate on a date that is within six months of the child's 18th birthday, the agreement will run afoul of the requirement that the payments cannot be reduced at a time clearly associated with the happening of a contingency relating to a child.

However, if the agreement provides instead that the payments will terminate on September 1 of that same year, since they will be reduced on a date that is more than six months before or after the date that the child is to attain the age of 18, they will fall within the "safe harbor" provisions of the regulations and will be protected from being treated as alimony. The same result would apply if, instead of terminating the payments on September 1 in the year in question, they were simply reduced, and then continued for the wife's benefit. Again, the only requirement is that if they are thereafter to terminate (be reduced), the second reduction must also avoid both of these proscriptions. In other words, the second reduction must also not run afoul of the conditions that will cause a portion of the alimony payments to be treated as child support. If the second reduction *does* run afoul of either of these two rules, however, the *entire* payment is not disallowed. Only the amount by which the payments are reduced by virtue of the second reduction is disallowed.

In applying these two tests (the happening of a contingency relating to a child and a time that can clearly be associated with a contingency relating to a child), it is important to keep in mind that the payment will be disallowed in two instances: (1) if, because it fails either of these two tests, it is treated as a payment for the support of a child, and (2) because it fails to comply with the recapture rule, it is disallowed as an alimony payment. Thus, if the payment is to be reduced on September 1 in the year in which the child graduates from high school, even if it will not be treated as a child support payment because that date is more than six months after the child's 18th birthday, it may still be disallowed if, because that date is within the three postseparation years, the payments run afoul of the recapture rule.

It must be remembered that the two rules (the happening of a contingency relating to a child and a time that can clearly be associated with a contingency relating to a child) simply create a presumption. Thus, the payments will not be disallowed, even though they violate either of these two tests, if it can be shown that the time at which the payments were to be reduced was determined independently of any contingency relating to the children. Be that as it may, it would be unwise to rely upon the fact that this presumption can be rebutted, as the onus will fall upon the taxpayer; and, as a practical matter, it may be as costly to rebut the presumption as it would be to pay the tax on the payments.

There is one potential problem with these planning devices that must be kept in mind. The agreement provides for a combined alimony and child support payment, designated as alimony, which will be reduced, either in part or completely, on the date on which the child will be either 18 years 7 months of age, or 21 years 7 months of age. The reduction is supposed to reflect the fact that the husband will no longer be obligated for the support of the child at that point. Suppose that the child dies prior to that date, or establishes his principal residence with the husband rather than with the wife.

If the payment in question had been denominated as a child support payment from the outset, then the agreement could have provided that the payment would terminate, or would be reduced, in either of those events. If the agreement were to do that *now*, however, it would run afoul of the Code's "happening of a contingency . . . related to a child" test. Does that mean that the husband will be obligated to continue to make the total payments to the wife until the date in question? The answer is *yes*; and this is one of the risks in employing this tax-saving device.

Structuring the agreement to meet the requirements of the six-month rule was fine when the couple only had one child. But suppose that they have two or more children. The six-month rule will not work then because it only applies when there is one child. If there are two or more children, then a second test, the multiple-reduction test, must also be met.

The multiple-reduction test is an extremely complicated test to apply. In fact, it is literally impossible to apply without a piece of graph paper. To illustrate this, we will use the example given by the Temporary Regulations of the Internal Revenue Code. It will be remembered that the regulations provide that there are two situations in which payments that would otherwise qualify as alimony will be presumed to be reduced at a time clearly associated with the happening of a contingency relating to a child of the person making the payments. "The second situation is where the payments are to be reduced on two or more occasions which occur not more than one year before or after a different child of the payor spouse attains a certain age between the ages of 18 and 24, inclusive. The certain age referred to in the preceding sentence must be the same for each such child, but need not be a whole number of years."[25] The Regulations then go on to give the following example.

"A and B are divorced on July 1, 1985, when their children, C (born July 15, 1970) and D (born September 23, 1972), are 14 and 12, respectively. Under the divorce decree, A is to make alimony payments to B of $2,000 per month. Such payments are to be reduced to $1,500 per month on January 1, 1991, and to $1,000 per month on January 1, 1995. On January 1, 1991, the date of the first reduction in payments, C will be 20 years, 5 months and 17 days old. On January 1, 1995, the date of the second reduction in payments, D will be 22 years 3 months and 9 days old. Each of the reductions in payments is to occur not more than one year before or after a different child of A attains the age of 21 years and 4 months. (Actually, the reductions are to occur not more than one year before or after C and D attain *any* of the ages 21 years 3 months and 9 days through 21 years 5 months and 17 days.) Accordingly, the reductions will be presumed to clearly be associated with the happening of a contingency relating to C and D. Unless this presumption is rebutted, payments under the divorce decree equal to the sum of the reduction ($1,000 per month) will be treated as fixed for the support of the children of A and therefore will not qualify as alimony or separate maintenance payments."[26]

FILING STATUS

A person's status determines which tax rate schedule he will use to arrive at the tax he will be required to pay on his income. Married couples have an option. They may either file a joint return or they may each file separate returns. Since the tax rate schedule for married couples filing separately is the highest, married couples usually file joint returns, even if only one of the parties has taxable income. Married couples may still file a joint return together even if they are separated. The only requirement is that they must still be married on December 31 of the year for which such joint income tax return is filed.[27] Thus, if it is the intention of the parties to file a joint income tax return for the year in question, it will then be necessary for them to postpone their divorce until January of the following year.

Another way that a taxpayer can reduce his or her income taxes is to file as the head of a household, and the parent with whom the children principally reside will generally be able to claim this status. However, head of household status is not generally available to a person who is still married. This does not mean that the person must have been divorced for the entire year. On the contrary, it is only necessary that they be divorced by the end of the year in question—in other words, on or before December 31.[28]

There is one exception to this. The taxpayer will be entitled to claim head of household status (will be considered unmarried for tax purposes) if (a) he files a separate return, (b) he maintain as his home, a home which is the principal residence of a child or stepchild for whom he is entitled to a dependency exemption and he provides over one-half of the cost of maintaining the home, and (c) his spouse is not a member of his household for the last six months of the year.[29]

To qualify for head of household status, a taxpayer must have paid more than half the cost of maintaining a home that was the principal residence of their (unmarried) child for more than half the year. [30] (They may also qualify for head of household status if they maintained a home that was the principal residence of a grandchild, stepchild, adopted child or foster child, or of a relative, provided that they can claim that person as a dependent, for the same period of time). [31]

In most instances, determining whether or not a party has maintained a home for their child for more than half the year is relatively easy. But what of the second test, which is that they must have paid half of the *cost* of maintaining that home? Here there are two questions that must be asked. The first is what costs are to be included. The second question is who paid for those costs.

In calculating the cost of maintaining a home to qualify as head of household, the party making the payments can include such costs as rent, mortgage interest, taxes, insurance on the home, repairs, utilities, domestic help, and food eaten in the home. [32] However, he can not include the cost of clothing, education, medical treatment, vacations, life insurance, transportation, or the value of his services as a homemaker. [33]

Let us suppose that the wife does not work outside of the home and that her children's primary residence is with her. Let us further assume that though she does pay half (and, in fact, *all*) the cost of maintaining the home for her children, that all of those payments are made from the money that she receives from her husband (or former husband) for her and their support. Who has paid for the cost of maintaining the home? The answer is that the wife has. The fact that the monies that the wife used for that purpose were derived from the husband, or from a third party (for example, her parents), would make no difference, unless those payments were made by her husband (or former husband) directly to the supplier of the services in question, and on a voluntary basis.

Suppose that the husband makes the mortgage payments directly to the bank. Can he use those payments to qualify for head of household status? The answer is no. Thus, if under the terms of their separation agreement, the husband is obligated to pay the mortgage payments on the marital residence directly to the bank, then, and although he may be entitled to a tax deduction for the payment (assuming it is not specifically denominated as child support and the couple's agreement does not specifically provide that it is not to be taxable to the wife or deductible by the husband), [34] the same payment does not qualify as a payment made by him to maintain a home for his children. The reason for this is that the home that he is maintaining is not his home. Secondly, even if it were, he would still not be entitled to claim head of household status, since his children do not live with him in that home for more than half of the year. Thus, it is not sufficient that the husband pays the cost of maintaining a home for his children or that that home is their principal residence for more than half the year. For him to claim head of household status it is also necessary that the home that he maintains for them be his home.

Can both the husband and the wife claim head of household status? The answer is *yes*; but not with respect to the same child. If the parties have one child, it is not possible for that child to live more than half of the year in two different homes. However, if they have two or more children, and particularly where their agreement provides for physical joint custody, both of them would be able to claim this status by simply having their agreement provide that one of the children will live an extra week during the year with one of the parties, and that the other child will live an extra week during the year with the other.

For a party to qualify for head of household status, it is not necessary that his (unmarried) child be his dependent—that he have the right to claim that child as an exemption.[35] Thus, it is possible for the parties' agreement to provide that the husband shall have the right to claim a child as an exemption; and his wife, based upon the fact that she pays for more than half of the cost of maintaining a home for that child, and that he resides with her for more than half the year, to base *her* head of household status on that same child.[36]

CHILD CARE CREDIT

On occasion, one of the parties may be entitled to a child care credit. To be entitled to this credit, the following conditions must be met:

(a) the party must maintain a home, which is his or her principal residence, and pay more than half of the costs of maintaining it.

(b) the residence in question must be the home of a child, under 15 years of age.

(c) the child in question must live with one or both parties for more than half of the year and must receive more than half of his or her support from one or both of the parties.

(d) the party claiming the credit must be employed or self-employed on either a full-time or part-time basis.

(e) The party claiming the credit must have incurred expenses for the care, well-being, or protection of the child in question.[37] (Typical expenses that would qualify would be the cost of a babysitter or housekeeper to care for a child while a party is at work or the cost of nursery school or a day care center employed for the same purpose.)[38]

If each of these conditions is met, then the party in question will be entitled to a child care credit. It is not necessary that the person claiming the child care credit be the person who is entitled to claim the child as an exemption.

The child care credit is not a deduction that is taken from the taxpayer's gross income, as is the case, for example, with an exemption. It is an amount that the taxpayer is permitted to deduct from the tax that he is required to pay on that income. That credit is 30% of the actual cost of the work-related expenses paid by the taxpayer during the year in question.[39]

There are two further limits that are placed upon the child care credit. The first is that the total amount of work-related expenses that are used to compute the credit may not exceed the person's earned income for the year in question.[40] The second limit is a dollar limit on the amount of the work related expenses that may be taken to figure the credit. If there is one child who qualifies, that limit is to $2,400. If there are two or more children that qualify, it is $4,800.[41] Thus, the most that a taxpayer can reduce his taxes in a year is $720 (30% of $2,400) if those expenses are for one qualifying child, and $1,440 (30% of $4,800) if it is for two or more children).

EXEMPTIONS

Every taxpayer is entitled to an exemption for himself and for each of his dependents.[42] For federal tax purposes, these exemptions are set at $2,000 for the tax year 1989 with the provision that they would be increased commensurate with the increase in the cost of living (Consumer Price Index) after that date.[43]

Until now, the question of who was entitled to claim these exemptions has probably not been an issue, since, in all likelihood, the parties have filed a joint return. Now that they are going to separate, however, and particularly if they are going to divorce, the issue will have to be addressed. The question is not whether the husband is entitled to claim the wife as an exemption, or she him, as each is only entitled to claim themselves. The question is who will have *the right to claim the children as exemptions.*

Prior to the enactment of the Tax Reform Act of 1984, these rules were rather complex and created some confusion. From the standpoint of the Internal Revenue Service, they represented a problem in that in many instances both of the parties claimed the children as exemptions of their income tax return. To eliminate this confusion in the future, the Internal Revenue Code established certain simple rules to determine who will have the right to claim the children as exemptions. There is one general rule, and one single exception to it.

The rule is that the parent with whom a child maintains his or her principal residence for more than half the year will be entitled to claim the child as an exemption.[44] In almost every instance, this will be the party designated in the agreement as the custodial parent or the parent with whom the child shall maintain his or her primary residence. The Code refers to this parent as the custodial parent. The one exception to this rule is when the custodial parent has signed a written declaration that he or she will not claim the child as a dependent for a particular year or years.[45]

In other words, the new Code gives the parties both the right and the ability to decide who will be entitled to claim each of their children as an exemption. Nor is it necessary that one of the parties be entitled to claim either all or none of the children as exemptions. On the contrary, the parties' agreement can provide that the wife will be entitled to claim one of the children as an exemption and the husband the other, and that she will sign the requisite written declaration with respect to the child that the husband is entitled to claim. Similarly, it is not necessary that if a parent is entitled to claim the child as an exemption that he be entitled to claim the child as an exemption each and every year. Thus the agreement can provide that the husband, who is not the custodial parent, will be entitled to claim the child in even years, and that the wife will sign the requisite written declaration with respect to the child for even years only.[46]

TRANSFERS OF PROPERTY

A couple's separation and divorce is often accompanied by a transfer of property by one of them to the other. Thus, the husband may transfer an automobile registered in his name to the wife. Or he may transfer his interest in their home to her. These transfers may or may not be accompanied by a cash payment. For example, there may be no consideration paid by the wife to the husband for the transfer of the automobile. On the other hand, the agreement may provide that the wife is to pay the husband $50,000 for his interest in their home.

Up until this point, there were no tax consequences in any of these transfers. Rather, they were simply treated as nontaxable gifts made by one of the parties to the other. Will these transfers be treated any differently now, simply because the couple are separating or divorcing?

Prior to the Tax Reform Act of 1984, they were. In fact, the transfers were treated as they would have been had they been made to a stranger. Thus, if by the terms of their separation agreement, a husband was to transfer to his wife his undivided one-half interest in a home that they had purchased ten years earlier at a price of $100,000 and which was now worth $200,000, the husband would be taxed on the transfer in the same manner, and to the same extent, as if he had sold the home to a third party.[47] Thus, since the husband was a one-half owner of the home, he would be taxed on one-half of the "profit" of $100,000, less, of course, one-half of any capital improvements that the parties had made to the home during the time that they had owned it together. When the wife later sold the home, she in turn would be taxed on the other half of the profit, plus, of course, any appreciation in the value of the home subsequent to her husband's transfer of his interest to her.

To illustrate this, let us assume that the wife had paid the husband $100,000 for his one-half interest in the home and that a few years later she had sold the home for $250,000. What would have been the tax consequences to each of the parties as a result of these transactions? Since the cost of the home had been $100,000 and since the husband had a one-half interest in the home, his cost (basis) would have been one-half of that amount, or $50,000. Since he received $100,000 for his interest in the home, and since he had only paid $50,000 for it, he would have realized a profit (gain) of $50,000 which would be taxable in the year he transferred the home to his wife. Since she had not transferred her interest at that time, there was no tax attributable to her.

However, five years later, when she sold the home, she would then have to pay the tax on her profit. What was her profit? As with her husband, one-half of the original cost of $100,000, or $50,000 was attributable to her. In addition, she had paid her husband $100,000 for his interest in the home. Thus, her total cost (basis) was $150,000. Since she received $250,000 upon its sale, her profit would be $100,000, and that would be the amount that she would have to report for tax purposes.

The 1984 Code changed these rules, and overruled the decisions of the Supreme Court of the United States which established them. Under the 1984 Code, all transfers between husbands and wives, and all transfers between former spouses which are incident to their divorce, are treated as nontaxable gifts.[48] Thus, in the above example, the transfer by the husband to his wife of his undivided one-half interest in their home will not be treated as a taxable event. As a result, the husband will not be required to pay tax on any portion of the $50,000 profit (the gain that accrued between the time that he and his wife bought the home and the date of his transfer of his interest in it to her) that he received when he transferred his interest in the home.

This does not mean that the husband's profit of $50,000 will not be taxed. It only means that it will not be taxed at this time (at the date of the transfer of the property from the husband to the wife), but, instead, when the wife later sells the home or otherwise transfers her interest in it. In short, the 1984 Code does not forgive the tax; it simply postpones it. However, in postponing the tax, the 1984 Code does something far more significant; and that is to shift the tax burden from (in this case) the husband to the wife. Thus when the wife later goes to sell the home, she will now be required to pay the tax, not only on her one-half ($50,000) of the profit, but on her husband's one-half ($50,000) as well. To put it another way, whereas under the Code prior to 1984 the husband would have been required to report and to pay tax on the $50,000 profit which he received, under the 1984 Code he receives this money tax-free.

How is this accomplished under the 1984 Code? Simply by not crediting the wife with the $100,000 that she paid to the husband for his one-half interest. Under the Code prior to 1984, that payment was deemed to increase the wife's cost for the home (deemed to step up her basis) from $50,000 to $150,000. Under the 1984 Code, however, it does not, and the wife simply takes over her husband's basis. That means that her cost for the home is deemed to have been the couple's original cost for the home, or $100,000. Since she is given no credit for the additional monies that she paid to her husband for his interest, her profit (gain) is deemed to be the difference between that cost (basis) of $100,000 and the selling price of $250,000, or $150,000. (Although the wife's basis is not increased by the $100,000 that she paid to her husband for his interest in the home, it is increased, in this example, by $50,000 of that payment since she takes over, and is given a credit for, her husband's basis in the home.)

The rules that we have been talking about are rules that apply to the transfer of property "incident to the divorce." The next question that must be answered, therefore, is when will such a transfer be treated as being "incident to the divorce" by the Internal Revenue Service. The Temporary Regulations provide that the transfer will be treated as being incident to the divorce in either of two circumstances: (1) if the transfer occurs within a year of the couple's divorce; or (2) if the transfer is "related" to the cessation of their marriage.

The first of these rules is clear. If the transfer occurs within a year of the couple's divorce, then it will be deemed "incident" to their divorce, regardless of the fact that there was nothing either in the parties' agreement or their divorce decree that called for such a transfer. If the transfer is made more than a year after the date of their divorce, however, it will only be deemed "incident" to their divorce if it is "related" to the cessation of their marriage. Again the Temporary Regulations provide guidelines by stating that the transfer will be deemed "related" to the cessation of their marriage if (a) it is made pursuant to the terms of either the couple's divorce decree or separation agreement and (b) if it occurs within six years of the date of their divorce.[49]

If the transfer is *not* made pursuant to the terms of their separation agreement or divorce decree, or if it occurs more than six years after their divorce, it is *presumed* not to be related to the cessation of their marriage. That presumption can be rebutted by the Internal Revenue Service, even if the transfer occurs beyond the six-year period, if it can be shown that the transfer was not made because of factors that hampered an earlier transfer of the property, and the property was transferred promptly after the impediment to the transfer was removed. Since that is the only way in which the presumption can be rebutted, however, no other transfer made beyond the six-year period will be deemed a transfer related to the cessation of the marriage.[50]

These rules create certain problems for a mediator. The most obvious one is that if there is to be a transfer, for example, of the husband's interest in the marital residence to the wife, the husband gets his money tax-free and the husband's tax obligation is thrown onto the wife's shoulders. An obvious way to deal with this situation is simply to factor this into their agreement. Thus, instead of receiving $100,000 for his interest in the home, the husband may perhaps be willing to take a little less. At other times he may not, however.

For example, he may argue that he would not be required to pay a tax, even if he had sold his interest to a third party, since he would have reinvested the money he received in a new home. [51] In other instances he may resist receiving a lesser amount by claiming that he does not know whether or not the wife will, in actual fact, be required to pay taxes on her profit from the sale of the home, or what those taxes will be. After all, she may be over 55 years of age at that time, and entitled to a lifetime exclusion of $125,000, [52] or she may herself reinvest the proceeds in a new home.

In some instances, however, it may not make any practical difference. Suppose, for example, that the wife were to accept a transfer of the husband's interest in the home in exchange for a release of her interest in his pension. While the husband's profit in the home would be taxable to her, so, for that matter, would have been that portion of his retirement benefits which she would have received from his pension.

The Sale of the Parties' Principal Residence

As a general rule, if a person sells property (stocks, his home, a parcel of vacant land, etc.) for an amount greater than he paid for it, he will be taxed on the appreciation in value (gain) that he receives. Thus, in the above example, if, instead of transferring his interest in the home to his wife, the husband and wife had sold the home and divided the proceeds equally, they would each be taxed on one-half the profit (appreciation in value) of $100,000 that they realized upon its sale (less, of course, one-half the cost of any capital improvements which they had made to it while they owned it, brokerage commissions, lawyers' fees, etc.).

The Internal Revenue Code provides for two exceptions to this general rule if the property that is being sold is the parties' principal residence. The first of these is that if they purchase a new home that will be used by either of them as their principal residence, and such new home is purchased no more than two years before, nor more than two years after, the sale of their present home, no gain will be recognized on the sale of their old home if the cost of their new home is at least equal to the sale price of their old home. [53] (If their new home does not cost as much as the sale price of their old home, the gain will be limited to the difference between the two prices). This rule was intended to recognize the inequity in leaving home owners in a position that they cannot afford to buy as nice a home as they previously had simply because they either had the desire or the need to move on with their lives.

If the home is owned by both parties, as is the common case with married couples, the same rules will be applied to each of them with respect to their one-half interest in the home. Thus, if the wife in this instance had purchased a new home (principal residence) for at least $100,000 within two years (before or after) the sale of this home, no tax will be imposed upon the profit at this time. If, on the other hand, the husband does not purchase a new home (principal residence) within this same period, he will be required to pay tax on his one-half of the profit.

It is important to note that the tax on the gain in this instance is not *waived*; it is simply deferred. In other words, rather than being taxed on that gain now, at the time of the sale of their home, if they are simply selling one home to purchase another one, the tax on the gain will be postponed (except to the extent that the new home costs less than the old home) until the new home is sold. At that point, they will be required to pay the tax on the gain that they realized from the sale of both the old home and the new home, unless, of course, they again purchase a new home that will be their principal residence within the prescribed period, or the tax is forgiven by another section of the Code.

As we have noted, the provisions of the Code that permit a taxpayer to defer the gain on the sale of their principal residence apply to them individually. Thus, if each of them receives one-half the proceeds from the sale of their home, they will each be entitled to reinvest those proceeds in a new home and thereby to defer the gain that they realized from the sale of their old home, provided that they meet the conditions prerequisite to such treatment.[54] These rules also apply if the home that they are either selling or buying is a condominium or cooperative apartment (i.e., the shares of stock in a cooperative housing corporation) rather than a private one- or two-family residence.

A second exception to the general rule occurs if they sell their home after they have attained the age of 55 years. If either of them has reached their 55th birthday at the time of the sale of their home, and if that home constituted their principal residence for periods totaling at least three years during the five-year period immediately preceding its sale, then—and if they have owned that home for periods totaling at least three years in such five-year period—they may elect to exclude up to $125,000 of the gain realized on the sale.[55] Unlike the previous provision of the Code, this section offers them not simply a postponement of the tax on the gain, but a forgiveness of that tax as well.

It is not necessary that both of the parties be over the age of 55 years at the time of the sale in order to qualify for this election.[56] It is only necessary that *one* of them has attained that age at the time of its sale (just as it is only necessary that one of them has owned the home, and used the home as their principal residence, for periods totaling at least three years in the five years immediately prior to its sale).[57] However, if they are not both 55 years of age, and if they do not file a joint return, only the party who is 55 years of age at the time of the sale can claim the exclusion, and it will then be limited to $62,500, or one-half (rather than the whole) of the gain, whichever is less.[58] In other words, if the profit is $200,000, and if the parties file a joint return, $125,000 of that profit will be forgiven. If they do not file a joint return, however, then the exclusion that can be claimed by the party who is 55 years of age is limited to $62,500.

If the couple is married at the time of the sale, they will not *each* receive a lifetime exclusion of $125,000 of the gain. Rather, they will each receive only an exclusion of $62,500 (for a combined exclusion of $125,000), and this is so even if they are both over the age of 55. However, if they divorce prior to the sale of the home, and if they are both over the age of 55 years at the time of the sale, then they will *each* be entitled to the full exclusion of $125,000 of the gain that they receive individually from the sale of the home.[59] If they are divorced, and if only one of them is 55 years of age at the time of the sale, then only that person will be entitled to make the election, and that election will only cover the gain on their one-half interest in the home. In that instance, the party who is not 55 years of age will not be entitled to claim the election, though it will again be available to him if, at a later time, he purchases a home which thereafter appreciates in value and he then sells it after attaining the age of 55 years.

But that is only if the parties are divorced. If the parties are married at the time, then, and even if they file separate returns, if the party who is over the age of 55 years claims the lifetime exclusion, then the other party will forever be barred from taking it.[60] Thus, the *timing* of the couple's divorce in relationship to the sale of their home can be very important. If they are both over the age of 55, it can double the exclusion. If one of them is under the age of 55, it can save for that person the right to claim the exclusion at a later date.

CHAPTER 23

THE COST OF RAISING A CHILD

One of the most formidable problems in mediation is to help a couple resolve an issue when there is not a ready yardstick to apply. If the issue is how long the wife should be permitted to live in the marital residence, and if the children are in their early teens, their graduation from high school, or at least college, will often appear to be a logical date, even if the wife may wish to live in the home *longer*, or the husband would like to see it sold *sooner*. But if the question is the amount of child support, a ready yardstick is not as easy to be found? On the face of it, it would seem sensible to say that the payment should reflect the children's needs and each of the parties' abilities to meet those needs. But how do you determine those needs? And how do you measure that ability?

In an effort to address these questions, there have been a number of studies in the last few years designed to assist decision makers and others interested in the question to determine the appropriate needs of children,[1] and they have already been relied upon by those who have wrestled with this problem. It can only be anticipated that there will be an even greater reliance upon these studies in the future, particularly since each of the states has been mandated to establish child support guidelines by the Child Support Enforcement Amendments of 1984.[2]

It is our purpose to summarize the latest, and one of the most authoritative, studies that has been made, that of Thomas J. Espenshade, a senior research associate in the Women and Family Policy Program at The Urban Institute published under the title *Investing in Children*.[3] Our purpose is threefold. First, to the extent that knowing what various socioeconomic groups spend in support of their children may be beneficial to mediators in helping couples arrive at an appropriate level of child support, to provide them with this information. Second, since it can be anticipated that his study, and particularly the conclusions that have been drawn from it, will be relied upon heavily in the future, to acquaint mediators with it. Finally, and perhaps most importantly, to give mediators a more sophisticated understanding of what this and other studies actually do represent and how they should be understood.

THE ESPENSHADE STUDY RESULTS

The Espenshade study broke down all of the husband/wife families into three socioeconomic groups.[4] For his purposes, he called these high, medium, and low. Families in the high group were those in which the husband had some college education and a white-collar job.[5] Medium families were those where the husband had a high school diploma and a blue-collar job. In low families the husband had less than a high school

TABLE 23-1. Parental Expenditures on Children
(Expressed in 1981 Dollars per Child per Week)

Socioeconomic status group	One-child families	Two-children families	Three-children families
Wife employed full-time full year			
High	$145	$112	$94
Medium	130	101	84
Low	123	95	79
Wife employed part-time full year			
High	$135	$105	$88
Medium	113	88	74
Low	103	80	67
Wife not employed			
High	$126	$ 98	$82
Medium	105	82	68
Low	96	74	62

education and a blue-collar job.[6] These three socioeconomic groups were in turn further divided into three groups based upon the wife's occupation. In the first group were those wives who did no market work at all outside of the home. In the second were those who worked outside of the home all year, on a part-time basis. In the third were those who worked outside of the home all year, on a full-time basis. The study thus resulted in nine groupings, three for each socioeconomic level. Each of these nine groups were then further divided into three more categories. In the first the couple had but one child, in the second two, and in the third, three. (The results of Espenshade's study are summarized in Table 23-1.)

As might be expected, the greatest expenditure per child was in the high group, where the wife worked full-time outside the home and the couple had one child. Here the total expenditure for the first 18 years of the child's life (until his 18th birthday) was $135,700, or $145 per week. (If a woman such as this had three children, the total expenditure was $262,700, or $94 per child per week.)[7] At the other end of the scale was the wife in the low category who did not work for pay and who had three children. There the total expenditure was $174,900, or $62 per week per child.[8]

Espenshade's conclusions were expressed in 1981 prices. Since the data for his study were taken from a 1972–1973 survey, however, Espenshade was required to update these figures to express them in terms of 1981 price levels. While it is possible to update these figures further to the present date with a fair degree of accuracy by applying a cost-of-living increase since that date, it is not as easy to project these figures into the future. To help decision makers and others interested in the question to do this, Espenshade then attempted to estimate a comparable expenditure for a child born in 1981. Since these figures are dependent upon the future rate of inflation, and since it is not possible to predict that rate, Espenshade projected his figures based upon three sets of assumptions. The first assumed a low rate of inflation (5.2%). The second assumed a medium rate of inflation (8.0%), and the third assumed a high rate of inflation (9.3%) (see Tables 23-2–23-4).

TABLE 23-2. Estimated Future Parental Expenditures on Children when 1st child is Born in 1981—Expressed in Dollars per child per Week—Low inflation scenario

Socioeconomic status group	One-child families	Two-children families	Three-children families
Wife employed full-time full year			
High	$248	$203	$179
Medium	221	181	159
Low	209	171	150
Wife employed part-time full year			
High	$232	$191	$169
Medium	194	159	141
Low	176	145	128
Wife not employed			
High	$218	$180	$159
Medium	180	148	131
Low	163	135	120

Using the examples that were given previously, the expenditures for a child ranged from a high of $342,800, or $366 per week, for a family in the high group with one child, where the wife worked outside the home on a full-time basis (assuming a high rate of inflation) to a low of $111,933, or $120 per week, for a family in the low group with three children, where the wife was not employed outside of the home (assuming a low rate of inflation).

TABLE 23-3. Estimated Future Parental Expenditures on Children when 1st child is Born in 1981—Expressed in Dollars per child per Week—Medium inflation scenario

Socioeconomic status group	One-child families	Two-children families	Three-children families
Wife employed full-time full year			
High	$322	$271	$246
Medium	287	241	220
Low	270	228	207
Wife employed part-time full year			
High	$302	$256	$233
Medium	251	213	195
Low	228	194	178
Wife not employed			
High	$284	$242	$221
Medium	233	198	182
Low	212	181	166

438

CHAPTER 23

TABLE 23-4. Estimated Future Parental Expenditures on Children when 1st child is Born in 1981—Expressed in Dollars per child per Week—High inflation scenario

Socioeconomic status group	One-child families	Two-children families	Three-children families
Wife employed full-time full year			
High	$366	$312	$286
Medium	325	277	254
Low	305	260	239
Wife employed part-time full year			
High	$344	$294	$271
Medium	284	243	224
Low	257	221	204
Wife not employed			
High	$323	$278	$257
Medium	263	226	209
Low	239	205	190

OBSERVATIONS

To understand Espenshade's conclusions, certain observations must be made. A number of factors affected the amount that a family spent for the support of their children. Principal among those were the parents' socioeconomic status, the wife's employment status, and the number of children in the family. Of the three, the number of children had the greatest impact on the amount spent. The second most important factor was the parents' socioeconomic status. While it still obviously impacted on the amount expended, the work status of the wife outside of the family had the *least* impact.[9]

In addition to analyzing the number of dollars expended by the various groups on their children, Espenshade's study also analyzed the percentage of total family consumption that was represented by the expenditures made for their children. Again, the most significant factor was the number of children in the family. Thus, whereas a family with only one child expended, on the average, about 30% of total family expenditures on their child, families with two children spent between 40 and 45% and families with three children spent 50%.[10]

Espenshade's study also indicated that the amount of dollars spent on children was not a constant throughout the first 18 years of their lives and that, as a rule, the expenditures gradually increased as they got older. Dividing the dollar expenditure into three equal groups of six years each, Espenshade found that approximately 26% of total child-related expenditures took place in the first six years, approximately 36% in the second six years, and approximately 38% in the last six years.[11]

The Espenshade study indicated that other factors also affected the expenditures made by a family for their children, although to a far less extent than the number of children in the family, the family's socioeconomic status, or the employment of the wife outside of the home. These factors related to black/white differences in child-related expenditures, differences related to residence in particular areas of the country, and differences related to residence inside and outside of large metropolitan areas. Thus, with families with two children, having a medium socioeconomic status, with the wife working full-time, white families spent $93,850 per child (or $100 per week) as compared to black families who spend $91,000 per child (or $97 per week).[12]

In families with the same characteristics, those living in the West spent $105,950 per child (or $113 per week), those in the Northeast, $98,150 per child (or $105 per week), those in the Northcentral, $97,700 per child (or $104 per week), and those in the South, $84,250 per child (or $90 per week).[13] Finally, families living in metropolitan areas expended more than those who lived outside of metropolitan areas. Thus, and again with families with the same characteristics, the total expenditure for families in metropolitan areas was $98,700 per child (or $105 per week) and in nonmetropolitan areas $83,500 per child (or $89 per week).[14]

Lastly, the Espenshade study examined the effect of certain other factors, in particular the age of the mother at the time that her first child was born and the interval between the birth of her children, on the expenditures made on children. Espenshade concluded that although expenditures increased per child as the length of the birth interval increased from one year to four years, and, although they also increased as the age of the mother at the time of the birth of her first child increased, these factors had far less affect upon parental expenditures than did the *number* of children in the family.[15]

CAVEAT

Does a mediator now know what it costs to raise a child, and can he rely upon the Espenshade study to support his conclusion? It would be comfortable to think that he does; but before jumping to that conclusion he had better keep certain considerations in mind.

1. The Espenshade study draws *no conclusions* as to the cost of raising a child.[16] In fact, as he himself states: "We emphasize that we are estimating parental expenditures on children, not the cost of raising them."[17] Moreover, these are expenditures made for children in intact families, and not those made by separated or divorced husbands and wives. In short, the fact that a married couple is *able* and *willing* to expend certain amounts in support of their children is not necessarily an appropriate basis to determine what a separated wife will *need* to support them.

Without question, the standard of living of the children will decrease if the husband and wife are no longer able to expend the same dollars for their support in the future that they were able to in the past. But they will *not*, any more than they will be able to spend the same amount on themselves. Thus, the amount previously expended on their children is not a necessary indication of what their reasonable *needs* are—unless one is prepared to maintain that those needs are synonymous with what they were *used* to receiving.[18]

2. The income and expenditure data relied upon by Espenshade were with respect to families and not individuals. As Espenshade himself acknowledges, this created a problem in terms of the apportionment of total family consumption (expenditures) to the individual family members.[19] It may be possible to apportion the cost of food among the

individual family members, and it may even be possible to apportion clothing. But how do you apportion the cost of an automobile or the cost of a home to particular family members? As Espenshade himself acknowledges, this is conceptually difficult. Thus, no matter how responsibly the expenditures are assigned, there cannot but be an arbitrary quality to that assignment.

Suppose, for example, that a husband and a wife live in a one-bedroom apartment that also contains a living room, a kitchen, and a dining area. Following the birth of their child, they decide to take larger living accommodations and rent a new apartment. It is almost identical to their present apartment except that it contains an additional bedroom. The rent for their new apartment is $750 per month as compared to $600 per month for their old one. Is the cost of housing (rent) attributable to their child one-third of the total cost, or $250 per month? Or is it simply the increased cost of their rent, or $150 per month? What is merely *difficult* in terms of certain expenditures, such as shelter, becomes almost *impossible* for others, such as transportation. While they rented a larger apartment after the birth of their child, they still continued to maintain the same automobile. Nor has there been any significant increase in its use following his birth. Does that mean that no portion of the family's transportation costs are assignable to their child? And, if they are, is it limited to the cost of those few additional miles that are attributable to him? There simply is no answer.

3. There is an even more serious problem in drawing any conclusions as to the cost of raising a child from Espenshade's study. As we have noted previously, the study is based upon expenditures, not costs. More importantly, however, it is based upon expenditures of both time and money. In other words, when Espenshade concludes that the expenditure of a Middle-American family with two children, having a medium socioeconomic status, with a wife who works outside the home on a part-time basis, is $82,400 per child (or $90 per week), he is not only including direct, out-of-pocket, maintenance expenses for such things as food, clothing, shelter, medical care, etc. He is also including expenditures of time or opportunity. While these opportunity expenditures, i.e., the income that the mother may give up by reducing the time that she works outside of the home in order to raise her children, may be "no less important," as Espenshade maintains, it would be *inappropriate*, nevertheless, to base the cost of raising a child, for the purpose of establishing child support payments, on these expenditures of both "time and money."

4. Without intending to detract from the integrity of Espenshade's study, statistical evaluations such as this must always be taken with a heavy grain of salt. As Espenshade himself acknowledges, the conclusions drawn from his present study differ from conclusions that he made only four years earlier.[20] He attributes these differences to "new data and improved methodology." The change in these conclusions are not simply reflections of more accurate data, however. They are also a reflection of a change in *the way this data was viewed*. But just as the 1980 estimates, that were taken at face value, and quoted without any forewarning that they would be revised based upon "new data and an improved methodology," were later reevaluated, so too can the present estimates be revised in the future. Using the terms "new" data and "improved" methodology suggests that we are *finally* using the "correct" data and methodology. However, it may also mean that we are only using *different* data and methodology. And, as Espenshade candidly acknowledges, other responsible estimators can and do use different data bases and different approaches.[21]

In this respect, Espenshade quotes the findings of the U.S. Department of Agriculture (USDA) which are also often cited as authority for the amount that parents spend on their children. While Espenshade maintains that the findings of USDA are close to his in terms of total expenditures, there are, nevertheless, some significant differences. For example, Espenshade finds clear evidence that a family's living standard *varies* over the life cycle of the family, whereas USDA finds it to be pretty much a constant.[22] Even more significantly, of the total amount expended, USDA attributes approximately 34% of the expenditure for housing and only 15% for transportation, while Espenshade attributes only about 24% to housing and 25% to transportation.[23] Espenshade attributes these differences simply to differences in data and estimation procedures. Unfortunately, this explanation will not do. Espenshade emphasizes that the conclusions of USDA are close to his own in terms of the total expenditures made for a child to age 18, as well as in terms of the distribution of that total in the six three-year periods, "despite differences in data bases and in approach," in support of the validity of his own conclusions. Nevertheless, he explains away the very significant differences in allocation in their study and his as far as housing and transportation are concerned based upon the same "differences in data and in estimation procedures. . . ."[24]

Espenshade cannot have it both ways. Either the different data bases and approaches are significant—in which case the similarity in his and USDA's conclusions as to total expenditures is simply coincidental—or they are *in*significant, in which case they cannot account for the different conclusions in the two reports as to the allocation for transportation and housing. To be sure, it is possible that the conclusions in one of the studies is correct and the other incorrect, either in whole or in part. However, it is far more likely that the differences are simply attributable to the fact that there are many *legitimate differences of opinion* as to *which of the facts are relevant*—not to mention different ways of approaching those facts. Facts never speak for themselves; and, particularly when they are as complex as the data that constitute the bases for these studies, they do not lead inevitably to one and only one conclusion.

5. Finally, the expenditures on children summarized in this study are estimates only, and Espenshade never pretends otherwise. On the contrary, he takes pains to underscore this fact. Thus, just as he distinguishes between the cost of raising a child and parental expenditures made for a child, he also carefully distinguishes between the actual amount of such expenditures and his "estimates" of them.

Does this mean that the conclusions drawn by Espenshade are without value? It is not our purpose to make these judgments. What is relevant is that the conclusions that Espenshade has drawn from his studies already have been, and undoubtedly will be, cited and relied upon by decision makers and other persons in the future. When mediators are faced with expressions of opinion based upon this or other studies, however, they should understand what they mean and how properly to evaluate them. They must also understand this before they rely upon them themselves.

FORMS AND LETTERS

TELEPHONE INFORMATION SHEET

Husband
    Name: _____
    Address: _____
    Telephone number: (home) _____ (work) _____
Wife
    Name: _____
    Address: _____
    Telephone number: (home) _____ (work) _____
Present status:
Living together _____   Separated _____
Marital residence: private home _____ apartment _____
Years married: _____
Children's ages: _____
Husband's occupation: _____
Wife's occupation: _____
Previous marriages: _____
How recommended: _____
Remarks: _____

INITIAL INTERVIEW SHEET

1. Wife's name _____ Age _____
   Birth: Date _____ Place _____
   Maiden name _____
   Address _____

   Phone number: Home _____ Work _____
   Race _____ Religion _____
   Education _____
2. Husband's name _____
   Birth: Date _____ Place _____
   Address _____

   Phone number: Home _____ Business _____
   Race _____ Religion _____
   Education _____
3. Marriage: Date _____ Place _____
   Date of Separation _____
4. Children
   Name   Date of Birth   Residence
   _____

5. Wife's Occupation _____
   Employer _____
   Direct Compensation: Gross Income _____
   Indirect Compensation:
   Medical Insurance yes _____ no _____   Life Insurance yes _____ no _____
   Pension yes _____ no _____   Automobile yes _____ no _____
   Other Income _____
6. Husband's Occupation _____
   Employer _____
   Direct Compensation: Gross Income _____
   Indirect Compensation:
   Medical Insurance yes _____ no _____   Life Insurance yes _____ no _____
   Pension yes _____ no _____   Automobile yes _____ no _____
   Other Income _____
7. Marital Residence—Owned
   Occupied by _____ Title _____
   First Mortgage—Bank _____
   Principal Balance _____ Present Value _____
   Monthly Payment _____
   Home Improvement Loans—Bank _____
   Principal Balance _____ Monthly Payment _____
   Marital Residence—Rented
   Occupied by _____ Security _____
   Rent _____
   Lease Commenced _____ Lease Ends _____
   Oral _____ Written _____
8. Medical History: _____
   _____
   _____

9. Previous Marriages and Support Payments: _____
   _____

Description of Mediation Practice Therapist/Attorney Team

Divorce mediation was born in the belief that disputes between husbands and wives, even disputes concerning their divorce, did not properly belong within the adversary system of the law, and that whatever might be its benefits in other areas, when it came to the resolution of marital disputes, those benefits were simply too far outweighed by the time, cost, and emotional injury that were inevitably its price. It was also born in the belief that many divorcing couples would like, and should be afforded, some other alternative.

Initial Interview

In a short while you will be interviewed by a member of our staff who will explain to you our work and answer any questions you may have at that time. At the conclusion of that interview, you will be asked to provide us with the necessary biographical and historical background of your family. Finally, you will be provided with a list of the financial information you will require in connection with your mediation.

If you decide to avail yourselves of our services, a second appointment will be scheduled with you. During this second appointment the divorce mediator with whom you will work will discuss with you the range of issues with which you will be dealing during the course of your mediation and will begin to address some of them. At the same time you will be given certain information that will be of help to you in the course of your mediation. This material has been prepared for you by our legal staff and will be yours to keep and to use during the course of your mediation. At the conclusion of this meeting, further appointments will be scheduled with you. These appointments are usually one week apart to give you an adequate opportunity to digest and review what has taken place at the previous meeting. During these subsequent meetings you will continue to work with the divorce mediator assigned to you, who will mediate the unresolved issues existing between you and help the two of you bring them to a resolution.

The Divorce Mediator

The divorce mediator's primary function is to help the two of you to work out an agreement between yourselves, and to mediate the differences between you that are standing in the way of that agreement. If there are emotional considerations that are making it more difficult for you to resolve your differences, he (or she) will try to help you deal with those too. Lastly, if your separation is having an adverse emotional affect upon other members of your family, he will also help you to better understand and deal with those problems, and you should not hesitate to discuss them with him. While the divorce mediator's primary professional background is in marital counseling, and although he will be happy to work towards a resolution of your marital problems should you wish, no attempt at reconciliation will be made unless both of you request it, and your decision to separate or divorce—whether that is a common decision or simply the decision of one of you—will at all times be respected.

The Advisory Attorney

While the divorce mediator to whom you will be assigned stands ready to assist you in any way that he can, you must keep in mind that he (or she) is not an attorney and that he will not be able to answer any legal questions which you may have. On the contrary, all such questions must be directed to the advisory attorney who will also be assigned to work with you. (It is the advisory attorney's policy to discuss and answer all such questions only in the presence of both of you together, and you may call and arrange for an appointment with him for that purpose at any time.)

Your Agreement

Once a tentative agreement has been reached, you may either take it to an attorney or attorneys of your own choice to have it reduced to a formal, written agreement or, should you wish, your advisory attorney will prepare that agreement for you.

In this regard, it must be kept in mind that the function of the advisory attorney is simply to reduce to a written agreement the understanding that the two of you have come to, either on your own or with the assistance of the divorce counselor to whom you were assigned. Although he will answer whatever questions you may have, explain to you the meaning and significance of any provisions in your agreement, and make whatever language changes you may feel are necessary to more clearly reflect your understanding, it is not his function to negotiate any of the terms of that agreement for either of you. In short, the advisory attorney does not represent either of you individually, and represents both of you only to the extent of reducing to writing the agreement that you have concluded between yourselves with our assistance.

Divorce Proceedings

Once an agreement has been reached, and provided that both of you would have him do so, the advisory attorney will prepare the necessary papers to permit you to obtain a divorce on the least offensive grounds available to you permitted by the law. However, he will only do that if both of you request him to do so, including your agreement as to who will be appearing as the plaintiff in that action, who will be appearing as the defendant, and the grounds upon which the divorce will be obtained.

Costs

One of our goals is to reduce the expenses which separating and divorcing couples normally face. In fact, we are committed to the principle of providing couples with an agreement of the highest quality, but at a cost they can afford.

In keeping with that goal, your total fee, for both of you, will be $-----. This will include not only the services of the divorce mediator assigned to you, but the fees, as well, of the advisory attorney through the preparation and execution of your agreement. If you should decide to obtain a divorce, there will be an additional fee of $-----, plus the actual out-of-pocket disbursements of the advisory attorney in connection with the filing of the necessary papers with the court. If you wish to retain your own attorney or attorneys to prepare your agreement, however, rather than have that agreement prepared by your advisory attorney (which is your absolute right), then your fee will be reduced by $-----.

PAYMENT OF FEES

If you decide to avail yourselves of our services, a second appointment will be scheduled for you. Prior to that meeting, you will be mailed a retainer agreement setting forth our fee arrangement, and you will be asked to sign and return that retainer agreement together with a deposit equal to 25% of your total fee.

Following this second meeting, additional meetings, each of which will be approximately one to one and one-half hours in length, will be scheduled until the two of you have concluded an agreement between yourselves. At the conclusion of each of these meetings, you will be asked to make an additional deposit toward your total fee of $-----. When you have concluded an agreement, and it is time to prepare the draft of that agreement, you will then be asked to pay the balance of your fee (if any balance is still owing). Again, if you choose to have that agreement prepared by your own attorney or attorneys, rather than by your advisory attorney, there will be a reduction in your fee of $-----.

Your initial retainer, as well as the additional payments made by you at each subsequent meeting, are not refundable should you decide not to continue with your mediation. However, the balance of your fee will not be due and owing unless we are successful in helping you to conclude an agreement between yourselves.

YOUR AGREEMENT

If you decide to have your advisory attorney prepare your written agreement, a draft of that agreement will be prepared and forwarded to you. After you have received that agreement, an appointment will be scheduled for you with your advisory attorney to review that agreement with him, for him to answer any questions you may have concerning it, and to make any changes or revisions that are required. Following this, your agreement will be put into final form and again sent to you, and an appointment will be scheduled with you to sign that agreement. (It is our policy to insist that each of you have that final agreement for at least a week to assure that each of you has had an adequate opportunity carefully to review and consider it, and to consult with such persons as you may wish, including independent attorneys of your own choosing, before you sign it.)

LETTER ACKNOWLEDGING INFORMATION PROVIDED AT INITIAL MEETING

January 1, 1988

Mr. & Mrs. John Smith
100 Main Street
Watertown, New York 12345

Dear Mr. & Mrs. Smith:

Before proceeding to assist the two of you to conclude an agreement between yourselves, we would ask that you acknowledge the following:

1. That during your initial appointment the procedures of divorce mediation were explained to you and you were given adequate opportunity to ask whatever questions you had at that time.

2. That after deciding to retain us you were given a divorce information manual prepared by our legal staff which contained, among other things, the questions which the two of you would have to answer in the course of your mediation in order to reach an agreement, a summary of the law of the State of New York as it pertains to the principal outstanding questions to be answered by the two of you, and excerpts from various statutes of the State of New York relating to those questions.

3. Following your initial meeting, a second appointment was made with the two of you. During that second meeting you were given the opportunity to ask any questions which you had in connection with the material contained in the divorce information manual and those questions were answered to your satisfaction.

4. That at one of these two meetings you had the opportunity of speaking with the advisory attorney assigned to you to ask him whatever legal questions you had. You were also advised that you could schedule further appointments with him at any time to discuss any other questions which might arise during the course of your mediation.

5. During your initial meeting, you were specifically advised of the following facts:

(a) That if you retain our services to mediate the issues incident to your separation and divorce, the two of you will be assisted by one attorney and one attorney alone, rather than each of you being represented by separate attorneys.

(b) That the advisory attorney assigned to assist the two of you will be representing neither of you except for the purpose of reducing to writing the agreement that the two of you will conclude between yourselves with the assistance of the mediator to whom you will be assigned.

(c) That it is not the function of your advisory attorney to negotiate an agreement for either of you, and although he will provide you with impartial legal information, and answer any legal questions which you may have, he will not take sides in any dispute between you, as it is not his purpose to be either of your advocates.

(d) That your advisory attorney will only answer questions which you may have in the presence of both of you. In fact, he will at no time meet or speak with either of you unless the other is present. For this reason, and although he will never voluntarily disclose to anyone else any information which either of you has told or given to him, your discussions are not confidential in the sense that they would be were they to take place between you and him alone without the presence of your spouse.

(e) That in keeping with the confidentiality which it has been agreed should extend to the discussions which will take place during the course of your mediation, you have each agreed that should your mediation fail to conclude in an agreement which is signed by the both of you, and should either of you thereafter institute any legal action or proceeding against the other, that neither of you will call any member of our staff, including the mediator that has been assigned to you, as a witness in that action or proceeding.

(f) That you have the absolute right to seek independent advice by counsel of your own choice before signing any agreement prepared for you by your advisory attorney, or at any other time during the mediation.

(g) That you may have your own attorney or attorneys prepare your written agreement, rather than have us prepare it for you, and that it is your absolute right to do so.

(h) That we will prepare the papers necessary for one of you to institute suit for an uncontested divorce following the completion of your agreement only if both of you agree to this.

(i) At no time, and under no circumstances, will your advisory attorney represent either of you individually, either during the course of your mediation or otherwise, regardless of the fact that such representation may not directly affect your husband or wife, and may have nothing to do with your separation or divorce.

If this letter accurately reflects your understanding, and what you have been told by us, please acknowledge that fact by signing your names where indicated below.

Very truly yours,

AGREED AND ACKNOWLEDGED:

_____

_____

LETTER SETTING FORTH FEE ARRANGEMENT

January 1, 1988

Mr. & Mrs. John Smith
100 Main Street
Watertown, New York 12345

Dear Mr. & Mrs. Smith:

The purpose of this letter is to set forth our agreement as to the fees to be paid by you for our assisting you to resolve your matrimonial differences and in then reducing your understanding to a formal written agreement.

The total fee to be paid by the two of you will be $_____. This includes the mediation fees as well as the fees of the advisory attorney who will assist you throughout the mediation. (If you should decide to have your own attorney or attorneys prepare your written agreement, that fee will be reduced by twenty-five (25%) percent.) At the present time, you will pay us the sum of $_____ representing your retainer fee. You will also be asked to make additional payments of $_____ toward the balance of our fee at each of the subsequent meetings scheduled for you following your second meeting. The balance of our fee will be due and payable when you have concluded a tentative agreement between yourselves and it is time for us (or for your own attorney or attorneys) to prepare the first draft of that agreement.

The retainer to be paid by you at the present time, as well as all additional fees paid by you, is nonrefundable, even if you are not able to reach an agreement between yourselves. However, the balance of our fee will not be due and payable unless the two of you reach a tentative understanding and we (or your own attorney or attorneys) are required to prepare a draft of that agreement.

If it is your desire to retain us for this purpose, and if this letter accurately reflects our understanding as to the fees to be paid by you in this regard, please sign your names at the place indicated below acknowledging this fact.

Very truly yours,

ACCEPTED AND AGREED

_____

_____

FINANCIAL DATA SHEET

INCOME (Husband and Wife)
 1. Wife's Occupation and Income
Employer: _____
Position Held: _____
Direct Compensation: Gross _____
Indirect Compensation: _____

 2. Husband's Occupation and Income
Employer: _____
Position Held: _____
Direct Compensation: Gross _____
Indirect Compensation: _____

ASSETS (Husband and Wife)
 3. Savings, Checking and Money Market Accounts:

Bank	Type of Account	Balance	Title

 4. Stocks and Mutual Funds

Name of Company	Number of Shares	Present Value	Title

 5. U.S. Savings Bonds

Certificate #	Date of Purchase	Face Value	Title

 6. Real Estate

Description	Present Value	Title

 7. Life Insurance

Name of Company	Insured	Type	Death Benefit	Title

 8. Business Interests

Nature of Interest	Present Value	Title

9. Personal Property (Automobiles, Boats, Jewelry, Antiques, etc.)

Description	Present Value	Title

10. Other Property

Description	Present Value	Title

ASSETS (Children)

Description	Present Value	Title

LIABILITIES

1. Mortgages on Real Property

Description	Present Balance	Monthly Payment

2. Notes Payable to Banks, etc.

Holder of Note	Balance	Monthly Payment	Debtor

3. Loans on Insurance Policies

Company	Amount of Loan

4. Credit Cards

Name of Company	Present Balance	Monthly Payment	Debtor

5. Other Debts

Description	Amount Owed	Debtor

Dated: _____

_____   _____
          Signature of Wife   Signature of Husband

STATE OF NEW YORK, COUNTY OF NASSAU : ss

Mary Smith, being duly sworn, deposes and says: I attest to the truth and accuracy of the information set forth on this financial data sheet with respect to my income, assets and liabilities. I further acknowledge that I believe that the income, assets and liabilities of my husband are true and accurate and that I have no information or belief that would suggest that his income, assets or liabilities are greater or other than as is set forth on this financial data sheet.

Sworn to before me this
12th day of June, 1985

_____

Mary Smith

STATE OF NEW YORK, COUNTY OF NASSAU : ss

John Smith, being duly sworn, deposes and says: I attest to the truth and accuracy of the information set forth on this financial data sheet with respect to my income, assets and liabilities. I further acknowledge that I believe that the income, assets and liabilities of my wife are true and accurate and that I have no information or belief that would suggest that her income, assets or liabilities are greater or other than as is set forth on this financial data sheet.

Sworn to before me this
12th day of June, 1985

_____

John Smith

QUESTIONS TO BE RESOLVED IN MEDIATION

Questions

(The following is a list of questions, broken down into categories, which must be answered by every separating and divorcing couple. While the ultimate agreement which the parties will sign will contain numerous other provisions, these can generally be left to the advisory attorney to add, at least in the initial draft.)

CHILDREN

1. Who will be the custodial or residential parent?

2. What rights will the noncustodial or nonresidential parent have to be and spend time with the children?

3. Will there be any restriction on where the custodial or residential parent may move with the children?

4. How will major decisions affecting the children's health, welfare and education be made?

5. If there are transportation expenses involved in the noncustodial or nonresidential parent's being and spending time with the children, who will be responsible to pay them?

MARITAL RESIDENCE (OWNED)

1. What disposition will be made of the home? (Will it be sold presently, will one of the parties deed his or her interest in it to the other, or will one of them have the right to continue to live in the home, and if so, for how long?)

2. If one of the parties will have the right to live in the home for a period of time, will he or she have the right to rent any portion of the home or to allow any other person to live there? (If rent will be received, who will have the right to keep it?)

3. If one of the parties will have the right to live in the home for a period of time, will that right be affected by that party's remarriage or by his or her living in the home, as if married, with another person?

4. If the home is to be sold, either now or in the future, who will be entitled to the proceeds upon its sale?

5. If the parties cannot agree upon any of the provisions of the sale (for example, the selling price, whether it will be sold privately or through a broker), how will this be determined?

6. Who will be responsible for the ordinary maintenance and carrying charges of the home until it is sold?

7. Who will be responsible for major repairs and the cost of preparing the home for sale?

8. If and when the home is to be sold, will either party have a first option to buy it?

9. Who will be entitled to deduct mortgage interest charges and real estate taxes for income tax purposes?

10. Who will be responsible for any income (capital gains) taxes which may be imposed as a result of the sale of the home?

MARITAL RESIDENCE (RENTED)

1. Who will have the right to continue to occupy the marital residence?

2. Who will be obligated to pay the rent and other carrying charges in the future?

3. What disposition will be made of any security on deposit?

4. Will the party who will not continue to occupy the marital residence have an obligation to join with the other party in renewing the present lease if the landlord will not renew it without his or her signature?

DEBTS

1. What debts (other than business debts or the mortgage on their home) do the parties have?

2. Who will be responsible to pay each of these debts?

PERSONAL PROPERTY

1. What disposition will be made of the furniture, household furnishings and other items of personal property in the marital residence?

2. What disposition will be made of any savings or checking accounts in either the joint or individual names of the parties?

3. What disposition will be made of any stocks, bonds or other securities in either the joint or individual names of the parties?

4. What disposition will be made of any automobiles, boats, motorcycles or other items of personal property in either the joint or individual names of the parties?

5. Will either party have the right to share in any pension or retirement benefits to which the other is or may be entitled, and if so, to what extent?

6. Will either party be entitled to a share of the value of any business, professional practice, royalties or other property owned by the other party and if so, to what extent?

SUPPORT

1. Will either party be required to make payment to the other for his or her support, and if so, in what amount and for how long?

2. Will either party be required to make payment to the other for the support of their children, and if so, in what amount and for how long?

3. If the parties have more than one child, by how much will the child support payments be reduced when the obligation for the support of one or more of the children terminates?

4. Will the support payments for the other party or for the children increase or decrease in the future due to the changed financial circumstances of either of the parties, economic conditions or other factors?

5. Who shall be entitled to claim the children as exemptions for income tax purposes?

LIFE INSURANCE

1. Will either party be obligated to maintain life insurance on his or her life for the benefit of the other, and if so, in what amount and for how long?

2. Will either party be obligated to maintain life insurance on his or her life for the benefit of their children, and if so, in what amount and for how long?

3. If either party is obligated to maintain insurance on his or her life for the benefit of their children, who will be the beneficiary of such insurance?

4. Will the obligation to maintain such insurance decrease (as to amount) in the future, and if so, when and in what amount?

MEDICAL INSURANCE

1. Will either party be obligated to provide medical or other insurance for the benefit of the other, and if so, what insurance and for how long?

2. Will either party be obligated to provide medical or other insurance for the benefit of their children, and if so, what insurance and for how long?

3. Who will be responsible to pay for any medical, dental or hospital expenses of the children that are not reimbursed by any policies of insurance which either of the parties may have?

COLLEGE

1. Will either or both of the parties be obligated to pay for the college education expenses of their children, and if so, what expenses, and to what extent?

2. If such expenses are financed, either in whole or in part, by loans, who will be responsible to repay them?

3. If one of the parties is obligated to make payment to the other for the support of the children, will there be any reduction in those support payments while any of the children are attending college?

INCOME TAXES

1. Who will be responsible for any deficiency which may be due on any past joint income tax returns filed by the parties?

2. Who will be entitled to receive any refund which may be due on any past joint income tax returns filed by the parties?

3. If permitted by law, will the parties file joint income tax returns for the present year? If so, who will be responsible to pay any taxes due and who will be entitled to receive any sums refunded?

MISCELLANEOUS PROVISIONS

1. Will the parties each waive whatever claims they may presently have in the other's estate?

2. Will either party be obligated to leave any portion of his or her estate to the other?

LETTER RECEIVED BY MEDIATOR FROM ATTORNEY FOR ONE OF THE PARTIES

James Wrong
Attorney at Law
22 Maple Avenue
Watertown, N.Y.

June 20, 1987

Lenard Marlow, Esq.
300 Garden City Plaza
Garden City, NY 11530

Dear Mr. Marlow:

I have reviewed some of the proposals for settlement and have suggested to Mr. Smith the following proposal for settlement:

$500 per month Maintenance
$500 per month Child Support

Such sums are to be stable and fixed until the children are emancipated. This would allow Mrs. Smith to plan five years ahead without being concerned with a drop or shifting of support upon the children's various life events.

Upon remarriage, maintenance would cease and child support of $200 per month per unemancipated child would commence.

I believe that five years of maintenance is more than a court would award and that the support is fair and reasonable. My advice to Mr. Smith is to go no higher and to go into quick litigation if this is not acceptable.

With regard to the marital property, I would prefer to have Mr. Smith keep his equity in the home and see it sold at emancipation and divide the net proceeds equally. I would tell him to offer Mrs. Smith a fixed monthly sum from his pension of $476 per month if, as and when he takes his pension.

That figure of $476 is based upon his estimated monthly pension fixed as of mid 1986 of $1,700 per month gross. We averaged the last three years' salaries per the plan to arrive at this figure. He will lose a minimum of 30% in taxes on the pension which would net to $1,190 per month. The courts are awarding between 30% and 40% of net pension to a nonworking wife, so we are offering 40% of net or $476 per month. The plan would be notified and when he takes his pension her check would be cut separately and sent to her for a lifetime, tax-free pension fund.

The courts are moving away from the concept of ordering an exchange of house equity for pension rights. Quite properly, they see that the pension is a "future" benefit for which survival is necessary for collection while the home equity is a "today" asset which both worked to achieve.

Please let me know your opinion on this matter.

Very truly yours,

James Wrong

Reply Sent by Mediator

January 1, 1988

Mr. John Smith
100 Main Street
Watertown, New York 12345

Dear Mr. Smith:

I am in receipt of a letter dated June 20, 1987 from James Wrong, Esq. I assume that you are familiar with its contents.

Frankly, I am somewhat at a loss to understand why this letter was addressed to us, or what I am supposed to do with it. The letter reflects advice which Mr. Wrong has given to you, and proposals which he has made on your behalf. The letter closes with the statement "Please let me know your opinion on this matter."

We have no "opinion" on this matter. We do not represent your wife, any more than we represent you, and it is not our business to take positions with respect to advice, opinions or proposals which have been given or made to you by the attorney with whom you have consulted. It is certainly not our business to do this on behalf of your wife.

Nor do I think it would be appropriate for me to act as a conduit of information between either you and your wife or Mr. Wrong and your wife. If you would like to continue to discuss these matters with your wife in a mediated setting, we would of course be glad to schedule a meeting for that purpose. However, and although you have every right to be guided by Mr. Wrong's advice and opinion, your wife is not bound by his opinion, and if you decide to continue with the mediation, you must understand this.

While it is not for me to express any opinion about the advice which Mr. Wrong has given to you (and I would not do so in any event), I can express the opinion that it is at least possible that if your wife were to consult with an attorney of her own, her attorney might not share Mr. Wrong's opinion. If he did, you and your wife would probably not have a problem in the first place. To put it another way, unless Mr. Wrong is successful in persuading either your wife or her attorney that he is correct, you and your wife are left with a problem. The question then is how that problem will be resolved, whether by continued mediation or by adversarial procedures, including possibly litigation. This is the decision that you and your wife must make.

You will excuse me if I do not reply to Mr. Wrong's letter. That is not meant as any impoliteness, and should not be so construed. It is simply a reflection of the fact that I do not consider it to be my business to be engaging in discussions, let alone negotiations, with your attorney.

For obvious reasons, a copy of this letter is being sent to Mrs. Smith. I have declined to enclose a copy of Mr. Wrong's letter for the reason that, as far as I am concerned, it does not exist as part of your mediation. It is simply a letter which reflects the advice which Mr. Wrong has given to you. However, and as I indicated previously, I do not believe that this has anything to do with me.

Sincerely,

Lenard Marlow

dd
cc: Mrs. Mary Smith

NOTES

PREFACE

1. O. J. Coogler, *Structured Mediation in Divorce Settlements: A Handbook for Marital Mediators,* (Lexington, MA: Lexington Books, 1978).
2. John Haynes, *Divorce Mediation: A Practical Guide for Therapists and Counselors,* (New York, NY: Springer, 1981).
3. While it might be assumed that there was also the question of what is a parent's obligation to his or her children, that has not been the case, as the increase in the rate of divorce in the 20th century has not required us to reexamine the responsibility of a parent to his or her child as it has the responsibilities of the parties to one another. The one exception to this—and this has had more to do with the fact that women increasingly work outside of the home than it has to the increased divorce rate—has been the gradual, but increasing shift in the responsibility for a child's support from the husband's shoulders alone to that of both parents, at least where they are both possessed of the ability to bear that responsibility.
4. The reader will note that we have talked about both individual as well as joint efforts, and about property that may be owned by the parties at or subsequent to the time of their divorce rather than simply property that was acquired by them during their marriage. The equitable distribution statutes enacted by the various states, however, have generally proceeded on just the opposite principles; namely, that *all* effort is joint effort, or marital effort, and that any property acquired by either of the parties subsequent to their divorce is not subject to distribution. *But see* Conn. Gen. Stat. Ann. §46b-81 (West 1986); Idaho Code §32-712 (1983); Ind. Code §31-1-11.5-11 (West 1979 & 1987 Supp.); Mont. Code Ann. §40-4-202 (1986); Neb. Rev. Stat. §42-366 (1984); Wis. Stat. Ann. §766.76 (West 1981 & 1986 Supp.); §861.01 (West 1971 & 1986 Supp.). Unfortunately, we have lost sight of the fact that these principles (the legal fictions that we have created to deal with the problem of divorce) are very arbitrary ones. The result is that the application of these principles, rather than any attempt to address, as far as the couple at issue is concerned, the considerations that gave birth to these legal fictions, has been substituted as the appropriate question that must be addressed and answered at the time of their divorce. This will be discussed further in Chapter 3, *Equitable Distribution and Divorce Mediation.*
5. While it might be assumed that these questions were both addressed and answered by the legislature in the equitable distribution statutes enacted by the various states, in point of fact they were not. On the contrary, rather than being reflective of any real serious consideration of these questions, those statutes are simply reflective of the feeling, on the one hand, that women should have a greater share in the assets that were acquired during the marriage than they previously did and, on the other hand, that men should not necessarily have a lifelong obligation to support their wives following their divorce. Nor have the courts addressed these questions in a comprehensive manner either. Instead, they have principally been concerned with attempting to construe and apply the equitable distribution statutes of their states, which were enacted to express these two considerations, on a case-by-case basis.

CHAPTER 1—WHAT IS DIVORCE MEDIATION?

1. Judith S. Wallerstein and Joan Berlin Kelly, *Surviving the Breakup: How Children and Parents Cope with Divorce,* (New York, NY: Basic Books, 1980).

2. The proceedings of this conference are contained in the American Bar Association publication *Alternative Means of Family Dispute Resolution*, (Washington, D.C., 1982).

3. Roger D. Fisher and William Ury, *Getting to Yes*, (Boston, MA: Houghton Mifflin Co., 1981).

4. Thomas S. Kuhn, *The Structure of Scientific Revolutions*, 2nd ed., (Chicago, IL: The University of Chicago Press, 1970).

5. One of the most important implications of Kuhn's thinking is expressed in his principle of incommensurability. Paradigm shifts do not merely result in our looking at the same phenomena and seeing them differently. They also result in the fact that certain questions that were considered relevant in terms of the old paradigm are not only irrelevant in terms of the new one, but simply do not appear as questions at all. This is an extremely important principle and we will return to it again in Chapter 11, *A Question of Choice*. For the time being, it is sufficient to say that one of our most important recurring themes will be that in failing to understand the sense in which divorce mediation represents a paradigm shift, its advocates, as well as its critics, have continued to ask questions of it which, though they may be relevant in an adversarial context, are not relevant in divorce mediation. Since divorce mediation is obviously not the kind of paradigm shift that Kuhn was talking about—and we only invoke the term to employ what we nevertheless consider to be an important analogy—we would not suggest that they are inappropriate questions in Kuhn's sense. But the analogy is sufficient enough to suggest, as we continually will, that they are still no longer appropriate or even relevant questions in the more limited sense of a paradigm shift that we are talking about. Since it will probably be easier for mental health professionals—and perhaps even those who are not—to see this in terms of marriage counseling rather than divorce mediation (divorce counseling), which is still seen as being basically a legal process, we would ask the reader, in each instance, to ask whether or not the question is one that a *therapist* would ask were the same couple to come to him for marriage counseling.

Chapter 2—Legal Myths

1. In the discussion that follows, we do not mean to suggest that there may not be important legal implications that flow from personal decisions. Thus, if during the course of their marriage a couple decide to buy a home, they may well need legal assistance to assure that they get good title. (In many states, California, for example, this will be done almost entirely without the intervention of lawyers, who will not even participate in the preparation of the contract of sale or be present when it is negotiated or signed.) However, if they retain an attorney for that purpose, that does not mean that the decisions incident to this will now become legal ones. Nor will their attorney question the fact that those decisions (including the community they will choose to live in, the kind of home that they will select, the price that they will pay for it, etc.) remain essentially personal ones. Even if their attorney were to offer advice, based upon his experience (just as a broker, a relative or a friend might), that advice will still be about decisions that all parties concerned recognize are personal ones, and for the couple alone to make. Unfortunately, and for reasons that will be discussed later, this basic distinction gets lost if the personal decision that one of the parties is considering or has made is the decision to separate or divorce.

2. In New York, for example, section 236 of the Domestic Relations Law provides that the court has the power, as well as the obligation, to make an equitable distribution of the parties' marital property "Except where the parties have provided in an agreement for the disposition of their property. . . ." When the parties conclude an agreement on their own, it is generally said that they have "opted out" of the statute— that they have opted to make a distribution of their property on their own rather than to have the court do it for them. While the court does, nevertheless, have the right to ignore the terms of the parties' agreement, and even to set it aside, it will not do this simply because, in making their determination, the parties did not follow the same rules that the court would have applied. Rather, it will only do so if it feels that the agreement was the result of fraud or duress, or that its terms were so unconscionable as to represent overreaching on the part of one of the parties. *See, e.g., Christian v. Christian*, 42 N.Y.2d 63, 365 N.E.2d 849, 396 N.Y.S.2d 817 (1977); *Johnson v. Johnson*, 67 N.C. App. 250, 313 S.E.2d 162 (1984); *Stockton v. Stockton*, 435 N.E.2d 586 (Ind. Ct. App. 1982); *Merritt v. Merritt*, 616 S.W.2d 585 (Mo. Ct. App. 1981).

3. The question of whether the application of legal rules will necessarily result in a fair agreement is one that will be addressed specifically in Chapter 4, *Is the Agreement Fair?* and, by implication, in Chapter 3, *Equitable Distribution and Divorce Mediation*.

4. The question of how lawyers actually apply legal rules in adversarial practice, and whether their purpose in applying them is to arrive at a fair agreement, will be discussed at greater length in Chapter 5, *The Rule of Law in Divorce Mediation*.

5. While it might be argued that the law's restraint here is based on respect for the principle of self-determination, and a compromise between that principle and its concern that justice be done in a particular instance, in a far more important sense it is based on the understanding that, first, the law is a very poor instrument by which to regulate the very delicate and intricate relations that exist between family members, and, second, and even more important, that the law cannot pretend to make more appropriate judgments and decisions in people's lives than they can make themselves and that, except in extreme situations, it is not its place to second guess them.

6. Although it is beyond the purview of our discussion, it is worth pointing out another inherent problem in the application of equitable distribution statutes, and of all laws for that matter. By definition, our laws embody general principles—for example, that all property acquired during a marriage is deemed derivative of marital effort and is therefore subject to distribution at the time of a couple's divorce. Unfortunately, and even if it is correct to say that their application will effectuate a just result when applied to separating and divorcing couples as a composite group, that is not to say that their application will necessarily do justice in any particular instance. It is for this reason that most of the statutes, rather than attempting to enunciate one rule that will be applied to all couples, direct the court to look more closely at the unique facts of each individual case so as to make an equitable distribution. Nevertheless, these general principles, which still tend to restrict the court's thinking, exert a very strong influence on its final determination. Moreover, they often cause the court to make decisions that, to the very extent that they mirror those general principles, do so at the expense of an equitable result in the given instance. (The incongruity between general legal principles, and equity and justice in any particular instance, and the implications of this for dispute resolution in mediation, will be discussed at greater length in Chapter 3, *Equitable Distribution and Divorce Mediation*.)

7. Given our legal mythology, which talks in terms of legal rights, it may be hard for some to accept the suggestion that it can be irresponsible to insist on going to court to resolve our disputes, especially when part of our legal mythology is the idea that everyone is entitled to his day in court. Nevertheless, it is at times no more responsible for a person to resort to legal combat than it is for a nation to resort to armed combat.

8. After all, the right to receive alimony for a fixed period, like the right to have to pay it for only a fixed period, is not, like the right to vote or speak, a right that cannot be abridged. *See, e.g., Marshall v. Marshall*, 394 N.W.2d 392 (Iowa 1986); *Edgar v. Edgar*, 366 Mich. 580, 115 N.W.2d 286 (1962). This is exactly what happened with the enactment of the various equitable distribution statutes in recent years. Until then, support was generally awarded to a dependent spouse (usually the wife) for life. The change in the climate of opinion that resulted in the enactment of our present equitable distribution statutes also brought with it a change in society's attitude toward alimony, a change that was reflected in the substitution of the term maintenance for that of alimony in many statutes. *See, e.g.,* Uniform Marriage and Divorce Act, § 308.

   While the statutes in the various states are not identical, the prevailing view is that except in marriages of very long duration, spousal support should be *rehabilitative*, and awarded only until the dependent spouse is reasonably able to provide for his or her own needs. *See, e.g.,* Ariz. Rev. Stat. Ann. § 25-319 (West 1976 & 1986 Supp.); Cal. Civ. Code § 4801 (West 1983 & 1987 Supp.); Colo. Rev. Stat. § 14-10-114 (1974 & 1986 Supp.); Del. Code Ann. tit. 13, § 1512 (1981 & 1986 Supp.); Fla. Stat. Ann. § 61.08 (West 1985 & 1987 Supp.); Haw. Rev. Stat. § 580.47 (1985); Idaho Code § 32-705 (1983 & 1987 Supp.); Ill. Ann. Stat. ch. 40, para. 504 (Smith-Hurd 1980 & 1987 Supp.); Ind. Code Ann. § 31-1-11.5-11(e) (West 1979 & 1987 Supp.); Iowa Code Ann. § 598.21 (West 1981 & 1987 Supp.); Kan. Stat. Ann. § 60-1610(b)(2) (1983 & 1987 Supp.); Ky. Rev. Stat. Ann. § 403.200 (Michie/Bobbs-Merrill 1984 & 1986 Supp.); La. Civ. Code Ann. art. 160 (West 1987 Supp.); Md. Fam. Law Code Ann. § 11-106 (1984 & 1986 Supp.); Minn. Stat. Ann. § 518.552 (West 1969 & 1987 Supp.); Mo. Ann Stat. § 452.335 (Vernon 1986); Mont. Code Ann. § 40-4-203 (1986); N.H. Rev. Stat. Ann. § 458.19 (1983 & 1986 Supp.); N.Y. Dom. Rel. Law § 236-B (McKinney 1986); Or. Rev. Stat. § 107.105 (1985); Pa. Stat. Ann. tit. 23, § 501 (Purdon 1987 Supp.); S.D. Codified Laws Ann. § 25-4-41 (1984 & 1987 Supp.); Tenn. Code Ann. § 36-5-101(d) (1984 & 1986 Supp.); Vt. Stat. Ann. tit. 11, § 752 (1984); Wash. Rev. Code Ann. § 26.09.090 (West 1986); Wis. Code Ann. § 767.26 (West 1981 & 1986 Supp).

9. *See, e.g., Fobes v. Fobes*, 124 Wis. 2d 72, 368 N.W.2d 643 (1985); *Simpson v. Simpson*, 134 Cal. App. 2d 219, 285 P.2d 313 (1955).

10. This one exception, as well as the place and function of legal rules in divorce mediation, will be discussed at greater length in Chapter 5, *The Rule of Law in Divorce Mediation*.

11. To blunt the implications of this fact, the legal community has repeatedly attempted to undermine the public's confidence in who it is that will replace lawyers if mediation is successful. Thus, rather than acknowledging that, based upon their legal background alone, they have no more special province here than does a bartender or a cab driver, they have instead attempted to intimidate the public with the suggestion that if divorcing couples turn away from lawyers and the adversarial system and toward mediation, they may find that all they will be left with is a bartender or a cab driver.

12. This, traditionally, has been the means employed by the legal profession to maintain its monopoly, and those who have attempted to infringe upon territory that the legal profession felt was within its own special province have done so under the threat that they might be subjected to a charge that they were engaged in the unauthorized practice of the law, which in most states is a crime. While such proceedings were employed in the early days of divorce mediation, they have proved less successful in recent years, particularly as mediators have learned the very few things they must avoid doing in order to protect themselves against this charge and particularly as they have increasingly worked with attorneys who, in addressing the legal issues involved in mediation, shelter them from this attack.

13. Most lawyers would have great difficulty in answering a question with both the husband and the wife present because they would not know whom to answer—they would not know who they are supposed to represent. Furthermore, they would not *question* this difficulty, but would instead accept it as being reflective of the fact that the *couple have conflicting interests*, rather than its simply being reflective of their own legal training and thinking.

    When lawyers begin to be trained to think otherwise than simply as advocates for the parties' conflicting interests, or when they begin to teach themselves this, they will come to understand that, although it may be impossible to advocate for parties who have conflicting interests, it does not follow from this that it is impossible, in a nonadversarial setting, to provide them with legal *information*. To be more accurate in terms of the choices that we insist have to be made here, they will learn that whatever the problems may be in attempting to provide legal information in a nonadversarial setting, those problems are not as great as are those posed by providing it in an adversarial setting. This will be discussed at greater length in Chapter 7, *Context*.

14. Strange as it may seem, it also sends shudders down the spines of many advocates of divorce mediation as well. Thus, standards of practice promulgated by divorce mediation advocates are replete with admonitions against this simple solution. Perhaps the most unfortunate of these is that contained in the *Professional Standards of Practice for Mediators* of the Mediation Council of Illinois, which provides that "Mediators, including attorney mediators, shall not advise either party as to their legal rights or responsibilities so as to direct the parties' decision on a given issue. Each party *must* be referred to independent legal counsel for that advise. A single attorney to advise the participants as to the law in the course of the mediation is not a substitute for independent legal counsel." (as quoted by Carl D. Schneider in A *Commentary on the Activity of Writing Codes of Ethics*, 8 Mediation Q. 83, 94 (June 1985)) (emphasis added).

    These ethical strictures are particularly unfortunate for two reasons. To begin with, they fly in the face of important advances that have been made in recent years by decisions such as that of the Court of Appeals in New York in *Levine v. Levine*, 56 N.Y.2d 42, 436 N.E.2d 476, 451 N.Y.S.2d 26 (1982), where the court, although acknowledging that agreements concluded with but one attorney would be more closely scrutinized, nevertheless affirmed that a couple had "an absolute right" to be represented by one attorney. Secondly, and perhaps more importantly for our purposes, in insisting upon the presence of separate representation, they have not only lent support to the idea that divorce is primarily a legal process but have also unwittingly reaffirmed the mythology that it has to be an adversarial one as well.

15. Notwithstanding this supposed impediment, attorneys represent parties having conflicting interests all the time. Nor has it necessarily been considered unethical for them to do so. In fact, it is more than likely that one attorney has previously represented both of the parties here, despite their conflicting interests. For example, if they were represented by an attorney when they bought their home, they undoubtedly used but one attorney. Suppose their attorney learned that, although title was to be taken in both of their names, the funds that were to be used to purchase it were the husband's own separate property. If the parties were to later divorce—and, at least statistically, that certainly had to be a very real possibility—taking title in their joint names might not be in the husband's best interests, as the court might now have the power to award the wife an interest in the property. *See, e.g., LaFleur v. LaFleur*, 395 So.2d 615 (Fla. 1981); *Carter v.*

Carter, 419 A.2d 1018 (Me. 1980); *In re Marriage of Moncrief*, 36 Colo. App. 140, 535 P.2d 1137 (1975); *Felkner v. Felkner*, 652 S.W.2d 174 (Mo. Ct. App. 1983); *Gist v. Gist*, 537 P.2d 460, (Okla. Ct. App. 1975); *Hampshire v. Hampshire*, 485 S.W.2d 314 (Tex. Ct. App. 1972).

Would it be unethical for the attorney to represent both of the parties at that point? If he did, would he be under an obligation to advise the husband of the implications of his using his own separate funds in this manner? One would certainly hope not. Nevertheless, and given the fact that we have been trained to accept only *adversarial* considerations, and to ignore all others, there will undoubtedly be some who will raise an objection. To those we would pose the following question. Suppose this husband lived in a state like New York which held that gifts made prior to a couple's marriage by one of them to the other were considered separate property not subject to distribution at the time of their divorce, while the same gifts made during their marriage *were*. Suppose also that the couple had come to this same attorney to buy the home in question prior to their marriage instead of afterwards. Would the attorney then be obliged to advise the husband that it might be in his best interest to postpone transferring the funds in question, and purchasing the home, until after they were married since, if he did so before, his wife would have an irrevocable one-half interest in the property, whereas, if he did so later, the court would have the power to return the funds in question to him should it deem it equitable to do so? For the same reason, should he advise the husband to postpone his gift of a wedding ring to his wife until after their marriage?

Chapter 3—Equitable Distribution and Divorce Mediation

1. In 1960, approximately 19 marriages per 1,000 were dissolved by death, whereas 9 per 1,000 were dissolved by divorce. After a slight increase in the 1960s, the rate of deaths declined through the 1970s until it reached a level of less than 18 per 1,000 marriages in 1980. Divorces, on the other hand, increased steadily throughout the 1960s and 1970s to the point that 23 marriages per 1,000 were dissolved by divorce in 1980. Arland Thorton and Deborah Freedman, *The Changing American Family*, 38 Population Bulletin 1, 7 (Washington D.C.: Population Reference Bureau, Inc., October 1983).
2. She was usually left with another disadvantage as well, since there has always been a great disparity between what women and men have been paid, even for the same work. Even today it has been estimated that a woman who works full-time, all year long, earns only about 60% of that earned by a man. Ralph E. Smith, Editor, *The Subtle Revolution—Women at Work*, (Washington D.C.: The Urban Press 1979), at 32-34.
3. Again, this is not to suggest that this solution solved the problem, for it did not. The reason for this is that although a husband's death did not affect his entitlement to his capital, it did terminate his (former) wife's right to support. Given the fact that husbands are generally older than their wives, and also have a shorter life expectancy, this exposed divorced women to a very considerable risk. In 1975, the average age of husbands in first marriages was 23.5 years, while their brides' average age was 21.1 years. U.S. Bureau of Census, *Current Population Reports*, Series P-20, No. 297 (Washington D.C., 1976). In 1976 his life expectancy was 71.6 years if he was white (66.8 years if he was black) while hers was 78.7 years if she was white (74.9 years if she was black). Smith, *The Subtle Revolution, Supra*, at 203. It has been suggested that the increased entry of women into the labor force, and their exposure to the competitive conditions that have traditionally affected men alone, may tend to equalize the life expectancies of men and women more in the future. *Id.*, at 110.
4. Thornton and Freedman, *The Changing American Family*, 38 Population Bulletin 10 (Washington, D.C.: Population Reference Bureau, Inc., October 1983). Of these Women, 60 to 70% marry within 5 years of their divorce. *Id.* Additionally, most divorces today are initiated by women. Martha Weinman Lear, *The New Marital Therapy*, New York Times Magazine, March 6, 1988, at 63, col. 1.
5. U.S. Bureau of the Census, *Current Population Reports*, Series P-20, No. 297 (Washington D.C., 1976).
6. As a general rule, in the absence of an agreement between the parties, a husband was not obligated by law to maintain insurance on his life for his wife's benefit. Moreover, in the absence of a statutory grant of authority, the court generally held that to require him to do so was to attempt to expand upon his legal obligation and to accomplish indirectly what it could not do directly. *Cf. Enos v. Enos* 41 A.D.2d 642, 340 N.Y.S.2d 783 (1973). Many equitable distribution statutes have now corrected this by giving the court specific authority to direct one of the parties to maintain insurance on his or her life for the other's benefit. N.Y. Dom. Rel. Law § 236 (McKinney 1986). *Cf. Wilbur v. Wilbur*, 130 A.D.2d 853, 515 N.Y.S.2d 636

(1987). *See also, Epperson v. Epperson*, 437 So.2d 571 (Ala. Civ. App. 1983); *Gallo v. Gallo*, 184 Conn. 36, 440 A.2d 782 (1981); *Brandenburg v. Brandenburg*, 425 So.2d 25 (Fla. Dist. Ct. App. 1982); *Ritchea v. Ritchea*, 244 Ga. 476, 260 S.E.2d 871 (1979); *Appelman v. Appelman*, 87 Ill. App. 3d 749, 410 N.E.2d 199, 43 Ill. Dec. 199 (1980); *Robbins v. Robbins*, 16 Mass. App. 576, 453 N.E.2d 1058 (1983); *In re Marriage of Young*, 26 Wash. App. 843, 615 P.2d 508 (1980); *Washington v. Hicks*, 109 Wis. 2d 10, 325 N.W.2d 68 (Ct. App. 1982).

7. For example, Title 12, Section 1289(D) of Oklahoma's Statutes provides, "The voluntary cohabitation of a former spouse with a member of the opposite sex shall be a ground to modify provisions of a final judgment or order for alimony as support." *See also*, Ala. Code § 30-2-55 (1983 & 1986 Supp.); Cal. Civil Code § 4801.5 (West 1983 & 1986 Supp.); Ga. Code Ann. § 19-6-19(b) (1982 & 1987 Supp.); Ill. Ann. Stat. ch. 40 para. 510(b) (Smith-Hurd 1980 & 1987 Supp.); La. Civ. Code Ann. art. 160 (West 1987 Supp.); N.Y. Dom. Rel. Law § 248 (McKinney 1986); Pa. Stat. Ann. tit. 23, § 507 (Purdon 1987 Supp.); Tenn. Code Ann. § 36-5-101(3) (1984 & 1986 Supp.); Utah Code Ann. § 30-3-5(5) & (6) (1984 & 1987 Supp.).

8. In 1983, 1.9 million single adults were sharing a household with an unrelated person of the opposite sex. This number was six times greater than in 1970. Thorton and Freedman, *The Changing American Family*, at 11. (It should be kept in mind, however, that these numbers include any two people who are unrelated and members of the opposite sex, including, for example, the situation where an elderly gentlemen and his full-time caretaker reside under the same roof.)

9. For example, in 1975, approximately 33% of ever-married men between the ages of 26 and 35 had divorced after second marriages, as opposed to 32% in the same age group who had divorced for the first time. Nearly 42% of women in the same age group had divorced for a second time, as compared to 36% who had divorced for the first time. U.S. Bureau of the Census, *Current Population Reports*, Series P-20, No. 297 (Washington D.C. 1976).

10. *See generally, Gevis v. Gevis*, 141 N.Y.S.2d 121 (Sup. Ct. 1955).

11. As of 1975, only 52% of all second marriages could be expected to last for ten years or more, as compared to 67% of first marriages. Andrew J. Cherlin, *Marriage, Divorce, Remarriage*, (Cambridge, MA: Harvard University Press, 1981), at 30. Most of the second marriages that ended in divorce in 1975 did so within two years. U.S. Bureau of the Census, *Current Population Reports*, Series P-20, No. 297.

12. In 1978, for example, 48% of all married women were participating in the labor force, as compared to a rate of only 20% in 1948. Smith, *The Subtle Revolution, Supra*, at 4. This rate increased to 51% by 1982. Thornton & Freedman, *The Changing American Family*, at 24. In addition, the labor force participation rate for women no longer married (divorced, separated, widowed) increased from 29% in 1890 to 42 percent in 1978. Smith, *The Subtle Revolution*, at 4.

13. As of 1975, the average age of the husband in a second marriage was 32.8 years, while that of the wife was 29.4 years. The average ages of a husband and wife in a first marriage were 23.5 and 21.1 years, respectively. U.S. Bureau of the Census, *Current Population Reports*, Series P-20, No. 297 (Washington D.C. 1976).

14. This is the general rule. Some states, such as Connecticut, do not use the term "marital property," and instead give the court the power to distribute any property owned by the parties at the time of their divorce, irrespective of when it was acquired. Conn. Gen. Stat. Ann. § 46b-81 (West 1986). *Cf.*, Haw. Rev. Stat. § 580.47(3) (1985) (court may order, divide, and distribute the parties' estate, "whether community, joint, or separate."); Ind. Code Ann. § 31-1-11.5-11 (West 1979 & 1987 Supp.) (property subject to equitable distribution upon divorce includes property acquired prior to the marriage as well as separate property); Mass. Gen. Laws Ann. ch. 3, § 208-34 (West 1958 & 1987 Supp.) (court may "assign to either the husband or wife all or any part of the estate of the other").

15. The law has generally recognized two exceptions to this. The first occurs when one of the parties takes separate property, which is in his or her own name alone, and puts it in both of their names jointly. This has been held to effectuate a transmutation of the property, changing the separate property into marital property. *See generally*, cases listed in Chapter 2, note 15. The second is where, although the property has remained in the individual name of the party whose separate property it is, it has appreciated in value during the course of the marriage. In those instances, and particularly where such appreciation can be attributed to the marital effort of either of the parties, that appreciation has been held to constitute marital property. *Price v. Price*, 69 N.Y.2d 8, 503 N.E.2d 684, 511 N.Y.S.2d 219 (1986). *See also, Halpern v. Halpern*, 256 Ga. 639, 352 S.E.2d 753 (Ga. 1987) (appreciation due to outside market forces is not marital property, but appreciation due to one party's active management is marital property). *Accord, Brooks v. Brooks*, 733 P.2d

1044 (Alaska 1987); *Lynam v. Gallagher*, 526 A.2d 878 (Del. 1987); *Rubin v. Rubin*, 204 Conn. 224, 527 A.2d 1184 (1987). *Cf.*, *In re Crislip*, 86 Or. App. 146, 738 P.2d 602 (1987). The question of transmutation and the appreciation in the value of separate property will be discussed at greater length in Chapter 16, *Assets and Liabilities*.

16. Thorton & Freedman, *The Changing American Family*, at 24.

17. Some states, like Delaware, limit alimony to a set number of years unless the parties have been married for a long duration, for example, more than 20 years. *See, e.g.*, Del. Code Ann. tit. 13, § 1512 (1981 & 1986 Supp.). Decisions in some states emphasize the fact that maintenance or alimony is supposed to be rehabilitative, that is, to provide for the needs of the ex-spouse, not to punish either party. *See, e.g.*, *Theiss v. Theiss*, 112 Idaho 681, 735 P.2d 992 (1987); *LaRue v. LaRue*, 304 S.E.2d 312 (W.Va. 1983).

18. This will also be discussed in Chapter 5, *The Rule of Law in Divorce Mediation*.

19. *O'Brien v. O'Brien*, 66 N.Y.2d 576, 489 N.E.2d 712, 498 N.Y.S.2d 743 (1985).

20. An argument could be made that the situation did not cry out for relief. While Dr. O'Brien was certainly left in a better position as a result of his marriage, and his wife's efforts, it is not clear that Mrs. O'Brien was left any worse off on that account. Although the Court of Appeals, wishing to find a peg to hang its hat on, suggested that Mrs. O'Brien had given up career opportunities in order to assist her husband to obtain his medical degree, the argument was rather strained. Mrs. O'Brien was a school teacher when she married her husband and she was a schoolteacher when she divorced him. The only thing that she gave up was the opportunity to obtain permanent certification. However, it was not something that she gave up permanently, and she could now obtain that certification in but a matter of months.

In short, there was not the *kind* of change in reliance upon the fact of the marriage here—as is so often the case when women give up their careers to raise a family—that is normally the occasion for our concern at where the divorce has left the wife and the motivation for a decision to compensate her in some way. For the purpose of the discussion that follows, however, we will accept the contention that the situation was one that cried out for relief.

21. In most, but not all states, the court only has the power to distribute property that was acquired during the marriage and prior to the commencement of the divorce action. *See, e.g.*, Pa. Stat. Ann. tit. 23, § 401(e)(4) (Purdon 1987 Supp.); Ind. Code Ann. § 31-1-11.5-11 (West 1987 Supp.). Property acquired subsequent to the commencement of the action, like property acquired prior to the marriage, is separate property and not subject to distribution. *Lentz v. Lentz*, 117 Misc.2d 78, 457 N.Y.S.2d 401 (N.Y. Sup. Ct. 1982).

22. In actual fact, Mrs. O'Brien had already remarried by the time the case reached the Court of Appeals.

23. Other states, such as New Jersey and Kentucky, had been willing to go part of the way, and to give recognition to at least the monetary contribution that had been made by the wife in these instances. *Mahoney v. Mahoney*, 91 N.J. 488, 453 A.2d 527 (1982); *Inman v. Inman*, 648 S.W.2d 847 (Ky 1982) What they had not been willing to do, however, was to go a step further and compensate the wife for the enhanced earning capacity that the license afforded the husband, since they could not find their way to do this without holding that his license was a species of property. *See also*, *Drapek v. Drapek*, 399 Mass. 240, 503 N.E.2d 946 (1987); *Hodge v. Hodge*, 513 Pa. 264, 520 A.2d 15 (1986); *Stevens v. Stevens*, 23 Ohio St. 3d 115, 492 N.E.2d 131 (1986); *Geer v. Geer*, 84 N.C. App. 471, 353 S.E.2d 427 (1987); *Peterson v. Peterson*, 737 P.2d 237 (Utah Ct. App. 1987).

24. While it might, at first blush, seem inappropriate to have used as an example a decision that is the law of but one or two states, this has been done purposely. It will be far harder for the reader to follow our argument, and to appreciate the very arbitrary character of the procedures employed by the law in dealing with the problems of divorce, were we to use as an example a principle that is the law in all of the states. (In addition to *O'Brien* in New York, the Michigan Court of Appeals may have reached a similar decision that a professional license will be considered marital property. *See*, *Woodworth v. Woodworth*, 126 Mich. App. 258, 337 N.W.2d 332 (1983). *Cf.*, *Olah v. Olah*, 135 Mich. App. 404, 354 N.W.2d 359 (1984)).

25. Alaska, *Nelson v. Nelson*, 736 P.2d 1145 (Alaska 1987); Alabama, *Jones v. Jones*, 454 So.2d 1006 (Ala. Civ. App. 1984); Arizona, *Pyeatte v. Pyeatte*, 135 Ariz. 346, 661 P.2d 196 (1982); *Wisner v. Wisner*, 129 Ariz. 333, 631 P.2d 115 (1981); California, *In re Marriage of Sullivan*, 134 Cal. App.3d 634, 184 Cal. Rptr 796 (1982); *In re Marriage of Aufmuth*, 89 Cal. App.3d 446, 152 Cal. Rptr 668 (1979), *overruled on other grounds*, *In re Marriage of Lucas*, 27 Cal. 3d 808, 614 P.2d 285, 166 Cal. Rptr. 853 (1980); *Todd v. Todd*, 272 Cal. App.2d 786, 78 Cal. Rptr. 131 (1969); Colorado, *In re Marriage of Graham*, 194 Colo. 429, 574 P.2d 75 (1978); *In re Marriage of McVey*, 641 P.2d 300 (Colo. App. 1981); Connecticut, *Zahler v. Zahler*, 8 F.L.R. (B.N.A.) 2694 (Conn. Super. Ct., New Haven Dist. 1982); Delaware, *Wright v. Wright*, 469 A.2d

803, (Del. Fam. Ct., 1983); District of Columbia, *Hill v. Hill*, 12 F.L.R. (B.N.A.) 1613 (D.C. Super Ct. 1986); Florida, *Hughes v. Hughes*, 438 So.2d 146 (Fla. Dist. Ct. App. 1983); *Severs v. Severs*, 426 So.2d 992 (Fla. Dist. Ct. App. 1983); Illinois, *In re Marriage of Weinstein*, 128 Ill. App. 3d 234, 470 N.E.2d 551, 83 Ill. Dec. 425 (1984); Indiana, *In re Marriage of McManama*, 272 Ind. 483, 399 N.E.2d 371 (1980); Iowa, *In re Marriage of Horstmann*, 263 N.W.2d 885 (Iowa 1978); Kentucky, *Inman v. Inman*, 648 S.W.2d 847 (Ky. 1982); *McGowan v. McGowan*, 663 S.W.2d 219 (Ky. Ct. App. 1983); *Leveck v. Leveck*, 614 S.W.2d 710 (Ky. Ct. App. 1981); Maine, *Sweeney v. Sweeney*, 534 A.2d 1290 (Maine 1987); Maryland, *Archer v. Archer*, 493 A.2d 1074 (Md. Ct. App. 1985); Massachusetts, *Drapek v. Drapek*, 399 Mass. 240, 503 N.E.2d 946 (1987); Minnesota, *DeLa Rosa v. DeLa Rosa*, 309 N.W.2d 755 (Minn. 1981); Missouri, *Lowrey v. Lowrey*, 633 S.W.2d 157 (Mo. Ct. App. 1982); New Hampshire, *Ruben v. Ruben*, 123 N.H. 358, 461 A.2d 733 (1983); New Jersey, *Mahoney v. Mahoney*, 91 N.J. 488, 453 A.2d 527 (1982); New Mexico, *Muckleroy v. Muckleroy*, 84 N.M. 14, 498 P.2d 1357 (1972); North Carolina, *Geer v. Geer*, 84 N.C. App. 471, 353 S.E.2d 427 (1987); Oklahoma, *Hubbard v. Hubbard*, 603 P.2d 747 (Okla. 1979); Pennsylvania, *Hodge v. Hodge*, 513 Pa. 264, 520 A.2d 15 (1986); South Carolina, *Helm v. Helm*, 289 S.C. 169, 345 S.E.2d 720 (1986); South Dakota, *Saint Pierre v. Saint Pierre*, 357 N.W.2d 250 (S.D. 1984); Tennessee, *Beeler v. Beeler*, 715 S.W.2d 625 (Tenn. Ct. App. 1986); Texas, *Frausto v. Frausto*, 611 S.W.2d 656 (Tx. Civ. App. 1980); Utah, *Rayburn v. Rayburn*, 738 P.2d 238 (Utah Ct. App. 1987); *Petersen v. Petersen*, 737 P.2d 237 (Utah Ct. App. 1987); Washington, *Washburn v. Washburn*, 101 Wash. 2d 168, 677 P.2d 152 (1984); *Gillette v. Gillette*, 101 Wash. 2d 168, 677 P.2d 152 (1984); Wisconsin, *Haugan v. Haugan*, 117 Wis. 2d 200, 343 N.W.2d 796 (1984); *In re Marriage of Lundberg*, 107 Wis. 2d 1, 318 N.W.2d 918 (1982); Wyoming, *Grosskopf v. Grosskopf*, 677 P.2d 814 (Wyo. 1984).

26. In a case decided following *O'Brien*, a lower court held that the wife's teacher's certificate, as well as her education and degree, all acquired during her marriage, were property subject to distribution at the time of the couple's divorce. *McGowan v. McGowan*, 136 Misc. 2d 225, 518 N.Y.S.2d 346 (Sup. Ct. 1987).

27. The court in *O'Brien* held that a professional license was property not because of any irresistible logic that led it to that conclusion, and not even because it wanted to; but because it had to if it was to be able to make any award to Mrs. O'Brien, as it obviously wished to. Unfortunately, however, and by creating a species of property in the process, the motivation that led the court to that conclusion has all but been forgotten, and all that has been left is a new species of property. The result is that if either of the parties has a professional license that was acquired during the course of their marriage, a court will no longer be able to view the equities, as did the Court of Appeals in *O'Brien*, which would dictate that one of them should share in the increased earning capacity that the other has by reason of that license. On the contrary, and having converted that license into money in the bank, those equities have now become largely irrelevant, and the sole issue is simply to place a value upon it and to then determine what an equitable distribution of that value would be. *See, e.g., McGowan v. McGowan*, 136 Misc. 2d 225, 518 N.Y.S.2d 346 (Sup. Ct. 1987).

    While it could be argued that those equities have not become entirely lost; that all that the court did in *O'Brien* was to hold that the license was property and not that the nontitled spouse necessarily had an interest in it; and that such interest, if any, still had to be determined based upon the equities of the particular case, this is not really so. Given the thrust of equitable distribution, there is an unexpressed presumption that the nontitled spouse should have some interest in it, and unless that presumption is rebutted by special circumstances, the only question is how much.

28. While a court in New York may have no authority to do this, the courts of some other states do. Minn. Stat. Ann. § 518.64, subd. 3 (West 1969 & 1987 Supp.) *See, e.g., Burr v. Burr*, 353 N.W.2d 644 (Minn. Ct. App. 1984) (payments may continue following the wife's remarriage where the divorce decree provides that payments are to be made until the wife reaches 62 or the husband retires at 62.); *Carruth v. Carruth*, 212 Neb. 124, 321 N.W.2d 912 (1982) (remarriage shall not automatically terminate alimony.); *accord, Ehrenworth v. Ehrenworth*, 187 N.J. Super. 342, 454 A.2d 895 (App. Div. 1982); *Perry v. Perry*, 551 P.2d 256 (Okla. 1976). *Cf., Marquardt v. Marquardt,* 396 N.W.2d 753 (S.D. 1986) (remarriage establishes a prima facie case for termination of maintenance, which divorced wife can overcome by showing extraordinary circumstances); *accord, In re Marriage of Shima*, 360 N.W.2d 827 (Iowa 1985); *Bauer v. Bauer*, 356 N.W.2d 897 (N.D. 1984). *But see, Voyles v. Voyles*, 644 P.2d 847 (Alaska 1982) (remarriage automatically terminates alimony).

29. Although the Court of Appeals ascribed to Dr. O'Brien the earning capacity of a general surgeon, this was extremely arbitrary. Putting aside for the moment Dr. O'Brien's contention that it was his intention to leave his residency in general surgery and to go back to his original residency in internal medicine, which would

provide him with less of an income in the future, the fact remained that Dr. O'Brien was neither a surgeon nor an internist. He was simply a general practitioner. Why the court then went and ascribed to Dr. O'Brien an income that he would (might) earn as a specialist in the future is extremely unclear, particularly since the court never attempted to defend the suggestion that Mrs. O'Brien would have anything to do with the efforts that he would expend in the future in becoming a specialist. Be that as it may, and for the purposes of the following discussion, we will accept this as the proper measure of the value of his medical license.

30. These are not inconsequential considerations. Prior to 1982, the maximum rate for an individual for federal tax purposes was 70 percent. Thereafter it was reduced to 50%. By the Tax Reform Act of 1986, that rate was then reduced to 28 percent for 1988. Similarly, the rate of inflation for 1980 was 13.5%. For 1983, it was 3.2%. U.S. Bureau of the Census, *Statistical Abstract of the United States: 1982–83* (103d ed.), (Washington D.C. 1982), at 461. *See also, World Almanac & Book of Facts 1988,* (New York, NY: Pharos Books 1987), at 109.

31. This distinction is far more significant than it may at first appear. More importantly, it underscores the terribly arbitrary character of all equitable distribution awards. Putting aside for the moment the question of whether a professional degree or license should be deemed property, what would have been the court's result had Dr. O'Brien been a pharmacist owning a drugstore, or simply a businessman who owned a business, instead of a physician? If he had been a businessman owning a business, the court would have held that Mrs. O'Brien had an interest in the present value of that business, not its future value. *Nehorayoff v. Nehorayoff,* 108 Misc. 2d 311, 437 N.Y.S.2d 584 (1981). In short, if she had supported her husband for the same length of time while he built up his business, her interest would have been limited to his present circumstances, not his future circumstances (his enhanced earning capacity).

32. *O'Brien,* 66 N.Y.2d at 591-2, 489 N.E.2d at 720, 498 N.Y.S.2d at 751 (Meyer, J., concurring).

33. *Moss v. Moss,* 639 S.W.2d 370 (Ky. Ct. App. 1982).

34. Although the Court of Appeals in *O'Brien* conveniently ignored it, the fact remains that it was Dr. O'Brien alone, and not Mrs. O'Brien, who was going to have to expend the effort necessary to convert that license into spendable dollars. Accordingly, while Mrs. O'Brien only had to work for nine years in order to be awarded 40% of its ultimate value, Dr. O'Brien would be required to work those same nine years plus an additional 32 more (five more years in order to complete his residency in general surgery, and then the anticipated 27 years in private practice.) Thus, although Mrs. O'Brien only contributed nine years of effort toward the total of 50 years that will ultimately have been devoted by both of them in achieving that degree and converting it into spendable dollars (although she will have only expended 18% of the effort), she was nevertheless awarded 40% of its value. Again, for the purposes of the discussion that follows, we will not take issue with this.

35. See Chapter 3, note 26, and accompanying text.

36. The mediator, after all, does not work under the same constraints that the Court of Appeals did. While the Court of Appeals may not have had the authority to direct that the payments to be made by Dr. O'Brien to his wife were to be tax-free, the parties, by their agreement, can so provide. I.R.C. § 71(b)(1)(B) (West 1988 Supp.).

37. *See, e.g.,* Fla. Stat. Ann. § 61.08(2) (West 1985) ("The court may consider any other factors necessary to do equity and justice between the parties"); N.C. Gen. Stat. § 50-20(c)(12) (1987) (the court may consider "[a]ny other factor which the court finds to be just and proper."); Va. Code Ann. § 20-107.3(E)(11) (1987 Supp.) (the court may consider "[s]uch other factors as the court deems necessary or appropriate to consider in order to arrive at equitable monetary award.").

38. Traditionally, state divorce laws were based upon the concept of *fault,* and even though the statutes of many states have been amended either to eliminate fault as the basis for a divorce or at least to diminish its importance, the law, nevertheless, has never been quite able to understand divorce apart from marital misconduct. As a result, the concept of fault is still a part of judicial thinking, even if to a much lesser extent. Thus, and while it may not be explicitly a part of the law of a particular state, it still often exists in the background.

39. The reasons for this are twofold. To begin with, there is an increased awareness on the court's part that the more modern view is one that discounts fault as a factor in divorce. Secondly, and perhaps more importantly, equitable distribution statutes have shifted the emphasis from fault to economics. To add to that burden the additional requirement that the court must now also assess the praise or blame that should be attributed to the conduct of each of the parties is only to compound the matter further. As a result, and unless specifically directed by statute to consider fault as a factor, courts have generally taken the position that

unless such fault is extreme, it will not be considered. *O'Brien v. O'Brien*, 66 N.Y.2d 576, 489 N.E.2d 712, 498 N.Y.S.2d 743 (1985).

However, and this will demonstrate the persistence of this ambivalence, the fact that the court will not consider fault as a factor in the distribution of property does not necessarily mean that they will not consider it as a factor in awarding spousal support. *See, e.g.*, Ala. Code § 30-2-52 (1983); Ark. Stat. Ann. § 9-12-301 (1987); Conn. Gen. Stat. Ann. § 46b-82 (West 1986); Fla. Stat. Ann. § 61.08 (West 1985); Ga. Code § 19-6-1 (1982); Idaho Code § 32-705 (1983); La. Civ. Code Ann. art. 160(A)(1) (West 1988); Md. Fam. Law Code Ann. § 11-106(b)(6) (1984); Mass. Gen. Laws Ann. ch. 208, § 34 (West 1987); Mo. Ann. Stat. § 452.335(2)(7) (Vernon 1986); N.C. Gen. Stat. § 50-16.6 (1987); Pa. Stat. Ann. tit. 23, § 501(b)(14) (Purdon 1987); R.I. Gen. Laws § 15-5-16 (1981); S.C. Code Ann. § 20-3-130 (Law. Co-op 1985); Tenn. Code Ann. § 36-5-101(d)(10) (1984 & 1987 Supp.).

CHAPTER 4—IS THE AGREEMENT FAIR?

1. Richard E. Crouch, *Divorce Mediation and Legal Ethics*, 16 Fam. L. Q. 228 (1982).
2. This was expressed by a well-known matrimonial lawyer in the following words, "I am in the business to win. . . . once I have been hired, . . . my sole aim is to gain victory. And in doing so, I will do anything and everything I think necessary to serve the interests of my client, to achieve his purpose—to gain him a divorce in which he will come out financially, psychologically—in every way—on top. That is what I have been hired to do and if in doing it I appear cold and calculating . . . , then that's the way it has to be. I am tough because I assume the lawyer who opposes me will also be tough. . . . When I take a case, I am not concerned with whether my client is right or wrong. As far as I am concerned, a client is always right." Raoul Felder, *Divorce—The Way Things Are, Not the Way They Should Be*, (New York, NY: World Publishing, 1971), at 1–2.
3. To be sure, judges are often called in before, and sometimes during, the trial, in an effort to help effectuate a settlement. But, and as any practicing attorney will attest, a judge is invariably more concerned over the fact of a settlement than he is in the quality of that settlement. By definition, he does not have all of the facts that the trial will reveal, as there has not been a trial, or at least not a completed one. He is thus not in a position to make sound, reasoned judgments. What he attempts to do is simply to get the parties to compromise and settle their differences and the device that he principally uses is that of banging heads together. Thus, and contrary to common mythology, the judge to whom we look as the safeguard of the system is, ironically, actually more interested in getting it done than in getting it right.
4. If this example seems somewhat fanciful, the reader is reminded of the contract entered into between Jacqueline Kennedy and Aristotle Onassis prior to their marriage, as reported by Christian Cafarakis, in his book, *The Fabulous Onassis—His Life and His Loves*, (New York, NY: William Morrow & Co., 1972), starting at page 110.
5. Although there are admittedly no published statistics concerning this, a number of mediators working in the private sector have corroborated the fact that clearly a majority of the divorces with which they have been involved were initiated by the wife. That is our experience as well.
6. This will be discussed at greater length in Chapter 7, *Context*.
7. In defending New York's Equitable Distribution Law against critics who have taken issue with whether or not it is fair to women, Henry H. Foster, Professor Emeritus of Family Law at New York University's Law School, stated, "The New York Equitable Distribution Law (EDL), which has been in effect since July 19, 1980, was the subject of extensive study and debate by members of the legislature and numerous bar association committees during its seven-year incubation period. *The final draft was the result of compromise, give and take, and represented what was legislatively possible at the time.* The EDL was not written in stone and indeed, some of its provisions may need clarification and change." *A Second Opinion: New York's EDL is Alive and Well and is Being Fairly Administered*, 17 Fam. L. Rev. 3 (N.Y. State Bar Assoc., Apr. 1985), (emphasis added).
8. La. Civ. Code Ann. art. 160 (West 1987 Supp.).
9. Mich. Comp. Laws Ann. § 552.23 (West 1967 & 1987 Supp.).
10. *Lapidus v. Lapidus*, 226 Va. 575, 311 S.E.2d 786 (1984).
11. N. Y. Domestic Relations Law, § 236 (McKinney, 1986).

12. *Gordon v. Gordon*, 10 F.L.R. (B.N.A.) 1473 (Del. Fam. Ct. 1984).
13. *Anderson v. Anderson*, 368 N.W.2d 566 (N.D. 1985), *rev'd on other grounds*, 390 N.W.2d 554 (N.D. 1986); *Winter v. Winter*, 338 N.W.2d 819 (N.D. 1983).
14. N. J. Stat. Ann. tit. 2A, § 34-23 (West 1952 & 1987 Supp.).
15. Ill. Ann. Stat. ch. 40, para. 503(c) (Smith-Hurd 1980).
16. Ala. Code, § 30-2-52 (1983 & 1986 Supp.).
17. Mo. Ann. Stat. § 452.330 (Vernon 1986).
18. *Brundage v. Brundage*, 100 A.D.2d 887, 474 N.Y.S.2d 566 (2d Dept. 1984) (citing N.Y. Fam. Ct. Act § 413 (McKinney 1983)).
19. *Grapin v. Grapin*, 450 So.2d 853 (Fla. 1984); *Keenan v. Keenan*, 440 So.2d 642 Fla. Dist. Ct. App. 1983).
20. Tex. Fam. Code Ann. §§ 3.59, 4.02 (Vernon 1987 Supp.). *See also, Price v. Price*, 591 S.W.2d 601 (Tex. Ct. App. 1979).
21. Pa. Stat. Ann. tit. 23, § 501 (Purdon 1987 Supp.).
22. Wash. Rev. Code Ann. § 26.09.090 (West 1986); *see, Mason v. Mason*, 40 Wash. App. 450, 698 P.2d 1104 (1985).
23. Neb. Rev. Stat. § 42-395 (1984); *see, Earl v. Earl*, 221 Neb. 574, 379 N.W.2d 261 (1986).
24. Utah Code Ann. § 30-3-5 (1984 & 1987 Supp.).
25. *Mahoney v. Mahoney*, 91 N.J. 488, 453 A.2d 527 (1982).
26. *Wisner v. Wisner*, 129 Ariz. 333, 631 P.2d 115 (1981).
27. *O'Brien v. O'Brien*, 66 N.Y.2d 576, 489 N.E.2d 712, 498 N.Y.S.2d 743 (1985).
28. *Moritz v. Moritz*, 10 F.L.R. (B.N.A.) 1534 (Pa. Ct. Comm. Pleas 1984).
29. *James v. James*, 248 S.W.2d 706 (Ky. 1982).
30. *Rubin v. Rubin*, 204 Conn. 224, 517 A.2d 1184 (1987); *Gregg v. Gregg*, 510 A.2d 474 (Del. Super. Ct. 1986); *Hashimoto v. Hashimoto*, 725 P.2d 520 (Haw. Ct. App. 1986); *In re Marriage of Meredith*, 394 N.W.2d 336 (Iowa 1986); *Burke v. Burke*, 733 P.2d 133 (Utah 1987).
31. *Gassaway v. Gassaway*, 489 A.2d 1073 (D.C. 1985).
32. While, as a general rule, it is normally the number of children that the two of them have together, it would also include any children that the husband had by a prior marriage.
33. N.Y. Est., Powers, & Trusts Law § 4-1.1(a)(1) (McKinney 1981 & 1987 Supp.).
34. In New York, the only exception to this is where a party is deemed to have abandoned his or her obligation to the other party completely. *In re Lamos' Estate*, 63 Misc. 2d 840, 313 N.Y.S.2d 781 (1970). *See also*, N.Y. Est., Powers, & Trusts Law § 5-1.2 (McKinney 1981 & 1987 Supp.).
35. In New York, for example, the Court is required to consider thirteen separate factors. Not only are the first twelve of these rather imprecise yardsticks to apply (e.g., number 6—"any equitable claim to, interest in, or direct or indirect contribution made to the acquisition of such marital property by the party not having title, including joint efforts or expenditures and contributions and services as a spouse, parent, wage earner and homemaker, and to the career or career potential of the other party") but the thirteenth factor only compounds the problem by permitting the court to then consider "any other factor which the court shall expressly find to be just and proper." N.Y. Dom. Rel. Law § 236-B (McKinney 1986).
36. Prior to the enactment of its equitable distribution statute, if a wife in New York consulted with an attorney and showed him a deed to a parcel of property in her husband's name, then, and with very minor exceptions (such as, for example, where she had previously deeded the property to her husband under circumstances that would suggest that a constructive trust should be imposed and he be deemed to hold it for her benefit), the lawyer could, with great assurance, advise the wife that she had absolutely no interest in the property. That might not have been *fair*, but it was *certain*.

    Today, and at least where the property was acquired by the husband during the period of the parties' marriage, the fact that the property is in the husband's name alone is totally irrelevant; and the circumstances of the couple's marriage might be such that a court might well find that the wife should be given an interest in it. Unfortunately, and unless the property in question is the parties' marital residence, the lawyer will be hard pressed to tell the wife exactly what her interest will be. In short, although the new law may well be *fairer*, to that very extent it is also far *less certain* (predictable).
37. *Putting It All Together—The Family Law Curriculum*, 14 Colum. L. Sch. Alum. Observer 6 (Oct. 1984).
38. This distinction is reflective of the very different attitudes—one might almost say *views of reality*—that are expressed by the law and in mediation. While, by definition, there had to be many legitimate ways in which most of the issues that were presented to the court under equitable distribution could be viewed—whether a

spouse should have an interest in the other's professional degree or license, his or her business, professional practice or retirement benefits, whether the appreciation is separate property should be considered marital property, etc.—and while different courts have come to very different conclusions on certain of these questions; once a definite decision has been made by the courts of a particular state, all other points of view are nullified and deemed without value.

From that point forward there is one, and only one, correct way to view the situation. (It is akin to an electoral college in a presidential election completely discounting and ignoring the millions of votes that may have been cast for all but one of the candidates and assigning all of them to the candidate with the most votes). While it may be necessary to adopt such a win/lose attitude toward competing points of view in politics and in the orderly administration of justice, it represents, nevertheless, a distortion of reality. More importantly, it is not a distortion that mediation is necessarily required to adopt. Since a mediator is not concerned with the administration of justice or, therefore, the precedential effect of the determination in this case upon the determination in other cases, he is not bound to hold that what was done in a previous instance (what was right there) must be done here. Nor is he bound, even in this instance, to choose between these competing points of view. On the contrary, he has the ability, which a court does not, to recognize the validity of both of the points of view being expressed and to attempt to effectuate an accommodation between them.

39. *See, e.g.*, John Lande, *Mediation Paradigms and Professional Identities*, 4 Mediation Q. 19 (June 1984).

Chapter 5—The Rule of Law in Divorce Mediation

1. R. H. Mnookin and L. Kornhauser, *Bargaining in the Shadow of the Law: The Case of Divorce in the Courts*, 88 Yale L. J. 950 (1979).
2. This is not to suggest that a mediator must be a legal expert or know exactly what these legal rules are and how to apply them. On the contrary, it will be our contention that there are very few legal rules that he need know in order to conduct mediation successfully.
3. This is also encouraged by the setting in which adversarial proceedings take place. This will be discussed at greater length in Chapter 7, *Context*.
4. In this regard, the reader is reminded of the attitude expressed by Raoul Felder, cited in Chapter 4, footnote 2.
5. The reader is reminded of the discussion of this in Chapter 3, *Equitable Distribution in Divorce Mediation*.
6. *Rubin v. Rubin*, 204 Conn. 224, 527 A.2d 1184 (1987); *Storm v. Storm*, 470 P.2d 367 (Wyo. 1970); *Loeb v. Loeb*, 261 Ind. 193, 301 N.E.2d 349 (1973); *Meeks v. Kirkland*, 228 Ga. 607, 187 S.E.2d 296 (1972). *But see, Rice v. Rice*, 372 Mass. 398, 361 N.E.2d 1305 (1977); *James v. James*, 248 S.W.2d 706 (Ky. Ct. App. 1952); *Moritz v. Moritz*, 10 F.L.R. (B.N.A.) 1534 (Pa. Ct. Comm. Pleas 1984). Again, what is fair under equitable distribution may depend upon the state that the parties live in at the time of their divorce.
7. For example, every state has a statute that requires mental health professionals to report instances where either of the parties may have physically abused their children. *See, e.g.*, Ala. Code § 26-14-3 (1986); Alaska Stat. § 47.17.020 (1984); Ariz. Rev. Stat. Ann. § 13-3620 (1978 & 1987 Supp.); Ark. Stat. Ann. § 12-12-506 (1987); Cal. Penal Code § 11166 (West 1982); Colo. Rev. Stat. § 19-10-104 (1986); Conn. Gen. Stat. Ann. § 17-38a (West 1975); Del Code Ann. tit. 16, § 903 (1983); D.C. Code Ann. § 2-1352 (1982); Fla. Stat. Ann. § 415.504 (West 1986); Ga. Code Ann. § 19-7-5 (1982); Haw. Rev. Stat. § 350-1.1 (1985); Idaho Code § 16-1619 (1976 & 1987 Supp.); Ill. Ann. Stat. ch. 23, para. 2054 (Smith-Hurd 1987 Supp.); Ind. Code Ann. § 31-6-11-3 (West 1979); Iowa Code Ann. § 232.69 (West 1985); Kan. Stat. Ann. § 38-1521 (1986 Supp.); Ky. Rev. Stat. Ann. § 199.335 (Michie/Bobbs-Merrill 1982 & 1986 Supp.); La. Rev. Stat. Ann. § 14:403 (West 1986); Me. Rev. Stat. Ann. tit. 22, § 4011 (1987 Supp.); Md. Fam. Law Code Ann. § 5-704 (1987 Supp. (eff. 7/1/88)); Mass. Gen. Laws Ann. ch. 119, § 51A (West 1987 Supp.); Mich. Comp. Laws Ann. § 722.623 (West 1987 Supp.); Minn. Stat. Ann. § 626.556 (West 1983); Miss. Code Ann. § 43-23-9 (1979); Mo. Ann. Stat. § 210.115 Vernon 1983); Mont. Code Ann. §41-3-201 (1987); Neb. Rev. Stat. § 28-711 (1985); Nev. Rev. Stat. Ann. §232B.220 (Michie 1986); N.H. Rev. Stat. Ann. § 169:40 (1978); N.J. Stat. Ann. § 9:6-8.10 (West 1972 & 1987 Supp.); N.M. Stat. Ann. § 32-1-15 (1986); N.Y. Soc. Serv. Law § 413 (McKinney 1983 & 1987 Supp.); N.C. Gen. Stat. § 7A-543 (1986); N.D. Cent. Code § 50-25.1-03 (1981 & 1987 Supp.); Ohio Rev. Code Ann. § 2151.42.1 (Baldwin 1976 &

1987 Supp.); Okla. Stat. Ann. tit. 21, § 846 (West 1983 & 1986 Supp.); Or. Rev. Stat. § 418.750 (1985); Pa. Stat. Ann. tit. 11, § 2206 (Purdon 1987); R.I. Gen. Laws § 40-11-3 (1984 & 1987 Supp.); S.C. Code Ann. § 20-7-510 (Law. Co-op. 1985); S.D. Codified Laws Ann. § 26-10-10 (1984 & 1987 Supp.); Tenn. Code Ann. § 37-1-403 (1984 & 1987); Tex. Fam. Code Ann. § 34.01 (Vernon 1986); Utah Code Ann. § 78-3b-3 (1987); Vt. Stat. Ann. tit. 33, § 683 (1987); Va. Code Ann. § 63.1-248.3 (1987); Wash. Rev. Code Ann. §26.44.020 (West 1986); W.Va. Code § 49-6A-2 (1986); Wis. Stat. Ann. §48.981 (West 1987); Wyo. Stat. § 14-3-205 (1987).

8. In commenting on the idea that manipulation was not only bad, but could and should be avoided, Watzlawick, Weakland, and Fisch, made the following observation:

    Nobody, unfortunately, has ever explained how this can be done. It is difficult to imagine how any behavior in the presence of another person can avoid being a communication of one's own view of the nature of one's relationship with that person and how it can, therefore, fail to influence that person. The analyst who silently sits behind his receiving patient, or the "non-directive" therapist who merely repeats the verbal utterances of his client, exert a fantastic amount of influences *by that very behavior*, especially since it is defined as "no influence." The problem, therefore, is not how influence and manipulation can be avoided, but how they can best be comprehended and used in the interest of the patient.

    Paul Watzlawick, John H. Weakland and Richard Fisch, *Change*, (New York, NY: W.W. Norton & Co. Inc., 1974), XV–XVI.

9. While, at first blush, it might be thought that a mediator is also under an obligation to assure that the couple's decision was not tainted by inappropriate emotional considerations, we would take issue with this. This is not to suggest that a mediator should proceed unmindful of these potential considerations. On the contrary, when the couple conclude an agreement very much at variance with the expectations created by the then given norms—and particularly when they come into mediation having already concluded such an agreement—the mediator should, of course, test out whether or not one or both of the parties is allowing these considerations to interfere with their own best interests.

    Suppose, for example, that a young couple with a one-year-old daughter come to a mediator and advise him that they have agreed that their daughter will live with her father. On the face of it, this is all that the mediator knows, and it may well be that it is a perfectly sensible and appropriate decision. Nevertheless, it flies in the face of the given norms of our society at the present time in that, absent very unusual circumstances, it would not be expected that a mother would agree to this. In fact, one would think that it would be very difficult for her even to entertain the idea. Without drawing any conclusions, the mediator must, nevertheless, keep a question mark in his mind. In the course of the mediation he will learn things that he does not now know that will either be consistent with that decision or call it into question.

    Suppose, for example, that he finds that the husband is a very indifferent father. Suppose, also, that he finds that the wife is very conflicted over the decision which she has made. If that is so, he will then be obligated to probe more deeply into that decision and to get the wife to examine the conditions that have led her to it. The mediator must be very careful here, however. It is not his function to *question* that decision, let alone to put the wife in the position of having to defend it. It is simply his function gently to probe at the decision to determine how comfortable or uncomfortable the wife is with it and, if necessary, to get the wife to reconsider the circumstances that have led her to it.

    While we would not suggest that this will necessarily always be the case, if a mediator does this carefully, and particularly if he slows down the pace of the mediation to assure that the wife has had an adequate opportunity to reconsider her decision, it is highly unlikely that, if she is seriously conflicted over her decision, that conflict will not surface or that the mediator will not have an opportunity to address it.

Chapter 6—In Whose Best Interests?

1. In considering the views expressed in this chapter, the reader is reminded of our comments with respect to the experience which has given birth to our conclusions, as was set forth in the first paragraph of the last section of the Preface, on page x.
2. Donald T. Saposnek, *Mediating Child Custody Disputes*, (San Francisco, CA: Jossey-Bass Inc., 1983), p. 38.
3. *Id.*, p. 37.

4. Me. Rev. Stat. Ann. tit. 19, § 214(5) (West 1986 Supp.).
5. This is not to suggest that it is necessarily wrong for a mediator to discuss the child's possible drug problem with the parents should they wish to, and should he be qualified to do so, any more than it is to suggest that it would necessarily be inappropriate for him to discuss their child's health problem, if he were a physician. It is only to say that this is outside of the purview of the mediation. Nor should mediators forget this simply because the issue relates to the parties' children rather than to some other problem in their lives.

Chapter 7—Context

1. That context is not simply critical to the issues that separating and divorcing couples must resolve, and that it is as important a factor in other areas of human understanding as well, was testified to by biologist Richard Lewontin in the closing page of his book, *The Genetic Basis of Evolutionary Change*, New York, NY: Columbia University Press, 1974). As he said, "The fitness of a single locus ripped from its interactive context is about as relevant to real problems of evolutionary genetics as the study of the psychology of individuals isolated from their social context is to an understanding of man's sociopolitical evolution. In both cases context and interaction are not simply second-order effects to be superimposed on a primary monadic analysis. Context and interaction are of the essence."
2. While it is not generally appreciated, one of the most important benefits of divorce mediation has been to correct this. To be sure, the husband may be a problem because he does not want a divorce or simply because he views the situation differently than the wife does. but that is very different from his being a problem for her because he has become her adversary. One of the great virtues of mediation is that it keeps the problem in the first sense from becoming a problem in the second.
3. It is perhaps understandable, and therefore excusable, that the critics of divorce mediation make this fundamental mistake. It is less understandable that its advocates do also.
4. There is another factor that unfortunately adds to this. If the wife—and this is equally true of the husband—should decide to retain her attorney's services, he is going to ask her for a retainer. If he specializes in matrimonial matters, and if the wife lives in a large metropolitan area, that retainer will probably be very substantial. The attorney in question cannot justify a retainer of this magnitude—which, after all, may only be a small portion of his actual fee—by presenting the matter to the wife as one that he and her husband's attorney will be able to sit down and resolve in a relatively short period of time. On the contrary, and regardless of how responsible he may be, he cannot help but send out signals to her that what they are talking about is both a large and long undertaking. To part the wife from her money, less responsible attorneys may very consciously emphasize this fact. They may then even go out and earn their fee by creating the very situation they have warned her about. In either event, it is almost impossible for the wife to leave without having her fears reinforced.
5. In their attempt to sing the praises of adversarial proceedings, and to answer their critics, divorce lawyers have generally muted this fact. Instead, they have emphasized the fact that probably no more than 10% of the cases that they handle result in a trial, let alone are resolved by a judge's decision. What they neglect to mention, however, is that in the overwhelming majority of instances the context in which their negotiations take place is such that it is impossible for the parties to conclude an agreement between themselves unless and until they have first resorted to litigation. Transposed over into the world of diplomacy, this would be as if a statesman were to claim that diplomacy had been successful in resolving all of the disputes between nations in the 20th century, with the exceptions of the first and second world wars, simply neglecting to count the hundreds and thousands of other instances of armed conflict as representing a breakdown in diplomatic efforts. The importance of litigation (as opposed to negotiations) in the resolution of the dispute between the parties, and as a weapon in the adversarial process, is belied by another fact that divorce lawyers generally do not mention, and that is that in a very large percentage of cases the very first thing that the attorney for one of the parties will do will be to institute suit, and this even before there has been any attempt at negotiations, let alone a breakdown in those negotiations.

      In some instances, this is justified in terms of legitimate adversarial concerns. In far too many instances, however, litigation is unthinkingly instituted simply as a matter of course, or because the attorney in question wants to negotiate from strength and believes that the institution of an action is a demonstration of that strength. In some instances it is instituted simply to prevent the client from turning back and to bind the client to the attorney and his fee.

6. It is not generally appreciated how much license each of the parties is given in adversarial practice by reason of the fact that they have someone else to do the accounting for them. The wife calls her attorney complaining about certain misconduct on her husband's part. He in turn calls the husband's attorney to make complaint. (This is the famous telephone game that matrimonial lawyers spend their lives playing.) Since the husband's attorney is generally ignorant of the situation, save for what the wife's attorney has just told him, all that he can do is tell the wife's attorney that he will get in touch with his client and then get back to him. What the wife's attorney is looking for is restitution, perhaps a solution to the problem, or at least an apology. He may even want and expect the husband's attorney to reprimand his client for his misconduct. Unfortunately, the husband's attorney was not hired by the husband to reprimand him, as his attorney full well knows. Thus, the husband's attorney will simply relate to him what he has been told as politely as he can and wait to hear what the husband has to say. In most instances, the story that he will get from the husband will be so at variance with the one that he has heard from the wife's attorney that he will wonder whether or not they are talking about the same case. Just as often, he will hear a counter complaint from the husband that he will be told to take back to the wife's attorney.

   Even if the husband is at fault, he will make some lame excuse and expect his attorney to put the best face on it that he can, which, after all, is what his attorney is being paid to do. And so his attorney will report back to the wife's lawyer that her husband denies the allegations, that he complains instead that it was the wife who was guilty of a breach of conduct, or that even if the husband may have been derelict in some respect, it was excusable or totally beyond his control. At times, and if he is more responsible, he may not attempt to give excuses for the husband that he does not deserve and will instead simply throw up his hands and acknowledge to the wife's lawyer that he has no control over his client. In any event, the husband will have been successful in using his attorney as a buffer between himself and his wife and in not having had to account for his actions.

7. Husbands and wives engaged in adversarial divorce proceedings are not generally aware of this. From their standpoint, what they have done has been to engage an attorney whose primary responsibility is to attempt to negotiate an agreement for them. However, in the overwhelming majority of instances, if they were to look at a record of their attorney's time sheets, they would be surprised to find that probably no more than 25% of his time has been devoted either to the preparation or conduct of these negotiations—and that would include, as well, the time that he has spent going over the husband's books and records, preparing a budget of the wife's expenses, etc. Rather, the bulk of his time will have been spent in the war of paper that attorneys forever engage in, but which has so little to do with the ultimate outcome of the case.

8. This is not generally appreciated. It is a fact nevertheless. Adversarial divorce proceedings represent a kind of institutionalized madness. Like war itself, each of the parties is required to engage in what would otherwise be considered irrational conduct. To get them to do this, and to accept it as appropriate, it is first necessary to give it official sanction. The healthier that a person is, however, the more he realizes just how crazy what he is involved in is, and just how much damage it does to him and to everyone around him. To end this madness, he is willing to make concessions and compromises. In fact, his ability and willingness to do this is a direct function of his emotional health. For the less healthy elements of society, however, and as unpleasant as it may be, that madness nevertheless serves a purpose. For them, it is more important to be *right* and to *get even* than it is to get *done* and *get on*. And this is so regardless of the injury that is caused to their spouse, to their children, and even to themselves in the process. Thus, they will persist to the bitter end, for as they see it what they are engaged in is a holy crusade, and whatever the costs or sacrifices may be, they are never too great. Again, their ability and willingness to do this is a direct function of their emotional ill health.

9. This exaggeration takes many forms. Thus, in traditional divorce proceedings, the year of the couple's divorce will invariably be the husband's worst year financially, and future prospects will look no better. Similarly, the wife's ability to contribute toward her own support will be literally nonexistent, and it is almost a cardinal rule in adversarial proceedings that a wife should never take a job while the proceedings are pending and thereby acknowledge her ability to earn income, let alone the fact that her children do not need her constant care and attention 24 hours a day. These claims are literally never made in mediation, as the parties do not feel the need to protect themselves with such counterproductive exaggerations.

10. In actual fact, however, these clues are more often found by questioning the wife herself, rather than in examining her husband. An appreciation of this fact is very important. If it is the wife, and not the husband, who provides most of the important information, she can provide it just as well in mediation as she can in an adversarial proceeding. Thus, just as she would not permit her husband to submit an affidavit in an

adversarial proceeding suggesting that his income is limited to that reported on his income tax return, nor would she sit by in mediation and permit him to make that same statement.

11. This is not to suggest that the couple will necessarily believe that they are mediating in a common cause. It is not even to suggest that the mediator will be successful in causing them to so view the enterprise. It is simply to suggest that this is the attitude that the mediator should project in all his dealings with the couple.

12. This is not to suggest that all women's groups are in opposition to mediation or that there is even unanimity of opinion within the same group. In this respect see *Divorce Mediation: A Guide for Women* written by Judith I. Avner and Susan Herman for the NOW Legal Defense and Education Fund.

13. This point was expressed by Lillian Kozak, Chair of the Domestic Relations Law Task Force of the New York State National Organization for Women (NOW) in presenting the views of that organization before the Judiciary Committee of the New York State Assembly in opposition to the proposed bill providing for the mediation of child custody disputes. She concluded her presentation by stating;

My contention has long been that there is not so much wrong with the law as with the practice of it. I can match horror stories of the legal system with those of any mediator. But—our efforts have been and are to assist in changing that system. This committee is certainly aware of our constant efforts to obtain fairer, more professional practice. Should this proposed bill pass, there will be two bureaucracies to monitor, two professions to educate, defects in each to correct.

. . . .

There is much to be done. Let us improve the legal system so that it lives up to the integrity and offers the protection which the citizenry are taught to expect and for which the public may gain some respect. The courts and the search for protection of rights and justice belong to the public as well as to Texaco, IBM and General Motors.

14. In this regard it is important to keep in mind that there will never be a consensus between men and women (or, for that matter, between those who have worked to build up professional practices and those who have not, between those who have stayed home to raise a family and those who have devoted their energies to supporting it, etc.) as to whether or not those rules are fair, and if a proper resolution of the issues that separating and divorcing couples face are seen to depend upon correcting those rules so that they are fair, then divorce is condemned to be a never ending struggle between the various competing groups to change and rechange those rules to their liking (in their favor).

Chapter 8—Power Imbalances

1. We do not mean to suggest by this that their husbands are really strong and powerful. On the contrary, they may only be very insecure and rigid bullies. We are simply willing to accept, for the sake of argument, the view being expressed that sees these traits as being strengths and the expression of power.

2. One of the ironies here is that the argument that men are more knowledgeable, more powerful, and better negotiators is not only usually made by women, but is also usually made by women who would not concede for a moment that a man is better or more competent than they are in any way.

3. To be sure, various factors, including societal norms, may provide men with certain advantages that women do not have. But this is not to say that these advantages have the results suggested by the argument, or that they are not balanced out in other ways. Consider the following. Men who married in the late 1950s, 60s and early 70s had an advantage over their wives in that the conventional norms at the time permitted them to ask their wives for a date, while it did not permit their wives to ask them for one. Given the tremendous advantage that this selection process afforded men, one would have to assume that the result would have been that while a vast majority of these men were able to marry someone whom they loved and wished to marry, only a small minority of these women were able to do the same. Since that was obviously not the case, other factors and considerations, less apparent, must have been at play.

4. See the discussion under the heading "Social Constructs" in Chapter 7, *Context*.

5. Suppose the more skillful and powerful husband here hires a more skillful and powerful attorney than his wife's. How will she be protected then? If one of the purposes of our adversarial system is to provide protection for those who need it—in this case, to provide a balance to the imbalances in power which exist

between the weak wife here and her strong husband—then instead of having each of the parties retain their attorneys freely and at random, adversarial proceedings would first assess the relative strengths and weaknesses of each of them, and if it did not then provide the less able of the two with a more skillful and competent attorney to balance out the superior strength of the other, it would at least see to it that the weaker party was assured of having an attorney of equal skill and competence. Needless to say, no member of the adversarial bar who professes his concern over these power imbalances has as yet proposed this solution.

6. Anyone who truly understands adversarial proceedings will also understand that the only protection they really offer is to prepare each of the parties to defend themselves in the inevitable conflict. However, the best protection they can be given is that which helps them to avoid it altogether. That is the kind of protection that mediation offers.

7. This will be discussed in Chapter 13, *The Initial Meeting.*

8. One of the most serious errors in current mediation thinking is its failure to appreciate that adversarial procedures are nothing more nor less then the expression of adversarial concerns and adversarial assumptions. One is the inevitable by-product of the other. It follows from this that if those same adversarial concerns and assumptions are carried over into mediation practice, then adversarial procedure will inevitably be carried over as well. In this regard, the reader is reminded of the various standards of practice that have been adopted by the advocates of divorce mediation, for example, those that insist that the parties must each have and receive independent (i.e. adversarial) legal representation and advice.

9. Lenore J. Weitzman, *The Economic Consequences of Divorce: An Empirical Study of Property, Alimony and Child Support Awards*; 8 F.L.R. (B.N.A.) 4037 (Aug. 1982). This study was eventually published by Professor Weitzman in her book, *The Divorce Revolution: The Unexpected Social and Economic Consequences for Women and Children in America*, (New York, NY: The Free Press, 1985).

10. Phyllis Chesler, *Mothers on Trial; The Battle for Children & Custody*, (New York, NY: McGraw Hill Book Co., (1986)

11. *Diagnosis Confirmed: EDL is Ailing*, 17 Fam. L. Rev. 3 (N.Y. State Bar Assoc., July, 1985). *But see, Vertigo v. Vertigo*, by Professor Henry H. Foster in response to this article, 18 Fam. L. Rev. 20 (N.Y. State Bar Assoc., Feb. 1986).

12. While these groups see mediation as leaving women without an attorney to protect their interests, they forget that it leaves their husbands in that same position also. If they really took their argument seriously, one would think that this trade-off would be to women's benefit. While this suggestion may not be taken seriously, it is as serious as is the concern being expressed for these women. After all, if their husbands have the power and sophistication that they are supposed to have, and that their wives lack, they also have an advantage in being better able to select an attorney to represent them. More importantly, they may well be in a better financial position to do so. The logic that expresses concern for these women in mediation thus leads to a very curious result. Rather than affording them the protection that it is supposed to, adversarial proceedings may simply widen the gap in power between the strong husband and the weak wife by providing him with more adequate representation. If that is the case, mediation may tend to narrow this gap by denying him this opportunity.

CHAPTER 9—WHOSE FAULT IS IT?

1. This element of punishment was exemplified, for example, in New York's divorce laws. For 180 years, from 1787 until 1967, the only grounds for divorce in New York was adultery. If adultery was proved, however, the penalty exacted by the law was that the guilty party was prohibited from remarrying during the lifetime of the other party. This prohibition was only removed in 1967. Even when that penalty was removed, however, and the grounds for divorce greatly expanded in the Divorce Reform Act of 1966, a party found guilty of marital misconduct, and against whom a divorce was granted, was still punished by being barred from receiving support, regardless of the length of the marriage or his or her financial need. This bar was only removed by the New York legislature in 1980.

2. Alabama, Arkansas, District of Columbia, Georgia, Hawaii, Indiana, Iowa, Kentucky, Louisiana, Maryland, Massachusetts, Michigan, Minnesota, Missouri, Montana, Nebraska, Nevada, New Hampshire, North Carolina, North Dakota, Oklahoma, Oregon, Pennsylvania, Rhode Island, South Dakota, Ten-

nessee, Utah, Virginia, Washington, West Virginia, Wisconsin, Wyoming. However, the issue of fault versus no-fault divorce laws is far from resolved. *See, e.g.*, R. Michael Redman, *Coming Down Hard on No-Fault*, 10 Fam. Advocate 6 (Fall 1987).

3. *See, e.g., Pacella v. Pacella*, 342 Pa. Super. 178, 492 A.2d 707 (1985); *Green v. Green*, 501 So.2d 1306 Fla. Dist. Ct. App. 1986 (citing *Vilas v. Vilas*, 153 Fla. 102, 13 So.2d 807 (1943)); *Tobey v. Tobey*, 165 Conn. 742, 345 A.2d 21 (1974); *Bollenbach v. Bollenbach*, 285 Minn. 418, 175 N.W.2d 148 (1970); *Tonjes v. Tonjes*, 24 Wis. 2d 120, 128 N.W.2d 446 (1964); *Errera v. Errera*, 332 Ill. App. 582, 76 N.E.2d 215 (1947); *McClung v. McClung*, 29 Tenn. App. 580, 198 S.W.2d 820

4. This is reflected in the fact that the equitable distribution statutes of a number of states still provide that fault is to be considered a factor in awarding alimony and in the distribution of marital property.

5. The states that consider it as a factor in making an award of alimony are set forth in footnote 11. Those that consider it a factor in the distribution of marital property are set forth in footnote 12.

6. Sigmund Freud, *Civilization and Its Discontents*, (New York, NY: W.W. Norton & Co., Inc., N.Y., 1961). (Originally published London: Hogarth Press, 1930.)

7. Jay Haley, *Strategies of Psychotherapy*, (New York, NY: Grune & Stratton, 1963.)

8. Catherine Frank, *Major Constructs of Contextual Therapy: An Interview with Dr. Ivan Boszormenyi-Nagy*, 12 Am. J. Fam. Therapy, 7 (Brunner/Mazel, Inc., Spring, 1984).

9. In a very real sense, it is a mistake to talk of a marriage that has lasted 23 years and produced two children to have been unsuccessful simply because it has resulted in a divorce. In fact, and given the reality that so many marriages, even those of long duration, end in divorce, we may well have to rethink the question of what it means to say that a marriage was successful or unsuccessful.

10. The description that follows as to why it is that people divorce is not to be taken as an attempt to explain all divorces. For example, it is insufficient to explain the many divorces that occur after but a few months, or even a year or two, when both parties are very young and immature. By the same token, it is insufficient to explain divorces that occur in marriages of much longer duration where the balance between the parties is assaulted by a serious life change that occurs, for example, due to serious illness, a dramatic change in financial circumstances (upward as well as downward), or the loss of someone very close. Thus, rather than intending to be a complete explanation of why a divorce occurs, its purpose is to contrast the therapist's attitude toward divorce, and his understanding of it, with the more traditional attitude and understanding of the law. Nevertheless, we believe that the explanation we have given will fit the experience of a majority of the couples whom a mediator will meet in private practice.

11. Alabama, Arkansas, Connecticut, Florida, Idaho, Louisiana, Maryland, Massachusetts, Missouri, North Carolina, Pennsylvania, Rhode Island, South Carolina, Tennessee, Virginia, and West Virginia.

12. Alabama, Arkansas, Connecticut, Maryland, Missouri, Rhode Island and Virginia.

CHAPTER 10—CONDUCTING MEDIATION

1. Roger Fisher and William Ury, *Getting to Yes*, (Boston, MA: Houghton-Mifflin, Co., 1981).

2. Lewis Browne Hill, *On Being Rather Than Doing in Psychotherapy*, 8 Int'l J. Group Psychotherapy 115 (April, 1958).

3. There will be some who will object to the suggestion that it is appropriate for a mediator to attempt to aid the couple here by providing them with a yardstick of what it could be expected that a court would or would not do, even assuming, as the example does, that the mediator in question is an experienced matrimonial attorney. Ironically, they will be the same group who are concerned that the parties may make decisions in mediation without being fully appraised of their legal rights. Their objection will be that it is not possible for the mediator to know this with any degree of certainty. Clearly, only one of two things is possible; either an experienced matrimonial attorney could know what it was to be expected that a court would or would not do, or he could not. If he could know this, then there is absolutely no reason to believe that this particular experienced matrimonial attorney would not know this. If, however, an experienced matrimonial attorney could not know this, then the law has failed to fulfill one of its most important functions, namely, to assist the parties in making decisions as to what is legally appropriate or inappropriate under the circumstances. If it fails in this respect, then in a very important sense it becomes irrelevant.

To extricate themselves from this conundrum, those who object may fall back upon the argument that our legal system will provide the correct answer, but only if appropriate adversarial proceedings are employed. Unfortunately, the argument begs the question. A court of law will not provide the correct answer; the correct answer will simply be whatever the court decides. (Put another way, the couple will resort to the court not to get the correct answer but because there is no correct answer.) The law is thus invoked not to decide the dispute, but simply to end it. If that is the case, then even if it is important in some sense that legal principles be invoked to end their disagreement, there is no reason that the parties should be required to pay the very heavy price that is involved in invoking those rules in adversarial proceedings. On the contrary, it makes far more sense for them to sit down with an experienced lawyer who can provide them with the benefit of these legal principles without having to pay that price.

4. *See, e.g., Christian v. Christian,* 42 N.Y.2d 63, 365 N.E.2d 849, 396 N.Y.S.2d 817 (1977); *Johnson v. Johnson,* 67 N.C. App. 250, 313 S.E.2d 162 (1984); *Stockton v. Stockton,* 435 N.E.2d 586 (Ind. Ct. App. 1982); *Merritt v. Merritt,* 616 S.W.2d 585 (Mo. Ct. App. 1981).

Chapter 11—A Question of Choice

1. *See, e.g., Divorce and Family Mediation—Standards of Practice,* §§ I(G), VI(A)(B). (A.B.A. Press, Chicago, IL, 1986).
2. The reader is reminded of the discussion in Chapter 5, *The Rule of Law in Divorce Mediation,* and in Chapter 7, *Context.*
3. *See, e.g.,* the views of Lawrence Gaughan, a devoted advocate of divorce mediation, as expressed in his article, *Taking a Fresh Look at Divorce Mediation,* 17 Trial 39 (April 1981).

Chapter 12—Starting Out

1. In the past, and particularly when divorce was grounded in fault, lawyers habitually admonished their clients not to leave their homes. The rationale for this was that their act of doing so could be used by their spouse as the basis for an action for divorce based upon abandonment. Whatever sense this advice may have made in the past—and it was rarely carefully thought out, and didn't make very much—there is little logic in it today, under modern divorce laws, where fault, particularly the very innocuous fault of leaving one's spouse, will have little if any effect upon the final outcome in most jurisdictions. The most that it will do will be to permit the party's spouse to sue him for a divorce, which is, after all, what he wants anyway. Nevertheless, a mediator may still find himself confronted with someone who has been given this advice and is very intimidated by it. The one instance where this advice made sense, and still makes sense, is where custody is in issue, as the party who leaves his home and children seriously undermines his chances of obtaining custody of the children at a later date.
2. A telephone information sheet, which may be used by a mediator for this purpose, will be found in the Appendix, on page 444.
3. A sample copy of just such a description for a therapist-attorney team will be found in the Appendix, on page 446.
4. Sample copies of these questions will be found in the Appendix, on pages 443–459.
5. The Internal Revenue Service has prepared a number of publications that can be extremely helpful to a mediator, and to the couple themselves. *See, e.g.,* publications 501 (exemptions), 503 (child and dependent care credit, and employment taxes or household employers) and 504 (tax information for divorced or separated individuals).
6. In this connection, see *Caring About Kids: When Parents Divorce,* published by the U.S. Department of Health and Human Services, Public Health Service, Alcohol, Drug Abuse, and Mental Health Administration.
7. *See, e.g.,* Emily Hancock, *The Dimensions of Meaning and Belonging in the Divorce Process,* 50 Am. J. Orthopsychiatry 18 (Jan. 1980).
8. All too often, adversarial attorneys' concern for the risks involved in an agreement that their respective clients are attempting to conclude tends to undermine the very possibility that an agreement will be

concluded between them at all. This is not particularly significant in nonmatrimonial matters where, for example, what is at issue may be a piece of property that one of the parties wishes to buy and the other party wishes to sell, as the only penalty for their failure to be able to conclude an agreement concerning its sale is that they each will have to look around for someone else to do business with. This, of course, is not the case with separating and divorcing couples. If they are unable to reach an agreement by one means, then they will be forced to reach it by another. Thus, the conclusion of an agreement between them legitimately becomes an end in itself. Viewing the situation as he does, a mediator, of course, understands this. Unfortunately, being disposed by training to concentrate more on the question of *risk*, and the *reduction* of that risk, rather than the *conclusion* of the matter (in this case an agreement), there is always the danger that adversarial attorneys will lose sight of this. Again, that is particularly unfortunate in matrimonial negotiations.

9. Address by Chief Justice Warren E. Burger on January 24, 1982 at the midyear meeting of the American Bar Association in Chicago as reported in the American Bar Association Journal, March, 1982, page 274.

10. A copy of a letter received by a mediator from one of the party's attorneys and his answer to that letter will be found in the Appendix, on pages 458–459.

Chapter 13—The Initial Meeting

1. A similar question arises when the couple initially comes to the therapist for marriage counseling, but it proves unsuccessful. We would not necessarily have the same objection here, particularly if both of the parties have come to the decision that a divorce is inevitable. To begin with, the therapist is not presenting the couple with multiple hats at the same time. On the contrary, he is only suggesting mediation because the couple have themselves come to the decision that the marriage cannot be saved. More importantly, he has probably already developed each of the parties' trust to the point that they will not question his new role as being inconsistent with his former one, but will instead view affirmatively the fact that he will still be able to help them, albeit in a different way. In addition, they will probably find comfort in the fact that they will not now have to find someone new for that purpose.

  We must also mention that the views of the parties in marital therapy are often very different, with one of them wanting to work to save the marriage and the other wanting to work toward a divorce. If, when it comes to a divorce, the one who wanted to save the marriage feels that the therapist had been allied with the one who wanted a divorce, distrust, rather than the necessary trust, may color his feelings. If that is the case, it would not be a good idea for the therapist then also to act as the mediator. Again, in each instance the decision will have to be made by balancing the possible advantages against the potential risks, and the answer in two different situations will not necessarily be the same.

2. *State v. Vennard*, 159 Conn. 385, 270 A.2d 837, *cert. denied*, 400 U.S. 1011 (1970); *Harter v. State*, 260 Iowa 605, 149 N.W. 2d 827 (1967).

3. While, from a therapist's standpoint, confidentiality is everything, from the standpoint of the law, that confidentiality does violence to the principle that there must be full disclosure in judicial proceedings to assure that there is not a miscarriage of justice. Accordingly, and from the standpoint of the law, there must always be a balancing of the equities between these two inconsistent principles.

4. *D. v. D.*, 108 N.J. Super. 149, 260 A.2d 255, (Ch. Div. 1969).

5. *People v. Sigal*, 235 Cal. App. 2d 449, 45 Cal. Rptr. 481 (1965).

6. *State v. Fagalde*, 85 Wash. 2d 730, 539 P.2d 86 (1975).

7. Rinteler v. Schaefer, 158 A.D. 477, 143 N.Y. 631 (2nd Dept. 1913).

8. The "Miranda warning" is the standard measure taken in order to safeguard the Fifth Amendment rights of a person taken into custody. Prior to interrogation, the person must be informed that he has the right to remain silent, that anything he says will be used against him in a court of law, that he has the right to consult with a lawyer and have him present during interrogation, and that if he cannot afford a lawyer, one will be appointed to him. *Miranda v. Arizona*, 384 U.S. 436, *reh'g denied*, 385 U.S. 890 (1966).

9. A copy of such a letter will be found in the Appendix, on page 449.

10. In a number of states, more than incompatibility or the fact that there has been an irretrievable breakdown in the relationship must be shown, especially if the divorce is contested. *See, e.g.*, Ariz. Rev. Stat. Ann. §

25-316 (West 1976); Del. Code Ann. tit. 13, § 1505 (1981); Mont. Code Ann. § 40-4-104 (1987); Neb. Rev. Stat. § 42-361 (1984); Wis. Stat. Ann. § 767.12(2)(b) (West 1981).

11. In many ways, this is true of our entire adversarial process. That a society's way of thinking can be afflicted by this kind of thinking was documented by Eric Fromm in *The Sane Society*, (New York, NY: Rinehart & Co., 1955).

12. A copy of such an initial interview sheet will be found in the Appendix on page 445.

13. A copy of such a financial data sheet will be found in the Appendix on pages 452–454.

CHAPTER 14—CHILDREN

1. The courts of the various states take very different views when the problem is presented to them for determination. The polar views are probably expressed by the courts of New York and New Jersey. In New York, "[d]isruption of the relationship between the non-custodial parent and the marital issue by relocation of the custodial parent in a distant jurisdiction will not be permitted unless a compelling showing of single 'exceptional circumstances' . . . or a 'pressing concern' for the welfare of the custodial parent and child . . . is made warranting removal of the child to a distant locale." *Courten v. Courten*, 92 A.D.2d 579, 580, 459 N.Y.S.2d 464, 466 (App. Div. 1983).

   In New Jersey, on the other hand, the custodial parent need only show that there is a real advantage to the move and that it is not inimical to the child's best interests. *Cooper v. Cooper*, 99 N.J. 42, 491 A.2d 606 (1984). As the court there stated, "If a noncustodial parent chooses to leave this state, or to alter his or her personal life style, the custodial parent cannot prevent his or her departure or change in life style even though it may severely disrupt the child's relationship with that parent. The custodial parent who bears the burden and responsibility for the child is entitled, to the greatest possible extent, to the same freedom to seek a better life for herself or himself and the children as enjoyed by the noncustodial parent." *Id.* at 55, 491 A.2d at 613 (citing *D'Onofrio v. D'Onofrio*, 144 N.J. Super. 200, 365 A.2d 27 (Ch. Div.), *aff'd*, 144 N.J. Super. 352, 365 A.2d 716 (App. Div. 1976)). For those who assume that what is fair is what the law says it is, this example should serve to demonstrate that it may have more to do with the rather fortuitous circumstance of which side of the Hudson River the parties happen to live on at the time of their divorce than on any necessary logic or equity.

2. The New York Times, October 26, 1989, C8.

3. The Maryland Court of Appeals has held that a child's non-adoptive stepparent may be awarded visitation rights on divorce. *Evans v. Evans*, 302 Md. 334, 488 A.2d 157 (1985). Other states have even gone further and held that the stepparent may be awarded custody. *See generally, Paquette v. Paquette*, 11 F.L.R. (B.N.A.) 1481 (Vt. 1985).

CHAPTER 15—MARITAL RESIDENCE

1. Although it is not generally appreciated, and rarely taken into consideration by the court in determining whether the custodial parent will be given the right to continue to live in the parties' marital residence, there are some potentially severe tax consequences for the party who will be vacating the marital residence prior to its ultimate sale. To begin with, and since it will not be his principal residence at the time of the sale, he will not be able to defer the taxes due on any gain realized as a result of the sale, by investing the proceeds that he will receive in a new principal residence. I.R.C. § 1034 (West 1988 Supp.). For the same reason, and since a portion of those proceeds will now have to go for income taxes, the amount that will be available to him to invest in a new principle residence will be reduced by that amount. Secondly, if the home is sold more than two years from the date that he vacates it, then, and if he is 55 years of age at the time of its sale, he will lose the benefit of the lifetime exclusion of $125,000 accorded to him by section 121 of the Internal Revenue Code, at least with respect to the profit derived from this residence. This will be discussed further in Chapter 22, *Income Taxes*.

2. In 1973, for example, the median price of an existing home was approximately $28,900. By 1984 it had risen to $72,300. In the same period, however, median family income, in constant dollars, dropped by more than $1,700. Translated in terms of spending power, this meant that whereas a median income family could afford a house priced $4,130 higher than the median price of an existing home in 1973, the same family was $28,236 dollars short of the amount that they needed in 1984. Michele Ingrassia, *Housing: Great Expectations are Falling Short*, Newsday, Part 2, June 2, 1976, at 3. Put another way, in 1973 the average 30-year-old male would have had to pay only 21% of his income for a mortgage on a median-priced home. In 1984 he would have had to pay 44% of his income for the mortgage on the same home. This is not to suggest that the average person is actually paying 44% of his income for that purpose, but simply that he would have to were he to buy the home. The answer, of course, is that he cannot afford to do so. Philip Longman, *The Mortgage Generation: Why the Young Can't Afford a House*, The Washington Monthly, April 1986, at 11. Part of the problem stems from the incredible increase in home prices in the last 30 years. Between 1955 and 1985, the increase in the cost of a median priced new home represented a real increase of more than 60 percent. *Id*. The other factor that accounted for the greater cost is the increase in the cost of financing the home. Thus, for example, a conventional first mortgage loan for the purchase of a single-family new home rose from 8.3% in 1970 to a high of 14.5% in 1982 before reducing to 11.9% in 1984. U.S. Bureau of the Census, *Statistical Abstract of the United States: 1986* (106th ed.), at 738. Finally, there were the record increases in the cost of fuel, which represented the largest increase in consumer goods since 1967 except for medical care services. Thus, the consumer price index for all urban consumers increased from $100 in 1967 to $469.20 by July of 1986. U.S. Department of Labor, Bureau of Labor Statistics, *CPI Detailed Report*, (Washington D.C. July 1986), at 8.

3. The problem that increased housing costs pose for the wife can be illustrated as follows: if the husband is the sole wage earner, if between 20 and 25% of his income has gone to pay for housing, and if, by their agreement, his wife is to receive half of his income for herself and their children, she will be required to spend between 40 and 50% of her income for housing. Suppose, instead, that the husband had been required to pay between 30 and 35% of his income for that purpose. Since these are largely fixed expenses over which the wife has no control, if she continues to live in the home she will now be required to spend between 60 and 70% of her income to meet those costs.

4. While this is still significant under the Tax Reform Act of 1986, it is less significant than it previously was. Under prior law, for a taxpayer in the 50% bracket, a deduction of $1 meant a savings of 50¢. With a maximum tax of 33%, that savings is now only 33¢. To put it another way, while, under previous law, a mortgage interest payment of $100 only costs this taxpayer $50, under the new law it will cost him $67.

5. This, of course, has all been changed by the Tax Reform Act of 1986, which now treats the profits on the home (the income received from its capital appreciation) as ordinary income. I.R.C. § 1(j) (West 1988 Supp.).

6. I.R.C. § 121 (West 1988 Supp.). This has not been changed by the Tax Reform Act of 1986. In that respect, the parties' investment in their home still represents sound financial planning from a tax standpoint.

7. Normally, if the husband and the wife were to sell their home to a third party, they would each be required to report one-half of the gain on their individual income tax returns (or the full gain on their joint return, if they are still married on December 31st of the year in question and file a joint return) and to pay the taxes on the gain so reported. If either of them should sell his interest in the home to the other, however, the situation may be very different, and the party purchasing the other's interest may be responsible for the entire tax, and the party whose interest is purchased, responsible for none of it. I.R.C. § 1041 (West 1988 Supp.). This will be discussed at greater length in Chapter 22, *Income Taxes*, starting at page 417.

8. *See, e.g., Diez-Arguelles v. Commissioner*, 1984 T.C.M. 356 (C.C.H.); *Finney v. Commissioner*, 1976 T.C.M. 329 (C.C.H.).

9. Again, he may deduct the full amount of the mortgage interest payments and taxes if the parties stipulate in their agreement that the payments the husband will make to the wife will be applied by her to make those payments.

CHAPTER 16—ASSETS AND LIABILITIES

1. Of the remaining states, virtually all are community property states which effectuate a division of property between the parties at the time of their divorce based upon community property concepts. Those states

(Arizona, California, Idaho, Louisiana, Nevada, New Mexico, Texas, Washington, and Wisconsin) generally provide that the property acquired during the marriage will be divided equally between the parties.

2. In this instance, the law generally holds that there has been a "transmutation" of the property from separate property to marital property. That does not mean, however, that a court will ignore the initial contribution of one of the parties and treat the property, for example, the marital residence, in the same manner that they would have had the original down payment been derived from savings that had been acquired by the parties during their marriage. On the contrary, the court will generally attempt to return to that party his or her contribution. In this regard, there are two approaches that have developed with respect to contributions made by a party, from their own separate funds, to property owned by them jointly. (For a discussion of the two approaches, see footnote 15 in Chapter 3, *Equitable Distribution and Divorce Mediation*.)

   Without necessarily intending to question either of these two approaches, a very strong argument can be made that neither of them is "fair." If the party who made the contribution had kept the property in his own name, the other party might not have had any interest in the appreciation in the value of that property, as they now will have in the appreciation in the value of the marital property in which it was invested. (In this respect, see the discussion dealing with the appreciation in the value of separate property in Chapter 3, *Equitable Distribution and Divorce Mediation*, at footnote 15, and the accompanying text). That the application of equitable distribution principles does not always lead to consistent results, let alone "equitable" ones, consider the following. Had the party here kept the money invested, in his own name, in passive, non-income producing property, the profit, in the form of increased value, would be considered separate property in those states that make this active/passive distinction. *See, e.g., Price v. Price*, 69 N.Y.2d 8, 503 N.E.2d 684, 511 N.Y.S.2d 219 (1986). On the other hand, had he invested it in passive, income producing property, the profit, in the form of current income, would be considered marital property. *See, e.g., Speer v. Speer*, 18 Ark. App. 186, 712 S.W.2d 659 (1986); *In re Reed*, 100 Ill. App. 3d 873, 427 N.E.2d 282, 56 Ill. Dec. 202 (1981); *Brunson v. Brunson*, 569 S.W.2d 173 (Ky. Ct. App. 1978); *Cartwright v. Cartwright*, 707 S.W.2d 469 (Mo. Ct. App. 1986).

3. This is the general rule. There are some states, however, where the court has the power to distribute any property owned at the time of the parties' divorce, including property owned by them at the time of their marriage. *See* footnote 14 of Chapter 3, *Equitable Distribution and Divorce Mediation*. *See also, Carlson v. Carlson*, 722 P.2d 222 (Alaska 1986); *Ernst v. Ernst*, 503 N.E.2d 619 (Ind. Ct. App. 1987); *Anderson v. Anderson*, 368 N.W.2d 566 (N.D. 1985).

4. *Price v. Price*, 69 N.Y.2d 8, 503, N.E.2d 684, 511 N.Y.S.2d 219 (1986). *See, e.g.,* Ky. Rev. Stat. Ann. §401.190 (Michie/Bobbs-Merrill 1984 & 1986 Supp.).

5. Although retirement benefits include more than simply pensions, the discussion that follows will be limited to pension benefits.

6. *See, e.g., Majouskas v. Majouskas*, 61 N.Y.2d 481, 463 N.E.2d 15, 474 N.Y.S.2d 699 (1984); *King v. King*, 9 F.L.R. (B.N.A.) 2273 (Pa. Ct. Comm. Pleas 1983).

7. *Majouskas v. Majouskas, Supra*. If the husband is no longer employed in the place of employment where he was previously accruing pension benefits (he stopped working there five years ago, at a time when his pension rights were vested), it is not necessary to resort to this formula as the calculation can be made at the present time.

8. The one exception to this would be where one of the parties wishes to offset the value of those pension benefits with other property they own. This would occur, for example, if one of the parties suggested an agreement whereby the husband will deed his interest in the parties' home to the wife and the wife will waive her interest in his pension. They know, or could easily determine, what the approximate present value of their home is. But what is the present value of the husband's future pension benefits?

9. While this may not be the case where the husband has a substantial salary, and his pension benefits will represent a very large percentage of that salary, it will be the case in the majority of situations, particularly where it required two incomes to support the parties prior to their retirement, but where only one of them has any substantial pension benefits that will be available to them following their retirement.

10. *See, e.g., Capponi v. Capponi*, 10 F.L.R. (B.N.A.) 1696 (Pa. Ct. Comm. Pleas 1984). It was this fact that caused Justice Meyer to express his concern in *O'Brien v. O'Brien* when he said, "[t]he equitable distribution provisions of the Domestic Relations Law were intended to provide flexibility so that equity could be done. But if the assumption as to career choice on which a distributive award payable over a number of years is based turns out not to be the fact . . . , it should be possible for the court to revise the distributive award to conform to the fact." 66 N.Y.2d 576, 592, 489 N.E.2d 712, 720, 498 N.Y.S.2d 743, 751 (1985) (Meyer, concurring). It was this same concern that caused the court in Kentucky to reject the idea that a

professional license was marital property. *Inman v. Inman*, 648 S.W.2d 847 (Ky. 1982). It is no answer to this to say that all that the court is doing is dividing marital property. What the court is doing is attempting to do equity between the parties, and dividing marital property is simply the means that is being employed for that purpose. But to become fixated over the means (the division of marital property) at the expense of doing equity between the parties (ignoring where that division may leave them in the future) is to take legal fictions too literally and to lose sight of why they were created in the first place.

11. *See, e.g.*, *O'Brien v. O'Brien*, 66 N.Y.2d 576, 489 N.E.2d 712, 498 N.Y.S.2d 743 (1985).

12. This is not to suggest that a Qualified Domestic Relations Order (QDRO) can be drafted to include all of these contingencies, or, more importantly, that it will be accepted by the plan administrator even if it does. On the contrary, it may be necessary for the agreement to contain a special provision (perhaps a provision for an alimony payment to be made by the wife to the husband equal to the amount of the pension benefits which she will receive under the QDRO) should any of those contingencies arise. It is only to suggest that it is possible to approach these problems more constructively in mediation (or in any private agreement, for that matter) than is the case when the decision is made by a court of law.

13. I.R.C. s 1034 (West 1988 Supp.)

14. It must also be remembered that the husband will lose a very substantial portion of his equity in the form of ta: es that will be imposed upon the gain he receives at that time, and will thus not have those monies available to him to reinvest in a new home, as will his wife. I.R.C. § 1034 (West 1988 Supp.).

15. Many pension plans do not contain the first of these three options.

16. A number of courts have held that they have the power to require the husband to choose an option which will provide survivorship benefits to his wife. *McDermott v. McDermott*, 119 A.D.2d 370, 507 N.Y.S.2d 390 (1986); *In re Marriage of Allison*, 189 Cal. App. 3d 849, 234 Cal. Rptr. 671 (1987).

17. Again, it may not be possible to provide this in the QDRO, or to get the plan administrator to accept it even if it is. However, this can again be accomplished by having the agreement provide that upon the husband's retirement, and commencing with the first pension payment, the wife will pay support to the husband, during his lifetime, equal to the difference in the amount of the pension payments which he actually receives and the amount of the pension payments which he would have received had he not elected that option.

Chapter 17—Support—Preliminary Considerations

1. Suppose, for example, the couple has two infant children. If the available dollars were distributed on a per capita basis, then, if the husband's after tax income was $20,000 and the wife's none, he would be allotted $5,000, she would be allotted $5,000, and each of their two children would be allotted $5,000. Since support payments are never made on this basis, then, and again from this standpoint, the husband will be left with more than his wife or either of their two children.

2. While the question of the disposition of the parties' marital residence is to a very great extent dependent upon the available dollars, as a general rule it is still best to ignore this fact and to proceed to a discussion of its disposition before the issue of support is taken up. (An obvious exception to this is where it is readily apparent to the mediator that the cost of maintaining the home is not consonant with the dollars that will be available to the parties following their separation.) The reason for this is that the mediator would first like to determine how each of the parties, and particularly the party with whom the children will not be living on a day-to-day basis—usually the husband—feels about their continuing to live in the home, and perhaps to get a commitment from him in this regard before the issue of support is addressed, as this will affect how the mediator will approach that question when it is taken up.

3. Before intervening, the mediator must first make a determination in his own mind as to whether or not it is realistic for the wife, in this case, to continue to live with the children in the home. In most instances, he should be able to do this quite easily with the information that he already has available to him. If he feels that it will help him to look at the wife's budget in making this determination, he can, of course, do that also.

4. This is not to suggest that "ability" is necessarily easier to determine than "need." (In fact, whether it should

be a relevant consideration or not, the husband's "willingness" to make the payment will often become as important a factor as his "ability.") It is simply to suggest that, in addressing the problem, adversarial lawyers tend to start with the husband's ability (income) rather than with the wife's needs (budget).

5. Child Support Enforcement Amendments of 1984, Pub. L. No. 98-378, (codified at 42 U.S.C. § 667 (1985)).

6. The reasons for this are set forth in Chapter 18, *Support and Maintenance—When, How Much, and How Long?*

CHAPTER 18—SUPPORT—WHEN, HOW MUCH, AND HOW LONG?

1. Weitzman, Lenore J., *The Divorce Revolution: The Unexpected Social and Economic Consequences for Women and Children*, (New York, NY: The Free Press, 1985), pages 338–9.

2. These guidelines, and the other guidelines which we will discuss, are summarized in Table 18-1 (pp. 353–356).

3. However, the wife can be given more money here by increasing the child support payment (e.g., by 40%) and by allocating a portion of the total (e.g., 60%) as maintenance.

4. Unfortunately, the partnership or co-venture theory of modern marriage will cause many to take issue with this conclusion. When it is the wife who is the recipient of the payments in question, they may even view it as patronizing. After all, why should the wife and children only have what they need, while the husband here is left with more then he needs? If the fictions created by modern matrimonial law are taken literally, and as if they were an inflexible part of reality, then obviously they should not be.

   We would argue, however, that those fictions were only created out of necessity to deal with the problem of divorce in modern marriages. To lose sight of the fact that they are but social constructs, or worse, to view them apart from the problems that they were intended to *solve*, is to lose sight of their purpose. It is also to make us slaves to those constructs and bind us to follow them wherever they may lead us. To go back to our example, if we are offended by the result, it is not because it is necessarily inequitable. It may offend us simply because it is inconsistent with the fictions we have created as a vehicle to achieve such equity, and which we have unthinkingly confused with it.

5. While the child support guidelines mandated by the Child Support Enforcement Amendments of 1984 are intended to address this problem, they will only reduce it, not eliminate it. Furthermore, they are concerned with child support, not spousal support, and will thus only address a portion of the problem. Then too, it is still too early to determine what application they will have when both child support and spousal support are at issue.

6. The different tax treatment for child support payments, on the one hand, and alimony or maintenance on the other hand, is discussed at greater length in Chapter 22, *Income Taxes*.

7. The following discussion assumes that the husband is obligated both for the support of the wife and for the support of their child or children.

8. Prior to 1984, that was always the case. Under the present code, however, it is possible that this is not true since, after peaking at 33%, the tax rate then reduces again to 28%. Thus a wife earning $65,000, and filing as head of household, is in a higher tax bracket, as far as her last taxable dollars, than is a husband who earns $200,000, regardless of his filing status. Tax charts, showing the federal tax rates for each filing status, are set forth at the conclusion of Chapter 22, *Income Taxes*.

9. If this is done, the mediator must be careful to provide that the support payment will stop more than six months before or more than six months after the 18th and 21st birthdays of the child. This will be discussed at greater length in Chapter 22, *Income Taxes*, starting at page 417.

10. In the past, it was very common to allocate a portion of the payment as alimony even when the husband's support obligation was only for the children, especially when the husband was in a very high tax bracket. This was because the child support payments were paid by him in after-tax dollars. If he could shift a portion of his income to the wife in the form of an alimony or maintenance payment, far less of the money would have to be paid in taxes, since the wife was usually in a much lower tax bracket and often had a significant portion of her income sheltered by the deductions for mortgage interest and real estate taxes that she was able to take in connection with the home. A husband's ability to do this was greatly curtailed by the Deficit Reduction Act of 1984. His motive for doing so was further reduced by the Tax Reform Act of 1986 which, by lowering the maximum tax bracket from 50 percent to 33 percent, also reduced the spread in the tax brackets of the husband and wife.

11. Most equitable distribution statutes provide that the amount of property distributed is a factor to be taken into consideration in making an award of spousal support. *See, e.g.*, Del. Code Ann. tit. 13, § 1512 (1981 & 1986 Supp.); Ill. Ann. Stat. ch. 40, para. 504 (Smith-Hurd 1980 & 1987 Supp.); Ind. Code Ann. §31-1-11.5-11(e) (West 1981 & 1987 Supp.); Iowa Code Ann. § 598.21(3) (West 1981 & 1987 Supp.); Minn. Stat. Ann. § 518.552(2) (West 1969 & 1987 Supp.).

12. Again, if the reader is bothered by this result it is because he has become a captive of the constructs created by the law to deal with the problem of modern marriage, and has taken them too literally. Since the value of the assets retained by the husband are equal to those that were distributed to the wife, and since his income is many times hers, it would seem that they have been left in very inequitable positions. To begin with, and legal fictions aside, to view the value assigned by a court to the husband's practice as being equal to the same number of dollars in the bank that were distributed to the wife would be wrong. It would only be to compound that error then to treat his income as an attorney as being separate and apart from the value that a court has assigned to that practice as, legal fictions aside once again, the only real value that the husband's practice has is the opportunity which it will afford him to earn income as an attorney in the future.

    (While it is possible to sell an interest in certain professional practices, and while partners in a professional practice may have an agreement between themselves in the event of one of the partner's retirement from the practice, the money that the husband will receive in this event is usually very small in relationship to the value of that practice as an ongoing businesses.) Just as importantly, it is not the purpose of equitable distribution statutes to leave the parties on an equal footing or, in this case, the wife with an income equal to that of her husband's. Its purpose is to see to it that their divorce does not leave them in grossly inequitable positions, based upon changes in position that took place as a result of their marriage, as was so often the case under previous law, and to narrow the gap in their respective circumstances when that is the case, particularly in marriages of long duration.

13. *See, e.g.*, Colo. Rev. Stat. § 14-10-114 (1974 & 1986 Supp.); Idaho Code § 32-705 (1983 & 1987 Supp.); Ky. Rev. Stat. Ann. § 403.200 (Michie/Bobbs-Merrill 1984 & 1986 Supp.); Mont. Code Ann. § 40-4-203 (1986); N.Y. Dom. Rel. Law § 236-B (McKinney 1986).

14. Again, for those who view the fictions created by the law to deal with the problem of divorce in modern marriage as literal truths, this will seem inconsistent with those fictions and, therefore, unfair. However, for those who understand that those fictions are only a means of doing equity, and are not to be confused with equity, it will not. Thus, the equitable distribution statutes of most states specifically direct the court to consider the separate property of each of the parties in effectuating an equitable distribution of their marital property. Some states—and this should hopefully put to rest the fiction once and for all—make a distinction between separate property acquired during a marriage and prior to the marriage, and will award an interest in the property acquired during the marriage to the non-titled spouse. *Cassiday v. Cassiday*, 716 P.2d 1145 (1985), *aff'd in part, rev'd in part*, 716 P.2d 1133 (1986), while others do not make this distinction and will grant the nontitled spouse an interest in the separate property that was owned at the time of the marriage as well. *See, e.g., Sayer v. Sayer*, 11 F.L.R. (B.N.A.) 1328 (Del. 1985).

15. There are certain states which apply a more elastic measuring stick. *See, e.g.*, Cal. Civil Code § 4700.7 (West 1983 & 1987 Supp.); Haw. Rev. Stat. § 580.47 (1985).

16. Some states, such as New York, provide for support until 21, although a child is emancipated for all purposes at age 18. *See, e.g.*, N.Y. Dom Rel. Law § 32(3) (McKinney 1988); Ind. Code Ann. § 31-1-11.5-17(b) (West 1979); Mo. Ann. Stat. § 452.370 (Vernon 1986). *See also, Harris v. Harris*, 670 S.W.2d 171 (Mo. Ct. App. 1984).

17. For a discussion of this, see Lawrence Stone, *The Family, Sex and Marriage in England, 1500–1800*, (New York, NY: Harper & Row, 1977), Chapter 8.

18. In 1947, 20 percent of all married women were working. By 1978, 48% of married women had entered into the labor force. Ralph E. Smith (ed.), *The Subtle Revolution: Women at Work*, (Washington D.C.: The Urban Institute, 1979).

19. In 1960, there were approximately 393,000 divorces in the United States, or 2.2 per thousand total population. By 1973, just thirteen years later, the rate had doubled to 4.4 per thousand total population. That translated into approximately 915,000 divorces. Two years later the figure exceed 1,000,000 and the rate climbed to 4.9 per thousand. National Center for Health Statistics: Advance Report of Final Divorce Statistics, 1981. *Monthly Vital Statistics Report*. Vol.32-No. 9, Supp. (2). DHHS Pub. No. (PHS) 84-1120, (Hyattsville, Md: Jan., 1984). Since 1978, the number of divorces has never been less than 1,100,000 and the rate has been between 4.9 and 5.2%.

20. This statement should not be taken literally, since to provide support for the wife which will end, for example, when the youngest child graduates from high school or college is to run afoul of Section 71(c)(2) of the Internal Revenue Code. This will be discussed in Chapter 22, *Income Taxes*.

21. *See, e.g.*, N.Y. Dom. Rel. Law § 248 (McKinney 1986); Okla. Stat. Ann. tit. 12, § 1289D.

22. While this has generally been the rule, in recent years a number of courts have broken with it and have directed that the support payments that one of the parties, usually the husband, is obligated to make to the other will increase as the cost of living increases. *See, e.g., In re Marriage of Nesset*, 345 N.W.2d 107 (Iowa 1984); *In re Marriage of Ortiz*, 108 Wash. 2d 643, 740 P.2d 843 (1987); *In re Marriage of Lamm*, 682 P.2d 67 (Colo. Ct. App. 1984); *Blomgren v. Blomgren*, 367 M.W.2d 918 (Minn. Ct. App. 1984).

23. Some courts have held that the mere increase in the cost of living, standing alone, is generally not sufficient to warrant an increase in payments. *See, e.g., Martin v. Martin*, 479 So.2d 51 (Ala. Ct. App. 1985); *Mandy v. Williams*, 492 So.2d 759 (Fla. Dist. Ct. App. 1986); *Crowell v. Crowell*, 742 S.W.2d 244 (Mo. Ct. App. 1987).

24. *See, e.g., In re Marriage of Cisek*, 409 N.W.2d 233 (Minn. Ct. App. 1987); *Gross v. Gross*, 355 N.W.2d 4 (S.D. 1984). Similarly, the husband has to show a decrease in earnings that will amount to a substantial change in his circumstances before his situation will warrant a reduction in the support payments. *In re Marriage of Richardson*, 693 P.2d 524 (Mont. 1985).

25. *See, e.g.*, N.Y. Dom. Rel. Law § 236(9)(b) (McKinney 1986).

26. *See, e.g., Weise v. Weise*, 699 P.2d 700 (Utah 1985); *Zaragoza v. Capriola*, 201 N.J. Super. 55, 492 A.2d 698 (1985); *Eckhardt v. Eckhardt*, 37 A.D.2d 629, 323 N.Y.S.2d 611 (1971); *Stahl v. Department of Social Services*, 43 Wash App. 401, 717 P.2d 320 (1986).

27. *See, e.g., Miller v. Miller*, 97 N.J. 154, 478 A.2d 351 (1984).

28. These same considerations will also bear on the question of visitation. In this respect, see the discussion in Chapter 14, *Children*, in Part II, on page 211.

29. *Fry v. Schwarting*, 4 Va. App. 173, 355 S.E.2d 342 (1987).

Chapter 19—Medical and Life Insurance

1. Until recently, she could also be turned down, at least in terms of her previous coverage. This has now been remedied, at least for a period of three years, by the Consolidated Omnibus Budget Reconciliation Act of 1985 (C.O.B.R.A.), Pub. L. No. 99-272, Title X.

2. To be sure, in many instances the wife could apply to the court to require her husband to assume all or a portion of these unreimbursed expenses. *Callen v. Callen*, 257 Ala. 226, 58 So.2d 462 (1952); *Harp v. McCann*, 97 A.D.2d 868, 469 N.Y.S.2d 266 (1983). However, as a general rule, the court will not grant the wife's application unless the expenses in question are extraordinary. *Grobleski v. Grobleski*, 408 So.2d 693 (Fla. Dist. Ct. App. 1982); *In re Marriage of Arnold*, 122 Ill. App. 3d 776, 462 N.E.2d 51, 78 Ill. Dec. 335 (1984); *Nuckols v. Nuckols*, 12 Ohio App. 3d 94, 467 N.E.2d 259 (1983).

3. It is for this reason that a husband was not generally obligated to maintain policies of insurance on his life for his wife, or even for his children. In recent years, however, and particularly with the enactment of equitable distribution statutes, many courts have now been given the authority to direct husbands (and, where appropriate, wives) to maintain policies on their lives. *See, e.g.*, Fla. Stat. Ann. § 61.08(3) (West 1985); N.Y. Dom. Rel. Law § 236 (McKinney 1986).

4. There is no estate tax on an estate of less than $600,000. I.R.C. § 2010 (West 1988 Supp.). If the husband's taxable estate, including the proceeds of such insurance, is less than $600,000, which is usually the case, the wife will not have to pay federal estate tax on the insurance policies.

Chapter 20—College

1. *See, e.g., Wolk v. Saidel*, 135 A.D.2d 987, 522 N.Y.S.2d 705 (1987); *Miller v. Miller*, 163 Ill. App. 3d 602, 516 N.E.2d 837, 114 Ill. Dec. 682 (1987).

2. It would be wrong to conclude from this that women who resort to mediation pay a larger portion of their children's college education expenses than do women who resort to traditional adversarial divorce proceedings. It is only the fact that college education expenses are included in mediated agreements so much more often than they are in agreements concluded through adversarial proceedings that would suggest this. Obviously, if the agreement contains no provision requiring the husband to contribute toward these expenses, it will be silent as to the wife's obligation as well. But this does not mean that she will not have any obligation. In fact, and as a practical matter, she may end up shouldering almost all of it.

3. A procedure that can be employed for this purpose is set forth in Chapter 21, *Memorandum of Agreement*, on pages 395–396.

CHAPTER 21—MEMORANDUM OF AGREEMENT

1. It is improper for a mediator, who is not a lawyer, to draw the final agreement that the parties will sign and to then administer its execution, and he does so at the risk of being accused of unauthorized practice of the law. *See, e.g.*, N.Y. Jud. Law § 478 (McKinney 1983).

2. We have previously had occasion to comment upon having the couple sign an agreement that they will be fair and equitable with one another, and will not comment upon it further at this point.

3. When a board of directors of a public corporation deliberates on an issue, takes a vote and comes to a result, the minutes simply reflect that the matter was discussed, a vote taken, and a resolution adopted or rejected. To leave in the minutes the minority's opinion is simply to provide dissident shareholders with ammunition should it later turn out that the minority was correct. Mediators should take note.

CHAPTER 22—INCOME TAXES

1. I.R.C. § 215 (West 1988 Supp.).

2. I.R.C. § 71 (West 1988 Supp.).

3. I.R.C. § 215(a) (West 1988 Supp.).

4. I.R.C. § 71(b)(1) (West 1988 Supp.). Payments made by check or money order will qualify as well. Temp. Treas. Regs. § 1.71-1T(b)Q-5 (1984).

5. I.R.C. § 71(b)(1)(A) (West 1988 Supp.).

6. *Id.*

7. I.R.C. § 71(b)(1)(D) (West 1988 Supp.).

8. It is only the payments that are to be made following the wife's death that will fail to qualify, not all of the payments. This will also apply to a substitute payment to be made after the death of the recipient spouse. If it is the intention of the parties to make a payment in a fixed amount, payable over a stated period, that will nevertheless qualify and be deductible by the husband, it is possible to achieve this by means of a life insurance policy (perhaps declining term) on the wife's life that will insure that she (and her estate) will receive the full amount bargained for, despite her death. The House Ways and Means Committee Report which was issued in connection with the 1984 Act suggests that the proceeds of the policy of insurance will not be considered a substitute for any such violative payment and that it would be permissible for the husband to pay the premiums on that policy. H.R. Rep. No. 98-432, Part 2, 98th cong., 2d Sess. 1496 (1984).

9. I.R.C. § 71(b)(1)(C) (West 1988 Supp.); Temp. Treas. Regs. § 1.71-1T(b)Q-9 (1984).

10. I.R.C. § 71(b)(1)(B) (West 1988 Supp.).

11. The Code also includes payments made to third parties on behalf of the spouse. Thus, if the agreement requires the husband to maintain medical insurance for his wife's benefit, premiums paid by the husband will be deemed alimony taxable to the wife and deductible by the husband. If the parties do not intend that result, it is again important that the agreement specifically provide that those payments will not be treated as alimony. I.R.C. § 71(b)(1)(B) (West 1988 Supp.).

12. The 1984 Act contained the requirement that if payments were to be made in excess of $10,000 in any calendar year, then no portion of such payments in excess of $10,000 paid in any year will be treated as

alimony unless the agreement or decree contained provision that payments (not necessarily in excess of $10,000 a year) would be made in each of the six post-separation years, unless the payments would otherwise terminate within the six year period by reason of the death of either of the parties, or by reason of the remarriage of the party receiving the payments. (If none of the payments in the first six post-separation years exceeded $10,000, there was no requirement that payments be made in each of the first six post-separation years.) This requirement was eliminated by the 1986 Act with respect to all instruments signed after December 31, 1986.

13. The 1984 Act related to payments made within the first six post-separation years. The 1986 Act, which applies to payments made under instruments executed after December 31, 1986, replaced this with a three-year recapture rule. I.R.C. § (71)(f) (West 1988 Supp.).

14. I.R.C. § 71(f)(3), (4) (West 1988 Supp.). The application of the recapture rules are rather complicated, and it is not very important that a mediator know how to apply them. What the mediator must know, however, is that the rule may be violated if there is a reduction in the payments within the first three post-separation years. Rarely will it be important for either the parties or the mediator to know what the penalty will be for violating the rules. After all, the point is to avoid the penalty, not to determine it. Therefore, if the proposed payment contains a reduction within the first three post-separation years, then, and unless the mediator is an attorney familiar with the application of the rules, the parties should be referred to either a qualified attorney or accountant for a determination as to whether or not the rule will be violated.

15. I.R.C. § 71(f)(6) (West 1988 Supp.).

16. I.R.C. § 71(f)(5)(C) (West 1988 Supp.).

17. I.R.C. § 71(f)(5)(A) (West 1988 Supp.). There is another exception to the recapture rule but it is not one which will normally concern mediators. That is that the rule does not apply when the support payments have been fixed by court order rather than by an agreement between the parties. I.R.C. § (f)(5)(B).

18. I.R.C. § 71(c) (West 1988 Supp.).

19. *Commissioner v. Lester*, 366 U.S. 299 (1961).

20. I.R.C. § 71(c)(2) (West 1988 Supp.).

21. I.R.C. § 71(c)(2)(B) (West 1988 Supp.).

22. Temp. Treas. Regs. § 1.71-1T(c)Q-18 (1984).

23. *Id.*

24. *Id.*

25. *Id.*

26. *Id.* (emphasis added). While it will not be difficult for an experienced mediator, even one who is not an attorney, to fashion an agreement that will not violate the contingency test when there is only one child involved, in no event should he attempt to meet the requirement of the multiple reduction test on his own. In fact, the test is a very complicated one, and its applications are so much narrower and its benefits so much smaller, that it is almost never employed by attorneys who negotiate agreements for separating and divorcing couples.

27. I.R.C. § 7703(a)(1) (West 1988 Supp.).

28. I.R.C. § 2(b)(1) (West 1988 Supp.).

29. I.R.C. § 7703(b) (West 1988 Supp.).

30. I.R.C. § 2(b)(1)(A) (West 1988 Supp.).

31. *Id.*

32. Treas. Regs. § 1.2-2(b)(6)(d) (1984).

33. *Id.*

34. Temp. Treas. Regs. § 1.71-1T(c) (1984).

35. I.R.C. § 2(b)(1)(A)(i) (West 1988 Supp.).

36. If they are still legally married at the close of the tax year in question, however, she must be entitled to claim the child as an exemption for that year. I.R.C. § 7703(b)(1) (West 1988 Supp.).

37. I.R.C. § 21 (West 1988 Supp.).

38. *Id.*

39. I.R.C. § 21(a)(2) (West 1988 Supp.).

40. I.R.C. § 21(d)(1) (West 1988 Supp.).

41. I.R.C. § 21(c) (West 1988 Supp.).

42. I.R.C. § 151(a), (b), (c). A dependent is generally defined as an individual who receives over half his support during the taxable year from the taxpayer, and who is related to the taxpayer in one of the following ways:

1. A son or daughter of the taxpayer, or a descendant of either,

2. A stepson or stepdaughter of the taxpayer,

3. A brother, sister, stepbrother, or stepsister of the taxpayer,

4. The father or mother of the taxpayer, or an ancestor of either,

5. A stepfather or stepmother of the taxpayer,

6. A son or daughter of a brother or sister of the taxpayer,

7. A brother or sister of the mother or father of the taxpayer,

8. A son-in-law, daughter-in-law, father-in-law, mother-in-law, brother-in-law, or sister-in-law of the taxpayer, or

9. An individual (other than an individual who at any time during the taxable year was the spouse, determined without regard to section 7703, of the taxpayer) who, for the taxable year of the taxpayer, has as his principal place of abode the home of the taxpayer and is a member of the taxpayer's household." I.R.C. § 152 (West 1988 Supp.).

43. I.R.C. § 151(d)(3) (West 1988 Supp.).

44. I.R.C. § 152(e)(1) (West 1988 Supp.).

45. I.R.C. § 152(e)(2) (West 1988 Supp.).

46. There is a problem that a mediator should expect in connection with the allocation of these exemptions. Many people who will come into mediation will know, or will have heard, that the law says that the custodial parent is entitled to claim the children as exemptions. Unfortunately, the custodial parent in this instance will tend to read more into the law than is appropriate. The rule established by the Code does not, and was not intended, to constitute a judgment by the Federal Government as to who should more appropriately be entitled to claim the children as exemptions. In fact, the former rule, which generally gave the exemption to the noncustodial parent if he or she made payments to the custodial parent for the support of the children, was far more appropriate (equitable), since the custodial parent received those payments without the obligation to pay taxes on them.

   The new rule was enacted simply for the convenience of the Internal Revenue Service, which did not want to be in the position of having to guess which of the parents was actually entitled to claim the children as exemptions. Thus, they wanted a simple rule that could be applied in all situations, namely, that the parent with whom the children principally resided (the custodial parent) was entitled to the exemption. More importantly, and rather than being dependent upon the couple's agreement, or any other extraneous document not necessarily in their possession, the Internal Revenue Service wanted to have to look to but one document, namely, the written declaration that had to be signed by the custodial parent and filed by the noncustodial parent with his tax return if he were to be given credit for the exemption which he claimed for a child. In short, there is nothing in the change effectuated by the Tax Reform Act of 1984 which should change the presumption which previously prevailed, which was that the exemption for a child would be given to the party who was obligated to make child support payments to the other party.

   More importantly, there is nothing in the change that should be deemed to suggest that the law has made a determination that the custodial parent should be the one who has the right to claim the child as an exemption, and a court of law, like the parties themselves, has the power to ignore the direction made by the Code, grant the exemption to the noncustodial parent, and direct the custodial parent to sign the necessary written declaration. *Cross v. Cross*, 363 S.E.2d 449 (W.V. 1987). There is also a minority view which holds that the Tax Reform Act of 1984 divested state courts of jurisdiction over which party could take the exemption. *Lorenz v. Lorenz*, 166 Mich. App. 58, 419 N.W.2d 770 (1988). *See also, Davis v. Fair*, 707 S.W.2d 711 (Texas 1986).

47. *U.S. v. Davis*, 370 U.S. 65 (1962). However, after 1984, the husband would recognize no gain or loss on such transfer. I.R.C. § 1041 (West 1988 Supp.); Temp. Treas. Regs. § 1.1041T(d)Q-10 (1984).

48. I.R.C. § 1041 (West 1988 Supp.).

49. Temp. Treas. Regs. § 1.1041-1T(b), Q7 (1984). This is an issue that can arise very often in mediation. By the terms of the parties' agreement, the wife is given the right to continue to live in the marital residence until either her remarriage or until the youngest child graduates from high school or college, whichever first occurs. At that time the home is to be sold, except that the wife is given an option to purchase the husband's interest rather than having it sold to a third party. The youngest child will not graduate from high school for eight more years and, since it is their intention to be divorced immediately, the sale by the husband to the wife at that time will not be related to the cessation of their marriage.

   But suppose that the wife should remarry and exercise her option within the six-year period? In that instance the husband will receive the consideration for his interest in the home tax free (just as would have been the case had the wife bought out his interest presently, and at the time of the signing of their agreement) and the wife will receive no credit, in terms of an increase in her basis, by reason of the payment which she has made to the husband for his interest in the home.

Quite obviously, in any discussions between the parties concerning the present or future transfer of property between them, they should be made aware of these tax implications. While the parties cannot obviously change the law in this respect (and the Internal Revenue Code represents one of the very few exceptions to the rule that the parties are free to make their own law as between themselves), there is nothing to say that their agreement cannot provide that the husband will share with the wife any tax obligation that she may later have in connection with her subsequent sale of the home.

50. Id.
51. I.R.C. § 1034 (West 1988 Supp.). This will be discussed in the next section, entitled *The Sale of the Parties' Principal Residence.*
52. I.R.C. § 121 (West 1988 Supp.). This will be discussed in the next section, entitled *The Sale of the Parties' Principal Residence.*
53. I.R.C. § 1034 (West 1988 Supp.).
54. If they are not selling the home presently, and if one of them (for example, the wife) is going to have the exclusive right to use it until it is sold, then they will not both meet the requirements, and only the wife, whose principal residence it will be at the time of its sale, will be able to avail herself of the right to roll over her portion of the gain. I.R.C. § 1034(a) (West 1988 Supp.).
55. I.R.C. § 121(a), (b). This exclusion can only be taken once in a lifetime.
56. I.R.C. § 121(d) (West 1988 Supp.).
57. However, if they are not both over 55, then to get the maximum exclusion of $125,000 they must file a joint return and both make the election. I.R.C. § 121(c), (d) (West 1988 Supp.).
58. I.R.C. § 121(b)(1) (West 1988 Supp.).
59. Id.
60. I.R.C. § 121(b)(2), § 121(d)(6) (West 1988 Supp.).

CHAPTER 23—THE COST OF RAISING A CHILD

1. *See*, Thomas J. Espenshade, *Investing in Children*, (Washington, D.C.: Urban Institute Press, 1984), Chapter 2, at 11–16.
2. Social Security Act, section 467 (codified as 42 U.S.C. § 667 et. seq.).
3. Espenshade, *Investing In Children, Supra.*
4. The study was based on 8,547 husband/wife families taken from the 1972–1973 consumer expenditure survey conducted by the United States Bureau of the Census on behalf of the Bureau of Labor Statistics.
5. In private mediation the overwhelming majority of couples will fit into this category.
6. The study assumed that the wives in each group had the same education as their husbands.
7. In every instance, where the couple had more than one child, the expenses for the first child were greater than for the second, and the second greater than for the third. Thus, the expenditure here was $99.89 per week for the first child, $91.98 per week for the second and $88.78 per week for the third. Espenshade, *Investing In Children*, at 26.
8. *Id*, at 28.
9. *Id*, at 3.
10. *Id*.
11. *Id*, at 4.
12. *Id*, at 35.
13. *Id*, at 41.
14. *Id*, at 48.
15. *Id*, at 5.
16. While this fact may not be readily apparent, it should be from the very classification of children into these various socioeconomic groups. It is also apparent from the different expenditures made for each of the

children in the same group. How can we say, for example, that the needs of a child in a one-child family are greater than the needs of each of the children in a two- or three-child family, or that the needs of the third child in a three-child family are not as great as the needs of the first child? Yet if needs are predicated on expenditures, that is the conclusion we are drawn to by Espenshade's study. Nor can you solve the problem by rejecting Espenshade's apportionment, and by saying that the amount spent on each of the children in a two or three child family is equal, and not disproportionate as he maintains. If we do that for the first two children in a three-child family, for example, then that logic leads to the inevitable conclusion that their needs decrease when their parents have a third child, since averaging in the expenditures made for the third child will reduce the average.

17. Espenshade, *Investing In Children*, at 2.
18. *Id.*
19. *Id*, at 19.
20. *Id*, at 1.
21. *Id*, at 5.
22. *Id.*
23. *Id.*
24. *Id.*

BIBLIOGRAPHY

Ady, Ronald W., *The Investment Evaluator*, (Englewood Cliffs, NJ: Prentice-Hall, 1984).

Alternative Means of Family Dispute Resolution, (Washington, D.C.: American Bar Association, 1982).

Pension Plans and Divorce, 8 Family Advocate 2 (Chicago, IL: American Bar Association, Fall 1985).

Aries, Philip, *Centuries of Childhood*, (New York, NY: Random House, Inc., 1962).

Avner, Judith I. and Herman, Susan, *Mediation: A Guide for Women*, N.O.W. Legal Defense and Education Fund.

Bahr, S. J., *An Evaluation of Court Mediation: A Comparison in Divorce Cases with Children*, 2 J. Fam. Issues 39 (1981).

Bahr, S. J., *Marital Dissolution Laws: Impact of Recent Changes for Women*, 4 J. Fam. Issues 455 (1983).

Bandler, Richard and Grinder, John, *The Structure of Magic*, (Palo Alto, CA: Science and Behavior Books, 1975).

Berger, Peter L. and Kellner, Hansfried, *Marriage and the Construction of Reality*, 46 Diogenes 1–24 (Summer 1964).

Berger, Peter L. and Luckman, Thomas, *The Social Construction of Reality*, (Garden City, NY: Doubleday & Co., 1966).

Blades, Joan, *Family Mediation*, (Englewood Cliffs, NJ: Prentice-Hall, 1985).

Blanck, Rubin and Blanck, Gertrude, *Marriage & Personal Development*, (New York, NY: Columbia University Press, 1968).

Bowman, M. E. and Ahrons, C. R., *Impact of Legal Custody Status on Fathers' Parenting Postdivorce*, 47 J. Marriage & Fam. 481 (1985).

Brown, D. G., *Divorce and Family Mediation: History, Review, and Future Directions*, 20 Conciliation Cts. Rev. 1 (1982).

Burger, Warren E., Chief Justice, address given on January 24, 1982 before the American Bar Association in Chicago, The American Bar Association Journal, March, 1982.

Cafarakis, Christian, *The Fabulous Onassis—His Life, His Loves*, (New York, NY: William Morrow & Co., 1972).

Cherlin, Andrew J., *Marriage, Divorce, Remarriage*, (Cambridge, MA: Harvard University Press, 1981).

Chesler, Phyllis, *Mothers on Trial; The Battle for Children & Custody*, (New York, NY: McGraw-Hill, 1986).

Cohen, Harriet N. and Hillman, Adria S., *Diagnosis Confirmed: EDL is Ailing*, 17 Fam. L. Rev. 3 (Family Law Section, N.Y. State Bar Assoc., July 1985).

Committee on the Family of the Group for the Advancement of Psychiatry, *New Trends in Child Custody Determination*, (NJ: Law and Business, Inc., Harcourt Brace Jovanovich, 1980.)

Coogler, O. J., *Structured Mediation in Divorce Settlements: A Handbook for Marital Mediators*, (Lexington, MA: Lexington Books, 1978).

Crouch, Richard E., *Divorce Mediation and Legal Ethics*, 16 Fam. L.Q. 228 (Fall 1982).

Espenshade, Thomas J., *Investing In Children*, (Washington D.C.: Urban Institute Press, 1984).

Espenshade, Thomas J., *Raising a Child Can Now Cost $85,000*, 8 Intercom 9 (Population Reference Bureau, Inc., September 1980).

Felder, Raoul, *Divorce—The Way Things Are, Not the Way They Should Be*, (New York, NY: World Publishing, 1971).

Fisher, Roger D. and Ury, William, *Getting to Yes*, (Boston, MA: Houghton Mifflin Co., 1981).

Folberg, Jay, (Editor), *Joint Custody and Shared Parenting*, (Washington, D.C.: The Bureau of National Affairs, Inc. and the Association of Family and Conciliation Courts, 1984).

Foster, Henry H., *Vertigo v. Vertigo*, 18 Fam. L. Rev. 20 (Family Law Section, N.Y. State Bar Assoc. Feb. 1986).

Foster, Henry H., *A Second Opinion: New York's EDL Is Alive and Well and Is Being Fairly Administered*, 17 Fam. L. Rev. 3, (Family Law Section, N.Y. State Bar Assoc., April 1985).

Francke, Linda Bird, *Growing Up Divorced*, (New York, NY: Simon & Schuster, 1983).

Frank, Catherine, *Major Constructs of Contextual Therapy: An Interview with Dr. Ivan Boszormenyi-Nagy*, 12 Am. J. Fam. Therapy 7, (New York, NY: Brunner/Mazel, Inc., 1984).

Freud, Sigmund, *Civilization and Its Discontents*, (New York, NY: W. W. Norton & Co., Inc., 1961). (Originally published London: Hogarth Press, 1930.)

Fromm, Eric, *The Sane Society*, (New York, NY: Rinehart & Co., Inc., 1955).

Gardner, Richard A., *Family Evaluation in Child Custody Litigation*, (Cresskill, NJ: Creative Therapeutics, 1982).

Gaughn, Lawrence, *Taking a Fresh Look at Divorce Mediation*, 17 Trial 39 (April 1981).

Goldstein, Joseph, Freud, Anna and Solnit, Albert J., *Beyond the Best Interests of the Child*, (New York, NY: The Free Press, 1979).

Gurman, Alan S. and Kniskern, Donald P., (Eds.), *Handbook of Family Therapy*, (New York, NY: Brunner/Mazel, 1981).

Haley, Jay, *Strategies of Psychotherapy*, (New York, NY: Grune & Stratton, Inc., 1963).

Hancock, Emily, *The Dimensions of Meaning and Belonging in the Process of Divorce*, 50 Am. J. Orthopsychiatry 18 (Jan. 1980).

Hawes, Gene R. and Brownstone, David M., *How to Get the Money to Pay for College*, (New York, NY: David McKay Co., 1978).

Haynes, John, *Divorce Mediations: A Practical Guide for Therapists and Counselors*, (New York, NY: Springer, 1981).

Hill, Lewis B., M.D., *On Being Rather Than Doing in Psychotherapy*, 8 Inter. J. Group Psychotherapy 115 (April 1958).

Howele, R. J. and Toepke, K. E., *Summary of the Child Custody Laws for the Fifty States*, 12 Am. J. Fam. Therapy 56 (Summer 1984).

Ingrassia, Michele, *Housing: Great Expectations are Falling Short*, Newsday, Part 2, June 2, 1976.

Isaacs, Marla, Montaivo, Braulio, and Abersohn, David, *The Difficult Divorce: Therapy for Children and Families*, (New York, NY: Basic Books, 1986).

Johnson, Sharon, *Divorce 101: Columbia Pioneering in Family Law*, The New York Times Style, Dec 31, 1984.

Kaslow, Florence W. and Schwartz, Lita Linzer, *The Dynamics of Divorce: A Life Cycle Perspective*, (New York, NY: Brunner/Mazel, 1987).

Kuhn, Thomas S., *The Structure of Scientific Revolutions*, 2d ed., (Chicago, IL: The University of Chicago Press, 1970).

Lande, John, *Mediation Paradigms and Professional Identities*, 4 Mediation Q. 19 (San Francisco, CA: Jossey-Bass, June 1984).

Lederer, William J. and Jackson, Don, *The Mirages of Marriage*, (New York, NY: W. W. Norton & Co., 1968).

Lemmon, John Allen, *Family Mediation Practice*, (New York: NY: Free Press, 1985).

Lemmon, John Allen (Ed.), *Mediation Quarterly*, (San Francisco, CA: Jossey-Bass, Inc., Volumes 1–17, 1983–1988).

Lewontin, Richard, *The Genetic Basis of Evolutionary Change*, (New York, NY: Columbia University Press, 1974).

Longman, Philip, *The Mortgage Generation: Why the Young Can't Afford A House*, The Washington Monthly (April 1986).

Lowery, C. R., *The Wisdom of Solomon: Criteria for Child Custody from the Legal and Clinical Point of View*, 8 L. & Human Behavior 371 (1984).

Marafiote, Richard A., *The Custody of Children: A Behavioral Assessment Model*, (New York, NY: Plenum Press, 1985).

Marlow, Lenard, *Divorce Mediation: Therapists in the Legal World*, 13 Am. J. Fam. Therapy 3 (New York, NY: Brunner/Mazel, Spring, 1985).

Marlow, Lenard, *Divorce Mediation: Therapists in Their Own World*, 13 Am. J. Fam. Therapy 3 (New York, NY: Brunner/Mazel, Fall, 1985).

Marlow, Lenard, *The Rule of Law in Divorce Mediation*, 9 Mediation Q. 5 (San Francisco, CA: Jossey-Bass, 1985).

Marlow, Lenard, *The Use and Misuse of Budgets*, 13 Mediation Q. 89 (San Francisco, CA: Jossey-Bass, 1986).

Marlow, Lenard, *Styles of Conducting Mediation*, 18 Mediation Q. 85 (San Francisco, CA: Jossey-Bass, 1987).

Mnookin, R. H. and Kornhauser, L., *Bargaining in the Shadow of the Law: The Case of Divorce*, 88 Yale L.J. 950 (1979).

Money, John, *Love and Love Sickness*, (Baltimore, MD: The Johns Hopkins University Press, 1980).

Moriarty, Robert B., *The Controversy Over O'Brien: The Problem and a Proposed Solution*, 18 Fam. L. Rev. 3 (Family Law Section, N.Y. State Bar Assoc., Aug. 1986).

Passell, Peter, *Where to Put Your Money 1986*, (New York, NY: Warner Books, 1986).

Piercy, Fred P. and Sprenkie, Douglas H., *Family Therapy Sourcebook*, (New York, NY: Guilford Press, 1986).

Pearson, J. and Thoennes, N., *Mediation and Divorce: The Benefits Outweigh the Costs*, 4 Fam. Advocate 26 (Winter 1982).

Rosenfeld, Jeffrey P., *Relationships: The Marriage and Family Reader*, (Glenview, IL: Scott, Foresman & Co., 1982).

Ross, Heather L. and Sawhill, Isabel V., *Time of Transition: The Growth of Families Headed by Women*, (Washington, D.C.: The Urban Institute, 1975).

Sager, C. J., *Marriage Contracts and Couple Therapy*, (New York, NY: Brunner/Mazel, 1976).

Saposnek, Donald T., *Mediating Child Custody Disputes*, (San Francisco, CA: Jossey-Bass, 1983).

Sauber, S. Richard, *It's All in the Name: A Language Guide for the Single, His Friends and Her Family*, (Hollywood, FL: Fredrick Fell, 1988).

Sauber, S. Richard, L'Abate, Luciano, and Weeks, Gerald R., *Family Therapy: Basic Concepts and Terms*, (Rockville, MD: Aspen Systems, 1985).

Sauber, S. Richard, and Panitz, D., *Divorce Mediation and Counseling*, in A. Gurman (Ed.) *Family Therapy*, (New York, NY: Brunner/Mazel, 1982).

Schneider, Carl D., *A Commentary on the Activity of Writing Codes of Ethics*, 8 Mediation Q. 83 (San Francisco, CA: Jossey-Bass, June 1985).

Shorter, Edward, *The Making of the Modern Family*, (New York, NY: Basic Books, 1977).

Silberman, Linda, *Professional Responsibility Problems of Divorce Mediation* 16 Fam. L.Q. 107 (Summer 1982).

Skolnik, Arlene S. and Skolnik, Jerome H., *Family in Transition*, (Boston, MA: Little, Brown and Company, 1971).

Smith, Ralph E., (Editor), *The Subtle Revolution: Women at Work*, (Washington, D.C.: Urban Institute, 1979).

Stapleton, Constance and MacCormack, Norma, *Caring About Kids: When Parents Divorce*, (U.S. Department of Health and Human Services, Public Health Service, Alcohol, Drug Abuse, and Mental Health Administration).

Stone, Lawrence, *The Family, Sex and Marriage in England 1500–1800*, (New York, NY: Harper & Row, 1977).

Putting It All Together—The Family Law Curriculum, 14 Colum. L. Alum. Observer 6 (Oct. 1984).

Thompson, Robert D., Report to the 132nd General Assembly, House of Representatives, State of Delaware, *The Delaware Child Support Formula—Study and Evaluation*.

Thompson, Robert D. and Paikin, Susan F., *Formulas and Guidelines for Support*, 36 Juv. & Fam. Court J. 33 (Fall 1985).

Thornton, Arland and Freedman, Deborah, *The Changing American Family*, 38 Population Bulletin 1 (Washington, D.C.: Population Reference Bureau, Inc., Oct. 1983).

Tufte, Virgin and Myerhoff, Barbara, (Eds.), *Changing Images of the Family*, (New Haven, CT: Yale University Press, 1979).

U.S. Bureau of the Census, *Current Population Reports*, (Series P-20, No. 297, 1976).

U.S. Bureau of the Census, *Statistical Abstract of the United States: 1982–83*, (103d Ed.), (Washington D.C. 1982).

U.S. National Center for Health Statistics, *Vital and Health Statistics*, Series 21, No. 29, "Divorces and Divorce Rates: United States," Table 1; and *Monthly Vital Statistics Report*, Vol. 27, No. 5 Supplement, "Advance Report Final Divorce Statistics, 1976," Table 1.

Visher, E. B. and Visher, J. J., *Old Loyalties, New Ties: Therapeutic Strategies with Stepfamilies*, (New York, NY: Brunner/Mazel, 1988).

Wallerstein, J. and Kelly J., *Surviving the Breakup, How Children and Parents Cope with Divorce*, (New York, NY: Basic Books, 1980).

Wallerstein, J. S., *Woman After Divorce: Preliminary Report from a Ten-Year Following*, 56 Am. J. Orthopsychiatry 65 (1986).

Watzlawick, Paul, Weakland, John W., and Fisch, Richard, *Change*, (New York, NY: W. W. Norton & Co., 1974).

Weiss, Robert S., *Marital Separation*, (New York, NY: Basic Books, 1975).

Weitzman, Lenore J., *The Economic Consequences of Divorce; An Empirical Study of Property, Alimony and Child Support Awards*, 8 F.L.R. 4037 (B.N.A., August 3, 1982).

Weitzman, Lenore J., *The Divorce Revolution: The Unexpected Social and Economic Consequences for Women and Children*, (New York, NY: Free Press, 1985).

Wheeler, Michael, *Divided Children: A Legal Guide for Divorcing Parents*, (New York, NY: W. W. Norton & Co., 1980.)

Williams, Robert G., *Child Support and the Cost of Raising Children: Using Formulas to Set Adequate Awards*, 36 Juv. & Fam. Court J. (Fall 1985).

World Almanac & Book of Facts 1988, (New York, NY: Pharos Books, 1987).

Name Index

In re Allison, Marriage of, 484
Anderson v. Anderson, 471, 483
Appelman v. Appelman, 466
Archer v. Archer, 468
In re Arnold, Marriage of, 487
In re Aufmuth, Marriage of, 467
Avner, Judith I., 476

Bauer v. Bauer, 468
Beeler v. Beeler, 468
Blomgren v. Blomgren, 487
Bollenbach v. Bollenbach, 478
Boszormenyi, Nagy I., 124
Brandenburg v. Brandenburg, 466
Brooks v. Brooks, 466
Brundage v. Brundage, 471
Brunson v. Brunson, 483
Burke v. Burke, 471
Burr v. Burr, 468

Cafarakis, Christian, 470
Callen v. Callen, 487
Capponi v. Capponi, 483
Carlson v. Carlson, 483
Carruth v. Carruth, 468
Carter v. Carter, 464–465
Cartwright v. Cartwright, 483
Cassiday v. Cassiday, 486
Cherlin, Andrew J., 466
Chesler, Phyllis, 477
Christian v. Christian, 462, 479
In re Cisek, Marriage of, 487
Cohen, Harriet, 119
Coogler, O.J., 461
Cooper v. Cooper, 481
Courten v. Courten, 481
In re Crislip, 467
Cross v. Cross, 490
Crouch, Richard E., 470
Crowell v. Crowell, 487

D. v. D., 480
Davis v. Fair, 490
Davis, U.S. v., 490

DeLa Rosa v. DeLa Rosa, 468
Diez-Arguelles v. Commissioner, 482
D'Onofrio v. D'Onofrio, 481
Drapek v. Drapek, 467, 468
Driscoll, State v., 480

Earl v. Earl, 471
Eckhardt v. Eckhardt, 487
Edgar v. Edgar, 463
Ehrenworth v. Ehrenworth, 468
Enos v. Enos, 465
Epperson v. Epperson, 466
Ernst v. Ernst, 483
Errera v. Errera, 478
Espenshade, Thomas J., 491
Evans v. Evans, 481

Falgade, State v., 480
Felder, Raoul, 470
Felkner v. Felkner, 465
Finney v. Commissioner, 482
Fisch, Richard, 473
Fisher, Roger D., 4, 128, 462, 478
Fobes v. Fobes, 463
Foster, Henry H., 470, 477
Frank, Catherine, 478
Frausto v. Frausto, 468
Freedman, Deborah, 465, 466, 467
Freud, Sigmund, 123, 478
Fromm, Eric, 481
Fry v. Schwarting, 487

Gallo v. Gallo, 466
Gassaway v. Gassaway, 471
Gaughan, Lawrence, 479
Geer v. Geer, 467, 468
Gevis v. Gevis, 466
Gillette v. Gillette, 468
Gist v. Gist, 465
Gordon v. Gordon, 471
In re Graham, Marriage of, 467
Grapin v. Grapin, 471
Green v. Green, 478
Gregg v. Gregg, 471

Grobleski v. Grobleski, 487
Gross v. Gross, 487
Grosskopf v. Grosskopf, 468

Haley, Jay, 123, 478
Halpern v. Halpern, 466
Hampshire v. Hampshire, 465
Hancock, Emily, 479
Harp v. McCann, 487
Harris v. Harris, 486
Harter v. State, 480
Hashimoto v. Hashimoto, 471
Haugan v. Haugan, 468
Haynes, John, 461
Helm v. Helm, 468
Herman, Susan, 476
Hill, Lewis B., 138
Hill, Lewis Browne, 478
Hill v. Hill, 468
Hillman, Adria, 119
Hodge v. Hodge, 467, 468
In re Horstmann, Marriage of, 468
Hubbard v. Hubbard, 468
Hughes v. Hughes, 468

Ingrassia, Michele, 482
Inman v. Inman, 467, 468

James v. James, 471, 472
Johnson v. Johnson, 462, 479
Jones v. Jones, 467

Keenan v. Keenan, 471
Kelly, Joan Berlin, 4, 461
King v. King, 483
Kornhauser, I., 63, 472
Kozak, Lillian, 476
Kuhn, Thomas S., 7, 462

LaFleur v. LaFleur, 464
In re Lamm, Marriage of, 487
In re Lamos' Estate, 471
Lande, John, 472
Lapidus v. Lapidus, 470
LaRue v. LaRue, 467
Lear, Martha Weinman, 465
Lentz v. Lentz, 467
Lester, Commissioner v., 489
Leveck v. Leveck, 468
Levine v. Levine, 464
Lewontin, Richard, 474
Loeb v. Loeb, 472
Longman, Philip, 482
Lorenz v. Lorenz, 490
Lowrey v. Lowrey, 468

In re Lucas, Marriage of, 467
In re Lundberg, Marriage of, 468
Lynam v. Gallagher, 467

McClung v. McClung, 478
McDermott v. McDermott, 484
McGowan v. McGowan, 468
Mahoney v. Mahoney, 467, 468, 471
Majouskas v. Majouskas, 483
Mandy v. Williams, 487
Marquardt v. Marquardt, 468
Marshall v. Marshall, 463
Martin v. Martin, 487
Mason v. Mason, 471
In re McManama, Marriage of, 468
In re McVey, Marriage of, 467
Meeks v. Kirkland, 472
In re Meredith, Marriage of, 471
Merritt v. Merritt, 462, 479
Meyer, Bernard, 31
Miller v. Miller, 487
Miranda v. Arizona, 480
Mnookin, R.H., 63, 472
In re Moncrief, Marriage of, 465
Moritz v. Moritz, 471, 472
Moss v. Moss, 469
Muckleroy v. Muckleroy, 468

Nehorayoff v. Nehorayoff, 469
Nelson v. Nelson, 467
In re Nesset, Marriage of, 487
Nuckols v. Nuckols, 487

O'Brien v. O'Brien, 27–34, 38, 467, 470, 471, 483, 484
Olah v. Olah, 467
In re Ortiz, Marriage of, 487

Pacella v. Pacella, 478
Paquette v. Paquette, 481
Perry v. Perry, 468
Petersen v. Petersen, 468
Peterson v. Peterson, 467
Price v. Price, 466, 471, 483
Pyeatte v. Pyeatte, 467

Rayburn v. Rayburn, 468
Redman, R. Michael, 478
In re Reed, 483
Rice v. Rice, 472
In re Richardson, Marriage of, 487
Ritchea v. Ritchea, 466
Robbins v. Robbins, 466
Ruben v. Ruben, 468
Rubin v. Rubin, 467, 471, 472

Saint Pierre v. Saint Pierre, 468
Saposnek, Donald T., 77, 473
Sayer v. Sayer, 486
Schneider, Carl D., 464
Severs v. Severs, 468
In re Shima, Marriage of, 466
Sigal, People v., 480
Simpson v. Simpson, 463
Smith, Ralph E., 465, 486
Speer v. Speer, 483
Stahl v. Department of Social Services, 487
Stevens v. Stevens, 467
Stockton v. Stockton, 462, 479
Stone, Lawrence, 486
Storm v. Storm, 472
In re Sullivan, Marriage of, 467
Sweeney v. Sweeney, 468

Theiss v. Theiss, 467
Thornton, Arland, 465, 466, 467
Tobey v. Tobey, 478
Todd v. Todd, 467
Tonjes v. Tonjes, 478

Ury, William, 4, 128, 462, 478

Vennard, State v., 480
Vertigo v. Vertigo, 477
Vilas v. Vilas, 478
Voyles v. Voyles, 468

Wallerstein, Judith, 4, 461
Washburn v. Washburn, 468
Washington v. Hicks, 466
Watzlawick, Paul, 473
Weakland, John H., 473
In re Weinstein, Marriage of, 468
Weise v. Weise, 487
Weitzman, Lenore J., 118, 477, 485
Wilbur v. Wilbur, 465
Winter v. Winter, 471
Wisner v. Wisner, 467, 471
Wolk v. Saidel, 487
Woodworth v. Woodworth, 467
Wright v. Wright, 467

In re Young, Marriage of, 466

Zahler v. Zahler, 467
Zaragoza v. Capriola, 487

SUBJECT INDEX

Activists, style of, 135–138
Adultery, 122–123
Advisory attorney, 168–175
  changes to agreement and, 169–170
  loss of control for mediators and, 170–171
  role of, 172–175
  selection by mediator, 171–172
Agreements, 175–176
  draft agreement, review of, 385–387
  fairness issue, 39–62
  ineffective agreements, examples of, 384
  memorandum of agreement, 387–415
  purposes of, 383
Alimony: *see* Support
Appreciated property, distribution of, 271–272
Assessment of couple for mediation, 195–200
Assets and liabilities
  appreciated property, 271–272
  bank accounts/stock, 262–263
  business interests, 266–271
  children's assets, 282–283
  contributions of parties to marriage and, 264–266
  debts, 283–284
  household furnishings, 281–282
  inherited money, 263
  pensions, 272–281
  short marriages, 266
Assumptions, by mediators, and mediation process, 143–144
Attire of mediator, 178
Attorney/divorce mediators, style of, 131–132
Attorneys
  confidentiality and, 192
  mediator's relationship with parties attorney, 181–183
  referrals from mediators, 66–67
  role of, 64

Budgets
  problems related to, 287–288
  procedure for use of, 291–294
  use in mediation, 285–294
Business interests
  complicating factors, 268–271

Business interests (*cont.*)
  distribution of, 266–271
  as marital property, 35–36

Careers, equitable distribution and, 28–29, 31–33, 35–36
Cash income, disclosure/proof of, 314–319
Childcare credit, 427
Children
  alternative custody arrangements, 213, 216
  as beneficiaries of life insurance, 369–371
  college costs, 373–381
  in context of mediation process, 13–14
  continuity and marital residence, 242
  cost of raising child, 435–441
  fairness of agreement and, 42–43
  graduate school, 379–380
  joint parental decision-making, 219–221
  medical insurance, 359–362
  meeting with parties separately and, 214 215
  participation in mediation, 180–181
  practical considerations, 67
  relations with grandparents and, 236–237
  relations with stepparents and, 237–238
  residence restriction, 233–236
  schedule for visitation, necessity of, 228–229
  third party relationships and, 229–232
  visitation, 222–228
  visitation as right v. obligation, 238–240
  see also Custody; Support
Children's assets, distribution of, 282–283
Child support, tax treatment, 421–425
Coercion, fairness and, 53–54
College education and children, 373–381
  graduate school, 379–380
  loans/financial aid, 380–381
  reduction in support payments and, 378–379
  very young children, 377–378
  wife's contribution, 375–377
Co-mediation, 178–180
  advantages/disadvantages of, 179
Confidentiality, 191–195
  legal profession and, 192
  mediator and, 192–195

Confidentiality (*cont.*)
  mental health profession and, 191–192, 193
Conflicting interests, 19–22
Consumer Price Index (CPI), 340–341
Context
  criticism of mediation and, 96–98
  divorce mediation and, 93–96, 99–101
  traditional divorce and, 89–93
Cost of living, escalation of support, 338–341
Custody
  alternative arrangements, 213, 216
  assumptions about family and, 80–81
  continuity and marital residence, 242
  custody disputes, 213–215
  divorce mediation and, 76–77
  joint custody, 215–219
  labels and custody, 212–213
  living arrangements, principles related to, 216–217
  mediator's qualifications and, 77–78
  mediator's role, 81–87
  shifts in custody, 221–222
  standards and, 78–79
  traditional divorce and, 73–76

Death, equitable distribution, 47
Debts
  distribution of, 283–284
  types of, 283
Decision-making, parents/child, post-divorce, 219–221
Deescalation clause, support, 341–344
Defense system, marital partners and, 124
Disclosure, and divorce mediation, 97–98
Divorce
  as legal event, 6–7, 11–22
  as personal event, 7–9
Divorce mediation
  choosing mediation vs. traditional divorce, 153–157
  criticisms of, 5, 10, 39, 57–58
  emotional climate and, 129–130
  as empowering situation, 110
  legal professions response to, 4–6
  legal rules and, 64–71
  negotiation process and, 99–101
  power imbalances and, 103–119
  quality of mediated agreements, 39
  referral of clients to attorneys, 66–67
  rise of, 3–5
  tasks of successful mediation, 132
Divorce mediation process
  advisory attorney and, 168–175
  attorneys for partners and, 181–183
  children's participation in, 180–181

Divorce mediation process (*cont.*)
  co-mediation, 178–180
  formal agreement with couple, 175–176
  formal material used in, 166–168
  initial conference, preparation for, 165–166
  initial contact, 161–165
  initial meeting, 185–209
  length and spacing of mediation sessions, 176–177
  setting for, 177–178
Divorce mediator, compared to judge, 38
Divorce proceedings
  lack of control of process, 205
  lawyers, role of, 64
  legal rules and, 64

Elective surgery, responsibilities for payment, 362
Emotional climate, and divorce mediation, 129–130
Equitable distribution, 23–38
  examples of, 28–29, 30–33, 35–36, 37
  issues related to, 27
  mediation and, 29–31, 34–38
  partnership law applied to, 26–27
  problem of, 23–26
Escalation clause, support, 338–341
Espenshade study, cost of raising children, 435–441
Exemptions, for dependents, 427–428

Fairness and agreements, 39–62
  absence of coercion and, 53–54
  conduct of divorcing partners and, 42–44
  couples' definition of fair, 52–53
  laws and fairness, 45–48
  mediator and, 44–45, 48–52, 54–62
  price of fairness, 57–59
  standards of fairness and, 39–42
Family, basic assumptions about, 80–81
Fees, discussion of, 206–208
Formal material, 166–168
  advantages to use, 166–168

Getting to Yes (Fisher and Ury), 4, 128, 131
Graduate school, 379–380
Grandparents, children's relations with, 236–237

Harvard Research Project, 4
Head of household tax status, 425–427
Honesty, and traditional proceedings, 96–97
Household furnishings, distribution of, 281–282

Income taxes
  alimony, tax law requirements, 417–419
  childcare credit, 427
  child support, 421–425

Income taxes (*cont.*)
  excess payments, 420
  exemptions, 427–428
  filing status, 425–427
  marital residence, 243, 257
  principal residence, sale of, 431–433
  recapture rule, 420–421
  transfers of property, 428–431
Income tax rates, 418
Indirect income issue, 319–322
Inherited money, 263
Initial contact
  mediator's preparation for, 165–166
  telephone contact, 161–165
Initial meeting
  arrival of couple, 185–186
  assessment of couples for mediation, 195–200
  concluding meeting, 204–206
  fees, discussion of, 206–208
  improper questions and, 189–190
  meeting parties separately, 200–204, 214–215
  position of mediator, 186–188
  questions of mediator, 188–189
Insurance
  life insurance, 363–373
  medical insurance, 359–362

Joint custody, 49, 215–219
  child support and, 347–250
Judgments, mediators, and mediation process, 146–151

Laws
  conflicting interests and, 19–22
  fairness and, 45–48
  legal rights, 15–16, 18–19
  legal rules, 13–14, 16–17
  use as reality principle, 65
Lawyers: *see* Attorneys
Legal myths, 13, 15–16
Legal profession, view of divorce mediation, 4–6
Legal rules
  and divorce mediation, 64–71
  and divorce proceedings, 64
  as legal weapons, 70
  self-determination and, 67–70
Life insurance, 363–372
  amount needed by husband, 364–366
  children as beneficiaries, 369–371
  increasing amount, 365–367
  new marital partner and, 370
  similarities/differences to medical insurance issues, 363
  time period for maintaining policy, 371–372
  whole life policy, 367

Life insurance (*cont.*)
  on wife's life, 368
Loans/financial aid, college education, 380–381

Maintenance/carrying charges, marital residence, 253–256
Marathon mediation sessions, 177
Marital property
  distribution and effect on support, 328–330
  as legal myth, 29
  state-to-state variation, 46
  see also Equitable distribution
Marital residence
  continuity for children and, 242
  cost of comparative housing, 242, 243–244
  division of proceeds, 256–257
  as forced savings, 243–244
  husband/boyfriend of wife and, 245–250
  length of occupancy for wife, 244–245
  maintenance/carrying charges, 253–256
  option to buy home, 251–252
  rented property, 259–260
  right to borrow on equity of marital property, 257–258
  right to rent home, 250–251
  sale of home, 252–253
  sale of, tax treatment, 431–433
  tax deduction issues, 243, 257
  wife and cost of house, 242–243
Mediating Child Custody Disputes (Saposnek), 77
Mediation styles
  activists, 135–138
  assumptions of mediator and, 143–144
  of attorney/labor mediators, 131–132
  judgments of mediator and, 146–151
  opinions of mediator, 144–146
  passivists, 135
  of therapist mediators, 132–135
  understanding of mediator and, 138–143
Medical insurance, 359–362
  for children, 359
  elective surgery, 362
  orthodontic treatment, 361
  psychotherapy, 361–362
  uncovered expenses, 360–361
  for wife, 359–360
Memorandum of agreement, 387–415
  example of agreement with related comments, 387–415
Mental health profession
  and confidentiality, 191–192, 193
  and power imbalances, 111–113
Misconduct and divorce, 121–126
Multiple reduction test, 424–425

Negotiation
  divorce mediation and, 99–101, 128
  skill of men vs. women, 108–109

Opinions, mediators, and mediation process, 143–
  144
Orthodontic treatment, responsibilities for payment,
  361
Overtime pay/bonuses, 322–323

Passivists, style of, 135
Pensions
  advantages of mediation and, 274–275
  distribution of, 272–281
  forms of, 279–280
  problems related to, 272–273, 274–277
Politicalization of divorce, and power imbalances,
  118–119
Power imbalances, 103–119
  divorce mediation and, 103–104, 113–118
  mental health professionals and, 111–113
  negotiating skill of men and, 108–109
  politicalization of divorce and, 118–119
  strong male vs. weak female, 105–108
  traditional divorce and, 109–111
Prenuptial agreements, 41–42
Professional license, as marital property, 28–29,
  30–33
Property transfers, tax treatment, 428–431
Psychotherapy, responsibilities for payment, 361–
  362

Rentals
  rented property as marital residence, 259–260
  right to rent marital residence, 250–251
Residence restriction, children and, 233–236
Retirement plans: see Pensions
Royalties, as marital property, 35

Safe harbor provisions, 422
Salary
  cash income issue, 314–319
  indirect income issue, 319–322
  overtime pay/bonuses, 322–323
Schedule, for visitation, 228–229
School holidays, visitation and, 225–226
Self-determination, 67–70
Self-fulfilling prophesy, 89
Setting for mediation, 177–178
Sexes
  attitudes toward, 48–49
  legal protection and, 42
  power imbalances, 103–119
Shared parenting, 213, 216

Standard of living, wife vs. husband, 307–308
State laws, marital property variations in, 46
Stepchildren, child support and, 347
Stepparents, children's relations with, 237–238
Summer recess, visitation and, 226–228
Support
  abatement and college payments, 378–379
  allocation of payments, 327–328
  basic questions in, 353–356
  budgets, use in mediation, 285–294
  cohabitation and wife and, 336–338
  deescalation in payments, 341–344
  distribution of marital property, effect of, 328–
    330
  duration of support, 332–336
  escalation in payments, 338–341
  grown children and, 313
  joint custody and, 347–350
  justification for, 310–313, 353–356
  problem solving in mediation, 309–310
  reduction in child support, 345–346
  rehabilitative perspective, 334
  salary considerations, 311–323
  scope of expenses, 351
  separate property, effect of, 330–332
  for stepchildren, 347
  support formulas, use of, 294–301
  suspension of payments, 344–345
  tax treatment, 417–421
  temporary support agreements, 301–306
  unequal allocation issue, 307–308
Surviving the Breakup (Wallerstein and Kelly), 4

Tax issues: see Income tax
Tax Reform Acts of 1984 and 1986, 418, 429
Temporary support agreements, 301–306
Therapist mediators, style of, 132–135
Third parties
  cohabitation of wife and support, 336–338
  custody/visitation issue, 229–232
  life insurance and new marital partner, 370
  new husband/boyfriend in marital residence,
    245–250
Time factors
  duration of support, 332–336
  length of mediation sessions, 176–177
  length of occupancy, marital residence, 244–245
Transfers of property, tax treatment, 428–431

Unallocated payment, 421
Uniform Gift to Minors Act, 282

Visitation, 222–228
  versus entertainment, 222

Visitation (*cont.*)
    principles related to, 222–224
    as right vs. obligation, 238–240
    schedule for visitation, necessity of, 228–229
    school holidays, 225–226
    summer recess, 226–228

Visitation (*cont.*)
    weekend variations, 224

Women, legal protection of interests, 42; *see also*
    Power imbalances

About the Authors

Lenard Marlow is past President of the New York State Council on Divorce Mediation and a Fellow of the American Academy of Matrimonial Lawyers. He is also past President of the Pederson-Krag Center, one of the largest outpatient mental health facilities in New York State. He is the founder and legal director of Divorce Mediation Professionals, one of the largest divorce mediation facilities in the country. He received his B.A. degree in philosophy from Colgate University in 1954 and his J.D. degree from Columbia University School of Law in 1958.

S. Richard Sauber, Ph.D. is in the private practice of family psychology and divorce mediation in Boca Raton, Florida. He was formerly an Associate Professor of Psychology in the Departments of Psychiatry at Brown and Columbia Universities. Dr. Sauber is the author of four other books on the subject and for the past 14 years he has been the Editor-in-Chief of the *American Journal of Family Therapy*. He was a founding board member of the Academy of Family Mediators and a founding board member of the association's journal, *Mediation Quarterly*.

ISBN 0-306-43286-2

90000

9 780306 432866